Emerging Research in Play Therapy, Child Counseling, and Consultation

Rheta LeAnne Steen
Loyola University New Orleans, USA

A volume in the Advances in Psychology, Mental Health, and Behavioral Studies (APMHBS) Book Series

IGI Global
DISSEMINATOR OF KNOWLEDGE

www.igi-global.com

Published in the United States of America by
IGI Global
Information Science Reference (an imprint of IGI Global)
701 E. Chocolate Avenue
Hershey PA, USA 17033
Tel: 717-533-8845
Fax: 717-533-8661
E-mail: cust@igi-global.com
Web site: http://www.igi-global.com

Library of Congress Cataloging-in-Publication Data

Names: Steen, Rheta LeAnne, 1971- editor.
Title: Emerging research in play therapy, child counseling, and consultation / Rheta LeAnne Steen, editor.
Description: Hershey, PA : Information Science Reference, [2017]
Identifiers: LCCN 2016056938| ISBN 9781522522249 (hardcover) | ISBN 9781522522256 (ebook)
Subjects: LCSH: Play therapy. | Counseling--Research. | Therapist and patient.
Classification: LCC RJ505.P6 E44 2017 | DDC 618.92/891653--dc23 LC record available at https://lccn.loc.gov/2016056938

This book is published in the IGI Global book series Advances in Psychology, Mental Health, and Behavioral Studies (APMHBS) (ISSN: pending; eISSN: pending)

British Cataloguing in Publication Data
A Cataloguing in Publication record for this book is available from the British Library.

For electronic access to this publication, please contact: eresources@igi-global.com.

Advances in Psychology, Mental Health, and Behavioral Studies (APMHBS) Book Series

Bryan Christiansen
PryMarke, LLC, USA

ISSN:pending
EISSN:pending

MISSION

The complexity of the human mind has puzzled researchers and physicians for centuries. While widely studied, the brain still remains largely misunderstood.

The **Advances in Psychology, Mental Health, and Behavioral Studies (APMHBS)** book series presents comprehensive research publications focusing on topics relating to the human psyche, cognition, psychiatric care, mental and developmental disorders, as well as human behavior and interaction. Featuring diverse and innovative research, publications within APMHBS are ideally designed for use by mental health professionals, academicians, researchers, and upper-level students.

COVERAGE

- Psychiatry
- Eating Disorders
- Addiction
- Counseling & Therapy
- Substance Abuse
- Mental Health & Disorders
- Trauma & Stress
- Anxiety
- Treatment & Care
- Developmental Disorders

IGI Global is currently accepting manuscripts for publication within this series. To submit a proposal for a volume in this series, please contact our Acquisition Editors at Acquisitions@igi-global.com or visit: http://www.igi-global.com/publish/.

Titles in this Series

For a list of additional titles in this series, please visit: www.igi-global.com

Workforce Development Theory and Practice in the Mental Health Sector
Mark Smith (Te Pou o te Whakaaro Nui: National Workforce Center for Adult Mental Health, Addiction and Disability, New Zealand) and Angela F. Jury (Te Pou o te Whakaaro Nui: National Workforce Center for Adult Mental Health, Addiction and Disability, New Zealand)
Information Science Reference • copyright 2017 • 378pp • H/C (ISBN: 9781522518747) • US $190.00 (our price)

Improving the Quality of Life for Dementia Patients through Progressive Detection, Treatment, and Care
Jinglong Wu (Okayama University, Japan)
Medical Information Science Reference • copyright 2017 • 353pp • H/C (ISBN: 9781522509257) • US $205.00 (our price)

Police Psychology and Its Growing Impact on Modern Law Enforcement
Cary L. Mitchell (Pepperdine University, USA) and Edrick H. Dorian (Los Angeles Police Department, USA)
Information Science Reference • copyright 2017 • 345pp • H/C (ISBN: 9781522508137) • US $190.00 (our price)

Seduction in Popular Culture, Psychology, and Philosophy
Constantino Martins (Nova University of Lisbon, Portugal) and Manuel Damásio (Lusófona University, Portugal)
Information Science Reference • copyright 2017 • 332pp • H/C (ISBN: 9781522505259) • US $175.00 (our price)

Chronic Mental Illness and the Changing Scope of Intervention Strategies, Diagnosis, and Treatment
Barre Vijaya Prasad (Dharwad Institute of Mental Health and Neurosciences, India)
Medical Information Science Reference • copyright 2017 • 404pp • H/C (ISBN: 9781522505198) • US $220.00 (our price)

Identifying, Treating, and Preventing Childhood Trauma in Rural Communities
Marion Baker (Center of Hope Arizona, USA) Jacqueline Ford (Center of Hope Arizona, USA & Walden University, USA) Brittany Canfield (Center of Hope Arizona, USA & Fielding Graduate University, USA) and Traci Grabb (Arizona's Children Association, USA & Center of Hope Arizona, USA)
Information Science Reference • copyright 2016 • 306pp • H/C (ISBN: 9781522502289) • US $185.00 (our price)

Handbook of Research on Diagnosing, Treating, and Managing Intellectual Disabilities
Rejani Thudalikunnil Gopalan (Gujarat Forensic Sciences University, India)
Information Science Reference • copyright 2016 • 496pp • H/C (ISBN: 9781522500896) • US $210.00 (our price)

Neuroeconomics and the Decision-Making Process
Bryan Christiansen (PryMarke LLC, USA) and Ewa Lechman (Gdansk University of Technology, Poland)
Business Science Reference • copyright 2016 • 354pp • H/C (ISBN: 9781466699892) • US $195.00 (our price)

This book is dedicated to Delilah and Anikah Morgan.

Editorial Advisory Board

Table of Contents

Foreword xvii

Preface xx

Acknowledgment xxvi

Chapter 1
Status of Play Therapy Research 1
Sue C. Bratton, University of North Texas, USA
Alyssa Swan, University of North Texas, USA

Chapter 2
The Impact of Trauma on Brain Development: A Neurodevelopmentally Appropriate Model for Play Therapists 20
Susan Stewart Bray, Wichita State University, USA
Jennifer P. Stone, Wichita State University, USA
Richard L. Gaskill, Wichita State University, USA

Chapter 3
Theraplay: The Evidence for Trauma-Focused Treatment for Children and Families 42
Catherine Tucker, Indiana State University, USA
Sondra Smith-Adcock, University of Florida, USA

Chapter 4
Integrating Interpersonal Neurobiology into the Play Therapy Process: Advancing Adlerian Play Therapy 60
Dalena L. Dillman Taylor, University of Central Florida, USA
Naomi Joy Wheeler, University of Central Florida, USA

Chapter 5
The Safe Space: An Examination of the Neurobiological Benefits of Play Therapy with Traumatized Children 81
Cary McAdams Hamilton, Antioch University, USA
Hannah E. Reas, Seattle Pacific University, USA
Megan E. Mansfield, Claremont Graduate University, USA

Chapter 6
Adlerian Play Therapy: Practice and Research 100
Kristin K. Meany-Walen, University of Northern Iowa, USA
Terry Kottman, Encouragement Zone, USA

Chapter 7
Pre-Therapy in Child-Centered Play Therapy: A Model for Treating Children with Autism 112
Karrie L. Swan, Eastern Washington University, USA

Chapter 8
A Cognitive-Behavioral Play Therapy (CBPT) Approach for Adolescents' Pro-Social Skill Development in the School Setting 124
Laura Jean Fazio-Griffith, Southeastern Louisiana University, USA
Reshelle Marino, Southeastern Louisiana University, USA

Chapter 9
Toy Guns in Play Therapy: An Examination of Play Therapists' Beliefs 140
Amanda Winburn, University of Mississippi, USA
Suzanne M. Dugger, University of Mississippi, USA
Jennifer Austin Main, University of Mississippi, USA

Chapter 10
Expanding the Range of Puppetry in Expressive Play Therapy 158
Michele J. Ferro, Lesley University, USA
Julia Gentleman Byers, Lesley University, USA

Chapter 11
Studying the Effectiveness of the Storytelling/Story-Acting (STSA) Play Intervention on Ugandan Preschoolers' Emergent Literacy, Oral Language, and Theory of Mind in Two Rural Ugandan Community Libraries 182
Geoff Goodman, Long Island University, USA
Valeda F. Dent, Long Island University, USA

Chapter 12
Ethics in Play Therapy Consultation and Supervision 214
Jeffrey S. Ashby, Georgia State University, USA
Laura Wood, Georgia State University, USA
Sarah Kiperman, Georgia State University, USA

Chapter 13
Integrating Play Therapy and Mental Health Consultation 232
Krystal Vaughn, LSUHSC New Orleans, USA
Erin Dugan, LSUHSC New Orleans, USA

Chapter 14
Multicultural Considerations in Play Therapy Caregiver Consultation 249
Kristy A. Brumfield, Immaculata University, USA
Celita J. Owens, Immaculata University, USA
Rheta LeAnne Steen, Loyala University New Orleans, USA
Renee M. Floer, Loyola University New Orleans, USA

Chapter 15
Consultation Strategies for Working with Professionals Supporting Foster Families 265
Kim Coggins, Austin Peay State University, USA
Kristie Opiola, UNC Charlotte, USA
Kara L. Carnes-Holt, University of Wyoming, USA

Chapter 16
Teachers Can Play Too: Teacher-Child Relationships, Social-Emotional Development, and Academic Engagement 288
Szu-Yu Chen, Central Michigan University, USA
Natalya A. Lindo, University of North Texas, USA

Chapter 17
Play and Speech Therapy in Schools: Toward a Model of Interprofessional Collaborative Practice. 314
Suzan E. Weishof, International School of Hamburg, Germany

Chapter 18
The Play Therapist in the Courtroom: Preparing Yourself and Your Client for Court 345
Jeffrey M. Sullivan, Sam Houston State University, USA
Sinem Akay, Sam Houston State University, USA

Compilation of References 367

About the Contributors 424

Index 433

Detailed Table of Contents

Foreword xvii

Preface xx

Acknowledgment xxvi

Chapter 1
Status of Play Therapy Research 1
Sue C. Bratton, University of North Texas, USA
Alyssa Swan, University of North Texas, USA

With today's focus on evidence-based treatment (EBT) for children, play therapists are ethically responsible to identify and deliver effective interventions as well as synthesize the considerable body of play therapy research to support their practice and to advocate for play therapy as an evidence-base practice. Play therapists' ability to articulate research findings is particularly important as they consult with the adults in children's lives who make decisions regarding children's wellbeing including parents, teachers, school administrators and other professionals. This chapter aims to present an up-to-date comprehensive review and synthesis of contemporary play therapy research with a focus on studies employing randomized control group designs in order to provide play therapy practitioners with a guide to understanding and utilizing the substantial research base for play therapy.

Chapter 2
The Impact of Trauma on Brain Development: A Neurodevelopmentally Appropriate Model for Play Therapists 20
Susan Stewart Bray, Wichita State University, USA
Jennifer P. Stone, Wichita State University, USA
Richard L. Gaskill, Wichita State University, USA

As many as four million children experience trauma every year, and some children experience multiple traumas over time. In this chapter, the authors provide an overview of the scope and the impacts of trauma on young children. The types of experiences that may be traumatizing to children and the potential effects of these experiences were included. A synopsis of the neurodevelopmental process was also provided along with the impact of trauma at the various neurodevelopmental stages. A neurodevelopmentally appropriate treatment model was described, and the model included the three neurosequential phases of regulate, relate, and reason. In the final section, a review of the impacts of trauma on school performance was provided, and suggestions for advocacy with classroom teachers were included.

Chapter 3
Theraplay: The Evidence for Trauma-Focused Treatment for Children and Families 42
Catherine Tucker, Indiana State University, USA
Sondra Smith-Adcock, University of Florida, USA

Theraplay® is a brief, attachment-based parent-child psychotherapy approach that uses interactional play to establish 'affectional' bonds between caregiver and child. Recent research related to Theraplay suggests it is an evidence-based practice for use in schools and clinical settings for a wide range of childhood problems, including those that are trauma-based. Of particular importance, Theraplay is emerging as an approach that is consistent with current neuroscience research on children's brain development and new understandings of attachment and disruption advanced by researchers. Young clients with some form of trauma-related symptoms comprise a large percentage of clinical cases, and present with complicated emotional and behavioral problems In this chapter, we will explore the basic theoretical underpinnings of Theraplay, the relevant mechanisms of change, and current evidence base. Although Theraplay can be used with a wide range of clients and problems, in this chapter, the focus will be on the applicatio with families with children who have experienced trauma.

Chapter 4
Integrating Interpersonal Neurobiology into the Play Therapy Process: Advancing Adlerian Play Therapy 60
Dalena L. Dillman Taylor, University of Central Florida, USA
Naomi Joy Wheeler, University of Central Florida, USA

Advancements in neuroscience provide theoretical support for principles and practices of counseling and play therapy intervention. Likewise, AdPT shares many conceptual similarities with IPNB and neuroscience research including emphasis on childhood experience, social interest and relationships, purposefulness of behavior, holism, and the internalized narrative or self-schema. This chapter per the authors will (a) develop connections from neuroscience and IPNB to play and play therapy, (b) review the IPNB model's domains of integration and their relationship to AdPT, and (c) provide an updated AdPT framework that encompasses the most recent neuroscience empirical support.

Chapter 5
The Safe Space: An Examination of the Neurobiological Benefits of Play Therapy with Traumatized Children 81
Cary McAdams Hamilton, Antioch University, USA
Hannah E. Reas, Seattle Pacific University, USA
Megan E. Mansfield, Claremont Graduate University, USA

This chapter illustrates the neurobiological effects of trauma on children, as well as the therapeutic benefits of play therapy as a stand-alone treatment for this population. The goal of this work includes providing a framework for the neurobiological effects of trauma on children, as well as the various advantages of play therapy as an effective intervention. Play, specifically, meets children where they are in their development, while also attending to the neurobiological effects that trauma can have on the brain. The primary neurobiological structures implicated and targeted by client-centered play-based interventions are discussed, as well as the impact play therapy has on neural integration, memory assimilation, and the limbic system. A clinical vignette from the principal author's practice and experience working with traumatized children is included to elucidate the healing nature of play.

Chapter 6
Adlerian Play Therapy: Practice and Research 100
Kristin K. Meany-Walen, University of Northern Iowa, USA
Terry Kottman, Encouragement Zone, USA

Many play therapists routinely use Adlerian theory as their primary mode of conducting therapy with children. In an age of evidenced-informed practices, research that supports or describes a treatment's effectiveness is important. Because of Adlerian play therapy's popularity and the emphasis for evidence of treatment effectiveness, researchers began investigating Adlerian play therapy. A brief description of Adlerian play therapy and a description of research is provided.

Chapter 7
Pre-Therapy in Child-Centered Play Therapy: A Model for Treating Children with Autism............. 112
Karrie L. Swan, Eastern Washington University, USA

Child-centered play therapy (CCPT) is widely used among practitioners as a developmentally responsive mental health treatment for children with a variety of behaviors and presenting problems, however for children with disabilities, modifications to CCPT may be warranted. Therefore, the purpose of this chapter is to present a model of pre-therapy in CCPT for treating children with ASD and other developmental disabilities. This chapter begins with an overview of person-centered therapy and pre-therapy; then moves to an explanation of using pre-therapy in CCPT. The chapter concludes with a synopsis for using therapeutic responses across three phases in pre-therapy. Recommendations for future research are discussed.

Chapter 8
A Cognitive-Behavioral Play Therapy (CBPT) Approach for Adolescents' Pro-Social Skill Development in the School Setting 124
Laura Jean Fazio-Griffith, Southeastern Louisiana University, USA
Reshelle Marino, Southeastern Louisiana University, USA

In this chapter, the authors will discuss the use of a cognitive-behavioral play therapy approach (CBPT) for teaching social skills to adolescents using expressive art techniques in a school setting. Expressive art techniques are integrated into an eight-week social skills curriculum, which represents a cognitive-behavioral play therapy approach for the development of pro social skills with adolescents. Consultation and collaboration with classroom teachers and parents are integrated into the pro social skills model. The inclusion of The American School Counselor Association (ASCA) National Model will provide applications to support the importance of pro social skills for adolescents in the school setting.

Chapter 9
Toy Guns in Play Therapy: An Examination of Play Therapists' Beliefs.. 140
Amanda Winburn, University of Mississippi, USA
Suzanne M. Dugger, University of Mississippi, USA
Jennifer Austin Main, University of Mississippi, USA

This chapter explores current trends related to play therapists' beliefs related to the decision of whether to include toy guns, as aggression-release toys, in the playroom. This issue is especially timely given the recent epidemic of mass shootings and heightened concerns about gun violence. The chapter presents the results of an original empirical study examining play therapists' views about gun violence and gun control; play therapist beliefs about aggressive play and toy guns; and play therapist practices with regard to toy selection and limit-setting. Recommendations for future research are offered.

Chapter 10
Expanding the Range of Puppetry in Expressive Play Therapy 158
Michele J. Ferro, Lesley University, USA
Julia Gentleman Byers, Lesley University, USA

This chapter focuses on expanding the therapeutic application of using puppetry as a communicative tool in the service of psychological growth and integration for children. A continuum of more than thirty descriptors of puppetry formats are presented that each hold specific value within therapeutic interventions. The types of materials used to construct the puppet and their cognitive, emotional, and sensory connections are explored, as is the impact of uniquely created productions versus commercial products. The authors also define the limitations and challenges of certain types of puppetry, which can evoke or incite different reactions within different stages and phases of psychosocial treatment. Examples of case vignettes are provided from a Child and Adolescent public services agency in an inner-city environment.

Chapter 11
Studying the Effectiveness of the Storytelling/Story-Acting (STSA) Play Intervention on Ugandan Preschoolers' Emergent Literacy, Oral Language, and Theory of Mind in Two Rural Ugandan Community Libraries... 182
Geoff Goodman, Long Island University, USA
Valeda F. Dent, Long Island University, USA

This study explored the impact of two rural village libraries in Uganda on preschool children's school readiness skills. Using two rural village libraries in Mpigi and Kabubbu as a backdrop, this study explored the effectiveness of a six-month play-based intervention known as the Storytelling/Story-Acting (STSA) activity. Children ages 3 to 5 at each library were randomly assigned to participate in either the STSA play intervention (n = 63) or a story-reading activity (n = 60) for one hour twice per week for six months. All children were administered school readiness skills measures before and after the six-month intervention. Caregivers were also administered an interview that assessed their educational level, quality of life, reading aloud to target child, social support, and total possessions. Children who participated in the STSA intervention had higher scores on the colors subtest of the emergent literacy measure than children who did not participate in this activity. Preschool children benefit from a story-reading activity with or without the STSA play intervention.

Chapter 12
Ethics in Play Therapy Consultation and Supervision.. 214
Jeffrey S. Ashby, Georgia State University, USA
Laura Wood, Georgia State University, USA
Sarah Kiperman, Georgia State University, USA

Ethics in play therapy consultation and supervision can be complex because of the "layered" nature of the relationships involved in each of these indirect services. In this chapter, we discuss the differential obligations the play therapy consultant or supervisor owes to the consulate/supervisee and the client. The ethical constructs of informed consent, competence, confidentiality, and dual relationships are discussed in relationship to the consultee/supervisee and the client. While the obligations are similar in these indirect services, there are also different obligations in each of these areas.

Chapter 13
Integrating Play Therapy and Mental Health Consultation 232
Krystal Vaughn, LSUHSC New Orleans, USA
Erin Dugan, LSUHSC New Orleans, USA

Many parents and teachers are often confounded when it comes to figuring out a child's presenting issues. Mental health consultants are able to note the frequency, proximity, duration and intensity of and in which the behavior(s) occur. These professionals are equipped with the tools, education, and experience and are able to gather information, observe, and assess the challenging behaviors or presenting issues in order to formulate and conceptualize a treatment plan for the child, their parent(s), and/or the school/center based setting. Additionally, mental health consultants may offer valuable feedback; increase of knowledge, skills and awareness; development of treatment plans; and implementation of the necessary interventions. This chapter seeks to provide professionals with the definitions, differences, structure, and implementation of a mental health consultation model.

Chapter 14
Multicultural Considerations in Play Therapy Caregiver Consultation.. 249
Kristy A. Brumfield, Immaculata University, USA
Celita J. Owens, Immaculata University, USA
Rheta LeAnne Steen, Loyala University New Orleans, USA
Renee M. Floer, Loyola University New Orleans, USA

The purpose of this chapter is to review the literature regarding parent consultation and to address special considerations when working across cultures and ethnicities. Understanding privacy expectations and how to meet the needs of families, without discouraging the caregivers or unintentionally breaking cultural guidelines, will be explored. This chapter is extremely important because mental health professionals must adhere to the diversity guidelines and ethical standards of practice in complex cases, with many involved caregivers at times. When consulting with caregivers from culturally diverse backgrounds, consultants need to consider the impact of culture on the caregiver, the child client, and on the consultation process.

Chapter 15
Consultation Strategies for Working with Professionals Supporting Foster Families 265
Kim Coggins, Austin Peay State University, USA
Kristie Opiola, UNC Charlotte, USA
Kara L. Carnes-Holt, University of Wyoming, USA

Children and families involved in the foster care system present with unique needs requiring support from diverse professionals. Because of the range of stakeholders involved with children and families in the foster care system, play therapists must become knowledgeable and skillful consultants and collaborators to best facilitate holistic wellness for these families. Through this chapter, the authors seek to provide play therapists with a strong foundation of knowledge and skills to draw upon when working with this population. First, readers are introduced to the mental health needs faced by foster care children and families. The authors then describe the diverse roles frequently fulfilled by play therapists as consultants and collaborators within various systems impacting children in foster care. Finally, a case study is included to provide a practical description of how play therapists can integrate a greater use of consultation, collaboration, and advocacy into their work to bet meet the needs of foster care children and families within their care.

Chapter 16
Teachers Can Play Too: Teacher-Child Relationships, Social-Emotional Development, and Academic Engagement 288
Szu-Yu Chen, Central Michigan University, USA
Natalya A. Lindo, University of North Texas, USA

Positive teacher-child relationships are key factors for children's social-emotional development and academic success in schools. Teachers' ability to provide children with emotional support and understand children's unique needs may improve challenging behaviors in the classroom. Play-based teacher intervention training models provide teachers opportunities to become therapeutic agents and learn how to use humanistic play therapy skills and language to communicate with children and respond to their unique needs. In this chapter, the authors introduce four play-based teacher intervention training models: Kinder Training, Child-Teacher Relationship Training, Relationship Enhancement for Learner and Teacher, and Teacher-Child Relationship Building. The authors also illustrate these models' goals, training structure, research support for their effectiveness with teacher-child relationships, children's behavioral issues, academic engagement, and teachers' classroom management skills.

Chapter 17
Play and Speech Therapy in Schools: Toward a Model of Interprofessional Collaborative Practice. 314
Suzan E. Weishof, International School of Hamburg, Germany

Research over the past eight decades has demonstrated strong correlations between the development of play and the development of language in young children. Play and speech therapists share a common child-centered, play-based approach to therapeutic interventions. The growing trend of service delivery within the school setting, along with professional ethical requirements, has led to the necessity of play therapists, speech therapists, teachers, and parents to work collaboratively in promoting holistic, comprehensive intervention plans that serve children's best interests. Based on the healthcare field's model of interprofessional collaborative practice, the purpose of this chapter is to define areas of common practice among speech and play therapists and to propose a model of interprofessional collaborative practice within a school-based context.

Chapter 18
The Play Therapist in the Courtroom: Preparing Yourself and Your Client for Court 345
Jeffrey M. Sullivan, Sam Houston State University, USA
Sinem Akay, Sam Houston State University, USA

This chapter addresses what is often the most anxiety inducing experience most play therapists will encounter in their professional career: appearing in court. Play therapists who work with cases of child abuse face a higher chance of appearing in court on behalf of their child client. The purpose this chapter is to detail some ways play therapists can best prepare for the court process, which often begins at the moment the client relationship is established, how to prepare for court once a subpoena is received, and best practices for testifying in court on behalf of the child client. Finally, this chapter discusses the effects of court on the child and how to best help children recover from courtroom experiences.

Compilation of References 367

About the Contributors 424

Index 433

Foreword

It was an honor to be asked to write the foreword for *Emerging Research in Play Therapy, Child Counseling, and Consultation.* For me, this was exciting, because the text covers areas that are near and dear to me: play therapy research, practice, and application. It is unique when compared with other play therapy primers, because it informs readers about the consultative process and thoroughly demonstrates this process, the settings we may use it in, and conceptualizes the impact of culture on consultation. It is also unique in the fact that it does not simply present play therapy theory and techniques. Instead it opens the door for the use of play therapy, as a tool in consultation, with teachers, allied health professionals, special populations, and those we might engage with in the legal system.

After having been a pharmacist for many years, it was not easy to find my place in the world of play therapy. Trying to blend the training of a medical model with a wellness model led to a dichotomous view of individuals rather than one of integration. It was through neuroscience research that integration occurred. My brain understood the neuroscience and play therapy components and I could tell and teach others how these components relate and support each other. In 2002, I began presenting at conferences about working with medicated children in play therapy. At this time, few states required mental health practitioners to know anything about psychopharmacology; now many require it as a course during graduate school. The attendees of these sessions said I made complex concepts easily digestible.

I had found my place in the world of play therapy. From this position, I could teach others about how to utilize play therapy, how to allow neuroscience to inform their practice, and how to blend the two parts to benefit children not only in the playroom but also when consulting with all of the other players within the systems of children. Although over the years the focus of my presentations and writings have evolved, my foundation remains clearly grounded in the fact that I understand the world and what occurs in play therapy by viewing it through a neuroscience lens. Therefore, if I can remain focused on my foundation, I can help other play therapists find their foundation, learn to focus it to help children, and to begin to harness this foundation to help those in a child's system to understand children and the circumstances that impact their existence, quality of life, and future.

As a play therapist and educator, I am encouraged because of the renewed focus on the value of play. After having utilized play therapy for more than 15 years, I am amazed when I read a news article or see a television report that focuses on the importance of play. This amazement comes from a place of "well duh", because as play therapist we know this. The question, "Why didn't others know this as well", comes to mind. For more than 100 years, theorists and developmental therapists have described for us, in research and books, that play is purposeful and meaningful; it is not simply a random act of fun. For so many, play is seen as a break from organized, constructive work. They see play as a reward for focused worked or good behavior. From this viewpoint, play is often eliminated when a child has not completed his or her work or when he or she has misbehaved. Play is negotiated. It is omitted when a task is deemed as more important. However, when it is minimized children suffer and those around them feel the repercussion. Classroom and home behaviors escalate and everyone in the system becomes stressed.

As play therapists, we differ from much of the world in that we see play as the work. We have defended our method of working with children for decades; while, much of the world around us focused on manuals and protocols. These competing viewpoints led to many debates, and at times, placed a wall between play therapists and other mental health practitioners. We assert that what we do in a playroom is not neat and cannot be easily reproduced in a scripted fashion. We operate from the philosophy that what occurs within a playroom needs to transpire in order for a child to heal.

Often our greatest challenge is to help others see the value of play and the need for play therapy. Texts like *Emerging Research in Play Therapy, Child Counseling, and Consultation* help us focus our foundation, explain our process, and support and encourage those within the systems of children to be a part of change rather than a hindrance to growth. We utilize our therapeutic skills, through consultation, to convey what we know about play therapy research, practice, and application. Through consultation and collaboration we try to add to a child's supportive army and provide them with allies outside the playroom.

When we are consulting with parents, teachers, administrators, other therapists, allied health professionals, and judges and attorneys, we know that most want to understand why something is the way it is, and that as humans, we try to make sense of the unknown. We peak the interest of our audience by taking them to a place of remembrance; we remind them that they once played, and that through it, they learned, experienced joy, and found release. In a sense, we have brought them to a place of universality, because as they reflect hope emerges. Now, in a receptive place, we begin to explain why children behave the way they do as a result of adversity. We utilize our knowledge of play therapy theory, our experience derived from collaborative practice, and our knowledge about how the brain develops under normal circumstances, and then, contrast it with development in the light of adverse experiences. We support our descriptions and definitions with the research of Perry, Schore, Siegel, van der Kolk, Zeanah, and countless others. Finally, we enumerate the many benefits of play and play therapy and confidently support this with our knowledge of neuroscience applications in play therapy. Our explanation is complete covering, cognitions, emotions, and behaviors. As a result, we have broken down the walls of skepticism, engaged our audience with facts about the brain, and conveyed our message. We have utilized everyone's fascination with the brain to win over our audience to become allies for our clients. Our team, the child's team, and play therapy has grown.

As a community of practitioners, from various branches of mental health, play therapists were among the first to acknowledge the relationship between the brain and play. In 1994, when neuroscience applications in mental health were in their infancy, in an *International Journal of Play Therapy* (IJPT) article, Kaufman (1994) initialed our interest about play and the developing brain. Since then, neuroscience research has been a frequent component of *IJPT* articles.

To date, few play therapy texts devote more than a single chapter to consultation and collaboration. However, *Emerging Research in Play Therapy, Child Counseling, and Consultation* changes this routine and extends it beyond caregivers and teachers to allied health professionals and those within the legal system.

Another unique facet of this text is it coverage of neuroscience applications in play therapy. Much of what we read about neuroscience applications in play therapy is an attempt to explain what we do as play therapist and that it is beneficial. In many ways, neuroscience has helped us justify the need for play and play therapy. It becomes a common ground that unites practitioners of different perspectives, modalities, and theories. Neuroscience acts as the bait and the hook: luring disbelieves in and capturing their attention. We utilize our neuroscience knowledge to help the non-play therapy world understand the world of children, how their development is altered by adverse experiences, and how play therapy helps them overcome adversity. These text's neuroscience chapters add to our arsenal of neuroscience applications in play therapy. Whether advancing theory, describing the impact of trauma on the brain, explaining a therapeutic modality, or exploring the safety of the playroom, the authors provide well-developed, reliable, and realistic evidence to support the use of play therapy. The authors and this text also set a new standard for play therapy texts that will be difficult to match.

Finally, within this text, readers will explore chapters that describe the pre-therapy process for children with Autism, debate the inclusion of toy guns in the playroom, deepen our knowledge and use of puppets, and demonstrate the use of play therapy with non-Western populations. Strategically placed in the text are theoretical chapters that support our collaborative practices. These chapters underpin our play therapy practice, and, as with other chapters, provide a blueprint.

I encourage readers to embrace *Emerging Research in Play Therapy, Child Counseling, and Consultation*, because I believe it will support our practice of play therapy, the clients we serve within the playroom, and all of those, which exist outside the playroom, that are tied to our clients.

Edward F. Hudspeth
Southern New Hampshire University, USA

REFERENCES

Kaufman, B. A. (1994). Day by day: Playing and learning. *International Journal of Play Therapy*, *3*(1), 11–21. doi:10.1037/h0089401

Preface

When I first had the idea for this book, I was really hoping to publish an edited book on just the consultation requirement in play therapy. I thought it would be amazing to focus the talent of our authors and researchers in understanding this aspect of our job, as play therapists and child counselors, that gets too little attention in the field: consultation.

What is consultation? Consultation is the work that we do outside of the playroom: when we seek professional supervision and case consultation; when we meet with caregivers and teachers; or call an allied health professional, pediatrician, or other professional working with the child whom we are seeing in play therapy and child counseling.

But, as I considered the book I realized, leaving out the important research, both conceptual and empirical, in play therapy would also deduce the reality of the consultation process. These factors, the work we do inside and outside of the play room, work in concert for the seasoned play therapist to create the best standard of care and continuity available to the child client, their caregivers, and family.

So, the purpose of this book is to consider that play therapy is an eco-systemic form of therapy, and integrating these topics is essential in modern day play therapy conceptualization. In saying that it is eco-systemic, I am not speaking of the actual relationship or interventions. I am talking about the reality of the complexity of working with children and their families. A play therapist is responsible for being competent to work with a variety of populations and to engage in consultive supervision, as is any counselor or therapist working with any individual clients. But, for play therapists, working with children, we are responsible for working with a variety of caregivers and professionals who are often connected to the child in meaningful ways.

Brofenbrenner (1979) first developed the concept of ecological systems theory as a means for understanding children developmentally, but within the context of their multi-systemic experience. The child is at the center (developmental age, gender identification, etc.); he or she is immediately surrounded by the *microsystem* (family/ caregivers, school church, friends); then the next layer surrounding the child is the *mesosystem* (the interconnections between microsystems like caregivers and teachers); then the *exosystem* (social services, neighbors, media, politics); and finally the *macro system* (culture and ideology).

The play therapist must attempt to join the child in their inner circle, by meeting the child both developmentally and with awareness of the relationships and systems impacting the child. Our role is to reach out to these caregivers and other professionals, to be the voice, to understand the services, to collaborate, to ensure there is not over duplication, and create supportive systems around the child. When working with caregivers, we need to engage them and respect their need for support and the diversity that they bring to the table too. As a child centered play therapist, I focus on my role in recognizing this multi-systemic reality and engaging within it, on behalf of the child, but my relationship with the child in the room follows child centered tenets. O'Conner (2015), however has outlined an entire play therapy theory based on the eco-systemic concept.

In this spirit, I have invited authors to write about emerging research in the field of play therapy, child counseling, and consultation. By including the consultative, I feel this book takes a more holistic perspective of the reality of play therapist's needs in the play therapy research and available literature. These are the practical implications, of being informed by the literature, as it pertains to the reality of play therapy. In addition, the book has a strong emphasis on the neurobiological implications in play therapy, and there are several chapters on specific theory and specific populations, including both empirical and conceptual studies that increase the evidence for best practice.

The target audience for this book includes play therapists, play therapy educators, students, and mental health providers of children and families.

Below, there are detailed short descriptions of each chapter. Here, I will outline the order and layout of the book. The opening chapter discusses the status of play therapy research. This chapter is very beneficial for play therapists who need to validate play therapy to individuals in the child's mesosystem, and exosystem. The next four chapters are from authors discussing the neurobiological interface with play therapy. I find it fascinating that the classic play therapy tenets, taught for decades, are being evidenced by research in neurobiology. The following five chapters are a combination of theory, research, empirical studies, and special populations.

The second half of the book is comprised of the chapters dedicated to consultation. The consultation portion of the book starts with a chapter outlining the ethics in play therapy supervision and consultation. Following the ethical exploration, there is a chapter on mental health consultation, including caregivers, and school settings. The following is a chapter on multicultural caregiver consultation. The final four chapters are focused on foster families, working with allied health professionals, teachers, and finally, preparing play therapists for court.

Here is a description of each chapter, outlining the importance for this book.

CHAPTER DESCRIPTIONS

The Status of Play Therapy Research

In this chapter, the authors present up to date and recent play therapy research, in particular, randomized control group studies. In this chapter, the authors promote the evidence based treatment of children using play therapy. It is important to note that the authors, in particular, are hoping to help practitioners promote play therapy to caregivers, school teachers, and other adults and professionals who interact with the children who may receive play therapy. There are two very helpful tables included in the chapter: Randomized Control Group Experimental Studies & another one outlining Studies by Target Outcome Variables. This chapter is a great resource for play therapists, in practice, consultation, and for play therapy promotion.

The Impact of Trauma on Brain Development: An Neurodevelopmentally Appropriate Model for Play Therapists

In this chapter, the authors describe the scope of trauma with children and outline a model for play therapists to understand children neurodevelopmentally, including: the impact of neurodevelopment stages & brain development; appropriate treatment strategies; and educational implications in the classroom. This chapter is exceptionally helpful in that play therapists have an opportunity to understand more about trauma as well as what that means, or how to apply practical adaptations in evidence based practice for trauma, in both the play room and classroom.

Theraplay: The Evidence for Trauma-Focused Treatment for Children and Families

In this chapter, the authors focus on evidence based use of Theraplay as an intervention for children who have experienced trauma. The authors argue that Theraplay has neural relevance in remediation of attachment disruptions. This chapter is especially important because of the focus on trauma and evidence based practice and expansion of understanding of attachment and parent-child psychotherapy, to include a neurobiological perspective. The authors also include a brief history of Theraplay and the theoretical and conceptual framework.

Integrating Interpersonal Neurobiology Into Play Therapy Process: Advancing Adlerian Play Therapy

In this chapter, the authors argue that Interpersonal Neurobiology (IPNB) and Adlerian Play Therapy are similarly conceptualized, therefore, understanding the IPNB of children will facilitate a neurobiological evidence based adlerian play therapy practice. In this chapter, basic tenets of Adlerian Play Therapy are explored as well as the primary tenets of IPNB. Practical implications are explored, including several integration strategies for play therapists that supports interpersonal neurobiology while increasing social interest.

The Safe Space: An Examination of the Neurobiological Benefits of Play Therapy With Traumatized Children

In this chapter, the authors discuss the neurobiological impact of trauma on children. They illustrate the neurobiological benefit in using client centered play based interventions and the benefit of play therapy on neural integration, memory assimilation, and the limbic system.

Adlerian Play Therapy: Practice and Research

In this chapter, the authors outline multiple studies where the findings indicate the efficacy of sustained change in children after participation gin Adlerian Play Therapy. Researchers in all of the studies examined used the Adlerian Play Therapy Treatment Manual procedures. All of the studies examined occurred between 2014 and the present. Additionally, the authors review some of the tenets of Adlerian Play Therapy tenets and practice.

Pre-Therapy in Child Centered Play Therapy: A Model for Treating Children With Autism

The authors outline a model for adapting Child Centered Play Therapy for children with Autism and other developmental disorders, using pre therapy. CCPT is hypothesized to facilitate functional communication and imitation and play in children with neurodevelopment disabilities. Three phases of pre-therapy are outlined, including therapeutic responses. The history of person centered therapy and child centered play therapy is included.

A Cognitive-Behavioral Play Therapy (CBPT) Approach for Adolescents' Pro-Social Skill Development in the School Setting

Using peer group orientation, the authors outline how to create a cognitive behavioral play therapy social skills group with adolescents in schools. The benefits of group therapy for adolescents, as well as applying play based interventions to develop pro-social skills in schools, is explored. Several CBPT Techniques for application are also explored and an eight week case study is included to exemplify the material. Self esteem is found to increase which furthers social and academic success in the school setting.

Toy Guns in Play Therapy: An Examination of Play Therapists' Beliefs

An empirical study outlining play therapists believes about the use of guns as an aggressive release toy in standard playrooms for play therapy. Four research questions were explored around play therapists beliefs regarding guns in the play room, gun violence, comfort with guns, and limit setting around toy guns. Findings indicate that play therapists have a variety of beliefs about guns and gun violence, however, most play therapists believe that guns and aggressive release toys are essential toys in play therapy.

Expanding the Range of Puppetry in Expressive Play Therapy

Case study design with a participant researcher conducting this pilot study. Vignettes are explored with a variety of child clients and adolescent clients. Field notes, artifacts, and session notes were analyzed in a four consecutive sessions. The purpose of the study is to highlight the use of puppetry as a communication tool in child and adolescent counseling an play therapy. The types of puppets, including homemade and commercial are thoroughly explored, as well.

Studying the Effectiveness of the Storytelling/Story-Acting (STSA) Play Intervention in Two Rural Ugandan Community Libraries: Effects on Ugandan Preschoolers' Emergent Literacy, Oral Language, and Theory of Mind

This empirical and Fullbright funded study of Uganda school children explored the effectiveness of using a play based intervention known as Story Telling/Story Acting (STSA). Children were randomly assigned to participate in the STSA intervention or a story reading activity for one hour, twice per week, for six months. Although this chapter is not specifically about play therapy or child counseling, I felt it was important to include as it discusses diversity, play based interventions for school readiness, and the caregiver's role. In the findings, the caregiver role is very important.

Ethics in Play Therapy Consultation and Supervision

The authors explore the nature of the play therapist in the consultant and supervision relationships, and supervisor responsibilities from an ethical perspective. Some of the topics include informed consent, competency exploration, confidentiality and dual relationships. This informative chapter is essential in understanding the complex variables and responsibilities evident in the supervisor and supervisee roles and responsibilities from an ethical and legal perspective.

Integrating Play Therapy and Mental Health Consultation

This chapter is unique in that the authors outline how the play therapist can act as a mental health and behavior consultant in the home and the school in order to help develop treatment plans and behavior plans for practice, home, and in the school setting. Step by step strategies are explained, including assessment strategies and using a strengths based perspective. Finally, challenges in consultation, including caregiver consultation and ethical considerations are explored.

Multicultural Considerations in Play Therapy Caregiver Consultation

In this chapter, the authors give up to date information regarding the literature, research, and practice of working with diverse clients in play therapy caregiver consultation. Ethical competency requirements are reviewed. Additionally, a thorough literature review is used to understand the special considerations necessary for the culturally competent play therapist and child counselor. Practical implications, including guidelines are included at the end of the chapter.

Consultation Strategies for Working With Professionals Supporting Foster Families

This chapter is very informative, including mental health needs of foster care children and their families, the involvement of advocates and the court system, roles of varying persons and systems, and multiple definitions in order to understand the complex nature of the foster care system and the courts. Additionally, play therapists and child counselors are given hands on practical application strategies for collaborative practice of holistic wellness. The chapter finalizes with an exemplary case study to facilitate understanding.

Teachers Can Play Too: Teacher-Child Relationships, Social-Emotional Development, and Academic Engagement

In this chapter, the authors introduce four play-based teacher intervention training models: Kinder Training, Child-Teacher Relationship Training, Relationship Enhancement for Learner and Teacher, and Teacher-Child Relationship Building. The authors also illustrate these models' goals, training structure, research support for their effectiveness with teacher-child relationships, children's behavioral issues, academic engagement, and teachers' classroom management skills.

Play and Speech Therapy in Schools: Toward a Model of Interprofessional Collaborative Practice

Based on the healthcare field's model of interprofessional collaborative practice, the purpose of this chapter is to define areas of common practice among speech and play therapists and to propose a model of interprofessional collaborative practice within a school-based context. Because the play therapist and the speech therapist share philosophical foundations in child centered approaches, and the importance and value of play in speech development is well researched, this chapter is extremely relevant in context of todays scholastic interventions for primary services.

The Play Therapist in the Courtroom: Preparing Yourself and Your Client for Court

Play therapists often work with children with a history of abuse which means play therapist are extremely likely to receive a subpoena for notes or testimony. This chapter outlines how to prepare for court, even from the first client session, and best practices when testifying in court. The impact of the court experience on the child is also explored as well as how to help children and families recover after court.

In conclusion, I am extremely excited about the impact of this book. I believe that the research and practical implication of the research are eminently important for play therapists. Indeed, I believe that this is the first edited book that takes into account holistic and eco-systemic nature of play therapy in inviting author to also speak about consultation from a multi-systemic perspective. I hope that this book will be helpful to practitioners, educators, academics, and students alike, due to this feature.

Thank you for buying the book. I hope you enjoy it.

Sincerely,

Rheta LeAnne Steen
Loyola University New Orleans, USA

REFERENCES

Brofenbrenner, U. (1979). *The ecology of human development: Experiments by nature and design.* Cambridge, MA: Harvard University Press.

O'Conner, K. (2015). Eco-systemic play therapy. In C. Schaefer & L. Braverman (Eds.), *Handbook of play therapy*. New York, NY: Wiley & Sons. doi:10.1002/9781119140467.ch9

Acknowledgment

When I first had the idea for this book, I was still a junior faculty, working for tenure, and thrusted unexpectedly into an overwhelming administrative position (Department Chair). I mapped out my plan and began contacting potential authors. I did not realize that it would be several years before I would be able to actually start the project and follow through with my idea. I was too overwhelmed with pregnancies, tenure development, and administrative requirements to fulfill my book project. Luckily, I was able to obtain tenure, retire from the chair position, and attain a sabbatical. So, to start with, I would really like to thank the authors who I invited when I first mapped out the idea and who were still willing to contribute to the book when I was able to finally find the time, years later to work on it. In particular, I would like to thank Sue Bratton, Kara Holt, Suzan Weishoff, Kristy Brumfield and Jeff Ashby. Thank you again for believing in me and my idea and being willing to participate after a long delay between the initial request, and follow through! I would also like to thank all of the contributing authors who came to be involved with this book. I appreciate your professionalism and attentiveness in working with a first time book editor.

I would like to thank IGI Global for accepting my book proposal and offering me a platform to develop the book and for recognizing the importance of this book. I also appreciate the patience of my publisher liaison, Courtney Tychinski, Assisting Managing Editor-Book Developer. You are a true gem and I appreciate your guidance and assistance.

I would like to acknowledge the Editorial Advisory Board, who tirelessly reviewed chapter proposals and chapters, gave expansive feedback, and spent many hours reading, thinking about, writing commentary, and basically just caring about this project. I could not have completed this project without the EAB. Your support, assistance, feedback, engagement, help, and patience is so appreciated and I am in awe of you for this level of service to the fields of play therapy and mental health, in general. You are true academics! Specifically, Franc Hudspeth, Rebecca Farrell, Adrianne Frischhertz, Kelly Camelford, Tom Foster, & Kristi Perryman, I appreciate you for being involved with this book and project.

To my colleagues at Loyola University New Orleans, I appreciate your being patient when I missed a few meetings, or forgot about the new student interviews. I was pretty busy with the final details and teaching classes after my sabbatical finished and this project was still in full swing. I am grateful that you were able to fill in for any gaps or weaknesses in the system that I might have created. THANK YOU! Tom Foster, John Dewell, Kevin Foose, Christine Ebrahim, and our amazing staff, Dianna Whitfield & Stephanie Robinson.

Acknowledgment

I would like to thank the Louisiana Association for Play Therapy Board and Membership! You have been very supportive of my growth and leadership.

Last, but definitely not least, I would like to thank my friends and family. For starters, my two beautiful daughters, Delilah & Anikah for inspiring me to be the best person I can be every single day. You are both amazing, intelligent, humorous, individual, & strong young women. I am in awe of you every day. I dedicated this book to you because I wanted to be play therapist because of you, before you were even conceived! I wanted to be the best mommy I could be and I loved you, already. Today, I love you more than you can possibly imagine. To my family, thank you for being supportive of me. For being a friend, and for hearing me out and for loving me (Steve Steen, Julie Steen, Paulette Steen, and in memoriam, my father, Joe Steen).

For my friends, you are the, "family that I choose" (Tiffany Vollmer), and I love you very much! You, my friends, have been loyal, caring, and supportive of me for many, many years. I cannot begin to name everyone here, but to name a few, Michael & Lisa Greene, Tiffany & Johnny Woodstock, Rachel & Shoel Ross, Crae & Judy Hillman, Emilie Mitchell, James Ewing, David Kozak, Shelly Sexton, Jeanne Charlebois, Barbara Wickland, Gene Luster, Danny & Maria Teresa Glick, Chad & Jennifer Shields, Josh & Jolene Nipper, Kimberly King, and my entire GONZO GANZA family.

Chapter 1
Status of Play Therapy Research

Sue C. Bratton
University of North Texas, USA

Alyssa Swan
University of North Texas, USA

ABSTRACT

With today's focus on evidence-based treatment (EBT) for children, play therapists are ethically responsible to identify and deliver effective interventions as well as synthesize the considerable body of play therapy research to support their practice and to advocate for play therapy as an evidence-base practice. Play therapists' ability to articulate research findings is particularly important as they consult with the adults in children's lives who make decisions regarding children's wellbeing including parents, teachers, school administrators and other professionals. This chapter aims to present an up-to-date comprehensive review and synthesis of contemporary play therapy research with a focus on studies employing randomized control group designs in order to provide play therapy practitioners with a guide to understanding and utilizing the substantial research base for play therapy.

STATUS OF PLAY THERAPY RESEARCH

With an increased focus on evidence-based treatment (EBT) for children, play therapists are ethically bound to identify and deliver appropriate and effective interventions. In addition, play therapists are charged with the responsibility of understanding and using the considerable body of play therapy research to support their practice and to advocate for play therapy as an evidence-base treatment for childhood disorders that interfere with children's day to day functioning. Play therapists' ability to articulate research findings is particularly important as they consult with the adults in children's lives who make decisions regarding children's wellbeing including parents, teachers, school administrators and other professionals.

National focus on the shortage of adequate mental health services for children (Center for Disease Control, CDC, 2013; Mental Health America, MHA, 2013; President's New Freedom Commission on Mental Health, 2003; U.S. Public Health Service, 2000), along with the evidence-based movement has heightened attention on disseminating information about EBT's for treating childhood mental health disorders and resulted in several texts (Baggerly, Ray, & Bratton, 2010; Chorpita, et al., 2011; Reddy,

DOI: 10.4018/978-1-5225-2224-9.ch001

Files-Hall, & Schaefer, 2016; Russ & Niec, 2011; Silverman & Hinshaw, 2008; Weisz & Kazdin, 2010) and websites (California Evidence Based Clearinghouse, CEBC, 2016; evidencebasedchildtherapy.com, 2015; Society of Clinical Child and Adolescent Psychology, SCCAP, 2016; National Center for Education and Evaluation, NCEE, 2016; SAMHSA National Registry of Evidence-Based Programs and Practices, NREPP, 2016) aiming to guide professionals to provide child interventions with evidentiary support. Although, with the exception of Baggerly et al. (2010) and evidencebasedchildtherapy.com (2015), these sources have paid little attention to play therapy interventions for children despite decades of research that supports the evidence base for play therapy.

Despite increased advocacy and research foci on providing EBT's for children over the past two decades, the number of children who go untreated continued to increase over this millennium (CDC, 2013; MHA, 2013; NCCP, 2014; U.S. Census Bureau, 2015). One possible explanation is the lack of currently recognized EBT's that are responsive to the developmental needs of children (Weisz & Kazdin, 2010; Bratton, 2015). Play therapy is widely recognized as a developmentally responsive mental health intervention for children (Landreth, 2012; Schaefer, 2011), yet continually criticized for lack of empirical support (Phillips, 2009; Russ & Niec, 2011). Our goal for this chapter is to respond to this misperception by presenting a comprehensive review of the evidence base for play therapy. Through synthesis of contemporary meta-analytic and systematic reviews and summaries of individual play therapy outcome studies meeting criteria for methodological rigor and treatment protocol, this chapter provides play therapy practitioners with a guide to understanding and utilizing the substantial research base for play therapy.

Contemporary Meta-Analytic and Systematic Reviews

Responding to previous lack of recognition of play therapy as an EBT, contemporary play therapy researchers have developed and disseminated a) comprehensive systematic reviews of outcome research (Bratton, 2010; Bratton, 2015; Bratton, Landreth, & Lin, 2010; Bratton & Ray, 2000; Landreth, 2012; Landreth & Bratton, 2006; Ray, 2011; Ray & Bratton, 2010; Ray & Bratton, 2015; Ray & McCullough, 2015), b) meta-analyses of controlled research studies (Bratton et al., 2005; LeBlanc & Ritchie, 2001; Lin & Bratton, 2015; Ray, Armstrong, Balkin, & Jayne, 2015), and c) online searchable play therapy research database (evidencebasedchildtherapy.com).

Meta-analyses and systematic reviews of controlled outcome studies are widely recognized as two of the most robust methods of evidentiary support for identifying evidence-based practices (Rubin, 2008). Researchers have conducted four meta-analytic reviews of play therapy in the 21st century. Bratton et al. (2005) conducted the largest meta-analysis of play therapy research to date which included a total of 93 controlled outcome studies spanning five decades. Play therapy, including filial therapy, demonstrated a large overall treatment effect (.80). Bratton and colleagues reported moderate to large treatment effects across presenting issue and target outcomes. LeBlanc and Ritchie (2001) reviewed 42 outcome studies from the same time period as Bratton et al. and found a moderate treatment effect (.66) for play therapy including filial therapy. Both Bratton et al. (2005) and LeBlanc and Ritchie (2001) identified parental involvement and duration of treatment as significant factors impacting children's treatment outcomes. Bratton et al. (2005) further pointed out that early studies in the field of play therapy were limited by lack of scientific rigor and recommended that contemporary play therapy researchers adhere to stringent research designs, sound methodology, and reporting guidelines.

Additionally, two meta-analyses (Lin & Bratton, 2015; Ray et al., 2015) were recently published focusing exclusively on the efficacy of child-centered play therapy (CCPT) approaches. Utilizing rigorous hierarchical liner modeling (HLM) methods, Lin and Bratton (2015) investigated the overall treatment effect of CCPT approaches including child-parent relationship therapy (CPRT)/filial therapy from a total of 52 controlled outcome studies published between 1995 and 2010. Findings demonstrated a statistically significant overall effect size of .47, indicating a moderate treatment (Lipsey & Wilson, 2001) effect for CCPT intervention. Using random effect model methodology, Ray et al. (2015) conducted a meta-analysis on the efficacy of CCPT conducted in elementary schools and included a total of 23 controlled outcome studies from 1975 to 2011. Results demonstrated a statistically significant effect sizes for outcome variables, including externalizing problems (d = 0.34), internalizing problems (d =0.21), total problems (d = 0.34), self-efficacy (d = 0.29), and academic progress (d = 0.36).

In effort to further explore the empirical support for play therapy, researchers have conducted several comprehensive systematic reviews. Due to space limitations, we include reviews published since 2010. Bratton (2010) reviewed 51 school-based play therapy intervention outcome studies published 1990 to 2009 conducted by mental health professionals (n = 30) or specially trained and supervised paraprofessionals (n = 21) and concluded that school-based play therapy demonstrated beneficial effects for a range of childhood disorders. Bratton reported that 75% of the investigations reviewed were conducted since 2000 which indicated a 100% increase compared to the previous 5 decades of research published on school-based play therapy. Ray and Bratton (2010) reviewed 25 experimental and quasi-experimental studies published 2000 to 2009 investigating impact of play therapy conducted by a mental health professional. Compared to their previous review of six decades of play therapy research (Bratton & Ray, 2000), Ray and Bratton (2010) concluded that methodological rigor and research productivity made considerable increases during the 21st century. Bratton (2015) conducted a systematic review, limited to randomized controlled trials (RCTs) in play therapy, and found 24 RCTs published since 2000 that met stringent inclusion criteria. Bratton offered a thorough review of strengths and limitations of the research base for play therapy and concluded that play therapy had strong evidentiary support to condone its use as an effective mental health intervention for children.

In 2015, Ray & McCullough in association with Association for Play Therapy (APT) published an evidence-based practice statement for play therapy, providing a comprehensive review of play therapy research and categorizing play therapy research into an evidentiary hierarchy pyramid from most credible research design (meta-analyses and systematic reviews) to least credible research design (case reports). Ray and McCullough reviewed 42 outcome studies published between 2000 and 2015, of which 21 were randomly controlled trials, 5 were quasi-experimental studies, 5 were single-case designs, and 11 were repeated measures single group designs.

The most comprehensive review of contemporary play therapy outcome research studies to date is accessible from an online data base at evidencebasedchildtherapy.com. The data base includes studies published 1995 to present and was created by Bratton, Dafoe, Swan, Opiola, McClintock, and Barcenas (2015) in association with the Center for Play Therapy (CPT) at the University of North Texas to provide a continually up-to-date means of accessing and disseminating the evidentiary support for play therapy as well as to serve as an international clearinghouse for play therapy research. As of this writing, the database includes 96 published studies, representing a total of 3,937 child participants. Of which, 73 studies were conducted by U.S. researchers and 23 studies were produced by researchers outside of the U.S. Publication patterns reveal a considerable increase in publications from 33 outcome research studies published 1995 to 2005 to 63 outcome studies published since 2006. The search and sort features allows viewers to examine the effects of play therapy by theoretical model, setting, research design, presenting issue/outcome variable, publication year, and author. To date, one-half of the included studies employed the gold standard in research methodology, randomized controlled group design (n = 48), with remainder of outcome studies investigating play therapy's effects using non-randomized controlled designs (n = 20), repeated measures single group designs (n = 19), and single case experimental designs (n = 9). Majority of studies are research investigations of the efficacy of CCPT (n = 44) and CPRT (n = 31), which is a CCPT model in which CPRT-trained therapists instruct and directly supervise parent and other significant caregivers, e.g. teachers and mentors in CCPT principles and skills. Other theoretical models represented include Adlerian play therapy (n = 3), cognitive behavioral play therapy (n = 3), sandtray play therapy (n = 3), activity play therapy (n = 4), theraplay (n = 3), gestalt play therapy (n = 2), and other/eclectic play therapy approaches (n = 3). A database sort by outcome variable reveals studies investigating play therapy's effectiveness on global behavior problems (n = 45 studies), externalizing problems (n = 39), internalizing problems (n = 31), caregiver-child relationship (n = 31), socio-emotional functioning (n = 16), self-concept (n = 12), trauma/attachment (n = 9), academic/language (n = 6), and development (n = 4).

Four additional reviews were conducted, narrowing systematic literature search to focus on specific theoretical models of play therapy. Landreth (2012) and Ray (2011) provided comprehensive research reviews of published and unpublished studies in their respective texts focused exclusively on CCPT approaches, independently concluding that CCPT research demonstrates sound evidence for its effectiveness with a variety of childhood disorders and presenting concerns. Landreth (2012) included 53 CCPT and CPRT studies 1995 to 2010 and Ray (2011) included 62 CCPT studies 1947 to 2010. Bratton et al. (2010) focused on CPRT, a filial play therapy intervention, in a comprehensive literature review of 32 controlled outcome studies published from 1995 to 2009. According to the APA standard for EBT's (Silverman & Hinshaw, 2008), Bratton et al. (2010) concluded that CPRT met criteria to be recognized in the "promising" or "probably efficacious" ranking categories as an EBT for childhood disorders. More recently, Ray and Bratton (2015) conducted a systematic review of 13 school-based CCPT studies that met stringent criteria for experimental research design and concluded that CCPT resulted in positive outcomes for academic achievement, disruptive behaviors including aggression and ADHD, internalizing behavior problems, speech, and functional impairment across diverse populations of children.

Several conclusions can be made from the results of these meta-analyses and systematic reviews regarding the research base and efficacy of play therapy. Research findings support play therapy as a developmentally responsive and viable intervention for a range of childhood disorders in real-world settings, particularly in schools. Play therapy demonstrates beneficial effects on childhood outcomes in relatively few number of sessions (10-13 sessions on average). Involving caregivers in children's play therapy treatment produces stronger outcomes, i.e., filial therapy/CPRT methodology. Authors reported notable improvements to contemporary play therapy research methods including larger sample sizes, manualized treatment protocols and procedures to ensure treatment fidelity, standardized assessments of child outcomes, and randomization to treatment groups. Despite communicating encouragement in the advancement in quality and quantity of play therapy research, authors unanimously called for the advancement of play therapy research by employing more stringent research methods and increasing productivity in order to elevate the credibility and dissemination of play therapy research.

Individual Outcome Studies

For the purpose of reporting on the current status of play therapy research, we conducted a comprehensive online and offline review of controlled outcome research studies published since 2000 to identify studies that demonstrated methodological rigor. Randomized controlled trials (RCT's) are typically referred to as the "gold standard" research design to determine treatment efficacy (Nezu & Nezu, 2008). Thus, in effort to conduct a rigorous systematic review of the play therapy literature, we decided to only review studies that used random assignment of participants to treatment groups. Inclusion criteria which further refined our search included: a) intervention was identified as play therapy, b) participants were children between the ages of 2 and 12; c) studies were published since 2000; d) studies were conducted by researchers in the United States; e) studies were published in English in a peer-reviewed journal or book; f) studies reported child outcome variables and used standardized assessments; g) studies provided descriptive information about the play therapy intervention and participants, and as noted previously, h) intervention used a randomized, control group design. Although studies conducted by non-U.S. research teams were excluded for the purpose of this review, there is a growing body of play therapy research being conducted internationally.

Studies coded as using randomized group assignment included block and stratified randomization to control for extraneous variables such as school or location in the case of multiple research sites, classroom environment, and to accommodate participants' schedules. The primary reasons for excluding studies from the final review was lack of random assignment to treatment groups and failure to meet the requirement for the intervention to be identified as "play therapy." Consistent with previous meta-analyses and systematic reviews of play therapy research, we restricted studies to those that used the term "play therapy" to describe the experimental treatment and appeared to meet the definition provided by the Association for Play Therapy (APT). APT defines play therapy as "the systematic use of a theoretical model to establish an interpersonal process wherein trained play therapists use the therapeutic powers of play to help clients prevent or resolve psychosocial difficulties and achieve optimal growth and development" (APT, 2016). Due to filial therapy's historical and current recognition as a play therapy intervention (L. Guerney, 1983; O'Connor & Schaefer, 1994, Schaefer, 2011), we included studies using child-centered filial therapy methodology.

Twenty-six studies meeting criteria are summarized in Table 1. We coded studies according to theoretical model/intervention type and control group type. Intervention models included 11 individual CCPT, 5 group CCPT, 8 child-centered filial therapy using the CPRT model, 1 individual Adlerian play therapy (AdPT), and 1 group sandtray play therapy. Consistent with previous systemic reviews of play therapy research (Bratton, 2015; Ray & Bratton, 2010), there remained a noticeable absence of research on other play therapy interventions using theoretical models traditionally used in child therapy, for example, Gestalt, Jungian, ecosystemic, prescriptive, existential, experiential, cognitive-behavioral, and theraplay (O'Connor & Braverman, 2009; Schaefer, 2011). Although the majority of studies reviewed utilized a no treatment control group (i.e., waitlist/delayed start control; n = 14), a noticeable shift in 21st century play therapy research is employing research designs that include active control (n = 8) or comparison treatment groups (n = 4).

We reported only original study data in instances where studies used duplicate participant data including follow-up studies. All but one investigation reported treatment providers' training, a significant improvement from Bratton et al.'s (2005) review. Except for CPRT studies in which paraprofessionals (i.e., parents, teachers, mentors) provided intervention under the direct supervision of a CCPT and CPRT/filial therapy-trained play therapist (noted in Table 1), researchers reported treatment was provided by doctoral or master's level play therapists or advanced play therapy graduate students under the supervision of a professional play therapist. All studies were conducted in the United States or by U.S. research teams. Only 3 studies failed to report the use of manualized protocols; 12 followed CCPT protocol (Ray,

Table 1. Experimental Play therapy research – randomized controlled studies

Study	Intervention Model/ Control Group Type # Sessions Frequency; Length Setting *Treatment provider	Sample Age Ethnicity Sex	Child Outcome Variable/ Target Problem	Findings
Baggerly & Landreth. (2001)	Modified CPRT / WC 10 play sessions 1/wk; 20 min School *CPRT-trained 5th-grade mentors	N = 29 Behaviorally at-risk students Age: 5-6; M=5.7 76% Cauc, 14% AfAm, 10% Lat 58% male	Internalized Behavior Problems; Self-esteem	Compared to the waitlist control, teachers and parents of experimental group children did not report statistically significant differences between groups across time. Results indicated positive trends in the adjustment of children who received the 10 weekly play sessions facilitated by peer mentors trained in modified CPRT. Further analysis of the experimental group's scores pre to post showed that according to parent report, children demonstrated statistically significant improvement in externalizing and delinquent behavior problems and child demandingness. *Companion study to Robinson, Landreth, & Packman, 2007.
Blanco, Muro, Holliman, Stickley, & Carter (2015)	CCPT / WC 16 sessions 2/wk; 30 min School	N = 59 Academically at-risk 1st graders Age: 6-7; M=6.5 69% Cauc, 17% Lat, 7% AfAm, 2% Asian, 5% other 53% male	Academic Achievement; Anxiety	Compared to the waitlist control group, children in the CCPT group demonstrated statistically significant increase in early achievement scores (YCAT). Additionally, children in the CCPT group demonstrated statistically significant lower mean scores on anxiety. Compared to the waitlist control group, children in the CCPT group demonstrated no significant difference on achievement test scores (WJIII ACH) between the groups.
Blanco & Ray (2011)	CCPT / WC 16 sessions 2/wk; 30 min School	N = 41 Academically at-risk 1st graders Age: M=6.4 46% Cauc, 34% Lat, 17% AfAm 63% male	Academic Achievement	Compared to the waitlist control, children in the CCPT group demonstrated statistically significant improvement on a standardized achievement test which indicated an increase in children's overall academic abilities with a medium effect size. Post hoc analysis showed that both groups demonstrated statistically significant improvement from pre to post test, however the treatment effect for the CCPT group was twice as large as the control group.
Bratton et al. (2013)	CCPT / AC 20 sessions 2/wk; 30 min Head Start school	N = 54 At-risk, low-income Pre-K students Age: 3-4; M=4.1 42% AfAm, 39% Lat, 18% Cauc 67% male	Clinical Disruptive Behaviors	According to teachers who were blinded to treatment groups, the CCPT group demonstrated statistically significant improvements and large treatment effects on disruptive behaviors, attention problems and aggression, compared to the active control (Mentoring) group over three points of measure; 78% of children in CCPT moved from clinical levels of concern to more normative functioning following treatment in 1 or more areas of concern.

continued on next page

Table 1. Continued

Carnes-Holt & Bratton (2014)	CPRT / WC 7 play sessions 1/wk; 30 min Community agency *CPRT-trained parents	N = 61 Adoptees Age: 2.5-10; M=5.7 47% Cauc, 15% Lat, 9% AfAm, 18% other 55% male	Attachment Difficulties; Clinical Comorbid Behavior Problems	Statistically significant findings and large treatment effects on all measures indicated the effectiveness of CPRT over the WC on 1) reducing adopted children's externalized behaviors and global behavior problems, and 2) increasing parental empathy as measured by objective raters blinded to the study.
Ceballos & Bratton (2010)	CPRT / WC 7 play sessions 1/wk; 30 min Head Start school *CPRT-trained parents	N = 48 At-risk, low-income PreK students Age: 3-4; M=4.3 100% Lat 56% male	Clinical Comorbid Behavior Problems;	Statistically significant findings and large treatment effects on all measures indicated the effectiveness of culturally-adapted CPRT over the WC on 1) reducing children's externalized and internalized behavior problems, and 2) decreasing parent-child relationship stress. 85% of children in the CPRT group moved from clinical levels of concern to more normative functioning. Cultural considerations discussed.
Cheng & Ray (2016)	Group CCPT / WC 15-16 sessions 2wk; 30 min School	N = 43 Kindergarten children Age: 5-6; M=5.1 44% Lat; 33% Cauc; 23% AfAm 70% male	Social-Emotional Functioning	Compared to the waitlist control group, children in CCPT group demonstrated statistically significant increases in parent reported total social-emotional functioning, social competence, and empathy with medium effect size. Teacher reports did not reveal statistically significant differences between groups.
Danger & Landreth (2005)	Group CCPT / AC (groups of 2) 25 sessions 1wk; 30 min School	N = 21 Speech-delayed PreK students Age: 4-6; M=4.9 81% Cauc; 19% Lat 86% male	Expressive Language; Receptive Language	Compared to the active control group (speech therapy), the CCPT group who also received speech therapy demonstrated non-statistically significant improvement from pre to post test with large treatment effects on receptive and expressive language and a small treatment effect on anxiety.
Fall, Navelski, & Welch (2002)	CCPT / WC 6 sessions 1/wk, 30 min School	N = 66 Special Educ. students Age: 6-10,; M=8.3 98.5% Cauc 64% male	Behavior & Social Problems	Case manager reports showed a statistically significant decrease for anxiety and social behaviors. Teachers' rating did not show statistically significant difference for classroom behaviors, anxiety, or social problems. No effect sizes were reported. Results also showed no statistically significant difference for self-efficacy.
Flahive & Ray (2007)	Group Sandtray / WC (groups of 3) 10 sessions 1/wk; 45 min School	N = 56 At-risk 4th-5th graders Age: 9-12 62% Lat, 9% AfAm, 28% Cauc 52% male	Comorbid Behavior Problems	According to teacher reports, children in the experimental group demonstrated statistically significant improvement on total behaviors with medium effect size. Parents' reports did not demonstrated statistically significant differences on overall behaviors with medium effect size. Parents and teachers' report demonstrated statistically significant differences on externalizing behaviors with medium effect sizes.

continued on next page

Table 1. Continued

Garza & Bratton (2005)	CCPT / COMP 15 sessions; 1/wk; 30 min School	N = 29 Behaviorally at-risk students Age: 5-11; M=7.4 100% Lat 59% male	Comorbid Behavior Problems	According to parents who were blinded to children's treatment group, culturally-responsive CCPT demonstrated a statistically significant benefit (large treatment effect) on externalizing behavior problems compared to the COMP treatment (empirically-supported manualized guidance intervention). CCPT demonstrated a medium beneficial treatment effect on children's internalizing problems, although not a statistically significant difference. Cultural considerations discussed.
Jones & Landreth (2002)	CCPT / AC 12 sessions 3/wk; 30 min Diabetic Summer Camp	N = 30 Insulin dependent children Age: 7-11; M=9.4 87% Cauc; 3%AfAm; 7% Lat 57% male	Diabetes Adaptation; Behavior Problems; Anxiety	According to parent report, children in the CCPT group demonstrated a statistically significant improvement in diabetes adaptation compared to the AC (Diabetic camp activities). At follow-up, there was no statistical significant between group differences, but the CCPT group continued to show greater improvement. Both groups reported decreased anxiety and improvement in behavior problems.
Jones, Rhine, & Bratton (2002)	Modified CPRT/ COMP 20 play sessions 1/wk; 20min School *11-12th grade CPRT-trained mentors	N = 26 Behaviorally at-risk PreK to K Age: 4-6; M=5.4 96% Cauc 57% male	Comorbid Behavior Problems	Parents who were blinded to children's treatment group reported CPRT group children demonstrated a statistically significant decrease in internalizing and total behavior problems, compared to the COMP group, PALS®, which used a manualized curriculum. According to blinded raters' direct observation, CPRT mentors demonstrated a statistically significant improvement in empathic interactions with their child of focus compared to PALS® mentors.
Meany-Walen, Bratton, & Kottman (2014)	Adlerian PT / AC 16 sessions 2/wk; 30 min School	N = 58 Students with disruptive behavior Age: 5-9; M=6.4 48% Lat, 33% Cauc, 19% AfAm 79% male	Clinical Disruptive Behaviors	Compared to the AC (Mentoring), 1) AdPT participants demonstrated a statistically significant and moderate to large decrease in disruptive behavior as reported by independent raters and teachers blinded to children's group assignment; and 2) teachers reported a statistically significant decrease in stress in their relationship with students receiving AdPT.
Morrison & Bratton (2010)	CTRT / AC 16 wks Daily center time play Head Start school *CPRT-trained teachers	N = 52 At-risk, low-income PreK students Age: 3-4; M=3.9 56% Lat, 31% AfAm, 13% Cauc 58% male	Clinical Comorbid Behavior Problems	Compared to the AC (Conscious Discipline®) across three points of measure, teacher-adapted CPRT (CTRT) demonstrated statistically significant benefits and large treatment effect on children's externalizing behavior problems and moderate effect on internalizing problems; 84% of CPRT group children moved from clinical to normal functioning.

continued on next page

Table 1. Continued

Ojiambo & Bratton (2014)	Group CCPT / AC (groups of 3) 16 sessions 2/wk; 30 min Ugandan orphanage school	N = 60 Ugandan orphans Age: 10-12; M=11.2 100% African 50% male	Comorbid Clinical Behavior Problems	According to teachers and housemothers who were blinded to treatment groups, Group CCPT demonstrated statistically significant improvement and moderate to large treatment effects on children's internalizing and externalizing behavior problems compared to the AC (Mentoring). Majority of children participating in CCPT moved from clinical concern to normal functioning following treatment.
Packman & Bratton (2003)	Group CCPT / WC (groups of 3) 12 sessions 1/wk; 1 hr School for Learning Differences (LD)	N = 24 Students diagnosed with LD Age: 10-12; M=11.4 92% Cauc; 4% Lat, 4% AfAm 75% male	Learning Differences; Comorbid Behavior Problems	According to parent report, Group CCPT demonstrated medium to large treatment effects on all outcome measures compared to the WC. The CCPT group demonstrated statistically significant improvement on internalizing problems as well as overall behavioral functioning compared with the WC. Between group differences were not significant for externalizing behaviors.
Ray et al. (2013)	CCPT / WC 12-16 sessions 2/wk; 30 min School	N = 37, Clinically impaired children Age: 5-8; M=6.3 38% Lat; 32% AfAm; 30% Cauc 78% male	Functional Impairment;	Phase I: CCPT demonstrated a medium treatment effect on children's functional impairment when compared to the WC, although between group differences were not statistically significant. Phase II (both groups received CCPT): within group difference indicated that children in both groups showed statistically significant improvement with large effect sizes as a result of CCPT.
Ray, Schottelkorb, & Tsai (2007)	CCPT / AC 16 sessions 2/wk; 30 min School	N =60 Students with ADHD symptoms Age: 5-11; M=7.5 35% Lat, 17% AfAm, 45% Cauc 80% male	ADHD;	According to teacher report, the CCPT group demonstrated statistically significant improvement on student characteristics, emotional lability, and anxiety/ withdrawal over the AC (Mentoring) group. No significant between group differences were found on children's ADHD symptoms. Post hoc within group analysis revealed that both groups demonstrated statistically significant improvement in ADHD, student characteristics, anxiety, and learning disability.
Schottelkorb et al. (2012)	CCPT / TF-CBT 17 sessions 2/wk; 30 min. School	N = 31 Refugees with trauma symptoms Age: 6-13; M=9.2 67.7% AfrAm; 16.1% Middle Eastern; 9.7% Asian; 6.5% Other 55% male	PTSD Symptom Severity	Results indicate both interventions, CCPT and TF-CBT (SCCAP evidence-based treatment for trauma symptoms), demonstrated a statistically significant reduction in PTSD symptom severity in a subset of study children who met stringent criteria for PTSD; findings indicate both treatments are equally effective for this population
Schumann (2010)	CCPT / COMP 12-15 sessions 1/wk; 30 min School	N = 37 aggressive K – 4th graders Age: 5-12; M=7.3 38% Lat, 24.4% AfAm, 37.8% Cauc 86% male	Aggression; Global Behavior Problems	According to parent and teacher report, Both CCPT and the COMP group (Second Step®, a SAMHSA evidence-based treatment) demonstrated statistically significant improvements in aggression, externalized problems, and internalized problems. Results indicate the effectiveness of both interventions for children identified with aggressive behavior. Qualitative feedback from parents was more positive for CCPT.

continued on next page

Sheely-Moore & Bratton (2010)	CPRT / WC 7 play sessions 1/wk; 30 min Head Start school *CPRT-trained parents	N = 23 At-risk, low-income Pre-K students Age: 3-5; M=4.2 100% AfrAm 62% male	Clinical Behavior Problems	Statistically significant findings and large treatment effects on all measures indicated the effectiveness of culturally-adapted CPRT over the WC on 1) reducing children's global behavior problems, and 2) decreasing parent-child relationship stress. Cultural considerations discussed.
Shen (2002)	Group CCPT / WC 10 sessions 2-3/wk; 40 min Taiwanese school	N = 30 Children at-risk for maladjustment following earthquake Age: 8-12; M=9.2 100% Taiwanese 47% male	Clinical Anxiety; Suicide Risk	Compared to the WC group, the CCPT group demonstrated statistically significant decreases in their overall anxiety, physiological anxiety, worry/ oversensitivity, and suicide risk. CCPT demonstrated large treatment effects on anxiety, worry, and oversensitivity and small to medium effect on reducing suicide risk.
Smith & Landreth (2004)	CTRT / WC 7 play sessions 1/wk; 30 min Preschool for Deaf *CPRT-trained teachers	N = 24 Deaf & hard of hearing Pre-K children Age: 2-6; M=4.1 33% Cauc; 42% Lat; 25% AfAm 54% male	Behavior Problems; Social-Emotional Functioning	Compared to the WC, 1) children whose teachers participated in teacher-adapted CPRT (CTRT) made statistically significant improvement in behavior problems and social-emotional functioning, and 2) CPRT-trained teachers demonstrated statistically significant gains in their empathic interactions with students according to direct observation by independent raters.
Stulmaker & Ray (2015)	CCPT / AC 15 play sessions 2/wk; 30 min School	N = 53 children who exhibited clinical or borderline levels of anxiety Age: 6-8; M = 6.5 45% Cauc, 21% AfAm, 19% Lat, 13% Biracial, 2% Asian 68% male	Clinical Anxiety	Compared to active control, CCPT demonstrated statistically significant decrease in worry and overall anxiety; treatment effects were large. Children in active control group increased their levels of anxiety and worry.
Yuen, Landreth, & Baggerly (2002)	CPRT / WC 7 play sessions 1/wk; 30 min Community agency *CPRT-trained parents	N = 35 Behaviorally at-risk immigrants Age: 3-10; M=6.4 100% Chinese Canadians 54% male	Comorbid Behavior Problems; Self-Concept;	Compared to the WC, the CPRT group demonstrated statistically significant improvements in 1) child behavior problems, parent-child relationship stress, and parental acceptance according to parent report, and 2) parental empathy according to raters blinded to treatment groups. CPRT group children also reported greater gains in perceived competence and social acceptance

Note: Control group type denoted by WC = waitlist control/delayed start, AC = active control, COMP = comparison treatment
AfAm = African American; Asian = of Asian descent living in U.S.; Cauc = Caucasian/European American; Lat = Latino/Hispanic
*Denotes play therapy intervention delivered by parent/teacher/mentor under direct supervision of a CPRT-trained play therapist

2011), 8 adhered to CPRT protocol (Bratton, Landreth, Kellam, & Blackard, 2006), 2 followed Group CCPT/Activity Therapy protocol (Ojiambo & Bratton, 2014), and 1 used AdPT protocol (Kottman, 2009). The majority of studies published since 2010 reported procedures for fidelity checks to ensure treatment integrity. Unless specified, active control and comparison groups participated in the same intensity and duration of intervention as the experimental group.

A large number of participants (total of 1087 with a mean of 42 participants per study), among the 26 studies reviewed, provides foundation to make several conclusions about play therapy based on the results of reviewing these studies. Outcome research indicated that children's participation in play therapy resulted in positive outcomes for externalized problems, disruptive behaviors, aggression, attention problems, internalizing problems, anxiety, academic achievement, speech problems, trauma symptoms, social emotional functioning, self-concept, co-morbid behavior problems and functional impairment. Table 2 provides a cross-reference of studies by target outcome variables.

Play therapy appeared effective across cultures including race, ethnicity, and gender. Majority of outcome studies included a diverse sample of ethnicities. Across the 26 studies, over 60% of the participants were non-Caucasian (27.3% Latina/o, 17.7% African American, 14.56% other/biracial/or international population, and 0.56% Asian American), 63% were male, and the vast majority of participants were identified as low-income. Play therapy's successful application across cultural groups is a unique feature of this intervention and is likely a factor of the large number of studies conducted in real-world settings, primarily low-income schools (n = 21). Participants' ages ranged from 2.5 to 13 years indicating play therapy's responsiveness to young children through preadolescence. In view of the shortage of EBTs for young children (Weisz & Kazdin, 2010), it is important to note that over 60% of studies reported a mean age of 6 and younger.

Findings also indicate that play therapy can be used as short-term intervention. The number of play sessions ranged from 7 to 25, with a mean of 13 and a mode of 16. The most frequently occurring format was 30-minute sessions conducted twice per week over approximately 8 weeks (total of 16 sessions)

Table 2. Cross-reference of Table 1 studies by target outcome variables

Child Outcome Variable/Target Problem	Studies
Internalized Problems including Anxiety	Baggerly & Landreth, 2001; Blanco et al., 2015; Ceballos & Bratton, 2010; Flahive, & Ray, 2007; Garza & Bratton, 2005; Jones et al., 2002; Morrison & Bratton, 2010; Ojiambo & Bratton, 2014; Packman & Bratton, 2003; Fall et al., 2002; Jones & Landreth, 2002; Shen, 2002; Stulmaker & Ray, 2015
Externalized Problems including Disruptive Behaviors, Aggression, ADHD	Ojiambo & Bratton, 2014; Bratton et al., 2012; Carnes-Holt & Bratton, 2014; Ceballos & Bratton, 2010; Flahive & Ray, 2007; Garza & Bratton, 2005; Meany-Walen et al., 2014; Morrison & Bratton, 2010; Ray et al., 2007; Ray et al., 2009; Schumann, 2010
Comorbid/Global Behavior Problems including Functional Impairment	Carnes-Holt & Bratton, 2014; Fall et al., 2002; Flahive & Ray, 2007; Jones et al., 2002; Packman & Bratton, 2003; Ray et al., 2013; Sheely-Moore & Bratton, 2010; Yuen et al., 2002
Trauma/Attachment/PTSD	Carnes-Holt & Bratton, 2014; Schottelkorb et al., 2012
Academic Achievement/ Speech Disorder	Blanco et al., 2015; Blanco & Ray, 2011; Danger & Landreth, 2005; Smith & Landreth, 2004
Social-Emotional Functioning	Cheng & Ray, 2016; Fall et al., 2002; Smith & Landreth, 2004
Self-Concept/Competence	Baggerly & Bratton, 2010; Yuen et al., 2002
Diabetes Adaptation	Jones & Landreth, 2002
Other Target Outcome Variables	Studies
Caregiver-Child Relationship Stress	Ceballos & Bratton, 2010; Sheely-Moore & Bratton, 2010; Yuen, Landreth & Baggerly, 2002
Caregiver Empathy	Carnes-Holt & Bratton, 2014; Jones et al., 2002; Smith & Landreth, 2004; Yuen et al., 2002

to conform to the needs of the school setting. Only 3 studies reported greater than 17 sessions. These findings represent a noticeable discrepancy from the meta-analytic results of Bratton et al. (2005) and LeBlanc & Ritchie (2001) who reported similar findings indicating optimal number of sessions ranging from 30 to 40 sessions. For the CPRT/filial therapy studies, we indicated session number as the total sessions in which children participated in CCPT-based therapeutic play sessions with their caregivers (mean = 7 sessions) in accordance with CPRT treatment manual and protocol (Bratton et al., 2006). Unless otherwise specified, caregivers and mentors participated in 10 two-hour group CPRT training sessions in addition to conducting 7 play sessions with their child.

The majority of included studies did not report direct caregiver (i.e., parent or teacher) involvement as a component of treatment (n = 16). This finding is due to the large number of school-based CCPT studies following CCPT protocol. Consistent with the foundational philosophical principle of CCPT, that children inherently possess the capacity to experience inward healing and develop coping strategies given the context of a safe and accepting therapeutic relationship, play therapy research supports that children are capable of demonstrating change in emotional and behavioral functioning without direct systemic intervention. Among EBT's recognized for young children under the age of 5 years old, there is a considerable dearth of early mental health interventions that do not require full parental participation (Weisz & Kazdin, 2010; SCAPP, 2016). This finding that young children are capable of change in therapy without direct intervention with caregivers addresses a gap in available EBT's for young children and, furthermore, positions play therapy as a particularly suitable intervention in school settings where it may be difficult to engage parents (Ray et al., 2015). However, the findings from the eight CPRT/filial play therapy studies included in this review, along with meta-analytic research results (Bratton et al., 2005; LeBlanc & Ritchie, 2001) and systematic literature reviews (Bratton et al., 2010; Bratton, 2015), demonstrate that including caregivers in the play therapy process results in stronger outcomes in fewer number of sessions than traditional individual play therapy.

Several well-designed play therapy outcome studies were omitted from this review based on failing to meet the inclusion criteria we established, due to: a) lack of randomization resulting from legitimate constraints of conducting clinical research in real world settings (e.g., Ray, Blanco, Sullivan, & Holliman, 2009; Shen, 2007); b) measuring caregiver-child variables without reporting child outcome variables (e.g., Lee & Landreth, 2003; Ray et al., 2007). Summaries of these studies and others omitted from the present review including studies employing non-randomized control group, single group, and single case experimental designs can be viewed at evidencebasedchildtherapy.com. Similar to previous literature reviews (Bratton, 2010; Bratton, 2015; Ray & Bratton, 2010; Ray & Bratton, 2105), we did not include RCT studies that failed to identify child intervention as play therapy, e. g. Parent-Child Interaction Therapy (PCIT; Eyberg, Nelson, & Boggs, 2008), Incredible Years (IY; Webster-Stratton, C., Reid, M., & Hammond, M., 2004), and Child Parent Psychotherapy (CPP; Lieberman, Van Horn, & Ghosh Ippen, 2005) and that had not been included in major contemporary texts on play therapy approaches (O'Connor & Braverman, 2009; Schaefer, 2011). Empirically-supported, play-based interventions that did not meet the criteria established for this review can be found in Reddy, Files-Hall, and Schaefer (2015) and Russ and Niec (2011).

Although individual studies included in this review demonstrated beneficial outcomes on a variety of childhood outcomes, play therapy research noticeably lacks replication and follow-up studies. Replication of well-designed studies targeting specific populations and outcomes, preferably by independent research teams (Chorpita et al., 2011), are needed to further confirm the efficacy of play therapy. Follow-up studies are essential to evaluate maintenance of therapeutic gains and provide information regarding adequate length of treatment relative the sample population. Furthermore, none of the studies reviewed involved multi-site sampling which could increase sample sizes and allow for greater generalizability of findings.

CONCLUSION

In today's climate of managed care and cost-control, mental health professionals are facing more pressure than ever before to deliver evidence-based intervention. In addition to the increased pressure from managed care systems to engage in evidence-based practice, play therapists are also challenged to serve as advocates for the profession in order to promote play therapy as an effective intervention for children who present with myriad difficulties that interfere with their day to day functioning. The current status of play therapy research demonstrated through this chapter's careful review of the most rigorous contemporary studies as well as meta-analytic and systematic reviews of the play therapy research literature indicates that play therapy can be considered an evidence-based approach for responding to the mental health needs of children. Although, as in all research, limitations exist, the body of research findings reviewed for this chapter shows that play therapy is a developmentally responsive and culturally sensitive intervention for children that has extensive scientific evidence to support its efficacy in a variety of settings and across a broad range of presenting concerns and childhood disorders. The empirical support for play therapy's effectiveness across diverse populations of children and its application in real-life settings are particular strengths. It is our hope that play therapists will use the research summaries provided in this chapter to support and defend their own practice as well as advocate for the profession of play therapy as they interact with adults who make decisions regarding children's holistic wellbeing.

REFERENCES

Association for Play Therapy. (2016, March). *Play therapy defined.* Retrieved from http://www.a4pt.org/ps.playtherapy.cfm?ID=1158

Baggerly, J., & Landreth, G. (2001). Training children to help children: A new dimension in play therapy. *Peer Facilitator Quarterly*, *18*(1), 6–14.

Baggerly, J., Ray, D., & Bratton, S. (2010). *Child-centered play therapy research: The evidence base for effective practice*. Hoboken, NJ: John Wiley & Sons. doi:10.1002/9781118269626

Blanco, P., Muro, J., Holliman, R., Stickley, V., & Carter, K. (2015). Effect of child-centered play therapy on performance anxiety and academic achievement. *Journal of Child and Adolescent Counseling*, *1*(2), 66–80. doi:10.1080/23727810.2015.1079117

Blanco, P., & Ray, D. (2011). Play therapy in the schools: A best practice for improving academic achievement. *Journal of Counseling and Development*, *89*(2), 235–242. doi:10.1002/j.1556-6678.2011.tb00083.x

Bratton, S. (2010). Meeting the early mental health needs of children through school based play therapy: A review of outcome research. In A. A. Drewes & C. E. Schaefer (Eds.), *School based play therapy* (2nd ed.; pp. 17–58). New York, NY: John Wiley & Sons. doi:10.1002/9781118269701.ch2

Bratton, S., Ceballos, P., Sheely-Moore, A., Meany-Walen, K., Pronchenko, Y., & Jones, L. (2013). Head start early mental health intervention: Effects of child-centered play therapy on disruptive behaviors. *International Journal of Play Therapy*, *22*(1), 28–42. doi:10.1037/a0030318

Bratton, S., Landreth, G., Kellam, T., & Blackard, S. (2006). *Child-parent relationship therapy (CPRT) treatment manual: A 10-session filial therapy model for training parents*. New York, NY: Taylor & Francis Group.

Bratton, S., & Ray, D. (2000). What the research shows about play therapy. *International Journal of Play Therapy*, *9*(1), 47–88. doi:10.1037/h0089440

Bratton, S., Ray, D., Rhine, T., & Jones, L. (2005). The efficacy of play therapy with children: A meta-analytic review of treatment outcomes. *Professional Psychology, Research and Practice*, *36*(4), 376–390. doi:10.1037/0735-7028.36.4.376

Bratton, S. C. (2015). Evidence Base for Play Therapy: Strengths and Limitations. In K. J. O'Conner, C. E. Schaefer, & L. D. Braverman (Eds.), *Handbook of Play Therapy* (2nd ed.). Hoboken, NJ: John Wiley & Sons. doi:10.1002/9781119140467.ch35

Bratton, S. C., Dafoe, E., Swan, A., Opiola, K., McClintock, D., & Barcenas, G. (2015). *Play Therapy Outcome Research Database*. Retrieved from http://evidencebasedchildtherapy.com/research/

Bratton, S. C., Landreth, G., & Lin, D. (2010). Child parent relationship therapy (CPRT): A review of controlled outcome research. In J. N. Baggerly, D. C. Ray, & S. C. Bratton (Eds.), *Child-centered play therapy research: The evidence base for effective practice* (pp. 267–294). Hoboken, NJ: John Wiley & Sons.

California Evidence-Based Clearinghouse for Child Welfare. (2016). *CEBC Program Registry*. Retrieved on July 24, 2016 from http://www.cebc4cw.org/

Carnes-Holt, K., & Bratton, S. (2014). The efficacy of child parent relationship therapy for adopted children with attachment disruptions. *Journal of Counseling and Development*, *92*(3), 328–337. doi:10.1002/j.1556-6676.2014.00160.x

Ceballos, P., & Bratton, S. (2010). Empowering Latino families: Effects of a culturally-responsive intervention for low-income immigrant Latino parents on childrens behaviors and parental stress. *Psychology in the Schools*, *47*(8), 761–775. doi:10.1002/pits.20502

Centers for Disease Control. (2013). *Children's mental health – New report*. Retrieved on July 24, 2016 from http://www.cdc.gov/Features/childrensmentalhealth/

Cheng, Y., & Ray, D. C. (2016). Child-centered group play therapy: Impact on social-emotional assets of kindergarten children. *Journal for Specialists in Group Work*, *41*(3), 209–237. doi:10.1080/01933922.2016.1197350

Chorpita, B., Daleiden, E., Ebesutani, C., Young, J., Becker, K., Nakamura, B., & Starace, N. et al. (2011). Evidence-based treatments for children and adolescents: An updated review of indicators of efficacy and effectiveness. *Clinical Psychology: Science and Practice*, *18*(2), 154–172. doi:10.1111/j.1468-2850.2011.01247.x

Danger, S., & Landreth, G. (2005). Child-centered group play therapy with children with speech difficulties. *International Journal of Play Therapy*, *14*(1), 81–102. doi:10.1037/h0088897

Eyberg, S., Nelson, M., & Boggs, S. (2008). Evidence based psychological treatments for children and adolescents with disruptive behavior. *Journal of Child and Adolescent Psychology*, *37*(1), 215–237. doi:10.1080/15374410701820117 PMID:18444059

Fall, M., Navelski, L., & Welch, K. (2002). Outcomes of a play intervention for children identified for special education services. *International Journal of Play Therapy*, *11*(2), 91–106. doi:10.1037/h0088866

Flahive, M., & Ray, D. (2007). Effects of group sandtray therapy with preadolescents. *Journal for Specialists in Group Work*, *32*(4), 362–382. doi:10.1080/01933920701476706

Garza, Y., & Bratton, S. (2005). School-based child-centered play therapy with Hispanic children: Outcomes and cultural considerations. *International Journal of Play Therapy*, *14*(1), 51–79. doi:10.1037/h0088896

Guerney, L. (1983). Client-centered (nondirective) play therapy. In C. Schaefer & K. J. O'Connor (Eds.), *Handbook of play therapy* (pp. 21–64). New York, NY: Wiley.

Jones, E., & Landreth, G. L. (2002). The efficacy of intensive individual play therapy for chronically ill children. *International Journal of Play Therapy*, *11*(1), 117–140. doi:10.1037/h0088860

Jones, L., Rhine, T., & Bratton, S. (2002). High school students as therapeutic agents with young children experiencing school adjustment difficulties: The effectiveness of a filial therapy training model. *International Journal of Play Therapy*, *11*(2), 43–62. doi:10.1037/h0088864

Kottman, T. (2009). *Treatment manual for Adlerian play therapy*. Unpublished manuscript.

Landreth, G. (2012). *Play therapy: The art of the relationship* (3rd ed.). New York, NY: Routledge.

Landreth, G., & Bratton, S. (2006). *Child-parent relationship therapy (CPRT): A 10-session filial therapy model*. New York, NY: Routledge.

LeBlanc, M., & Ritchie, M. (2001). A meta-analysis of play therapy outcomes. *Counselling Psychology Quarterly*, *14*(2), 149–163. doi:10.1080/09515070110059142

Lee, M., & Landreth, G. (2003). Filial therapy with immigrant Korean parents in the United States. *International Journal of Play Therapy*, *12*(2), 67–85. doi:10.1037/h0088879

Lieberman, A., Van Horn, P., & Ghosh Ippen, C. (2005). Toward evidence-based treatment: Child-Parent Psychotherapy with preschoolers exposed to marital violence. *Journal of the American Academy of Child and Adolescent Psychiatry*, *44*(12), 1241–1248. doi:10.1097/01.chi.0000181047.59702.58 PMID:16292115

Lin, Y., & Bratton, S. (2015). A meta-analysis of child-centered play therapy outcome research. *Journal of Counseling and Development*, *93*, 45–58. doi:10.1002/j.1556-6676.2015.00180.x

Meany-Walen, K., Bratton, S., & Kottman, T. (2014). Effects of Adlerian play therapy on reducing students disruptive behaviors. *Journal of Counseling and Development*, *92*(1), 47–56. doi:10.1002/j.1556-6676.2014.00129.x

Mental Health America. (2013). *Recognizing mental health problems in children*. Retrieved from http://www.mentalhealthamerica.net/farcry/go/information/get-info/children-s-mental-health/recognizing-mental-health-problems-in-children

Morrison, M., & Bratton, S. (2010). Preliminary investigation of an early mental health intervention for Head Start programs: Effects of Child Teacher Relationship Therapy (CTRT) on childrens behavior problems. *Psychology in the Schools*, *47*(10), 1003–1017. doi:10.1002/pits.20520

National Center for Children in Poverty. (2014). *Children's mental health*. Retrieved from http://nccp.org/publications/pub_929.html

National Center for Education Evaluation, U.S. Department of Education. (2014). *What Works Clearinghouse*. Retrieved from http://ies.ed.gov/ncee/wwc/

Nezu, A. M., & Nezu, C. M. (2008). *Evidence-based outcome research*. New York: Oxford Press.

O'Connor, K., & Schaefer, C. (1994). *Handbook of play therapy: Advances and innovations* (Vol. 2). New York, NY: John Wiley & Sons.

O'Connor, K. J., & Braverman, L. D. (Eds.). (2009). *Play therapy theory and practice: Comparing theories and techniques* (2nd ed.). Hoboken, NJ: John Wiley & Sons.

Ojiambo, D., & Bratton, S. (2014). Effects of group activity play therapy on problem behaviors of preadolescent Ugandan orphans. *Journal of Counseling and Development*, *92*(3), 355–365. doi:10.1002/j.1556-6676.2014.00163.x

Packman, J., & Bratton, S. (2003). A school-based group play/activity therapy intervention with learning disabled pre-adolescents exhibiting behavior problems. *International Journal of Play Therapy*, *12*(2), 7–29. doi:10.1037/h0088876

Phillips, R. D. (2009). How firm is our foundation? Current play therapy research. *International Journal of Play Therapy*.

President's New Freedom Commission on Mental Health. (2003). *Achieving the promise: Transforming mental health care in America final report (DHHS Publication N. SMA-03-3832)*. Rockville, MD: Department of Health and Human Services.

Ray, D. (2011). *Advanced play therapy: Essential conditions, knowledge and skills for child practice*. New York, NY: Routledge.

Ray, D., Armstrong, S., Balkin, R., & Jayne, K. (2015). Child centered play therapy in the schools: Review and meta-analysis. *Psychology in the Schools*, *52*(2), 107–123. doi:10.1002/pits.21798

Ray, D., Blanco, P., Sullivan, J., & Holliman, R. (2009). An exploratory study of child-centered play therapy with aggressive children. *International Journal of Play Therapy*, *18*(3), 162–175. doi:10.1037/a0014742

Ray, D., & Bratton, S. (2010). What the research shows about play therapy: 21st century update. In J. Baggerly, D. Ray, & S. Bratton (Eds.), *Child-centered play therapy research: The evidence-base for effective practice*. New York, NY: John Wiley.

Ray, D., & McCullough, R. (2015). *Evidence Based Practice Statement: Play Therapy*. Retrieved from https://c.ymcdn.com/sites/a4pt.site-ym.com/resource/resmgr/About_APT/APT_Evidence_Based_Statement.pdf

Ray, D., Schottelkorb, A., & Tsai, M. (2007). Play therapy with children exhibiting symptoms of attention deficit hyperactivity disorder. *International Journal of Play Therapy*, *16*(2), 95–111. doi:10.1037/1555-6824.16.2.95

Ray, D., Stulmaker, H., Lee, K., & Silverman, W. (2013). Child-centered play therapy and impairment: Exploring relationships and constructs. *International Journal of Play Therapy*, *22*(1), 13–27. doi:10.1037/a0030403

Reddy, L., Files-Hall, T., & Schaefer, C. (2016). *Empirically based play intervention program* (2nd ed.). Washington, DC: American Psychological Association. doi:10.1037/14730-000

Rubin, A. (2008). *Practitioner's guide to using research for evidence-based practice*. Hoboken, NJ: Wiley.

Russ, S., & Niec, L. (2011). *Play in clinical practice: Evidence-based approaches*. New York, NY: Guilford Press.

Schaefer, C. (2011). *Foundations of play therapy*. Hoboken, NJ: John Wiley & Sons.

Schaefer, C., & O'Connor, K. (1983). *Handbook of play therapy*. John Wiley & Sons.

Schottelkorb, A., Doumas, D., & Garcia, R. (2012). Treatment for childhood refugee trauma: A randomized, controlled trial. *International Journal of Play Therapy*, *21*(2), 57–73. doi:10.1037/a0027430

Schumann, B. (2010). Effectiveness of child centered play therapy for children referred for aggression in elementary school. In J. Baggerly, D. Ray, & S. Bratton (Eds.), *Child-centered play therapy research: The evidence base for effective practice* (pp. 193–208). Hoboken, NJ: Wiley.

Sheely-Moore, A., & Bratton, S. (2010). A strengths-based parenting intervention with low income African American families. *Professional School Counseling*, *13*(3), 175–183. doi:10.5330/PSC.n.2010-13.175

Shen, Y. (2002). Short-term group play therapy with Chinese earthquake victims: Effects on anxiety, depression, and adjustment. *International Journal of Play Therapy*, *11*(1), 43–63. doi:10.1037/h0088856

Shen, Y. (2007). Developmental model using gestalt-play versus cognitive-verbal group with Chinese adolescents: Effects on strengths and adjustment enhancement. *Journal for Specialists in Group Work*, *32*(3), 285–305. doi:10.1080/01933920701431784

Silverman, W. K., & Hinshaw, S. P. (2008). The second special issue on evidence-based psychosocial treatments for children and adolescents: A 10-year update. *Journal of Clinical Child and Adolescent Psychology*, *37*(1), 1–7. doi:10.1080/15374410701817725

Smith, D., & Landreth, G. (2004). Filial therapy with teachers of deaf and hard of hearing preschool children. *International Journal of Play Therapy*, *13*(1), 13–33. doi:10.1037/h0088883

Society of Clinical Child and Adolescent Psychology. (2014). *Effective Child Therapy*. Retrieved from http://www.effectivechildtherapy.com/

Stulmaker, H., & Ray, D. (2015). Child-centered play therapy with young children who are anxious: A controlled trial. *Children and Youth Services Review*, *57*, 127–133. doi:10.1016/j.childyouth.2015.08.005

Substance Abuse and Mental Health Services Administration, U.S. Department of Health and Human Services. (2014). *National Registry of Evidence-Based Programs and Practices*. Retrieved from http://www.nrepp.samhsa.gov/

U.S. Census Bureau. (2015). *Quick Facts*. Retrieved from https://www.census.gov

U.S. Public Health Service. (2000). *Report of the surgeon general's conference on children's mental health: A national action agenda*. Washington, DC: U.S. Department of Health and Human Services.

Webster-Stratton, C., Reid, M., & Hammond, M. (2004). Treating children with early-onset conduct problems: Intervention outcomes for parent, child, and teacher training. *Journal of Clinical Child and Adolescent Psychology*, *33*(1), 105–124. doi:10.1207/S15374424JCCP3301_11 PMID:15028546

Weisz, J., & Kazdin, A. (2010). *Evidence-based psychotherapies for children and adolescents*. Guilford Press.

Yuen, T. C., Landreth, G. L., & Baggerly, J. (2002). Filial therapy with immigrant Chinese parents in Canada. *International Journal of Play Therapy*, *11*(2), 63–90. doi:10.1037/h0088865

KEY TERMS AND DEFINITIONS

Child Parent Relationship Therapy (CPRT): A filial play therapy approach in which a CPRT-trained mental health professional trains and directly supervises parents/caregivers in the principles, attitudes and skills of child-centered play therapy (CCPT).

Controlled Outcome Research: Research conducted to study treatment effectiveness using a control group design and examining pre to posttest differences, at a minimum, to measure between group differences over time.

Early Mental Health: A term that conveys the holistic view of young children's cognitive, emotional, social, and behavioral functioning, typically between the ages 2 to 9 years old.

Evidence-Based Treatment: A mental health approach that has been recognized by a governing body as an approach with rigorous controlled outcome research to support its effectiveness.

Filial Therapy: A play therapy approach based on the principles of child-centered play therapy (CCPT) that fosters parents/caregivers to become therapeutic agents in their children's lives.

Meta-Analysis: A research method used to investigate overall treatment effectiveness for a particular intervention by combining treatment effects on specific outcomes across multiple controlled research studies employing the target intervention.

Play Therapy: A developmentally-appropriate mental health intervention for children in which play is acknowledged as children's natural medium of communication and play therapists strive to provide an environment for children in which they can feel fully heard, understood, and unconditionally accepted by returning responsibility, encouraging children's self-directed process, facilitating creativity, and utilizing therapeutic limit setting and choice giving.

Randomized Controlled Trials: Experimental research studies using random group assignment to determine the effectiveness of a treatment compared to a control group by examining pre to posttest differences to measure between group differences over time.

Chapter 2
The Impact of Trauma on Brain Development:
A Neurodevelopmentally Appropriate Model for Play Therapists

Susan Stewart Bray
Wichita State University, USA

Jennifer P. Stone
Wichita State University, USA

Richard L. Gaskill
Wichita State University, USA

ABSTRACT

As many as four million children experience trauma every year, and some children experience multiple traumas over time. In this chapter, the authors provide an overview of the scope and the impacts of trauma on young children. The types of experiences that may be traumatizing to children and the potential effects of these experiences were included. A synopsis of the neurodevelopmental process was also provided along with the impact of trauma at the various neurodevelopmental stages. A neurodevelopmentally appropriate treatment model was described, and the model included the three neurosequential phases of regulate, relate, and reason. In the final section, a review of the impacts of trauma on school performance was provided, and suggestions for advocacy with classroom teachers were included.

INTRODUCTION

The National Child Traumatic Stress Network (NCTSN) defines trauma as a single time-limited event (acute trauma) or as multiple events occurring over time (chronic trauma). Trauma occurs as the result of violence, abuse, neglect, loss, disaster, war and other emotionally harmful experience. Perou et al. (2012) stated in a report titled *National Survey on Children's Health* that nearly 50%, or 1 in 2, children

DOI: 10.4018/978-1-5225-2224-9.ch002

experience at least one traumatic event in their lifetime. Many children experience multiple traumatic events over their childhood (Anda et al., 2006; Kalmakis & Chandler, 2013).

Anda et al. (2006) reported as the number of adverse childhood events in a child's life increases so does the likelihood of mental health disorders and physical health problems (including panic reactions, depressed affect, anxiety, hallucinations, sleep disturbance, severe obesity, multiple somatic symptoms). The neurodevelopmental effects of maltreatment and trauma on the developing brain became visual to affective neuroscientists beginning in the 1990's, with the introduction of complex imaging techniques. The neuroscientists noted trauma related changes in brain architecture as well as processing alterations within the brain and persist over a lifetime (Anda et al., 2006; DeBellis, 2001; Delima & Vimpani, 2011; Perry & Pollard, 1998; Perry, Pollard, Blakely, Baker, & Vigilante, 1995; Watts-English et al., 2006). In addition, trauma adversely impacts cognitive, emotional, behavioral, social, sensory-motor, and physical health functions (Felitti et al., 1998; Perry, 2006, 2008, 2009; Perry & Dobson, 2013; van der Kolk, 2002).

The United States General (U. S. Public Health, 2000) estimated that 4 million children experience trauma each year. In 2010, The Centers for Disease Control and Prevention (CDC) estimated the lifetime economic consequences of the maltreatment of children in the United States at $124 billion dollars (Fang, Brown, Florence, & Mercy, 2012). These costs lead the Substance Abuse and Mental Health Services Administration (SAMHSA, 2014) to describe trauma as "a widespread, harmful, and costly public health problem." (p. 2).

Children become traumatized due to a variety of experiences. These experiences include obvious traumas such as physical, emotional, sexual abuse, neglect, experiencing a natural disaster or becoming the victim of a criminal act (Felliti et al., 1998). Children can also be traumatized by witnessing domestic violence, witnessing neighborhood or community violence and other adverse childhood events such as living in a home where mental or physical illness is present, having an incarcerated parent or family member, and by living in a family where substance abuse is occurring (Felliti et al., 1998; Edwards, Holden, Anda, & Felitti, 2003).

In this chapter, the authors describe a neurodevelopmentally-informed play therapy approach. In the first section of the chapter, an overview of childhood trauma, neurodevelopment and the effects of trauma on children's brain development will be provided. In the second section of the chapter, the authors include suggestions for the incorporation of play therapy and play activity adaptations based in neuroscience. The second section also provides possible activities for each of Perry's (2008) three-step treatment approach: Regulate, Relate, and Reason. In the final section, information regarding special considerations for school-based play therapists will be included and a discussion will be provided for practical school classroom adaptations for traumatized children.

BACKGROUND

Childhood Trauma

The Federal Child Abuse Prevention Act (CAPTA, 2010) defines child abuse and neglect as "a recent act or failure to act on the part of a parent or caretaker which results in death, serious physical or emotional harm, sexual abuse or exploitation" or "an act or failure to act, which presents a imminent risk of serious harm." (p. 6)

Abused and neglected children suffer from changes in brain function and neurodevelopmental changes which potentially contribute to lifelong dysfunction along emotional, cognitive, behavioral, and health dimensions (Gaskill & Perry, 2012). Anda et al. (2006) reported children do not experience one type of child abuse in isolation from other types of abuse. The effects of abuse on the development of children vary by the type of abuse the child has suffered.

Types of Traumatic Experiences

Physical Abuse

Wilson and Scarpa (2014) reported as many as 16% of children in the United States experience physical abuse at some point in their childhood. The Federal Child Abuse Prevention and Treatment Act (2010) defines physical abuse as "nonaccidental physical injury (ranging from minor bruises to severe fractures or death) as a result of punching, beating, kicking, biting, shaking, throwing, stabbing, choking, hitting (with a hand, stick, strap or other object) burning, or otherwise harming a child, that is inflicted by a parent, caregiver, or any other person who has responsibility for the child" (p. 3) (Child Welfare Information Gateway, 2013). Hyperarousal (e.g. being watchful of caregiver or teacher anger) and feeling unsafe are common symptoms of physical abuse (Soomro, Abbasi, & Lalani, 2014).

Neglect

Perry (2002) describes neglect as one of the "most destructive yet least understood area[s] of child maltreatment" (p. 88). Childhood neglect can impact cognitive development, causing significant developmental delays in the development of speech and language as well as other areas. In addition, neglect during the first three years of life can cause the brain structures regulating socio-emotional functioning to be dysfunctional (Perry, 2002). Nelson, Fox and Zeanah (2014) studied the effects of neglect in Romania's abandoned orphans and found significant cognitive and social behavior impairments in the institutionalized children.

Emotional neglect is a specific subcategory of neglect in young children (Perry, 2002), which can hinder the formation of healthy relationships or healthy attachment. Perry defined emotional neglect as "mistimed, abnormal or absent caregiving interactions" (p. 94). An emotionally neglected child will likely have an inability to form healthy relationships and have poor attachment.

Sexual Abuse

The World Health Organization (WHO) defines child sexual abuse as a situation where an adult uses a child for his or her own sexual satisfaction (Runyan, Wattam, Ikeda, Hassan, & Ramiro, 2002). It is not uncommon for children who have been sexually abused to exhibit symptoms of sexually transmitted infections, genital injury, abdominal pain, constipation, chronic or recurrent urinary tract infections, or behavioral problems. Detecting child sexual abuse requires a high index of suspicion and familiarity with the verbal, behavioral, and physical indicators of abuse. Many children will spontaneously disclose sexual abuse to caregivers, though there may also be indirect physical or behavioral signs.

Exposure Trauma

Children are sensitive to their environment and can be traumatized by stressors or adverse childhood experiences (Anda et al., 2006). These direct or indirect traumatic incidents include witnessing domestic violence, parental substance abuse, criminal activity by a household member, a parent's chaotic lifestyle, parental relationship discord, the incarceration of a family member, or parental mental illness. Other types of childhood exposure trauma may include exposure to the events of war, experiencing natural disasters, and the effects of refugee status (Osofsky, Kronenberg, Bocknek, & Hansel, 2015).

Trauma disrupts the pattern, processes or cues in neurodevelopment, and the timing, nature, and pattern of the disruption(s) determine the nature and severity of the neurological dysfunction (2008). Research on the neurodevelopmental processes suggests there are key principles in brain development that can provide a deeper understanding of the impact of trauma on a child's future.

Children's Reactions to Trauma

Children's response to trauma may be quite different from the well-known fight or flight response (Perry, Pollard, Blakley, Baker, &Vigilante 1995). Children are too small and weak to effectively defend themselves or get away from a threat and may retreat physically or mentally when faced with trauma. Perry et al. (1995) identified two adaptive response patterns when children are faced with a threat: the hyperarousal continuum (fight or flight) and the dissociative continuum (surrender).

Hyperarousal

Children who exhibit behaviors along the hyperarousal continuum have significantly increased activity in their sympathetic nervous system, causing increased heart rate, blood pressure, and respiration (Perry et al., 1995). The over activation of the sympathetic nervous system causes an increase in muscle tone, a sense of hypervigilance, and the tuning out of information noncritical to survival. A child in the hyperarousal state may experience impairments in the regulation of emotion, behavior, and stress. Traumatized children with behaviors on the hyperarousal continuum may exhibit hyperactivity, anxiety, behavioral impulsivity, and maladaptive responses to normal stimuli.

Dissociation

Traumatized children may also respond to perceived threats by dissociation, also known as freezing (Perry et al., 1995). Children who have the freezing response shut down physically and cognitively, and often do not respond to adult directives. Adults often label the freezing response oppositional defiant behavior and respond with threats such as "if you don't, I will." These responses, however, often cause the child to feel more threatened, which may lead to an increase in the freezing response and eventually dissociation.

Dissociation is defined as disengaging from the external world and instead attending to an internal world by daydreaming, imagining fantasies, or depersonalization (experiencing a sensation of "floating"; Perry et al., 1995). Perry and colleagues reported that children might exhibit dissociative behaviors, such as numbing, compliance, avoidance, and restricted affect, both during the trauma and post trauma phases. Children often report these dissociations as 'going to a different place,' 'watching a movie,' or 'floating.' Observers may describe dissociative children as robotic, daydreamers, or nonreactive.

NEURODEVELOPMENT

Perry (2002) stated that in the span of just a few years a child develops from a single cell into a functional thinking and feeling human being. However, genetics, environmental factors, and childhood experiences impact development, including the development of the human brain (Anda et al., 2006; Nelson, 2007). An understanding of the neurodevelopmental process leads to an appreciation of the link the between exposure to trauma and the emotional, behavioral, and cognitive difficulties experienced by traumatized children (Creeden, 2009). The following section provides a brief overview of brain development and the impacts of trauma on children's brain development.

Brain Developmental Process

Neurogenesis

The first stage of brain development, neurogenesis, begins in utero shortly after an embryo is conceived (Holt & Mikati, 2010; Perry, 2002, 2008). Brain and nerve cells (i.e. neurons) are generated during neurogenesis, which begins soon after conception. The process continues after birth to begin the creation of the functional neural networks of the brain (Perry, 2002). Stress and trauma during early childhood can inhibit the process of neuron development (Anda et al., 2006).

Migration

The process of migration begins in utero and continues through the developmental process (Perry, 2008). During the migration phases of neurodevelopment, gilal cells and chemical markers guide neurons to "cluster, sort, move and settle in a location in the brain that will be their final 'resting' place" (Perry, 2002, p. 83). Any stress or trauma such as alcohol exposure, lack of oxygen, or infections has an impact on future brain function (Anda et al., 2006).

Differentiation

The development of neurons continues throughout childhood and is also influenced by environmental cues (Belsky & de Hann, 2011; Holt & Mikati, 2010; Perry, 2002). Neurons express genetic potential and specialize in the differentiation process, and for example, develop into functional brain areas or neurotransmitters. Traumatic experiences may alter crucial neurochemical processes during development (Perry, 2008). These alterations influence neuron differentiation, alter neurochemical signals, and change the functional capability of the brain (Beck, 2008; Perry, 2002).

Apoptosis

All humans are born with more neurons than are needed to develop a functional brain (Perry, 2002). The processes of apoptosis and arborization remove the unneeded neurons and neuronal connections. The apoptosis process removes redundant neurons through cell death. Abuse and neglect can increase the rate of neuron death.

Arborization

Neurons connect with one another through fiber-like processes. Neurons that do not connect into the neurological network or do not become activated will die in a true 'use it or lose it' fashion (Perry, 2002). Dendrites, one type of neuron connection are tree-like structures in the brain. The development of dendrites is dependent upon the activation of the brain through sensory experiences. Similar to the apoptosis process, during arborization neurons that are not used will be reabsorbed (Beck, 2008; Perry, 2002).

Synaptogenesis

Other fiber-like connections develop during synaptogenesis and become axons and synapses (Perry, 2002). Neurons use neurotransmitters, neuromodulators, or neurohormones for communication, and the neural connections or synapses are guided by genetic and environmental cues, that organize the brain (Herlenius & Lagercrantz, 2001). Anda et al. (2006) reported a lack of developmentally appropriate environmental experiences reduces synaptic connections, neurotransmitter production, and can influence neuron survival.

Synaptic Sculpting

The synaptic sculpting process is the foundation of learning and memory (Beck, 2008). Neurotransmitters cause the synaptic sculpting process to become more efficient by reducing the gaps between synapses. Abuse, neglect, and trauma during the period of synaptic sculpting decrease the amount of neurotransmitter activity causing synaptic connections to disappear (Perry, 2002).

Core Principles of Neurodevelopment

Genetics and Environment

Human brain development is a complex interaction of genetic influences, epigenetic processes, and environmental influences (Leckman & March, 2011). Genetic factors include the child's DNA sequence (Champagne, 2015). The child's DNA creates the building blocks of human anatomy.

Champagne (2015) defined epigenetics as the developmental process of the expression of gene activity or turning genes off and on without altering the DNA sequence. A child's genes develop potential according to environmental experiences, and a child who lack developmentally appropriate experiences structured in a predictable routine fails to develop to his or her genetic potential (Beck, 2008; Blesky & de Hann, 2011). It is now clear that our genes are not our destiny. Early experiences can turn genes on or off, even determining whether they are expressed at all. Early life experiences and environmental influences can shape brain architecture and the trajectory of development (Bales et al, 2010).

Sequential and Hierarchical Development

The brain develops in a hierarchical and sequential manner (Perry, 2002). During sensitive periods of hierarchical and sequential brain development, trauma may have critical impacts on brain organization (Beck, 2008). MacLean (1990) described the brain as triune or divided into three major regions. The three brain regions develop in a hierarchical manner from the least complex or low brain areas (brainstem), to the most complex (limbic and cortical). The low brain or the brainstem controls heartbeat and respiration necessary for survival, the child's level of arousal, and some reflexes (Creeden, 2009; Perry, 2002). The limbic system or the emotional brain contains several important brain structures including the amygdala (threat monitoring system), the hippocampus (learning and memory), the thalamus (sensory processing), and the hypothalamus or the center for the exchange of information between the brain and the body (Creeden, 2009). Perry (2002) calls the thalamus and the hypothalamus the midbrain. The cortical area or the thinking brain allows for thinking, reasoning, and abstract cognition to take place (Perry, 2002). Children who experience traumatic experiences may develop overly sensitized low brain neural Children who have dysregulated and disorganized low brain centers may experience symptoms related to core physiological symptomatology such as abnormalities in heart rate, blood pressure, respiration, sleep difficulties, eating feeding, and appetite problems, as well as balance, and motor problems. Low brain regulatory disruption results in later emotional and cognitive difficulties in limbic and cortical structures.

The brain also organizes into left and right hemispheres connected by the corpus collosum (Creeden, 2009). In most adults, the left hemisphere is dominant for analytical and sequential thinking, while the right hemisphere provides a more global perspective and processes verbal and non-verbal communication. Generally, the right hemisphere processes more negative emotions, and is implicated in the experience and recall of trauma.

Activity Dependent Development

Brain development is also dependent on environmental and microenvironmental cues (Beck, 2008; Perry, 2002). These cues can be favorable (e.g., patterned and repetitive physical activity) or negative (e.g., a chaotic and unpredictable environment), and are also reliant upon the quantity, pattern, and nature of the sensory experiences of the child. Adverse experiences such as loss, threat, injury, or neglect may disrupt neural development and cause dysfunction throughout life.

The structural effects of trauma on the child's developing brain can be observed with neuroimaging (Rinne-Albers, van der Wee, Lamers-Winkelman, & Vermeiren, 2013). On neuroimaging, the effects of traumatic events may be evident in decreased hippocampal volume, which inhibits socially inappropriate behavior, and in structural abnormalities of the amygdala, which may account for dysregulation in traumatized children.

MAIN FOCUS OF THE CHAPTER

Neurodevelopmentally-Informed Treatment of Traumatized Children

Perry (2008) proposed a neurodevelopmental and neurosequential model for the treatment of traumatized children. The model divides the treatment approaches into three brain regions targeted for intervention: the low brain, the midbrain, and the cortex. The appropriate brain regions targeted for intervention are assessed using detailed developmental interviews, and brain mapping (Perry & Dobson, 2013). The low brain areas targeted include the brain stem and the diencephalon, which controls functions such as arousal, self-regulation, physiological functioning, sleep, and appetite. The target midbrain area includes the limbic system also known as emotional processing center of the brain. The limbic system controls functions such as affect, mood, and the threat response systems, etc. The cortex or upper brain region includes the cerebral cortex and the frontal cortex, which controls functions such as reasoning, memory, insight, and morality. Neurodevelopment treatments focusing first on the cerebral cortex and frontal cortex are verbally mediated and are referred to as top down treatments. Treatments that focus on low brain areas first are referred to as bottom up treatments.

Top Down Trauma Treatment

Traditional evidence based therapies such as cognitive behavioral therapy (CBT) experiential therapies, or psychodynamic approaches can work with traumatized children. However, most of these therapies use a verbal and cortically mediated focus on higher order brain functioning or a top-down approach (Neuchterlein, Ventura, Subotnik, & Hayata, 2014). The traditional evidence-based therapies require skills such as reasoning, memory, and other executive functions of the upper brain, and emphasize understanding, emotional processing, insight, and problem solving. These therapies when used with traumatized children may include an over emphasis on cognitive coping strategies before lower order brain development is in place (Gaskill & Perry, 2012, 2014, 2016).

The premature use of higher order brain region (top down) interventions common in the evidence-based therapies are less likely to succeed (Perry, 2006). Traumatized children often have disorganized and dysregulated neural brain networks. These dysfunctional neural networks cause changes in the child's autonomic physical sensation and in the child's physiology (Perry, 2006). Children suffering from complex trauma first require bottom-up therapeutic work to organize and regulate extremely the disorganized and dysregulated low neural networks in the brain stem and diencephalon regions. Failure to understand this neurobiological concept becomes "blaming the victim" and failed child management, counseling, therapy, and play therapy interventions (Perry, 2006; Gaskill & Perry, 2016).

Bottom-Up Trauma Treatment

Bottom-up treatment strategies are those that help calm and regulate the lower brain regions, which control functions such as sensory processing, perception, and movement (Neuchterlein, Ventura, Subotnik, & Hayata, 2014). Such strategies offer the best chance to organize or re-organize the regulatory neural networks in the lower brain regions through primary sensory, somatic, movement, and rhythmic activities. The reorganization of the regulatory networks offers the best opportunity to establish basic state regulation. Basic state regulation allows treatment advance to target midbrain or cortex brain regions (Perry, 2006; Gaskill & Perry, 2016).

It is of vital importance for parents, teachers, administrators, and others to maintain developmentally appropriate relational, language, and cognitive expectations for the child's developmental age. Adults, parents, teachers, therapists, and counselors often push chronologically based developmental expectations on a traumatized child who is ill prepared to meet the expectations due to the impact of trauma.

PLAY THERAPY

The Association for Play Therapy (APT, 2015) defined play therapy as the "systematic use of a theoretical model to establish an interpersonal process wherein trained play therapists use the therapeutic power of play to help clients prevent or resolve psychological difficulties and achieve optimal growth and development. The play therapy process helps a child develop his or her develop to his or her full potential.

Play therapists help the whole child by providing an accepting environment, sending a message of confidence in the child's abilities, and by building a relationship with the child. Developmentally appropriate toys are used to communicate with the child in his or her own language, play (Landreth, 2002). The toys assist the child in expressing feelings, to test reality, and provide opportunities for creativity. The relationship with the play therapist and their client is often different than the child's relationship with other adults in that no directives are given, permission does not have to be sought, and limits are set only when needed (Landerth, 2002).

Credentials available to the play therapist include the registered play therapist (RPT) and the registered play therapist supervision (RPT-S) designations (APT, 2015). In addition in January of 2016, the Association for Play Therapy created a new play therapy credential the school-based play therapist designation (SB-RPT) intended for school counselors and school psychologists. The school-based credential allows licensed or certified professionals who are trained in play therapy to share their knowledge, training, and expertise in play therapy with school children, parents, administrators, and the general public (Blanco, 2009; Eigsti & Cicchetti, 2004).

Play Therapy with Traumatized Children

Language based or verbally facilitated therapies may be problematic for all young children, especially young children displaying serious language delays or impairments (Eigsti & Cicchetti, 2004). Language deficiencies can impede the play therapist's therapeutic relationship with the child and therefore the therapeutic process. Maltreatment may place speech and language development at risk including language production, articulation, comprehension, as well as school readiness issues (McConachy, Bartlett, Biddle, & Lunken, 2013). Such communication problems have been strongly associated with educational delays, attachment problems, and a poor sense of self and others (Kleim & Jones, 2008). While play therapy has frequently been recognized as a helpful treatment of choice for children, recent affective neuroscience research suggests modifications in the play therapy approach may improve the usefulness of the technique in children with complex trauma due to the cognitive limitations and language problems common with traumatized children.

Neurodevelopmentally Appropriate Play Interventions for Traumatized Children

Perry (2008) stated trauma informed interventions must adhere to these neurobiological principles for optimal outcomes. The efficacy of this neurodevelopmentally-informed approach to healthy social emotional development has been validated across a number of studies (Barfield, Dobson, Gaskill & Perry, 2011; Hansen, 2011; Miranda, Arthur, Mahoney, & Perry, 1998; Miranda, Schilick, Dobson, Hogan, & Perry, 1999; van der Kolk, 2001; 2007). Perry (2008) stated healthy developmental change for traumatized children was maximized through three sequential steps for the progression of treatment: Regulate, Relate, and Reason. Perry further specified the steps must be relevant or developmentally matched to the child's current level of functioning, rather than the chronological age of the child.

Perry's treatment approach starts where the child is at, not where parents, teachers, or counselors want the child to be developmentally and behaviorally (Gaskill & Perry, 2016). In Perry's treatment model, the child moves from one step to the next based on mastery of the steps, and the child's progression through the steps must be sequential or hierarchical. Each step is nested in the developmental neurobiology of childhood (Elkind, 2001). The steps cannot be skipped or speeded up, as each step is the foundation for the next step. The steps must also occur in a repetitive and patterned way over time, woven into the daily routines, rituals, and relationships in the child's life.

Perry's approach is most effective when the child is in a safe, nurturing relationship with caregivers. Perry's approach requires the caregiver or parent to work toward the neurobiological processes of synchronization or entrainment between child and adult. The synchronization process requires the child along with the parent or caregiver to mirror each other's movements and share emotional states. As the synchronization process develops, the child's social and emotional capacity grows and develops.

SOLUTIONS AND RECOMMENDATIONS

Regulate, Relate, and Reason: A Bottom Up Play Therapy Treatment Approach

Trauma-informed Play Therapy™ is defined as neurodevelopmentally-informed play therapy approaches using interventions matched and sequenced to the neural networks and brain areas that have been altered by trauma and/or maltreatment. This requires activation of the symptom mediating brain region, promoting organization and mature functioning of that region. The concept of bottom up treatment is grounded in the hierarchical nature of brain development (mastery of lower levels first). It is critical that lower areas function properly; otherwise, lower brain regions will defectively process information, effectively corrupting the ability of higher centers to accurately interpret, process, and act on the information. Successful treatment will require decreased arousal, establishing body regulation, and establishing healthy homeostasis.

Regulate Treatment Approaches for Traumatized Children

A somatosensory focus is the focus of the Regulate step. Maltreatment during the development of low brain regions (brain stem and diencephalon originating neural networks) is often marked by poor regulation of core body functions, over/under arousal, impulsivity, sleep problems, attention difficulties, or irregularities in sensory perception. Children who have experienced trauma and underdevelopment of low brain regions frequently display appetite, feeding, or metabolism problems, chronic bodily dysregulation, motor movement or balance difficulties, endocrine anomalies, or chronic sensory misperceptions.

The treatment approach for children experiencing dysregulation related to trauma in the low brain region should include copious amounts of somatosensory experience, self-regulatory activity, and movement interventions (Gaskill & Perry, 2016). The treatment approaches for dysregulated children should deemphasize verbal language, reasoning, logic, and understanding. While verbal communication in the play therapy session will necessarily occur, the play therapist should recognize verbal communication is not the focus of the play session. The play therapist must recognize the critical importance of conducting the somatosensory interventions in a positive relational context. Without the positive relational interaction between therapist and child, the somatosensory activity alone is incapable of creating positive developmental growth and neural organization.

Somatosensory activities should be scheduled at specific times each day for short periods of 10 to 15 minutes. For somatosensory interventions to be effective many repetitions will be required. While the play therapist may not be able to carry out all of the repetitive, patterned practice his or herself, a supportive web of counselors, family, teachers, and other therapists can provide support.

It is important to note, the low brain does not learn as quickly as the cortex, but it does learn though repetitive experience. For somatosensory interventions to be effective the child must enjoy the activity. Play therapists can return to basic play therapy skills of letting the child lead and find his or her own unique ways to play out the activity during this step of treatment. However, activities must be supervised closely to prevent over stimulation causing dissociation and hyperarousal (Kranowitz, 2010).

The regulate somatosensory activities should include soothing and calming play activities such as: gentle touches, swinging in a swing/glider, using a rocking chair, putting lotion on boo boos, face painting, listening to music, natural sounds, hugs, stroking, massage, use of comforters, pillows, stuffed animals, fidgets, sensory bags, wiggle cushions, reading stories, poetry, rhyming songs, playing with clay, sand, or texture boxes with many textures to feel (Gaskill & Perry, 2016). Other suggestions for activities include games or active play with piggyback rides, swings, exercise equipment, beanbags, playing catch, or running an obstacle course. The list of activities is only limited by the adult and child's imagination. Children will frequently reinvent and alter the activities once they understand that such somatosensory play is acceptable and enjoyable.

The wise play therapist will welcome and support the child's play innovations as these changes in play indicate the child's commitment to treatment (Gaskill & Perry, 2016). Furthermore, this creative process helps the child understand and use activities he or she finds enjoyable. The goal for the interventions at the regulate step is for the child to sense his or her own body and for the child to sense the world around them. The traumatized child needs to sense opposites (fast/slow, big/small, energized/tired and other opposite comparisons), and to experience calmness, quiescence, pleasure, and relaxation with a trusted caregiver.

Relate

The brain's limbic region processes and interprets affective stimuli such as relational behavior, attunement, reward, and pleasure (Perry, 2006). In addition, the limbic region is the area of the brain responsible for comprehension of emotional experiences of both self and others. The comprehension of emotion includes emotional skills such as responding empathically, forming lasting relationships, taking turns, sharing, and general psychosocial growth and development (Gaskill & Perry, 2016). Comprehension of emotion is both semi-conscious and conscious process, which makes these skills available for both behavioral and verbal expression. The limbic brain region, while conscious and verbal is not capable of logic, planning, or reason.

Children who have experienced trauma may have an underdeveloped limbic region, and therefore the child uses his or her affective experience of the child to guide behavioral decisions (Perry, 2006). Traumatized children struggling with affective and relational difficulties may not display the normal range of emotion, do not regulate their emotions well, do not martial words carefully, misperceive the social cues of others, have difficult relationships with others, or may feel little pleasure or reward from normal experience. Age appropriate empathy, delaying gratification, or learning or memory problems are difficult for traumatized children who have underdeveloped limbic brain regions.

In the Relate step of the intervention process focuses on processing emotional experience (Gaskill & Perry, 2016). The intervention does not emphasize cortical functions of abstraction, conceptual understanding, problem solving, or planning. The principal focus of the play therapist at the relate step of intervention is empathy, attachment, attunement, and positive relational reward. The play therapist's work is related to interpersonal relationships with an emphasis on synchronicity. Synchronicity includes face-to-face gaze, eye-to-eye contact, matching facial expression, matching tone of voice, and using reflective responses.

The focus on mutual relationship is of critical importance at this step of intervention as shared emotional experiences are key to the child's social and emotional growth and development (Gaskill & Perry, 2016). Examples of activities to be included in play therapy and play activities include: singing, music, enjoyable social activities, playing with a dog or cat, telling stories, special handshakes, and playing with stacking blocks, Other examples include playing with *Legos*, or manipulatives, playing games that allow taking turns, playing with a cardboard box maze, playing social games (*Red Light Green Light, Mother May I, Simon Says, Duck Duck Goose, Sorry, Candy Land*), dramatic play, and reading stories of social experiences (*Aesop's fables*, *Annie's Stories*, *Berenstain Bears,* and so forth). Other possible activities include puppet plays, family rituals, cooperation games, memory games, sociodramatic play. In summary, any play activity helping the child express their internal experiences in a warm relational environment are appropriate.

As the child begins to understand the relationship and time spent with the play therapist these activities will evolve naturally, often as an expression of the child's understanding of the play routine and rituals of the relationship (Gaskill & Perry, 2016). Seriously emotionally disturbed children have far fewer positive emotional experiences than his or her peers; therefore, the play therapist needs to promote positive relational activities with the therapeutic web designed by the play therapist, family, and school. Ideally, everyone involved in the life of the child will participate in the relational activities so as to provide the appropriate number of experiences for change (Perry & Hambrick, 2008).

Reason

Upon completion of the regulate step and the relate step, the lower brain networks are more organized and developmentally functional and cognitively mediated interventions are applicable (Gaskill & Perry, 2016). These cognitively mediated interventions include executive function approaches, which typically include understanding, labeling, categorizing, conceptualizing, planning, problem solving and creativity. The upper brain (neocortex) is the last region to mature and is responsible for highly evolved mental activities, maximizing intellectual potential as well as making the individual more human (Szalavitz & Perry, 2010). The cortical region of the brain or upper brain reprocesses information from the lower brain regions, and the cortical region is responsible for analyzing and understanding this information and as necessary, acting on the information and input provided by lower regions. The cortex allows us to integrate, organize, classify, order, and manipulate multiple sensory stimuli into unitary concepts: such as relationships between time, space, and matter. The cortical region also provides our understanding of others and ourselves morally, ethically, and spiritually (Gaskill & Perry, 2016). Authors further stated when lower brain regions are fully functional; the cortical region of the brain is capable of moderating, controlling, and regulating the neural networks of the lower brain.

However the cortex is also capable of being overwhelmed, disorganized and even shut down by highly overactive and dysregulated neural networks in the lower brain. Authors (2016) concluded when the cortex is struggling the person may have difficulties with communication and language, understanding causality, motivation, academics, conservation of matter, ordering events, classifying, forming hypotheses, problem solving, or moral and ethical judgment can be noted.

In the reason step of intervention, the play therapist may now focus on cognitive, behavioral, language, and insight oriented interventions (Gaskill & Perry, 2014, 2016). All developmentally appropriate therapeutic modalities are available to the play therapist (Gaskill & Perry, 2012, 2014, 2016). The top-down strategies are mediated by cortical and limbic areas and are predicated on regulatory competence of lower brain regions to succeed (Cook et al., 2005). Gaskill and Perry (2012, 2014, 2016) concluded when the play therapist begins treatment at the cortical level and fails to understand the contribution of the dysregulated networks of the lower brain regions, the play therapy is not very likely to not be helpful to the traumatized child.

Examples of interventions which might be considered cortically-targeted are many play therapies, bibliotherapies, behavioral management, individual talk and family therapies, storytelling games, books, stories, chess, checkers, *Battle Ship, Clue, Concentration* as well as various therapeutic games (, deleted to maintain the integrity of the review process 2016). The performing arts and other expressive mediums become much more powerful interventions, as do discussion about morality, values, and spirituality.

IMPACT OF TRAUMA ON CHILDREN'S SCHOOL PERFORMANCE

The New Commission on Mental Health (2003) which noted children with mental/emotional difficulties fail school or drop out of school at a higher rate than their non-traumatized age mates. Traumatized children are frequently incapable of meeting age appropriate norms due to the ravaging effects of trauma on academic, language, and social/emotional skills (Elias, 2006). The powerful relationship between emotional health and academic success, clearly points to the need for mental health services in the school setting if schools hope to comply with academic standards for students (New Freedom Commission on Mental Health, 2003). The findings of several researchers indicate improving children's emotional functioning can improve academic achievement as well (Packman, & Bratton, 2003; Watson, 2007; Zins, Wessberg, Wang, & Walberg, 2004). In the recent Peter P. v. Compton Unified School District et al. (2015) case, the court found that complex trauma can create disability, and in such cases, schools must address the barriers to learning just as they would any other physical or mental disability. The court finding has raised awareness of the importance for schools to attend to the whole child.

Impacts of Trauma on School Performance

Regardless of disability status or Individuals with Disabilities Education Act (IDEA) qualifications, the identification of young children who have been exposed to trauma is important in order to begin the process of recovery (Stone & Bray, 2015). Exposure to traumatic events can affect children's cognitive development and abilities. Specifically, student's achievement in reading is affected by exposure to loss and violence (Duplechain, Reigner, & Pakcard, 2008). Children exposed to trauma in their early years are also more likely to be diagnosed with ADHD, have lower IQs than their nontraumatized peers, and have negative symptoms related to cognitive development.

Social emotional competence is tied directly to school readiness for young children (Ashdown & Bernard, 2012). As children who have experienced trauma develop gaps in developmentally appropriate social emotional skills, they are likely to have further setbacks in academic and cognitive growth. Young traumatized children can experience attachment issues associated with separating from the parent or primary caregiver. This may make it difficult for children to form bonds and establish trust in a school environment with counselors, teachers and peers (Klein, Devoe, Miranda-Julian, & Linas, 2009). Furthermore, children who have experienced trauma may not have the neurodevelopmental capacity to meet the same social emotional benchmarks as their typically developing non-traumatized peers. When a child experiences trauma, their neurological development cannot only halt, their skills can often regress. The lack of developmentally appropriate social emotional skills can result in unwanted classroom behaviors such as avoidance, aggression, withdrawal, and further skill regression.

Traumatized Children and Special Education Services

Traumatized children have higher rates of inclusion in special education services (Lee & Jonson-Reid, 2009). The most recent available data show 6,429,000 students being served under IDEA (2004) in U.S. public schools (NCES, 2014). Of those students, 362,000 qualify for services under the category Emotional/Behavioral Disturbance. Under IDEA (2004) students must show an academic need in order to qualify for these educational services. IDEA (2004,) defines an emotional disturbance as:

A condition exhibiting one or more of the following characteristics over a long period of time and to a marked degree that adversely affects a child's educational performance:

1. An inability to learn that cannot be explained by intellectual, sensory, or health factors.
2. An inability to build or maintain satisfactory interpersonal relationships with peers and teachers.
3. Inappropriate types of behavior or feeling under normal circumstances.
4. A general pervasive mood of unhappiness or depression.
5. A tendency to develop physical symptoms or fears associated with personal or school problems (Part 300.A Sec. 300.8(c)(4)(ii)(A-E) and Sec. 300.8(c)(4)(ii))

Emotional disturbance includes schizophrenia. However, the term emotional disturbance as used in education does not apply to children who are socially maladjusted.

School counselors, especially those with the school-based play therapy credential, can use his or her advocacy skills with classroom teachers to assist traumatized children in the classroom. School counselors who have acquired an understanding of neurodevelopmental principles, and the effects of trauma on children can educate other school professionals with classroom adaptations for traumatized children. School counselors can assist classroom teachers in the development of individualized social and emotional goals and instruction for children who have experienced trauma and for whom age-appropriate standards are not applicable (Dahir, Burnham, & Stone, 2009; Walsh, Barrett, & De Paul, 2007).

Counselors can assist students who have experienced trauma by helping facilitate the culture shift necessary to initiate the focus to a trauma-informed school environment. Trauma-informed schools add compassionate and restorative solutions to disruptive behaviors and other discipline issues (Morgan, Pendergast, Brown, & Heck, 2015; Oehlberg, 2008). The benefits of a trauma informed school includes improved academic performance, improved teacher safety and teacher job satisfaction, and a reduction in the need for special education and counseling services (Oehlberg, 2008).

Assisting Teachers

- Helping teachers understand the common educational practice of varying materials may be stressful to a child who has experienced trauma (Ryan & Needham, 2001).
- Highly decorated classroom environments can be over stimulating to traumatized children. Counselors can speak with teachers regarding balancing the developmentally appropriate practice (DAP) of displaying a variety of learning materials on the walls of classroom with providing an environmental appropriate for the needs of traumatized children (Copple & Bredekamp, 2009).
- Counselors can also help teachers learn appropriate communication practices with children who have experienced trauma. For example, helping teachers understand eye contact may be threatening to a child who has experienced trauma (Clemens, 2007; Kottman, 2010).
- Coach teachers to talk to children who do not talk about traumatic events including those who will not talk about incidents in the classroom. For example: teachers may not understand that a student who is avoiding eye contact is not doing so out of disrespect. Teachers need to be coached in the methods needed to work with students who do not have the developmental capability to know what is being asked of them as mentioned in earlier in the "Neurodevelopment" section of this chapter.
- Counselors can share the purpose and benefits of repeated re-enactments of traumatizing events through play with teachers (Kottman, 2010; Ryan & Needham, 2001).
- Counselors can help teachers to know, no subject is taboo. Teachers may be afraid of inappropriate subject matter and may punish expression of emotion with a reprimand, removal of privileges, a time out, an office referral, etc. (Stone & Bray, 2015). Teachers need to be made aware of the therapeutic nature of these expressions, and counselors can help teachers note the difference between a child working through trauma and a behavioral incident.
- Additionally, counselors can assist teachers in recognizing post-traumatic play where children are agitated or retraumatized by repetitive play. In such cases, appropriate teacher intervention strategies will need to be taught (Kottman, 2010).
- Provide teachers with alternatives to socially inappropriate play or behavior (Kottman, 2010; Ogawa, 2004).

CONCLUSION

The U. S. Surgeon General (U.S. Public Health Service, 2000) estimates four million children a year experience trauma. The effects of trauma include impacts on the individual child's brain development, and therefore the creation of many lifelong problems such as increased potential for issues such as mental health disorders, physical health disorders, incarceration, and high school dropout. An understanding of neurodevelopment principles is crucial to all practitioners who work with traumatized children. In this chapter, the authors have provided an overview of neurodevelopment, the effects of traumatic experiences on children, and a three-step model for the treatment of traumatized children. Finally, suggestions for providing a trauma sensitive approach in schools were discussed.

REFERENCES

Anda, R. F., Felitti, V. J., Bremner, D. J., Walker, J., Whitefield, J. D., Perry, B. D., & Giles, W. G. (2006). The enduring effects of childhood abuse and related experiences. *European Archives of Psychiatry and Clinical Neuroscience, 256*(3), 174–186. doi:10.1007/s00406-005-0624-4 PMID:16311898

Ashdown, D. M., & Benard, M. E. (2012). Can explicit instruction in social and emotional learning skills benefit the social-emotional development, well-being, and academic achievement of young children? *Early Childhood Education Journal, 39*(6), 379–405. doi:10.1007/s10643-011-0481-x

Association for Play Therapy. (n.d.). *What is play therapy?* Retrieved from http://www.a4pt.org/?page=PTMakesADifference

Bales, S. N., Fisher, P. A., Greenough, W., Knudsen, E., Phillips, D., & Roineck, A. J. (2010). *Early experiences can alter gene expression and affect long-term development*. Working paper no. 10. National Scientific Council on the Developing Child. Retrieved from www.developingchild.net

Beck, L. E. (2008). *Infants and children: Prenatal through middle childhood* (6th ed.). Boston, MA: Pearson Education.

Belskey, J., & de Hann, M. (2011). Parenting and children's brain development. *Journal of Child Psychology and Psychiatry, and Allied Disciplines, 52*, 409–429. doi:10.1111/j.1469-7610.2010.02281.x PMID:20626527

Blanco, P. J. (2009). *The impact of school-based child centered play therapy on academic achievement, self-concept, and teacher-child relationship stress* (Doctoral Dissertation). University of North Texas.

Champagne, F. A. (2015). Epigentics of the developing brain. *Zero to Three, 35*, 2–8. Retrieved from http://search.ebscohost.com.proxy.wichita.edu/login.aspx?direct=true&db=cmh&jid=QQT&site=chc-live

Child Abuse Treatment and Prevention Act. (2010). *As Amended by P. L. 111-320 The CAPTA Reauthorization Act of 2010. U. S. Department of Health and Human Services*. Retrieved from https://www.acf.hhs.gov/sites/default/files/cb/capta2010.pdf

Child Welfare Information Gateway. (2013). *What is child abuse and neglect? Recognizing the signs and symptoms*. Washington, DC: U.S. Department of Health and Human Services, Children's Bureau.

Clemens, E. (2007). Developmental counseling and therapy as a model for school counselor consultation with teachers. *Professional School Counseling, 10*(4), 352–359. doi:10.5330/prsc.10.4.t142010klu723434

Cook, A., Spinazzola, J., Ford, J., Lanktree, C., Blaustein, M. B., Cloitre, M., & van der Kolk, B. (2005). Complex trauma in children and adolescents. *Psychiatric Annals, 35*(5), 390–398.

Cook, L., & Friend, M. (1995). Co-teaching: Guidelines for creating effective practices. *Focus on Exceptional Children, 28*(3), 1–16.

Copple, C., & Bredekamp, S. (2009). *Developmentally appropriate practice in early childhood programs serving children from birth through age 8* (3rd ed.). Washington, DC: National Association for the Education of Young Children.

Creeden, K. (2009). How trauma and attachment can impact neurodevelopment: Informing our understanding and treatment of sexual behaviors problems. *Journal of Sexual Aggression*, *15*(3), 261–273. doi:10.1080/13552600903335844

Dahir, C. A., Burnham, J. J., & Stone, C. (2009). Listen to the voices: School counselors and comprehensive school counseling programs. *Professional School Counseling*, *12*(3), 182–192. doi:10.5330/PSC.n.2010-12.182

De Bellis, M. D. (2001). Developmental traumatology: The psychobiological development of maltreated children and its implications for research, treatment, and policy. *Development and Psychopathology*, *13*(3), 539–564. doi:10.1017/S0954579401003078 PMID:11523847

De Bellis, M. D., Keshavan, M. S., Clark, D. B., Casey, B. J., Giedd, J. N., Boring, A., & Ryan, N. D. (1999). Developmental traumatology part II: Brain development. *Society of Biological Psychiatry*, *45*(10), 1271–1284. doi:10.1016/S0006-3223(99)00045-1 PMID:10349033

Delima, M. D., & Vimpani, G. (2011). The neurobiological effects of childhood maltreatment: An often overlooked narrative related to long term effects of early childhood trauma? *Family Matters (Melbourne, Vic.)*, *89*, 42–52.

Edwards, V. J., Holden, G. W., Felitti, V. J., & Anda, R. F. (2003). Relationship between multiple forms of childhood maltreatment and adult mental health in community respondents: Results from the adverse childhood experiences study. *The American Journal of Psychiatry*, *160*(8), 1453–1560. doi:10.1176/appi.ajp.160.8.1453 PMID:12900308

Eigsti, I. M., & Cicchetti, D. (2004). The impact of childmaltreatment on expressive syntax at 60 months. *Developmental Science*, *7*(1), 88–10. doi:10.1111/j.1467-7687.2004.00325.x PMID:15323121

Elias, M. (2006). The connection between academic and social-emotional learning. In M. Elias & H. Arnold (Eds.), The Educator's guide to emotional intelligence and academic achievement (pp. 4-14). Thousand Oaks, CA: Corwin Press.

Elkind, D. (2001). *The hurried child: Growing up too fast too soon* (3rd ed.). Cambridge, MA: Perseus.

Fang, X., Brown, D. S., Florence, C. S., & Mercy, J. A. (2012). The economic burden of child maltreatment in the United States and implications for prevention. *Child Abuse & Neglect*, *36*(2), 156–165. doi:10.1016/j.chiabu.2011.10.006 PMID:22300910

Felitti, V. J., Anda, R. F., Nordenberg, D., Williamson, D. F., Spitz, A. M., Edwards, V., & Marks, J. S. et al. (1998). Relationship of childhood abuse and household dysfunction to many of the leading causes of death in adults: Adverse Childhood Event Study. *American Journal of Preventive Medicine*, *14*(4), 245–258. doi:10.1016/S0749-3797(98)00017-8 PMID:9635069

Gaskill, R., & Perry, B. (2014). The neurobiological power of play: Using the Neurosequential Model of Therapeutics™ to guide play in healing process. In C. Malchoidi & D. Crenshaw (Eds.), *Creative arts & play therapy for attachment trauma*. New York: Guilford Press.

Gaskill, R., & Perry, B. (manuscript in preparation). *NMT guided play, play therapy and activities for children who won't talk.*

Gaskill, R. L., & Perry, B. D. (2012). Child sexual abuse, traumatic experiences, and their impact on the developing brain. In P. Goodyear-Brown (Ed.), *Handbook of child sexual abuse: Identification, assessment, and treatment* (pp. 30–47). Hoboken, NJ: John Wiley & Sons, Inc.

Gysbers, N. (2001). School guidance and counseling in the 21st century: Remember the past into the future. *Professional School Counseling*, *5*(2), 96–106.

Hansen, T. W. (2011). Prevention of neurodevelopmental sequelae of jaundice in the newborn. *Developmental Medicine and Child Neurology*, *53*, 24–28. doi:10.1111/j.1469-8749.2011.04059.x PMID:21950390

Herlenius, E., & Lagercrantz, H. (2001). Neurotransmitters and neuromodulators during early human development. *Early Human Development*, *65*(1), 21–37. doi:10.1016/S0378-3782(01)00189-X PMID:11520626

Holt, R. L., & Mikati, M. A. (2010). Care for child development: Basic science rationale and effects of interventions. *Pediatric Neurology*, *44*(4), 239–253. doi:10.1016/j.pediatrneurol.2010.11.009 PMID:21397164

Individuals With Disabilities Education Act, 20 U.S.C. § 1400 (2004).

Kalmakis, K. A., & Chandler, J. A. (2014). Adverse childhood experiences toward a clear conceptual meaning. *Journal of Advanced Nursing*, *70*(7), 1489–1501. doi:10.1111/jan.12329 PMID:24329930

Kleim, J. A., & Jones, T. A. (2008). Principles of experience-dependent neural plasticity: Implications of rehabilitation after brain damage. *Journal of Speech, Language, and Hearing Research: JSLHR*, *51*(1), 225–239. doi:10.1044/1092-4388(2008/018) PMID:18230848

Kottman, T. (2010). *Play therapy: Basics and beyond* (2nd ed.). Alexandria, VA: American Counseling Association.

Kranowitz, C. S. (2010). *The out-of-sync child.* New York, NY: Tarcher Penguin.

Landreth, G. L. (2002). *Play therapy: The art of the relationship.* New York, NY: Brunner-Routledge.

Leckman, J. F., & March, J. S. (2011). Editorial: Developmental neuroscience comes of age. *Journal of Child Psychology and Psychiatry, and Allied Disciplines*, *52*(4), 333–338. doi:10.1111/j.1469-7610.2011.02378.x PMID:21410471

Lee, M. Y., & Jonson-Reid, M. (2009). Needs and outcomes for low income youth in special education: Variations by emotional disturbance diagnosis and child welfare contact. *Children and Youth Services Review*, *31*(7), 722–731. doi:10.1016/j.childyouth.2009.01.005 PMID:19714226

MacLean, P. D. (1990). *The triune brain in evolution: Role in paleocerebral functions.* New York, NY: Plenum Press.

McConachy, J., Bartlett, J., Biddle, D., & Lunken, T. (2013). *Small talk final report: Identifying communication problems in children, developing a problem identification tool.* Richmond, Victoria: Berry Street, Take Two Research Project.

Miranda, L. A., Arthur, A., Mahoney, O., & Perry, B. D. (1998). The art of healing: The healing arts project, early childhood connection. *Journal of Music and Movement-Based Learning*, *4*, 35–40.

Miranda, S. S., Dobson, C., Hogan, L., & Perry, B. D. (1999). *The developmental effects of brief music and movement program at a public preschool: A pilot project* (Abstract). Retrieved from www.childtrauma.org/ctaServices/neigh_artsasp

Morgan, A., Pendergast, D., Brown, R., & Heck, D. (2015). Relational ways of being an educator: Trauma-informed practice supporting disenfrancised young people. *International Journal of Inclusive Education, 19*(10), 1037–1051. doi:10.1080/13603116.2015.1035344

National Center for Education Statistics. (2014). *Children 3 to 21 years old served under Individuals with Disabilities Education Act (IDEA), part B, by type of disability: Selected years, 1976-77 through 2012-2013* [Data file]. Retrieved from http://nces.ed.gov/programs/digest/d14/tables/xls/tabn204.30.xls

Nelson, C. A. (2007). A neurobiological perspective on early human development. *Child Development Perspectives, 1*(1), 13–18. doi:10.1111/j.1750-8606.2007.00004.x

Nelson, C. A., Fox, N. A., & Zeanah, C. H. (2014). *Romania's abandoned children: Deprivation, brain development, and the struggle for recovery*. Cambridge, MA: Harvard University Press. doi:10.4159/harvard.9780674726079

Neuchterlein, K. H., Ventura, J., Subotnik, K. L., & Hayata, J. N. (2014). Developing a cognitive training strategy for first episode schizophrenia: Integrating bottom-up and top-down approaches. *American Journal of Psychiatric Rehabilitation, 17*(3), 225–253. doi:10.1080/15487768.2014.935674 PMID:25489275

New Freedom Commission on Mental Health. (2003). Achieving the promise: Transforming mental health care in America. Final Report. DHHS Pub. No. SMA-03-3832. Rockville, MD: Author.

Oehlberg, B. (2008). Why schools need to be trauma informed. *Trauma and Loss Research and Interventions, 8*(2), 1–12.

Ogawa, Y. (2004). Childhood trauma and play therapy intervention for traumatized children. *Journal of Professional Counseling, Practice, Theory, & Research, 32*(1), 19–29.

Osofsky, J. D., Kronenberg, M., Bocknek, E., & Hansel, T. C. (2015). Longitudinal impact of attachment-related risk and exposure to trauma among young children after hurricane Katrina. *Child and Youth Care Forum, 44*(4), 493–510. doi:10.1007/s10566-015-9300-7

Packman, J., & Bratton, S. (2003). A school-based group play/activity therapy intervention with learning disabled preadolescents exhibiting behavior problems. *International Journal of Play Therapy, 12*(2), 7–12. doi:10.1037/h0088876

Perou, R., Bitsko, R. H., Bloomberg, S. J., Pastor, P., Ganhdour, R. M., Gfroefer, J. C., . . . Huang, L. N. (2013). *Mental Health Survelience Among Children – United States, 2005-2011*. Retrieved from: http://www.cdc.gov/mmwr/preview/mmwrhtml/su6202a1.htm

Perry, B. D. (2002). Childhood experience and the expression of genetic potential: What childhood neglect tells us about human development. *Brain and Mind, 3*(1), 79–100. doi:10.1023/A:1016557824657

Perry, B. D. (2006). Applying principles of neurodevelopment to clinical work with maltreated and traumatized children. In N. B. Webb (Ed.), *Working with traumatized youth in child welfare*. New York, NY: Guilford Press.

Perry, B. D. (2008). Child maltreatment: A neurodevelopmental perspective on the role of trauma and neglect in psychopathology. In T. Beachaine & S. P. Hinshaw (Eds.), *Child and adolescent psychopathology* (pp. 93–129). Hoboken, NJ: John Wiley & Sons.

Perry, B. D. (2009). Examining child maltreatment through a neurodevelopmental lens: Clinical application of the Neurosequential Model of Therapeutics. *Journal of Loss and Trauma*, *14*(4), 240–255. doi:10.1080/15325020903004350

Perry, B. D., & Dobson, C. (2013). The Neurosequential Model (NMT) in maltreated children. In J. Ford & C. Courtois (Eds.), *Treating complex traumatic stress disorders in children and adolescents* (pp. 249–260). New York, NY: Guilford Press.

Perry, B. D., & Hambrick, E. (2008). The neurosequential model of therapeutics. *Reclaiming Childhood and Youth*, *17*(3), 38–43.

Perry, B. D., & Pollard, R. (1998). Homeostasis, stress, trauma, and adaptation: A neurodevelopmental view of childhood trauma. *Child and Adolescent Psychiatric Clinics of North America*, *7*, 33–51. PMID:9894078

Perry, B. D., Pollard, R., Blakley, T., Baker, W., & Vigilante, D. (1995). Childhood trauma, the neurobiology of adaptation and the use-dependent development of the brain. How states become traits. *Infant Mental Health Journal*, *16*(4), 271–291. doi:10.1002/1097-0355(199524)16:4<271::AID-IMHJ2280160404>3.0.CO;2-B

Peter P. v. Compton Unified School District et al., Compton, California Case 2:15-cv-03726-MWF-PLA Document 41 (07/09/15)

Rinne-Albers, M. A. W., van der Wee, N. J. A., Lamers-Winkelman, F., & Vermeiren, R. R. J. M. (2013). Neuroimaging in children, adolescents and young adults with psychological trauma. *European Child & Adolescent Psychiatry*, *22*(12), 745–755. doi:10.1007/s00787-013-0410-1 PMID:23553572

Runyan, D., Wattam, C., Ikeda, R., Hassan, F., & Ramiro, L. (2002). Child abuse and neglect by parents and other caregivers. In *World report on violence and health* (pp. 57–82). Geneva, Switzerland: World Health Organization.

Ryan, V., & Needham, C. (2001). Non-directive play therapy with children experiencing psychic trauma. *Clinical Child Psychology and Psychiatry*, *6*(3), 437–453. doi:10.1177/1359104501006003011

Soomro, S., Abbasi, Z., & Lalani, F. (2014). An indepth insight into child abuse and its impact on personality of victims. *International Research Journal of Art and Humanities*, *10*(40), 53–68.

Stone, J., & Bray, S. (2015). Trauma and young children: How the problem plays out. *Discussions on Sensitive Issues: Advances in Early Education and Day Care*, *19*, 177–211. doi:10.1108/S0270-402120150000019012

Substance Abuse and Mental Health Services Administration. (2014). *SAMHSA's concept of trauma and guidance for a trauma-informed approach.* Retrieved from http://store.samhsa.gov/shin/content/SMA14-4884/SMA14-4884.pdf

Szalavitz, M., & Perry, B. D. (2010). *Born for love: Why empathy is essential and endangered.* New York, NY: Harper Collins Publishers.

U.S. Public Health Service. (2000). *Report of the Surgeon General's conference on children's mental health: A national action agenda.* Washington, DC: U.S. Public Health Service.

Van der Kolk, B. A. (2001). The psychobiology and psychopharmacology of PTSD. *Human Psychopharmacology: Clinical and Experimental, 16*(S1), 49–64. doi:10.1002/hup.270 PMID:12404535

van der Kolk, B. A. (2002). The assessment and treatment of complex PTSD. In R. Yehuda (Ed.), *Psychological trauma.* Arlington, VA: American Psychological Press.

Van der Kolk, B. A., & Fisler, R. (2007). Dissociation and the fragmentary nature of traumatic memories: Overview. *British Journal of Psychotherapy, 12*(3), 352–361. doi:10.1111/j.1752-0118.1996.tb00825.x

Walsh, M. E., Barrett, J. G., & DePaul, J. (2007). Dat-to-day activities of school counselors: Alignment with new directions in the field of the ASCA national model. *Professional School Counseling, 10*(4), 370–378. doi:10.5330/prsc.10.4.47p342040286mw72

Watson, D. (2007). An early interventions approach for students displaying negative externalizing behaviors associated with childhood depression: A study of the efficacy of play therapy in school. *Dissertation Abstracts International.*

Watts-English, T., Fortson, B. L., Gibler, N., Hooper, S., & DeBellis, M. D. (2006). The psychobiology of maltreatment in childhood. *The Journal of Social Issues, 62*(4), 717–736. doi:10.1111/j.1540-4560.2006.00484.x

Wilson, L., & Scarpa, A. (2014). Childhood abuse, perceived social support, and posttraumatic stress symptoms: A moderation model. *Psychological Trauma: Theory, Research, Practice, and Policy, 6*(5), 512–518. doi:10.1037/a0032635

Zins, J., Weissberg, R., Wang, M., & Walberg, H. (Eds.). (2004). *Building academic success and emotional learning: What does the research say?* New York, NY: Teachers College Press.

KEY TERMS AND DEFINITIONS

Bottom-Up Trauma Treatment: Trauma treatment approaches designed to calm and regulate the lower brain regions, which control functions such as sensory processing, perception, and movement.

Neurodevelopmentally Appropriate Trauma Treatment Approaches: A childhood trauma treatment using recent discoveries and understandings in neuroscience and neurodevelopment to provide treatment of traumatized children using a bottom-up treatment methods.

Reason Treatment Phase for Traumatized Children: The third and final phase of a bottom-up childhood trauma treatment approach concentrating on the development and organization of the cortical or upper-level brain regions. The reason treatment approach requires the organization and development of the lower brain regions in the regulate and relate phases of trauma treatment.

Regulate Treatment Phase for Traumatized Children: The first phase of a bottom-up childhood trauma treatment developed by Bruce D. Perry of the Child Trauma Academy, focusing on development and organization of the brain stem and diencephalon low brain regions with a somatosensory focus.

Relate Treatment Phase for Traumatized Children: The second phase of a bottom-up childhood trauma treatment approach focused on processing emotional experience developed by Bruce D. Perry of the Child Trauma Academy, concentrating on the development and organization of the limbic system, which is the emotional processing area of the brain.

Top-Down Trauma Treatment: Trauma treatment approaches using verbal and cognitive strategies, which require the use of higher order brain functioning.

Trauma-Informed Play Therapy™: Neurodevelopmentally appropriate play therapy approaches using interventions matched and sequenced to the neural networks and brain areas altered by trauma and/or maltreatment.

Chapter 3
Theraplay:
The Evidence for Trauma-Focused Treatment for Children and Families

Catherine Tucker
Indiana State University, USA

Sondra Smith-Adcock
University of Florida, USA

ABSTRACT

Theraplay® is a brief, attachment-based parent-child psychotherapy approach that uses interactional play to establish 'affectional' bonds between caregiver and child. Recent research related to Theraplay suggests it is an evidence-based practice for use in schools and clinical settings for a wide range of childhood problems, including those that are trauma-based. Of particular importance, Theraplay is emerging as an approach that is consistent with current neuroscience research on children's brain development and new understandings of attachment and disruption advanced by researchers. Young clients with some form of trauma-related symptoms comprise a large percentage of clinical cases, and present with complicated emotional and behavioral problems In this chapter, we will explore the basic theoretical underpinnings of Theraplay, the relevant mechanisms of change, and current evidence base. Although Theraplay can be used with a wide range of clients and problems, in this chapter, the focus will be on the applicatio with families with children who have experienced trauma.

HISTORY AND EVOLUTION OF THERAPLAY

In 1965, the Head Start program began in the United States, offering free pre-school to underprivileged children. Dr. Ann Jernberg, a Clinical Psychologist, was hired to develop a treatment program that could serve the hundreds of children entering the program in Chicago who needed help with behavioral and social-emotional issues that left them ill-prepared to integrate into the program. At that time, the only mental health services available to young children were at private psychological practices, an impractical model to deliver services to these children in poor neighborhoods. Theraplay was born out of this need

DOI: 10.4018/978-1-5225-2224-9.ch003

for mental health care for young children and families, and has since evolved to a more central focus on attachment and the importance of caregiver attunement and co-regulation based on co-creator Phyllis Booth's studies with John Bowlby and at the Tavistock Institute. Attunement, or the adult's ability to recognize and respond to the child's internal emotional state, and co-regulation, the adult's ability to soothe a child who is distressed and engage a child who is distracted or bored, are essential to achieving healthy attachment and social-emotional development (Schore, 2009; Schore & Schore, 2008).

The Theraplay Institute was organized in Chicago in 1971, originally as a private psychological practice, where parents who had heard of the success of Theraplay in Head Start sought treatment for their own children and families. Theraplay® was registered as a service mark in the United States in 1976, to protect the integrity of the model. During this time, professionals had begun coming to the Institute to get trained in Theraplay, and a fledgling certification program was developed. Within a few years, people from Canada, Germany, and Finland traveled to Chicago to train in the Theraplay method. Realizing that the Institute was becoming more of an international training organization than a local clinical practice, it was reincorporated as a non-profit organization in 1995. A rigorous protocol for certification as a Theraplay therapist and further training to become a Theraplay Trainer and Supervisor were developed, and Booth wrote the second edition of the Theraplay text, published in 1999. She published the third edition of the Theraplay text in 2010. Theraplay is now used in over 60 countries.

Over the intervening four decades since its inception, Theraplay has evolved considerably. Among the changes are; adaptations for working with adolescents and adults (Kyung, 2011), adaptations for involving parents/caregivers (Bennett, Shiner, & Ryan, 2006; Weir, Lee, Canosa, Rodrigues, McWilliams, & Parker, 2013), adaptations for children with developmental disabilities (Siu, 2014). Adaptations have also been made specifically for treating trauma, which lends credibility to its use as a trauma-focused intervention (Bennett et al., 2006; Cort & Rowley, 2014; Robison, Lindaman, Clemmons, Doyle-Buckwalter, & Ryan, 2009; Wier et al., 2013). Several studies have been published on the efficacy of Theraplay with children on the autism spectrum (Franklin, Moore, Howard, Purvis, & Lindaman, 2007; Fuller, 1995) and internalizing disorders (Makela & Vierikko, 2005; Siu, 2009). Readers with a special interest in these populations should seek out those works.

Currently, a growing number of Theraplay clients are children who have experienced significant early relational traumas (Booth & Jernberg, 2010). Several agencies that focus on adoption and foster care have chosen Theraplay as their primary mode of therapy based on successful outcomes with complex and difficult cases (Cort & Rowley, 2015). As this particular application of Theraplay has expanded, The Theraplay Institute has invested more time and staff resources to discovering the change mechanisms that may account for this success, and to offering specific modifications for the treatment of trauma (Booth & Jernberg, 2010). Simultaneously, new evidence from researchers in cognitive science and brain biology has begun to identify underlying mechanisms within the human brain and body that may explicate some of the reasons that Theraplay has long been a successful clinical intervention for young children who have had traumatic experiences.

As it is currently and most frequently practiced, Theraplay is a dyadic therapy involving parents or caregivers and children between the ages of 2 to 12 (Lender, Booth, & Lindaman, 2012). Children with a variety of social, emotional and behavioral difficulties benefit from Theraplay, including those with withdrawn or depressed behavior, overactive- aggressive behavior, temper tantrums, phobias, and difficulty socializing and making friends (Wettig, Coleman & Gleder, 2011; Siu, 2009, 2014; Hong, 2004). Theraplay is also indicated for children with behavior and interpersonal problems resulting from learning disabilities, developmental delays, and pervasive developmental disorders (Franklin, et al. 2007), although treatment may extend over a longer period of time for children with developmental delays, pervasive developmental disorders, or autism. In recent years, Theraplay treatment has been modified so that more time is spent in sessions preparing the caregivers for the attachment work involved in the treatment of the child (Booth & Jernberg, 2010; Weir, et al., 2013). This is of utmost importance in the care of children who have been traumatized because caregivers who are not themselves securely attached can have a great deal of difficulty providing a secure base or attuned engagement to a child (Bowlby, 1988). Encouraging increased time spent actively engaged in enjoyable play activities appears to be a key to helping children who have experienced trauma to learn to regulate their affect and bodies more appropriately, and to develop trust in caring adults. To be able to provide this secure relationship, parents and caregivers need to be able to regulate their own emotional reactions consistently (Bolwby, 1988). Depending on the severity of the parents' mental health needs, the Theraplay therapist may conduct a few sessions with the adult caregivers only in order to help them model and engage appropriately with the child, or refer the parent to additional personal therapy.

Another recent shift in the practice of Theraplay is an increasing demand from teachers and school-based therapists for additional training in group counseling applications. Although Theraplay group models have existed for quite some time (Rubin & Tregay, 1989), an increased awareness of trauma-informed education and therapies along with a recent emphasis on social and emotional development in early education have likely driven this change. Sunshine Circles (Schieffer, 2013), and other Theraplay-based groups for young children are adaptations of the Theraplay approach for use in school settings (Rubin, & Tregay,1989; Siu, 2009). However, few studies have examined the effectiveness of these school-based Theraplay approaches. One exception is a controlled study of a weekly classroom-based Sunshine Circles group intervention with 206 at-risk students, which demonstrated strong gains across developmental pathways (Tucker, Schieffer, Willis, & Hull, n.p.).

THEORETICAL AND CONCEPTUAL FRAMEWORK FOR THERAPLAY

Theraplay places emphasis on developing the caregiver- child relationship by recreating the sensitive, responsive and playful interactions that would naturally occur between parents and their children facilitating the development of secure attachment and long term mental health (Booth & Jernberg, 2010). Bowlby (1969) and Ainsworth (1969) defined attachment as an emotional tie to a specific person or persons that endures across space and time. In recent years, advances in neuroscience have provided evidence to confirm that early attachment relationships have a significant impact on the developing brain, more specifically neural development involved with the individual's ability to regulate emotions. Thus, modern Attachment Theory (Schore & Schore, 2008) expands on Bowlby's core ideas to integrate this new research. Schore and Schore (2008) explain, "...at this point in time, any theory of development and its corresponding theory of therapy must include these psychobiological findings, regarding how precisely early emotional transactions with the primary object impact development of the psychic structure, that is how affective attachment communications facilitate the maturation of brain systems involved in affect and self- regulation" (Shore & Shore, 2008, p.9). Love and attachment create a sense of security and belonging. Further, love and attachment are essential for the healthy development of the right hemisphere of the brain, and hence, as contemporary neuroscience suggests, drives our ability to regulate emotions and promote positive mental wellbeing.

Theraplay Core Concepts

Theraplay is perhaps best understood through an exploration of its seven core concepts and four dimensions. The core concepts underlay all Theraplay treatment. They describe both how treatment is done, and why. The activities or techniques in Theraplay sessions are relational, playful, and are congruent with the goals of one or more of the four Theraplay dimensions. In combination, the seven core concepts and four dimensions give a foundational understanding of the approach. All of the concepts and dimensions are described in more detail in Booth (2010):

- **Theraplay is Interactive and Relationship Based:** The healthy parent-child relationship, and the felt safety and joy of that connection provide the base layer for all Theraplay work. Treatment goals and interventions are designed with the facilitation of this relationship in mind. In cases where the child does not live with his or her parents, another caregiver may be involved. Even when the literal parent-child bond is irretrievably broken, the child's inner working model, or cognitive schema of the parental bond, can be strengthened and repaired (Pace & Zavattini, 2011).
- **Theraplay Provides a Direct, Here and Now Experience:** The activities that comprise Theraplay sessions are not rehearsals for something else, nor are they discussions about past events (although these discussions may occur at times). The repair and/or strengthening of the dyadic relationship are practiced in session. As a result, the child and adult both feel the physical and psychological relief of reduced distress and increased positive affect during the session in real time, rather than having to wait for opportunities to practice skills learned in the session later.
- **Theraplay is Guided by the Adult:** In order to mimic "good enough parenting" in the session, the therapist chooses activities and leads them. The child, who is not developmentally mature enough to feel comfortable in this role, is not allowed to lead. Having the adult make the decisions within the session allows the child to relax and enjoy the activities without having to be anxious about taking on tasks beyond his/her years. The authoritative, but not aggressive, stance of the therapists' also presents an appropriate model for the parent, who may be overly permissive or overly controlling.
- **Theraplay is Responsive, Attuned, Empathic, and Reflective:** Parents who are securely attached are able to meet the basic needs of their infants. In Theraplay, the therapist uses careful observation of the child's behaviors and expressions in order to tune in to his or her needs. This responsive, empathic engagement reduces the child's anxiety about having his or her immediate needs met, presents a model for the parent, and for traumatized children, helps to co-regulate their affect and behavior (Kinniburgh, Blaustein, Spinazzola, & van der Kolk, 2005).
- **Theraplay is Geared Towards the Preverbal, Social, Right-Brain Centers of Development:** Because Theraplay mimics healthy early attachment relationships; nonverbal interactions form the base of interventions across all four domains. As Schore (2012) points out, the right brain is dominant for the first two years of life when primary attachments are formed. Therefore, in replicating the sense of felt safety and care of those early relationships, Theraplay relies on the types of interaction available to very young children: eye contact, mutual facial expressions, patty-cake games, etc. Language-based therapies draw more from higher-level cortical and left-brain processes, which may cause them to be less effective in resolving early relational traumas (van der Kolk, 2014).

- **Theraplay is Multisensory:** At various points, Theraplay sessions draw on all five senses. This serves not only to engage the client, but also to use multiple pathways to experience connection, much like infants do. The use of gentle touch is the key to the effectiveness of Theraplay, especially in assisting clients who have experienced trauma to learn to self-soothe and self-regulate.
- **Theraplay is Playful:** Although serious work is accomplished in Theraplay sessions, the activities are designed to be joyful. Laughter is very common during sessions and does not diminish the gravity of the work being performed. This concept is especially important when considering Porges' (2011) work on the neurobiology of play. Porges theorizes that in order to be able to play, an animal (including people) must first feel safe, and secondly, must engage the sympathetic nervous system, the basic fight or flight instinct. This combination of relaxation and arousal allows a unique window of opportunity to open up and play, wherein the player might learn to read social cues and facial expressions of others without fear of serious harm, and to practice self-regulation (Kestley, 2014).

The Four Dimensions of Theraplay

The four Theraplay dimensions are *Structure, Engagement, Nurture* and *Challenge* (Jernberg and Booth, 1999). The therapist is able to adapt the therapeutic process, drawing interactive play activities from one or more of the dimensions to address the presenting needs of the child. The activities are familiar; hold hands and play 'row- row – row your boat,' play 'patty cake,' pretend to paint a flower on your partner's hand, thumb wrestle with your partner. Applying activities using the four dimensions help to organize the therapists' goals and strategies, and allow for significant variation of activities within and between sessions. What results is a lively relational and therapeutic playful interaction that is based on the needs of children and caregivers.

According to Booth and Jernberg (2010) activities based on the dimension of *Structure* promote the child's experience of the caregiver as 'trustworthy and predictable and provide safety, organization and regulation' (p.21). Through Engagement the caregiver provides attuned, playful experiences that create a strong connection, an optimal level of arousal and shared joy. Nurture activities encourage parents to respond empathically to the child's attachment and regulatory needs by being warm, tender, calming and comforting. They provide a safe haven and create feelings of self-worth. Challenge, as Booth and Jernberg (2010) suggest, creates a secure base through structure, engagement and nurture, to encourage the child to extend beyond their comfort zone, "to take risks, to explore, to feel confident and to enjoy mastery" (p.21). Theraplay activities are organized in terms of which dimension or dimensions they encompass, and the traditional Theraplay assessment, the Marshak Interaction Method (MIM), leads to treatment plans that address the unique strengths and limitations of the relationship dyad. In these ways, the four dimensions are building blocks upon which the treatment protocol is built.

HOW TO CONDUCT DYADIC AND GROUP THERAPLAY

There are three stages in the family Theraplay treatment process: assessment, treatment, and follow-up. Each stage will be described briefly here. Further information about each stage and other aspects of treatment can be located in the Booth (2010) textbook. This description is not intended to replace professional training in Theraplay. Therapists who wish to use this approach in their practices should seek out appropriate training before attempting to use it. When implemented by a well-trained therapist, Theraplay can successfully help traumatized children gain a neuroception, or felt sense, of safety, allowing them to no longer feel constantly on guard for danger. Theraplay in this context can also help children widen their window of tolerance for taking in new information and participating in gently challenging activities, and build a stronger bond with his or her caregivers (Booth & Jernberg, 2010).

Assessment

In the United States, and in many other countries where Theraplay is used, the primary tool for assessment is the Marshack Interaction Method (MIM) (Marschak, 1960). The MIM is a highly structured observational technique usually performed in the first or second session with a family. The child is assessed first with one caregiver or parent, then the second if appropriate, and then as a triad. The parent-child or caregiver-child pairs or triad are given a series of simple tasks to complete. Some examples include: "comb each other's' hair; tell the child about when s/he was a baby; try on silly hats." Each task is coded according the four dimensions (structure, engagement, nurture, and challenge). The tasks can be modified for different ages, ability levels, cultures, and conditions. Once the tasks are completed, the therapist reviews the audio/video recording she made of the session and reflects on it based on a scoring system and training. At the next session, the therapist gives the family feedback on the MIM, praising their strengths and creating one or two goals for improvement. This forms the basis of the treatment plan. The treatment plan may also be informed by data gathered from an extensive developmental history, and scores on standardized assessments such as the Behavior Assessment Scales for Children, 3rd edition (Reynolds & Kamphaus, 2015) and the BASC Parent Relationship Questionnaire, which are used in the clinic at The Theraplay Institute.

Theraplay treatment can vary widely in duration and intensity, but is most often comprised of 18-24 sessions and four to six follow-up sessions. Session length is largely determined by the practice setting, but is normally somewhere between thirty and fifty minutes, once a week. The therapist designs each session to reflect the goals identified in the assessment phase. Activities are selected based on the four dimensions, as well as the child's personal preferences and abilities. Activities should be slightly challenging but not difficult, and are always designed to be fun and to build the parent-child relationship. Parent(s) or caregivers are expected to participate in each session. In early sessions, the parent or caregiver may observe the therapist interact with the child, and over time, may be gradually given the primary role in interactions (although the therapist still guides the interactions and choses the activities). Typical activities might include: rubbing lotion on the child's hands (nurture), play "Simon Says" (structure and challenge), making a stack of hands (structure and engagement), measuring the child's arms and legs with crepe paper (structure), and closing with feeding the child a small snack (nurture). Lists of activities by dimension are featured in the Booth (2010) textbook. The lists are exhaustive and a great resource for child and family therapists.

As the child makes progress, assessments are repeated to gauge the efficacy of treatment. Usually, at around the eighth to tenth session, the MIM, BASC-3 and PRQ are repeated. The treatment plan is adjusted based on findings, and treatment continues if needed. This process should be repeated at fairly even intervals until all parties conclude that goals have been met and treatment can be suspended. When treating children with more severe problems, such as PTSD or Reactive Attachment Disorder, it is important to leave open the possibility of returning for further therapy if needed when the child moves into another developmental stage or if life circumstances become difficult again. Regardless of the original reason for seeking therapy, follow-up appointments should be scheduled at increasing intervals to ensure that gains are maintained.

Group Theraplay or Sunshine Circles

In addition to the form of Theraplay described above, children can also benefit from Theraplay in groups. As mentioned in the earlier section, this brief description is not intended to replace professional training. Essentially, the same core concepts and dimensions are used in group work as in the family therapy model. In group Theraplay, mental health care providers make individual treatment plans and goals for each child, and typically use the groups as one aspect of a treatment plan. Group Theraplay is used regularly in residential treatment facilities and in therapeutic schools to treat children who have experienced some form of trauma (e.g., Makela & Vierikko, 2005).

Sunshine Circles, which is closely related to Group Theraplay, is a preventative, whole-class intervention designed for use by teachers in Head Start, preschools and elementary schools, and day care facilities. Sunshine Circles use many of the same activities as Theraplay groups, but are less intense and intended for use as universal classroom interventions. All children can benefit from the joyful, developmentally-appropriate intervention. Furthermore, Sunshine Circles are intended to help foster classroom environments that are nurturing as well as challenging, and to promote interpersonal skills in young children. In a recent study of 206 Head Start students, children exposed to thirty minutes of Sunshine Circles one time per week at school made significant gains in social-emotional and academic goals as compared to a control group (Tucker et al., n.p.). Though further studies are needed to confirm findings of the Tucker et al. study, years of anecdotal evidence indicates that Sunshine Groups improve classroom climate, child-child relationships, and teacher-child relationships (Booth, 2010; Tucker et al.).

Group applications of Theraplay, whether intended as part of a general education curriculum or as part of clinical treatment, are again based on the four dimensions of nurture, engagement, structure, and challenge. The core concepts also are applied, with a few exceptions. In group work, there are three rules to teach the children, and one unspoken rule. The unspoken rule is that the adult(s) is in charge (generally, one adult per three to four children is advisable). The other three rules are: no hurts, stick together, and have fun. After recalling the rules, the adult moves the group into a fun, moderately-paced series of developmental play activities. Some favorites are; passing a smile around the circle, singing any number of nursery rhymes with motions, doing the Hokey-Pokey, sharing a small snack, and check-ups. Check-ups in group are a key component, representing the nurturing dimension. During check-ups, each adult creates a small circle with 3-4 children and attends to any "hurts" they may have that day. This may be done by applying non-allergenic lotion to the child's "hurt" (although never in an open wound of any kind), rubbing a cotton ball near the area, or blowing kisses. Children generally enjoy the check-up time, which is a non-judgmental child-adult exchange.

THERAPLAY AS A TRAUMA-INFORMED PRACTICE

Beginning with the early research on attachment between infants and parents (Ainsworth, 1969; Bowlby, 1969, Main & Goldwin, 1984), scientists have sought physiological explanations for how infants and young children learn or develop social behavior, and what can cause it to be derailed. Adler- Tapia (2012) highlights, "With this evidence of the profound impact of attachment, the therapist has a foundation from which to conceptualize child psychotherapy and create treatment plan goals. It is within this attached relationship that children develop, cope, learn and acquire resiliency to the stressors in the world" (p. 39). Mapping recent discoveries on brain development to the newly recognized power of attachment theory emphasizes the crucial role of the parent-infant relationship to the development of emotionally healthy children and adults. In the 2010 edition of the Theraplay textbook by Booth & Jernberg, an entire chapter is dedicated to the treatment of trauma. In this chapter, the authors detail the mechanics of modifying Theraplay practice for traumatized clients, and should be studied by therapists before attempting these modifications. Therapists not yet trained in the use of Theraplay are ethically bound not to attempt to use it with clients.

Figure 1 attempts to illustrate how the varying levels of arousal, the concept of neuroception, and the domains of Theraplay are articulated in the treatment of trauma. It may be helpful to the reader to keep the chart within sight while reading the next section of this chapter. In recent years, researchers such as Bessel van der Kolk (2014), Stephen Porges (2011), Jan Panskeep (2011), Allan Schore (2012), and others have reinvigorated theories about how early development can be compromised by relational trauma, such as abuse and neglect. These cutting-edge, neurobiological theories are often complex and highly technical. For the purposes of this chapter, we have identified a handful of findings that seem most clearly related to the mechanisms of change processes seen in Theraplay, including: the idea of *hierarchical brain development* and information processing (Panksepp & Biven, 2012; Perry 2009, 2014); developmental trauma research findings that explain the physical and functional changes to the *developing brain when exposed to trauma* (Cloitre, Stolbach, Herman, van der Kolk, Pynoos, Wang, & Petkova, 2009; Lester, Wong, & Hendren, 2003; Perry, 2009; Schore, 2001) the concept of *neuroception* (Porges, 2004); and the concept of the *window of tolerance* (Ogden, Minton & Pain, 2006; Porges, 2011). The first two concepts are used to help Theraplay therapists understand common brain-based

Figure 1. Using Theraplay in the window of tolerance
Adapted from: Ogden, P., Minton, K., & Pain, C. (2006). p. 32

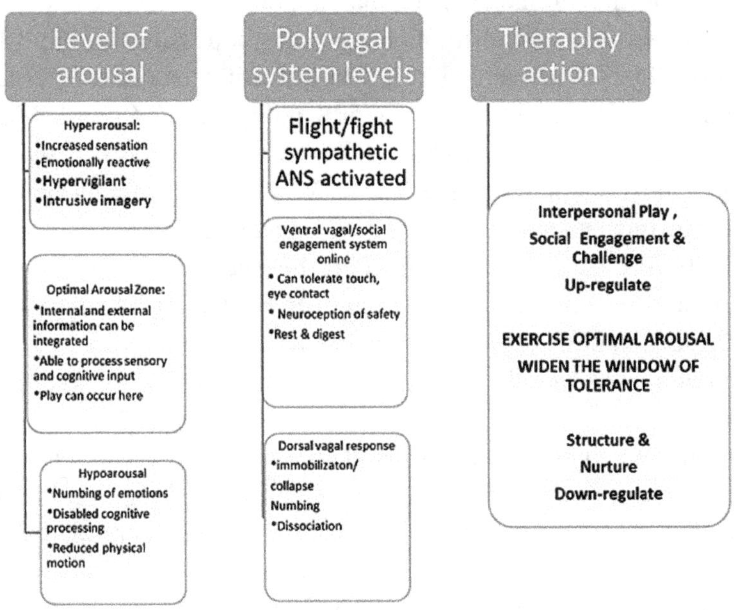

symptoms in children who have experienced trauma, and the second set of concepts are crucial in helping Theraplay therapists plan effective treatments. Each of these ideas are briefly explained and related to Theraplay below.

Hierarchical Brain Development and Information Processing

Unlike most models of psychotherapy, which are largely verbal and therefore draw heavily on the client's cortices and left-brain thinking, Theraplay is primarily motor-based and relational, drawing on the more primitive parts of the brain that develop earliest in life. By avoiding the need for complex higher-order thinking, Theraplay can help the client strengthen the basic building blocks of relating to others and the felt sense of safety. Often, in early relational trauma, it is these circuits that are most damaged and in need of repair (Schore, 2012).

The mammalian brain develops from the bottom up; from brain stem to mid brain, to limbic system and cortex (Perry, 2006; Panksepp, 2007). Healthy development requires appropriately timed and patterned responses at each stage of development. The organization of the different areas of the brain occurs in direct response to life experiences. In the first year of life, fight-flight- freeze responses to trauma come from the brain stem and override higher level thinking processes. When children experience trauma early in life, the brain can continue to miscue a threat, even when there is none. Importantly, these miscues can mean that the child's behavior seems erratic and many misunderstand their outward behavior (Perry, 2009). Often, children who have experienced early trauma may react towards neutral environmental cues as if there is a clear and present threat. For example, a child may mistake his peer's tossing a ball to him as an act of aggression and may punch the other child, when the action was meant to be an invitation to play. The traumatized child might well report later that the ball was thrown at him in anger, as a weapon.

During early brain development, the right brain limbic system, in conjunction with the developing orbito-frontal cortex attunes to the social environment and regulates the internal state of the body. It is the center for social cognition and understanding of others. Attachment patterns, including inner working models, are stored in the procedural memory system, which is nonverbal and movement oriented. New procedural memories are formed in moments of shared, positive, affective experience (Schore, 2012). The affective attunement between a mother and baby makes it possible for the baby to understand the feelings of others (Stern, 2002). The ongoing experience of being together allows the sensitive parent to attune to the level and tone of the child's emotion, or "vitality affect" (Stern, 2002). Furthermore, this attunement can soothe the young child's fight-flight-freeze reaction. An infant learns about her own feelings by seeing them mirrored in her mother's face (Winnicott, 2005). The parent makes it clear she is mirroring the child's feeling and not expressing her own feelings through exaggeration (Fonagy et al., 2002), or cross modality matching (Stern, 2002). Play, between child and caretaker, also creates new neural connections in the child's brain that may strengthen her feeling of safety when with the adult, as depicted in the middle section of Chart A (Cozolino, 2010).

Rapid neuronal growth, especially in the right, social-emotional brain structures, takes place in the first two years when attachment is being formed. Neurons are activated during interactive experience with caregivers. Neurons and connections between them are pruned away or eliminated if they are not activated by the age of three or four (Cozolino, 2010). Although the brain is now understood to be more plastic or changeable than previously believed, it is likely that neurons pruned away in the early years due to a lack of stimulation may not be replaceable (Cozolino, 2010). The brain of the newborn is shaped by the world of relationships into which they are born for better or worse (Gerhardt, 2004). Attention, care, and nurturing build robust, resilient brains, while neglect and abuse lead to underdeveloped attachments, sense of self, and ability to regulate emotion (Kestley, 2014). Therefore, the parent's role is crucial in creating the child's capacity to respond to positive and negative experiences without losing her sense of self. Failures of affect regulation between caregiver and child (dyadic regulation) result in developmental psychopathology (Schore, 2009). Theraplay's emphasis on right-brain dominant, tactile, sensory activities help clients use the most primitive parts of the brain which may not have developed adequately during the first years of life if neglect and/or abuse were occurring, allowing them to catch up some of the basic relational and self-regulatory skills they lack (Dozier, Bick, & Bernard, 2011).

The Impact of Trauma on Brain Development

Healthy caregiver- infant relationships are supported by two important innate drives that create safety and connection, one drive to stay close in order to stay safe, and second a drive to share the meaning and joy of companionship (Booth, 2010). The goal of Theraplay is to create a felt sense of safety for both parent and child. These overlapping elements support this instinctual drive and are basic to the Theraplay approach: intersubjectivity, the social engagement system, imitation and the use of mirror neurons, resonance, rhythm and synchrony, and affect attunement. Taken together, these interwoven elements provide gentle stimulation of neural circuitry in the brains and bodies of both children and caregivers which allow the dyad to fully engage with each other in an atmosphere of perceived safety and comfort. Theraplay's focus on nurturing, gentle touch, and non-verbal play match recent models of improving self-regulation and reducing symptoms of complex trauma in young children by triggering the child's brain to perceive safety, reducing hypervigilance and reactivity, allowing for increased cortical activity and learning (Porges, 2011; Perry, 2014).

When people experience trauma, they often lose the ability to fully relax in the presence of others, which can in turn cause people to distance themselves from crucial sources of social support due to the anxious discomfort residual to the traumatic experience, which in turn intensifies and prolongs suffering (Cloitre et al., 2009; Olff, Koch, Nawijn, Frijling, Van Zuiden, & Veltman, 2014). This concept is also referred to as "collapse without fear" in the neurobiology literature, and is thought to be a key component of restoration of health following a traumatic event (Sahar, Shalev, & Porges, 2001). In Theraplay, quiet nurturing activities are used to approach this state, which helps the child relax and become less hypervigilant. For example, a child who screams and clings to an adult when a fire alarm sounds might, over time with practice participating in nurturing, learn to maintain a calmer state of arousal during fire drills.

When clinicians use brain development as a guide for treatment, therapeutic approaches must be rooted in an awareness of the centrality of early dyadic regulation, right hemisphere emotional development, and the dynamics of implicit procedural memory (Schore & Schore, 2008). Theraplay accomplishes all of these tasks. The focus of treatment is the parent/child dyad, sessions are largely non-verbal and movement-oriented, and the therapist repeats activities often in order to allow for new neuronal pathways to be created (Booth & Jernberg, 2010).

Neuroception

Neuroception is a concept generated by Stephen Porges in his explorations of the evolution of the fight/flight/collapse response in mammals (Porges, 2004). The levels associated with neuroception are depicted in Chart A. In essence, neuroception is the mammal's nervous system's detection of threat from that is not consciously controlled. In other words, when you feel anxious or on edge in a place but you have not immediately taken notice of your surroundings, you are experiencing a neuroception of threat. This appears to be an evolutionary adaptation that allows mammals to sense danger on a very basic, non-cognitive level of awareness (Porges, 2011). Most of the time, neuroception is a helpful adaptation that helps us be alert to danger when we are primarily focused on other tasks. However, when a person has experienced trauma, sometimes his or her alarm system is reset to give a warning of danger even when there is no immediate threat. This can result in what clinicians see as hypervigilance, exaggerated startle response, inattention, and anxiety (Porges, 2011). In these cases, people are much less likely to operate with what Porges calls the neuroception of safety. It is important to note that neuroception of safety may not correlate with any actual threat in the environment. People who have experienced trauma may perceive or have a neuroception of threat even in perfectly neutral settings. Neuroception is not a conscious function.

The neuroception of safety is a crucial state for humans to engage. It allows the individual to rest and restore his or her health, allows the person to learn new cognitive material and motor tasks, and allows for new relationships and connections to be made (Geller & Porges, 2014). When a person is not able to access the state of the neuroception of safety, he or she is also not able to engage these other brain and body functions.

Therefore, when working with clients who have experienced trauma, it is important for the clinician to be aware that the client's body may be reacting to threats that are not present in the current environment. In these cases, sensorimotor soothing activities, such as the nurturing activities of Theraplay, need to be employed to encourage the client's body and brain to resume a state of neuroception of safety. Activities such as, rubbing lotion on the client's hand or arm with a firm touch, singing a lullaby together, or doing a simple rhythmic activity like playing "Patty-Cake" can help to soothe the client's body. Of course, the therapist should ask the client how comfortable he/she is with these activities before beginning.

Window of Tolerance

All mammals have varying levels of arousal and attention which are largely dependent on the level of risk versus safety in the environment (Porges, 2004). As seen in Chart A, some of the time, mammals may be hyper-aroused or hyper-alert, as when there is a threat in the environment and the animal needs to run or fight, or may be hypo-aroused, such as when an attack has occurred, death is imminent, and the animal loses consciousness. Between these two states exists the window of tolerance. In this middle state of arousal, animals are able to rest, to learn, and to play and relate to others (Porges, 2011). This middle state is where clients need to be in order to take in new information during therapy sessions. However, for clients who have a trauma history, most of their days and nights are spent in a state of hyper-arousal, which does not allow for the intake and processing of new ideas and actions. Clients who have dissociative symptoms are often stuck in the hypo-active state (Porges, 2011). Theraplay, through its specific focus on nurturing the safety of the parent-child relationship deactivates the fight or flight response and allows the child to begin to relax and allow the adults to be in charge. Conversely, when children are hypoaroused, engaging and challenging activities can be introduced to help bring the child into the window of tolerance. Over time, most children gain the ability to remain in the zone of optimal arousal for longer periods of time. This generally correlates to a reduction in angry, controlling behaviors in hyperaroused children, and an uptick in time on task in hypoaroused children.

In early childhood, parents who meet their children with joy and interest generate a sympathetic arousal state in the child's nervous system that promotes attachment formation by engaging and widening the window of tolerance. Without early experiences of high levels of positive affect and co-regulation with an attuned caregiver, children cannot develop a sense of connectedness and empathy, and are more frequently either hyper- or hypo-aroused. The better the nervous system is at handling high arousal levels without disintegrating, the more flexible and resilient the child will become. Theraplay provides experiences of high arousal followed by experiences of calm and quiet and thus "trains" the vagus system to regulate arousal levels (Porges, 2011, Kestley, 2014). This increased flexibility of arousal levels widens the window of tolerance and allows the child to spend more of the day in the middle state of arousal where rest and learning can occur.

The Evidence for Theraplay as a Trauma-Focused Intervention

The evidence for Theraplay as a trauma-focused treatment is emerging and there are some promising results in a few studies (Makela & Vierikko, 2005; Bennett, et al, 2006; Robison, Lindaman, Clemmons, Doyle-Buckwalter, & Ryan, 2009; Cort & Rowley, 2015). Though all of these were case studies, pre-post-test study designs, without controls, each was conducted in settings that serve children in foster or shelter care, and reported positive results using dyadic and small group Theraplay.

In a qualitative study conducted in England, Cort and Rowley (2015) examined the effects of a group Theraplay intervention among a sample of five preschool children and their mothers residing in a shelter following experiences of domestic abuse. Using a group case study format, findings suggested that both mothers and children had positive experiences with Theraplay. In addition to focus group interviews with the mothers, the researchers measured the group's progress using the Parenting Stress Index 4 Short Form (Abidin, 1995) and the Tool of Parenting Self-Efficacy (Kendall & Bloomfield, 2005). These two formal measures were given to mothers before and after the intervention were implemented.

Importantly, mothers related increased level of play with their child, reported increased parenting self-efficacy and positive maternal identity, self-acceptance, and positive perceptions of the child. Clinical assessments also showed marked improvement in parent-child interactions on a number of parenting dimensions including affection, positive discipline, self-acceptance, and knowledge of childcare. Mothers also reported strong satisfaction at a 3-month follow-up using a ten point Likert scale assessing their satisfaction with a variety of parenting domains.

Similarly, Mäkelä and Vierikko (2005), in a study of Theraplay with 15 children and their caregivers (who completed), ranging in age from 2 to 13, in foster care in Finland. In this study, weekly sessions were modified for some families to an intensive small group format, in which Theraplay sessions were provided for families (who had to travel) to two, four-day sessions (2 dyads at a time), about 6 weeks apart. A modified case study design tracked each dyad across a length of treatment that varied according to the needs of the child/family. Pre- and post-tests of children's behavior, using the Child Behavior Checklist (CBCL) and the related Teacher Report Form (TRF), measures of parent-child interactions [MIM and the VAS (Finnish interpretation of Interaction Scale], and a follow-up questionnaire all showed positive outcomes of the treatment. Qualitative findings also illustrated the positive perspectives of children, parents, and childcare workers toward the program. Though this study also was not controlled, these case-specific results point to the clinical utility of Theraplay for this particular group of children and their significant others.

Bennett et al. (2006) conducted an evaluation of a group Theraplay program called Family Connections, at a center for children and families experience family violence in Canada. Ten mothers and fifteen children participated in this study. The six-week, two times a week, Family Connections program was evaluated using formative process evaluation based on close observation of the sessions by research assistants. Findings suggested a number of promising outcomes, which included a high level of involvement of the children, parents and children valued the high activity level of the group, and a change was reported in how the center staff understood the needs of the families and approached their work.

In a single-case design peer-reviewed article, Robinson et al (2009) explore the course of treatment used with a single adolescent male. This young man had suffered chronic and complex traumas, beginning with his biological mother's use of drugs during pregnancy. She was thirteen years old when she gave birth to the boy, and his biological father was also in his teens. Following multiple reports of abuse and neglect by the biological mother, the boy was taken into foster care before his first birthday. For the next several years, he was placed in multiple homes and was reported to have been a victim of sexual and other physical abuse and neglect. He arrived at residential treatment at 14 with severe emotional and behavioral problems. After 23 months of ongoing Theraplay and other complementary treatments, the boy was placed in a therapeutic foster home. At a follow-up visit one year later, the boy was still in the same home and was continuing to make progress: he had not been involved with juvenile justice and was able to make a solid connection with his new foster family, especially the foster mother.

Even though this single-case study is unique to the individuals involved, the information about how the residential treatment facility went about meeting the needs of this badly traumatized young man describes a successful and hopeful process. The methods used by the treatment team, which were built around Theraplay, can be used by staff at other residential facilities given adequate staff education, supervision, and support. Interested readers should contact the authors of that article to learn more about how this outcome was achieved and might be duplicated.

Though strongly positive, the experiences and satisfaction of participants in these studies only generalize to the samples being studied, and cannot be generalized to other populations. Rigorous research is needed to support the generalizability of these outcomes. Further studies on both group and dyadic Theraplay are needed to further support the efficacy of the approach. There is much promise from these studies and anecdotal findings from therapists who use Theraplay in many settings and countries. Additionally, much of research is conducted in countries outside of the U.S. (England, Canada, & Finland) and these findings should be replicated within care settings in the U.S.

CONCLUSION AND FUTURE DIRECTIONS

New findings building on those explained earlier in this chapter will continue to shape the practice of Theraplay throughout the twenty-first century. Although no one can know what science has yet to teach us about early brain development, the impact of trauma on youth, or the best pathways to recovery following trauma, we expect that Theraplay will advance as an evidence-based treatment for childhood trauma based on the serve-and-return interaction between caring adults and children. The attachment relationship exists within all species of mammals, and is critical in the social-emotional development of all higher primates, including ourselves (Panksepp & Biven, 2012; Porges, 2011; Schore, 2001).

Research on Theraplay now ongoing and planned for the near future includes randomized controlled studies in multiple settings (schools, residential treatment facilities and outpatient therapy). Results from these studies will potentially support claims of Theraplay's efficacy as an intervention for children with traumatic histories. Trauma-informed Theraplay interventions will be refined as research results point toward the most promising practices.

One study, currently underway in the Midwestern United States, examines the correlation between Adverse Childhood Experiences (ACES), as reported by both parent and children, on parent's perceptions of children's emotional and behavioral problems. By surveying families visiting a family practice medical care clinic, the researchers hope to learn about familial patterns of ACEs and how adverse experiences in a family may contribute to children's acting out or withdrawn behaviors. The second phase of this study will introduce a randomized controlled trial of Theraplay versus traditional family counseling for families who report both high numbers of ACEs and children with emotional and/or behavioral problems. Families who desire treatment will be seen weekly in an outpatient, integrated health setting by mental health therapists. Families who participate will be randomly assigned to a Theraplay or trauma-focused cognitive behavioral therapy. Standardized assessments will be gathered from parents and teachers at intake, mid-point, and exit in order to evaluate treatment efficacy.

A large mental health service organization in the northeast is also pursuing a randomized controlled trial of Theraplay versus traditional family therapy delivered by in-home therapists. In this study, all of the prospective families have children with moderate to severe externalizing behaviors. To compare treatments, new clients in the in-home therapy program will be randomly assigned to therapists trained in Theraplay, or to family therapists who are not trained in Theraplay. Multiple pre- and post-test measures of the children's behaviors will be taken at intake, mid-point, and exit to determine the relative efficacy of each treatment approach for these families.

In the United Kingdom, a school that has adopted Theraplay as its guiding approach to classroom management is also evaluating children's response to the intervention. Multiple outcome measures of specific groups in the school, including regular and special education students, teachers, and parents will be collected and analyzed.

Research also continues in labs around the globe on identifying the structures in the brain that are impacted by trauma and on how best to treat the damage done by adversity. Importantly, innovative counseling programs designed to prevent trauma in young children are also being designed, implemented, and evaluated. Prevention and treatment programs with a two-generation (parent and child) focus are of great interest to The Theraplay Institute, and have potential for reducing or potentially ending the need for counseling treatment for early relational trauma.

REFERENCES

Abidin, R. R. (1995). Parenting Stress Index: Professional Manual (3rd ed.). Odessa, FL: Psychological Assessment Resources, Inc.

Adler-Tapia, R. (2012). *Child psychotherapy: Integrating developmental theory into clinical practice.* New York, NY: Springer.

Ainsworth, M. D. (1969). Object Relations, dependency and attachment: A theoretical review of the infant mother relationship. *Child Development*, *40*(4), 969–1025. doi:10.2307/1127008 PMID:5360395

Anda, R. F., Felitti, V. J., Bremner, J. D., Walker, J. D., Whitfield, C., Perry, B. D., & Giles, W. H. (2006). The enduring effects of abuse and related adverse experiences in childhood: A convergence of evidence from neurobiology and epidemiology. *European Archives of Psychiatry and Clinical Neuroscience*, *256*(3), 174–186. doi:10.1007/s00406-005-0624-4 PMID:16311898

Bennett, L., Shiner, S., & Ryan, S. (2006, October). Using Theraplay in shelter settings with mothers & children who have experienced violence in the home. *Journal of Psychosocial Nursing and Mental Health Services*, *44*(10), 38–48. PMID:17063889

Booth, P., & Jernberg, A. (2010). *Theraplay: Helping parents and children build better relationships through attachment-based play* (3rd ed.). San Francisco, CA: Jossey-Bass.

Bowlby, J. (1969). Attachment and loss: Vol 1 Attachment. New York, NY: Avery (Penguin Group).

Bowlby, J. (1988). *A secure base: Parent-child attachment and healthy human development*. New York: Basic Books.

Cloitre, M., Stolbach, B. C., Herman, J. L., van der Kolk, B., Pynoos, R., Wang, J., & Petkova, E. (2009). A developmental approach to complex PTSD: Childhood and adult cumulative trauma as predictors of symptom complexity. *Journal of Traumatic Stress*, *22*(5), 399–408. doi:10.1002/jts.20444 PMID:19795402

Cort, L., & Rowley, E. (2015, September). A case study evaluation of a Theraplay intervention to support mothers and preschool children following domestic abuse. *Debate.*, *156*, 33–41.

Cozolino, L. (2010). *The neuroscience of psychotherapy*. New York: Norton.

Dozier, M., Bick, J., & Bernard, K. (2011). Attachment-based treatment for young, vulnerable children. In J. Osofsky (Ed.), *Clinical Work with Traumatized Young Children* (pp. 75–95). New York: Guilford.

Dube, S. R., Feletti, V. J., Dong, M., Giles, W. H., & Anda, R. F. (2003). The impact of adverse childhood experiences on health problems: Evidence from four birth cohorts dating back to 1900. *Preventive Medicine*, *37*(3), 268–277. doi:10.1016/S0091-7435(03)00123-3 PMID:12914833

Fonagy, P. (1999). Psychoanalytic Theory from the viewpoint of attachment theory and research. In J. Cassidy & P. Shaver (Eds.), *Handbook of attachment theory and research* (pp. 595–624). New York: Guilford Press.

Franklin, J., Moore, E., Howard, A., Purvis, K., Cross, D., & Lindaman, S. (2007). *An Evaluation of Theraplay Using a Sample of Children Diagnosed with Pervasive Developmental Disorder (PDD) or Mild to Moderate Autism*. Poster presentation at the American Psychological Association Conference, San Francisco, CA.

Fuller, W. (1995). Theraplay as treatment for autism in a school-based day treatment setting. *Continuum. Journal of the American Association for Partial Hospitalization*, *2*(2), 89–93.

Geller, S. M. & Porges, S. W. (2014). Therapeutic presence: neurophysiological mechanisms mediating feeling safe in therapeutic relationships. *Journal of Psychotherapy Integration*, *24*(3), 178-192.

Gerhardt, S. (2004). *Why Love Matters: How affection shapes a baby's brain* (2nd ed.). New York: Routledge.

Hong, R., & Mason, C. (2016). Becoming a neurobiologically-informed play therapist. *International Journal of Play Therapy*, *25*(1), 35–44. doi:10.1037/pla0000020

Jernberg, A. M., & Booth, P. (1999). *Theraplay: Helping Parents and Children Build Better Relationships* (2nd ed.). San Francisco, CA: Jossey Bass.

Kendall, S., & Bloomfield, L. (2005). Developing and validating a tool to measure parenting self-efficacy. *Journal of Advanced Nursing*, *51*(2), 174–181. doi:10.1111/j.1365-2648.2005.03479.x PMID:15963189

Kestley, T. A. (2014). *The Interpersonal Neurobiology of Play*. New York, NY: Norton.

Kinniburgh, K. J., Blaustein, M., Spinazzola, J., & van der Kolk, B. A. (2005). Attachment, Self-Regulation, and Competency. *Psychiatric Annals*, *35*(5), 424–430.

Kyung, K. Y. (2011). The effect of group Theraplay on self-esteem and depression of the elderly in a day care center. *Korean Journal of Counseling*, *12*(5), 1413–1430.

Lender, D., Booth, P., & Lindaman, S. (2012). The Theraplay treatment program: Description and implementation of an attachment-based play for children and caregivers. In A. Rubin (Ed.), *Programs and Interventions for maltreated children and families at risk*. New York: Wiley and Sons.

Main, M., & Goldwin, R. (1984). Predicting rejection of her infant from mothers representation of her own experience: Implications for the abused/abusing intergenerational cycle. *Journal of Child Abuse & Neglect*, *8*(2), 203–217. doi:10.1016/0145-2134(84)90009-7 PMID:6539642

Makela, J., & Vierikko, I. (2005). From heart to heart: Interactive therapy for children in care. Report on the Theraplay project in SOS Children's Villages in Finland 2001-2004. The SOS Children's Villages Association, Finland, Annual Report.

Marshack, M. (1960). A method for assessing child-parent interactions under controlled conditions. *The Journal of Genetic Psychology*, *97*(1), 3–22. doi:10.1080/00221325.1960.10534309 PMID:14421486

Ogden, P., Minton, K., & Pain, C. (2006). *Trauma and the body: A sensorimotor approach to psychotherapy*. New York: Norton.

Olff, M., Koch, S. J., Nawijn, L., Frijling, J. L., Van Zuiden, M., & Veltman, D. J. (2014). Social support, oxytocin, and PTSD. *European Journal of Psychotraumatology*, *51*. doi:10.3402/ejpt.v5.26513 PMID:25511718

Pace, C. S., & Zavattini, G. C. (2011). Adoption and attachment theory: The attachment models of adoptive mothers and the revision of attachment patterns of their late-adopted children. *Child: Care, Health and Development*, *37*(1), 82–88. doi:10.1111/j.1365-2214.2010.01135.x PMID:20637017

Panksepp, J. (2007). Can play diminish ADHD and facilitate the construction of the social brain? *Journal of the Canadian Academy of Child and Adolescent Psychiatry*, *16*(2), 57–66. PMID:18392153

Pankseppp, J., & Biven, L. (2012). *The archaeology of the mind: Neuroevolutionary origins of human emotions*. New York, NY: Norton.

Perry, B. (2009). Examining child maltreatment through a neurodevelopmental lens: Clinical applications of the neurosequential model of therapeutics. *Journal of Loss and Trauma*, *14*(4), 240–255. doi:10.1080/15325020903004350

Perry, B. (2014). The neurosequential model of therapeutics: Application of a developmentally sensitive and neurobiologically-informed approach to clinical problem-solving in maltreated children. In K. Brandt, B. Perry, S. Seligman, & E. Tronick (Eds.), *Infant and early childhood mental health: Core concepts and clinical practice*. Washington, DC: American Psychiatric Publishing.

Porges, S. (2004). Neuroception: A subconscious system for detecting threats and safety. *Zero to Three*.

Porges, S. (2011). *The polyvagal theory: Neurophysiological foundations of emotions, attachments, communications, self-regulation*. New York: Norton.

Reynolds, C., & Kamphaus, R. (2015). *Behavioral Assessment Scales for Children* (3rd ed.). San Antonio, TX: Pearson Assessments.

Robison, M., Lindaman, S., Clemmons, M., Doyle-Buckwalter, K., & Ryan, M. (2009). I Deserve a Family: The evolution of an adolescents behavior and beliefs about himself and others when treated with Theraplay in residential care. *Child & Adolescent Social Work Journal*, *26*(4), 291–306. doi:10.1007/s10560-009-0177-x

Rubin & Tregay. (1989). *Play with them: Theraplay groups in the classroom*. Springfield, IL: Charles Thomas.

Sahar, T., Shalev, A. Y., & Porges, S. (2001). Vagal modulation of responses to challenge in PTSD. *Biological Psychiatry*, *49*, 635–647. doi:10.1016/S0006-3223(00)01045-3

Schieffer, K. (2013). *Sunshine Circles: Interactive playgroups for social skills development and classroom management: Teacher Manual*. Evanston, IL: The Theraplay Institute.

Schore, A. N. (2001). The effects of early relational trauma on right brain development, affect regulation, and infant mental health. *Infant Mental Health Journal*, *22*(1/2), 201–269. doi:10.1002/1097-0355(200101/04)22:1<201::AID-IMHJ8>3.0.CO;2-9

Schore, A. N. (2009). Right-brain affect regulation: An essential mechanism of development, trauma, dissociation and psychotherapy. In D. Fosha, D. J. Siegel, & M. Solomon (Eds.), The healing power of emotion: Affective neuroscience development and clinical practice (pp. 112–114). Academic Press.

Schore, A. N. (2012). *The science of the art of psychotherapy*. New York, NY: Norton.

Schore, J. R., & Schore, A. N. (2008). Modern Attachment Theory: The central role of affect regulation in development and treatment. *Clinical Social Work Journal*, *36*(1), 9–20. doi:10.1007/s10615-007-0111-7

Shahmoom-Shanok, R. (1997). Giving back future's promise: Working resourcefully with. parents of children who have severe disorders of relating and communicating. *Zero to Three*, *17*(5), 37–48.

Siu, A. F. Y. (2009). Theraplay in the Chinese world: An intervention program for Hong Kong children with internalizing problems. *International Journal of Play Therapy*, *18*(1), 1–12. doi:10.1037/a0013979

Siu, A. F. Y. (2014). Effectiveness of Group Theraplay on Enhancing Social Skills among Children with Developmental Disabilities. *International Journal of Play Therapy*, *23*(4), 187–203. doi:10.1037/a0038158

Stern, D. N. (2002). *The first relationship: Infant and mother*. Cambridge, MA: Harvard University Press.

Sunderland, M. (2006). *The Science of Parenting*. New York, NY: DK Publishing Inc.

Tucker, C., Schieffer, K., Willis, T., & Hull, C. (2016). *Teacher-led groups foster social- emotional development in at-risk preschools students.* In process.

van der Kolk, B. (2014). *The body keeps the score: Brain, mind, and body in the healing of trauma.* New York: Viking.

Weir, K. N., Lee, S., Canosa, P., Rodrigues, N., McWilliams, M., & Parker, L. (2013). Whole Family Theraplay: Integrating Family Systems Theory and Theraplay to Treat Adoptive Families. *Adoption Quarterly*, *16*(3-4), 175–200. doi:10.1080/10926755.2013.844216

Wettig, H. G., Coleman, A. R., & Geider, F. J. (2011). Evaluating the effectiveness of Theraplay in treating shy, socially withdrawn children. *International Journal of Play Therapy*, *20*(1), 26–37. doi:10.1037/a0022666

Winnicott, D. W. (2005). *Playing and reality*. New York, NY: Tavistock Publications.

KEY TERMS AND DEFINITIONS

Attachment: A psychological theory that examines the development of interpersonal or social relationships in human development, especially the early parent-child relationship.

Attunement: An adult caregiver's ability to recognize and respond to the child's internal emotional state, and co-regulation.

Challenge: A dimension of parenting that encourages the child to explore new things, to take risks and to increase in confidence.

Co-Regulation: An adult caregiver's ability to soothe a child who is distressed and engage a child who is distracted or bored.

Engagement: A dimension of parenting that helps parents to be present with (attuned) and provide interactions that create connection and mutual enjoyment.

Nurture: A dimension of parenting in which parents respond empathically to the child's attachment and regulatory needs by being warm, tender, calming and comforting. Nurture activities provide a safe haven and create feelings of self-worth.

Play Therapy: A collection of counseling modalities that employ play process and play media to facilitate change in individuals and families.

Structure: A dimension of parenting that facilitates the child's experience of the caregiver as someone who is trustworthy and can keep the child safe.

Theraplay: A play-based family therapy for building healthy parent-child relationships. Theraplay is based on attachment theory and focuses on dimensions of healthy parenting that include nurture, engagement, structure and challenge.

Chapter 4
Integrating Interpersonal Neurobiology into the Play Therapy Process:
Advancing Adlerian Play Therapy

Dalena L. Dillman Taylor
University of Central Florida, USA

Naomi Joy Wheeler
University of Central Florida, USA

ABSTRACT

Advancements in neuroscience provide theoretical support for principles and practices of counseling and play therapy intervention (Badenoch & Kestley, 2015; Siegel, 2012). Likewise, AdPT shares many conceptual similarities with IPNB and neuroscience research including emphasis on childhood experience, social interest and relationships, purposefulness of behavior, holism, and the internalized narrative or self-schema. This chapter per the authors will (a) develop connections from neuroscience and IPNB to play and play therapy, (b) review the IPNB model's domains of integration and their relationship to AdPT, and (c) provide an updated AdPT framework that encompasses the most recent neuroscience empirical support.

NEUROSCIENCE, IPNB AND PLAY: ADVANCING ADLERIAN PLAY THERAPY

The first six years of life are the most influential period of neuronal growth, as well as, the most vulnerable to maltreatment (National Scientific Council on the Developing Child, 2010; U.S. Department of Health and Human Services, 2013). This period of vulnerability makes early childhood a critical and influential time in development and learning. Recent advancements in neuroscience provide evidence that our environment, early life experiences, and relationships contribute to physical and psychological health (Kandel, 1998; Panksepp & Biven, 2012; Porges, 2011; Siegel, 2012). Negative and positive experiences exert a differential impact to how our brains are formed, function, and integrate information.

DOI: 10.4018/978-1-5225-2224-9.ch004

The Interpersonal Neurobiology model (IPNB; Siegel, 2012) incorporates several theories from neuroscience that address (a) memory encoding, (b) the polyvagal theory (Porges, 2011), (c) neuroplasticity (Kandel, 1998), and (d) the midbrain's affective emotional-motivational systems (Panksepp & Biven, 2012). These theories underscore the value of new experiences and interaction in our social environment to reshape and restructure both brain and behavior. Therefore, this introduction begins with a review of neuroscience theory within the framework of the IPNB model, play, and play therapy, specifically Adlerian play therapy.

IPNB

In the Interpersonal Neurobiology (IPNB) model, Siegel (2012) postulates that health is influenced by the integration of the brain, mind, and in interactions with others in our social environment. All relationships have the potential to inhibit or contribute to neural integration. IPNB addresses nine domains of neural integration: *consciousness, bilateral, vertical, memory, narrative, state, interpersonal, temporal,* and *transpirational* or *identity integration* (refer to IPNB domains of integration and Adlerian Play Therapy section below). Each domain contributes to overall health and requires attention in therapeutic and educational intervention (Siegel, 2012), because each domain also produces energy and information flow through the nervous system and body. We are constantly receiving information, interpreting and incorporating messages into conscious and unconscious responses. Likewise, energy and information are shared between nervous systems with others in the social environment. We are impacted by those around us and respond in accordance to the integrated messages experienced from within (internal cues) and between (our system in interaction with others in the environment).

Similarly, Alfred Adler (1998) identified early childhood influences to personality and lifestyle development from the social system (e.g. family constellation, gender roles, parental attitudes, and family economic position) and inherited qualities (i.e. health and appearance). Adler noted the importance of a person's perceptions of childhood experiences for adult life and the value of social interest for well-being. He theorized that our beliefs and logic about self, others, and the world are created in childhood and serve as the foundation for future attitudes and behavior. We are wired to seek integration among brain, mind, and in interactions, which contributes to growth, health, and restoration. Principles emerging from IPNB provide theoretical support for many prevention and intervention strategies with adults as well as children.

Play

Children are able to work through experiences and make meaning of their life events, environment, and relationships through play. In fact, play contributes to neurobiological development as well as cognitive, socio-emotional, physical development, acquisition of social skills, and capacity for self-regulation (Berk, 2012; Erickson, 1963; Greenspan, 1993; Ray, 2011). Play is the first, natural language for children whereby needs, emotions, and thoughts are communicated (Landreth, 2012). Through play, children interpret their experiences and relationships to cultivate social skills, self-regulation, and a nervous system responsive to life. Play contributes to secure relationships and social connection that provides safety for exploration and engagement with the world. However, when a child experiences trauma or poor attachment to significant caregivers, development can be interrupted resulting in heightened stress responses, immobilization, and developmental delays (Badenoch, 2008; Kestley, 2015). Therefore, when challenging or traumatic events occur in early childhood, appropriate assessment and intervention may be crucial to influence maladaptive health trajectories and schemas initiated.

When untreated, posttraumatic stress symptoms persist at six-month follow-up in young children exposed to a traumatic event (Meiser-Stedman, Smith, Glucksman, Yule, & Dalgleish, 2008). Children exposed to trauma seem to be more sensitive to subsequent stressors. This heightened sensitivity contributes to an increased risk for problematic internalizing and externalizing behaviors (Grasso, Ford, & Briggs-Gowan, 2013). When poor attachments exist, education regarding the neurological underpinnings of disrupted attachment may be helpful to parents and the child alike. Neuroeducation may help to facilitate understanding between family members and contribute to responses that promote safety and facilitate healthy neurological growth. Further, many theories of play therapy, such as Adlerian play therapy, involve the parent/guardian in the therapeutic process of a child.

Play Therapy and Adlerian Play Therapy

Play therapy is a developmentally responsive approach to therapeutic work with children based in empirical support (Bratton, Ray, Rhine, & Jones, 2005; Landreth, 2012; Lin & Bratton, 2015; Ray, 2011). Children are able to express themselves symbolically and through play, supporting their needs while in therapy (Landreth, 2012; Ray, 2011). Research supports play therapy as an efficacious intervention for children with problematic or disruptive behaviors (Bratton et al., 2005; Lin & Bratton, 2015). Additionally, play therapy is an effective intervention for treatment of several different presenting issues: (a) externalizing or disruptive behaviors (i.e., aggression, ADHD symptoms, anger, impulsivity; Flahive & Ray, 2007; Garza & Bratton, 2005; Ojiambo & Bratton, 2014; Packman & Bratton, 2003; Ray, Blanco, Sullivan, & Holliman, 2009; Ray, Schottelkorb, & Tsai, 2007), (b) academically at-risk (Blanco & Ray; 2011; Blanco, Ray, & Holliman; 2012), and (c) functional impairment (Ray, Stulmaker, Lee, & Silverman, 2013). The therapeutic relationship between therapist and child can facilitate greater levels of awareness and regulation.

Adlerian Play Therapy (AdPT) shares many conceptual similarities with IPNB and neuroscience research including emphasis on childhood experience, social interest and relationships, purposefulness of behavior, holism, and the internalized narrative or self-schema. AdPT is empirically supported as effective (e.g., Meany-Walen, Bratton, & Kottman, 2014; Dillman Taylor & Meany-Walen, 2015; Meany-Walen, Bullis, Kottman, & Dillman Taylor, 2015). Additionally, AdPT is one of the leading approaches to play therapy (Lambert et al., 2007), emphasizing social interest and connection, subjective perspectives, a holistic approach to working with children, and the purposefulness of behavior – adaptive or maladaptive – to meet one's needs (Kottman & Meany-Walen, 2016). Due to the influence of early childhood experiences, children develop subjective perspectives about self, others, and the world (e.g., life style) and how to form relationships through this lens. Children enter therapy with mistaken beliefs in their lifestyle, and behaviors that once helped them to feel safe, secure, and significant are no longer feasible. Additionally, relationships with significant others – parents, caregivers, and/or teachers – are strained. Adlerian play therapists holistically conceptualize children that enter therapy, considering the child's (a) assets, (b) Crucial C's (e.g. perception of self as connected, capable, count as a human being, courageous; Lew & Bettner, 2000), (c) life tasks, (d) family constellation, (e) family atmosphere, (f) early recollections, (g) goal of misbehavior, (h) personality priorities, (i) lifestyle convictions, (j) private logic, and (k) play themes. AdPT "is further distinguished from other models of play therapy by specific techniques used in the play process, critical role of encouragement, emphasis on collaboration with caregivers, and type of information gathered through play themes" (Dillman Taylor & Bratton, 2014, p. 208).

Advancements in neuroscience provide theoretical support for the principles and practices of counseling and play therapy intervention (Badenoch & Kestley, 2015; Siegel, 2012). However, in spite of the theoretical connections between play therapy and neuroscience (Wheeler & Dillman Taylor, 2016), further research is needed to examine this relationship. Additionally, outside of the scope of this chapter, applications of IPNB informed play therapy intervention with diverse and/or special needs populations may be a useful next step. This chapter will (a) develop connections from neuroscience and IPNB to play and play therapy, (b) review the IPNB model's domains of integration and their relationship to AdPT, and (c) provide an updated AdPT framework that encompasses the most recent neuroscience empirical support.

INTEGRATING PLAY THERAPY AND NEUROSCIENCE

The interpersonal neurobiology (IPNB) model incorporates several theories from neuroscience to explain the connections among the brain, mind, and relationships with others (Siegel, 2012). Also, in the IPNB model, integration is based in neuroscience research regarding how memories are developed and the influence of biological instinctual responses for emotion and survival. Basic summaries for neuroscience theories including (a) memory encoding, (b) polyvagal theory, and (c) affective emotional-motivational systems will be provided; however, this review is not exhaustive, nor replacement for review of the original scholarly works (See Kandel, 1998; Panksepp & Biven, 2012; Porges, 2011; Siegel, 2012 for a detailed explanation of the aforementioned theories).

Memory Encoding

Encoding is a biological process whereby memories are created (Siegel, 2012). Events perceived by our senses are given attention and create or strengthen neural pathways. Implicit memory refers to unconscious recalled mental models of emotions, images, or behaviors that influence our reactions. Implicit memories begin to develop prenatally; and once born, the caregiver attachment influences neural development and the child's view of self. According to Adler (1998), attachment and the parent-child relationship are influenced by parental attitudes such as rejecting, democratic, or overprotective. The parent-child dynamic contributes to feelings of equality, inferiority, or superiority.

Conversely, explicit memory appears around age two. Explicit memory requires focused attention for conscious encoding of events and to be able to add a sense of time to the memory. The development of explicit memory contributes to autobiographical recollection where storytelling can help children learn and attach meaning. Autobiographical memories are often more easily recalled due to their strong connection to enhanced emotional states and neural activity.

At the core, an implicit and nonverbal process often guides play. We are wired at a primitive level motivated for play (Panksepp, 2010). This natural process occurs repeatedly in play therapy where preverbal implicit memories may emerge (Kestly, 2014). In response, the play therapist attunes to the child's needs and experiences through the restoration and reconsolidation process of the implicit. Implicit interpretations of the world and its rules are often reflected in play behaviors (Marks-Tarlow, 2012). Similarly, children are provided the opportunity for implicit learning through play.

Implicit learning occurs through engagement in the implicit world and by making sense of the implicit explicitly (McGilchrist, 2009). Children engage in metaphorical play that emerges naturally in the play therapy process, thus grounding this experience in nonverbal storytelling. Additionally, in play therapy, the therapist verbally communicates the child's process, thereby connecting the metaphoric and verbal worlds. In so doing, autographical and metaphorical understanding of the child's embodied story increases (Kestly, 2014; McGilchrist, 2009). When facilitated in a safe environment and safe attachment, play moves from implicit to explicit and contributes to autonomy and social engagement (Marks-Tarlow, 2012). Through the safety of the therapeutic relationship, children engage in the right-left-right progression of integration (McGilchrist, 2009). The progression from processing between the right and left hemispheres of the brain (i.e. right-left-right) facilitates integration of implicit memories and narrative into the explicit, conscious world.

Polyvagal Theory

According to the polyvagal theory (Porges, 2011), our neural systems are continuously assessing our experience and environment to match a response as a means of survival. Of the three neural system responses, the most primitive is 'immobilization' or more commonly called the 'freeze' response where an individual feigns death for survival. Second, the 'fight-or-flight' response allows us to take action or exit a perceived challenge or threatening situation. Finally, higher order processes, such as social engagement or self-soothing behaviors, can only be employed once the sympathetic nervous system (SNS) is calm. The SNS facilitates the 'fight-or-flight' response, whereas the parasympathetic nervous system stimulates 'rest-and-digest' and a return to homeostasis. Our physiological state influences our options for behavioral response because we are wired to seek safety. Additionally, older circuits are engaged sequentially to regain a sense of safety, responding from more developed circuits first. As a result, in counseling, the polyvagal response allows for development of safety and trust in the therapeutic relationship once both systems are receptive.

To experience the benefits of play discussed to this point, the child's SNS must first enter a calm state. As Porges (2011) outlines in the polyvagal theory, every human is wired to seek out a sense of safety, limiting behavioral options depending on which neural system is engaged. In play therapy, the polyvagal response allows for development of safety and trust within the playroom as well as in the therapeutic relationship.

The playroom should be designed and maintained in a way to promote stability and predictability for the child (Axline, 1964; Kestley, 2014; Landreth, 2012; Ray, 2011). Kestly (2014) refers to this room as the "play sanctuary," in which the environment is designed to create a calm, safe space that is inviting and welcoming of the child. Therapist considerations for creation of a play sanctuary outlined by Kestly (2014) include that it: (a) is inviting, (b) is organized and predictable, (c) includes special play areas for nurturing, aggressive, make-believe, reality, and creative toys, and (d) presents flexible boundaries. However, the child must *perceive* the environment as safe in order to calm his or her SNS and engage in the circuitry of *PLAY* (Panksepp & Biven, 2012). The perception of a threat to safety may be influenced by an individual's style of life including attitudes towards self, others, the world and challenges encountered in any of those domains. As the *PLAY* circuit is engaged and safety is felt, children are capable of accessing their implicit memories in play for integration into their autobiographical story (Kestly, 2014)

Affective Emotional-Motivational Systems

Instinctual drives for survival also contribute to the basic emotional networks in the brain or affective neuroscience (Panksepp, 2010). These primitive networks are located in the subcortical regions of the brain, yet inform higher order psychological processes and motivate behavior. There are seven basic emotional processes including *SEEKING, RAGE, FEAR, LUST* (seen in adolescence), *CARE, PANIC/GRIEF*, and *PLAY*. The emotional processes are indicated with capital letters to designate the associated systems fundamentally engaged across species without conditioning. These emotional responses allow us to interpret safety or survival concerns in the environment.

Several of these systems, including *SEEKING, PLAY*, and *CARE*, underscore the significance of play and play-based interventions. Oftentimes when children are in internal distress, their disruptive behaviors can create challenges for parents/caregivers to recognize the underlying need for connection and safety. By engaging the circuitry of play, children can explore their world and internal interpretation through the safety of a symbolic medium. Likewise, in play therapy children can begin to "widen the window of tolerance" by experiencing safety in the playroom and within the therapeutic relationship while processing and integrating disturbances.

Neuroplasticity

New neural connections are developed across the lifespan through exposure to novel stimuli. Also known as neuroplasticity (Kandel, 1998), the brain continues to adapt and grow in response to experience. Similarly, reparative experiences can enhance neural development contributing to hope for change.

New ways of thinking, feeling, and experiencing prior memories or beliefs can be created through novel and repetitive experiences (Kandel, 1998; Siegel, 2012). In play therapy, children explore their world and experiences through play while maintaining safety in both the physical space and relationship with the therapist. AdPT (Kottman & Meany-Walen, 2016) posits the experience of safety while exploring past disturbances can challenge previous beliefs of self or others. Over time, these experiences in the playroom can alter beliefs about self, others, and the world. Ultimately, such schema modification creates a more accurate and complex depiction of the world that incorporates both positive and negative components.

Interpersonal Neurobiology (IPNB)

Relationships, experiences, and interaction with the environment exert bi-directional influences, each informing the next experience throughout our lifetime. In IPNB the focus is on how this interplay contributes to the overall development of the nervous system. Regulation of information and energy between the brain, mind, and interpersonal experience is called integration (Siegel, 2012). Oftentimes, the greater the integration between these systems, the more functional and healthy the individual. Therefore, all relationships and experiences have the potential to inhibit or contribute to integration and health. Furthermore, therapeutic relationships can facilitate integration by seeking to enhance awareness and build from experiences of co-regulation.

IPNB DOMAINS OF INTEGRATION AND ADLERIAN PLAY THERAPY

The IPNB model (Siegel, 2012) addresses nine domains of neural integration including: *consciousness, bilateral, vertical, memory, narrative, state, interpersonal, temporal,* and *transpirational* or *identity integration*. We will briefly outline each domain of integration, as well as, related neuroscience theory with application to AdPT below.

Consciousness Integration

Integration of consciousness is a teachable skill that aims to increase intentional attention to each of the senses. Consciousness can be practiced through awareness to the present moment and each of the four areas of sensation (Siegel, 2014). In the 'wheel of awareness' Siegel addresses (a) the five senses (touch, taste, smell, sight, hearing); (b) the sixth sense or the sensations of the interior of the body; (c) the seventh sense or mental activities including thoughts, feelings and beliefs; and (d) the eighth sense, or interconnectedness to others, the earth, the past, and future. Although just one form of consciousness integration, the wheel of awareness underscores the linkage between sensations, thoughts, feelings, and connection as contributors to mindfully experiencing the here-and-now. Present moment awareness can only be accomplished as the SNS is calmed and diffuse physiological arousal is reduced. In play therapy, intentional coordination and organization of the 'play sanctuary' can convey comfort, safety and invite children to explore the space and toys (Kestley, 2014; Landreth, 2012). Similarly, the therapeutic presence and relationship can enable the connection between self and others (Crenshaw & Kenney-Noziska, 2014; Geller & Porges, 2014). The first phase of AdPT focuses on development of the therapeutic and egalitarian relationship.

In AdPT, the therapeutic relationship between the therapist and child creates a feeling of safety and security in the playroom, thus opening up the child to experience and begin integration of consciousness. The play therapist will direct attention to the current moment through reflections of sensory experiences including the sights, sounds, and tactile sensations. In the Adlerian playroom, toys and materials are displayed in an open arrangement that is inviting to children. The structure of an Adlerian playroom allows the child to engage all five senses. Kottman and Meany-Walen (2016) identified appropriate materials and toys that encourage exploration. To engage touch, children can use water, sand, paints, and others. Children can engage their sound sense by playing instruments, popping the bubble wrap, etc. Visual stimuli in a playroom include the lights and the variety of colors of the toys and materials. Children can also engage in the sense of smell (i.e., the smell of paints, markers) and taste (e.g. baby bottle, water, or other toys). See Kottman and Meany-Walen (2016) for a complete list of playroom materials.

Bilateral Integration

Bilateral integration refers to the connection between the left and right hemispheres of the brain. Although each hemisphere performs similar functions, each attends to information in unique ways. Autobiographical memory, symbols, and creativity are primarily held in the right hemisphere (Siegel, 2010); whereas, the left hemisphere adds logical, linear, and literal processing including the addition of words and context to memories. When bilateral integration has not occurred, the individual may be challenged to incorporate emotions and cognitions in communication. Therefore, Siegel (2010) proposes connecting with other's on the emotional level and then redirecting cognitions to facilitate bilateral integration – connect to redirect.

Adlerian play therapists use specific skills to encourage bilateral integration. A unique Adlerian skill in conducting this level of integration is metacommunication. Kottman and Meany-Walen (2016) defined metacommunication as "the counselor step[ping] outside the interaction and communicat[ing] about the communication taking place in the relationship" (p. 111). In other words, the therapist notices the emotion, underlying meaning, or pattern being expressed by the child then reflects that information to the child. Through this interaction, the therapist is helping the child bring the emotional, abstract level to the forefront in a cognitive manner (i.e., metacommunication, reflection). When the child recognizes or "owns" this reflection, the child has established insight into his or her own patterns of viewing self, others, and the world (e.g., lifestyle) and thus, bilateral integration.

Vertical Integration

Vertical integration refers to the incorporation of higher (prefrontal cortex) brain functions with lower (subcortical) brain functions and body sensations. An individual responds to a triggering event by activating the emotional circuitry, FEAR and SEEKING. In response to the sensory input, the limbic region ("downstairs brain") is engaged with the goal of re-establishing safety. However, the individual can also engage higher order thinking from the prefrontal cortex ("upstairs brain"). In so doing, integration supports a shift from a state of reactivity to receptivity and openness to new information and experience. The play therapist can provide opportunities for learning and incorporate vertical integration by teaching children about their upstairs and downstairs brain through the *hand model of the brain* (Siegel & Payne Bryson, 2012).

Play therapists integrate many interventions into the play therapy modality to best meet each child's needs. In AdPT, Kottman and Meany-Walen (2016) outlined several metaphoric techniques such as (a) designing therapeutic metaphors, (b) mutual storytelling, and (c) directing role-plays; all that can help children retell experiences that were challenging or created anxiety. The therapist initiates storytelling to help the child connect his or her limbic area to the prefrontal cortex. When these two areas are not integrated, they may impede the child's progress in play therapy. Through storytelling, the therapist uses a custom-designed therapeutic metaphor that relates to the child's own experiences but creates distance for the child to establish safety as needed (Kottman & Meany-Walen, 2016). In turn, the use of metaphoric storytelling engages the *PLAY* circuitry (Panksepp & Biven, 2012). Storytelling includes a beginning, middle, and end – in that the main character overcomes the problem in a clear, concrete process. The child witnesses the therapist telling the story first, engaging the child's "upstairs brain" (i.e., prefrontal cortex). For younger children, their developmental level may not warrant this level of cognitive processing; however, repetition of the story can still encourage vertical integration. For older children, this process can be more explicit. By reading a child's non-verbal signals to assess his or her level of readiness to process, the therapist can purposefully discuss the obstacles and resolution in the story to enhance vertical integration. The therapist can also invite the child to tell/re-tell the story depending on his or her expressed interest in participating. When the child retells the story, this narrative directly relates to the process of vertical integration – using the prefrontal cortex to make sense of a triggering/challenging event.

Memory Integration

Memory integration distinguishes explicit from implicit and incorporates factual with autobiographical memory to create an awareness of self across time. Recall that implicit memories are based on experience and contribute unconsciously to options in behavioral response. Memory integration supports differentiation between past and present, so that an individual can avoid flooding responses and experience the past as the past. Additionally, through memory integration, an individual can become more aware when expectations for the world or mental models are triggered and attach factual reasoning before responding (Siegel & Payne Bryson, 2012).

Adlerian play therapists can utilize metacommunications to increase awareness of these mental models. Small nuances (i.e, body language – shrugs, downward glances; body position – toward or away from the therapist; verbal noises – sighs, heavy/shallow breathing) that the child communicates during session tend to relate to an internal struggle that he or she is experiencing and cannot cognitively articulate. Through use of metacommunications, the therapist is drawing the child's attention toward these nuances. Once the child is aware, the therapist can begin using interventions to make the implicit, explicit.

Further, Adlerian play therapists can also implement a specific intervention to recall emotions associated with memories – early recollections (Kottman & Meany-Walen, 2016).

Each early recollection elicited by the counselor should be a single, specific incident preferably occurring before the age of 10. Early memories are not coincidences; they are often projections. In large measure, what we selectively attend to from the past is reflective of what we believe and how we behave in the present, and what we anticipate from the future (Watts, 2013, p. 464).

Early recollections provide insight into the child's lifestyle – view of self, others, and the world. Therapists may find it more challenging to engage younger children in the memory process necessary for this activity. Therefore, the child needs to be at least six or seven years old when using early recollections in play therapy (Kottman & Meany-Walen, 2016). The therapist works with the child to develop his or her autobiographical memory, recalling up to seven early life memories. This activity should be conducted over several sessions versus the one session used for adults given the developmental level of children who are appropriate for play therapy (e.g., 3-10 years).

Narrative Integration

Narrative integration supports an individual's meaning-making process of their lived experiences. Violated expectations influence the adaptation of inaccurate and skewed schemas of the self, other, or the world, especially where trauma may have occurred. Storytelling can integrate thoughts, sensations, and feelings (Siegel & Payne Bryson, 2012). Likewise, narrative integration provides context for our experience, allowing negative events to remain in the past instead of intruding on the present (Collie, Backos, Malchiodi, & Spiegel, 2006; Siegel, 2012). However, storytelling and development of a self-narrative begins before language development (Badenoch, 2008). Therefore, storytelling activities can enable the externalization of internal challenges (Butler, Gutterman, & Rudes, 2009). Art, dance, sandplay, puppetry, music or free play may all be useful play therapy interventions that facilitate storytelling, depending on the developmental level of the child and his or her readiness to engage.

Unlike the custom-designed metaphor described earlier, the Adlerian therapist can also implement mutual storytelling, an intervention that allows *the child* to direct the story. Kottman and Meany-Walen (2016) suggested encouraging:

...the child [to] invent a story that has not happened in real life or been the plot of a television show, movie, video game, or book. This keeps the story in the 'made-up' realm, which lets children process their experiences without evoking their defenses (p. 237).

During the storytelling process, the therapist carefully listens for how the story is similar or what aspects of the story are similar to the child's presenting issues. The therapist then tells the child that he or she will tell another story using the same characters. The therapist retells the story using the same characters, same setting, and same beginning; however, she changes the middle and end to demonstrate more socially appropriate ways to handle the situation with a more positive outlook on life. This activity allows for narrative integration in a developmentally appropriate manner. Children feel safer when their internal struggles are explored in metaphor. Through the use of mutual storytelling, they can begin to see their own strengths, identify positive ways to build relationships, and learn strategies to enhance their own feelings of connectedness, capability, significance, and courageousness.

State Integration

State integration addresses the temporary nature of feelings experienced in life, relationships, and external events that can influence how we view or identify ourselves internally. Personality, character, and a sense of identity are generally persistent over time; however, experiences of a particular state may create internal conflict seeming incongruent or at odds with how an individual views him/herself. In response, play therapists can support resolution of this internal tension by bringing awareness to other choices or truths within the current moment.

The therapist can develop the client's understanding of state transience throughout the AdPT process (e.g. across phases) by validating a child's emotional state with reflection of feeling or metacommunications and acknowledging the fluidity of feelings about our experiences. In the fourth phase of Adlerian play therapy (i.e. reeducation/reorientation), the therapist teaches the child new, socially appropriate behaviors and provides opportunities for the child to try out new or learned feelings, thoughts, and behaviors that he or she has developed over the course of therapy. Within this phase, the therapist can teach children how to differentiate between thoughts that "I feel angry" (state) and "I am angry" (trait). Distinguishing between state and trait can contribute to more adaptive narrative for the self as described above, thus, promoting the reorientation aspect of therapy.

Interpersonal Integration

Human brains are wired for connection and interaction with others in the environment (Siegel & Payne Bryson, 2012). Therefore, once one system becomes integrated and differentiated within, interpersonal integration can occur between, through the introduction of another system. Interpersonal integration links the individual to a bigger purpose and degree of intimacy by incorporating input from others – movement from a 'me' to a 'we' perspective. We are attuned when we respond to the perceived and interpreted emotional states of those around us accurately. Mirror neurons allow us to predict and respond to inferred patterns in others and demonstrate connections to the human capacity for empathy. In response to the 'felt connection', neural firing becomes more coherent. In play therapy, attunement and coherence with another person contribute to the development of self-regulation within the therapeutic relationship.

In AdPT, the interaction between child and therapist encourages the natural healing that occurs when two systems resonate with one another. Facilitative responses communicate a trust and overall belief in the potential of the child to be *inter*dependent, learning to collaborate and work with the therapist to achieve therapeutic goals (Kottman & Meany-Walen, 2016). The therapeutic relationship is defined as a shared partnership, in that both the therapist and child share the responsibility and power in the play sessions. This nurturing, collaborative relationship is essential for the growing mind and child. AdPT interventions such as returning responsibility and allowing the child to take the lead empower interpersonal integration within the playroom. These skills communicate to the child that he or she is capable, competent, counts, and is courageous (four C's, Lew & Bettner, 1996) to try new tasks. By encouraging the child's four C's, the therapist builds the child's confidence in oneself and in the therapeutic relationship. Unlike other play therapy theories/approaches, AdPT emphasizes the importance of others in the process of change. Kottman and Meany-Walen (2016) stressed the critical nature of not only building an egalitarian relationship with the child, but also with the parents/caregivers and teachers. This systemic, interpersonal approach has been deemed most useful for integration (i.e., mental health). For instance, AdPT techniques applied in family therapy seem to not only increase involvement by the child, but also enhance positive emotional experiences within the family during family therapy sessions (Willis, Walters, & Crane, 2014). Related, children participating in group AdPT demonstrate improvements in socio-emotional competence and skills through interactions and cooperation between members (Chinekesh, Kamalian, Eltemasi, Chinekesh, & Alavi, 2014).

Temporal and Transpirational Integration

Developmentally, young children may be limited in their experience of the last two domains of integration – temporal and transpirational integration. Temporal integration examines the existential tensions between our desire for certainty and immortality versus the reality of uncertainty and death. Similarly, transpirational integration focuses on the larger belonging, connection, and purpose at the social, community, or planetary level. The capacity for abstract and hypothetical thought does not develop until adolescence (Berk, 2012; Piaget, 1951). Additionally, young children lack the cognitive ability to conceptualize personalized understandings of death (Himebauch, Arndol, & May, 2008). However, temporal integration also incorporates the connection of self in time related to the past, present and anticipated future (Siegel, 2012). Self-knowledge is increased by experiences and interactions with others that create our life story.

Children can communicate stories (as discussed with narrative integration), developing a stronger sense of their experiences as having a beginning, middle, and end, thus developing a stronger sense of their autobiographical memory. Adlerian play therapists provide a safe, nonjudgmental environment *with* the child; this environment is co-created. In this space, children can play out events from their past as a way to process and integrate those events into their life story (Siegel, 2012). Children involved in play therapy can use the facilitative responses of an Adlerian play therapist (including tracking, reflection of content, metacommunication) to make sense of both internal and external experiences (Kottman & Meany-Walen, 2016).

PUTTING IT ALL TOGETHER: NEUROSCIENCE-INFORMED ADLERIAN PLAY THERAPY

AdPT consists of four unique phases, although not rigid or linear. At any time, the therapist can transition to an early phase to meet the needs of the child client. Kottman and Meany-Walen (2016) outlined the four phases as (a) building an egalitarian relationship, (b) investigating the lifestyle, (c) gaining insight, and (d) reorientation/reeducation. The therapist role is fluid in this process, alternating between directive and non-directive approaches (Dillman Taylor & Bratton, 2014). Adlerian play therapists consider the therapeutic relationship to be a critical element in the change process for the child client. The purpose of this section is to provide an updated AdPT framework that is inclusive of neuroscience research (Table 1). We outline the nature of people, therapeutic goals, the role of the therapist, and the four therapeutic phases of Adlerian theory through a neuroscience lens.

Nature of People

Adlerian theorists view individuals as "indivisible, social, creative, decision-making beings whose beliefs and behavior have a purpose" (Carlson & Slavik, 1997, p. xi). Current neuroscience research supports this view of individuals – highlighting the importance of holism, social connection, purposefulness of behavior, and creativity (Miller & Dillman Taylor, 2016). Individuals strive to belong, gain significance, and develop social interest within their family of origin first, then generalizing this approach to other important relationships. This process of conceptualization is defined as the lifestyle – "the use of the personality, traits, temperament, and psychological and biological processes in order to find a place in the social matrix of life" (Maniacci, Sackett-Maniacci, & Mosak, 2014, p. 66). Lifestyles create predictability and emotional safety, thus, paving the path for involvement in the social engagement system.

Table 1. Integrating Adlerian play therapy and interpersonal neurobiology

	AdPT	AdPT and IPNB
Nature of People	Indivisible, social, creative, purposeful behavior, decision-makers	Holistic, social, purposeful behavior, creative, subjectivity
Therapeutic Goals	Primary: Increase social interest	Primary: Striving for well-being, mental health, and social interest (i.e., neural integrational, differentiation and linking)
Role of the Therapist	Fluid and fluctuating according to the need of the client and phase of therapy	Fluid and fluctuating according to the need of the client and phase of therapy
Phase I	Building an egalitarian relationship between therapist and client	Building an egalitarian relationship between therapist and client with a focus on conscious, interpersonal, and bilateral levels of integration
Phase II	Investigating the lifestyle	Investigating the lifestyle with a focus on memory and narrative levels of integration
Phase III	Gaining insight	Gaining insight with a focus on vertical, narrative, and memory levels of integration
Phase IV	Reeducation/Reorientation	Reeducation/Reorientation with a focus on interpersonal integration and neuroeducation

Even if a child is responding in a negative manner (e.g., one lacking in social interest), this behavior provides a sense of safety and manages to calm the SNS due to the predictability of others' reactions to this behavior. Adlerians' theorize that family members often develop a fixed view for who the child is and how he or she will behave by the age of six or seven. This view of the child acts as a 'psychology box' that can encapsulate the child. However, current neuroscience research supports Adlerians' view that these boxes can be modified through a trusting, collaborative therapeutic relationship with the child client and his or her family.

Further, social interest, a critical piece to Adlerian theory, "describes a person's connection to and appreciation of others' contributions to the betterment of the entire community" (Kottman and Meany-Walen, 2016, p. 21). "Social interest is consistent with a neurobiological view of optimal wellbeing" (Miller & Dillman Taylor, 2016, p. 113). Reflective of neural integration is the selfless response of having concern for and acting in the benefit of others (Siegel, 2010).

Adlerian therapists view individuals as goal-directed and their behaviors as achievement towards one's desire for significance and belonging. Clients in therapy, in collaboration with the therapist, transition from goals of misbehavior (inadequacy, revenge, power, and attention) to positive goals of behavior (involvement, independence, fairness, and competence) that can aid as a barometer of mental health and increased improvement (Kottman & Meany-Walen, 2016). Neuroscience defines goals of human growth and development as survival and belonging (Baumeister & Leary, 1995; Cozolino, 2010; Immordino-Yang & Damasio, 2007; Siegel, 2012; Spielberg et al., 2012). Individuals consistently assess risk and engage protective instincts of fight, flight, or freeze. In early childhood, children learn to adapt to their environment utilizing key behaviors that may create obstacles in adulthood when bids for connection are made; thus, the individual struggles to connect with others in an emotionally supportive, interpersonal relationship – another important goal. Therefore, to remain consistent with current literature, we advise Adlerian therapists to embrace the goal of survival in the conceptualization of clients due to the hierarchical relationship between establishing safety and the goals of belonging and significance.

In addition, people view life subjectively – this perspective aids in the development of the client's worldview and how he or she strives to achieve the goals as listed above. Rudolf Dreikurs is credited for once stating, children are keen observers, but poor interpreters. They tend to develop inaccurate beliefs about events and interactions. These inaccurate interpretations and goals of misbehavior contribute to the development of mistaken beliefs – a belief based on one's biased perception of self, others, and the world. People are also considered creative. The concept of neuroplasticity validates individuals' ability to adapt and change over time (Siegel, 2012). Adlerian therapists view the client holistically, focusing on the big picture based on the information gathered, and not singling out one aspect of his or her worldview. Therapists, within session and through the conceptualization process, focus on encouraging an individual's assets, uniqueness; exploring one's Crucial c's, goals, personality priorities, private logic, thought, emotions, and behaviors through a holistic manner; and examining the client's uniqueness across the five life tasks (work/school, friends, love, finding meaning in life, and coming to terms with oneself [self - self-regulation]; Kottman & Meany-Walen, 2016). This approach of viewing the client as indivisible is supported by neuroscience (e.g., interpersonal neurobiology; Siegel, 2012).

Goals of Therapy

The overarching goal of Adlerian therapy is to increase social interest. Given that social interest is a marker for mental health, this goal ties directly to IPNB (Miller & Dillman Taylor, 2016). For example,

Fredrickson et al. (2013) found a correlation between individuals' healthier gene expression and meaningful happiness (e.g., eudemonia). Therefore, preliminary neuroscience research supports that social interest and mental well-being go hand-in-hand, acknowledging the need to strive for social interest as priority in therapy. However, Miller and Dillman Taylor (2016) recommended that the Adlerian definition of mental health (e.g., degrees of social interest and discouragement) should be expanded to include brain-based understanding of mental health, particularly the definition proposed by Siegel (2012). From the IPNB perspective, "the mind as a complex, self-organizing, non-linear system that achieves wellbeing when aspects of the system (e.g., parts of the embodied brain, interpersonal relationships) are allowed to sufficiently differentiate (i.e., specialize) and then link with other aspects of the system" (Miller & Dillman Taylor, 2016, p. 122-123). In keeping this more holistic view of mental health in mind when working towards achievement of goals in AdPT, therapists will be able to address the whole person and his or her system as Adler first proposed.

According to Kottman and Meany-Walen (2016), secondary goals within AdPT aim to continue advancing the client's mental health. Some of these goals include: (a) decrease feelings of inferiority; (b) overcome feelings of discouragement while recognizing and using personal resources; (c) make changes in life goals and mistaken beliefs about self, others, and the world; (d) alter negative motivation to achieve significance and belonging; (e) gain a sense of equality with others; and (f) become cooperative, contributing members of society. Neuroplasticity adds support grounded in neuroscience for the possibility of change and achievement towards these goals within a supportive, encouraging therapeutic relationship.

Role of the Therapist

In AdPT, the therapist role is fluid, fluctuating according to phase of therapy. Within the first phase of therapy, the therapist responds to the child in a non-directive manner and power is shared between the therapist and client (Dinkmeyer, Dinkmeyer, & Sperry, 1987; Kottman & Meany-Walen, 2016). The therapist's role in phase two transitions to a more directive approach, acting as a detective to gain information regarding the client's lifestyle (Kottman, 2011). In phase three, the therapist's role is more fluid alternating between non-directive and directive approaches to challenge the child's mistaken beliefs and to increase insight (Kottman & Meany-Walen, 2016). During the last phase of therapy, the therapist shifts to a more active role, teaching and encouraging the child to integrate, practice, and incorporate new skills and perceptions about self, others, and the world.

Four Phases of Adlerian Play Therapy

Adlerian theory consists of four phases of therapy: (a) building an egalitarian relationship, (b) investigating the lifestyle, (c) gaining insight, and (d) reeducation/reorientation. Each of the four phases builds on the former, allowing the therapist to revisit a previous phase as needed. To advance Adlerian theory to current day practice, Miller and Dillman Taylor (2016) recommended therapists incorporate a developmental framework (outlined in phase two below) and neuroscience informed interventions (across the four phases, with emphasis in phases three and four).

Phase I: Building an Egalitarian Relationship

A strong, collaborative relationship is the foundation for change to occur and for the child to move towards *conscious integration* within the therapeutic process. This phase lays the foundation for the other three; thus, the therapist is consistently working on the maintenance of the therapeutic relationship and *interpersonal integration* for the duration of therapy (Kottman & Meany-Walen, 2016). To develop safety in the playroom, Kottman and Meany-Walen (2016) stated that the therapist treats the child client as an equal from the first meeting by: (a) getting on the child's level and introducing self to child client prior to the parent/caregiver in the waiting room, (b) asking the child client what he or she was told regarding play therapy, (c) demystifying the counseling process, (d) giving the child a business card, and (e) communicating in a developmentally appropriate manner the nature of confidentiality. Once safety is established, the child's play is free to move from the implicit to explicit, engaging in the right-left-right progression of integration. Further, the therapist utilizes several skills in order for *conscious integration* to occur – awareness of non-verbal behavior – such as tracking behavior, restating content, metacommunicating, reflecting feelings, answering and asking questions, returning responsibility to the child, and interacting actively with the child. Metacommunication is a particularly important skill in AdPT. This skill is interwoven into all four phases to help the client gain insight into his or her lifestyle. The use of metacommunication aids in *bilateral integration*, connecting the right hemisphere (dominated by emotions) to the left hemisphere (dominated by language).

Phase II: Investigating the Lifestyle

Early childhood experiences contribute to one's overall physical and psychological health (Kandel, 1998; Panskeep & Biven, 2012). Therefore, the therapist works with caregivers, teachers, and the child to understand early life experiences and their influence on the child's development of lifestyle. Further, as Miller and Dillman Taylor (2016) recommended, therapists should take inventory of the child's early life experiences through a developmental theory such as attachment theory. Through the integration of attachment theory into AdPT, therapists will be better equipped to conceptualize the whole child and his or her relational influences to one's worldview as Adler intended. Therefore, the therapist takes a detailed developmental history (Kottman & Meany-Walen, 2016; Ray, 2011). The child's lifestyle is multifaceted, consisting of several components that together formulate the overall conceptualization of how the child views self, others, and the world. The therapist explores with the child and significant others the following aspects: (a) assets, (b) functioning at life tasks, (c) play themes, (d) psychological birth order, (e) family constellation, (f) family atmosphere, (g) early recollections, (h) goals of misbehavior, (i) crucial c's, and (j) personality priorities. In particular, early recollections aid in *memory integration*. As the client is able to describe and piece together early childhood memories, he or she links these early recollections into an autobiographical narrative, thus increasing *memory* and *narrative integration*. In this phase, the therapist gathers information to formulate tentative hypotheses regarding the client's worldview. In the next phase, the client begins to gain insight into his or her lifestyle, thus aiding further integration.

Phase III: Gaining Insight

A child begins to develop an internalized narrative or mistaken beliefs about self, others, and the world from early experiences. Therapists, in this phase, work to provide the client with insight into this internalized framework. As noted earlier in the chapter, Kottman and Meany-Walen (2016) outlined several metaphoric techniques to aid in *vertical* and *narrative integration* such as (a) designing therapeutic metaphors, (b) mutual storytelling, and (c) directing role-plays; all that can help the child retell experiences that were challenging or created anxiety. Further, the therapist uses the collection of early memories from phase two to provide the client with tentative hypotheses regarding his or her worldview and increase the client's *memory* and *narrative integration*. The therapist uses retelling of early memories and/or storytelling techniques to attach meaning to memories and help further implicit learning through play, the child's natural language.

Phase IV: Reorientation/Reeducation

The child learns to develop new ways to think, behave, feel, and experience prior memories and beliefs through novel and repetitive experiences. In this phase, the therapist collaborates with the client to modify mistaken beliefs and private logic to more socially useful ways of seeing self, others, and the world. Through repetition of practicing new behaviors and thoughts, the client can begin to internalize and experience his or her world more accurately. The therapist uses this phase to educate the client on more socially useful approaches to engaging and interacting with others – both to increase in social interest and *interpersonal integration*. Further, as Miller and Dillman Taylor (2016) recommended, inclusion of *neuroeducation* is impactful for clients to begin understanding how their behaviors relate to brain development. Siegel and Payne Bryson (2011) found that teaching children the hand model of the brain was helpful in providing insight, increasing recognition of cues preceding "flipping their lid," and implementing mindfulness strategies to regain control. Similarly, Siegel and Payne Bryson (2011) suggested education to teach calming skills, skills to redirect attention, and skills to integrate states, feelings, and desires as methods of state integration. Adlerian play therapists can integrate various techniques to help the child focus on his or her breath as it fits with the child's presenting issue, such as (a) use of pinwheels to demonstrate deep breathing, (b) bubbles for slow controlled breaths, or (c) deep belly breaths while balancing a toy on a child's stomach. These activities can be generalized for use in other settings including home or school.

SUMMARY

Current neuroscience research provides theoretical support for the principles and practices of play therapy (Badenoch & Kestley, 2015; Siegel, 2012). Specifically, AdPT shares many conceptual similarities with IPNB, including an emphasis on childhood experience, social interest and relationships, purposefulness of behavior, holism, and the internalized narrative or self-schema. The connections between neuroscience principles and play therapy were demonstrated, reviewed the IPNB model's domains of integration and their relationship to AdPT, and provided an updated AdPT framework that encompassed current neuroscience empirical support. Therefore, the integration of AdPT with IPNB demonstrates significant promise given the ease of connection between these two therapeutic models. It is likely that therapists who integrate AdPT with IPNB can help facilitate healthy brain development and interpersonal and intrapersonal relationships; although, future research is needed on the efficacy of this approach.

REFERENCES

Adler, A. (1998). *Understanding human nature.* London: Oneworld Publications. (Original work published 1927)

Axline, V. M. (1964). *Dibs: In search of self - personality development in play therapy*. Boston, MA: Houghton Mifflin.

Badenoch, B. (2008). *Being a brain-wise therapist: A practical guide to interpersonal neurobiology*. New York, NY: Norton.

Badenoch, B., & Kestly, T. (2015). Exploring the neuroscience of healing play at every age. In D. Crenshaw & A. Stewart (Eds.), *Play therapy: A comprehensive guide to theory and practice* (pp. 524–538). New York, NY: Guildford Press.

Baumeister, R. F., & Leary, M. R. (1995). The need to belong: Desire for interpersonal attachments as a fundamental human motivation. *Psychological Bulletin, 117*(3), 497–529. doi:10.1037/0033-2909.117.3.497 PMID:7777651

Berk, L. (2012). *Infants and children: Prenatal through middle childhood* (7th ed.). Boston, MA: Pearson Allyn and Bacon.

Blanco, P. J., & Ray, D. C. (2011). Play therapy in elementary schools: A best practice for improving academic achievement. *Journal of Counseling and Development, 89*(2), 235–243. doi:10.1002/j.1556-6678.2011.tb00083.x

Blanco, P. J., Ray, D. C., & Holliman, R. (2012). Long-term child centered play therapy and academic achievement of children: A follow-up study. *International Journal of Play Therapy, 21*(1), 1–13. doi:10.1037/a0026932

Bratton, S. C., Ray, D., Rhine, T., & Jones, L. (2005). The efficacy of play therapy with children: A meta-analytic review of treatment outcomes. *Professional Psychology, Research and Practice, 36*(4), 376–390. doi:10.1037/0735-7028.36.4.376

Butler, S., Guterman, J. T., & Rudes, J. (2009). Using puppets with children in narrative therapy to externalize the problem. *Journal of Mental Health Counseling, 31*(3), 225–233. doi:10.17744/mehc.31.3.f255m86472577522

Carlson, J., & Slavik, S. (1997). *Techniques in Adlerian Psychology*. New York, NY: Routledge.

Chinekesh, A., Kamalian, M., Eltemasi, M., Chinekesh, S., & Alavi, M. (2014). The effect of group play therapy on socio-emotional skills in pre-school children. *Global Journal of Health Science, 6*(2), 163–167. PMID:24576376

Collie, K., Backos, A., Malchiodi, C., & Spiegel, D. (2006). Art therapy for combat-related PTSD: Recommendations for research and practice. *Art Therapy: Journal of the American Art Therapy Association, 23*(4), 157–164. doi:10.1080/07421656.2006.10129335

Cozolino, L. (2010). *The neuroscience of psychotherapy: Healing the social brain* (2nd ed.). New York, NY: W. W. Norton & Co.

Crenshaw, D. A., & Kenney-Noziska, S. (2014). Therapeutic presence in play therapy. *International Journal of Play Therapy*, *23*(1), 31–43. doi:10.1037/a0035480

Dillman Taylor, D., & Bratton, S. C. (2014). Developmentally appropriate practice: Adlerian play therapy with preschool children. *Journal of Individual Psychology*, *70*(3), 205–219. doi:10.1353/jip.2014.0019

Dillman Taylor, D., & Meany-Walen, K. (2015). Investigating the effectiveness of Adlerian Play Therapy (AdPT) with children with disruptive behaviors: A single-case research design. *Journal of Child and Adolescent Counseling*, *1*(2), 81–99. doi:10.1080/23727810.2015.1081519

Dinkmeyer, D., Dinkmeyer, D. Jr, & Sperry, L. (1987). *Adlerian counseling and psychotherapy* (2nd ed.). Columbus, OH: Merrill.

Erickson, F. (1963). Viewpoints on children in hospitals. *Hospitals*, *1*, 37–47.

Erickson, F. (1963). Viewpoints on children in hospitals. *Hospitals*, *1*, 37–47.

Flahive, M. W., & Ray, D. (2007). Effect of group sandtray therapy with preadolescents. *Journal for Specialists in Group Work*, *32*(4), 362–382. doi:10.1080/01933920701476706

Fredrickson, B. L., Grewen, K. M., Coffey, K. A., Algoe, S. B., Firestine, A. M., Arevalo, J. G., & Cole, S. W. et al. (2013). A functional genomic perspective on human well-being. *Proceedings of the National Academy of Sciences of the United States of America*, *110*(33), 13684–13689. doi:10.1073/pnas.1305419110 PMID:23898182

Garza, Y., & Bratton, S. C. (2005). School-based child-centered play therapy with Hispanic children: Outcomes and cultural consideration. *International Journal of Play Therapy*, *14*(1), 51–80. doi:10.1037/h0088896

Geller, S., & Porges, S. (2014). Therpeutic presence: Neurophysiological mechanisms mediating feeling safe in therapeutic relationships. *Journal of Psychotherapy Integration*, *24*(3), 178–192. doi:10.1037/a0037511

Grasso, D., Ford, J., & Briggs-Gowan, M. (2013). Early life trauma exposure and stress sensitivity in young children. *Journal of Pediatric Psychology*, *38*(1), 94–103. doi:10.1093/jpepsy/jss101 PMID:23008502

Greenspan, S. (1993). *Playground politics: Understanding the emotional life of your school-aged child.* Reading, MA: Harvard University Press.

Himebauch, A., Arnold, R., & May, C. (2008). Grief in children and developmental concepts of death #138. *Journal of Palliative Medicine*, *11*(2), 242–243. doi:10.1089/jpm.2008.9973 PMID:18333739

Immordino-Yang, M., & Damasio, A. (2007). We feel, therefore we learn: The relevance of affective and social neuroscience to education. *Mind, Brain, and Education*, *1*(1), 3–10. doi:10.1111/j.1751-228X.2007.00004.x

Kandel, E. (1998). A new intellectual framework for psychiatry. *The American Journal of Psychiatry*, *155*(4), 457–469. doi:10.1176/ajp.155.4.457 PMID:9545989

Kestly, T. (2015). Sandtray and storytelling in play therapy. In D. A. Crenshaw & A. L. Stewart (Eds.), *Play therapy: A comprehensive guide to theory and practice* (pp. 156–170). New York, NY: Guilford Press.

Kestly, T. A. (2014). *The interpersonal neurobiology of play: Brain-building interventions for emotional well-being*. New York, NY: W.W. Norton & Company.

Kottman, T. (2011). *Play therapy: Basics and beyond* (2nd ed.). Alexandria, VA: American Counseling Association.

Kottman, T., & Meany-Walen, K. K. (2016). *Partners in play* (3rd ed.). Alexandria, VA: American Counseling Association.

Lambert, S. F., LeBlanc, M., Mullen, J. A., Ray, D., Baggerly, J., White, J., & Kaplan, D. (2007). Learning more about those who play in session: The National Play Therapy in Counseling Practices Project (Phase 1). *Journal of Counseling and Development*, *85*(1), 42–46. doi:10.1002/j.1556-6678.2007.tb00442.x

Landreth, G. (2012). *Play therapy: The art of the relationship* (3rd ed.). New York, NY: Brunner Routledge.

Lew, A., & Bettner, B. L. (1996). *Responsibility in the classroom: A teacher's guide to understanding motivating students.* Connexions Press.

Lew, A., & Bettner, B. S. (2000). *A parent's guide to motivating children.* Connexions Press.

Lin, Y., & Bratton, S. C. (2015). A meta-analytic review of Child-Centered Play Therapy approaches. *Journal of Counseling and Development*, *93*(1), 45–58. doi:10.1002/j.1556-6676.2015.00180.x

Maniacci, M., Sackett-Maniacci, L., & Mosak, H. (2014). Adlerian psychotherapy. In D. Wedding & R. J. Corsini (Eds.), *Current psychotherapies* (10th ed.; pp. 55–94). Belmont, CA: Thomson Brooks/Cole.

Marks-Tarlow, T. (2012). The play of psychotherapy. *American Journal of Play*, *4*(3), 352–377.

McGilchrist, I. (2009). *The master and his emissary: The divided brain and the making of the western world.* New Haven, CT: Yale University Press.

Meany-Walen, K., Bratton, S., & Kottman, T. (2014). Effects of Adlerian play therapy on reducing students disruptive behaviors. *Journal of Counseling and Development*, *92*(1), 47–56. doi:10.1002/j.1556-6676.2014.00129.x

Meany-Walen, K., Kottman, T., Bullis, Q., & Dillman Taylor, D. (2015). Effects of Adlerian play therapy on childrens externalizing behavior. *Journal of Counseling and Development*, *93*(4), 418–428. doi:10.1002/jcad.12040

Meiser-Stedman, R., Smith, P., Glucksman, E., Yule, W., & Dalgleish, T. (2008). The posttraumatic stress disorder diagnosis in preschool- and elementary school-age children exposed to motor vehicle accidents. *The American Journal of Psychiatry*, *165*(10), 1326–1337. doi:10.1176/appi.ajp.2008.07081282 PMID:18676592

Miller, R., & Dillman Taylor, D. (2016). Does Adlerian theory stand the test of time? Examining individual psychology from a neuroscience perspective. *Journal of Humanistic Counseling*, *55*(2), 111–128. doi:10.1002/johc.12028

National Scientific Council on the Developing Child. (2010). *Early experiences can alter gene expression and affect longterm development* (Working paper 10). Retrieved from http://developingchild.harvard.edu/resources/reports_and_working_papers/working_papers/wp10/

Ojiambo, D., & Bratton, S. C. (2014). Effects of group activity play therapy on problem behaviors of preadolescent Ugandan orphans. *Journal of Counseling and Development*, *92*(3), 355–365. doi:10.1002/j.1556-6676.2014.00163.x

Packman, J., & Bratton, S. C. (2003). A school-based group play/activity therapy intervention with learning disabled preadolescents exhibiting behavior problems. *International Journal of Play Therapy*, *12*(2), 7–29. doi:10.1037/h0088876

Panksepp, J. (2010). Affective neuroscience of the emotional BrainMind: Evolutionary perspectives and implications for understanding depression. *Dialogues in Clinical Neuroscience*, *12*(4), 533–545. Retrieved from http://www.ncbi.nlm.nih.gov/pmc/articles/PMC3181986/pdf/DialoguesClinNeurosci-12-533.pdf PMID:21319497

Panksepp, J., & Biven, L. (2012). *The archaeology of mind: Neuroevolutionary origins of human emotions*. New York, NY: Norton.

Piaget, J. (1951). *Play, dreams, and imitation in childhood*. New York, NY: Norton.

Porges, S. (2011). *The polyvagal theory: Neurophysiological foundations of emotions, attachment, communication, and self-regulation*. New York, NY: Norton.

Ray, D. C. (2011). *Advanced play therapy: Essential conditions, knowledge, and skills for child practice*. New York, NY: Routledge/Taylor & Francis Group.

Ray, D. C., Blanco, P. J., Sullivan, J. M., & Holliman, R. (2009). An exploratory study of child-centered play therapy with aggressive children. *International Journal of Play Therapy*, *18*(3), 162–175. doi:10.1037/a0014742

Ray, D. C., Schottelkorb, A., & Tsai, M. (2007). Play therapy with children exhibiting symptoms of attention deficit hyperactivity disorder. *International Journal of Play Therapy*, *16*(2), 95–111. doi:10.1037/1555-6824.16.2.95

Ray, D. C., Stulmaker, H. L., Lee, K. R., & Silverman, W. K. (2013). Child-centered play therapy and impairment: Exploring relationships and constructs. *International Journal of Play Therapy*, *22*(1), 13–27. doi:10.1037/a0030403

Siegel, D., & Payne Bryson, T. (2012). *The whole-brain child: Twelve revolutionary strategies to nurture your child's developing mind*. New York, NY: Delacorte Press.

Siegel, D. J. (2010). Commentary on integrating interpersonal neurobiology with group psychotherapy: Reflections on mind, brain, and relationships in group psychotherapy. *International Journal of Group Psychotherapy*, *60*(4), 483–485. doi:10.1521/ijgp.2010.60.4.483 PMID:21028973

Siegel, D. J. (2012). *The developing mind: How relationships and the brain interact to shape who we are* (2nd ed.). New York, NY, US: Guilford Press.

Siegel, D. J. (2014, August 1). *Mindfulness as integration* [blog post]. Retrieved from http://www.drdansiegel.com/blog/2014/08/01/mindfulness-as-integration/

Spielberg, J. M., Miller, G. A., Warren, S. L., Engels, A. S., Crocker, L. D., Sutton, B. P., & Heller, W. (2012). Trait motivation moderates neural activation associated with goal pursuit. *Cognitive, Affective & Behavioral Neuroscience*, *12*(2), 308–322. doi:10.3758/s13415-012-0088-8 PMID:22460723

U.S. Department of Health and Human Services, Administration on Children, Youth, and Families, Children's Bureau. (2013). *Child Maltreatment 2012*. Retrieved from http://www.acf.hhs.gov/sites/default/files/cb/cm2012.pdf#page=31

Watts, R. E. (2013). Adlerian counseling. In B. J. Irby, G. Brown, R. Lara-Alecio, S. Jackson, B. J. Irby, G. Brown, & S. Jackson (Eds.), *The handbook of educational theories* (pp. 459–472). Charlotte, NC: IAP Information Age Publishing.

Wheeler, N., & Dillman Taylor, D. (2016). Integrating interpersonal neurobiology with play therapy. *International Journal of Play Therapy*, *25*(1), 24–34. doi:10.1037/pla0000018

Willis, A., Walters, L., & Crane, D. (2014). Assessing play-based activities, child talk, and single session outcome in family therapy with young children. *Journal of Marital and Family Therapy*, *40*(3), 287–301. doi:10.1111/jmft.12048 PMID:24118088

KEY TERMS AND DEFINITIONS

Adlerian Play Therapy (AdPT): A developmentally responsive approach to therapeutic intervention with children based upon the tenants and ideas of Alfred Adler. AdPT follows four phases of intervention including: (a) building an egalitarian relationship, (b) investigating the lifestyle, (c) gaining insight, and (d) reeducation/reorientation.

Affective Emotional Motivational Systems: The seven emotional processes (i.e. SEEKING, RAGE, FEAR, LUST, CARE, PANIC/GRIEF, PLAY) that motivate behavior across species and as a component of survival.

Interpersonal Neurobiology (IPNB): A model for neural integration developed by Daniel Siegel that addresses the associations between the brain, mind, and interpersonal interactions for an individual's health and well-being.

Memory Encoding: The physiological process of memory formation whereby experiences contribute to neural pathways for (a) implicit or unconscious and (b) explicit and conscious responses.

Neural Integration: The process of connection for the parts of the brain and mind within an individual as well as between others in the environment that contribute to a healthy mind.

Neuroplasticity: The ability of the brain to continue neural growth and development across the lifespan through new experiences.

Play: The first natural language for human beings that (a) is a primitive emotion that motivates behavior when safety is perceived, (b) may reveal implicit and nonverbal interpretations of the world, (c) allows for exploration of the world, and (d) facilitates learning, neural development and skill acquisition.

Polyvagal Theory: A component of human beings' survival response whereby the sympathetic and parasympathetic nervous systems are engaged to respond to a perceived threat (i.e. fight, flight, or freeze) or return to homeostasis respectively, as a means to assess and obtain safety.

Chapter 5
The Safe Space:
An Examination of the Neurobiological Benefits of Play Therapy with Traumatized Children

Cary McAdams Hamilton
Antioch University, USA

Hannah E. Reas
Seattle Pacific University, USA

Megan E. Mansfield
Claremont Graduate University, USA

ABSTRACT

This chapter illustrates the neurobiological effects of trauma on children, as well as the therapeutic benefits of play therapy as a stand-alone treatment for this population. The goal of this work includes providing a framework for the neurobiological effects of trauma on children, as well as the various advantages of play therapy as an effective intervention. Play, specifically, meets children where they are in their development, while also attending to the neurobiological effects that trauma can have on the brain. The primary neurobiological structures implicated and targeted by client-centered play-based interventions are discussed, as well as the impact play therapy has on neural integration, memory assimilation, and the limbic system. A clinical vignette from the principal author's practice and experience working with traumatized children is included to elucidate the healing nature of play.

INTRODUCTION

Millions of children are exposed to stressful and traumatic events each year. Internationally, approximately 25% of youth are affected by sexual abuse, physical assault, or domestic violence, among other traumatic stressors (Cohen & Mannarino, 2008). According to the United States Department of Health and Human Services (2014), approximately 1,580 children died as a result of abuse and neglect in

DOI: 10.4018/978-1-5225-2224-9.ch005

2014, and over 3 million suspected cases of child maltreatment were reported to authorities that same year. After a traumatic event children often develop clinically distressing or impairing symptoms that may manifest into various affective and anxiety-related disorders, such as post-traumatic stress disorder (PTSD). Furthermore, after the traumatic stressor has passed, the memory of the event, in conjunction with a sense of helplessness and lost autonomy, continues to cause extreme distress in the individual (Cohen & Mannarino, 2008; Cohen, Perel, Debellis, Friedman, & Putnam, 2002; van der Folk, 1994).

As the rate of traumatized children continues to rise, it is imperative to understand the neurobiological effects of trauma on survivors and to address these developmental realities and implications for children (Hong & Mason, 2016; Perry, 2009). Play therapy is a *neurobiologically informed* treatment in which emotionally disturbed children are encouraged to act out their fantasies and express their feelings through play with the guidance of a trained therapist (Schaefer & Drewes, 2014; Kestly, 2014; Gil, 2006; Wheeler & Taylor, 2016). Play, specifically, meets children where they are in their development, while also attending to the neurobiological effects that trauma can have on the brain. As a result, this chapter will broadly focus on the benefits of using play therapy with traumatized children. The conversation of trauma will focus on PTSD, as this disorder is becoming a common diagnosis for children and adolescents suffering from psychological and behavioral difficulties following a traumatic event (Ackerman, Newton, McPherson, Jones, & Dykman, 1998; Cohen & Scheeringa, 2009; Schwarz & Perry, 1994). This chapter will begin with a brief overview of PTSD, from a clinical perspective, and then will continue onto the neurobiological symptoms of the disorder. Subsequently, foundational components of play therapy will be detailed, followed by an explanation of how the play process addresses the neurobiological symptoms of children with a history of trauma. A clinical vignette will make up the final portion of the chapter to elucidate the healing properties and neurobiological benefits that occur in the therapeutic play therapy process.

PTSD Basics

Post-traumatic stress disorder is one of the most complex and pervasive mental health conditions afflicting survivors of trauma (McDonald, Borntrager, & Rostad, 2014; van der Kolk, 2005; Ryan & Needham, 2001). One of the unique characteristics of PTSD, in terms of diagnosis, is that the presenting symptoms must be tied to a causal, traumatic event (Van Hooff, McFarlane, Baur, Abraham, & Barnes, 2009; Rothschild, 2003). Traumatic events are "psychologically overwhelming because they potentially threaten a [person's] sense of safety and security and lead to subjective feelings of terror, fear, shame, anger, helplessness, and/or worthlessness" (Cohen, Mannarino, & Deblinger, 2012, p. 1). These experiences can be direct or vicarious in nature, but what truly defines them as traumatic and relevant for a PTSD diagnosis is the presence of "actual or threatened death, serious injury, or sexual violence" (APA, 2013, p. 271).

The severity of any one event will vary between children depending on several protective and risk factors, such as social support, preexisting coping strategies, the nature of the trauma and previous trauma exposures, and comorbid mental health conditions (Cohen & Mannarino, 2008; Caffo & Belaise, 2003; Pfefferbaum, 1997). However, several studies have shown that children having experienced trauma will invariably develop symptoms that may manifest into various affective, anxiety, or trauma-related disorders (Ackerman et al., 1998; Balaban, 2006; Grych, Jouriles, Swank, McDonald, & Norwood, 2000; McFarlane, Policansky, & Irwin, 1987). Some common symptoms of PTSD, which must persist for over one month to be clinically diagnosed, include:

- Intrusion symptoms (e.g., re-experiencing through memories, dreams without recognizable content, flashbacks, and repetitive play in which themes or aspects of the traumatic event(s) are expressed),
- Avoidance symptoms (e.g., avoiding internal and external reminders of the trauma, such as conversing about the event),
- Negative alterations in cognitions and mood (e.g., inability to recall salient aspects of the trauma, persistent negative self-talk and affect dysregulation),
- Alterations in hyperarousal and reactivity (e.g., hypervigilance, aggressive or irritable behavior) and
- Associated symptoms of dissociation. (APA, 2013, pp. 271-274)

This definition of what constitutes a traumatic event, specifically for child populations, has been fervently debated (McDonald et al., 2014; van der Kolk, 2005; Ryan & Needham, 2001). For example, children who experience pervasive social neglect, or reside with caregivers with mental disorder(s), may not qualify for a diagnosis of PTSD (van der Folk, 2005; D'Andrea, Stolbach, Ford, Spinazzola, & van der Kolk, 2012). Parenting styles and insecure parent-child relationships, such as disorganized attachment relationships characterized by terror, domination, and an incoherent sense of self (due to parenting that is chaotic, frightening, and generally abuse), may not be accurately captured in the diagnostic picture of PTSD (McDonald et al., 2013; Chaffin et al., 2006; Siegel & Hartzell, 2003). In addition, traumatic events can be isolated and time-limited, or chronic and multi-faceted, which adds another layer of clinical complexity to assessing trauma reactions (Perry, Pollard, Blakley, Baker, & Vigilante, 1995; van der Folk, 2005).

To ameliorate this diagnostic uncertainty, van der Kolk (2005) argues for the inclusion of Developmental Trauma Disorder in the *DSM-5,* asserting, "...classification of traumatic events may need to be defined more broadly, and treatment may need to address directly the sequalae of these interpersonal adversities, given their prevalence and potentially severe negative effects on children's development and emotional health" (p. 406). Although *developmental trauma* was not formally accepted into the diagnostic nomenclature, the APA task force for the *DSM-5* expanded their definition of severe social neglect, defined as "patterns of extremes of insufficient care;" this recognition is demonstrated in reactive attachment disorder, disinhibited social engagement disorder, as well as social anxiety and separation disorders (American Psychiatric Association, 2013, p. 265). A full discussion of the nuances between PTSD and these disorders is beyond the scope of this chapter, although it is imperative to note that trauma should be captured from a multifaceted and clinically informed framework.

The psychological effects of trauma can significantly impact the emotional and behavioral well-being of the survivor (van der Folk, 1996, 2005; Findling, Bratton, & Henson, 2006; Cohen & Mannarino, 2008). Children may experience affective dysregulation, which is characterized by heightened levels of sadness, anger, fear, and confusion (APA, 2013). They may be stimulated/triggered by innocuous cues (e.g., loud sounds) that instill fright and prompt an exaggerated startle response (Ryan & Needham, 2001; APA, 2013). This extreme hypervigilance is an expression of children's attempts to recapture a sense of security and control over their environment. As van der Folk (2005) asserts:

These [traumatic] experiences engender intense affects, such as rage, betrayal, fear, resignation, defeat, and shame, and efforts to ward off the recurrence of those emotions, including the avoidance of experi-

ences that precipitate them or engaging in behaviors that convey a subjective sense of control in the face of potential threats. (p. 406)

Children might also have difficulty expressing their emotions and begin internalizing or projecting these feelings onto themselves. This tendency correlates with cognitive dimensions that include "distorted ideas about why the traumatic event happened, who was responsible (including self-blame), shame or worthlessness, and/or a loss of trust" (Cohen & Mannarino, 2008, p. 159). These beliefs cloud children's views of themselves, others, and the world and contradict basic assumptions of a "just world" (Shapiro et al., 2006, p. 481). Children's behaviors can also be oppositional, regressive, sexualized, or unresponsive (van der Folk, 2005; Cohen & Mannarino, 2008; Foa, Keane, Friedman, & Cohen, 2009). These symptoms may present as children gravitating away from peers, aggressing toward others, re-enacting behaviors reminiscent of the original trauma, creating maladaptive coping mechanisms (e.g., smoking, overeating), freezing when faced with minor stressors, and/or engaging in more disruptive behaviors that can lead to conflict between parents and children. Physiological reminders of the trauma may also be present, such as heightened arousal, sleep difficulties, enuresis, headaches, stomach pains, and other somatic complaints (Ryan & Needham, 2001; van der Folk, 2005; Cohen, Mannarino, & Deblinger, 2012). The myriad of responses to trauma reflects children's inability to restore homeostasis to the body and mind, which are no longer functioning at their optimal baseline levels (van der Folk, 2005; Cohen et al., 2002). In addition, trauma also has long-term implications for the brain as its development and ability to integrate information is significantly impaired.

The Traumatic Response and Resulting Symptoms

Some of the symptoms described in the previous section can be tied to the body's response to the experience of a traumatic event. This section will describe the traumatic response, focusing on the neurobiological implications and how such implications contribute to the symptoms common to PTSD. Specifically, irregularities in the physical nature of key brain structures, memory functions, and limitations to *hemispheric integration* will be elucidated.

The Fear Response and the Amygdala

In response to a traumatic event, the brain's *limbic system* activates the sympathetic nervous system (a branch of the autonomic nervous system (ANS)), preparing the body to face the threat. During this time of extreme stress and potential lethal danger the body primes muscles to react quickly (Carlson, 2010; Rothschild, 2003). This intrinsic fight-or-flight response of the sympathetic system is characterized by dilated pupillary responses, increased heart rate, respiration, and blood flow to the vital organs, and is constantly at work in children who have experienced repeated traumas, which results in a continuous state of hyperarousal (Rothschild, 2003; Stewart, Field, & Echterling, 2016). Another branch of the ANS, the parasympathetic nervous system, is engaged when hypo-arousal occurs (Porges, 2011). Specifically, the vagus nerve, which modulates stress responses and sends inhibitory messages to the heart, may not respond adequately in excessively stressful situations, resulting in dysregulated cardiac vagal control (Carlson, 2010). This dysregulation can result in the fight or flight response described above, or hypo-arousal symptoms like dissociation and immobilization—generally, the individual freezes when this system is over-engaged (Porges, 2011).

A child's exposure to trauma initiates sensory stimuli (e.g., sights, smells, sounds) to be transmitted to the amygdala, a structure of the limbic system associated with emotional memory, detection of fear, and threats to survival (Rauch et al., 2000; Shin et al., 2005; Cohen et al., 2002; Ward, 2010; Carlson, 2010). The amygdala stores the sensory stimuli for later recall and assigns emotional meaning to it. Therefore "emotions occur not by conscious choice…[rather] limbic structures, such as the amygdala, sort incoming stimuli and determine their emotional significance" (Schaefer & Drewes, 2014, p. 27).

PTSD adversely affects the structural integrity and functioning of the amygdala. Physically, the volume of the amygdala in those who suffer from PTSD is abnormal, perhaps impacting its role in the assessment of danger cues (Rogers et al., 2009; Pezawas et al., 2005; Carlson, 2010). So when the amygdala communicates information about danger to other brain regions the information becomes too generalized, resulting in hypersensitivity to innocuous stimuli (Cohen et al., 2002). This process is further explained by disruption in communication between the amygdala and ventromedial prefrontal cortex (vmPFC), which exerts inhibitory signals to the amygdala in healthy functioning individuals (Koenigs & Grafman, 2009; Koenigs et al., 2008; Carlson, 2010). Gold et al. (2011) found decreased cerebral blood flow in this PFC region, illustrating the poignant impact of hypofrontality on down-regulation of the amygdala. This impaired communication between brain structures leads to the presentation of "conditioned fear" responses (Vasterling & Brewin, 2005, p. 60), and results in a habituated perception of the world as a fearful and dangerous place wherein no one, not even friends and family, can be trusted.

Because of the amygdala's role in identifying and labeling the emotional significance of stimuli it, additionally, has a place in altering affective responses to stressors. Of specific interest in this context of PTSD is fear extinction, which involves the amygdala along with the vmPFC, hippocampus, and anterior cingulate cortex working towards regulating responses to fear (Rogers et al., 2009; Koenigs et al., 2008; Carlson, 2010). A classic example of this working would be when one sees a stick and for a moment thinks it's a snake. A fear response is initiated, as evidenced by an increase in heart rate, but as the person realizes the stimuli is not actually a snake, but a stick, they are able to calm back down—extinguishing the fear response. However, again perhaps due to the hyper-reactivity of the amygdala, in conjunction with hypo-activation of the medial PFC and other salient brain structures, those suffering from PTSD cannot regulate their responses to fear (Cohen et al., 2002; Carlson, 2010; Rogers et al., 2009).

Trauma and Memory

In close proximity to the amygdala is the hippocampus, the primary brain region involved with learning and memory (Carlson, 2010). There are two forms of memory related to the functions of the hippocampus and amygdala in the context of trauma: implicit and explicit memory (Kestly, 2014). The process of encoding, storing, and retrieving memories, particularly explicit memories, may be impacted by both physiological abnormalities of the hippocampus and how the hippocampus processes traumatic events. Studies of Vietnam combat veterans with PTSD demonstrated a decrease in the size and activity of the hippocampus, as compared to non-combat veterans with no history of the disorder, perhaps impacting their abilities to recall aspects of their trauma (Bremner et al., 1995; Gurvits et al., 1996; Hayes et al., 2011; Gilbertson et al., 2002). Additionally, in the hippocampus, traumatic memories are processed differently than non-traumatic memories. As Rothschild (2003) argues:

[During a traumatic event], when the arousal in the ANS becomes very high, the activity of the hippocampus can be suppressed by the wealth of stress hormones released...The results may be that the traumatic event is prevented from becoming a "memory" in the usual sense of the word. (p. 11)

Therefore, the traumatic memories may not be successfully processed in the hippocampus, meaning they will never be fully encoded or retrieved due to high levels of stress and fear. Instead, the memories remain in the survivor's implicit memory. Implicit memory involves memories that are beneath the surface of conscious awareness (Kestly, 2014; Rothschild, 2003). These memories are consolidated from birth on through life and may manifest in many nonverbal behavioral responses, bodily sensations, mental schemas, and working models of self and others (Kestly, 2014; van der Folk, 2005).

PTSD, specifically, involves implicit memories that continue to affect a person without their conscious awareness (Carlson, 2010). In many cases, the survivor cannot access the explicit memories, which are memories that are consciously recalled, that would otherwise clarify the expressions of their implicit memories (Kestly, 2014). These expressions of implicit memories include flashbacks and re-experiencing of the trauma, which feel as though they are happening during the present moment rather than a memory of the past. These involuntary flashbacks are often distorted or fragmented due to the high levels of stress that occurred during the traumatic event and often cause severe distress (Vasterling & Brewin, 2005).

Dan Siegel (2009, 2010, 2012) discusses the impact of trauma disrupting the neural integration of the cerebral hemispheres. Integration of the right and left hemispheres of the brain is also necessary for memories to be successfully integrated from implicit to explicit neuronal pathways. For this to occur information must be transferred along the corpus callosum, a band of neuronal fibers, that connects the two hemispheres. The corpus callosum is involved in communicating "information between the right and left cerebral hemispheres of the brain and is important in integrating perceptions, cognitive processing, and responses" (Cohen et al., 2002, p. 99). Successful integration of right and left-brain functioning is imperative for children because it promotes coherence—something that is often lost in the experience of trauma (Kestly, 2014).

The Developing Brain of Children with Trauma

The human brain is organized and develops in a sequential, hierarchical manner from the most basic and primitive areas to more complex areas that mediate human functions (Carlson, 2010). A conceptual framework developed by Perry (1997) organizes the brain into four areas: the brainstem, midbrain, limbic system, and cortical region of the prefrontal cortex. The brainstem develops first and regulates vital functions, such as blood pressure, respiration, and heart rate. Then comes the midbrain, which is responsible for appetite, sleep, motor movements, attention, and arousal. Next, the limbic system responds to emotional stimuli, attachment and interpersonal functioning, and learning. The prefrontal cortex develops last, engaging high executive functions, such as abstract thinking, decision-making, judgment, social behaviors, and planning (Carlson, 2010; Perry, 1997, 2009; Ward, 2010).

Especially where children are concerned, there are three limitations to the use of the prefrontal cortex during, and following, a traumatic event. First, the prefrontal cortex does not completely form until the mid-20s (Ward, 2010). Therefore, children exposed to trauma may not be developmentally capable of processing the event unfolding before them with clarity and fully functioning executive processing abilities. Second, the prefrontal cortex and other higher order regions of the brain (e.g., limbic system) are not always in synchrony with the lower regions (e.g., the brainstem and midbrain) during or following formation. When these systems are not able to function together and build on one another they often default to the lower regions of the brain (i.e., bottom-up processing) (Perry, 2009). This generally results in hyper/hypo arousal system response of tantrums, high reactivity, and loss of emotional and/or bodily control (Siegel & Bryson, 2011). Third, during a traumatic event the normal functioning of the prefrontal cortex is impaired by the release of stress hormones (Carlson, 2010). As these hormones (e.g., norepinephrine, cortisol) flood the brain it becomes impossible for a person to think clearly, inhibiting memory formation in the developing brain.

Like other brain structures discussed, the prefrontal cortex shows structural abnormalities in those suffering from PTSD that point to the region being under-reactive (Carlson, 2010; Koenigs et al., 2008; Rauch et al., 2006). For example, when presented with trauma-related words and examples, clients with PTSD displayed or experienced decreased blood flow and activation in the medial prefrontal cortex region (Bremner et al., 1995; Shin et al., 1999). This phenomenon may be linked to dopamine activity in the brain region. Excessive dopamine in the medial prefrontal cortex contributes to the "persistence and overgeneralization of conditioned fear responses seen in childhood PTSD" (Cohen et al., 2002, p. 94). Perhaps the excessive dopamine in the prefrontal cortex leaves the brain region under-reactive and thus people suffering from this are not able to think critically about what they are experiencing. This in turn leaves them unable to regulate their fear response, which may be related to problems in their cardiac vagal control system described earlier (Porges, 2011).

To summarize, PTSD is a complex psychological condition that continues to impact sufferers long after the traumatic event has passed. Part of the reasoning for this is the neurobiological implications of the condition. The signs of physical irregularities in key brain structures of the fear response leave people unable to accurately assess cues for danger and regulate their reactions to stimuli. These irregularities may also have implications for memories related to the traumatic event, leading to incomplete encoding of explicit memories, which are thus unable to be recalled later. This becomes problematic when implicit memories of the event continue to influence survivors. Without the explicit memories to make sense of these flashbacks and re-experiencing of the trauma people are often left feeling confused and distressed. For children and adolescents these neurobiological implications are further complicated and concerning given the developmental state of their brains (Perry, 2009). Thus, the rest of the chapter will focus on a developmentally sensitive therapeutic modality, play therapy, and how it addresses these neurobiological implications of trauma.

Play Therapy Foundations

Traditional, talk-based therapies often do not honor the developmental level of children, presupposing the child's ability to engage in a verbal, cognitive, and abstract manner. These modalities require verbal capacities, self-awareness, and a willingness to remain seated for long periods of time. These are skills and/or behaviors that of which children are not necessarily developmentally capable (Stewart et al., 2016). Play therapy, however, is an alternative therapeutic modality, which is primarily characterized by its ability to reach clients where they are in terms of their trauma and/or overall overdevelopment. Play therapy is a modality with various theoretical perspectives and a description of them all is beyond the scope of this chapter (for a comprehensive review see Landreth, 2012 and Schaefer, 1995). This chapter will focus on *Child Centered Play Therapy* (CCPT), which is operationalized, by Landreth (2012), as:

A dynamic interpersonal relationship between a child (or person of any age) and a therapist trained in play therapy procedures who provides selected play materials and facilitates the development of a safe relationship for the child (or person of any age) to fully express and explore self (feelings, thoughts, experiences, and behaviors) through the child's natural medium of communication, play. (p. 16)

Play is a universal, natural, and fundamentally kinesthetic, neurobiological activity that meets children where they are by entering their worldview. This is possible through the developmentally appropriate use of play instead of words, allowing children to reveal salient information about what they have experienced, their reactions and affective understanding of their circumstances, and insight into their needs and self-concept (Landreth, 2012). Play is symbolic in nature (Axline, 1969), which can help traumatized children externalize their experiences via psychological distancing. Findling et al. (2006) describe this process, asserting that "[the child]...is shielded from the intensity of their own feelings because the play allows the child to indirectly express feelings that might be overwhelming if expressed directly" (p. 9). In CCPT the child is thought to be the expert of his or her world, thereby eliminating any hierarchical relationship between the child and therapist. In addition, through the safe and secure therapeutic alliance and explorative nature of the play therapy process, the child "restores the powers of his individual nature and affirms his real self" (Moustakas, 1959, p. 3).

In terms of neurobiology, play works to align and integrate the child's brain by moving them from implicit to explicit memory via a method that is non-verbal in function (Perry, Hogan, & Marlin, 2000). This further leads to external and internal processing and cognitive understanding of the child's traumatic experiences. These integrative aspects also allow for "active control and mastery of experience, and... assimilation of the experience by repetitive play" (Schaefer & Drewes, 2014, p. 89). Through this experience a sense of agency (autonomy over one's actions), self-efficacy (belief that one can accomplish tasks), and control over one's environment is fostered within the child that is reparative to their sense of identity. Play is also implicated in divergent thinking and improvement of self-regulation, which is especially beneficial in traumatized populations, as engaging the prefrontal cortex allows for clearer decision making and problem solving to occur in these children's' daily lives (Kestly, 2014).

Neurobiology and The Play Process

The purpose of this section is to articulate the general nature of CCPT. Pertinent approaches and tools will be explored. Some outcomes and neurobiological implications will be mentioned but further developed in later sections.

The process of play in children mirrors the way the human brain develops and facilitates healthy development of vital brain structures (Perry et al., 2000). Specifically, the repetitive, exploratory, and sensation seeking aspects of play allow for neuronal growth and improved connectivity between brain regions. For example, babies repeatedly play with their mothers' nipples and engage in sleep and feeding routines, which regulates vital functions. Toddlers develop their motor skills while exploring their environments, which addresses somatosensory integration. Children develop socio-emotional and cognitive maturity as they use metaphors, symbols, and fantasy play to understand their world (Perry et al., 2000). As children continue to develop, the complexity of their play continues to shift and expand. This is observed in their advances from solitary, parallel, and dyadic play, to finally group play. As Perry and colleagues (2000) posit, "at each stage of development, it is the repetitive element of play that helps organize neural systems which will ultimately mediate more complex motor, social, emotional, and cognitive skills" (p. 10).

In CCPT the play therapist leverages the natural, sequential progression of play to build rapport with the child and thus the play therapy process looks similar to the natural development of the child as expressed through play. First, the play therapist "establish[es] state regulation", a vital stage of regulating bodily states (i.e., breathing, heart rate) for children with hyper- or hypoactive neural systems" (Perry et al., 2000, p. 10). In this stage nondirective interventions of tactile play and "peek-a-boo" encourage this state regulation in a safe and secure way. Throughout this process children do not need to verbalize their experiences. Instead, they learn to ground themselves in the present, nonthreatening moment with the play therapist. Additionally, due to the lack of verbalization the child is able to engage his or her lower brain to further help gain state regulation and build a firm foundation for further therapeutic development.

As the child's play progresses in the playroom, the therapist can integrate somatosensory activities, such as creative play with miniatures. This facilitates large and fine motor movements within the midbrain, as well as attentional processes (Perry et al., 2000). Through this process children learn how to regulate their emotions and establish a secure, team-oriented and egalitarian relationship with the therapist. Naturally, the relationship development that occurs in the playroom mirrors how play is used in everyday life, as Schaefer and Drewes (2014) assert: "In game play, children play together around games and rules…[this] fosters various social skills, including turn-taking, following rules, cooperation, problem solving, sharing, good sportsmanship, empathy, and reciprocity" (p. 188).

The cortical structures of the brain are integrated through complex play opportunities, such as fantasy, dramatic, and role-play. These practices foster abstract thought, decision-making abilities, and increased verbal skills as the right and left hemispheres of the brain begin to integrate. The safety of the playroom and secure relationship established with the therapist are key to allowing this integration to occur.

With trauma specifically in mind, there are various aspects of CCPT that allow the child to work through their trauma from a neurobiological perspective. The sections that remain will detail how CCPT addresses hemispheric integration, memory, and the limbic system.

Hemispheric Integration

Play facilitates integration of the most complex structures of the brain, namely the right and left hemispheres of the cerebral cortex. Successful integration is imperative in the process of resolving trauma, as Siegel and Bryson (2011) assert: "Using only the right or left brain would be like trying to swim using only one arm. We might be able to do it, but wouldn't we be a lot more successful—and avoid going in circles—if we used both arms together?" (p. 18). The right brain is tapped via the creative, instinctive, and nonverbal aspects of play (Kestly, 2014). When children are able to communicate their internal world through stories, symbols, fantasy, and other metaphoric mediums they are further engaging their right brain. The analytical, linear, and linguistic-oriented left-brain can then begin to logically organize and conceptualize the information manifested through play (Kestly, 2014; Siegel & Bryson, 2011). Kestly (2014) eloquently illustrates this process:

In the left hemisphere, the right hemisphere experiences are "unpacked," using narrative and analytical processes to deepen conscious understanding. The left hemisphere loves to tell stories about what the right experiences. In the absence of experience, the left hemisphere has no story to tell—at least, not an authentic one. (pp. 172-173)

In essence, successful hemispheric integration leads to healthier and more adaptive cognitive functioning. This occurs through what Kestly (2014) terms as the "spiral of play," wherein the right-brain mechanisms ground the child in the immediate environment, connecting and developing with the left-brain properties—including linguistic abilities. Though a child, at first, may demonstrate as nonverbal and distant, verbalization and dialogue will enter the playroom as integration occurs. This is witnessed through the child actively engaging the therapist directly in play and storytelling. Through repeated play and unconditional positive regard from the therapist the child is "able to tell more and more of his or her autobiographical story, becoming ever more conscious of who he or she is in the world" (Kestly, 2014, p. 124).

Memory

The power of implicit memories can be expressed through play and within the safety of the therapeutic space as they are transformed into explicit memories. The play process facilitates externalization, wherein the child is less subject to triggers as they are no longer in a state of heightened physiological arousal (Schaefer & Drewes, 2014). As previously demonstrated, play down-regulates the systems that allow for physiological arousal (e.g., heart rate, breathing). Therefore, play therapy allows a child's brain to adapt and access the implicit memories of the traumatic event, which contributes to the child's internal working models and schemas (Hong & Mason, 2016; Kestly, 2014). Though processing of traumatic events can be difficult due in part to the affective fear and biological stress hormones that are present—play is able to work through all of these barriers (Schaefer & Drewes, 2014). This is possible because play allows the expression of these memories without verbal articulation and conscious thought. Through the act of play the implicit memories can be accessed and eventually become explicit. This process then allows for further integration of memories and understanding of traumatic experiences.

The Limbic System

As previously articulated, the limbic system is addressed via exploratory and game-like play, which, in turn, fosters social-emotional development. As children begin to develop a trusting, secure relationship with the play therapist and begin to regulate their emotions better they also begin to reestablish control. Attachment and healthy relationships contribute substantially to health organization of the brain, specifically in the limbic system regions (e.g., the amygdala and hippocampus) as well as hemispheric integration (Kestly, 2014; Siegel, 2009). Although hemispheric integration is a primary component of CCPT such neurobiological growth cannot occur without establishing a sense of security and safety through the therapeutic alliance between the play therapist and child. This relationship is paramount for children with trauma background, as Hughes (1999) illustrates:

Traditional therapy presupposed that the child has the readiness and ability to form a therapeutic relationship that can be utilized to resolve past traumas and form a more stable and positive sense of self. (p. 554)

This assertion highlights the challenge that therapists encounter when working with traumatized populations. Within the therapeutic space of CCPT, children are given a medium to express themselves with full acceptance and unconditional positive regard on the part of the therapist. Furthermore, the play therapy space is specifically structured to allow for consistent expectations in regards to boundaries and limits. These promote safety for the traumatized child. Thus, in the playroom, children can test and retest safe limits in their environments and within themselves (Landreth, 2012). For example, if the child feels uncomfortable playing with a specific miniature toy, she can lead the play in another direction. This action lays the groundwork for future *abreaction* (tolerating and expressing emotions) and cognitive processing to develop (Gil, 2006).

Through this reestablishment of affective control, the child and therapist are nonverbally and innately aligned to each other's internal state(s), defined as *limbic resonance* (Lewis, Amini, & Lannon, 2000; Siegel, 2012).

When the child plays and experiences extreme distress, the therapist also experiences empathic synchrony and subjective stress similar to the child. This process is linked to mirror neurons in the brain, which also contribute to learning processes of imitation and modeling. The therapist's ability to enter the world of the client and establish an attachment relationship with them, which may be reminiscent of unhealthy relationships initially, allows the limbic system to be revised and adapted. Over time, the therapist's healthier limbic system reshapes the client's attachment system, resulting in reorganization of their cognitive and emotional frameworks. The child, in essence, "borrows" and models the healthier limbic system of the therapist in modifying her own. A new neural functioning pattern is created throughout this process and the client's behaviors and affective states are able to change (Lewis, Amini, & Lannon, 2000).

In summary, exploration and discovery in the playroom allow for abreaction, mastery, self-control, and catharsis to occur naturally through the child's means of communication—play. As the child begins to feel secure and safe within the playroom and therapeutic alliance the limbic system activates, developing new pathways that increase social-emotional skills (e.g., trusting relationships, emotional regulation, increased self-efficacy). As the child is able to express her implicit memories through play she can begin to make them explicit—allowing for a more complete processing of the traumatic event. Learning and coping mechanisms continue to be established and repeated in order to develop healthy neural integration. All of this is possible through the power of play, which is its innate ability to reach children with their own language and in their own space.

Clinical Vignette

The purpose of this section is to illustrate how to use play therapy techniques with a client that has experienced trauma. This vignette also works to depict how to involve and educate parents and families as the child goes through his or her process in play therapy. Though this vignette is modeled after real experiences, client-identifying information has been changed to maintain confidentiality. The vignette will begin with details about the playroom before moving onto background details about the client. Next, the therapy process will be depicted, ending with comments regarding parent involvement in the play therapy process.

The Playroom

The playroom is equipped with the necessary categories of toys, including: real-life toys (e.g., dolls, kitchen), aggressive toys (e.g., Bobo doll, handcuffs), creative expression materials (e.g., coloring paper, play doh), and make believe/imaginative toys (e.g., puppets, dress up).

Client Background

MacKenzie is a six-year-old Caucasian girl in kindergarten. After being referred by a primary care doctor MacKenzie's mother, Patricia brought her into therapy. MacKenzie witnessed domestic violence targeted at her mother, which concluded in her father's incarceration. His trial occurred six months following the initiation of therapy. MacKenzie, in addition to talking about these events daily, has demonstrated symptoms related to anxiety and fear since her father's removal. Some symptoms include separation anxiety, inappropriate boundaries, irrational fears, and regression of previously gained behavioral developmental milestones (e.g., toilet training, baby talk, etc.). Patricia is receiving her own individual psychotherapy treatment, and is very dedicated to obtaining treatment and further supporting her daughter.

The Therapy Process

During the initial session, MacKenzie was very excited and notably engaged in her environment. Her play was exploratory as she involved herself with a variety of toys without any particular concentration. She eventually went to the kitchen area and started making food. Her play demonstrated a nurturing theme as she fed the therapist and informed her on "how to have manners." This nurturing theme was present throughout her session but was also intermixed with aggressive/agitated and quiet/contemplative behaviors, which frequently occurred while she was transitioning from one area to another. Aggressive play occurred in the form of hitting the Bobo doll, while quiet behaviors presented in her hiding in a tent with her previously prepared food. She stated that this was to "escape and go on a trip." MacKenzie did engage the therapist at times, but always took the lead, generally showing the therapist how to do a variety of things. Otherwise, MacKenzie's play was independent and sought little attention from the therapist. The variety of behaviors presented in MacKenzie's play is typical of children who have the ability to experiment and tryout new behaviors. At times it became necessary for the therapist to set limits in order to maintain the psychological and physical safety of the playroom. MacKenzie would occasionally become irritated and attempt to strike the clinician or break toys. It was during these times MacKenzie had difficulty regulating her emotions and inhibiting her actions but did eventually conform to the established limits of the playroom.

Over nine weeks MacKenzie and the therapist developed a trusting relationship during which MacKenzie was eager to come to therapy sessions. At this point in the therapy process the therapist suggested moving sessions to bi-weekly occurrence, hoping to see further improvement in behaviors outside the playroom.

At the time of her father's trial there was a noticeable increase in MacKenzie's anxious behaviors. This included a developmentally appropriate mirroring of her mother's anxieties. During this time MacKenzie used the playroom as a way to express her confusion. She moved from providing care to a baby (nurturing theme) to becoming aggressive with the Bobo doll, then hiding in tents. These were all behaviors previously noted as being present when MacKenzie's anxieties were high. The ease with which she flowed between these behaviors and play-tasks demonstrated that she felt safe and comfortable enough to work through and process conflicting emotions. This was made possible through the healthy, trusting bond with the therapist and the limits and security of the playroom. Neurobiologically, the abreaction and catharsis demonstrated by MacKenzie in the playroom allowed for integrative brain development.

As a result of MacKenzie's experiences with play therapy, her behaviors outside of the playroom were significantly healthier and self-regulated. She engaged in problem solving activities at home and in daycare. The playroom provided MacKenzie the environment she needed to work through her anxieties and challenges using tools and skills in a developmentally appropriate fashion.

As MacKenzie's treatment came towards a close the therapist worked to provide an easy, smooth transition out of therapy for MacKenzie. She accomplished this by providing a therapy countdown for three consecutive weeks, wherein the termination of therapy was discussed with MacKenzie. During these times MacKenzie demonstrated moments of aggression and agitation.

As often happens with children, MacKenzie struggled with saying goodbye to the therapist at the end of the final session. She was able to engage and inquire why therapy was stopping. The therapist articulated an age appropriate reflection of MacKenzie's desire to continue with therapy, recognizing that she was uncomfortable and stressed by the ending of therapy. At this juncture the therapist reflected back to MacKenzie how this conversation demonstrated that she had learned to communicate her wants and needs well with the therapist, a skill she can continue using with other adults in her life. This skill, additionally, allows MacKenzie to be able to cope with changes and future transitions in her life.

MacKenzie left therapy confident in her own capacities and decision-making. The therapist reminded MacKenzie that she is welcome to come back at anytime and that she just needs to ask her mom to set up an appointment. This reminder provided additional comfort for MacKenzie and she was able to leave the playroom giving the therapist a fist-bump on the way.

Parent Involvement in the Therapy Process

Prior to beginning therapy with MacKenzie, Patricia was provided with psychoeducation on play therapy so that she could provide informed consent for MacKenzie's treatment in the playroom.

After approximately seven sessions Patricia reported significant improvement in MacKenzie's behavior overall with less anxiety present at home and at daycare. MacKenzie also demonstrated no further regression in her developmental tasks (e.g., no further soiling events or behavioral challenges going to bed).

Around the time of Patricia's husband's trial, the therapist provided further psychoeducation regarding play therapy. Patricia was eager to learn an alternative way of interacting and promoting MacKenzie's psychological well-being. This education was used to help Patricia allow MacKenzie more freedom in her play, something normal to the playroom but different from the expectation at home. Though allowing MacKenzie to lead the play and establishing few limitations on behaviors in the play space was a challenge for Patricia, through practice and perseverance she was able to overcome her own fear and anxieties of "not having enough control." Patricia became quite adept in using and incorporating the principles of child play therapy and facilitative techniques, which she observed the therapist modeling in the playroom. For example, Patricia demonstrated great attunement in following MacKenzie's lead in play, verbally tracking MacKenzie's behavior, demonstrating a neutral emotional affect, and presenting a calming presence in order to balance and soothe MacKenzie when needed.

Patricia inquired as to how play therapy can be of benefit to MacKenzie so quickly. The therapist's explanation stated that, unlike an adult, children are unable to use executive functioning to consistently direct their behavior and help modulate their emotions. Therefore, a child is more likely to communicate with their body in play and with nonverbal expression because spoken language, at this level and complexity, is not available yet. Through play MacKenzie was able to express her anxiety and fear regarding the domestic violence she witnessed. During this expression the therapist demonstrated unconditional positive regard and nonjudgmental acceptance while witnessing MacKenzie's experience through empathic verbal tracking of her play behaviors. The therapist also provided safety in the playroom by setting therapeutic limits. All of these factors facilitated a therapeutic relationship to develop between the therapist and MacKenzie, encouraging and developing her self-regulation and catharsis through abreaction in her play. In being present with MacKenzie during these times, the therapist provided a soothing presence from which MacKenzie could use to regulate her emotions by attuning to the therapist's calm state.

The therapist conducted a final session with Patricia without MacKenzie present in order to review MacKenzie's progress and to explain future expectations now that therapy was imminently terminating. The therapist explained that, although MacKenzie had worked through much of her trauma and moved towards integration of these emotional events, it is likely she will continue to struggle with events or discussions related to the trauma. The therapist encouraged Patricia to continue weekly therapy sessions at home to provide congruence and an ongoing relational bond between mother and child. It is through this repetition of playing in the home that positive coping behaviors are learned, made automatic, and integrated via MacKenzie's neural pathways. The therapist also reviewed specific techniques for the mother, such as effective listening and verbal tracking of nonverbal behaviors. The therapist encouraged Patricia to continue using the skills they had learned in play therapy to support MacKenzie in her ongoing development and regulation of appropriate emotional and behavioral expression. At the conclusion of the session, Patricia reported increased understanding and confidence in her own ability to prepare MacKenzie and support her in future challenges and transitions.

REFERENCES

Ackerman, P. T., Newton, J. O., McPherson, W. B., Jones, J. G., & Dykman, R. A. (1998). Prevalence of post traumatic stress disorder and other psychiatric diagnoses in three groups of abused children (sexual, physical, and both). *Child Abuse & Neglect*, *22*(8), 759–774. doi:10.1016/S0145-2134(98)00062-3 PMID:9717613

American Psychiatric Association. (2013). *Diagnostic and statistical manual of mental disorders* (5th ed.). Washington, DC: American Psychiatric Association.

Axline, V. (1964). *Dibs in search of self.* New York, NY: Random House Publisher.

Balaban, V. (2006). Psychological assessment of children in disasters and emergencies. *Disasters*, *30*(2), 178–198. doi:10.1111/j.0361-3666.2006.00314.x PMID:16689917

Bremner, J. D., Randall, P., Scott, T. M., Bronen, R. A., Seibyl, J. P., Southwick, S. M., & Innis, R. B. et al. (1995). MRI-based measurement of hippocampal volume in patients with combat-related posttraumatic stress disorder. *The American Journal of Psychiatry*, *152*(7), 973–981. doi:10.1176/ajp.152.7.973 PMID:7793467

Caffo, E., & Belaise, C. (2003). Psychological aspects of traumatic injury in children and adolescents. *Child and Adolescent Psychiatric Clinics of North America*, *12*(3), 493–535. doi:10.1016/S1056-4993(03)00004-X PMID:12910820

Carlson, N. R. (2010). *Physiology of behavior* (10th ed.). Boston, MA: Allyn and Bacon.

Chaffin, M., Hanson, R., & Saunders, B. E. (2006). Report of the APSAC Task Force on attachment therapy, reactive attachment disorder, and attachment problems: Reply to letters. *Child Maltreatment, 11*(4), 381–386. doi:10.1177/1077559506292636 PMID:17043315

Cohen, J. A., & Mannarino, A. P. (2008). Trauma-focused cognitive behavioral therapy for children and parents. *Child and Adolescent Mental Health, 13*(4), 158–162. doi:10.1111/j.1475-3588.2008.00502.x

Cohen, J. A., Mannarino, A. P., & Deblinger, E. (Eds.). (2012). *Trauma focused CBT for children and adolescents: Treatment applications*. New York, NY: The Guilford Press.

Cohen, J. A., Perel, J. M., Debellis, M. D., Friedman, M. J., & Putnam, F. W. (2002). Treating traumatized children: Clinical implications of the psychobiology of posttraumatic stress disorder. *Trauma, Violence & Abuse, 3*(2), 91–108. doi:10.1177/15248380020032001

Cohen, J. A., & Scheeringa, M. S. (2009). Post-traumatic stress disorder diagnosis in children: Challenges and promises. *Dialogues in Clinical Neuroscience, 11*(1), 91–99. PMID:19432391

DAndrea, W., Stolbach, B., Ford, J., Spinazzola, J., & van der Kolk, B. A. (2012). Understanding interpersonal trauma in children: Why we need a developmentally appropriate trauma diagnosis. *The American Journal of Orthopsychiatry, 2*(2), 187–200. doi:10.1111/j.1939-0025.2012.01154.x PMID:22506521

Findling, J. H., Bratton, S. C., & Henson, R. K. (2006). Development of the trauma play scale: An observation-based assessment of the impact of trauma on play therapy behaviors of young children. *International Journal of Play Therapy, 15*(1), 7–36. doi:10.1037/h0088906

Foa, E. B., Keane, T. M., Friedman, M. J., & Cohen, J. A. (Eds.). (2009). *Effective treatments for PTSD: Practice guidelines from the International Society for Traumatic Stress Studies* (2nd ed.). New York, NY: The Guilford Press.

Gil, E. (2006). *Helping abused and traumatized children: Integrating directive and nondirective approaches*. New York, NY, US: Guilford Press.

Gilbertson, M. W., Shenton, M. E., Ciszewski, A., Kasai, K., Lasko, N. B., Orr, S. P., & Pitman, R. K. (2002). Smaller hippocampal volume predicts pathologic vulnerability to psychological trauma. *Nature Neuroscience, 5*(11), 1242–1247. doi:10.1038/nn958 PMID:12379862

Gold, A. L., Shin, L. M., Orr, S. P., Carson, M. A., Rauch, S. L., Macklin, M. L., & Pitman, R. K. et al. (2011). Decreased regional cerebral blood flow in medial prefrontal cortex during trauma-unrelated stressful imagery in Vietnam veterans with post-traumatic stress disorder. *Psychological Medicine, 41*(12), 2563–2572. doi:10.1017/S0033291711000730 PMID:21733221

Grych, J. H., Jouriles, E. N., Swank, P. R., McDonald, R., & Norwood, W. D. (2000). Patterns of adjustment among children of battered women. *Journal of Consulting and Clinical Psychology, 68*(1), 84–94. doi:10.1037/0022-006X.68.1.84 PMID:10710843

Gurvits, T. V., Shenton, M. E., Hokama, H., Ohta, H., Lasko, N. B., Gilberton, M. W., & Pitman, R. K. et al. (1996). Magnetic resonance imaging study of hippocampal volume in chronic, combat-related post-traumatic stress disorder. *Biological Psychiatry, 40*(11), 1091–1099. doi:10.1016/S0006-3223(96)00229-6 PMID:8931911

Hayes, J. P., LaBar, K. S., McCarthy, G., Selgrade, E., Nasser, J., Dolcos, F., & Morey, R. A. (2011). Reduced hippocampal and amygdala activity predicts memory distortions for trauma reminders in combat-related PTSD. *Journal of Psychiatric Research*, *45*(5), 660–669. doi:10.1016/j.jpsychires.2010.10.007 PMID:21047644

Hong, R., & Mason, C. M. (2016). Becoming a neurobiologically-informed play therapist. *International Journal of Play Therapy*, *25*(1), 35–44. doi:10.1037/pla0000020

Hughes, D. A. (1999). Adopting children with attachment problems. *Child Welfare*, *78*(5), 541–560. PMID:10501012

Kestly, T. A. (2014). *The interpersonal neurobiology of play: Brain-building interventions for emotional well-being*. New York, NY: W. W. Norton.

Koenigs, M., & Grafman, J. (2009). Posttraumatic stress disorder: The role of medial prefrontal cortex and amygdala. *The Neuroscientist*, *15*(5), 540–548. doi:10.1177/1073858409333072 PMID:19359671

Koenigs, M., Huey, E. D., Raymont, V., Cheon, B., Solomon, J., Wassermann, E. M., & Grafman, J. (2008). Focal brain damage protects against post-traumatic stress disorder in combat veterans. *Nature Neuroscience*, *11*(2), 232–237. doi:10.1038/nn2032 PMID:18157125

Landreth, G. L. (2012). *Play therapy: The art of the relationship* (3rd ed.). New York, NY: Routledge.

Lewis, T., Amini, F., & Lannon, R. (2000). *A general theory of love*. New York: Random House.

McDonald, M. K., Borntrager, C. F., & Rostad, W. (2014). Measuring trauma: Considerations for assessing complex and non-PTSD criterion a childhood trauma. *Journal of Trauma & Dissociation*, *15*(2), 184–203. doi:10.1080/15299732.2014.867577 PMID:24410287

McFarlane, A. C., Policansky, S. K., & Irwin, C. (1987). A longitudinal study of the psychological morbidity in children due to a natural disaster. *Psychological Medicine*, *17*(3), 727–738. doi:10.1017/S0033291700025964 PMID:3628633

Moustakas, C. (1959). *Psychotherapy with children: The living relationship*. Greeley, CO: Carron.

Perry, B. D. (1997). Incubated in terror: Neurodevelopmental factors in the 'cycle of violence. In J. D. Osofsky (Ed.), *Children in a violent society* (pp. 124–149). New York, NY: Guilford Press.

Perry, B. D. (2009). Examining child maltreatment through a neurodevelopmental lens: Clinical applications of the neurosequential model of therapeutics. *Journal of Loss and Trauma*, *14*(4), 240–255. doi:10.1080/15325020903004350

Perry, B. D., Hogan, L., & Marlin, S. J. (2000, August). Curiosity, pleasure, and play: A neurodevelopmental perspective. *Houston Area Association for the Education of Young Child,* 9–12.

Perry, B. D., Pollard, R. A., Blakley, T. L., Baker, W. L., & Vigilante, D. (1995). Childhood trauma, the neurobiology of adaptation, and use-dependent development of the brain: How states become traits. *Infant Mental Health Journal*, *16*(4), 271–291. doi:10.1002/1097-0355(199524)16:4<271::AID-IMHJ2280160404>3.0.CO;2-B

Pezawas, L., Meyer-Lindenberg, A., Drabant, E. M., Verchinski, B. A., Munoz, K. E., Kolachana, B. S., & Weinberger, D. R. et al. (2005). 5-HTTLPR polymorphism impacts human cingulate-amygdala interactions: A genetic susceptibility mechanism for depression. *Nature Neuroscience*, *8*(6), 828–834. doi:10.1038/nn1463 PMID:15880108

Pfefferbaum, B. (1997). Posttraumatic stress disorder in children: A review of the past 10 years. *Journal of the American Academy of Child and Adolescent Psychiatry*, *36*(11), 1503–1511. PMID:9394934

Porges, S. W. (2011). *The polyvagal theory: Neurophysiological foundations of emotions, attachment, communication, and self-regulation*. New York, NY: W.W. Norton & Company.

Rauch, S. L., Whalen, P. J., Shin, L. M., McInerney, S. C., Macklin, M. L., Lasko, N. B., & Pitman, R. K. et al. (2000). Exaggerated amygdala response to masked facial stimuli in posttraumatic stress disorder: A functional MRI study. *Biological Psychiatry*, *47*(9), 769–776. doi:10.1016/S0006-3223(00)00828-3 PMID:10812035

Rogers, M. A., Yamasue, H., Abe, O., Yamada, H., Ohtani, T., Iwanami, A., & Kasai, K. et al. (2009). Smaller amygdala volume and reduced anterior cingulate gray matter density associated with history of post-traumatic stress disorder. *Psychiatry Research: Neuroimaging*, *174*(3), 210–216. doi:10.1016/j.pscychresns.2009.06.001 PMID:19914045

Rothschild, B. (2003). *The body remembers casebook: Unifying methods and models in the treatment of trauma and PTSD*. New York, NY: W. W. Norton.

Ryan, V., & Needham, C. (2001). Non-directive play therapy with children experiencing psychic trauma. *Clinical Child Psychology and Psychiatry*, *6*(3), 437–453. doi:10.1177/1359104501006003011

Schaefer, C. E. (1995). *The therapeutic powers of play*. Northvale, NJ: J. Aronson.

Schaefer, C. E., & Drewes, A. A. (Eds.). (2014). *The therapeutic powers of play: 20 core agents of change*. Hoboken, NJ: Wiley.

Schwarz, E. D., & Perry, B. D. (1994). The post-traumatic response in children and adolescents. *The Psychiatric Clinics of North America*, *17*(2), 311–326. PMID:7937362

Shapiro, J. P., Friedberg, R. D., & Bardenstein, K. K. (2006). *Child and adolescent therapy: Science and art*. Hoboken, NJ: Wiley.

Shin, L. M., Wright, C. I., Cannistraro, P. A., Wedig, M. M., McMullin, K., Martis, B., & Rauch, S. L. et al. (2005). A Functional Magnetic Resonance Imaging Study of Amygdala and Medial Prefrontal Cortex Responses to Overtly Presented Fearful Faces in Posttraumatic Stress Disorder. *Archives of General Psychiatry*, *62*(3), 273–281. doi:10.1001/archpsyc.62.3.273 PMID:15753240

Siegel, D. J. (2009). Mindful awareness, mindsight, and neural integration. *The Humanistic Psychologist*, *37*(2), 137–158. doi:10.1080/08873260902892220

Siegel, D. J. (2010). *The mindful therapist: A clinician's guide to mindsight and neural integration*. New York, NY, US: W W Norton & Co.

Siegel, D. J. (2012). *The developing mind: How relationships and the brain interact to shape who we are* (2nd ed.). New York, NY: Guilford Press.

Siegel, D. J., & Bryson, T. P. (2011). *The whole-brain child: 12 revolutionary strategies to nurture your child's developing mind.* New York, NY: Delacorte Press.

Siegel, D. J., & Hartzell, M. (2003). *Parenting from the inside out: How a deeper self-understanding can help you raise children who thrive.* New York, NY: J. P. Tarcher/Penguin.

Stewart, A. L., Field, T. A., & Echterling, L. G. (2016). Neuroscience and the magic of play therapy. *International Journal of Play Therapy*, *25*(1), 4–13. doi:10.1037/pla0000016

Sunderland, M. (2006). *The science of parenting.* New York, NY: DK Publishing.

US Department of Health and Human Services, Administration on Children, Youth, and Families, Children's Bureau. (2014). *Child maltreatment.* Retrieved from http://www.acf.hhs.gov/sites/default/files/cb/cm2014.pdf#page=21

van der Kolk, B. A. (1996). The body keeps score: Approaches to the psychobiology of posttraumatic stress disorder. In B. A. van der Kolk, A. C. McFarlane, L. Weisaeth, B. A. van der Kolk, A. C. McFarlane, & L. Weisaeth (Eds.), *Traumatic stress: The effects of overwhelming experience on mind, body, and society* (pp. 214–241). New York, NY: Guilford Press.

van der Kolk, B. A. (2005). Developmental Trauma Disorder: Toward a rational diagnosis for children with complex trauma histories. *Psychiatric Annals*, *35*(5), 401–408.

Van Hooff, M., McFarlane, A. C., Baur, J., Abraham, M., & Barnes, D. J. (2009). The stressor Criterion A-1 and PTSD: A matter of opinion? *Journal of Anxiety Disorders*, *23*(1), 77–86. doi:10.1016/j.janxdis.2008.04.001 PMID:18511232

Vasterling, J. J., & Brewin, C. R. (Eds.). (2005). *Neuropsychology of PTSD: Biological, cognitive, and clinical perspectives.* New York, NY: The Guilford Press.

Ward, J. (2010). *The student's guide to cognitive neuroscience* (2nd ed.). New York, NY: Psychology Press.

Wheeler, N., & Dillman Taylor, D. (2016). Integrating interpersonal neurobiology with play therapy. *International Journal of Play Therapy*, *25*(1), 24–34. doi:10.1037/pla0000018

KEY TERMS AND DEFINITIONS

Abreaction: The ability of the child to tolerate and express her emotions through psychic reworking of the traumatic event.

Developmental Trauma: Adverse traumatic events that impact the emotional, cognitive, behavioral, and interpersonal aspects of children's development, with associated neurobiological changes.

Child-Centered Play Therapy: An approach to play therapy that assumes children have the ability to self-direct and self-heal when provided with unconditional positive regard, empathic understanding, and congruence from the therapist.

Hemispheric Integration: The process through which play facilitates integration of the most complex structures of the brain, namely the right and left hemispheres of the cerebral cortex.

Limbic Resonance: Defined by Lewis, Amini, and Lannon (2000), this process occurs when a child plays and experiences extreme distress, and the therapist subsequently experiences empathic synchrony and subjective stress similar to the child.

Limbic System: A complex brain system, including structures such as the amygdala and hippocampus, which are involved in emotional stimuli responses, attachment, interpersonal functioning, memory formation, and learning.

Neurobiology-Informed Treatment: Neurobiologically informed play therapy in which emotionally disturbed children are encouraged to act out their fantasies and express their feelings through play with the guidance of a trained therapist.

Play Therapy: The use of the therapeutic powers of play to aid clients in preventing and/or resolving psychosocial difficulties and achieve optimal growth and development.

Therapeutic Powers of Play: The agents of change through the play process, such as abreaction, that facilitate adaptive functioning of the child.

Chapter 6
Adlerian Play Therapy:
Practice and Research

Kristin K. Meany-Walen
University of Northern Iowa, USA

Terry Kottman
Encouragement Zone, USA

ABSTRACT

Many play therapists routinely use Adlerian theory as their primary mode of conducting therapy with children (Lambert et al., 2007). In an age of evidenced-informed practices, research that supports or describes a treatment's effectiveness is important (Chambless & Ollendick, 2001). Because of Adlerian play therapy's popularity and the emphasis for evidence of treatment effectiveness, researchers began investigating Adlerian play therapy. A brief description of Adlerian play therapy and a description of research is provided.

INTRODUCTION

Adlerian play therapy is a popular method of working with children, adolescents, and families and been identified as one of the top three most widely used play therapy approaches by people who work therapeutically with children (Lambert et al., 2007). It was developed by one of the authors (TK) in the late 1980s, merging the concepts and strategies of Individual Psychology and the skills of play therapy to a developmentally responsive intervention for children (Kottman & Meany-Walen, 2016). Its philosophical tenants follow those of Alfred Adler and his theory, Individual Psychology, emphasizing that people are socially embedded, goal directed, and striving for belonging (Adler, 1927/1998). Although Adler stressed the importance and influence of childhood on human development and personality, he did not provide specific strategies in which to work with children. We believe he would endorse Adlerian play therapy as he wrote,

DOI: 10.4018/978-1-5225-2224-9.ch006

[Play] should be seen as educational aids and as stimuli for the child's psyche, imagination and life skills. Every game is a preparation for the future....In observing children at play, we can see their whole attitude towards life; play is the utmost importance to every child. (Adler, 1927/1998, p. 83)

The Adlerian play therapist and client move through four phases of counseling: building a collaborative and egalitarian relationship, investigating the child's lifestyle, helping the child gain insight, and reorienting/reeducating the child to more productive and socially responsible ways of thinking, feeling, and behaving in various situations (Kottman & Meany-Walen, 2016). In the process of Adlerian play therapy, the therapist uses directive and nondirective interventions and toys, play, metaphor, storytelling, art, sand tray experiences, and movement to learn about, communicate with, and educate the child client. Because Adlerian theory holds that people are socially embedded and cannot be understood in isolation, parents or other important adults such as teachers are involved throughout the process. They provide information about their relationship with the child, the child's history, current functioning, and changes.

In the first phase, the therapist and client begin to develop a relationship in which the child is and feels valued and encouraged. The goal of this phase is for the child to feel cared for, safe, and hopeful about the potential for positive change. As these feelings become activated in the child, the child becomes more free and open to express him or herself, available to gain insight, and less resistant to making changes. The therapist shares power with the child as both parties exchange information, make decisions, and interact with one another. The play therapist uses basic play therapy skills of tracking, restating content, and reflecting feelings as a way to build a relationship with the child. Using some directive techniques (i.e., art, movement, sand trays, puppet shows), the Adlerian play therapist also actively engages the child in games and activities designed to build trust, foster the emerging relationship, and set the stage for the therapeutic process. One examples of a directed technique is to play a relatively simple and common game such as Jenga®, tic tac toe, or checkers. This can be helpful to assess the child's ability to take turns, follow pre-set rules, win or lose gracefully, and stay focused. During the game, and based on what the counselor knows about the child, the counselor may or may not insist that the child follow the traditional rules of the game, or might brainstorm with the child new ways of playing the game. Essentially, the goal is to build trust and practice sharing power. Metacommunicating about themes and underlying issues throughout this process, the Adlerian play therapist deepens the relationship. Although the primary focus of the first phase is building an egalitarian alliance with the child, the Adlerian play therapist continues to strengthen the therapeutic relationship throughout all phases of the play therapy process.

In the next phase, investigating the child's lifestyle, the play therapist works to understand the child's lifestyle--his or her unique way of being and beliefs about self, others, and the world and the behaviors that accompany those beliefs (Kottman & Meany-Walen, 2016). The lifestyle is at the center of Adlerian theory and the following constructs are frequently used by Adlerian play therapists: family constellation (Kottman & Meany-Walen, 2016), personality priorities (Kfir, 1981, 2011), goals of misbehavior (Dreikurs & Soltz, 1964), Crucial Cs (Lew & Bettner, 1998, 2000), life tasks (Adler 1927/1998; Maniacci, Sackett-Maniacci, & Mosak, 2014), mistaken beliefs (Sweeney, 2009), and assets (Kottman 2009; Kottman & Meany-Walen, 2016). The therapist uses this information to conceptualize the client and his or her assets, issues, and patterns of thinking, feeling, and behaving and develops a treatment plan. Treatment plans are designed to encourage and strengthen the child's assets, and shift the child's feelings of inferiority, mistaken beliefs, and socially deconstructive behaviors into socially useful and constructive self-perceptions, attitudes, and behaviors (Kottman & Meany-Walen, 2016).

The Adlerian play therapist uses directive strategies as well as child-lead play to help gather the information necessary to form tentative hypotheses about the child's lifestyle. Children will naturally reveal some lifestyle patterns during the session such as how a child approaches activities, the counselor, and making decisions. For example, a child who readily makes decisions and takes charge might have a need to be in control. A child who becomes easily frustrated when she makes a mistake might lack courage to be imperfect and have a personality priority of superiority. Additionally, directive interventions are valued and used to gather other information about the child, his or her family, and patterns of his or her emotions, beliefs, behaviors, and attitudes. An example of a directed activity is asking the child to do a family drawing, a puppet show about school, or a sand tray about the child's friends or a problem situation.

The third phase is dedicated to helping the child gain insight (Kottman & Meany-Walen, 2016). The therapist's goal in this phase is to help the child to have a better understanding of his or her patterns of thoughts, feelings, and behaviors. To help the child gain insight, the therapist is directive and active. He or she uses developmentally responsive activities that can include play, art, crafts, sand tray, music, dance or movement, games, puppet shows, mutual story-telling, custom-designed metaphors, bibliotherapy, and/or other intentionally designed interventions that help the child better gain insight into his or her emotions, thoughts, and behaviors. Metacommunicating to the child his or her patterns of communicating, solving problems, and building or maintaining relationships, the Adlerian play therapist helps the child develop an understanding of what is and what is not working well for him or her. The Adlerian play therapist believes that when the child has awareness of his or her lifestyle dimensions, the child is better able to make changes that will be personally and socially advantageous.

Lastly, in the reorienting/reeducating phase, the therapist creates opportunities for the child to learn and practice new behaviors that reflect his or her changed thoughts and attitudes. The therapist may teach new skills through modeling, having the child "act as if" they possessed particular qualities, or playing red light-green light. In red light-green light the therapist intermittently says "right light" or "green light" throughout the session, and the child practices stopping and staying still as he or she plays. This intervention might be used with children with goals of increasing skills of listening, following directions, or being still. The play therapist may invite the child to play games that were played in the earlier phases of the relationship to see if changes in attitudes or behaviors developed, such as if a child is better able to share, take turns, or win or lose with grace. Other children or family members might be included in the sessions during this phase to practice newly developed skills or to provide information to the therapist about changes they have noticed outside of the playroom. Adults can be coached in child development and strategies that can encourage positive change for the child. For complete description of theoretical underpinnings and process of Adlerian play therapy, readers are referred to *Partners in Play: An Adlerian Approach to Play Therapy* (3rd ed.) (Kottman & Meany-Walen, 2016).

While Adlerian play therapy is practiced by many people and is recognized as a leading play therapy intervention, research that uses Adlerian play therapy as the independent variable has only recently been published. The movement for counseling interventions to be evidenced-based created the impetus for Kottman to develop a treatment protocol for her model. As a student and mentee of Kottman, and a practitioner of Adlerian play therapy, Meany-Walen conducted the first published Adlerian play therapy research. Results of this research suggested that Adlerian play therapy is effective at reducing children's problem behaviors, increasing their classroom on-task behaviors, and reducing teacher stress (Meany-Walen, Bratton, & Kottman, 2010). A more thorough description of the research is described within this chapter.

ADLERIAN PLAY THERAPY RESEARCH

Rigorous research requires the intervention follow a treatment protocol (Chambless & Ollendick, 2001). The *Treatment Manual for Adlerian Play Therapy* (Kottman, 2009) contains an explanation of the theoretical rationale for Adlerian play therapy, the role of the therapist, the therapeutic skills used throughout the four phases, and goals of treatment. Using live observation or video recording, therapists and supervisors can establish whether the play therapist adheres to the procedure outlined in the manual in observed play therapy sessions, creating a procedure for conducting treatment fidelity checks.

As stated previously, Adlerian play therapy research is relatively new. In fact, 2014 was the year of the first published account of the effects of Adlerian play therapy. Since then, a number of studies have been published or submitted for publication. Each is briefly described below. The studies have many similarities including: (a) most (all but one) used an objective observation form for assessing changes in the child's behaviors, (b) all of them took place at the participants' schools, (c) all of them followed procedures of the *Treatment Manual for Adlerian Play Therapy* (Kottman, 2009), (d) and all of them included fidelity checks by comparing sessions to the skills matrices (Kottman, 2009).

Published accounts of Adlerian play therapy used either a randomized control trial (RCT) or a single case design (SCD). A RCT is considered the gold standard of research in which there are at least two groups of participants (Chambless, & Ollendick, 2001; Rubin, 2008). One group receives the intervention under investigation (i.e. experimental group) and the other group(s) receives no treatment, comparison treatment, or alternative treatment design (i.e. control group). Each group usually has a minimum of 15 participants. Researchers typically use a pre/post- test design to assess the treatment effectiveness of the intervention over time (pre-post text) and between groups (experimental group vs. control group). Adlerian play therapy has one published RCT.

The greatest number of published research accounts of Adlerian play therapy used SCDs as the design method and data analysis. SCDs have become popular and emphasized in the helping professions because of its practicality for practitioner researchers (Lundervold & Belwood, 2000; Purswell & Ray, 2014; Ray, 2015; Rubin, 2008). This type of design allows for fewer participants, with each participant's baseline data serving as an independent control. Data is collected frequently (e.g. daily or weekly). Study findings can provide readers with information about the timing of change and intervention variables that might contribute to noted change in the dependent variable (Ray, 2015). To date, one dissertation used a SCD, four SCD studies have been published, and four more are under peer-review for publication. Overall, the results suggest individual and group Adlerian play therapy is an effective intervention at reducing problematic behavior and improving desired behaviors. A brief description of each study follows.

Meany-Walen conducted her dissertation research in 2010 and published results of the study in 2014 (Meany-Walen, Bratton, & Kottman, 2014). She created a randomized control trial study to investigate the effectiveness of Adlerian play therapy on children's externalizing behaviors and teachers' teaching stress. In addition to obtaining parental consent, to be included in the study children had to score in the borderline or clinical range on the Direct Observation Form (DOF; McConaughy, & Achenbach, 2009) Total Behaviors scale, the Teacher Report Form (TRF; Achenbach & Rescorla, 2001) Externalizing Problem scale or one of the following TRF subscales: Attention Problems, Rule Breaking, Aggressive Behavior, ADHD, Oppositional Defiant Problems, or Conduct Problems. Participants were randomly assigned to the Adlerian play therapy or reading mentoring group. Reading mentoring was used as an active control group to account for effects of attention. Children in both groups received 30 minute sessions, twice weekly for 16 sessions and were removed from their classrooms for the same amount of time, which increased the rigor of the study by blinding teachers to the treatment grouping of their students (Meany-Walen et al., 2014). An additional strength of this study was the use of blinded and objective observers. Trained observers who were blinded to the study design and grouping of the participants conducted pre and posttest observations using the DOF. Thus, assessments were completed by teachers who had relationships with the children, and by observers who did not have relationships with the children.

The dependent variables for this study included: TRF Externalizing Problems, DOF Total Behaviors and On-task Behaviors, and Index of Teaching Stress (ITS; Abidin, Greene, & Konold, 2004) Total Stress. Results indicated that children who received Adlerian play therapy showed a statistically significant interaction effect for time and group membership on each of the dependent variables (Meany-Walen et al., 2014). Results from the TRF Externalizing Behaviors and ITS Total Stress data revealed a moderate treatment effect for children who received Adlerian play therapy, and a large treatment effect for improving DOF Total Behaviors and On-task Behaviors. Notably, assessment completed by objective observers showed the strongest treatment effect, which may be a more accurate indication of students' behavioral change (Volpe, DiPerna, Hintze, & Shapiro, 2009).

Akay (2013) investigated the effects of Adlerian play therapy on children's maladaptive perfectionism and anxiety using a SCD. Two children completed the study, which is sufficient for SCD. To qualify, they scored in the borderline or clinical range on the Conners Rating Scales-Revised (CRS; Conners, Siteranios, Parker, & Epstein, 1998) for anxiety and were identified by teachers as having qualities of perfectionism. Participants received 30 minute, bi-weekly Adlerian play therapy sessions for 16 sessions, and their parents and teachers received consultation throughout the intervention period.

The Self-Oriented Perfectionism (SOP) and Socially-Prescribed Perfectionism (SPP) scales of the Child–Adolescent Perfectionism Scale (CAPS; Flett, Hewitt, Boucher, Davidson, & Munro, 2002), Revised Children's Manifest Anxiety Scale (RCMAS-2; Reynolds & Richmond, 2008), and CRS were used as dependent variables in this research (Akay, 2013). The percentage of data exceeding the median (PEM) statistic was used to assess the treatment effect size during the intervention and follow-up periods of the study. CRS completed by the children's parents and teachers revealed a reduction in both children's anxiety and perfectionism behaviors from the pretest to the posttest. However, statistical analysis suggested that Adlerian play therapy was ineffective at reducing perfectionistic qualities in both children. Per RCMAS-2 scores, one child showed a reduction in anxiety and the other showed an increase in anxiety over the study phases. Dependent variables for both children moved from atypical levels of concern at the beginning of the study to a normal range of functioning during follow-up. This suggests that parents and teachers noticed an improvement in desired functioning of the children following the Adlerian play therapy intervention despite the lack of statistical evidence suggesting change as a result of Adlerian play therapy (Akay, 2013).

Meany-Walen, Kottman, Bullis, and Dillman Taylor (2015) studied children referred to counseling due to teachers' concerns with the children's classroom behaviors. The children's behaviors scored in the borderline or clinical range of the Total Problem Behaviors scale on the DOF and qualified them for inclusion in the study. A total of five children between the ages of five and seven participated in the study. Three received Adlerian play therapy and two were in a control group. Control groups are not a requirement of SCDs, but can provide information about a typical trajectory of behaviors without intervention. They can also help to explain unexpected changes in data in the intervention group. Children in both groups were assessed using the DOF by an observer who was blinded to the treatment groups and was uninformed of the intervention start dates. Children started intervention on staggering weeks, which created multiple base lines and increased the rigor of the study (Ray, 2015; Rubin, 2008). Participants in the treatment group received 30-minute, bi-weekly sessions for 15-17 sessions. Visual analysis and percentage of non-overlapping data (PND) statistic were used to determine Adlerian play therapy's impact on the children's behaviors.

Of the three children in the experimental groups, visual analysis showed a steady improvement in behaviors across assessment periods (i.e. intervention and follow-up) for two children on the DOF Total Problem scale, and all three children showed steady improvement on the DOF On-task behavior scale. On the Total Problem scale, statistical analysis revealed ineffective treatment effect during intervention phase for one child, effective treatment effect during intervention phase for one child, and very effective treatment effect during the intervention phase for one child. During the follow-up phase, all three children resulted in very effective treatment effects. Statistical analysis of the On-task scale revealed ineffective treatment effect during intervention phase for one child, questionably effective treatment effect during the intervention phase for one child, and effective treatment effect during the intervention phase for one child. During the follow-up phase, two children showed questionable treatment effect and one resulted in very effective treatment effect. Despite confounding statistical results, each of the three children in the experimental group showed improvement in their behaviors as evidenced by a reduction of their initial clinical scoring behaviors, resulting in behaviors that scored in the normal range according to the DOF Manual (McConaughy, & Achenbach, 2009). The children in the control group, who did not receive an intervention, demonstrated consistent disruptive behavior or a decline of desired behavior over the study period (Meany-Walen, Kottman et al., 2015).

Dillman Taylor and Meany-Walen (2015) also investigated Adlerian play therapy with children's externalizing behaviors. Three children between the ages of five and ten qualified for the study by scoring in the clinical or borderline range on the TRF (Achenbach & Rescorla, 2001), which is a complimentary assessment to the DOF. Two children received bi-weekly Adlerian play therapy for 30-minute sessions for a total of 8 sessions. One child was in a waitlist control group. The DOF's Total Problems and On-task Behavior scales were used to measure effectiveness of the intervention.

Dillman Taylor and Meany-Walen (2015) used visual analysis and the PEM statistic to calculate the treatment effect for each of the dependent variables in the intervention and follow-up phases for each child. The children's visual analysis showed a steady improvement in behaviors during the intervention and follow-up periods. During the intervention phase on the Total Problems scale one child showed moderate treatment effects and one child showed questionable treatment effects. The follow-up phase of the Total Problems scale resulted in very effective treatment effects for one child and ineffective treatment effects for the other child. Statistical analysis of the children's scores during the intervention phase on the On-task scales revealed moderate treatment effects for one child and questionable effects for the other child; during the follow-up phase one child's scores suggested moderate treatment effects and the other suggested ineffective treatment effects. Both children showed an improved level of behaviors during the follow-up phase compared to the baseline phase despite inconsistent and questionable statistical results. The child who did not receive intervention showed a consistent decline of desired behaviors across the study period.

Exploring Adlerian play therapy's effectiveness on symptoms related to attention deficit hyperactivity disorder (ADHD), Meany-Walen and Teeling (2016a) used a SCD with four early-elementary aged participants who qualified for inclusion in the study by scoring in the borderline or clinical range of functioning on the DOF ADHD scale. The researchers strengthened their study design by staggering participants' intervention start times and by including additional children in the observation process – the additional children had consent to be observed but did not receive intervention – to blind observers from knowing which students received treatment and at what point their treatment began. Participants received weekly Adlerian play therapy for eight weeks at their elementary school.

Meany-Walen and Teeling (2016a) used visual analysis and the PEM statistic to analyze participant's data. Visual analysis was consistent among the four participants. On their On-task scales, they each showed steady improvement from baseline, intervention, and follow-up phases. The PEM statistic also revealed a very effective treatment effect during the intervention phase and the follow-up phase for all four participants. On the ADHD scale, each participant showed an initial undesirable change in behaviors during the intervention phase with an improvement in desired behaviors during the follow-up phase. During the intervention phase the PEM statistic was questionably effective treatment effect for two participants and no treatment effect for two participants. The follow-up phase, according to the PEM statistic, revealed very effective treatment effect for one participant, questionably effective treatment effect for two participants, and no treatment effect for one participant.

Group Adlerian play therapy has also received attention, and six studies have explored the effectiveness of group intervention or the combination of group and individual sessions on children's behaviors using a SCD. Play groups can include as few as two participants (Sweeney, Baggerly, & Ray, 2014). Meany-Walen and Teeling (2016b) used a mixed intervention approach to investigate Adlerian play therapy on children's externalizing behaviors and their social skills. Three participants in first and second grade who were reportedly disruptive in the classroom and had social skill deficits and scored in the borderline or clinical range of concern on the DOF On-task scale qualified for the study. The participants received sessions twice weekly. They received 30 minute individual sessions on Mondays and 45 minute group sessions on Thursdays for a total of 10-12 sessions throughout the seven week intervention period.

Visual analysis and PEM statistic were used to measure the mixed intervention effects on the children's behaviors. Participants' scores visually represented improvement on on-task behaviors during the intervention and follow-up periods. Two of the three children's scores resulted in an effective treatment effect and one child's scores resulted in a very effective treatment effect for the intervention during the intervention period. All children's scores resulted in a very effective treatment effect during the follow-up period (Meany-Walen & Teeling, 2016b). Teacher reports and therapist observation during group sessions also suggested improvement in the children's ability to appropriately interact in social settings with peers and adults.

In another mixed intervention study, two, second grade elementary students received individual and group Adlerian play therapy twice weekly for six weeks (Meany-Walen, Teeling, Davis, Artley, & Vignovich, 2016) in their elementary school. Students were referred to the study based on off-task classroom behaviors that aligned with characteristics commonly used to diagnose attention deficit hyperactivity disorder (ADHD). The dependent variables in this study were the DOF's On-task, Total Problems, and ADHD scales.

Using visual analysis and the PEM statistic, results suggested the combined interventions were effective at improving the participants' behaviors. One participant's scores resulted in very effective treatment effects for each of the dependent variables (On-task, Total Problems, and ADHD scales) during the intervention and follow-up phases (Meany-Walen et al., 2016). The other participant's results resulted in very effective treatment effects for the intervention phase on the On-task and ADHD scales and questionably effective treatment effects on these scales during the follow-up phase. For this participant, there was no treatment effect during the intervention or follow-up phase on the Total Problems scale (Meany-Walen et al., 2016). Visual analysis for each of the participants on each scale showed improvement, and anecdotal evidence supported desired change in the children's behaviors from the beginning of the intervention to the weeks following the intervention.

Dillman Taylor, Nelson, Gungor, and Meany-Walen (2016) used group Adlerian play therapy as the independent variable with three children between the ages of six and eight. Participants qualified for the study after referral from their teacher for classroom disruptive behaviors and scoring in the borderline or clinical range on the Externalizing subscale of the TRF. Participants received eight, weekly, 45-minute sessions of group intervention. Visually, one child showed improvement on the DOF Total Problem and On-task scales, the other child showed inconclusive results.

Using the PEM statistic on the Total Problems scale during the intervention phase, one child showed very effective treatment effects, and one showed ineffective treatment effects. Total Problems scale results during the follow-up period revealed very effective treatment effects for one child and moderate effective treatment effects for the other child. PEM statistic on the DOF On-task scale during the intervention phase revealed one child with very effective treatment effects and one child with moderate treatment effects. On-task scale results during the follow-up period revealed very effective treatment effects for one child and ineffective treatment effects for one child. The child who did not receive treatment during this observation period showed a projection of undesirable behaviors. Results were similar to other studies that indicated behaviors falling in the normal range of functioning during the follow-up period even when statistical analysis did not support effectiveness of the intervention (Dillman Taylor et al., 2016).

Meany-Walen (2016) used a combined intervention approach in which participants received a series of individual Adlerian play therapy sessions followed by a series of group Adlerian play therapy sessions. Three participants in first and second grade qualified for the study based on teachers' referrals for disruptive classroom behaviors. The participants received approximately eight weeks of 30-minute, biweekly interventions followed by four weeks of 45-minute, once weekly group intervention.

Visual analysis and the PEM of the children's DOF On-task scores were used to assess children's behavioral changes across the study period (Meany-Walen, 2016). While the On-task scores seemed to fluctuate between the individual intervention and the group intervention phases, the concluding follow-up scores were an improvement from the baseline phase for two of children and remained stable for the third child. Statistical analysis resulted in two children's behaviors showing effective treatment effect and one child's behaviors showing very effective treatment effect during the individual Adlerian play therapy phase. Two children's behaviors showed very effective treatment effect, and one child's behaviors revealed no treatment effect during the group Adlerian play therapy phase. Each child's scores resulted in very effective treatment effect during the follow-up phase.

In a study in which participants received only group Adlerian play therapy, two six year-old boys participated in six, weekly, 45-minute sessions (Meany-Walen, Bullis, Kottman, & Dillman Taylor, 2015). The participants scored in the borderline or clinical range of functioning on the On-task domain on the DOF to qualify for inclusion in the study. Both participants showed very effective treatment effects during the intervention. One student's behaviors revealed questionable treatment effect and the other student revealed ineffective treatment during the follow-up phase. Importantly, both participants' scores fell in the normal range of functioning during the post-intervention assessment period.

In sum, a total of nine articles are published or in review for publication that report the effectiveness of Adlerian play therapy with children with behaviors deemed adverse by their teachers or parents. Participants were between the ages of five and ten were included in the studies, and they received Adlerian play therapy in individual, group, or a combination of both formats. Notably, a strong improvement in children's behaviors were found with as few as six sessions (i.e. Meany-Walen, Bullis et al., 2015).

Randomized control trials are considered to be the most desired and rigorous research design (Chambless, & Ollendick, 2001; Rubin, 2008) and can be quite difficult to conduct for practitioners and researchers in the helping professions due to the logistics involved in creating and carrying out such a design. Of the number of research publications that investigate Adlerian play therapy, only one article featuring this research design exists (i.e. Meany-Walen et al., 2014). Meany-Walen et al. (2014) found strong evidence that suggests Adlerian play therapy is effective at reducing children's externalizing behaviors and assuaging teachers' teaching stress. The remainder of the published Adlerian play therapy research accounts were SCDs, and the authors reported visual analysis and statistical data from the intervention and follow-up phases, and anecdotal evidence when available. Whereas results were not consistent across the entirety of the studies, the majority of results suggested that Adlerian play therapy was effective at reducing children's externalizing behaviors, and researchers most often reported effective or very effective treatment effects during the follow-up phases. This is particularly important as the goal of counseling interventions is for clients to maintain positive changes after the direct intervention is no longer being implemented (Ray, 2015).

A couple of considerations must be examined for a comprehensive and objective understanding of the data. First, each of the studies took place in a school setting. While this is important and noteworthy given the increase in school-based mental health services, no Adlerian play therapy research has been published that accounts for treatment delivered in an agency or clinic setting. Second, Meany-Walen is an author of nine of the ten studies. She has a deep interest in Adlerian play therapy and co-authored the leading Adlerian play therapy text with Adlerian play therapy creator, Terry Kottman. Her published articles describe the research methods and appear to have strategies in place to account for researcher bias (i.e. blinded observers and staggering start times), and yet readers are wise to consider her contributions to the number of Adlerian play therapy research manuscripts. Lastly, the majority of studies described were SCDs. While SCD is a respected research method and those outlined here appear to have a rigorous design, organizations charged with proclaiming treatments as evidenced-based typically reject SCDs as evidence for treatment effectiveness or require multiple published SCD accounts to carry the same weight as a randomized control trial (Chambless, & Ollendick, 2001). Because of these considerations, diversity of authorship, exploration of intervention setting, and more studies that use a randomized control trial design are recommended.

Helping professionals are under pressure to provide evidence-based treatment interventions to their clients. Over the last few decades, Adlerian play therapy has become a leading play therapy intervention for children (Lambert et al., 2007) and up until recently had no available research that supported its efficacy and effectiveness. Of late, Adlerian play therapy practitioners and researchers have made great strides in beginning to provide confirmation for professionals who use this approach and their clients who benefit from the intervention. Preliminary research has suggested that the use of Adlerian play therapy with children's externalizing behaviors can be efficacious and effective, and continued exploration is necessary.

REFERENCES

Abidin, R., Greene, R., & Konold, T. (2004). *Index of teacher stress: Professional manual.* Lutz, FL: Psychological Assessment Resources.

Achenbach, T. M., & Rescorla, L. A. (2001). *Manual for the ASEBA school-age forms & profiles.* Burlington, VT: University of Vermont, Research Center for Children, Youth, & Families.

Adler, A. (1998). *Understanding human nature.* Academic Press. (Original work published 1927)

Akay, S. (2013). *The effects of Adlerian play therapy on maladaptive perfectionism and anxiety in children* (Unpublished doctoral dissertation). University of North Texas, Denton, TX.

Chambless, D. L., & Ollendick, T. H. (2001). Empirically supported psychological interventions: Controversies and evidence. *Annual Review of Psychology, 52*(1), 685–716. doi:10.1146/annurev.psych.52.1.685 PMID:11148322

Conners, C. K., Sitarenios, G., Parker, J. D. A., & Epstein, J. N. (1998). Revision and restandardization of the Conners Teacher Rating Scale (CTRS-R): Factor structure, reliability, and criterion validity. *Journal of Abnormal Child Psychology, 26*(4), 279–291. doi:10.1023/A:1022606501530 PMID:9700520

Dillman Taylor, D., & Meany-Walen, K. K. (2015). Investigating the effectiveness of Adlerian play therapy with children with disruptive behaviors: A single-case research design. *Journal of Child and Adolescent Counseling, 93*, 418–428. doi:10.1080/23727810.2015.1081519

Dillman Taylor, D., Nelson, K. M., Gungor, A., & Meany-Walen, K. K. (2016). *Group Adlerian play therapy with children with externalizing behaviors.* Manuscript submitted for publication.

Dreikurs, R., & Soltz, V. (1964). *Children: The challenge.* Hawthorn Dutton.

Flett, G. L., Hewitt, P. L., Boucher, D. J., Davidson, L. A., & Munro, Y. (2002). *The Child–Adolescent Perfectionism Scale: Development, validation, and association with adjustment.* Unpublished manuscript.

Kfir, N. (1981). Impasse/priority therapy. In R. Corsini (Ed.), *Handbook of innovative psychotherapies* (pp. 400–415). New York: Wiley.

Kfir, N. (2011). *Personality and priorities: A typology.* Bloomington, IN: Author House.

Kottman, T. (2009). *Treatment manual for Adlerian play therapy.* Unpublished manuscript.

Kottman, T., & Meany-Walen, K. K. (2016). *Partners in play: An Adlerian approach to play therapy* (3rd ed.). Alexandria, VA: American Counseling Association.

Lambert, S. F., LeBlanc, M., Mullen, J. A., Ray, D., Baggerly, J., White, J., & Kaplan, D. (2007, Winter). Learning more about those who play in session: The national play therapy in counseling practices project (phase 1). *Journal of Counseling and Development, 85*(1), 42–46. doi:10.1002/j.1556-6678.2007.tb00442.x

Lew, A., & Bettner, B. L. (1998). *Responsibility in the classroom: A teacher's guide to understanding and motivating students.* Connexions Press.

Lew, A., & Bettner, B. L. (2000). *A parent's guide to understanding and motivating children.* Connexions Press.

Lundervold, D. A., & Belwood, M. F. (2000). The best kept secret in counselling: Single-case (*N*= 1) experimental designs. *Journal of Counseling and Development, 78*(1), 92–102. doi:10.1002/j.1556-6676.2000.tb02565.x

Maniacci, M., Sackett-Maniacci, L., & Mosak, H. (2014). Adlerian psychotherapy. In D. Wedding & R. J. Corsini (Eds.), *Current psychotherapies* (10th ed.; pp. 55–94). Belmont, CA: Thomson Brooks/Cole.

McConaughy, S. H., & Achenbach, T. M. (2009). *Manual for the ASEBA Direct Observation Form.* Burlington, VT: University of Vermont, Research Center for Children, Youth, & Families.

Meany-Walen, K. K. (2015). *Individual and group Adlerian play therapy with children with externalizing behaviors: A single case research design.* Manuscript submitted for publication.

Meany-Walen, K. K., Bratton, S., & Kottman, T. (2014). Effects of Adlerian play therapy reducing students disruptive behaviors. *Journal of Counseling and Development, 92*(1), 47–56. doi:10.1002/j.1556-6676.2014.00129.x

Meany-Walen, K. K., Bullis, Q., Kottman, T., & Dillman Taylor, D. (2015a). Group Adlerian play therapy with children with off-task behavior. *Journal for Specialists in Group Work, 40*(3), 294–314. doi:10.1080/01933922.2015.1056569

Meany-Walen, K. K., Kottman, T., Bullis, Q., & Dillman Taylor, D. (2015). Adlerian play therapy with children with externalizing behaviors: Single case design. *Journal of Counseling and Development, 93*, 418–428. doi:10.1002/jcad.12040

Meany-Walen, K. K., & Teeling, S. (2016a). Adlerian play therapy with children with disruptive behaviors and poor social skills. *International Journal of Play Therapy, 25*, 64–77. doi:10.1037/pla0000022

Meany-Walen, K. K. & Teeling, S. (2016b). *Effects of Adlerian play therapy on children's off-task behaviors and ADHD symptoms.* Manuscript submitted for publication.

Meany-Walen, K. K., Teeling, S., Davis, A., Artley, G., & Vignovich, A. (2016). *Effects of a play therapy intervention on children's on-task behaviors, total problems, and ADHD symptoms.* Manuscript submitted for publication.

Purswell, K. E., & Ray, D. C. (2014). Research with small samples: Considerations for single case and randomized small group experimental designs. *Outcome Research Design, 5*, 116–126. doi:10.1177/2150137814552474

Ray, D. C. (2015). Single-case research design and analysis: Counselling applications. *Journal of Counseling and Development, 93*(4), 394–402. doi:10.1002/jcad.12037

Reynolds, C. R., & Richmond, B. O. (2008). *The Revised Children's Manifest Anxiety Scale manual.* Los Angeles, CA: Western Psychological Services.

Rubin, A. (2008). *Practitioner's guide to using research for evidenced-based practice*. Hoboken, NJ: John Wiley & Sons, Inc.

Sweeney, D. S., Baggerly, J. N., & Ray, D. C. (2014). *Group play therapy: A dynamic approach*. New York, NY: Routledge.

Sweeney, T. J. (2009). *Adlerian counseling and psychotherapy: A practitioner's approach* (5th ed.). New York, NY: Taylor & Francis.

Volpe, R. J., DiPerna, J. C., Hintze, J. M., & Shapiro, E. S. (2009). Observing students in classroom settings: A review of seven coding schemes. *School Psychology Review*, *34*, 454–474.

Chapter 7
Pre-Therapy in Child-Centered Play Therapy:
A Model for Treating Children with Autism

Karrie L. Swan
Eastern Washington University, USA

ABSTRACT

Child-centered play therapy (CCPT) is widely used among practitioners as a developmentally responsive mental health treatment for children with a variety of behaviors and presenting problems, however for children with disabilities, modifications to CCPT may be warranted. Therefore, the purpose of this chapter is to present a model of pre-therapy in CCPT for treating children with ASD and other developmental disabilities. This chapter begins with an overview of person-centered therapy and pre-therapy; then moves to an explanation of using pre-therapy in CCPT. The chapter concludes with a synopsis for using therapeutic responses across three phases in pre-therapy. Recommendations for future research are discussed.

RATIONALE

Children that meet diagnostic criteria for Autism Spectrum Disorder (ASD) and other developmental disabilities have imparied funtioning in all areas of their lives (Dekker, Koot, Ende & Verlhulst, 2002; Dykens, 2005; Matson, Fostad & Rivet, 2009; Rogers & Pennington, 1991). Children with neurodevelopmental disorders have deficits in communication, self-regulation, and executive functioning. As a result, children with ASD have difficulty forming peer and familial relationships, demonstrating appropropriate social skills and displaying classical play behaviors (Rogers & Pennington). For many children with developmental disabilities, play follows an atypical pattern, which is characterized by a lack of pretense, spontaneity, creativity, and social interaction. The upshot of the array of impairments is observed through children's peer interactions; their lack of perspective-taking, recipricol communication, and social flexibility, all of which are requisites to the development of imitation and play. Without

DOI: 10.4018/978-1-5225-2224-9.ch007

early support, deficits in appropriate socialization, communication, and play remain constant (Green, O'Reilly, Itchon, & Sigafoos, 2004).

Treating children with ASD is complex and for children with stunted functional communication, treatment options are limited because most interventions are dependent on childrens' ability to verbally express their thoughts and emotions. Specifically, practitioners serving children with ASD primarily utilize psychopharmacology and behavioral methods to modify children's behaviors and alter their deficiencies. As an outgrowth of recent outcome studies, scholars have highlighted the importance of developing interventions that not only address children's behavioral difficulties but also their emotional, social, and developmental needs (Goodman & Linn, 2003; Seltzer & Krauss, 2001). In response, numerous directive and non-directive interventions have been developed for teaching children social skills and play behaviors. However, to date, a humanistic counseling intervention that is adapted for working with children with ASD has not been developed.

Because contact work in person-centered therapy has been found to increase social skills and speech, contact work in child-centered play therapy (CCPT) may increase functional communication, imitation and play for children with developmental disabilities. Support for children with ASD is important and play therapists are not only positioned to help children process their thoughts and feelings, but also provide an attachment relationship that helps children communication and play development. This chapter begins with an overview of person-centered therapy and pre-therapy; then moves to an explanation of using pre-therapy in CCPT. The chapter concludes with a synopsis for using pre-therapy in practice and research.

THEORETICAL BACKGROUND

Person-Centered Therapy

Person-centered therapy (PCT) is considered to be one of the leading relational approaches to therapy (Cooper, O'Hara, Schmid and Wyatt, 2007). PCT is a theory of psychological growth that promotes the notion that all people naturally move towards development and differentiation in unique ways. Specifically, an emphasis is placed on growth producing social environments and relationships and as such, the person-centered therapist aims to provide a mutually facilitative climate comprised of specific affirming conditions. The resultant presumption is that the growth producing environment allows for clients to reestablish contact with their core self, which ultimately leads to self-direction, change and growth.

Central to the formation of the therapeutic relationship, Rogers (1957) held that specific conditions were necessary for client change to occur. Specifically, Rogers emphasized that (a) the client and therapist engage in psychological contact, (b) the client demonstrates incongruence (c) the therapist demonstrates congruence, (d) the therapist experiences unconditional positive regard for the client, (e) the therapist experiences and communicates empathy to the client, and (f) the client receives the therapists use of empathy and unconditional positive regard. In describing the first condition, Rogers contended that relationship formation was contingent on psychological contact, which is defined as mutual, reciprocal communication. In PCT, one displays contact through meaningful verbal and non-verbal dialogue, relational interactions, and self-awareness.

For many client populations, including children with ASD and other developmental disabilities, psychological contact is difficult to maintain and social relationships are impaired.

Pre-Therapy in PCT

To prepare contact impaired clients to enter PCT, Garry Prouty established pre-therapy, an approach that helps clients establish contact and mutual communication so they can begin talk therapy. Prouty (2001) explained that pre-therapy was achieved through use of the following contact reflections: situational, facial, word-for-word, body, and reiterative (Prouty). According to Prouty, a therapist selects situational reflections to reflect a client's moment-to-moment behaviors and relies on facial reflections to reflect a client's facial expressions. To show a client that their message is heard, a therapist uses word-for-word reflections and reiterative reflections to echo the client's exact words (Prouty). Last, a therapist may use body reflections for helping a client become aware of his or her body movements and shifts.

By focusing on the clients' concrete experience, Prouty believed that contact impaired clients would demonstrate a growth in contact behaviors by increasing engagement with people (interactive contact), expanding verbal and non-verbal communication (communicative contact), and developing awareness of their emotional states (affective reality) and environment (reality contact). Research conducted in the realm of pre-therapy suggests that contact impaired clients benefit from concrete, reality-based reflections. Specifically, studies indicate that pre-therapy improves functional communication, social adjustment, and imitative behavior for clients with dementia and schizophrenia (Brooks & Patterson; Dinacci, 2001, Peters, 1999; Prouty, 2001).

Child-Centered Play Therapy

Virginia Axline developed non-directive play therapy, known today as child-centered play therapy (CCPT). CCPT is a therapeutic approach that helps children move from a state of fragmentation and confusion to wholeness, growth, and responsibility. Through the process, play therapists create an environment congruent with children's developmental needs by encouraging children to engage in self-expression through play rather than words.

In accordance with the tenets of CCPT, counselors provide an empathic, caring, non-directive environment so that children will reveal their experiences, thoughts, and feelings through play. In believing that children will tap into their own internal resources, play therapists encourage children to engage in a self-directed therapeutic journey. Therefore, play therapists attend to children's expression of needs and experiences as expressed through symbolic play, rather than on symptoms or behaviors.

As a result of the facilitative relationship and through symbolic expression, children develop mastery over their experiences and move towards autonomy, socialization and responsibility (Landreth, 2012). Although the therapeutic relationship and expression of symbolic transformations are identified as effectuating change, little is known about the conditions that impact children's growth in CCPT, especially for children with limited or no communicative ability or delayed play behaviors. In CCPT, psychological contact is fundamental to establishing a therapeutic alliance, and for clients with contact impairments, the process of pre-therapy may facilitate growth and prepare children for CCPT.

Research

There is ample support for use of CCPT with a variety of populations. Research has shown that CCPT has the potential to improve ADHD behaviors (Farahzadi, Bahramabadi & Mohammadifar, 2011; Ray, Schottelkorb, & Tsai, 2007), behavioral problems (Ray, Blanco, Sullivan, & Holliman, 2009; Schumann,

2010), language development (Danger & Landreth, 2005) academic achievement (Blanco & Ray, 2011) and trauma symptomology (Schottelkorb, Doumas, & Garcia, 2012).

To examine the effectiveness of child-centered play therapy, Lin and Bratton (2015) reviewed results from 52 controlled outcome studies completed between 1995 and 2010. In their meta-analysis, Lin & Bratton found a statistically significant medium effect (.47) for child-centered play therapy. The researchers also detected statistically significant effect sizes for internalizing behaviors (ES = 0.42), externalizing behaviors (ES = 0.33), self-efficacy (ES = 0.63), academic achievement (ES = 0.46), and parent child relationship stress (ES = 0.59).

Although an abundance of evidence shows that CCPT is an effective approach for children with a range of difficulties, limited research exists regarding the effectiveness of play therapy for children with neurodevelopmental disabilities. Nonetheless, two recent studies revealed promising results. Ware and Ray (2015) specifically investigated the impact of CCPT on social competence, self-regulation, and empathy for children with ASD. In their single case design study, the authors found that all five participants showed improvements in social competence and three children demonstrated increases in self-regulation and empathy.

In a separate single subject research design, researchers found that 15 sessions of CCPT with 2 children diagnosed with an intellectual disability significantly reduced symptoms of hyperactivity and irritability (Swan & Ray, 2014). The authors concluded that the therapeutic relationship and conditions of acceptance and permissiveness helped child participants develop play behaviors, thereupon raising questions about the need to teach play behaviors to children with disabilities. To further investigate the process of change in CCPT, Swan and Schottelkorb (2014) used a task analytic case method to assess the influence of pre-therapy on a child's exhibition of contact behaviors. The authors found that therapeutic responding in pre-therapy had the greatest impact on the client's exhibition of affective and interactive behaviors and had the smallest effect on communicative contact (Swan & Schottelkorb). The authors concluded that the child's speech impairment may have impacted his ability to verbally and non-verbally engage with the therapist, thereby influencing psychological contact (Swan & Schottelkorb).

PRE-THERAPY IN CCPT

Developmental Rationale

Play is an integral aspect of child development. Through play, children develop language, social skills, creativity, problem-solving skills, and empathy (Garner, 1998). Piaget, a cognitive developmental theorist postulated that cognitive stages of play occur through a sequence of object play, functional play, symbolic play, and games with rules. Through object play, children explore and manipulate objects and learn about causal relationships. However, children with developmental disabilities struggle to engage in motor and sensory experiences through toy play and consequently fail to understand how to use toys in appropriate ways. As typically developing children move from object play to functional play, toys and objects are used in socially appropriate ways. Although pretense is still lacking during this stage, children begin to name and use objects in accordance with their function. For children with ASD, naming, classifying, and using toys in a functional manner is limited.

As children's cognitive development increases, play moves from being functional to symbolic. Through symbolic play, children use language and action sequences to manipulate their experiencing of the world. Typically developing children create elaborate, emotive play scenes that represent their understanding of social relationships, cause-effect events, reality, fantasy, and the future. In contrast, children with neurodevelopmental disorders tend to display play sequences that lack emotion and appear mechanical. In essence, children that struggle to engage in symbolic play have difficulty expressing ideas symbolically and abstractly. Because CCPT is based on children's expression of symbolic play, pre-therapy may be necessary for children operating at lower levels of play development. This thought converges with studies that indicate children with limited functional language benefit from naturalistic play techniques and imitation training. (Howard, Shaughnessey, Sanger, & Hux, 1998; Kaiser & Delaney, 2001).

The Method

Drawing on attachment theory, the approach incorporates attunement and how to concretely demonstrate to a child that their way of being in the world is fully accepted. According to Siegel (2011), attunement is shown by how "we connect deeply with another person and allow them to feel felt" (p. 481). A play therapist using pre-therapy will exemplify the heart of attunement by feeling their client's internal state and by experiencing their emotions, eye contact, vocalizations, and body language. The attuned therapist will also fully accept, see, interpret and respond to the child's unique means for expressing their emotions, needs, and desires. Through this special dance of attunement, the child begins to trust the therapist and engage in self-regulatory behaviors. As a result, the child demonstrates increased contact with people and objects and shows varying degrees of emotional responsiveness (Siegel).

Another important aspect of using pre-therapy in CCPT is to follow the child's lead in the playroom. The therapist does not use direct or guided instruction in play skills, rather the child is allowed to engage in play behaviors consistent with his or her level of cognitive functioning and development. Through the process, the play therapist will combine attunement with specific therapeutic responses to help the child increase contact behaviors. Table 1 provides an illustration of contact behaviors in pre-therapy.

Therapeutic Responses

Pre-therapy in CCPT consists of three imitative responses and two reflections. Table 2 depicts examples of therapeutic responding in pre-therapy. Accordingly, imitation is central to the development of language and play and many children with ASD tend to have deficits in body imitation, object imitation, and action imitation. To better understand the effect of imitation on children's development, researchers have found that imitation predicts the acquisition of language and the development of play skills (Stone & Yoder, 2011). Therefore, in this approach, therapist use of imitation responses are used to garner children's attention and encourage imitative responsiveness.

Body Movement Imitation

Imitation of body movements help children establish reality contact with self, others, and the world. Because children with ASD often present with limited communication skills and play skills, body movement imitation is used as a primary means for connecting and communicating with clients. Counselors use body movement imitation to follow children's specific movements in space and time. For example, if a child begins to rock back and forth while sitting in a chair, the counselor would imitate the child's behavior and rock back and forth. The counselor could also combine an imitative response with a concrete reflection by stating, "you are rocking back and forth and I am rocking back and forth."

Object Imitation

Imitating children's exhibition of object play assists children to gain awareness of motor and sensory experiences. Play therapists use object imitation to follow children's actions and engagement with objects. For example, if a child bangs two miniature trucks together, the counselor would imitate the child's actions by banging two objects together. To further expand the therapeutic response, the counselor could verbally reflect the child's actions by stating, "you are banging the trucks together." "I am banging the trucks together."

Verbal Imitation

Imitating children's gestures and vocalizations that are both meaningful or lacking in context assists children to develop communicative contact and functional play. In therapy, a contact impaired client might randomly state intelligible and unintelligible words. For example, if a child states, "car" and "ma-da", the counselor would copy the client's words and utterances in order to communicate to the client that their message was heard.

Facial Reflection

Reflecting facial expressions at a concrete level assists children to develop an understanding of how facial responses are related to the expression of feelings. Examples of facial reflections include: "You are smiling." "You look happy." These concrete reflections help children to establish affective contact by increasing awareness of emotional responses.

Linguistic Mapping

In pre-therapy, linguistic mapping is used to help children gain an understanding of their immediate experiencing and to provide a verbal connection between their words and actions. As such, a counselor provides verbal commentary on the client's moment-by-moment emotions and behaviors. The counselor also concretely labels play objects and materials. An example of linguistic mapping used in pre-therapy is as follows. "You are putting the car in the sand. You sound happy as you move the car in the sand and sing: da-da-da." Through linguistic mapping, children are provided a context for understanding cause-effect responses, all of which leads to increases in reality and communicative contact.

Pre-Therapy Phases

Engagement

Typically, the engagement phase is comprised of the first 6 sessions. This phase accounts for the development of the therapy relationship, wherein the therapist demonstrates attunement and empathy. The client may present as having difficulty connecting and maintaining contact with the therapist and the child's play behaviors are characterized by a lack of focus, pretense, or function. The counselor's primary goal in the engagement phase is to create an empathic relationship and to qualitatively assess the child's developmental functioning and stage of play behaviors. The following questions are posed to assist the therapist in the assessment process.

1. Does the child exhibit stereotyped patterns of play behavior?
2. Does the child show little interest in playing with a range of materials?
3. Does the child demonstrate repetitive motor behaviors?
4. Does the child exhibit repetitive language and gestures?
5. Does the child display unusual perceptual responses?
6. Does the child have difficulty initiating and sustaining in play?
7. Does the child avoid social contact?

Affirmative responses to the previously posed questions reveal the presence of a contact impairment and indicate a need for the therapist to primarily use body movement imitation, object imitation, and verbal imitation to establish psychological contact. Through the first phase, the child may begin to show an increase in receptive communication, hand-eye coordination, fine and gross motor skills, and imitation.

Contact Reparation

The contact reparation phase generally extends across 20 sessions. The primary purpose of using therapeutic responses in this phase is to bring about growth in affective, communicative, interactive, and reality contact. During this phase, the child may present as having limited functional play behaviors and stunted communication. Therapeutic skills used in this phase include body movement imitation, object imitation, verbal imitation and reflection, facial and affect reflection, and linguistic mapping. Throughout this phase, the child may begin to label toys and play with items in functional ways. The child may also exhibit an increase in gestures and verbal communication.

Contact Maintenance

Once a child begins to exhibit growth in contact behaviors, the therapist will primarily use affect reflection and linguistic mapping to help the child maintain psychological contact. During this phase, the child's play behaviors become increasingly functional and/or constructive and symbolic play behaviors may begin to emerge. Additionally, the child may begin to show increases in attention, turn-taking skills, and spontaneous play.

As this phase draws to a close, the child may be ready to enter CCPT and the play therapist may begin to use tracking, reflection of content and feelings, and reflection of meaning to help the child flourish socially and cognitively.

MATERIALS FOR PRE-THERAPY

Setting/Toys

Because children's acquisition of language skills lags behind their cognitive skills, play therapists use a variety of toys so that children have a means for emotional and behavioral expression. In this approach, counselors are generally encouraged to follow Landreth's (2012) guidelines for creating a play space, however, to create a space that is sensitive to the unique needs of exceptional children, accommodations are warranted. Specifically, use of pre-therapy in CCPT requires acquisition of toys that enhance manipulation or object play. Object and sensory toys that enhance language, coordination, and exploratory manipulation include: peg board, peg puzzle, shape sorting, latch and lock sets, pounding bench, sensory block set, and squeezie animals. Because play behaviors among children with ASD are often impeded by their social, emotional, and physical impairments, it is important for play therapists to include adaptive materials and equipment in the form of adaptive paintbrushes, crayons, and pencils (Carmichael, 1993). In addition, counselors should incorporate play materials that promote children's understanding of cause-effect relationships. Suggested toys include a remote control car, pop up toys, see and say toy, play bowling set, and toys that involve sounds and movements when activated.

Format and Ethical Considerations

In clinical settings, it is recommended for play therapists to offer three 30-minute sessions per week, rather than the traditional 50-minute session for the purpose of establishing and maintaining psychological contact. Additionally, counselors are encouraged to practice within their scope of competence by obtaining appropriate training and supervision in conducting CCPT. Prior to using pre-therapy in CCPT, play therapists educate parents about the benefits and limitations of using CCPT with children with ASD, noting that there is scant literature on the effectiveness of CCPT with this population.

RECOMMENDATIONS FOR FUTURE RESEARCH

In the realm of CCPT, little is known about the particular factors effectuating outcomes, thus process research is needed. Additionally, pre-therapy in CCPT has only been examined in one case study, therefore researchers are encouraged to examine the efficacy of this model through experimental research. Researchers should conduct single subject research to investigate the effectiveness of using pre-therapy with children with ASD. Future research using a larger sample should investigate differences between this particular model and CCPT on improving children's emotions and behaviors.

Table 1. Illustration of contact behaviors

Contact Behavior	Example
Reality (awareness of environment/others)	Child sustains attention, interacts with others, shows concept of space, and demonstrates turn-taking skills.
Affective (awareness of self)	Child expresses self through verbal and non-verbal communication, feelings, responds to the therapist, shows increases in flexibility, coping, and adaptability.
Interactive (relational)	Child uses increased eye contact, gestures and speech to engage with therapist.
Communicative (non-verbal/verbal)	Child uses utterances or gestures to communicate, uses spontaneous or purposeful speech.

Table 2. Examples of therapeutic responses in pre-therapy

Therapeutic Response	Example
Body movement imitation	Raising arm up and down
Object imitation	Lining up miniature army men and knocking them down
Verbal imitation	"Cat, grr, cat"
Facial/affect reflection	You have tears coming down your face. You are sad.
Linguistic mapping	You are putting the car in the sandbox.

CONCLUSION

Children with developmental disabilities have difficulty communicating, initiating and maintaining play, and relating to others, all of which leads to deficits in reality, affective, interactive, and communicative contact. Because psychological contact is fundamental to change in CCPT, pre-therapy as a therapeutic approach may help children establish contact and improve play behaviors. Using pre-therapy, play therapists use specific therapeutic responses for impacting children's exhibitions of contact behaviors, ultimately preparing children to enter CCPT.

REFERENCES

Blanco, P., & Ray, D. (2011). Play therapy in the schools: A best practice for improving academic achievement. *Journal of Counseling and Development*, *89*(2), 387–396. doi:10.1002/j.1556-6678.2011.tb00083.x

Brooks, S., & Patterson, G. (2011). Using contact work in interactions with adults with learning disabilities and autistic spectrum disorders. *British Journal of Learning Disabilities*, *39*(2), 161–166. doi:10.1111/j.1468-3156.2010.00643.x

Carmicheal, K. D. (1993). Play therapy and children with disabilities. *Issues in Comprehensive Pediatric Nursing*, *16*(165), 165–173. doi:10.3109/01460869309078273 PMID:8119836

Cooper, M., O'Hara, M. O., Schmid, P. F., & Wyatt, G. (2007). Preface. In M. Cooper, M. O'Hara, P. Schmid, & G. Wyatt (Eds.), The handbook of person-centered psychotherapy and counseling (pp. xxi-xxiv). New York, NY: Palgrave Macmillan.

Danger, S., & Landreth, G. (2005). Child-centered group play therapy with children with speech difficulties. *International Journal of Play Therapy*, *14*(1), 81–102. doi:10.1037/h0088897

Dekker, M. C., Koot, H. M., Ende, J., & Verhulst, F. (2002). Emotional and behavioral problems in children and adolescents with and without intellectual disability. *Journal of Child Psychology and Psychiatry, and Allied Disciplines*, *43*(8), 1087–1098. doi:10.1111/1469-7610.00235 PMID:12455929

DeVre, R. (1992). *Prouty's Pre-Therapy* (Master's Thesis). Department of Psychology, University of Ghent, Belgium.

Dinacci, A. (2001). Objective evaluation criterion for the Pre-Therapy interview. *International Pre-Therapy Review*, *1*(1), 21–30.

Dykens, E. M. (2000). Annotation: Psychopathology in children with intellectual disability. *Journal of Child Psychology and Psychiatry, and Allied Disciplines*, *41*(4), 407–417. doi:10.1111/1469-7610.00626 PMID:10836671

Farahzadi, M., Bahramabadi, M., & Mohammadifar, M. (2011). Effectiveness of gestalt play therapy in decreasing social phobia. *Journal of Iranian Psychologists*, *7*, 387–395.

Garner, B. P. (1998). Play development from birth to age four. In D. Fromberg & D. Bergen (Eds.), *Play from birth to twelve and beyond: Contexts, perspectives, and meanings* (pp. 137–153). New York: Garland.

Goodman, J. F., & Linn, M. I. (2003). Maladaptive behaviors in the young child with intellectual disabilities: Reconsideration. *International Journal of Disability Development and Education*, *50*(2), 137–148. doi:10.1080/1034912032000089648

Green, V. A., OReilly, M., Itchon, J., & Sigafoos, J. (2004). Persistence of early emerging aberrant behavior in children with developmental disabilities. *Research in Developmental Disabilities*, *26*(1), 47–55. doi:10.1016/j.ridd.2004.07.003 PMID:15590237

Howard, S., Shaughnessy, A., Sanger, D., & Hux, K. (1998). Lets talk! Facilitating language in early elementary classrooms. *Young Children*, *53*(3), 34–39.

Kaiser, A. P., & Delaney, E. M. (2001). Responsive conversations: Creating opportunities for naturalistic language teaching. In M. Ostrosky & S. Sandall (Eds.), *Young Exceptional Children Monograph Series No. 3: Teaching Strategies: What to do to support Young Children's Development* (pp. 13–23). Longmont, CO: Sopris West.

Landreth, G. (2012). *Play Therapy: The Art of the Relationship* (3rd ed.). New York, NY: Routledge.

Lin, D., & Bratton, S. (2015). A meta-analytic review of child-centered play therapy approaches. *Journal of Counseling and Development*, *93*(1), 45–58. doi:10.1002/j.1556-6676.2015.00180.x

Matson, J. L., Fodstad, J. C., & Rivet, T. T. (2009). The relationship of social skills and problem behaviors in adults with intellectual disability and autism or PDD-NOS. *Research in Autism Spectrum Disorders*, *3*(1), 258–268. doi:10.1016/j.rasd.2008.07.001

Murphey, G. H., Beadle-Brown, J., Wing, L., Gould, J., Shah, A., & Holmes, N. (2005). Chronicity of challenging behaviors in people with severe intellectual disabilities and/or autism: A total population sample. *Journal of Autism and Developmental Disorders*, *35*(4), 405–418. doi:10.1007/s10803-005-5030-2 PMID:16134027

Peters, H. (1999). Pre-Therapy: A client-centered/experiential approach to mentally handicapped people. *Journal of Humanistic Psychology*, *39*(3), 8–29. doi:10.1177/0022167899394002

Peters, H. (2005). Pre-Therapy from a developmental perspective. *Journal of Humanistic Psychology*, *45*(1), 62–81. doi:10.1177/0022167804269404

Prouty, G. (2001). The practice of Pre-Therapy. *Journal of Contemporary Psychotherapy*, *1*(31), 31–40. doi:10.1023/A:1010226814792

Prouty, G., Van Werde, D., & Portner, M. (1998). *Prae-Therapie*. Stuttgart: Klett-Cotta.

Ray, D., Schottelkorb, A., & Tsai, M. (2007). Play therapy with children exhibiting symptoms of attention deficit hyperactivity disorder. *International Journal of Play Therapy, 16*(2), 95-111.

Ray, D. E., Blanco, P., Sullivan, J. M., & Holliman, R. (2009). An exploratory study of child-centered play therapy with aggressive children. *International Journal of Play Therapy*, *18*(3), 162–175. doi:10.1037/a0014742

Rogers, C. R. (1957). *Client-centered therapy: Its current practice, implications, and theory*. Oxford, UK: Houghton Mifflin.

Rogers, S., & Pennington, B. (1991). A theoretical approach to the deficits in infantile autism. *Developmental Psychology*, *3*(02), 137–162. doi:10.1017/S0954579400000043

Schottelkorb, A., Doumas, D., & Garcia, R. (2012). Treatment for childhood refugee trauma: A randomized, controlled trial. *International Journal of Play Therapy*, *21*(2), 57–73. doi:10.1037/a0027430

Schumann, B. (2010). Effectiveness of child-centered play therapy for children referred for aggression. In J. Baggerly, D. Ray, & S. Bratton (Eds.), *Child-centered play therapy research: The evidence-base for effective practice*. Hoboken, NJ: John Wiley. doi:10.1002/9781118269626.ch11

Seltzer, M., & Krauss, M. (2001). Quality of life of adults with mental retardation/developmental disabilities who live with family members. *Mental Retardation and Developmental Disabilities Research Reviews*, *7*(2), 105–114. doi:10.1002/mrdd.1015 PMID:11389565

Siegel, D. J. (2011). *The whole-brain child*. New York: Delacorte Press.

Stone, W. L., & Yoder, P. J. (2001). Predicting spoken language level in children with autism spectrum disorders. *Autism*, *5*(4), 341–361. doi:10.1177/1362361301005004002 PMID:11777253

Swan, K., & Ray, D. (2014). Effects of child-centered play therapy on irritability and hyperactivity behaviors of children with intellectual disabilities. *Journal of Humanistic Counseling*, *53*(2), 120–133. doi:10.1002/j.2161-1939.2014.00053.x

Swan, K., & Schottelkorb, A. (2014). *Contact work in child centered play therapy: A case study*. Person-Centered and Experiential Psychotherapies.

Ware Balch, J., & Ray, D. C. (2015). Emotional assets of children with autism spectrum disorder: A single-case therapeutic outcome experiment. *Journal of Counseling and Development*, *93*(4), 429–439. doi:10.1002/jcad.12041

Whiten, A., & Brown, J. (1998). Imitation and the reading of minds: Perspectives from the study of autism, normal children, and non-human primates. In S. Braten (Ed.), *Intersubjective communication and emotion in early ontogency* (pp. 260–281). Cambridge, UK: Cambridge University Press.

KEY TERMS AND DEFINITIONS

Attachment Theory: The conception that a strong emotional connection between infant and caregiver is essential to one's developmental functioning.

Attunement: A harmonious emotional response and behavioral reaction to another's needs, desires, and emotions.

Autism Spectrum Disorder: A disorder characterized by impaired communication and social interactions that results in abnormal developmental functioning.

Child Centered Play Therapy: A relational counseling approach used to aid children communicate their thoughts and feelings through use of play.

Person Centered Theory: A humanistic view that human beings are innately self-actualizing and internally resilient in the presence of an open, accepting, and emotionally responsive environment.

Pre-Therapy: A counseling approach aimed at fostering one's aural, ocular, affective, and relational connections with others and their surroundings.

Psychological Contact: A present-centered awareness of relating to self, others, and the environment.

Chapter 8
A Cognitive-Behavioral Play Therapy (CBPT) Approach for Adolescents' Pro-Social Skill Development in the School Setting

Laura Jean Fazio-Griffith
Southeastern Louisiana University, USA

Reshelle Marino
Southeastern Louisiana University, USA

ABSTRACT

In this chapter, the authors will discuss the use of a cognitive-behavioral play therapy approach (CBPT) for teaching social skills to adolescents using expressive art techniques in a school setting. Expressive art techniques are integrated into an eight-week social skills curriculum, which represents a cognitive-behavioral play therapy approach for the development of pro social skills with adolescents. Consultation and collaboration with classroom teachers and parents are integrated into the pro social skills model. The inclusion of The American School Counselor Association (ASCA) National Model (2012) will provide applications to support the importance of pro social skills for adolescents in the school setting.

INTRODUCTION

Social development is crucial to the identity formation of adolescence, second only to infancy. Social skills that are taught in childhood are honed, defined, and refocused during adolescence (Feldman, 2014). Adolescents' social skills development can alternate between superficial and intimate relationships, developing advanced levels of empathy, learning to accept rules, structure and negotiating issues of separation and dependence with their primary caregivers can be profoundly challenging for a number of adolescents (Vickers, 2002). Pro social skills are defined as: socially acceptable learned behaviors

DOI: 10.4018/978-1-5225-2224-9.ch008

that enable children and adolescents in a school environment to interact with their peers and teachers in ways that elicit positive responses and assist in avoiding negative responses as a result of these interactions (McClelland, Morrison, & Holmes, 2000). The peer group connection for an adolescent can be viewed as a natural and effective setting to enhance and maintain pro social skills (Warner, Fisher, Shrout, Rathor & Klein, 2007).

Adolescents can have great difficulty in developing and maintaining pro social skills, such as: following instructions, using self-control, responding to teasing, and avoiding fighting that can occur when feelings of awkwardness and uncertainty regarding changes, which are occurring both individually and socially are present (Goldstein & McGinnis, 1997). These difficulties with social skills experienced by adolescents can lead to thoughts of negative expectations, self-deprecation, and physiological arousal. The aforementioned difficulties can contribute to dysfunctional social performance, which can lead to a major social skill and academic deficits. These deficits could cause an adolescent to avoid social situations, and foster feelings of isolation and depression.

SOCIAL SKILLS GROUPS AND PLAY THERAPY WITH ADOLESCENTS

Social Skills Groups

The group process, especially smaller groups, is particularly useful in facilitating the development of social skills, and decision making skills to help adolescents be more successful in their lives (Trotzer, 2006). According to Gladding (2012), groups of all kinds can be helpful to adolescents in making a successful transition from childhood to adulthood. They are valuable because they allow members to experience a sense of belonging, share common problems, to find and provide support, to facilitate new learning, to help ease internal and external pressures, and to offer hope and models for change (p.266). Peer relationships provide an important context for social learning and support individual development. These relationships are strongly related to social, emotional, and cognitive functioning during adolescence (Parker et al. 2006). Social interaction, in a group setting, during adolescence in particular have distinctive impact on long-term patterns of both intra-and interpersonal functioning (Hartup, 1983; Piaget, 1954; Savin-Williams and Berndt, 1990; Sullivan, 1953).

The importance of pro social skills training for adolescents in a group setting is well defined in the literature (Hemphill & Littlefield, 2001, Fisher, Masia-Warner, & Klein, 2004, Cartwright-Hatton, Techernitz & Gomersall, 2005, Flanagan, Allen & Henry, 2010, Ellis, 2002). McGinnis (2012), along with Goldstein and McGinnis (1997), have developed a prosocial skills curriculum, facilitated in a group setting, using a cognitive-behavioral model. The curriculum includes teaching skills that address the following topics: dealing with feelings, alternatives to aggression, dealing with stress, and planning skills (McGinnis, 2012). A meta-analytic study conducted by Spence (2003), suggest that social skills training interventions that combine behavioral modeling with instruction in social perception skills, self-regulation techniques, and social problem skills produce the most positive treatment effects. These elements should be included in school social skills training programs to maximize efficacy (Harrell, Mercer, & DeRosier, 2008).

Play Therapy with Adolescents

Play therapy with adolescents can be deemed effective in group settings to facilitate pro social skills. Play is an excellent way of assessing how adolescents function in the world (Gallo-Lopez & Schaefer, 2005). For adolescents with social skills deficits and behavioral concerns, playing can maximize the number of positive interactions experienced with their peer group, which is often encouraged as a means of changing dysfunctional behavior patterns (Delaney, 1994).

Group cognitive-behavior play therapy techniques have been successful with adolescents, not only with social skills training but in alleviating anxiety, fears, phobias, socialization difficulties, and impulse control disorders (Gladding, 2012). Adolescents who perceive themselves as different from their peers, or who have poor social interaction skills, can benefit from group play therapy. Group play therapy provides an especially effective modality for them to learn new social skills and to discover that they are capable of peer acceptance, self-control, and self-acceptance (Shechtman & Pastor, 2005). One additional benefit of group cognitive-behavior play therapy is adolescents' interaction with each other becomes positive, and a sharing of belief systems, actions, and consequences for their irrational beliefs are discussed and examined during the group process (Gonzalez, Nelson, Gutkin, Saunders, Galloway & Shewery, 2004).

A small group counseling intervention can strengthen the development of social skills through positive peer relationships (Kayler & Sherman, 2009). Group counseling combined with a cognitive behavioral play therapy (CBPT) approach is valuable because it allows students to experience a sense of belonging, share common problems, find and provide support, facilitate new learning, help ease internal and external pressures, and offer hope and models for change. Group work is efficient, effective, and multifaceted (Akos & Milsom, 2007), an ideal method to meet the needs of at-risk students, which includes those with social skills deficits. Group counseling allows students to develop and maintain connections to others while exploring factors that influence achievement.

The group setting provides a safe haven for adolescents to practice social skills and explore irrational beliefs without experiencing negative consequences. Social skill development can be enriched by successful interactions with skillful peers, as well as appropriate interventions by teachers and school counselors. When students exhibit poor social skills it is important to provide interventions that can enhance self-concept and promote impulse control and healthy growth and development. In employing the CBPT approach, the adolescents are offered an opportunity to feel connected to their peers, to develop life skills, and practice behaviors in the group that will increase their self-esteem as they provide feedback for each other and view each other as active members and resources (Kottman, 2011).

THE AMERICAN SCHOOL COUNSELORS ASSOCIATION MODEL (ASCA) AND PRO SOCIAL SKILLS

Teachers and school administrators continue to report their greatest challenge is to reduce classroom and school disruption, often occurring in the form of student aggression and violence. Educators have cited discipline as the most serious issue in today's schools, second only to the lack of financial support (McGinnis, 2012). It is further estimated that between 2 and 7 percent of students have significant emotional or behavior problems, which often includes anger and aggression (Kauffman, 2005).

The American School Counselor Association (ASCA) recommends that professional school counselors allocate 80% of their time to providing direct student services, with facilitating groups as a component of those direct services (ASCA, 2014). Gysbers and Henderson (2011) identified four components of a comprehensive school guidance program in conjunction with the ASCA model (2013). The components include: guidance curriculum, responsive services, individual planning, and systems support. At the middle school level, the majority of the school counselors' time (75%) should be spent developing and facilitating guidance curriculum and responsive services. Individual planning and systems support should comprise only 25% of the school counselors' time. ASCA acknowledges that schools are playing increasingly larger roles in assisting students with their development of social skills and has endorsed group work as a vital component in a comprehensive school counseling program. Simply defined, social skills are socially acceptable learned behaviors that enable adolescents in a school environment to interact with their peers and teachers in ways that elicit positive responses and assist in avoiding negative responses as a result of these interactions. The responsive services provided by school counselors' focus on the social and interpersonal development of students, which can in turn, bolster academic success (McClelland, Morrison, & Holmes, 2000).

According to ASCA, "Today's school counselors are vital members of the education team. They help all students in the areas of academic achievement, social/emotional development and career development ensuring today's students become the productive, well-adjusted adults of tomorrow" (ASCA *National Model*, 2013). The role of the school counselor in utilizing the cognitive-behavioral play therapy approach is as important as the actual group process. The school counselor "needs to understand that adolescents are changing cognitively the way they see and evaluate themselves, and he or she needs to facilitate this rather than criticize it as inappropriate or describe it as instability" (Blyth & Traeger, 1995, p.95). The school counselor, while assisting the adolescent in recognizing his or her belief system also needs to help them find and develop competencies they feel good about so positive self-growth can occur. The professional school counselor will address the student competencies in the social/emotional domain under Standard A of the ASCA Student Standards (2013). "Students will acquire the knowledge, attitudes and inter- personal skills to help them understand and respect self and others related to acquiring self-knowledge" (ASCA, 2013). Specifically, social skills groups will address the following competencies: PS:A1.4: understand change is a part of growth; PS:A1.6: distinguish between appropriate and inappropriate behavior; PS:A1.8: understand the need for self-control and how to practice it; PS:A1.9: demonstrate cooperative behavior in groups; PS:A1.10: identify personal strengths and assets; PS:A1.11: identify and discuss changing personal and social roles; PS:A2.3: recognize, accept, respect, and appreciate individual differences; PS:A2.6: use effective communication skills; PS:A2.7: know that communication involves speaking, listening and nonverbal behavior; PS:A2.8: and learn how to make and keep friends (ASCA, 2013).

COGNITIVE BEHAVIOR THERAPY AND PRO SOCIAL SKILL DEVELOPMENT

Cognitive behavior therapy (CBT) is a structured, goal-oriented therapy with a strong rationale for its use with children and adolescents (Knell, 2009). CBT emphasizes teaching skills that directly links assessment, intervention, and evaluation. The focus of CBT is deficits or distortions in thinking, which are postulated to interfere with appropriate social skills and other life skills needed to function effectively at home and in school. The main concept for CBT is that all behavior is learned. A key component for

CBT is discovering factors that reinforce and maintain behavior that is deemed inappropriate which is very common in adolescents who present with social skills deficits. It is imperative to work with these adolescents to change these factors, thus changing the behavior. Behavior is mediated through verbal and cognitive processes. According to Beck (1976) and Knell (2009), there are three key ideas in cognitive therapy, (a) thoughts influence emotions and behaviors, (b) beliefs and assumptions influence perceptions, and interpretations of events, (c) most individuals who are having psychological problems have errors in logic, irrational thinking, or cognitive distortions.

Increasingly, CBT interventions, are effective individually and are being adapted for delivery to groups of children and adolescents in the therapeutic and school settings (Flanagan, Allen, & Henry, 2010). CBT used with children and adolescents in the group setting can have beneficial effects such as peer modeling, interpersonal learning, or group cohesiveness (Yalom, 2005). Several global goals exist for CBT interventions in relation to working with adolescents with social deficits who lack the necessary skills needed for optimal functioning. These goals may include increasing the student's ability to express feelings, decreasing maladaptive thoughts and perceptions, increasing adaptive and realistic assessment of relationships, increasing positive self-talk, and increasing appropriate use of problem-solving skills (Kottman, 2011). CBT can be an integral piece for improving this populations social and academic skills both individually and in a group counseling setting.

COGNITIVE-BEHAVIORAL PLAY THERAPY (CBPT) APPLICATION TO PRO SOCIAL SKILLS GROUPS IN THE SCHOOL SETTING

Cognitive-behavioral play therapy (CBPT) is a theoretical framework based on cognitive-behavioral principles and integrates these principles in a developmentally appropriate manner (Knell, 2009). CBPT incorporates cognitive and behavioral interventions (Corey, 2013), within a play therapy paradigm. CBPT integrates ideas from behavior therapy, cognitive therapy, and cognitive-behavioral therapy, which was the impetus for formulating the concepts and theoretical basis for CBPT. Play activities and verbal and nonverbal forms of communication are used to resolve problems. In CBPT, there are some global goals in addition to the individual goals of each student. The general goal for the student is to increase the ability to cope with problem situations and stressors, master difficult tasks, decrease faulty thinking patterns, and/or assist in achieving developmental milestones that have been delayed for some reason (Wolpe, 1982).

CBPT places a very strong emphasis on the student's involvement in the process of developing appropriate social skills. According to Knell (2009), CBPT has six specific properties, or tenets, that provide the foundation for positive outcomes. The tenets are as follows:

1. CBPT involves the child in counseling via play.
2. CBPT focuses on the child's thoughts, feelings, fantasies, and environment.
3. CBPT provides a strategy or strategies for developing more adaptive thoughts and behaviors.
4. CBPT is structured, directive, and goal-oriented, rather than open ended.
5. CBPT incorporates empirically demonstrated techniques such as modeling and role playing.
6. CBPT allows for empirical evaluation of treatment which can enhance the involvement of parents and stakeholders in the school environment.

Although CBPT is very different from traditional play therapy approaches, the development of the relationship and communication patterns established through play are important tenets of this approach. CBPT establishes concrete, objective goals, and movement towards these goals is an important part of the group process. The process of CBPT, promotes collaboration between parties as the students and the school counselor work together to select the play materials and activities.

CBPT TECHNIQUES

The following CBPT techniques can be facilitated by school counselors in a group setting to help adolescents/students develop and hone their social skills:

Modeling

Most of the techniques in CBPT are delivered by modeling, for example, using a variety of expressive art materials such as: finger puppets, clay, paint, and other art supplies to demonstrate the appropriate social skills to adolescents. Several other examples of modeling with clay can include shaping/positive reinforcement during the social skills group (Knell, 2009). The school counselor selects two of the clay creations made by the adolescents in the group, along with a social skill to introduce to the small group and may say, "We are going to practice listening skills with each other. One first student explains his or her clay piece and the second student listens and demonstrates appropriate listening skills and is provided with encouragement and positive feedback as he or she exhibits the steps for appropriate listening skills. This activity is repeated until everyone in the group has participated in demonstrating appropriate listening skills.

Behavioral Rehearsal

Behavioral rehearsal provides an opportunity for school counselors to help adolescents' master difficult situations by utilizing appropriate social skills. By rehearsing, new more functional behaviors are observed and practiced by the students. The goal of behavioral rehearsal is for students to recognize and modify social skills deficiencies and ways of responding by role playing a variety of alternative responses. When using behavioral rehearsal, school counselors can provide immediate, concrete feedback, followed by continued rehearsal of problem situations (Knell, 2009).

School counselors can use finger puppets to coach more adaptive responses. In this way social skills are modeled for the students, and the students can rehearse the new skills. For example, school counselors may choose to focus on dealing with anger and recognizing others anger as the targeted social skills. The selected puppets are having a dialogue about a situation at school that has made them angry. Schools counselors coach the puppets on the appropriate responses regarding expressing anger in appropriate ways. The students are then given the opportunity to practice with the puppets. School counselors provide feedback regarding the interaction of the puppets and the appropriate responses. The students continue rehearsing until all are satisfied that appropriate responses for expressing anger in the school environment have been expressed.

Behavioral Contingencies

Behavioral contingencies can be used by school counselors to provide rewards in the group setting for acquiring new skills. For example, school counselors can ask the students in the group to pick three rewards they would like to earn during the group. Once the students have mastered the skills, rewards will be given. A chart can be displayed during the group that would indicate the social skills that need to be mastered with each student's name by the specific skills and the rewards once the students master the specific skills. Examples of rewards include: homework passes, selection of music to play during the group, and time added to break time during the school day.

Coping Self-Statements

The way in which adolescents interpret events, and not the events themselves, affects their ability to cope and function effectively, both socially and academically. Adolescents' perception of events can negatively influence their social skill development (Knell, 2009). Negative thoughts lead to negative self-statements, which can lead to poor decision making and interactions with peers and adults. For example, an adolescent who predicts no one will want to socialize with her at social time, supported by her negative self-statements, "I do not wear the right clothes, and have the right things to say in a group, I always say something stupid, so no one wants to talk me during social time." This negative self-talk can lead to poor social interactions and hinder the development of social skills. School counselors can work with students in the group setting to teach them coping self-statements. Students need to learn simple statements about themselves, such as, "I can contribute to the group conversation as well as my peers." These positive affirmations can be written down during the group, and the students can apply these affirmations to learning the different social skills.

Bibliotherapy

Bibliotherapy is used to provide a story telling approach for adolescents in a group setting. Adolescents' stories have an abundance of messages regarding specific problems or traumatic events such as divorce, death, or moving (Knell, 2009). School counselors may use these stories or excerpts from these stories to convey a message indirectly, with the hope that the students will learn something through the main character(s) in the book. The literature is rich with stories of amazing characters that have successfully coped with problems such as aggression, bullying, anger, and friendship. Examples of books that can be used to help adolescents develop their social skills can be found in Appendix A.

CBPT techniques provide an excellent intervention for school counselors to utilize in small groups with adolescents needing to develop, remediate, or enhance their social skills. CBPT provides the opportunity for adolescents to experience positive social skills in the presence of their peers through modeling, rehearsing, or learning from fictional characters in a story. This ongoing support and encouragement can be invaluable, especially for adolescents who are struggling socially and academically. School counselors should make every effort to incorporate an intervention of this type in to their comprehensive school counseling programs. The following is an example of a pro social skills group that exemplifies the effectiveness of using CBPT techniques with adolescents in a group setting.

Case Study

Carla Black, a school counselor, in an urban middle school in the Southwest United States, consulted and collaborated with teachers to identify and screen eight students to participate in a group designed to enhance social skills through self-image enhancement, feeling expression, stress management, and the development of friendships. To best identify potential group members, Ms. Black requested the teachers complete the Teacher/Staff Skillstreaming Checklist (McGinnis & Goldstein, 2011, p.1-11), which is designed to evaluate prosocial skills. Teachers assessed the potential group members for the following: difficulty in following classroom rules, low self-esteem, isolates self during social interactions, does not have a peer group, and has inconsistent grades. Students earning low scores were included as potential members for the group and were chosen to participate in the group. These students demonstrated some inappropriate behaviors such as: bullying, ineffective communication skills, and an inability to identify feelings and emotions.

In addition to teacher input, the Ms. Black collaborated with the parent/guardian by personally calling them to inform them about the nature of the group, invite them to ask any questions and provide input into their child's strengths and areas for growth. This engagement could encourage the parent(s)/guardian(s) to discuss the group topics at home with the child weekly and reinforce the skills learned at home. One way to encourage a transfer of learning to the home environment would be to involve the parent(s)/guardian(s). The ethical standards for school counselors B.2.b. suggests that professional school counselors recognize that working with minors in a school setting requires school counselors to collaborate with students' parents/guardians to the extent possible (ASCA, 2013).

The group met for 50 minutes each week for 8 weeks, during school hours, on-site, in a confidential location, during a nonacademic period, and focused on social skills development using a cognitive-behavioral play therapy (CBPT) approach. The eight selected students were in grades 7 and 8, and were comprised of two Black male, two Caucasian males, two Caucasian females and two Black female. After obtaining parental consent, Ms. Black met with each student individually to explain the purpose of the group. Each of the following sessions demonstrates CBPT techniques designed to enhance the social skill development of each student and to further their academic and social success, which addresses the ASCA standards.

Session 1: Pro Social Skill: Getting Acquainted, Building Rapport, and Trust

Establishing group rules, developing rapport, and building trust were the goals of the first group session, skills essential for forming friendships and peer relationships. The group rules and norms such as: be respectful, talk one at a time, listen, stay in your seat, and participate are discussed and integrated as part of the eight-week process. The students agreed to the following rules: be respectful, talk one at a time, listen, stay in your seat, and participate. The first skill, getting acquainted and building rapport and trust, can be illustrated by utilizing an expressive art activity with the students. Ms. Black introduced the first skill by announcing, "We are going to learn about each other by introductions." Each student will be given some modeling clay and asked to sculpt something that represents something he or she would like the group to know. For example, a student who enjoys reading may sculpt a book". Ms. Black, gives the students ample time to sculpt with their clay. She then utilized the technique of modeling by stating, "I have sculpted a beach umbrella and a beach ball, because the beach is where I love to be, especially during the summertime." Each group member followed her example by discussing his or her sculpture and describing to the group how the sculpture is representative of self.

Session 2: Pro Social Skill: Identification of Feelings

Ms. Black checks in with the students by asking them to identify one positive interaction they had during the week at school. Ms. Black informs the students of the skill, identification of feelings. Feeling charades is a game that assists adolescents in identifying and discussing feelings. Ms. Black divides the students into dyads. She gives each dyad a sealed envelope. Inside each envelope are six feeling words: frustrated, disappointed, embarrassed, elated, worried, and discouraged. She conveys the following, "one member of the dyad picks from the envelope and is instructed to act out the feeling for their partner, without using any words. The dyad that guesses all six words correctly first is the winner." The prize is a homework pass for any class the student chooses to select. Once the game is over, Ms. Black asks the group members to process the feelings in terms of how each feeling can affect their thoughts and behaviors in the classroom.

Session 3: Pro Social Skill- Choosing Appropriate Options

Ms. Black welcomes the students back to group and introduces the skill for the week, "This week we are going to work on choosing appropriate options." Ms. Black passes out booklets and on each booklet is written a title of a story. Examples of some of the titles include: Julie's Interaction with her Science Teacher, Mark Goes to the Office, and Ginny faces her Bully. Ms. Black instructs each student to "develop their own story with two endings; one ending that is appropriate and an ending that is not appropriate for the main character." She then directs each group member to create their own ending to the story, based upon the choices they would make. Once the students are finished creating their story, Ms. Black, begins the discussion, by asking group members to share their appropriate choices that might change the story's ending. Ms. Black then askes the group, "which ending to your story do you prefer and why?' The group discusses the perceived appropriate versus inappropriate endings to the story.

Session 4: Pro Social Skill- Replacing Negative Self-Defeating Behaviors

Ms. Black begins the session by reviewing the skills that have been discussed over the past three sessions. She then begins by stating the goal for session 4. "The goal of session 4 is to help you replace negative self-defeating behaviors by utilizing coping self-statements." Ms. Black explains, "We are going to learn how to be positive about ourselves and present a positive self-image." She pairs the students in dyads and gives each dyad a shoe box, glue stick, glitter, markers, crayons, and yarn, along with appropriate magazines. She then gives the instructions for the activity, "In your dyads, as a pair, you are going to create a positively positive box both inside and out. You are going to cut out pictures and words in the magazines that describe your positive qualities, things you like, and activities you like to do when you are not in school. She continues, the goal of the activity is to develop a positive place that celebrates who you are on the outside and who you are on the inside." Once boxes are completed Ms. Black invites each student to share their part of the box both outside and inside the box and discuss the pictures and words that are representative of themselves. She and the group discuss how different things can look on the outside from the inside. What did the group members place on the outside of their box versus the inside of the box? Each group member discusses why certain pictures and words were chosen and how they work to create a positive self-image inside and out. Ms. Black closes the group by asking the group members to share one positive from inside and one from outside their box.

Session 5: Pro Social Skill - Stress Management

Ms. Black welcomes the students and informs the students of the skill for session 5, "The skill we are going to introduce today is stress management." Ms. Black begins to facilitate a discussion with the students about stress. She proposes the following questions to the group members: "What is stress?" What happens when you feel stress?" What do you think about when you feel stress?" Ms. Black tells the group, "Stress can interfere with being productive in the classroom and at home." She explains the expressive art activity for the session. She states, "This activity is designed to assist the group members in dealing positively with stress. The activity is called,' Welcome to My Music World.' She gives each student a piece of paper and markers. A big circle has been drawn on each paper. She tells the group, "Write your name and the word 'Music World' at the top. Then divide your paper into four quadrants and label them North, South, East, and West. Please draw in each specific quadrant a source of stress for you at home, in school, with their friends, and alone. In each of your quadrants, please place a song that signifies that source of stress. Ms. Black asks the group members to share their four quadrants, specifically their song. Ms. Black plays the songs on her iTunes and askes the group members to discuss the song and how the song relates to their particular stressor. Ms. Black models for the group members some stress reduction activities like breathing exercises, guided imagery, and listening to music. Ms. Black asks the group members to discuss some of their strategies for managing stress such as using positive self-coping statements, as well as how to apply these strategies to the different environments. Ms. Black closes the session by asking each group member to disclose how one of their selected songs can assist them in managing stress in their life.

Session 6: Pro Social Skill- Positive Self-Image

Ms. Black begins the session by reminding the students that only two groups remain. She positively reinforcing the group members for coming to the group each week and being active participants. Ms. Black introduces the skill for the week, "This week we are going to work on building our self-esteem by creating a positive self-image using coping self-statements." Ms. Black asks each group member to say one negative thought they have about themselves. Some examples of group members negative thoughts are, "I am stupid, I get D's and C's in school." No one talks to me during the day, I must not be a good friend." "My dad did not pick me up this weekend for our visit and it is my fault, if only I played sports" She addresses the negative thoughts the members think about themselves. She explains, "The goal of this session is to learn how to change the negative thinking to positive behaviors that can be used in the classroom and at home." She asks each group member to draw a self-portrait on one side of the paper. Ms. Black instructs the group members to "draw on one side of the paper what you see when you look in the mirror. Turn your paper over, and draw how you believe your friends, teachers, and family members see you. What do they see in the mirror?" Once the group members have completed their drawings, Ms. Black asks each group member to share their pictures and discuss the differences and similarities between the two pictures. Ms. Black has the group members realize how their perception is usually very different from how others perceive them. Ms. Black asks the students, "How do you think your pictures will influence your actions at home and in school?" Ms. Black closes with each member sharing one thought about self that will help them have a positive interaction during class time or at home.

Session 7: Pro Social Skill- How to Manage Anger

Ms. Black welcomes the group back and explains that the group will end next week. She begins the discussion with ways to end the group and celebrate the work that the members have done collectively and individually. The group members decide they would like to show their appreciation for each other by creating a keepsake for each group member. She then introduces the skill "The focus for our group today will be on expressing anger in appropriate ways, by having each member design their anger montage. She provides a sheet of poster board, magazines construction paper, glitter, yarn, paint, and markers for each member. Ms. Black asks members to look through the magazines and select pictures and words that represent what makes them angry. She gives the students some time to decorate their montage with glitter and makers. Once the montage is completed Ms. Black models the activity by explaining, "I am going to begin and tell the group about my anger montage. After I explain to you what is on my montage, we are going to discuss what I can do to effectively manage what I am angry about. Then it will be your turn, please tell us what you did when you got angry, and what you could have done instead." Ms. Black asks each student to write their alternatives on construction paper and glue them onto their montage. Ms. Black and the group discuss how to choose appropriate options to manage anger. She asks the group members to leave their issues on their montage, but take the list of positive coping alternatives with them. Ms. Black tells the group that by leaving their anger issues on their montage, they do not carry them outside the group. The group discusses what happens when one carries around their anger without healthy alternatives to anger expression. Ms. Black closes the group by asking the members to disclose one positive coping alternative they will use this week when they get angry.

Session 8: Pro Social Skill: Ending Relationships- Integration of Skills Learned

Ms. Black begins the final session by thanking members for their active participation and for adhering to the group rules for the past eight weeks. She tells the group what she appreciates about them and how she has enjoyed watching each of them grow and develop their own set of social skills. She then employs the technique of behavioral rehearsal. The group members are given the opportunity to practice appropriate ways of building relationships and saying goodbye. Ms. Black introduces the final activity that integrates the final skill, building interpersonal relationships and saying goodbye. She states, "Each member will leave with a keepsake from the group. The activity is called an appreciation booklet. Each of you will receive a piece of construction paper and markers. Fold the paper in half and on one side write your name and you can take some time to decorate the front side any way you would like. Now, open the booklet. Please finish the following sentences: My proudest moment in this group was __________. The skill I have mastered in this group is __________. My biggest accomplishment during this group was_________. I will leave this group with_______" She instructs the members to close the booklet and pass it to the person on their right. Each group member will write one thing he or she appreciates about the members book in their possession. Once they have completed their appreciation note, the group member will pass the booklet to the next person and so it continues until everyone is in possession of their own booklet. Ms. Black gives the members' time to read the appreciation notes written from fellow group members. Ms. Black gives the group members the chance to reflect upon their work and gain closure by experiencing appropriate ways to end relationships with each member. Each member will take their booklet with other group members appreciation notes with them as a reminder of the work accomplished during the group .Ms. Black closes the group by asking each member to reflect upon one skill that they have learned and utilized in the classroom or at home and what they will miss about the group.

Teacher and School Counselor Follow-Up

Four weeks after the last group session, Ms. Black collaborates with the teachers to complete the Teacher/Staff Skillstreaming Checklist (McGinnis & Goldstein, 2011, p.1-11), the same checklist that they completed on each student before the group sessions began. Ms. Black consults with the teachers to compares the results of the post-checklist to the pre-checklist to determine the students' progress during the duration of the group and the application of appropriate social skills beyond the group. The assessment will be based on the adolescents' understanding of the concept of social skills and for behavioral change, which will be indicated by post test results and teacher observations of behavior. In evaluating the adolescents, Ms. Black can pay close attention to their thought process, beliefs, and consequences about these beliefs. She should be able to recognize whether any belief systems, actions, and feelings have changed. Ms. Black works with the teachers weekly to encourage the continued progress of all group members in implementing appropriate social skills to increase academic, social, and emotional growth in the school environment.

Ms. Black will initiate follow-up phone calls to parent(s)/guardian(s) and administer the post-test to receive input from the home environment. She will collaborate with the parent(s)/guardian(s) and to make any additional suggestions or recommendations for the student to increase social, and emotional growth at school. Additionally, Ms. Black will submit a written report to the school administration detailing the results of the pro social skills group and the level of improvement, to collaborate with the stakeholders to identify needed changes in the curriculum or school policy.

IMPLICATIONS

The use of a cognitive-behavioral play therapy approach, coupled with play therapy techniques, to teach pro social skills with adolescents in a school setting can result in a higher level of self-esteem at school, home and with involvement in social, recreational, and athletic areas, with the result being increased academic and social success. .Coping behaviors will increase hence emotions such as anxiety, and depression can be handled appropriately and interactions in social situations should be enhanced and improved. An integral part of the pro social skills group, is to teach adolescents, through CBPT, how to dispel irrational beliefs and faulty thinking. Once irrational beliefs and faulty thinking is removed, positive interactions will occur with peers, teachers, and school administrators.

CONCLUSION

A cognitive-behavioral play therapy approach, coupled with play therapy techniques, when working with adolescents is especially effective in teaching them pro social skills in the school setting. Many middle school children have maladaptive social skills. These skills may include poor interpersonal relationships, inability to make friends, issues with controlling emotions, negative and self-defeating thoughts, anger and stress management. These deficiencies can negatively affect their academic, personal, social and emotional functioning in and outside the classroom. It is imperative that school counselors and teachers recognize these maladaptive skills and consult with the idea of collaboration to provide responsive services in the form of individual or small group counseling services. School counselors can adapt the cognitive behavioral play therapy approach when teaching social skills in small group settings. The CBPT approach will teach adolescents varying social skills and how to apply these social skills to relationships in and outside the classroom. As adolescents learns to change their thoughts, actions and feelings, as a result of the group, the social interaction with his or her peers and teachers will improve in the classroom and interactions with parents and siblings should improve in the home environment.

Additionally, classroom guidance lessons can also provide an opportunity to teach social skills that will improve academic and social functioning. For the purpose of this chapter, CBPT was demonstrated in a series of eight group sessions to improve social skills. School counselors should consider the flexibility needed in comprehensive school counseling programs when examining how to improve a student's social skills. Individual and group counseling, as well as classroom guidance, can be beneficial when using this approach.

REFERENCES

Akos, P., & Milsom, A. (2007). Introduction to special issue: Group work in K-12 schools. *Journal for Specialists in Group Work*, *32*(1), 5–7. doi:10.1080/01933920600977440

American Counseling Association. (2014). *Code of ethics and standards of practice*. Alexandria, VA: Author.

American School Counselor Association. (2013). *Ethical standards for school counselors*. Alexandria, VA: Author.

Blyth, D. A., & Traeger, C. M. (1995). The self-concept and self-esteem of early adolescents. *Theory into Practice*, *22*(2), 91–98. doi:10.1080/00405848309543045

Cartwright-Hatton, S., Tschernitz, N., & Gomersall, H. (2005). Social anxiety in children: Social skills deficit or cognitive distortion? *Behaviour Research and Therapy*, *43*(1), 131–141. doi:10.1016/j.brat.2003.12.003 PMID:15531358

Corey, G. (2013). *Theory and practice of counseling and psychotherapy* (9th ed.). New York: Brooks/Cole Publishing Company.

Delany, R. J. (1994). *Fostering changes: Treating attachment-disordered foster children*. Fort Collins, CO: Walter J. Corbett Publishing.

Feldman, R. S. (2014). *Development across the life span* (7th ed.). Upper Saddle River, NJ: Prentice Hall.

Fisher, P., Masia-Warner, C., & Klein, R. (2004). Skills for social and academic success: A school-based intervention for social anxiety disorder in adolescents. *Clinical Child and Family Psychology Review*, *7*(4), 241–249. doi:10.1007/s10567-004-6088-7 PMID:15648278

Flanagan, R., Allen, K., & Henry, D. J. (2010). The impact of anger management treatment and rational emotive behavior therapy in a public school setting on social skills, anger management, and depression. *Journal of Rational-Emotive & Cognitive-Behavior Therapy*, *28*(2), 87–99. doi:10.1007/s10942-009-0102-4

Gallo-Lopez, L., & Schaefer, C. E. (Eds.). (2005). *Play therapy with adolescents*. New York: Jason Aronson.

Gladding, S. T. (2012). *Counseling a group specialty* (6th ed.). Upper Saddle River, NJ: Pearson.

Goldstein, A. P., & McGinnis, E. (1997). *Skillstreaming the adolescent: New strategies and perspectives for teaching prosocial skills*. Champaign, IL: Research Press.

Gonzalez, J. E., Nelson, J. E., Gutkin, T. B., Saunders, A., Galloway, A., & Shwery, C. S. (2004). Rational emotive therapy with children and adolescents: A meta-analysis. *Journal of Emotional and Behavioral Disorders*, *12*(4), 222–235. doi:10.1177/10634266040120040301

Gresham, F. M., & Elliot, S. N. (1993). Social skills intervention guide: Systematic approaches to social skills training. *Special Services in the Schools*, *8*(1), 137–158. doi:10.1300/J008v08n01_07

Gysbers, N., & Henderson, P. (2011). *Developing & managing your school guidance program* (5th ed.). Alexandria, VA: American Counseling Association.

Harrell, A. W., Mercer, S. H., & DeRosier, M. E. (2008). Improving the social-behavioral adjustment of adolescents: The effectiveness of a social skills group intervention. *Journal of Child and Family Studies*, *18*(4), 378–387. doi:10.1007/s10826-008-9241-y

Hartup, W. W. (1983). Peer relations. In Handbook of child psychology: Socialization, personality, and social development (vol. 4, pp. 103-196). New York: Wiley.

Hemphill, S. A., & Littlefield, L. (2001). Evaluation of a short-term group therapy program for children with behaviour problems and their parents. *Behaviour Research and Therapy*, *39*(7), 823–841. doi:10.1016/S0005-7967(00)00058-9 PMID:11419613

Kauffman, J. M. (2005). *Characteristics of emotional and behavioral disorders of children and youth* (9th ed.). Upper Saddle River, NJ: Pearson.

Kayler, H., & Sherman, J. (2009). At-risk ninth grade students: A psychoeducational group approach to increase study skills and grade point averages. *Professional School Counseling*, *12*(6), 434–439. doi:10.5330/PSC.n.2010-12.434

Knell, S. M. (2009). *Cognitive-behavioral play therapy*. Northvale, NJ: Jason Aronson Inc.

Kottman, T. (2011). *Play therapy basics and beyond* (2nd ed.). Alexandria, VA: American Counseling Association.

McClelland, M., Morrison, F., & Holmes, D. (2000). Children at risk for early academic problems: The role of learning related social skills. *Early Childhood Research Quarterly*, *8*(3), 327–329.

McGinnis, E. (2012). *Skillstreaming the adolescent: A guide for teaching prosocial skills*. Champaign, IL: Research Press.

Parker, J. G., Rubin, K. H., Erath, S. A., Wojslawowicz, J. C., & Buskirk, A. A. (2006). Peer relationships, child development, and adjustment: A developmental psychopathology perspective. In D. Cicchetti & D.J. Cohen (Eds.), Developmental psychopathology: Theory and methods (2nd ed.; pp. 96-161). New York, NY: Wiley.

Piaget, J. (1954). *The construction of reality in the child*. New York, NY: Basic Books. doi:10.1037/11168-000

Savin-Williams, R. C., & Berndt, T. S. (1990). Friendship and peer relations. In S. S. Feldman & G. R. Elliot (Eds.), *At the threshold: The developing adolescent* (pp. 277–307). Cambridge, MA: Harvard University Press.

Shechtman, Z., & Pastor, R. (2005). Cognitive-behavioral and humanistic group treatment for children with disabilities: A comparison of outcome and process. *Journal of Counseling Psychology*, *52*(3), 322–326. doi:10.1037/0022-0167.52.3.322

Sullivan, H. S. (1953). *The interpersonal theory of psychiatry*. New York, NY: Norton.

Trotzer, J. P. (2006). *The counselor and the group* (4th ed.). New York, NY: Routledge.

Vickers, B. (2002). Cognitive behaviour therapy for adolescents with psychological disorders: A group treatment programme. *Clinical Child Psychology and Psychiatry*, *7*(2), 249–262. doi:10.1177/1359104502007002011

Warner, C. M., Fisher, P. H., Shrout, P. E., Rathor, S., & Klein, R. G. (2007). Treating adolescents with social anxiety disorder in school: An attention control trial. *Journal of Child Psychology and Psychiatry, and Allied Disciplines*, *48*(7), 676–686. doi:10.1111/j.1469-7610.2007.01737.x PMID:17593148

Wolpe, J. (1982). *The practice of behavior therapy* (3rd ed.). Oxford, UK: Pergamon.

Yalom, I. D., & Leszcz, M. (2005). *The theory and practice of group psychotherapy*. Cambridge, MA: Basic Books.

KEY TERMS AND DEFINITIONS

Adolescent: A process that occurs in childhood around the age of 13 and continues until the age of 17.

American School Counseling Association (ASCA): An organization established to meet the needs of all professional school counselors as it relates to professional school counseling.

Cognitive-behavioral play therapy (CBPT): A structured therapeutic intervention that utilizes play to develop appropriate social skills with children and adolescents.

Expressive Arts: Using creative arts such as clay, sand, markers, paint, and other art supplies to facilitate the therapeutic process.

Group Counseling: Consists of 8-10 individuals coming together for a common goal to develop positive interactions with the assistance of a counselor.

Pro Social Skills: Positive skills utilized to interact with others including peers, teachers, family members, and administrators.

Susan Knell: Creator of Cognitive-behavioral play therapy (CBPT).

APPENDIX

Bibliotherapy Resources for Pro Social Skills Development with Adolescents

Albom, M. (1997). *Tuesdays with Morrie: An old man, a young man, and life's greatest lesson*. Random House Publishers.

Albom, M. (2003). *The five people you meet in heaven*. New York: Hyperion.

Collins, S. (2010). The hunger games. New York: Scholastic Books. (Any in the Hunger Games series)

Forman, G. (2009). *If I stay*. New York: The Penguin Group.

Frank, A. (1995). The diary of a young girl: The definitive edition (O. H. Frank & M. Pressler, Eds.; S. Massotty, Trans.). Doubleday. (This edition, a new translation, includes material excluded from the earlier edition.)

Gaines, E. J. (1993). *A lesson before dying*. New York: Vintage Books.

Grant, M. (2008). *Gone*. New York: Harper-Collins Children's Books.

Green, J. (2008). *Paper towns*. New York: The Penguin Group.

Green, J. (2012). *The fault in our stars*. New York: The Penguin Group.

Palacio, R. J. (2012). *Wonder*. New York: Random House.

Roth, V. (2011). *Divergent*. New York: Harper-Collins Children's Books. (Any in the Divergent series)

Snicket, L. (1999). *A series of unfortunate events: The bad beginning*. New York: Harper-Collins.

Zusak, M. (2005). *The book thief*. New York: Random House.

Chapter 9
Toy Guns in Play Therapy:
An Examination of Play Therapists' Beliefs

Amanda Winburn
University of Mississippi, USA

Suzanne M. Dugger
University of Mississippi, USA

Jennifer Austin Main
University of Mississippi, USA

ABSTRACT

This chapter explores current trends related to play therapists' beliefs related to the decision of whether to include toy guns, as aggression-release toys, in the playroom. This issue is especially timely given the recent epidemic of mass shootings and heightened concerns about gun violence. The chapter presents the results of an original empirical study examining play therapists' views about gun violence and gun control; play therapist beliefs about aggressive play and toy guns; and play therapist practices with regard to toy selection and limit-setting. Recommendations for future research are offered.

INTRODUCTION

A key element of play therapy involves the intentional selection of toys for the playroom (Axline, 1947; Kottman, 2011; Landreth, 2012; Moustakas, 1959; Ray et al., 2013; Trotter, Eshelman & Landreth, 2003). With the exception of "play therapists who use Theraplay and ecosystemic play therapy" (Kottman, 2011, p. 90), playrooms tend to be well stocked with a wide variety of toys. Summarizing the extant literature, Ray and colleagues (2013) concluded that play therapists agree that "children use toys to express themselves symbolically through the language of play" (p. 43). Regardless of theoretical orientation, play therapists view toys as vehicles for expression and as facilitators for the counseling process.

Landreth (2012), for example, described play as a child's communication and likened toys to a child's vocabulary. He called for the intentional selection – not collection – of toys and specifies that well-equipped playrooms should include real-life toys, acting-out-aggressive-release toys, and toys for

DOI: 10.4018/978-1-5225-2224-9.ch009

creative expression and emotional release. Similarly, Moustakas (1959) called for the inclusion of toys that allow children to express hostility, toys that facilitate the expression of emotions, and noncommittal toys which allow children to avoid the expression of feelings. Expanding upon these groupings, Kottman conceptualized play therapy toys in five categories: "family/nurturing toys, scary toys, aggressive toys, expressive toys, and pretend/fantasy toys" (2011, pp. 90-91).

Although Ray and colleagues found that "play therapists, to a large degree, have agreed on the essential materials to be included in a play therapy room" (2013, p. 45), some disagreement within the field continues to exist. One specific area of disagreement involves the facilitation of and reaction to aggressive behavior by children in the playroom (Laue, 2015; Trotter, Eshelman & Landreth, 2003). Play therapists differ in their beliefs both about aggressive behavior and aggressive toys in the playroom.

On the one hand, some theorists argue that aggression is natural in a child's developmental process and that play therapists need to facilitate aggressive expressions. Landreth (2002), states that children have internalized emotions and may not have the verbal ability to express these emotions. Aggression is a natural emotion in a child's developmental process, and as children age they learn how to channel these aggressive thoughts and feelings into more appropriate and productive behaviors (Ray, 2011). But, until the child learns these appropriate ways of expression, it should be expected that a child be drawn to aggressive toys or use body motions or signals that would express the child's feelings. For example, Moustakas (1959) contended that children find "structured items such as guns, knives, swords, [and] darts" appropriate because such toys allow them to "express strong aggression in socially acceptable ways" (p. 7). Similarly, Landreth (2012) stated that aggressive-release toys give children permission to release aggressive feelings in a safe environment and by doing so the children are able to move on and ultimately experience more positive self-enhancing feelings. Kottman (2003) claimed that the use of aggressive toys provides a child the ability to test limits within a safe therapeutic environment and improve self-control. She explained that aggressive toys can aid a child in building a sense of competence, confidence, and self-efficacy (Kottman, 2003). Ray (2011) maintained that the inclusion of aggressive toys in the playroom is critical to the child's expression of aggression and cautioned that, when these toys are not included, the child may assume that his or her feelings and expression of aggression are not allowed.

On the other side of this controversy, there are play therapists who argue that the inclusion of some aggressive toys – specifically, toy guns – are both unnecessary and potentially harmful (Fuhrman & Franz, 2010; Laue, 2015). For example, Drewes (2008) cautioned that the presence of aggression-releasing toys in the play therapy room increases a child's likelihood of demonstrating aggressive behavior, in turn requiring the play therapist to set more limits due to the child's limited ability to self-regulate or self-soothe. The functionality of the aggressive toy may elicit a particular type of behavior and potentially structure the behavior of the child, increasing the likelihood that he or she will demonstrate aggression (Drewes, 2008). Drewes (2008) explained that the inclusion of a toy gun is unnecessary to children's ability to express their feelings or tell their story. Children are able to use other mediums or toys to express internal feelings and desires (Drewes, 2008). Although Landreth (2002, 2012) recommended the inclusion of toy guns in the playroom, he also acknowledged that toy guns are unnecessary as a large variety of toys can be used to express and represent aggression, frustration, or hostility.

This issue of whether the inclusion of toy guns in a play therapy room is necessary and/or advisable is complicated by the recent epidemic of mass shootings. Although mass killings with the use of guns have been viewed historically as isolated incidents punctuated by long periods of calm and safety, they have become so frequent that gun violence is now epidemic. According to the Mass Shooting Tracker (Gun Violence Archive, 2016), there have been 354 mass shootings in the United States in 2015, leaving

462 dead and another 1,312 injured. In response, many elementary schools have adopted a zero-tolerance policy prohibiting even toy weapons at school. Elementary school counselors who conduct play therapy are thereby barred from including toy guns in their play therapy rooms. Additionally, play therapists practicing in community settings may have heightened sensitivity to the controversy surrounding toy guns and may therefore revisit the issue of whether to include toy guns in their play therapy rooms.

Prior to this controversy, research on decisions about whether to include toy guns in play therapy rooms focused on treatment considerations. Past research was based on an assumption that play therapists make these decisions based upon their theoretical orientation or upon the needs of each individual client. Research has not yet explored the role of more fixed beliefs related to gun violence and/or gun policies in decisions about toy selection for the play therapy room. It is possible that some play therapists base decisions about which aggressive toys to include in a play therapy room not simply upon treatment considerations or theoretical beliefs but rather upon their own ideologies related to second amendment rights and gun policies.

MAIN FOCUS OF THE CHAPTER: AN EMPIRICAL STUDY

This chapter presents an original, empirical study examining play therapists' beliefs about gun violence and gun control, their beliefs about toy guns in the play therapy room, and the limits they set on aggressive play in their sessions.

Purpose of the Study

The purpose of this quantitative, descriptive study was to examine play therapists' beliefs about guns, their beliefs about toy guns in the play therapy room, and the limits they set on aggressive play when children use toy guns in the play therapy room. More specifically, the following research questions guided the design of the study.

Research Questions

1. What are play therapists' beliefs about guns, gun violence and gun control?
2. How comfortable are play therapists with real guns and toy guns?
3. What are play therapists' beliefs about aggressive play and toy guns in the play therapy room?
4. What types of limits do play therapists set on aggressive play using toy guns?

Instrumentation

To study these topics, the authors created a questionnaire that allowed for the collection of descriptive data regarding play therapists' beliefs about guns, level of comfort with guns, beliefs about toy guns in the playroom, and the limits they set on aggressive play using toy guns in their play therapy sessions. The survey consisted of 45 items, which were divided into three sections. The first section contained 10 items requesting basic demographic and work place information. These items are specified in Table 1.

The second section contained 19 items regarding participants' personal beliefs about real guns and gun policies and their level of comfort with real guns. These items are specified in Table 2.

Table 1. Questionnaire items related to real guns

Demographic Information:
- Gender
- Age
- Ethnicity

Education and Credentials:
- Highest level of education
- Current licenses and certifications

Experience and Practice Settings:
- Are you currently employed or working as a play therapist?
- Number of years working as a play therapist
- What type of community do you serve?
- Do you work at a school or clinical mental health setting?
- Please identify your current client population.

Table 2. Questionnaire items related to real guns

Factual Items:
- Do you personally own a gun or does someone else in your household own a gun?
- Have you, or any close personal friends or relatives of yours, ever been a victim of a crime involving a gun?
- Are you comfortable with guns?

Beliefs about Gun Violence:
- Do you think gun violence is a current issue in U.S. culture?
- What do you think contributes to gun violence? (Click all that apply)
- Do you consider gun violence to be an issue in the area in which you currently live?
- Do you consider gun violence to be an issue for your play therapy clients?
- Do you think having a gun in the house makes it a safer place to be or a more dangerous place to be?
- Is it safer or more dangerous to live in the United States than in most other countries?
- Which do you think is most likely to reduce gun violence: stricter gun control laws for everyone, better mental health services, or better parenting?

Beliefs about Gun Rights and Gun Control:
- Do you think it is too easy to buy a gun in the U.S. today?
- In general, do you think laws covering the sale of guns should be made more strict, less strict, or kept as they are now?
- How much do you think stricter gun laws would help prevent gun violence? Would stricter laws help a lot, some, not much, or not at all?
- If someone has a mental disability, should they be required to go through an additional background check in order to purchase a gun?
- Do you think it's more important to protect gun rights or control gun violence?
- What would you say is your general stance on firearms?

Beliefs about Open Carry:
- What is your stance on open carry laws?
- Are you comfortable with licensed gun owners carrying a weapon into your work place? (Only applicable for those living in states with open carry laws)
- Do you favor or oppose allowing teachers and school officials to carry guns in schools?

The final section contained 16 questions specifically focused on participants' approaches to toy selection for their play therapy rooms, to their beliefs about aggressive toys in general and about toy guns specifically, and about their limit-setting practices. These items are specified in Table 3.

Data Collection

After receiving approval from the university's institutional review board, the researchers utilized Qualtrics software to collect data through the electronic dissemination of the questionnaire described above. The Qualtrics link led to a letter of explanation, informed consent document, and the research instrument questions. To maximize the response rate, follow up emails were sent out to potential participants two and four weeks after the original mailing.

Table 3. Questionnaire items related to toy selection for and limit setting in the play therapy room

Toy Selection in General:
- Do you have the same toys for each client, or do you exclude or include certain toys based upon the client's needs?

Aggressive Toys in General:
- Do you think children should be allowed to play with aggressive toys?
- Do you feel that aggressive toys are necessary in the playroom to facilitate children's emotions?
- Do you feel that aggressive toys such as toy guns are essential to a child's ability to express a certain range of emotions?
- Are you comfortable with children playing with aggressive toys such as knives or swords in the playroom?

Toy Guns:
- Do you think children should be allowed to play with toy guns?
- Do you feel that toy guns should be allowed in schools?
- Do you feel that play therapists should allow toy guns in the playroom?
- Do you currently have toy guns in the playroom in which you see clients?
- If yes, how many toys guns are in your playroom?
- Do you feel that toys guns within the playroom should be realistic or obviously fake?
- Do you feel like the inclusion of toys guns in the playroom is potentially harmful to your clients?
- Are you comfortable with toy guns?
- Are you comfortable with children playing with toy guns in the playroom?

Limit Setting:
- Do you feel like you facilitate or discourage aggressive play behavior in your playroom?
- Do you set limits on your clients when they are playing with aggressive toys?
- Do you set limits on your clients when they are playing with toy guns?
- What types of limits do you set on clients when they are using aggressive toys?
- Are you more or less likely to set limits when clients are using toy guns?

Population and Sample

The target population for this study was all play therapists in the United States, and the study population consisted of all active members of the Association for Play Therapy (APT) who were actively seeing clients at the time of the study. Specifically, the researchers invited approximately 2,000 play therapists, identified by the APT membership list, to participate in the study.

Results

Description of the Sample

Three hundred and eleven individuals started the survey. Because only those participants who identified as play therapists and were seeing clients at the time of study were included in the sample, the sample size was reduced to a total of 307 participants. This represented a 15.3% response rate.

Demographic Characteristics of the Sample

The first section of the questionnaire requested demographic information from the participants. Table 4 summarizes the demographic characteristics of this sample.

As shown in Table 4, 307 participants provided data regarding their sex and age. Of this sample, 280 were female (91%) and 27 were male (9%). This is consistent with the overall APT membership, in which 93% of members are female. The largest proportion of participants were 55 years of age or over (28%), with another 21% in the 45-54 age range, 22% in the 35-44 age range, and 16% in the 25-34 age range. 273 participants responded to the question about ethnic diversity. Of these respondents, the vast

Table 4. Demographic characteristics of the sample

Sex			Age			Race/Ethnicity		
Sex	**n**	**%**	**Age**	**n**	**%**	**Race/Ethnicity**	**n**	**%**
Female	280	91	18--24	1	0	White/Caucasian	252	92
Male	27	9	25-34	49	16	Asian American	0	0
Total	307	100	35-44	68	22	African American	9	3
			45-54	66	21	Pacific Islander	0	0
			55-64	86	28	Hispanic/Latino	10	3
			65 +	37	12	Native American	2	1
			Total	307	100	Other/No Response	5	2
						Total	273	

majority (92%) identified as Caucasian, with the remaining respondents identifying as Latino/Hispanic (4%), African-American (3%), Native-American (1%), or Asian-American (<1%), Other (2%).

Education and Credentials of the Participants

The first section of the questionnaire also asked participants to provide information about their education and credentials. Table 5 summarizes this information. Because participants may hold more than one credential, no total percentage was calculated for that column.

As shown in Table 5, all but one participant held graduate degrees. The vast majority of participants (81%) identified as master's level practitioners. Another three percent held specialist degrees and 17% held doctoral degrees. All but three of the respondents held a license of some kind. The pool of respondents consisted predominately of licensed professional counselors (51%) and licensed clinical social

Table 5. Education and credentials

Highest Degree			Credential		
Degree	n	%	Credential	n	%
Bachelor	1	0	Licensed Professional Counselor	134	51
Master	221	81	Licensed Clinical Social Worker	76	28
Specialist	8	3	Marriage/Family Therapist	32	12
Doctorate	47	17	Licensed School Counselor	18	7
Total	274	100	Certified School Psychologist	3	1
			Licensed Psychologist	3	1
			No license	3	1
			Registered Play Therapist	78	29
			Registered Play Therapist/Supervisor	79	30
			National Certified Counselor	39	15
			Board Qualified Supervisor	20	8

workers (28%). Another 12% of participants reported licensure as marriage and family therapists, and seven percent identified as licensed school counselors. The remaining two percent of respondents were evenly split between certified school psychologists and licensed psychologists. With regard to certifications beyond licensure, approximately two thirds of respondents reported holding the RPT and/or RPT-S credential, 15% held the National Certified Counselor credential, and 8% of the participants identified themselves as Board Qualified Supervisors.

Experience and Practice Settings of the Participants

This section of the questionnaire also included items to better understand our participants' professional experience, work environments, and practice settings. Table 6 summarizes this information.

As shown in Table 6, participants were asked about the number of years they had worked as a play therapist. Approximately a third of the respondents stated that they had 16 years or more experience, 19% of them reported 11-15 years of experience, 29% had 6-10 years of experience, and 19% reported no more than 5 years of play therapy experience. When asked about the type of community participants were currently serving, 48% of respondents described their community setting as suburban, 28% described their community setting as urban, and 24% described their community setting as rural. The vast majority of respondents reported working in a community setting, with 66% working primarily in a private practice and another 26% practicing in a clinical mental health agency. Another 16% of them identified K-12 schools as their primary practice setting. Only 2% of respondents reported working primarily in a university based clinic, and 9% reported working in another type of setting.

Beliefs about Guns and Gun Policies

The second section of the questionnaire examined participants' beliefs about and level of comfort with guns. Questions within this section sought to elicit participants' view of guns, attitudes toward gun policies, and beliefs about the impact of guns in our society. As shown in Table 2, the 19 items in this section included factual items; items assessing participants' beliefs about gun violence in the United States as well as in the communities in which they and their clients reside; items assessing participants' beliefs about gun rights and gun control; and items assessing participants' beliefs about open carry.

Table 6. Experience and practice settings

Experience			Community Setting			Practice Setting		
Years	**n**	**%**	**Setting**	**n**	**%**	**Practice Setting**	**n**	**%**
0-5	52	19	Urban	77	28	K-12 School	44	16
6-10	80	29	Suburban	131	48	Agency	69	26
11-15	51	19	Rural	67	24	University	5	2
16+	90	33	Total	275	100	Private Practice	177	66
Total	273	100				Other	23	9
						Total	270	100

Factual Items

In order to better understand participants' actual experiences with guns, respondents were asked about gun ownership, their personal experiences as victims of gun violence, and their comfort with guns. The results are presented in Table 7.

As shown in Table 7, nearly two-thirds of the participants denied owning a gun or having a gun in their home, whereas the remaining third reported that at least one person in the household owns a gun. Approximately one quarter of participants reported that they themselves, a close personal friend, or a relative had been a victim of gun violence. Only 27% of respondents expressed comfort with guns, and a combined 55% described themselves as uncomfortable or very uncomfortable with guns.

Beliefs about Gun Violence

The survey also included eight items assessing participants' beliefs about gun violence. Responses to these items are summarized in Table 8.

Interestingly, although 94% of respondents agreed that gun violence is a current issue in the United States, a far smaller proportion viewed gun violence as an issue in their own communities or in the lives of their play therapy clients. Specifically, only 54% of participants expressed a belief that gun violence is an issue where they currently live and only 32% believe gun violence is an issue for their play therapy clients. Also, although 94% of respondents agreed that gun violence is a current issue in the United States, responses to the item about whether it is safer or more dangerous to live in the U.S. were distributed relatively evenly. Regarding the impact of having a gun in the house on safety, respondents were also divided. Nine percent expressed a belief that having a gun in the house makes it a safer place to be, 36% expressed a belief that having a gun in the house makes it a more dangerous place to be, and the remaining 54% either said it depends or expressed uncertainty. When asked to identify factors contributing to gun violence, more than 70% of participants agreed that drugs, gangs, availability of guns and mental illness were contributing factors. Approximately half of the participants also identified poverty and video games as contributing factors, and approximately a third identified movies and television shows as contributing factors. Only 13% viewed boredom as contributing to gun violence.

Table 7. Factual items

Question	Responses	
Do you personally own a gun or does someone else in your household own a gun?	62% 7% 8% 23%	No Yes – Personally Yes – Both Yes – Someone Else
Have you, or any close personal friends or relatives of yours, ever been a victim of a crime involving a gun?	69% 26% 5%	No Yes Not Sure
Are you comfortable with guns?	9% 18% 18% 28% 27%	Very Comfortable Comfortable Neutral Uncomfortable Very Uncomfortable

Table 8. Beliefs about gun violence

Question	Responses	
Do you think gun violence is a current issue in U.S. culture?	94% 3% 3%	Yes No Not Sure
Is it safer or more dangerous to live in the United States than in most other countries?	37% 34% 29%	Safer More Dangerous About the Same
Do you consider gun violence to be an issue in the area in which you currently live?	54% 36% 10%	Yes No Not Sure
Do you consider gun violence to be an issue for your play therapy clients?	32% 50% 18%	Yes No Not Sure
Do you think having a gun in the house makes it a safer place to be or a more dangerous place to be?	9% 36% 50% 4%	Safer More Dangerous Depends Not Sure
What do you think contributes to gun violence? (Click all that apply)	73% 80% 74% 71% 51% 48% 32% 13% 30%	Availability of guns Drugs Gangs Mental Illness Poverty Video Games Movies Boredom Television Shows
Which do you think is most likely to reduce gun violence: stricter gun control laws for everyone, better mental health services, or better parenting?	8% 12% 10% 64% 6%	Stricter Gun Laws Better Mental Health Services Better Parenting All of the Above Not Sure

Beliefs about Gun Rights and Gun Control

The survey also included six items assessing participants' beliefs about gun rights and gun control. Responses to these items are summarized in Table 9.

The majority of participants (79%) expressed a belief that purchasing a gun in the United States is too easy and that laws governing the sale of guns should be made stricter (76%). Consistent with these beliefs, most participants agreed that stricter regulations on gun sales would help with gun violence in our country "a lot" (24%) or at least "some" (41%). Participants were torn between controlling gun violence (50%) or controlling both gun rights and gun violence (42%), but very few were concerned primarily with protecting gun rights (5%). When asked about their general stance on gun ownership 47% stated that firearms should be restricted to those who are able to pass a safety class; 25% stated firearms should be unrestricted to those who are not felons or mentally ill; 20% stated firearms should be restricted only to people in the military or law enforcement; 5% stated firearms should be completely removed; and finally 4% stated firearms should only be unrestricted to those who are not felons.

Table 9. Beliefs about gun rights and gun control

Question	Responses	
Do you think it is too easy to buy a gun in the U.S. today?	79% 6% 15%	Yes No Not Sure
In general, do you think laws covering the sale of guns should be made more strict, less strict, or kept as they are now?	76% 3% 21%	More Strict Less Strict Kept as they are now
How much do you think stricter gun laws would help prevent gun violence? Would stricter laws help a lot, some, not much, or not at all?	24% 41% 16% 13% 5%	A lot Some Not much Not at all Not sure
If someone has a mental disability, should they be required to go through an additional background check in order to purchase a gun?	72% 5% 23%	Yes No Not Sure
Do you think it's more important to protect gun rights or control gun violence?	5% 50% 3% 42%	Gun Rights Gun Violence Not Sure Both, gun rights & gun violence
What would you say is your general stance on firearms?	0%	Firearms should be completely unrestricted to anyone in the U.S.
	4%	Firearms should be unrestricted to those who are not felons
	25%	Firearms should be unrestricted to those who are not felons or mentally ill
	47%	Firearms should be restricted to those who are able to pass a safety class
	20%	Firearms should be restricted only to people in the military or law enforcement
	5%	Firearms should be completely removed

Beliefs about Open Carry

Finally, this section he survey also included two items assessing participants' beliefs about open carry. Responses to these items are summarized in Table 10.

Responses to the question about open carry were rather divided, with 56% expressing a belief that open carry should not be allowed and 45% believing it should be allowed. In contrast, only 16% of respondents expressed comfort with open carry when this question was placed in the context of their workplace.

Toy Selection and Limit-Setting in the Play Therapy Room

The third section of the questionnaire examined factors related to toy selection and limit-setting in the play therapy room. Participants were asked about their approach to toy selection; their beliefs about and comfort with aggressive toys in general; their beliefs about and comfort specifically with toy guns in the play therapy room; and their limit-setting practices.

Table 10. Beliefs about open carry

Question	Responses	
What is your stance on open carry laws??	43% 2% 56%	Should be allowed for licensed owners Should be allowed to anyone Should not be allowed
Are you comfortable with licensed gun owners carrying a weapon into your work place? (Only applicable for those living in states with open carry laws)	16% 62% 11% 11%	Yes No Not sure Does not apply to me

Approach to Toy Selection

This portion of the questionnaire focused on toy selection with a single question. The results are displayed in Table 11. As seen in the table below, the majority of participants (77%) stated that they use the same toys for all clients.

Aggressive Toys

Participants also responded to items focused on their beliefs about and comfort with aggressive toys. Table 12 presents the results.

Table 11. Toy selection

Question	Responses	
Do you have the same toys for each client, or do you exclude or include certain toys based upon the client's needs?	77% 19% 4%	Same toys Select toys based upon client Other

Table 12. Aggressive toys

Question	Responses	
Do you think children should be allowed to play with aggressive toys?	86% 8% 6%	Yes No Not Sure
Do you feel that aggressive toys are necessary in the playroom to facilitate children's emotions?	81% 16% 3%	Yes No Not Sure
Do you feel that aggressive toys such as toy guns are essential to a child's ability to express a certain range of emotions?	61% 32% 7%	Yes No Not Sure
Are you comfortable with children playing with aggressive toys such as knives or swords in the playroom?	78% 10% 12%	Yes No Not Sure

The majority of participants (86%) believe that children should be allowed to play with aggressive toys and most (78%) described themselves as comfortable with children using some form of aggressive toy in the play therapy room. Although 81% agreed that aggressive toys are necessary in the play therapy room to facilitate children's expression of emotions, a small but notable percentage (16%) feel that children do not need to use aggressive toys for emotional release. Further, only 61% endorsed the idea that aggressive toys such as toy guns are essential to a child's ability to express a certain range of emotions.

Toy Guns

At the heart of this study were questions related to participant beliefs about and comfort with toy guns. A summary of the results from this portion of the questionnaire are presented in Table 13.

Table 13. Toy guns

Question	Responses	
Do you think children should be allowed to play with toy guns?	78% 11% 11%	Yes No Not Sure
Do you feel that toy guns should be allowed in schools?	11% 71% 18%	Yes No Not Sure
Do you feel that play therapists should allow toy guns in the playroom?	84% 9% 7%	Yes No Not Sure
Do you currently have toy guns in the playroom in which you see clients?	78% 22% 0%	Yes No Not Sure
If yes, how many toys guns are in your playroom?	74% 19% 7%	1-3 4-5 6+
Do you feel that toys guns within the playroom should be realistic or obviously fake?	5% 58% 29% 7%	Realistic Fake Doesn't matter Not Sure
Do you feel like the inclusion of toys guns in the playroom is potentially harmful to your clients?	8% 82% 10%	Yes No Not Sure
Are you comfortable with toy guns?	33% 38% 13% 10% 6%	Very Comfortable Comfortable Neutral Uncomfortable Very Uncomfortable
Are you comfortable with children playing with toy guns in the playroom?	37% 39% 9% 6% 9%	Very Comfortable Comfortable Neutral Uncomfortable Very Uncomfortable
Are you comfortable with children pointing toy guns at you in the playroom?	19% 17% 16% 27% 21%	Very Comfortable Comfortable Neutral Uncomfortable Very Uncomfortable

Whereas the majority of participants (78%) expressed a belief that children should be allowed to play with toy guns, most (71%) did not believe toy guns should be allowed in schools. Although 84% of respondents indicated that play therapists "should allow" toy guns in the play therapy room, only 78% actually did so. This discrepancy may be related to our finding that only 71% of respondents described themselves as comfortable or very comfortable with toy guns and only 76% of respondents described themselves as comfortable or very comfortable with toy guns in the playroom. This level of comfort decreased dramatically when children point the toy duns directly at the play therapist, with only 36% describing themselves as comfortable or very comfortable in this situation. Also, eight percent of participants expressed a belief that the inclusion of toy guns in the play therapy room could be potentially harmful to children.

When play therapists do include toy guns in their playroom, their play therapy rooms tend to have 1-3 toy guns and rarely more than 5 toy guns. A slight majority of participants (58%) expressed a belief that the toy guns in a play therapy room should obviously be "fake," but nearly a third of participants contended that it doesn't matter whether the toy guns look "fake" or real.

Limit-Setting

The survey also queried respondents about their limit-setting practices. The results are displayed in Table 14.

Most play therapists (65%) indicated that they consider the unique needs of each child when deciding whether to facilitate or discourage aggressive play in the play therapy room. Many play therapists (29%) even encourage aggressive play, perhaps because they believe that aggressive play serves a therapeutic purpose. Surprisingly, although 30% of the participants indicated that they were more likely to set limits when a child is using a toy gun, more play therapists stated that they place no limits on a child's aggressive play involving toy guns (16%) than those who place no limits on aggressive play in general

Table 14. Limit-setting

Question	Responses	
Do you feel like you facilitate or discourage aggressive play behavior in your playroom?	29% 4% 65% 3%	Facilitate Discourage Depends on client Not Sure
Do you set limits on your clients when they are playing with aggressive toys?	48% 10% 42%	Yes No Depends on client
Do you set limits on your clients when they are playing with toys guns?	46% 16% 38%	Yes No Depends on client
Are you more or less likely to set limits when clients are using toy guns?	30% 62% 2% 6%	More likely No difference Less likely Not Sure
What types of limits do you set on clients when they are using aggressive toys? (open-ended)	54% 25% 15% 6%	Cannot hurt themselves or therapist Cannot point gun at therapist Cannot break or destroy toys Other

(10%). In response to an open-ended question about what types of limits play therapists set on clients using toy guns, the most frequent responses were (a) that they will not allow children to hurt themselves or the therapist; (b) that clients are not allowed to point the toy gun at themselves or the therapist; and (c) clients cannot break or destroy toys.

Discussion of Results

The descriptive data yielded by this study afford some insights but also raise additional questions. In addition to exploring possible interpretations and insights supported by the data, this section will acknowledge limitations to the study and offer suggestions for future research.

Insights and Intrigue

Play therapists represent a group of mental health professionals dedicated to improving the lives of children. Given the epidemic of gun violence, even at the hands of youthful perpetrators, it is reasonable to speculate that play therapists may face new dilemmas related to the inclusion of toy guns in their play therapy rooms and to their approach to aggressive behavior manifested by their play therapy clients. This study sought to better understand the current beliefs of play therapists with regard to guns and gun violence, to aggressive toys and behavior in the play therapy room, and to the limit-setting behaviors they should demonstrate in response to aggressive behavior by their play therapy clients.

Perceptions of Gun Violence as an Issue

The data from this study suggest that, although the vast majority of play therapists consider gun violence a major issue in contemporary society, they are less concerned with gun violence in their own communities and even less concerned that gun violence may be an issue affecting the lives of their child clients. More specifically, only a third of the respondents who agreed that gun violence is a major issue in contemporary society expressed a belief that it is also an issue for their play therapy clients. How closely these beliefs parallel reality, however, remains unknown. It is possible that the children seen by these play therapists live in communities which are safer than the communities in which the play therapists themselves live and far safer than most communities across the United States. It is also possible that the communities in which play therapists and their clients live are equally susceptible to gun violence and that other, perhaps psychological, factors better explain their disparate recognition of gun violence as an issue in various settings. This discrepancy could reflect a state of denial in which respondents, although recognizing gun violence as an abstract issue affecting the nation as a whole, have yet to internalize the possible impact of gun violence on their own communities and in the lives of their clients. This interpretation would be consistent with our finding that only 26% of respondents affirmed that they themselves or someone close to them had been a victim of a crime involving a gun. Yet another possibility is that respondents interpreted the question about whether gun violence is "an issue for [their] play therapy clients" more narrowly than intended by the researchers. Whereas this question was intended to explore beliefs about the potential for gun violence to affect the lives of play therapy clients for wide variety of reasons, it is possible that respondents interpreted the question as about whether they considered their play therapy clients at risk of becoming perpetrators of gun violence.

Beliefs about Gun Rights and Gun Control

The data suggest that study participants collectively agreed that it is too easy to buy a gun in the United States, that laws governing the sale of guns should be stricter, and that stricter gun laws would help combat gun violence at least to some extent. Surprisingly, fewer than half of the respondents expressed a belief that individuals should be required to pass a safety class before purchasing a firearm.

In contrast, three quarters of respondents agreed that access to firearms should be unrestricted – meaning no license, permit, background checks or safety class requirements – for individuals as long as they are not felons or mentally ill. It is difficult to reconcile this finding with the fact that 76% of the respondents expressed a belief that laws governing the sales of guns should be stricter, especially given that federal law, via the Brady Handgun Violence Prevention Act of 1993 and the Gun Control Act of 1968, already prohibit the sales of firearms to felons and require background checks using the National Instant Criminal Background Check System (NICS) prior to the sale of handguns by a federally licensed arms dealer (ATF, 2016a, 2016b, 2016c). Explanations for these conflicting findings include the possibility that the study participants did not fully understand the concept of "unrestricted," the possibility that the study participants were exceptionally well versed in loopholes in current gun laws, and the possibility that the respondents are ambivalent about these issues and therefore responded inconsistently to items.

Toy Selection and Limit-Setting Practices

Whereas the majority of study participants expressed concerns about gun violence and perceived a need for stricter gun laws, these concerns did not seem to translate into the play therapy room. The majority of respondents expressed a view of aggressive toys, including toy guns, as important to children's ability to express their emotions. With the notable exception of school settings, participants expressed a belief that children should be allowed to play with toy guns both within and outside the play therapy room, and most reported having at least one gun in their play therapy room.

This fact, combined with our finding that fewer respondents expressed comfort with toy guns than those who believe they should be included in the play therapy room, may suggest that play therapists base their toy selection decisions on perceived therapeutic value rather than on personal beliefs about gun control or on personal feelings of comfort. It would be interesting to examine this issue in greater depth to determine the factors contributing to these decisions. For example, the researchers wonder the extent to which contemporary play therapists subscribe to the catharsis theory of aggression and view aggression in the play therapy room as ultimately important to affect regulation (Bresin & Gordon, 2013) despite considerable debate about the issue (Bushman, Baumeister & Stack, 1999; Schaefer & Mattei, 2005).

The data regarding limit-setting was particularly intriguing. As noted earlier, although 30% of the participants indicated that they were more likely to set limits when a child is using a toy gun, more play therapists stated that they place no limits on a child's aggressive play involving toy guns (16%) than those who place no limits on aggressive play in general (10%). Additional research into this issue is warranted to better elucidate current trends in limit-setting by play therapists.

Limitations and Recommendations for Future Research

Although this study provides useful, descriptive information for play therapists, the results should be interpreted cautiously, due to the nature of the sample, research design, and the sometimes conflicting and ambiguous nature of the findings. With regard to the sample, the sample size was relatively small (n = 307) and the 15.3% response rate may also limit the generalizability of the results. Additionally, the majority of the participants identified as White/Caucasian (92%) and only 3% of the sample identified as African American. This study did not ask participants for data regarding the demographic composition of their play therapy clients. Especially given the recent spate of highly publicized, racially charged events involving gun violence, one must question the generalizability of these results to a diverse population of potential clients in play therapy. Future researchers should seek a larger and more representative sample, and future research on the perspectives of minority play therapists and/or play therapists whose clientele is diverse is advisable.

The data analysis for this exploratory study was limited to descriptive statistics. Future studies should utilize instrumentation and methods which will allow for the use of inferential analyses. This would allow for greater insight into the relationship of play therapist decisions regarding toy selection and limit setting, demographic variables, their personal beliefs about gun violence, and their theoretical orientations and beliefs.

Finally, recommendations for future research include a follow-up study to determine implications for practice. Future studies might explore the relationship between aggressive toy use and a child's presenting problem and/or diagnosis, potentially yielding useful treatment recommendations for the selective inclusion of toy guns in the play therapy room. Further research exploration could also examine children's depth of expression when using aggressive toys, specifically toy guns, as well as the impact of this play on aggression outside the counseling setting. Such exploration of aggressive toy use in play therapy might prove useful in supporting intentional, evidence-based decisions about toy selection and may contribute to the discussion and debate about the therapeutic value of aggressive toys or behaviors in play therapy sessions.

CONCLUSION

The current study served as a starting point for the exploration of play therapists' beliefs and practices regarding toy guns in the playroom. This study yielded information about play therapist views about gun violence and gun control; play therapist beliefs about aggressive play and toy guns; and play therapist practices with regard to toy selection and limit-setting. On the basis of the results and limitations of this study, one may conclude that issues related to the inclusion or exclusion of toy guns in the play therapy room are complex and require additional investigation to better understand potential interactions or confounding variables. It is our hope that this chapter inspires additional research into this important topic.

REFERENCES

ATF. (2016a). *Brady law*. Washington, DC: Bureau of Alcohol, Tobacco, Firearms and Explosives. Retrieved from https://www.atf.gov/rules-and-regulations/brady-law

ATF. (2016b). *Gun Control Act*. Washington, DC: Bureau of Alcohol, Tobacco, Firearms and Explosives. Retrieved from https://www.atf.gov/rules-and-regulations/gun-control-act

ATF. (2016c). *National Firearms Act*. Washington, DC: Bureau of Alcohol, Tobacco, Firearms and Explosives. Retrieved from https://www.atf.gov/rules-and-regulations/national-firearms-act

Axline, V. M. (1947). *Play therapy*. New York, NY: Ballantine.

Bresin, K., & Gordon, K. H. (2013). Aggression as affect regulation: Extending catharsis theory to evaluate aggression and experiential anger in the laboratory and daily life. *Journal of Social and Clinical Psychology*, *32*(4), 400–423. doi:10.1521/jscp.2013.32.4.400

Bushman, B. J., Baumeister, R. F., & Stack, A. D. (1999). Catharsis, aggression, and persuasive influence: Self-fulfilling or self-defeating prophecies? *Journal of Personality and Social Psychology*, *76*(3), 367–376. doi:10.1037/0022-3514.76.3.367 PMID:10101875

Drewes, A. (2008). Bobo revisited: What the research says. *International Journal of Play Therapy*, *17*(1), 52–56. doi:10.1037/1555-6824.17.1.52

Fuhrman, K., & Franz, D.A. (2010, March). Toy guns in the playroom: Yes or No? *Play Therapy*, p. 5.

Gun Violence Archive. (2016). *Mass shootings in 2015*. Retrieved from http://www.gunviolencearchive.org/reports/mass-shooting

Kottman, T. (2003). *Partners in play: An Adlerian approach to play therapy* (2nd ed.). Alexandria, VA: American Counseling Association.

Kottman, T. (2011). *Play therapy: Basics and beyond* (2nd ed.). Alexandria, VA: American Counseling Association.

Landreth, G. (2002). *Play Therapy: The art of the relationships* (2nd ed.). New York, NY: Brunner-Routledge.

Landreth, G. (2012). *Play therapy: The art of the relationship* (3rd ed.). New York, NY: Brunner-Routledge.

Laue, C. E. (2015). *Toy guns in play therapy: Controversy and current practice* (Doctoral Dissertation). Available from ProQuest Dissertations and Theses database. (UMI No. 3688574)

Moustakas, C. (1959). *Psychotherapy with children: The living relationship*. New York, NY: Ballantine Books.

Ray, D. C. (2011). *Advanced play therapy: Essential conditions, knowledge, and skills for child practice*. New York, NY: Routledge.

Ray, D. C., Lee, K. R., Meany-Walen, K. K., Carlson, S. E., Carnes-Holt, K. L., & Ware, J. N. (2013). Use of toys in child-centered play therapy. *International Journal of Play Therapy*, *22*(1), 43–57. doi:10.1037/a0031430

Schaefer, C. E., & Mattei, D. (2005). Catharsis: Effectiveness in childrens aggression. *International Journal of Play Therapy*, *14*(2), 103–109. doi:10.1037/h0088905

Trotter, K., Eshelman, D., & Landreth, G. (2003). A place for Bobo in play therapy. *International Journal of Play Therapy*, *12*(1), 117–139. doi:10.1037/h0088875

KEY TERMS AND DEFINITIONS

Aggression: Hostile attitudes or behaviors that express the intent or wiliness to harm another individual.
Aggressive Toys: Playroom items typically used by children to express aggression.
Gun Control: The act of limiting or restricting gun sales or gun possession within a community.
Gun Violence: Violence that is committed with the use of a gun.
Limit-Setting: The enforcement of boundaries or structure by a play therapist.
Open Carry: The act of openly carrying a gun within a public space.
Self-Efficacy: Confidence in one's ability to accomplish a goal or successfully complete a task.

Chapter 10
Expanding the Range of Puppetry in Expressive Play Therapy

Michele J. Ferro
Lesley University, USA

Julia Gentleman Byers
Lesley University, USA

ABSTRACT

This chapter focuses on expanding the therapeutic application of using puppetry as a communicative tool in the service of psychological growth and integration for children. A continuum of more than thirty descriptors of puppetry formats are presented that each hold specific value within therapeutic interventions. The types of materials used to construct the puppet and their cognitive, emotional, and sensory connections are explored, as is the impact of uniquely created productions versus commercial products. The authors also define the limitations and challenges of certain types of puppetry, which can evoke or incite different reactions within different stages and phases of psychosocial treatment. Examples of case vignettes are provided from a Child and Adolescent public services agency in an inner-city environment.

INTRODUCTION

This chapter focuses on advancing the therapeutic application of puppetry as a communicative tool in the service of psychological growth and integration for children. Initially inanimate, the puppet can be brought to life through words and movement echoing the motions made by humans. Accordingly, puppetry has long been used and recognized as a vital projective and communication tool in therapy allowing for the safe disclosure of thoughts, emotions, affective responses, and physical expressions (Bromfield, 1995; Carter & Mason, 1998; Hartwig, 2014; Irwin, 2002; Ivon, 2014; Jenkins & Beckh, 2002; Lebedeva, 2012; Oaklander, 2007; and Steinhardt, 1994). Related literature (Bromfield, 1995; Burneikaite, 2009; Carter & Mason, 1998; Hartwig, 2014; Irwin, 2002; and Jenkins & Beckh, 1995) has highlighted the importance of choosing puppets that are suitable for therapeutic use. Despite these

DOI: 10.4018/978-1-5225-2224-9.ch010

explorations, there is limited research integrating therapeutic issues within a continuum of the range of puppetry available to clients in play therapy.

The understanding of the physicality of puppetry and its range of therapeutic applications can be expanded through the proposed "Puppetry in Play Therapy Continuum" (PPTC) framework that considers the elements of structure, materials, process, and symbolic and metaphoric content. Carter & Mason (1998) defined puppetry into four basic commercially made formats – 1) Hand puppets, 2) Marionettes, 3) Muppets, and 4) Ventriloquist dummies. The authors propose an amplification of that premise naming at least thirty different descriptors of puppet making that hold specific value within therapeutic applications. Within the chapter, the PPTC of different puppets is outlined and explored. The authors also create a framework of therapeutic materials that define different uses of commercial and uniquely created products that meet specific treatment goals and provide opportunities for a range of diagnoses. For purposes of the chapter, examples of case vignettes from a pilot research project designed to explore the potentiality of this expansion using a non-directive, humanistic, and relational approach, are presented and examined.

BACKGROUND AND LITERATURE REVIEW

Therapeutic Use of Puppets

Puppets allow for freedom of expression, providing opportunities for connection with others. Inherently creating metaphor, they are designed to communicate and have the ability to voice wants, needs, and desires that the individual who creates or operates them may fear to express (Ackerman, 2005). Current professional literature suggests that soft hand puppets, which are easy to manipulate, are purported to be the type of puppet best suited for therapeutic purposes (Bromfield, 1995; Carter & Mason, 1998; Hartwig, 2014: and Oaklander, 2007). The authors recognize the benefit of soft hand puppets and deepen this posture, examining the importance of the physicality of the puppets including the structure, materials, and mode of construction. Bromfield (1995) discussed elements of physicality and briefly considered this concept when he stated, "All aspects of puppet play - including form, manifest and latent content are fair game for observation and examination" (p.442). He supported his recommendation of soft hand puppets based in part on his observation that the hard rubber wolf in his collection was rarely used. Since rubber is hard and non-pliable, and the "personality" of the wolf "aggressive", the authors are curious about when and how puppets, such as the hard rubber wolf, or puppets of other materials, are used and how this correlates with the client's presentation and diagnosis. The authors contend that examining the use of puppets made of a variety of materials and puppet types are needed in order to explore a full range of expression and affect.

The expanded range of puppetry encompasses the symbolic and metaphoric meanings of the puppets as well as the materials and mode of construction. The authors found minimal research exploring these elements together or in the creation of self-made puppets and toys. In addition to proposing soft hand puppets, the literature supports selecting puppets based on personality and roles (Carter & Mason, 1998: Hartwig, 2014; and Irwin, 2002). Hartwig (2014) proposed specific puppet categories - friendly, foolish, and frightening - and recommended choosing puppets from each category to allow clients to fully communicate an extensive range of thoughts, emotions, and experiences.

A brief further exploration of the professional literature discusses the therapeutic use and benefits of puppets within the disciplines of play therapy, art therapy, and expressive arts therapy. The authors are promoting the concept of integrating the modalities for the benefit of the client with the understanding that each of the therapeutic disciplines has considerable merit on its own.

Play Therapy

Play therapy is a developmentally appropriate process for children to express emotions, and "act out" disturbing, conflicting, and confusing situations. Lacking the verbal acumen to express their inner feelings, children communicate most naturally through play. Play therapy allows children the space to work through and resolve inner conflicts, make sense of new experiences, learn new coping skills, gain self-control, increase decision-making skills, and make responsible choices (Axline, 1969; Kottman, 2011; Landreth, 2012; and Moustakas, 1959). The use of toys and expressive arts materials allows for self-expression and emotional distance, and creates a forum for the therapist and child to communicate and build a vital therapeutic alliance. The therapist provides an environment of acceptance, trust, and safety that allows children to address difficult issues. Children's communication through their play becomes imbued with symbols and metaphoric information. The themes that emerge are rich and relevant to the child's thoughts, feelings, and perspectives.

Puppets are a natural fit in play therapy. Immediately metaphoric and with the ability to speak (Ackerman, 2005), puppets fulfill the role of a distinct mode of communication while also allowing for significant emotional distance.

Art Therapy

Art therapy awakens the power of the image and the materials used to express in metaphor what words alone cannot (Malchiodi, 2002; Malchiodi, 2007; Moon, 2007; and Rubin, 2010). Providing an alternate mode of expression of thoughts, feelings, and emotions, art created in a therapeutic context provides a space to safely confront old ideas and create new possibilities. Many of the images that emerge in therapy may have their roots in preverbal or taboo consciousness (Rubin, 2010). As expressions of visual thought, images are multi-layered and can help communicate hidden or unconscious issues and concerns along with the exploration of a client's future potential (Rubin, 2011).

Both the symbolic expression expressed in the art product and the art making process itself have significant merit. Art making is a key part of human experience and a healing process. In addition, the art making process creates a transitional object, which allows for projection and distance (Rubin, 2010). As in play therapy, the pleasurable process helps build the therapeutic bond. Moon (2007) stated, "The therapeutic alliance is fostered when the focus is placed on the art process" (p.v). The creation of puppets in an art therapy context provides for a deepening of the therapeutic relationship, the creation of metaphor during the puppet-making process, and the metaphor established when the client gives the puppet a "voice".

Expressive Arts Therapy

Expressive arts therapy includes the modalities of various creative art forms such as dance/movement, painting, sculpture, drama, improvisation, poetry/creative writing, and music where the process of creation and expression is the focus as opposed to the finished product (Malchiodi, 2005; Rogers, 1993). Self-expression through the arts has the ability to hold authentic understanding of deep inner wisdom. The opportunity for tangible understanding is provided as clients are actively engaged and involved in the process of creating (Malchiodi, 2005). Imagination is rekindled since the process is highlighted versus the product.

All the different modalities lend themselves to different expressions, allowing for the expansion of multiple feelings (Dhaese, 2011; Knill, 2005). "All the arts complement and interact with each other to unify play and imagination" (Knill, 1994, p.320). Puppets are one of the few techniques that traverse the various expressive art disciplines. Made of a multitude of materials, puppets incorporate all of the arts and are a "means of communication, an extension of human expression" (Baird, 1965, p13). Puppets can be created, danced, moved and spoken through in the creation of narrative and story. Each of the modalities has unique value and allows for the self-expression of unconscious thoughts, feelings, and conflicts to emerge, providing self-understanding and a deepening of communication between client and therapist.

Importance of Integrating Play Therapy with the Expressive Arts

Self-made toys have been purported to deepen the therapeutic connection (Bratton, Ceballos, Ferebee, 2009; Byers, 2013; Byers, 2016; Gerity, 2005; Lebedeva, 2012; and Steinhardt, 1994). Recognizing the integrity of the individual therapeutic disciplines, the authors encourage integrating these disciplines into the puppet spectrum to strengthen the function of the puppet as a communication tool. Choosing the type and style of puppet to create adds additional levels of understanding and self-exploration. Art and puppetry is a fairly new form of integration in play therapy with children. Bernier (2005a) specifically promoted the creation of self-made puppets, which are subsequently used in therapeutic play with the understanding that puppets are an extension of the creator and thus portray different aspects of the self. In addition, Steinhardt (1994) explored the combination of puppetry and art therapy as part of an art therapy graduate program, recognizing the connection between the self-made puppet and the catharsis and growth that occurred as a result of the process. The authors promote integrating play therapy with the expressive arts, introducing the PPTC, a continuum of different types of puppets, all of which elicit different responses.

Meanings of Materials and Media

Contemplating the aspects of the media's impact on the client as part of the materials/structural facet of the client's puppet making is essential. The choice or "style" of puppets, the structure and materials the puppet is made of, and the level of control each media provides impacts the character/role of the puppet and the symbolic and metaphoric meanings. "Different media… provoke different kinds of messages" (Robbins, 1994, p. 206). The understanding of materials and media in art therapy has been explored in multiple sources (Bratton, Ceballos, Ferebee, 2009: Dhaese, 2011; Fenner, 2016; Hinz, 2009; Hinz, 2016; Malchiodi, 2002; Moon, 2010; Robbins, 1994; and Rubin, 2011) but rarely applied to the creation and use of puppets in a therapeutic context. The diverse art materials available all have fundamental qualities from highly controllable materials, such as pencils or pens used for drawing, to loose fluid media, such as watercolor paint or wet clay. Inherently, fluid media correlates with emotional/affective experiences and resistive media are connected to more cognitive responses (Hinz, 2009). Considering the emotional and cognitive responses suggested by the various art media, the authors also explore a range of additional materials such as string, tape, and glue and observe how these elements correlate with the client's puppet-making expression.

THE PHYSICALITY OF PUPPETRY

Five Facets of Meaning

Focusing on the importance of the physicality of puppetry, the therapeutic application can be explored through five different facets of meaning. These facets include 1) the structure (type of puppet), 2) materials (physicality and structural components), 3) process (method of puppet construction), 4) symbolic (therapeutic issues), and 5) metaphor/projection (way of working in therapy). These applications are considered in conjunction with the client's diagnosis and developmental level to provide deeper significance and understanding.

The Structure (Type of Puppet)

The authors have outlined the PPTC, a continuum of different types of puppets that hold therapeutic value within therapeutic applications. The PPTC is categorized based on the body parts used to manipulate the puppet and ranges from the intimacy of a single finger puppet to large carnival puppets that may require multiple individuals to manipulate. Table 1 lists the various puppets and includes simple descriptors for each type. Figure 1 presents illustrations of many of these puppets. Despite the linear presentation of the PPTC, the stages and phases of puppetry development do not necessarily have a specific order. The relative size, ease of flexibility and manipulation, the degree and direction of control that a person can utilize, the degree of intimacy relationally with the therapist, the degree of positive and negative behaviors as seen through the puppets, and the use of projection all enhance the therapist's awareness of therapeutic and symbolic structure and design of the puppetry that can meet the specific needs of a client.

Finger Puppets

Finger puppets are predominantly small and worn on the finger. Movement created by a finger is fairly limited which leads to more intimate connections and reflections. The degree to which a child needs to build fine motor capacities, sensory exploration, or build trust with the therapist is executed through the intimate nature of fingers that give or take within the expression of the emotional therapeutic alliance. Each type of finger puppet outlined on the PPTC has additional qualities. For example, the tangible sustained nature of a tattoo/painted on finger puppet keeps the objects literally with a client beyond the session, as a very intimate transitional object (Winnicott, 1971).

Hand Puppets

Hand puppets cover the hand including part of the arm and are manipulated by the hand within the puppet. They are the most common type of puppet used in therapy. There are many different types that create nuances within the therapeutic response. Because "hand puppets" are universally known and understood within the cultural context of early childhood experiences, the familiarity, comfort, and ease at

Table 1. Puppetry in Play Therapy Continuum (PPTC)

Puppet types are categorized by body parts used to manipulate puppet							
FINGER	HAND		HAND & ARM	FACE	TORSO	LEG/FOOT	BODY
1. Tattoo/Painted on finger	6. Traditional hand puppet (Papier maché or plastic head)	11. Pop-up	14. Hand and glove	19. Mask (tied on head)	22. Marionette	26. Foot (Surprise/Disorienting dilemma)	28. Humanette
These puppets are literally affixed onto the fingers.	A traditional hand puppet is a simple puppet with a cloth body and a 3D papier maché or plastic head.	The pop-up puppet rests inside a cup or cone and "pops up" when an attached rod is pushed up.	This is a hand puppet that is controlled with one hand inside the head and the other hand inside a glove that is part of the puppet.	This is a facial disguise that covers all or part of the face and is tied onto the head.	A marionette is a puppet that is brought to life using strings that are attached to the puppet's head and limbs.	This type of puppet is placed on the foot or the foot itself designed as a puppet.	A humanette puppet uses the human head of the puppeteer as the head of the "puppet" with a small puppet body hung from the puppeteer's neck. Limbs can be moved using rods or the puppeteer's hands.
2. Traditional (around finger)	7. Sock	12. Reversible	15. Human arm puppet	20. Mask (on stick)	23. Bunraku	27. Planchette	29. Full body suit
This is a small puppet worn and controlled by a single finger and made from a variety of materials such as fabric, yarn, pipe cleaners, paper, or rubber.	A sock puppet is a hand puppet fashioned from a sock, which can be easily created and animated.	A reversible puppet form holds two puppets in one and has the ability to flip or transform from one character to another.	This is a large hand puppet that requires two people to operate and uses the puppeteers' arms as part of the puppet. Also known as a two-man puppet.	This mask is similar to the mask (tied on head), except it has a stick attached to the mask instead.	Bunraku is a Japanese puppet form. The puppets are each controlled by rods by three puppeteers onstage.	A planchette is a pair of puppets, on a plank controlled by the puppeteer's leg, which is attached to the puppets on a horizontal string that runs through the puppet's body.	A full body suit is a puppet costume operated from within. It can be worn by one person or group of people.
3. Multiple fingers	8. Cookie cutter	13. Paper	16. Simple rod puppet	21. Full head	24. Pull string		30. Carnival/Uber
Multiple fingers puppets include gloves that have a different character attached to each finger, or simply wearing an assortment of puppets on different fingers.	A cookie-cutter puppet is a simple 2D hand puppet of the head and body of a human or animal figure. The three middle fingers are generally placed in the head with the thumb and pinkie finger in alternate arms.	A paper puppet is often made from a simple paper bag where the fold of the bag becomes the mouth of the puppet.	The simplest rod puppet is called a Marotte and has a head, and possibly a torso, affixed to the top of a stick or rod. Additional rods may be added to manipulate the puppet's arms.	A full head mask completely encompasses the head and disguises it completely.	A pull string puppet/toy is a flat, 2D puppet with jointed limbs that are tied to a pull string at the bottom. When the string is pulled, the arms and legs go up. It is often constructed from paper, cardboard, or wood.		A carnival/uber puppet is often larger than life and takes a number of people to manipulate. It can be manipulated from within or without using rods or strings.
4. Ticklebug	9. Stuffed animal/3D		17. Hand and rod		25. Shadow/Black light		
A ticklebug puppet uses the hand as the body with the fingers representing the "legs". Also included in this type are frames made of wood or cardboard that the fingers "poke through" as legs.	A stuffed animal/3D puppet looks like a stuffed animal or doll prior to animation. Most of these types of puppets have movable mouths and are made of soft fuzzy fabric.		A hand and rod puppet is similar to a hand puppet and includes additional thin rods that can be used to move the puppet's limbs.		A shadow puppet is a 2D rod puppet placed in front of a light source projecting the puppet's shadow onto a screen. Black light puppets are a technique that uses ultraviolet light so that the only the puppet is seen.		
5. Clothespin/Peg	10. Tattoo/Painted on hand		18. Ventriloquist figure				
A clothespin/peg puppet uses a clothespin or peg that opens and closes to create the "puppet".	Similar to tattooed or painted fingers, this type of puppet has images affixed to the skin of the hands that allows the hand itself to become the puppet.		The ventriloquist figure has a moveable mouth and is controlled from inside the puppet's body, using hands and levers.				

Figure 1. Puppetry in Play Therapy Continuum (PPTC) with illustrations

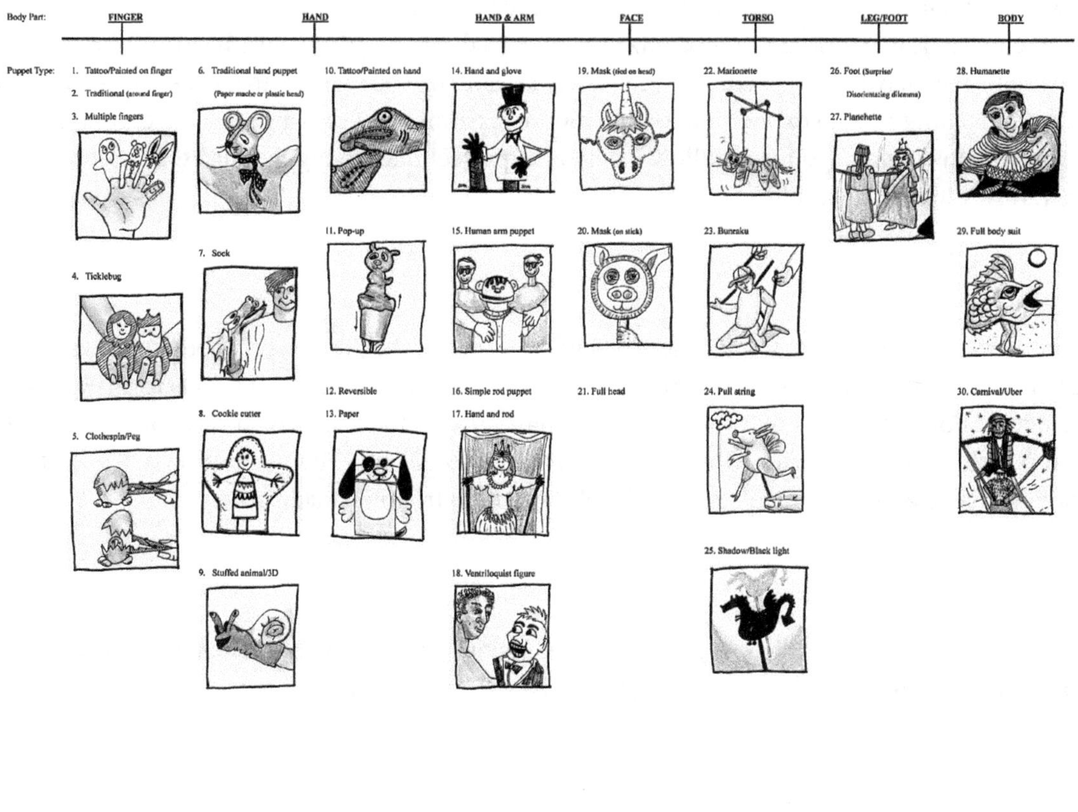

which a client can quickly take on different roles in the emotional affect of the character directly relates to the metaphoric language of play. Qualities of the different types of hand puppets have variations of meanings. Of special import and consideration within this category are the pop-up and reversible puppets. The pop-up puppet is often used with younger children to help separation anxiety issues, akin to the "peek-a-boo" stage in human development, allowing a child to relearn appropriate attachment issues and develop coping skills of object constancy, permanence, and internalized imagination. The reversible puppet allows for another character to emerge when "flipped over". Testing elements of safety, the reversible puppets allows opportunity for surprise and encouragement to see multiple emotional elements within psychological character development. However, if sexual abuse is suspected, this type of puppet can potentially incite or over stimulate the client. The therapist chooses the degree to which a client is prepared for the fun or scary elements within the flip over action.

Hand and Arm

The hand and arm puppet builds on the hand puppet allowing for more movement of the body and the head. Often both hands and arms are used, either to hold a rod or to become the hand or arm of the puppet itself. The relative action of moving away from a small movement to a larger authority and sense of power in expressing voice and action is made possible through extending a person's sense of agency. With the hand and arm puppets, the movements are stronger and portray more of the individual's sense of control as witnessed by others.

Face

Masks are often recognized within the realm of puppetry and hold a great deal of therapeutic significance. Masks allow for the exploration of different aspects of the self, including masks people may unknowingly wear in their lives. Wearing the mask on the face allows individuals to give voice to the persona behind the mask. It is important to recognize that masks that are tied onto the head can feel constrictive to individuals who have been sexually or physically assaulted. The mask with a stick attached is a simple and less threatening way to express alternate emotions. Similar yet dynamically different than a whole body ventriloquist, animated masks allow a person to project underlying feelings that want to be stated, yet are rarely allowed "in public".

Torso

Many puppets require more manipulation and involve more of the puppeteer's body to move. They may require more practice and skill to control. It is also important to explore the various forms of puppets in this category. For example, a marionette literally has strings attached, which can correlate to relationships in people's lives. Learning when and how to use the "strings" helps develop a sense of mastery and independence and may correlate with the ability to control the attachment.

Leg/Foot

This is an unexpected use of the body to manipulate the puppet. As such, it creates surprise and potentially a disorientating dilemma. The concept of a disorientating dilemma in the field of transformative education/therapy (Mezirow, 1995) works best when used with puppets that are animated using body parts that are unexpected. The surprise element and the degree to which a person can take risks may feed a sense of courageousness in being different than others expect of him/her, or that others "expect" of themselves.

Body

There are a variety of full body puppets that can both be worn by a person, or multiple people, or be manipulated by them using rods or strings. Of all the puppets the variety of bodysuits or carnival type costumes are generally more akin to drama therapy or theater performance. Often the narrative life stories are played out and the opportunity to role-play different scenarios are evident within the production. For the purpose of this chapter, the authors have included the humanette form of puppetry to denote an "all in" embodied response to creating and wanting change. The end plot of a story becomes more expected by an audience and the individual anticipates choices in the outcome of the action. Because the life-size puppets are created with others, all aspects of group dynamics and understanding of self in relation to others is the therapeutic goal of the interaction.

Materials (Physicality and Structural Components)

Puppets are made of a variety of materials including soft fabric, hard rubber, papier maché, clay, wood, metal, and recycled materials. The materials used to construct the puppet and the method of construction all impact the issue or symbolic meaning of the puppet. Table 2 lists various materials and symbolic associations. The different materials provide a metaphoric avenue for therapeutic bonding. The authors examine the impact of the different material choices made by the research participants in the discussion section of the chapter.

Time is also a consideration in the process of the therapeutic relationship. The choice to complete the making of a puppet in a session or multiple sessions highlights what issues need to be worked through.

Process (Method of Puppet Construction)

The type of puppet and the materials used both impact the method of construction. Whether glued, stapled, taped, sewn, carved, or hammered, this method can be explored therapeutically and symbolically. Each execution or rendering of the art objects can signify ways in which relationships are felt or experienced. The degree of permanency is evident in the way something is loosely taped or glued versus firmly sewn or carved. Beyond the opportunity for self-expression, sewn, carved, and other structurally created products provide the possibility for grounding and ego strengthening (Dhaese, 2011). The investment and commitment (level of engagement) to the process of the therapeutic alliance or relationship can be monitored in the ongoing interactions. The making of puppetry allows for a fuller assessment of attachment issues beyond the relative skills acquired or needed to create the imagined product.

Symbolic (Therapeutic Issues)

Time, space, and place have been used as cornerstones of the play therapy room and setting (Kottman, 2011; Landreth, 2012; and Moustakas, 1959). Although there are many designs and uses of the play

Table 2. Puppet materials: physicality and structural components

Material	Symbolic Connections
1. Stick	The stick moves the puppet away from the body and often expresses the need for distance and/or autonomy.
2. Soft fabric	Soft fabric reveals a need for nurturance and comfort. Its use may indicate possible attachment issues.
3. Papier maché	The layering process of papier maché can mirror layers of meaning. When it hardens, the resulting material is closer to molded plastic.
4. Paper	Paper is accessible and can be used quickly with low technical needs or expanded to extreme detail with cut designs. Paper allows for extreme control as in shadow puppets. It is also easily destructible for the ventilation of emotions.
5. Paint	Paint adds emotional content and can be used to cover up elements. It is important to observe how thinly or thickly the paint is applied.
6. Rubber	Rubber can be a playful sensory object with the ability to bounce back. It's surface is hard and difficult to destroy. It is most often used to borrow a specific object to metaphorically or symbolically express a relationship to someone or something.
7. Molded plastic	Molded plastic is more rigid in structure than rubber and is less adaptable. Use tends to represent clear messages and direct communication.
8. Wood	When used as sticks, wood provides minor or more manipulative structure. When carved, the use of wood adds risk and courage in the process of forming an object. It can also easily frustrate clients due to the heavy time commitment; There is a long process of carving, sandpapering, and then applying lacquer or paint.
9. Loose objects/Recycled (Includes Toilet paper rolls, pipe cleaners, cookies, soda bottles, clothes pins, slime)	Loose and recycled objects encourage imagination, providing access to problem solving and creative skills. It is good for joint work to build the therapeutic relationship, in asking or gaining help in the process.
10. Tin foil or metal	Tin foil is very malleable and flexible, and can act as a reflective surface. It can be used as structural base but can also be easily destroyed. Metal objects within puppet parts are permanent, offering object constancy.
11. String - thick & thin (Includes wire, rubber bands, yarn)	String is metaphoric in assessing the level of attachment within relationships. It is important to recognize whether it is tightly wound, knotted, loosely scrabbled, unattached, etc.
12. Glue	Glue relates to the degree to which objects are sticky, loosely attached or permanently applied. This can be used as an assessment tool in building connections and trust.

space according to different theoretical tenets, the commonality of understanding play therapy experiences is predicated on the development of the therapeutic relationships. The authors identified five major issues and concerns based on clinical experience that need to be recognized when working with children in order to achieve a more integrated state. These factors include 1) aggressiveness, 2) love/attachment including safety and the importance of relationship, 3) empathy towards others, 4) social role/engagement with others, and 5) coping skills (both positive and negative). Using multiple forms of puppetry provides the therapist with direct exploration into attachment issues, building the therapeutic alliance, trust, and safety to reveal more problematic or symptomatic expressions of the human condition. Puppets have the unique form to expect or anticipate an interaction. Cultural divides are lessened around the universal human need to 'play' with another. The actual making of puppets allows a further dimension of creation myths around what and how people live their lives. As a result, the therapist has the opportunity to interact with a corrective emotional experience in which to offer different scenarios of life experiences. The fact that the projected toys are generally more "fun" aids in the likelihood that a client will come back for more in a trusting new environment.

Metaphor/Projection (Way of Working in Therapy)

Metaphoric representations of actual people or characters behind the puppets allow the puppeteer to demonstrate clear actions and behaviors. Using body part sizes and choice, a client chooses what is best for her/him symbolically to represent dimensions of life experiences, real or imagined. Being able to gently and metaphorically hold the fire of a dragon can be experienced without actually harming another. Since puppets are often so close to being human, especially when clients animate them, puppets are more confrontational in dealing with emotions and the regulation of impulses. The ability of the puppets to express their fears, hopes, and aspirations before a client can incorporate them into a more balanced individual is paramount. "When symbols are animated, as in puppetry, they take on even more of a life of their own with multi-leveled meanings, which can become integral parts of the therapeutic process. Everything that occurs in psychopuppetry can be understood symbolically" (Bernier, 2005b, p.126). The case vignettes in this chapter are provided to illustrate significantly different ways the puppets evoke affect.

METHOD

Participants

For purposes of the chapter, examples of case vignettes are provided from individual clinical sessions from a Child and Adolescent community mental health services agency in an urban environment. Participants represent low-socioeconomic-status (SES) boys and girls, aged 6-14, from different ethnicities. All participants are in therapy for different challenges and diagnoses including behavioral issues, attention deficit hyperactivity disorder (ADHD), posttraumatic stress disorder (PTSD), anxiety, depression, and disruptive mood disorders. Informed consent for the pilot research study was obtained by the agency and the parents of the participants. All client names and key identifying information has been changed to protect the participants' identities. One participant researcher led the individual clinical sessions with a caseload of 20 clients – 13 boys and 7 girls - with the average age of 9.

Materials

The researcher supplied a range of necessary art and play therapy materials to make puppets. Some elements, such as soft hand puppet templates, clothespins, and marionette frame tops were provided to facilitate client-made toys. In addition, the researcher provided a range of puppets from the frightening, foolish, and friendly categories recommended by Hartwig (2014). The puppets available included commercially made stuffed animal type/3D puppets, soft cookie cutter hand puppets, rubber monster finger puppets, soft fabric finger puppets, and researcher made soft cookie cutter hand puppets, sock puppets, and finger puppets. The hand puppets specifically provided in the playroom included a snake, shark, dragon, lion, and witch in the frightening category, a couple of sock puppets with googly eyes in the foolish category, and a giraffe, dog, baby chick, elephant, turtle, owl, baby lion, doctor, construction worker, policeman, fireman, and a people puppet created by the researcher in the friendly category. Multiple finger puppets in each domain were also provided. One of the benefits of making puppets allows for the creation of whatever category or personality the client wants or needs.

Study Design

The research was designed as a generalized study to explore the PPTC and the facets of meaning proposed by the authors. A pilot research project was explored using a participant observation qualitative method. One researcher met with clients individually once per week for 45 minutes for four consecutive weeks using a primarily non-directive, humanistic, and relational approach. As a result, the puppets were offered to each client as an option as opposed to a directive. The importance of the therapeutic relationship was emphasized and the researcher provided unconditional positive regard and used core non-directive play therapy skills such as tracking, restating content, reflecting feelings, and returning responsibility to the child (Kottman, 2011; Landreth, 2012). Field notes, artifacts, and session notes were collected and analyzed with respect to the PPTC, the expanded framework that contains facets of meaning including structure, materials, process, as well as symbolic and metaphoric content. Puppet usage for each participant was noted on a working chart (Table 3) that explored the level of puppet engagement (mild, moderate, high), the method of construction and materials used, symbolism, metaphors, and themes that emerged in individual sessions, and emotions expressed through puppet play. Observations and some recorded sessions were shared in supervision. Triangulation occurred by combining the supervisor observer and a neutral professional through the study of recorded observations, sessions, and created toys. The researcher recorded sessions and clinical impressions at the beginning, middle, and end of the research period and highlighted what was noticed in the range of applications. Questions such as how and when puppets are used were also considered and noted. The authors chose three case vignettes with clients that are all in the working through stage in order to amplify the nature and focus of the puppet making process.

Case Vignettes

Case Vignette 1: Lucia

Lucia, 8, is of Spanish and Puerto-Rican descent. She was referred to the agency by the school for disturbing behavior, including an incident of tying herself to a chair during class. Both her mother and the school shared concerns about her behavioral outbursts and struggles with peer relationships. There were reports of Lucia being bullied at school and in the neighborhood. Lucia physically hit other children when she was upset or when she felt they were laughing at her. At the time of the study, Lucia lived with both biological parents although her father often left for extended periods of time to return to the country of his birth. The first time he left was when Lucia was 4 and he did not return for a year. These departures were often followed by escalated behavioral outbursts.

At the point of the pilot research project, the researcher had been working with Lucia for eight months. Originally diagnosed with an adjustment disorder with disturbance of conduct, some of the play prior to the pilot research project indicated the possibility of trauma beyond the abandonment issues but none had been disclosed or reported. Treatment goals included increasing self-esteem, working through abandonment issues, helping the client recognize triggers to emotional outbursts, and learning coping skills to manage symptoms. Lucia's behavioral outbursts had decreased dramatically since the beginning of therapy; there were fewer reports of being bullied, and some improved social relationships.

Table 3a. PPTC: puppet usage/level of engagement

PARTICIPANT	AGE	SEX	SELF-IDENTIFIED ETHNICITY	DIAGNOSIS	TIME IN THERAPY PRIOR TO STUDY	WEEK #	TYPE OF PUPPETS	MATERIALS	LEVEL OF ENGAGEMENT WITH PUPPETS	METHOD OF CONSTRUCTION	SYMBOLISM/ METAPHOR	THEMES EXPRESSED	EMOTIONS EXPRESSED	OTHER NOTES
Art	8	M	Caucasian American	ADHD/ODD	10 months	1	*		N/A					
						2	Rubber monster finger puppets & Dragon 3D/stuffed animal hand puppet	Rubber; Fabric	High	N/A - Commercial	Monstrous tendencies/ Thwarted flight (Dragon)	Aggression & bullying / Helplessness	Angry / Dejected	Client shut down when therapist reflected feelings
						3, 4	OUT SICK / SUSPENDED		N/A					
Arnie	9	M	Cape Verdean/ Portuguese	Anxiety	3 months	1, 2, 3, 4	*		N/A					
John	10	M	Caucasian American	ADHD/ODD	9 months	1, 2, 3, 4	*		N/A					
Natalia	10	F	African American	Anxiety	1 year	1	Created Cookie cutter hand puppet	Fabric, sequins, googly eyes, "gem"stones, glue gun	High	Glue gun	Self-representation	Identity	Satisfied	
						2	Created Cookie cutter hand puppet(2)	Fabric, sequins, thread	High	Sewing, gluing	Superhero elements - Flight	Power & Control / Identity	Frustrated & Annoyed / Proud	Client did not want to complete puppet started previous week or engage with it.
						3	Snake sock puppet and 'girl' cookie cutter hand puppet (researcher made)/ Created Cookie cutter hand puppet (2)	Fabric, sequirs, thread, gliter glue	High	Sewing, gluing	Snake (Hissing and Biting)	Aggression / Identity	Angry & Frustrated / Satisfied	Returned responsibility (Client wanted researcher to sew for her).
						4	Created/completed Cookie cutter hand puppet (2)	Fabric, sequins, thread	High	Sewing, gluing	Superhero - Flying above	Escapism/ Aggression & Anxiety	Glad/ Frustrated & Annoyed	Storytelling therapy- slowed client down for reflection.
Carl	11	M	Caucasian American	ADHD/ASD	10 months	1, 2	*		N/A					
						3	OUT SICK		N/A					
						4	Lion, witch, dog, and dragon 3D/stuffed animal hand puppets; hedgehog finger puppet	Rubber, Fabric, Video	High	N/A - Commercial	Searching for treasure and finding true self	Isolation (Feeling left out and different) / Aggression	Lost, Sad, Confused, Agitated	Videoed story using puppets. Client used humor to hide from difficult emotions.
David	7	M	African American	Anxiety/ PTSD	11 months	1	Dragon, Snake, Shark, and Lion 3D/stuffed animal hand puppets	Fabric	High	N/A - Commercial	Intense hunger	Aggression	Excited	Session strengthened therapeutic bond
						2	Dragon, Snake, Shark, and Lion 3D/stuffed animal hand puppets	Fabric	Moderate	N/A - Commercial	Hunger	Aggression / Sadness	Moody	Less intensity than previous week
						3	*		N/A					
						4	Dragon and Dog 3D/stuffed animal hand puppets	Fabric	Mild	N/A - Commercial	Projection of self	Identity	Proud	Used puppets to play ball
Mariah	8	F	African American/ Haitian	Anxiety	11 months	1	Created Masks (tied on)	Paper, paint	High	Drew, painted, and cut	Kitty cat (tame animal nature)	Identity	Proud, Happy	
						2	Created Masks (tied on)	Paper, paint, yarn	High	Tied	Tame & Wild animal nature	Fear, Trickery, Danger, Intrusion. Mother & daughter relationship issues.	Sad, Scared, Confused, Misunderstood	Created and illustrated story inspired by masks
						3	Finger puppet (Researcher made), Witch hand puppet, Dog 3D/stuffed animal hand puppet, Rubber monster finger puppets, plus a range of other hand and finger puppets, and other toys/figurines.	Fabric, rubber	High	N/A - Commercial	Good versus Evil (Witch & Monsters)	Aggression / Power & control / Loneliness / Trickery / Protection	Scared, Threatened/ Determined	Client became averse to touching rubber monster finger puppets as session progressed
						4	Story related to Created Masks (tied on)	Paper painted masks	High	N/A - Completed masks	Tame & Wild animal nature	Identity. Mother & daughter relationship issues.	Distressed	Returned to story related to masks
Fred	8	M	Caucasian American	PTSD	9 months	1	*		N/A					
						2	Dog puppet and giraffe 3D/stuffed animal hand puppets; Created Finger puppet	Fabric, felt, thread, glitter glue, googly eyes	High	Sewing, gluing	Loyalty/Connection	Trust/Relationship/Attachment	Connected/ Excited/ Frustrated	Struggled with sewing. Enjoyed using glitter glue.
						3, 4	*		N/A					
Jack	7	M	Cape Verdean	DMDD	1 year	1	Shark and Lion 3D/stuffed animal hand puppets plus a variety of other animals. Witch hand puppet.	Fabric	High	N/A - Commercial	Hunger/ Naming (puppets)	Aggression & Love/Attachment	Angry, Excited, Connected	Client loved all the puppets except he didn't like the witch.
						2	Shark, Lion, Dragon 3D/stuffed animal hand puppets plus a variety of other animals. Witch hand puppet.	Fabric	Moderate	N/A - Commercial	Hunger/ Naming (puppets) / Punishment	Aggression	Angry, Excited, Connected	Puppets used at start and end of session. They were in "time out" during session for hitting him.
						3	Shark, Snake, Lion 3D/stuffed animal hand puppets plus a variety of other animals.	Fabric	Moderate	N/A - Commercial	Naming (puppets)	Relationships	Angry, Bored	Puppets used at start and end of session. They watched session in between.
						4	Variety of animal hand puppets. Witch hand puppet.	Fabric	Moderate	N/A - Commercial	Punishment	Aggression, Power & control	Angry, Scared	Puppets used at start and end of session. They were in "time out" forever. He threw witch in trash.
Donald	10	M	Caucasian American	ADD/ ODD	10 months	1, 2, 3	*		N/A					
						4	Shark, snake, dragon, dog, giraffe, lion, turtle, and witch 3D/stuffed animal puppets. Cookie cutter occupation puppets.	Fabric	Moderate	N/A - Commercial	Exploration	Identity	Tentative, Unsure	Sporadic puppet use throughout session.
Nick	7	M	Portuguese/ Puerto Rican	ADHD	1 year	1	Stuffed animal/3D Dragon puppet	Fabric	Mild	N/A - Commercial	Good versus Evil	Identity, Power & control	Cautious	
						2, 3, 4	*		N/A					
Francis	11	M	African American	Depression with AV & VH/ Anxiety/ PTSD	1 month	1, 2, 3, 4	*		N/A					

Lucia is artistic and imaginative. She fully engaged in the puppet making during the four-week process, animating the puppets and the materials. In Lucia's first session she chose to have the researcher help her affix fairy tale finger tattoos onto every finger, creating a personality for each one as it was adhered. Thus, a mixture of a tattoo puppet and multiple fingers puppet was created. Some of her characters, among others, included Shy, Sadness, a light-hearted princess named Flutter, a Frog who no one could get to know because he had no name, and a lonely misunderstood Witch. The intimacy of the finger puppets allowed the client to share deep feelings along with different aspects of herself, using the "glue" to literally affix these various images to her skin. Once affixed, all the puppets went behind the castle and spoke with each other quite fervently, in gibberish. There was an intimacy to the session and a level of autonomy. Lucia's language regressed and she did not clearly share what was happening behind the castle walls.

In the second session, Lucia chose to make a cookie cutter hand puppet and focused first on the head. She attached the felt pieces together with glue, and she also glued the sparkling sequin hair strips in multiple colors along the side of the puppet's face. Lucia worked with care and personified the sequin strips as she worked – one strip cried out that it was being hurt as it was being cut, and another was shy when it fell on the ground and somebody looked at it. Lucia drew the features on the face with fabric markers, converting an initial smile into fully closed lips. She shared with the researcher that the lips were glued shut from eating glue and that this was creating tornados in her lungs. The prominence of

Table 3b. PPTC: puppet usage/level of engagement

PARTICIPANT	AGE	SEX	SELF-IDENTIFIED ETHNICITY	DIAGNOSIS	TIME IN THERAPY PRIOR TO STUDY	WEEK #	TYPE OF PUPPETS	MATERIALS	LEVEL OF ENGAGEMENT WITH PUPPETS	METHOD OF CONSTRUCTION	SYMBOLISM/ METAPHOR	THEMES EXPRESSED	EMOTIONS EXPRESSED	OTHER NOTES
Lucia	8	F	Columbian/ Puerto Rican	Adjustment Disorder Conduct/ PTSD R/O	8 months	1	Attached tattoo fairy tale finger puppets onto each finger (both hands)	Temporary tattoo with glue, water	High	Glued	Naming (puppets)	Identity, Relationship, Attachment, Loneliness	Shy, Sad, Lonely, Cautious	Client personified each figure as it was affixed to her finger
						2	Created Cookie cutter hand puppet	Fabric, glue, sequin strings, fabric markers	High	Cut, glued	Secrets - "glued lips"	Sadness, Confusion, Secrecy	Hurt, Shy, Uneasy	Client animated materials as she created
						3	Created Cookie cutter hand puppet/ Researcher made girl hand puppet and snake sock puppet; and 3D/stuffed animal commercial hand puppets	Fabric	High	Cut, Sewn	Biting / Broken promises	Aggression (accompanied by excitement), Trickery, Betrayal, Lack of trust	Angry, Excited, Sad, Shy	Placed researcher made puppet in role of victim
						4	Created/completed Cookie cutter hand puppet/ Researcher made girl hand puppet	Fabric	High	Sewn	Relationship betrayals and reconnections.	Trust, Relationship, Violation, Protection/Safety, Aggression	Angry, Scared, Cautious	Played with kinetic sand between completing puppet and playing with it
Rey	9	M	Cuban/ Puerto Rican	ADHD/ PTSD	1 year	1	Giraffe 3D/stuffed animal puppet and giraffe finger puppet	Fabric	Moderate	N/A - Commercial	Relationships/ Being stuck	Abandonment, Relationship, Trapped, Loneliness, Betrayal	Upset, Lonely, Confused	Used sand tray figures in addition to puppets
						2	Owl 3D/stuffed animal puppet/ Created slime mask	Slime	Moderate	Sculpture	Exploring new perceptions	Abandonment, Relationship, Trapped, Aggression, Nurturing, Death	Worried, Confused	Client commented that looking through slime made things look different
						3	Shark 3D/stuffed animal puppet/ Created a wig	Fabric/ Yarn	High	Tied	Self-exploration	Abandonment, Adjustment/Change	Shy, Happy	Client transformed personality when he put on the wig
						4	Giraffe, Lion, Shark,, and Turtle 3D/stuffed animal puppets	Fabric	High	N/A - Commercial	Running away/Intense hunger	Aggression, Power & control, Confusion	Angry, Confused	Expressed anger through Shark/ Confusion with Turtle
Amy	6	F	Portuguese/ Dominican	Adjustment Disorder with Depression and Anxiety	1 year	1	*							
						2	Created finger puppet/ Researcher made finger puppet and Barbie doll	Fabric	High	Sewing, gluing	Superhero - Helping	Bullying, Protection	Upset, Relieved, Regretful (bully)	Client created mini "puppet show" about bullying
						3	Researcher made girl cookie cutter hand puppet/ Witch puppet. Elephant 3D/stuffed animal puppet, and Barbie dolls	Fabric	Moderate	N/A - Commercial	Relationship exploration - Nice versus Mean	Relationships, Anxiety, Identity	Angry, Misunderstood	Used puppets in pretend play and role play
						4	*							
Susan	9	F	Caucasian American	ADHD/ Adjustment Disorder with Mixed Mood	10 months	1	*		N/A					
						2	Created cookie cutter hand puppet	Fabric, thread	High	Sewing	Mother/Daughter Relationship	Identity, Self-empowerment	Calm, Content	Struggled somewhat with time commitment
						3	Created cookie cutter hand puppet / Dog 3D/stuffed animal puppet	Fabric, thread	High	Sewing	Mother/Daughter Relationship	Identity, Self-empowerment, Loyalty	Calm, Satisfied	
						4	Created cookie cutter hand puppet/ Researcher made snake puppets	Fabric, trim, thread	High	Sewing	Family relationships/ Limitations	Boundaries, limitations, anxiety	Worried, Unsure	
Joe	9	M	Cape Verdean	Mood Disorder NOS	1 week	1, 2, 3	*		N/A					
						4	3D/stuffed animal puppets and finger puppets	Fabric	Moderate	N/A - Commercial	Misbehavior & punishment/ Feeling trapped	Aggression/ Power & control	Angry, Overwhelmed	All of the puppets were angry and aggressive including friendly animal puppets
Tim	11	M	Caucasian American	Anxiety/ Mild Mental Retardation	8 months	1	*		N/A					
						2	Dragon, Dog, Giraffe, Turtle 3D/stuffed animal puppets	Fabric	High	N/A - Commercial	Puppets biting each other (hurt not dead)/ Treasure	Anger, Rejection, Loyalty, Attachment, Safety	Angry, Sad, Content	Found Dog puppet comforting
						3	Dog, Giraffe, Dragon, Shark, Turtle, Lion, Elephant 3D/stuffed animal puppets	Fabric	Moderate	N/A - Commercial	Good versus Evil	Identity, Relationship, Attachment	Embarrassed	Played with puppets first half of session
						4	*		N/A					
Jessica	9	F	Caucasian American	Adjustment Disorder with Depression and Anxiety	5 months	1	*		N/A					
						2	Dog, Giraffe, Dragon, Shark, Turtle, Lion, Elephant 3D/stuffed animal puppets/ Created finger puppet	Fabric, glue, glitter glue, feathers	High	Sewing, gluing	Exploration	Safety/ Relationship	Content	Client tried puppets on. She responded well to creative process and struggled to project onto puppets.
						3	*		N/A					
						4	Miscellaneous friendly finger puppets	Fabric	Moderate	N/A - Commercial	Playing store - The price of the relationship	Power & control/ Trust/ Relationship	Satisfied, Timid	
Samantha	14	F	Chose not to self-identify	Anxiety	7 months	1	*		N/A					
						2	Created Pig puppet	Fabric, thread	High	Sewing	Relationships & Identity	Identity	Satisfied, Content	Talked about tattoo she designed and wants to get at 18. "Listen to your heart" with an image of a heart & infinity sign
						3	Created Pig puppet and Puffball puppets/ Researcher made snake sock puppets	Fabric, thread	High	Sewing	Personifying comfort (puff ball puppets)/ Biting (snake)	Nurturing & Protection/ Aggression	Excited	Surrounded herself with puff ball puppets. This felt "safe". Pretended to bite researcher with snake puppet.
						4	*		N/A					

glue throughout this session repeats to some extent the stickiness of the first puppet session in conjunction with the speculation that Lucia has secrets she feels she can't share, even in play.

Lucia continued creating her puppet in the third session. She glued additional strands of sequin hair to her puppet and stated that she wanted legs on her puppet. Once the body and legs were cut, Lucia stopped making her puppet, and began playing with a researcher made cookie cutter girl puppet, and a commercially made stuffed snake puppet. The snake bit the girl puppet repeatedly so she needed to go to the doctor. The doctor was also the snake and bit her again. Additional animals became the doctor and each of them bit the girl puppet. In this session, the focus shifted from lips that were glued together to lips that bit. The stuffed animal/3D puppets were perpetrators but also provided a level of comfort. Their victim was a puppet made by the researcher, placing the researcher in the important role of understanding the child as victim.

Once her puppet was sewn together in the final session, Lucia was excited about having it play with the cookie cutter puppet created by the researcher. She stated that her puppet was going to be mean, and then they were going to become friends again. This was verbally relayed but not played out. Instead, Lucia started playing with kinetic sand and created a story about leprechauns whose world had been ripped apart. The leprechauns spoke angrily in a gibberish language and Lucia shared their anger and concerns with the researcher. She shared that they grouped together to hide and keep themselves safe, and then she showed the researcher the passageway into the mountain. Lucia said, "You have to be careful who you say things to". Then, animating her newly created puppet for the first time, it pulled the hair of the researcher's puppet. This scene is portrayed in Figure 2, which further provides an illustration of the degree of work that went into creating the puppet, and the size of the puppet's mouth that is "sealed tight".

In the final session, there was a return to gibberish but at this point Lucia was willing to translate for the researcher. The puppet play she proposed appeared to echo bullying situations that the client had experienced. It's possible that the puppets were not projective enough for a nine-year-old girl not to recognize the correlation with her own life. The story about the leprechauns was more fantastical and the story unfolded as she played with the sand. The play became small and intimate again as images were created in the sand, fingers were pushed through mountains to break them apart, and then pushed together again. Lucia continued to metaphorically and symbolically allude to unexpressed difficulties, victim and perpetrator, unspoken words, suppressed anger and hurt, and a need for trust. Her intimate play, especially the use of the snake and glue, conjointly with play prior to the study demonstrating aggressive bedroom activity, indicated the possibility of sexual abuse and highlighted the need for further investigation.

Case Vignette 2: Rey

Initially referred to the agency by his father for coping skills for ADHD, learning disorders, and behavioral outbursts, Rey, 9, truly needed a safe trusting environment to process feelings of grief and trauma. When this researcher started meeting with Rey, who is of Cuban and Puerto Rican descent, he lived with his father and fraternal twin brother. His father's girlfriend of 4 years had just left along with her two sons and a half-brother. This was Rey's second loss of a maternal figure and he was emotionally impacted by this departure. His father left his mother when Rey was four because she was addicted to drugs and the children have had no contact with her since that time.

Figure 2. Lucia's cookie cutter hand puppet

Rey loves animals, has positive peer relationships, and displays kindness and understanding to others. The researcher had been working with Rey for a year at the point of the pilot research project during which time he had been actively processing complicated grief, loss, and family dynamics using sand tray and play therapy applying primarily animals to represent significant people. About six months after the initial session, his father's girlfriend, stepbrothers, and half-brother rejoined the family, but Rey shared being worried that she'll leave again. Shortly after their return, his cat, which he loved dearly, was given away, adding another loss to his life.

During the research period, Rey continued his use of sand tray while also interspersing the use of puppets in his play. Rey's first session in the study involved simply putting on a large plush giraffe stuffed animal/3D puppet that he called the Mom, and a small giraffe finger puppet he called the baby. Setting the puppets aside, he picked up a large and small giraffe from the sand tray toys. He placed the plastic mother giraffe in the slime and had a baby plastic giraffe help it become unstuck so they could be together and free. Further themes of play in this session included feeling left out, hiding, not wanting to go home, and having his brothers and friends turn against him and bury him. He cried, "We're supposed to get along. We're supposed to be friends." Rey's need for nurturance with respect to the Mom was reflected in his use of the soft plush puppet. The finger puppet was smaller and had less ability to move. The switch to plastic figurines allowed for more direct communication and expressed a projection of the baby saving the mother instead of the other way around.

In the second session, Rey used a commercial stuffed animal/3D puppet that accompanied the plastic figurines, sand tray, and slime. The owl puppet trapped all the animals of various species when their parents were out getting food. He then trapped all the parents, caught them in poisoned slime, and killed and buried them. The kids were all worried about their parents when they didn't return but engaged in a game of hide and seek while they waited. A black horse arrived looking for its mother, and the horse's mother arrived shortly after that, and they were happy together. The other animal parents all returned, not dead after all, and were reunited with their children. "And everything was normal again", stated Rey. Rey then took the slime, put it on his face, poked holes in it, and exclaimed that he had made a mask. In this session, the stuffed animal was the perpetrator, not a comfort object. The loss of parents was felt by all of the children. The slime's stickiness correlates in many ways to glue. It poisoned the parents, but ultimately did not kill them, and became a temporary mask, not one tied on or attached to a stick, but literally affixed to Rey's skin.

Putting on the stuffed animal/3D shark puppet was how Rey started the third session. He opened the mouth a couple times but neither he nor the shark said anything. This session was the first departure from the themes of abandonment and reunification in a few months. Rey announced that he wanted to make a wig and he created one with long multicolored hair with some support from this researcher. The yarn was tied together, tying together different aspects of his life and more tightly securing the therapeutic alliance. Rey was excited when it was completed but seemed a bit shy when he first put it on. He shared that he was a girl named Emma who was 18 years old and loved animals. He picked up the soft plush dog puppet while wearing the Emma wig. The researcher asked if the dog had anything to say to Emma and the dog said, "I love you". Similar to a mask, although not covering the facial features, the wig allowed Rey to explore gender identity and other facets of his personality but it was much more vulnerable than a mask. That he felt safe to express another aspect of himself was conveyed through the words "I love you" by the soft comforting dog puppet. Despite the losses in his life, Rey appeared able to make attachments and was actively working through internal issues.

The final session during the research pilot project with Rey was significant because since the third session he had been told that his family was moving to another state at the end of the school year and he attempted to run away. Rey ventured out into a dangerous urban environment after ten o'clock at night with $9 and two bags filled with clothes, books, stuffed animals, and a cat dish. Luckily, a shopkeeper who knew the family saw Rey and called the police, who brought him safely home. Rey shared verbally some of what occurred and then switched to play. He played primarily with the commercially made stuffed animal/3D puppets. He started with a lion and a giraffe and directed the researcher to be the giraffe and try to run away. Then he grabbed the shark puppet who was really angry and started eating all of the other puppets. He had difficulty owning his feelings of anger and allowed the shark to express his frustration and rage. At the end of the session, Rey took a turtle puppet and tossed it off the table and onto the floor saying, "The turtle jumped in the deep end but he doesn't know how to swim". This is an apt metaphor given his recent runaway attempt. Rey also asked the researcher to walk him back to his classroom after the session, something he hadn't done in a few months. The soft stuffed animal puppets seemed necessary to appease his anger, fear, and need for comfort in a way the plastic animals and sand tray were too structured and rigid to allow.

Case Vignette 3: Mariah

Mariah, 7, is of African American and Haitian decent. Although reports from the client's mother included obstinance and refusal to cooperate, there were fewer concerns reported by the school. Mariah is diagnosed with anxiety and exhibits a great deal of anxiety and worry both at home and school. Her struggles with emotional control are more prominent at home. Mariah lives with her mother and six siblings, of whom she is the second youngest. She lived with both of her parents at the start of our work together, 11 months prior to the onset of the pilot study, but her father left the family to live with his girlfriend 6 months ago. Mariah stills sees him occasionally and shares that she has a difficult relationship with her mother who she feels does not understand her. Mariah is kind, thoughtful, highly imaginative, and tries hard to please.

Mariah was very excited about the idea of puppets at the initial session of the project and asked if we could create kitten masks. Mariah was insistent that this researcher should have a mask as well so two kitten masks were created on paper, painted with a thin layer of paint, and cut out. Mariah and this researcher both donned the masks during the next session using ribbon to tie the masks on. Mariah wrote and illustrated a story about the 2 kittens, a baby kitten that had her name, and a mama kitten, who often didn't believe or trust the baby kitten. Both of them were trying to escape from foxes and were ultimately victorious. Paper was a good material for Mariah since the project could be more quickly completed. The wearing of the mask allowed her to enter a different world that paralleled her relationship with her mother. Despite the simplicity of the masks, illustrated in Figure 3, the creation of them gleaned substantial information and provided more depth than ready-made masks. In addition, the therapeutic alliance was enhanced through the process of creating masks together.

During the third session Mariah initially stated that she wanted to make a puppet but instead she started playing. She commenced play with a little finger puppet made by this researcher that she called "Mr. Office" and added a multitude of finger puppets, hand puppets, and other items to her play. A witch commanded the rubber monster finger puppets to freeze the good puppets. Mariah put on all the rubber monster finger puppets to obey the command but hastily took them off, visibly and audibly disturbed by wearing them. Good and evil battled, with good being ultimately victorious, and the rubber monster

Figure 3. Mariah's kitten masks

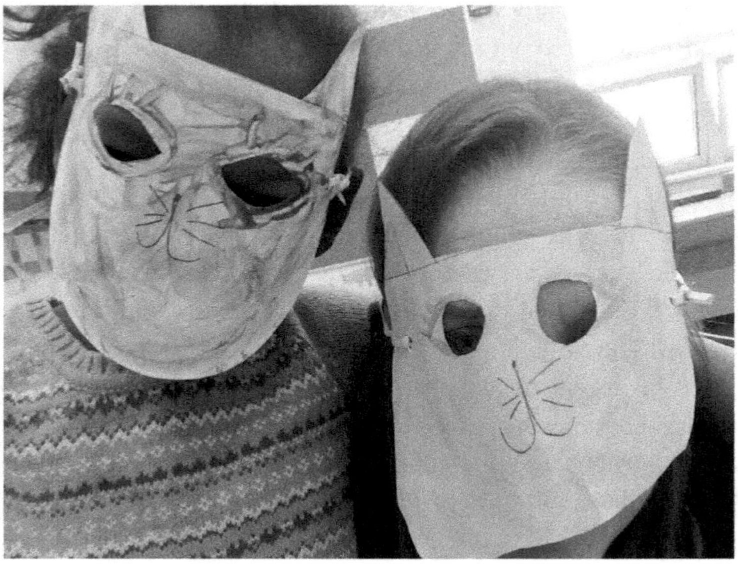

finger puppets were locked in in a small box with a note saying, "Do not open the evil box". Mariah asked for help to place the monsters in the box because she didn't want to touch them at all as the session progressed. She did not have any issues placing the soft evil witch puppet in the box with them. This speaks directly to the impact of the materials on the psyche.

The final session returned to the story Mariah had written. She wanted to read it aloud to this researcher and turn it into a book. She said she wished her mother understood her and asked if we could share the story with her.

RESULTS

Participant Engagement

The opportunity to create and use puppets was offered to the clients during the research period, but participation was not required. In the pilot study 85% of the clients, or 17 out of 20, engaged in playing with or creating puppets, including 77%, 10 out of 13, of the boys and 100%, 7 out of 7, of the girls. The level of engagement in the puppet play ranged from mild (5%) to moderate (27%) to high involvement (68%). Gender and developmental level appeared significant in the utilization of and creation of puppets. All of the girls in the study created their own puppets and also used the puppets provided. In contrast, only two boys created their own puppets; most of the boys used the ready-made puppets instead. 95% of participants who engaged in puppet making had high levels of engagement in the process. Three boys, two of whom were aged 10 or older, chose not to create or use puppets when offered. Participants often combined playing with available puppets while creating their own.

Reflection of Feelings

Reflected feelings were noted and analyzed by intensity of emotion and counted once per session regardless of the number of times the feeling was expressed. Anger, sadness, happiness, fear, and shame were the main emotions explored with variations within each marked as high, medium, or low intensity feelings. In the pilot study, 30% of the emotions were happy although 82% of these were medium and low intensity feelings such as satisfied and content, 22% were afraid, 21% were angry, 20% were sad, and 7% were ashamed.

Emerging Themes

In the context of this pilot exploration of the PPTC, themes of aggression, love/attachment, and identity/relationship issues emerged which correlated with some of the main clinical issues proposed by the authors. Aggression was the most prominent at 32% including themes of trickery, betrayal, and power and control. Aggression was expressed through the puppets by children with a range of diagnoses from ADHD to Anxiety to PTSD. The combined themes of relationships, love/attachment, and protection/safety was 29% showing an almost equal need to feel safe, secure, and accepted. Identity and relationship issues were 26% and included issues of loneliness and abandonment. Other common themes included fear and danger (8%), boundaries and limitations (2%), self-empowerment (2%), and secrecy (1%).

Each of the case studies explored themes of aggression and love/attachment, which are common concerns in clinical situations. Summaries of themes within the case studies are presented to better understand the exploration of the PPTC and the impact of materials on client expression and presentation.

Lucia started with naming and acknowledging different aspects of herself in the first puppet session. She moved to explore relationships and attachment both with the therapist and with someone else in her life using glue as a prominent feature. By creating a cookie cutter hand puppet, she explored the "norm" or what is expected of her from others. During this process, one string cried out that it was being hurt, thereby revealing that a part of her is hurting. This is followed by a string that was shy, which reflects a level of secrecy inherent in her sharing. Using the fabric markers, Lucia shows how she is trying to contain her thoughts and feelings within by drawing a large mouth whose lips are tightly sealed. Aggression is shown through the snake persona biting others.

Rey used the sticky substance of slime to echo attachment issues that are embodied and enmeshed. Dealing with themes of abandonment and loss, he also explores aggression and the need for love and protection. Exploring the concepts of desire and reality, using the wig as mask, he portrays inner desires and gender confusion.

Mariah opted for the flexibility and ease of paper in the creation of her mask that led to a story filled with trickery and traps that explored her relationship with her mother. Aggression was expressed through the story, as was the battle of good versus evil between "Mr. Office" and the Witch. The rubber monster finger puppets shared a level of aggression with her to the point that she had difficulty putting them on after they obeyed the evil wishes of the witch, desiring to distance herself from her aggressive thoughts and behaviors.

DISCUSSION

Concept of Puppetry

Puppets are powerful play tools, expressing the real emotions and behaviors of the client behind a projected story. The clients exhibited the ability to express a multitude of emotions, issues, and behavioral concerns through the puppets. Content and feelings were immediately revealed through the engagement with the puppets. In all of the case vignettes presented, collectively with those explored through the study, an expression of feelings and exploration of deeper issues was revealed. The creation and engagement with puppets sparked the imagination of the participants and allowed them to safely project thoughts and emotions. Genuine communication transpired as a result of the accessible and non-threatening nature of the puppets, deepening the therapeutic connection and allowing the therapist clearer insight into the client's perspective and true behaviors.

The Making of Puppetry

The shape, role, or structural components of the puppets examines different explorations of client issues. For clients that exhibit mood disorders, or anxiety or depressive disorders, the choice of specifically made play therapy objects are designed to emphasize different aspects of the animated interactive therapeutic tool. The manner in which puppets are made parallels the process of the therapeutic relationship. The clients in the study sometimes explored the idea of puppet beyond the PPTC created by the authors. Rey interspersed the use of puppets and sand tray miniatures showing fluidity between forms of play. He created variations on the extensive list of puppets provided in the PPTC – a mask made of slime, and a wig, which transformed him from male to female. Themes of unresolved grief, abandonment, separation from parents, and seeking to integrate aspects of himself and those around him were evident in the play.

Many of the participants in the pilot research project were in the working stage of therapy and had been working with this researcher for months prior to the introduction to puppet making. Commercially made finger puppets and hand puppets had been available prior to the study. However, puppets were used more extensively once the pilot study began and puppet making materials and puppets created by the therapist were provided. A few of the participants created simple finger puppets. Most made cookie cutter hand puppets, personifying themselves through their creations. More complex than finger puppets, these puppets required multiple sessions to complete. This involved patience and learning a skill, thus enhancing personal agency. More peripheral discussions occurred as a result that also provided insight into client behaviors. The therapeutic alliance was deepened through gluing, sewing, and creating the puppets.

Impact of Materials

The impact of materials chosen differed between individuals and had different metaphoric meaning. The participants' use of materials included yarn, fabric, paper, slime, felt, and feathers, among others. As seen in Lucia's case vignette, glue was a prominent metaphoric feature, literally exposing the "stickiness" or complexities within her significant relationships. Sticky and non-permanent, glue was used not only to create the puppet, but also the concept of glue was echoed in Lucia's words regarding her puppet whose lips had been glued shut. Lucia expressed a need to keep her mouth glued shut, even in play. Another theme in her puppet play was that her puppets often communicated with each other using gibberish, another way of holding secrets inside. It was not until the final session that the client, acting as translator, interpreted some of the gibberish for the therapist, and relayed concerns of safety along with providing a clue to the issues that had been buried deep within.

Mariah utilized both cognitive and emotional elements through the process of her "puppets". The use of paper to create the masks allowed for a quick expression of the form. Painting the mask helped her access her emotions more easily, and wearing the mask helped provide access to a deeper story that echoed her maternal relationship.

Many of the materials and types of puppets the authors presented were not utilized or created by the participants in the study. With the exception of the slime mask, the paper tied on mask, and the wig, the majority of created puppets were the cookie cutter type and a few simple finger puppets. Other puppets, such as marionettes, were not created during the pilot study although materials were available to do so. Perhaps they required more instruction and level of mastery and there wasn't significant time available. Given more time with the children and a more structured study, it is possible that a greater range of puppets would have been created.

Limitations

The expanded range of therapeutic applications in puppetry focused on the therapeutic application of commercial and self-made objects along the designed PPTC and client led projections. The authors are focusing on the visual perspectives and the value of the relationship in knowing more about the process of integrating art, image making and symbolic representations under a spontaneous application. The PPTC is presented predominantly as a concept to be further considered and explored. For the purposes of this chapter, the authors do not highlight the value of the separate therapeutic disciplines, each of which has separate modality integrity. In addition, the authors only lightly explore the use of puppetry in drama therapy, as puppetry has traditionally been viewed under the umbrella of theatre, drama therapy, and psychodrama.

Limitations in the pilot study include the small sample size with primarily low-income minority clients, many of whom were in the working through stage of therapy at the time of the study. Ideally, a larger sample size with clients in various stages of therapy would yield a broader understanding of the PPTC. In addition, more than half of the clients are either Hispanic or African American and the researcher is a middle-aged Caucasian woman of Italian descent. As a result, the authors are aware of and responded to the need for multicultural competencies although these issues are not addressed within the chapter.

RECOMMENDATIONS

The pilot research study recognized the value of puppets and use of puppets to enhance the therapeutic relationship. The creation of the pilot research study and framework of the PPTC yielded higher participation with the children than previously observed. Puppetry is a creative response and 85% of the participants engaged to some extent in the study. Claymation, and film animation puppetry are elements of puppetry that may be able to reach more gender/developmental issues especially with older boys who were primarily the ones who did not participate.

Additional studies are recommended to allow for a greater understanding of the potentials of the PPTC. The pilot research study had a small number of participants, a short research period, and was primarily non-directive. As a result, only a small portion of the different types of puppets, puppet construction, and materials could be examined with respect to metaphoric and symbolic content. It would be beneficial to extend the time frame and create a more directive study to allow for the creation of a broader range of the puppets on the PPTC. In addition, studies exploring the creation of puppets with children who have similar diagnoses would provide a more complete comparison of the impact of the PPTC. This could be examined through individual sessions or small groups.

FUTURE RESEARCH DIRECTIONS

The proposed PPTC pilot research project barely scratched the surface of the potential of the concept. The framework creates a powerful tool to continue to explore in the context of art and play therapy. A larger sample size would be needed to generate a fuller understanding of the PPTC. It would be important to track the physicality of the form compared to the communication it evokes. A tracking instrument, such as the sample chart provided (Table 4), would be important to indicate the different puppet types, levels of engagement, construction methods, materials used, and themes that emerged. In the pilot pro-

Table 4. PPTC: session chart per week

PARTICIPANT	AGE	SEX	ETHNICITY	DIAGNOSIS	TYPE OF PUPPET	MATERIALS	LEVEL OF ENGAGEMENT	METHOD OF CONSTRUCTION	SYMBOLISM/ METAPHOR	THEMES	EMOTIONS	OTHER NOTES

gram, themes emerged such as aggression and love/attachment. Further research could also narrow the implications of the PPTC of specific body parts to a focused exploration.

Future research should provide a longer research period as a result of the amount of time needed for clients to create puppets. In the authors' viewpoint, therapists are encouraged to create the various puppets on the PPTC to understand the complexity and metaphysical value of different categories and material choice. The creation of puppets should also be explored with respect to specific diagnoses, different stages of the therapeutic relationship, and a smaller age range in order to yield more comparable results. Another interesting study would be to compare individuals with access to both commercially made puppets and puppet making materials versus individuals with access solely to commercially made products.

CONCLUSION

Exploring the PPTC of puppet type, construction process, materials, and symbolic and metaphoric meaning, the process of making puppets deepened the quality of the working through process, slowing things down to say more. The proposed PPTC allowed for the expansion of opportunities within play therapy by providing a framework that considered physicality as a key element. Integrating art materials and play objects expanded the language of play and deepened the therapeutic connection. Expression was communicated at multiple levels through the creation of the puppets, the animation of the created or ready-made puppet, and through the story/metaphor conveyed by the puppet. A broader repertoire of projected behaviors and stories helped the researcher more deeply understand the client. Although additional research is needed to explore this concept more fully, the brief study of the PPTC helped provide a more empathic stance, improving interpersonal dynamics, and enhancing the therapeutic relationship.

REFERENCES

Ackerman, T. (2005). The puppet as a metaphor. In M. Bernier & J. O'Hare (Eds.), *Puppetry in education and therapy* (pp. 5–11). Bloomington, IL: Authorhouse.

Axline, V. M. (1969). *Play therapy*. New York, NY: Houghton Mifflin Company.

Baird, B. (1965). *The art of the puppet*. New York, NY: The Macmillan Company.

Bernier, M. (2005a). Introduction to puppetry in therapy. In M. Bernier & J. O'Hare (Eds.), *Puppetry in education and therapy* (pp. 109–115). Bloomington, IL: Authorhouse.

Bernier, M. (2005b). Psychopuppetry: Animated symbols in therapy. In M. Bernier & J. O'Hare (Eds.), *Puppetry in education and therapy* (pp. 125–133). Bloomington, IL: Authorhouse.

Bratton, S. C., Ceballos, P. L., & Ferebee, K. W. (2009). Integration of structured expressive activities within a humanistic group play therapy format for preadolescents. *Journal for Specialists in Group Work*, *34*(3), 251–275. doi:10.1080/01933920903033487

Bromfield, R. (1995). The use of puppets in play therapy. *Child & Adolescent Social Work Journal*, *12*(6), 435–444. doi:10.1007/BF01875812

Burneikaite, S. (2009). Possibilities of puppet therapy and their use in puppeteers projects. *Socialinis Ugdymas*, *7*(18), 112–122.

Byers, J. (2013). Integrating play and expressive art therapy into communities: A multimodal approach. In E. J. Green & A. A. Drewes (Eds.), *Integrating expressive arts and play therapy with children and adolescents* (pp. 283–301). Somerset, NJ: John Wiley & Sons.

Byers, J. G. (2016). Expressive arts in play therapy. In K. J. O'Connor, C. E. Schaefer, & L. D. Braverman (Eds.), *Handbook of Play Therapy* (pp. 277–288). Hoboken, NJ: John Wiley & Sons.

Carter, R. B., & Mason, P. S. (1998). The selection and use of puppets in counseling. *Professional School Counseling*, *1*(5), 1–13.

Dhaese, M. (2011). Holistic Expressive Play Therapy: An integrative approach to helping maltreated children. In A. A. Drewes, S. C. Bratton, & C. E. Schaefer (Eds.), *Integrative play therapy* (pp. 75–93). Hoboken, NJ: John Wiley & Sons Inc.; doi:10.1002/9781118094792.ch5

Fenner, L. B. (2016). Constructing the self: Three-dimensional form. In D. E. Gussak & M. L. Rosal (Eds.), *The Wiley handbook of art therapy* (pp. 154–162). Chichester, UK: John Wiley & Sons, Ltd.

Gerity, L. (2005). Trauma, puppet making, and narrative: Creating moments of reprieve. In M. Bernier & J. O'Hare (Eds.), *Puppetry in education and therapy* (pp. 139–146). Bloomington, IL: Authorhouse.

Hartwig, E. K. (2014). Puppets in the playroom: Utilizing puppets and child-centered facilitative skills as a metaphor for healing. *International Journal of Play Therapy*, *23*(4), 204–216. doi:10.1037/a0038054

Hinz, L. D. (2009). *Expressive therapies continuum: A framework for using art in therapy*. New York, NY: Routledge.

Hinz, L. D. (2016). Media considerations in art therapy: Directions for future research. In D. E. Gussak & M. L. Rosal (Eds.), *The Wiley handbook of art therapy* (pp. 135–145). Chichester, UK: John Wiley & Sons, Ltd.

Irwin, E. C. (2002). Using puppets for assessment. In C. E. Schaefer & D. Cangelosi (Eds.), *Play therapy techniques* (2nd ed., pp. 101–113). Lanham, MD: Jason Aronson.

Ivon, H. (2014). Features of children's play and developmental possibilities of symbolic puppet play. *Croatian Journal Educational / Hrvatski Casopis Za Odgoj I Obrazovanje, 16,* 161-180.

Jenkins, R. L., & Beckh, E. (2002). Finger puppets and mask making. In C. E. Schaefer & D. Cangelosi (Eds.), *Play therapy techniques* (2nd ed.; pp. 115–122). Lanham, MD: Jason Aronson.

Knill, P. J. (1994). Multiplicity as a tradition: Theories for interdisciplinary arts therapies – An overview. *The Arts in Psychotherapy*, *21*(5), 319–328. doi:10.1016/0197-4556(94)90059-0

Knill, P. J. (2005). Foundations for a theory of practice. In P. J. Knill, E. G. Levine, & S. K. Levine (Eds.), *Principles and practice of expressive arts therapy: Toward a therapeutic aesthetics* (pp. 75–170). Philadelphia, PA: Jessica Kingsley Publishers.

Kottman, T. (2011). *Play therapy: Basics and beyond* (2nd ed.). Alexandria, VA: American Counseling Association.

Landreth, G. L. (2012). *Play therapy: The art of relationship* (3rd ed.). New York, NY: Routledge.

Lebedeva, L. (2012). Animated treatment: The method of art therapy used with children having communication problems. *Social Welfare Interdisciplinary Approach*, *2*(1), 123–130.

Malchiodi, C. A. (2002). *The Soul's palette: Drawing on art's transformative powers for health and well-being*. Boston, MA: Shambhala.

Malchiodi, C. A. (Ed.). (2005). *Expressive therapies*. New York, NY: Guilford Press.

Malchiodi, C. A. (2007). *The art therapy sourcebook*. New York, NY: McGraw Hill.

Mezirow, J. (1995). Transformation Theory of Adult Learning. In M. R. Welton (Ed.), *In defense of the lifeworld* (pp. 39–70). New York, NY: SUNY Press.

Moon, B. L. (2007). *The role of metaphor in art therapy: Theory, method, and experience*. Springfield, IL: Charles C Thomas Publisher.

Moon, C. H. (2010). *Materials & media in art therapy: Critical understandings of diverse artistic vocabularies*. New York, NY: Taylor and Francis.

Moustakas, C. E. (1959). *Psychotherapy with children: The living relationship*. Greeley, CO: Carron Publishers.

Oaklander, V. (2007). *Windows to our children*. Gouldsboro, ME: The Gestalt Journal Press.

Robbins, A. (1994). *A multi-modal approach to creative art therapy*. Bristol, PA: Jessica Kingsley Publishers.

Rogers, N. (1993). *The creative connection: Expressive arts as healing*. Palo Alto, CA: Science & Behavior Books, Inc.

Rubin, J. A. (2010). *Introduction to art therapy: Sources & resources*. New York, NY: Taylor & Francis Group.

Rubin, J. A. (2011). *The art of art therapy: What every art therapist needs to know* (2nd ed.). New York, NY: Routledge.

Steinhardt, L. (1994). Creating the autonomous image through puppet theatre and art therapy. *The Arts in Psychotherapy*, *21*(3), 205–218. doi:10.1016/0197-4556(94)90050-7

Winnicott, D. W. (1971). *Playing and reality*. London: Tavistock Publications.

Chapter 11
Studying the Effectiveness of the Storytelling/Story-Acting (STSA) Play Intervention on Ugandan Preschoolers' Emergent Literacy, Oral Language, and Theory of Mind in Two Rural Ugandan Community Libraries

Geoff Goodman
Long Island University, USA

Valeda F. Dent
Long Island University, USA

ABSTRACT

This study explored the impact of two rural village libraries in Uganda on preschool children's school readiness skills. Using two rural village libraries in Mpigi and Kabubbu as a backdrop, this study explored the effectiveness of a six-month play-based intervention known as the Storytelling/Story-Acting (STSA) activity. Children ages 3 to 5 at each library were randomly assigned to participate in either the STSA play intervention (n = 63) or a story-reading activity (n = 60) for one hour twice per week for six months. All children were administered school readiness skills measures before and after the six-month intervention. Caregivers were also administered an interview that assessed their educational level, quality of life, reading aloud to target child, social support, and total possessions. Children who participated in the STSA intervention had higher scores on the colors subtest of the emergent literacy measure than children who did not participate in this activity. Preschool children benefit from a story-reading activity with or without the STSA play intervention.

DOI: 10.4018/978-1-5225-2224-9.ch011

INTRODUCTION

Children in the developing world are at far greater risk for all sorts of emotional, psychological, and health challenges; at the same time, they have little access to therapy, clinical interventions, and other types of support services. There are precious few resources, so traditional approaches to play therapy that might include toys and other props are not available. The intervention presented in this study is a low-cost, play-based intervention that we believed could help to address some early learning and developmental challenges using the child's natural inclination toward flexing his or her imagination and play muscles. The intervention also builds on the local practice of oral storytelling. We believe that play therapists, educators, and philanthropic foundations in the West need to be aware of these efforts to improve the socioemotional, educational, and financial well-being of sub-Saharan African preschool children. Perhaps this study will inspire others to implement play-based interventions in rural village libraries and schools in Uganda and other sub-Saharan African countries to produce a dramatic difference in the lives of these preschool children as well as their families and communities.

One of the legacies of colonialism on the African continent is the widespread illiteracy and entrenched poverty that interfere with its people's full participation in the global economy. A historical snapshot illustrates the scope of the problem: as of March, 2014, 38% of all Africans were illiterate (United Nations Educational, Scientific and Cultural Organization [UNESCO], 2014). Africa is also the poorest region in the world and the only major developing region with negative growth in income per capita during 1980 to 2000 (Sachs et al., 2004). In sub-Saharan Africa, the per capita gross domestic product is less than it was in 1974 (Artadi & Sala-i-Martin, 2003), and recently, the average per capita income declined from \$608 to \$556 (Lakner & Milanovic, 2015). The average life expectancy is 59 years (World Bank Sub-Saharan Africa Statistics, 2014), while the average child mortality rate (deaths before the age of 5 per 1,000 live births) is 92 (You, Hug, & Chen, 2014). Improvement in the literacy rate could provide the necessary conditions for an economic renaissance in Africa through mass dissemination of information that people could then use to produce goods and services in demand in other parts of Africa and overseas (Dent, 2007). The role of literacy in the functioning of the democratic process has also been noted (Kranich, 2001; Stilwell, 1989, 1991).

Uganda is a sub-Saharan landlocked country enduring the same struggles as its African neighbors. With a population of 37 million (World Bank Country Statistics, 2014), Uganda's literacy rate is 86% for men (World Bank Literacy Indicators Male, 2014) and 62% for women (World Bank Literacy Indicators Female, 2014). The average life expectancy is 58 years (World Bank Country Statistics, 2014), and the scourge of AIDS orphaned more than 1 million children in the 1990s alone (World Bank, 2014). Eighty-eight percent of the population live in rural villages and earn an average daily wage of 77¢ (Dent, 2006, 2007). Having gained independence from Great Britain in 1962, Uganda is ranked 163rd out of 188 countries on the Human Development Index (Human Development Reports, 2014). Since coming to power in 1987, the current Ugandan government has attempted to redress illiteracy and its devastating effects by instituting the policies of universal primary education in 1997 and universal secondary education in 2007 (Parry, 2007, 2014). These policies seem to be bearing early fruit; the current literacy rate for young adults is approximately 10% higher than for older adults (UNESCO, 2007).

School Readiness Skills

The goal of this study is to improve Ugandan preschool children's school readiness skills, which would logically improve the literacy rate and, in turn, improve the economic outlook of this developing country (for a broader overview of this project, see Dent, Goodman, & Kevane, 2014). School readiness skills have been defined as skills that adequately prepare children for academic success, which obviously includes literacy acquisition (Kagan & Lowenstein, 2004). Assessing school readiness skills poses challenges for the researcher. The child's nascent linguistic and cognitive abilities necessitate adopting creative methods to discover a child's readiness for school-based learning. Nicolopoulou and her colleagues (Nicolopoulou, de Sá, Ilgaz, & Brockmeyer, 2010; Nicolopoulou, Schnabel Cortina, Ilgaz, Brockmeyer Cates, & de Sá, 2015) have identified three broad domains of school readiness that collectively reflect a child's confident exploration of the environment: 1) emergent literacy skills, 2) oral language skills, and 3) social competence (specifically, theory of mind skills). Instruments have been developed to assess each of these domains in preschool children. These instruments have then been used to assess the effectiveness of preschool intervention programs designed to facilitate linguistic development and literacy acquisition (e.g., Barnett et al., 2008; Nicolopoulou & Cole, 2010; Nicolopoulou et al., 2015; Zigler, Singer, & Bishop-Josef, 2004). These three domains of school readiness represent the outcome variables.

Emergent Literacy

This domain reflects the skills required by preschool children to begin the process of reading words. These skills include but are not limited to having a receptive knowledge of colors, letters, numbers and counting, sizes and comparisons, shapes, and words. Any assessment of emergent literacy in preschool children would include these basic skills because reading consists of recognizing letters and numbers and putting them together into words already known to the child. Emergent literacy seems to be a necessary but not sufficient condition for the development of later forms of literacy (Adams, 1990; Catts, Fey, Zhang, & Tomblin, 1999; Dickinson & Neuman, 2006; Hecht, Burgess, Torgesen, Wagner, & Rachotte, 2000; Pullen & Justice, 2003; Storch & Whitehurst, 2002; Whitehurst & Lonigan, 2001). Emergent literacy is necessarily transmitted within a context of human relationships and narrative activities that provide meaning to these foundational skills.

Oral Language Skills

This domain reflects the skills required to comprehend stories. The mastery of oral language is crucial to school readiness because it contributes to emergent literacy and later reading development (e.g., Snow, 1991; Snow & Dickinson, 1990, 1991; Wells, 1985, 1986; Westby, 1991). Oral language skills occupy a continuum, which ranges from listening to and comprehending oral and written stories, to telling stories embedded in the child's surrounding context such as enactments with characters (e.g., doll play) or visual aids (e.g., picture sequences), to telling spontaneously generated stories. In young children whose symbolic capacities are just coming online, external verbal and nonverbal cues are required to contextualize their stories. We used a measure of receptive vocabulary skills as a proxy for oral language skills.

Social Competence

This domain reflects the skills required to understand social interactions and to regulate one's own behavior, attention, and emotions. Social competence plays a key role in the development of school readiness skills because social interactions both facilitate and promote cognitive development, learning, and academic success (Blair et al., 2007; Bronson, 2000; Coolahan, Fantuzzo, Mendez, & McDemott, 2000; Fantuzzo, Sekino, & Cohen, 2004; Raver, Garner, & Smith-Donald, 2007). Classroom learning requires children to attend to the information presented by the teacher. Children need to regulate their attention, emotions, and behavior to retain this information and acquire school-based skills such as reading, writing, and arithmetic. Children also need to develop theories about the intentions and feelings of their teachers, classmates, and themselves. Verbal communication depends on one's understanding of the mental states of others—what they know and do not know about what one knows. Understanding social interactions provides a necessary context for learning, not only in the classroom but also in children's peer groups. Without this understanding, children might avoid social interactions and therefore lose the benefits of pretend play experiences provided by the peer group. These benefits include the development of symbolic capacities required for reading and writing and the construction of a shared set of rules of peer-group engagement (Nicolopoulou et al., 2015). We used theory of mind skills as a proxy for social competence.

Caregiver Influences on School Readiness Skills

Caregivers play a monumental role in their children's development of school readiness skills. For example, a caregiver's verbal responsiveness to a child's gestures, communication, or other initiation of communication influences the child's development of oral language skills (Tamis-LeMonda, Bornstein, & Baumwell, 2001). A caregiver's use of words to describe the infant's and young child's mental states also predicts later theory of mind and oral language skills (Meins et al., 2002). We were interested in exploring whether five caregiver variables would moderate the relation between the STSA play intervention and the three child outcome variables: 1) Educational Level, 2) Quality of Life, 3) Reading Aloud to Target Child, 4) Social Support, and 5) Total Possessions. Each of these caregiver variables has support in the literature for its potential impact on the development of school readiness skills.

Educational Level

A caregiver's educational level impacts the child's school readiness skills, probably because educational level is associated with a wider vocabulary, which in turn is associated with exposure to more words. By age 4, children of professional caregivers hear about four times the total number of words as children whose caregivers receive welfare benefits (Hart & Risley, 1999). Unsurprisingly, caregiver's educational level also predicts school readiness (Quirk, Mayworm, Furlong, Grimm, & Rebelez, 2015), reading trajectories (Aikens & Barbarin, 2008), and academic and behavioral outcomes (Ferguson, Jimerson, & Dalton, 2001). This association between caregiver educational level and school readiness skills holds across cultures: caregivers' educational and vocabulary levels accounted for their children's vocabulary levels and cognitive development in general in Ecuador (Schady, 2011) and reading achievement in South Africa (Hungi & Thuku, 2010).

Quality of Life

Caregivers whose basic physical health is compromised cannot provide a secure base for their children to rely on during anxiety-provoking situations. In Uganda, where the average life expectancy is 48 years, and the scourge of AIDS has orphaned 940,000 children (Dent, 2006, 2007), caregiver health is often severely compromised. In their study conducted in Kampala, Uganda, Nuwagaba-Biribonwoha and her colleagues (Nuwagaba-Biribonwoha, Mayon-White, Okong, Carpenter, & Jenkinson, 2006) found that pregnant HIV-positive women scored significantly lower than pregnant HIV-negative women on the dimensions of Feelings, Daily Activities, Pain, Overall Health, and Quality of Life. In addition, pregnant HIV-positive women have a 70% higher likelihood of having major morbidity than pregnant HIV-negative women (Nuwagaba-Biribonwoha, Mayon-White, Okong, Brocklehurst, & Carpenter, 2012). HIV, malaria, and malnutrition seem to be a way of life for many Ugandans. The effect of Ugandan caregivers' health on their children's development, however, is poorly understood. Other family members assume the primary caregiving role when the initial primary caregiver is no longer able to complete the caregiving responsibilities. In the current study, some grandmothers as well as four fathers had assumed the primary caregiving role for the target child.

Adverse childhood experiences such as abuse and household dysfunction are known to have debilitating effects on adults' physical health (Felitti et al., 1998), and recent evidence suggests that these same adverse childhood experiences also impact children's well-being such as obesity and learning and behavioral problems (Burke, Hellman, Scott, Weems, & Carrion, 2011). It seems plausible to suggest that caregivers' quality of life would not only reflect an exposure to some of these same adverse childhood experiences but also pose a risk for their children's well-being, which in turn would impact on their development of school readiness skills.

Social Support

A caregiver's social support is expected to be associated with the child's school readiness skills. Social support has been associated with more emotionally responsive parenting and more favorable child health and developmental outcomes (Oyserman, Bybee, Mowbray, & MacFarlane, 2002; Sheppard, 2009; Simons, Beaman, Conger, & Chao, 1993). Crockenberg (1981) found that caregiver social support moderated the relation between infant irritability and anxious-resistant attachment at 12 months, which in turn has been shown to predict early school performance (Sroufe, Egeland, Carlson, & Collins, 2005).

Total Possessions

A caregiver's total possessions impact the child's school readiness skills in some of the same ways that educational level does (Aber, Jones, & Cohen, 2000). For example, household income was conflated with educational level when Hart and Risley (1999) discovered that by age 4, children of professional caregivers hear about four times the total number of words as children whose caregivers receive welfare benefits. Caregiver total possessions also predict school readiness (Quirk et al., 2015), reading trajectories (Aikens & Barbarin, 2008), and academic and behavioral outcomes (Ferguson et al., 2001). More possessions might also reflect a less stressful, more harmonious household environment that facilitates a higher level of attention paid to conversational discourse and thus greater absorption of school readiness skills from caregivers as well as the preschool environment.

Patterns of Caregiver Reading Aloud to the Child

The developmental researcher Meins (1997) has investigated specific aspects of caregiver sensitivity responsible for promoting both secure attachment and early linguistic capabilities in young children. Mothers of securely attached infants were more likely to treat their 19-month-olds' vocal utterances as meaningful than mothers of insecurely attached infants. She used this finding to account for the significant correlation of $r = .28$ between attachment and language development found in a meta-analysis (van IJzendoorn, Dijkstra, & Bus, 1995). Meins's (1997) research is consistent with other studies (e.g., Fonagy & Target, 2005; Meins, Fernyhough, Russell, & Clark-Carter, 1998; Slade, Grienenberger, Bernbach, Levy, & Locker, 2005) that suggest that a caregiver's treatment of a child as a thinking, feeling, desiring agent—in other words, a person possessing a mind—is associated with children's attachment security and predicts later indices of socioemotional competence. Notably, the children in Meins's (1997) study could not have cognitively understood their mothers' verbal responses to them because of their limited receptive vocabularies but rather probably experienced the accompanying affective communication as subjective evidence that their mothers were understanding their needs (see also Grienenberger, Kelly, & Slade, 2005). These mentalizing (Fonagy, Gergely, Jurist, & Target, 2002) interactions between mother and child serve to stretch the child's linguistic capabilities (Belsky & Fearon, 2002). By ages 4 to 6, exposure to stories read aloud predicts theory of mind skills (Mar, Tackett, & Moore, 2010).

We are suggesting that a caregiver's reading aloud to her child will facilitate that caregiver's treatment of her child as a mentalizing agent, which in turn will foster the child's theory of mind skills. In other words, reading aloud to a child provides an ideal opportunity for a caregiver to communicate her sensitivity (or insensitivity) to her child by treating him or her as a child with a thinking, feeling, desiring mind, which he or she can then use to explore and understand the world around them. Through reading stories, caregivers are exposing their children to narrative structure and emotional understanding and facilitating these children's self-regulation skills through the act of listening.

Anecdotally, Ugandan caregivers complain that they have less time to tell stories to their children than their caregivers did because they are struggling just to make ends meet. Of course, reading to one's child depends on a caregiver's literacy skills, and some of the caregivers in the current study were illiterate. We found, however, that reading aloud to the target child was not correlated with a caregiver's wealth, social support, or overall quality of life but only with a caregiver's educational level.

Storytelling/Story-Acting (STSA) Play Intervention

While many preschool interventions have been effective at improving school readiness skills (e.g., Barnett et al., 2008; Weiland & Yoshikawa, 2013; Zigler et al., 2004), this study selected the Storytelling/Story-Acting (STSA) play intervention because it has been shown to be effective, requires few materials, and is easy to conduct. Developed by Paley (1990), a Chicago educator, the STSA play intervention capitalizes on oral storytelling (which has a venerable tradition in sub-Saharan African culture) to enhance children's cognitive and linguistic development. The STSA play intervention consists of two phases: 1) young children's dictation of spontaneously generated stories (storytelling phase), and 2) young children's acting out these stories on a makeshift stage (story-acting phase). During a period of unstructured time for children in the library, a child can approach the librarian with a story. The librarian then writes down the story verbatim with minimal intervention and reads it back to the child to ensure accuracy. The librarian also underlines all the characters in the story, and the child author assigns child actors to all the characters. After four or five stories have been collected, the librarian assembles all the children around a large rectangle on the floor, instructing them to sit behind the lines. The librarian then calls up the first child author, who selects from the group those child actors who will be acting out the story characters. The librarian reads the story first to acquaint the children with it, and then reads it again with the child actors acting it out. Each child author's story is read and acted out in the same fashion.

Paley's (1990) STSA play intervention combines narrative and play that can be deeply engaging to children and, in the process, helps them to develop strong oral language skills. Paley discussed this play intervention and some of its effects, usually in conjunction with other aspects of her classroom environment, producing rich, vivid, and engrossing ethnographic studies during the period she taught at the Chicago Laboratory School (e.g., Paley, 1990). For about 15 years, Nicolopoulou and her research team have been implementing and evaluating this play intervention in classroom settings both similar to and different from Paley's (e.g., Nicolopoulou, 2002). While a strong ethnographic dimension was always included, principles of evidence-based research involving quantitative measures of intervention outcomes also guided their efforts. In an effort to promote an evidence base for this powerful educational intervention that includes principles of play, Nicolopoulou and her research team conducted five iterative studies in the US building on Paley's research: (1) a two-year study of two middle-income preschool classrooms; (2) a three-year study of two middle-income preschool classrooms in a different setting; (3) a one-year study of a Head Start classroom using another classroom for comparison; (4) a two-year study of four Head Start classrooms in a large urban center using two other classrooms as comparisons; and (5) a two-year study where a total of seven experimental and seven control classrooms serving low-income families were studied. Each of these studies yielded significant results that validate the effectiveness of the STSA play intervention in promoting school readiness skills (for a summary of findings, see Nicolopoulou & Cole, 2010).

Our goal in studying preschool children from Uganda was to determine whether six months of participation in the STSA play intervention could improve children's school readiness skills in comparison with a control group of children who received only stories being read aloud to them. A significant finding would support the idea that this play intervention could make preschool children more prepared to enter the school environment. We wanted to demonstrate that this finding holds true even when caregivers are not providing optimal learning environments at home such as infrequent reading patterns with their children, or optimal supports because of a poor quality of life. In other words, can the STSA play intervention buffer these children from their emotionally and materially impoverished home environments and facilitate the development of school readiness skills?

METHOD

Participants

We collected data from two groups of Ugandan villagers: caregivers and children ages 3 to 5 from Mpigi ($n = 61$) and Kabubbu ($n = 62$). Both groups of children were randomly assigned to participate in either the STSA play intervention ($n = 63$) or a story-reading activity ($n = 60$) for one hour twice per week for six months. Inclusion criteria for caregivers included having a child between the ages of 3 and 5 ($M =$ 58.4 months, $SD = 8.7$) over whom she had primary caregiving responsibilities. Caregivers were either the mother or grandmother of the target child; four fathers participated as caregivers. Eleven caregivers had two children enrolled in the study, and one caregiver had three children enrolled. One set of twins participated. The caregivers of these 123 children were informed of the study by word of mouth spread by the librarians and project coordinator. All caregivers who satisfied the inclusion criteria consented to their participation and the participation of their children and were enrolled in the study. Caregivers in both conditions tended to be living in economically poor conditions with their spouses or partners in large households and were graduates of primary school. Children were 43.1% male and had not yet begun primary school.

Caregiver Measures

At Time 1 (January, 2014), all caregivers completed an hour-long semistructured interview designed by the authors. Interviews were videotaped and transcribed verbatim for coding purposes.

Educational Level

Educational level was assessed by asking caregivers about their highest level of educational attainment. Seventeen levels ranged from "none" to "graduate of university".

Quality of Life

The Dartmouth Primary Care Cooperative Information Charts (COOP Charts; Nelson et al., 1987) is a 10-minute, 9-item survey that assesses the quality of the person's physical health and its effects on their quality of life on nine 5-point items ("not at all" to "extremely"): 1) Feelings, 2) Daily Activities, 3) Pain, 4) Physical Fitness, 5) Change in Health, 6) Social Activities, 7) Social Support, 8) Overall Health, and 9) Quality of Life. The five anchor points for each item are visually displayed on a chart shown to the person. Adequate convergent and discriminant validity was established with the RAND scales (Nelson et al., 1987). This instrument was used previously in Uganda (Nuwagaba-Biribonwoha, Mayon-White, Okong, Carpenter, & Jenkinson, 2006). HIV-positive pregnant women scored higher on five of the nine items than HIV-negative pregnant women (Nuwagaba-Biribonwoha et al., 2006). The nine items were summed so that total scores could range from 9 to 45. In the present study, the internal consistency of the COOP Charts was .67.

Reading Aloud to Target Child

We attempted to establish the extent of caregivers' reading to the target child. Whether the caregiver read aloud to the target child (rated 2 = "yes"; 1 = "no") and the frequency of reading aloud to the target child (rated 1 = "less than 1 day/wk"; 2 = "1 day/wk"; 3 = "2-3 days/wk"; 4 = "4-5 days/wk"; 5 = "greater than 5 days/wk"), were variables used in the exploratory analyses.

Social Support

To determine the quality of social support, caregivers were read three vignettes, modified from the work of Schaefer, Coyne, and Lazarus (1981), related to emotional, financial, and childcare support, and then asked to name three persons in their lives who could provide each of the three kinds of social support. Each item was assigned 1 point for every person named. Scores could thus range from 0 to 9.

Total Possessions

The Africa Centre Demographic Information System (ACDIS; Tanser et al., 2008) is a 10-minute, 18-item survey originally designed to assess the demographic, social, and health impact of the HIV epidemic in South Africa. Socioeconomic status was positively correlated with HIV incidence in the regions of South Africa surveyed (Tanser et al., 2008). One item, caregiver's Total Possessions in the household, included 18 possessions. We selected 12 possessions and added one item—cement floors in the home. Possessions received 1 point each and were then summed.

Child Measures

At both Time 1 (January, 2014) and Time 2 (August, 2014), all children completed three measures designed to assess three indices of school readiness: 1) Emergent Literacy, 2) Oral Language, and 3) Theory of Mind skills. These measures were selected because they are easy to administer and do not depend heavily on expressive vocabulary skills.

Bracken School Readiness Assessment: Third Edition (BSRA-3; Bracken, 2007)

The BSRA-3 is a 10-minute, 85-item interview that assesses school readiness skills in five domains: 1) colors, 2) letters, 3) numbers/counting, 4) sizes/comparisons, and 5) shapes. The child is shown a series of four pictures and instructed to point to the picture corresponding to the correct response. Split-half reliabilities for children ages 3 to 5 ranged from .96 to .97 (Bracken, 2007). The BSRA-3 was also shown to distinguish language-impaired and intellectually disabled children from a normative sample that included a range of ethnicities, US geographical locations, and socioeconomic status (SES; Bracken, 2007).

Each item was assigned 1 point for each correct response. A subtest was discontinued when the child received three consecutive scores of 0. Items were then summed both within and between domains so that total scores could range from 0 to 85. Raw scores rather than norm-referenced standard scores were used in the statistical analyses because we were not comparing this sample to a normative sample in the US. The BSRA-3 was used as a measure of Emergent Literacy skills.

Kilifi Picture Vocabulary Test (Holding et al., 2004; Nampijja et al., 2010)

The Kilifi is a 4-minute, 24-item measure of receptive vocabulary adapted and translated into Luganda, the native language of the children in this sample, by Maggie Nampijja, a Ugandan child development researcher (Nampijja et al., 2010). The child is shown a series of four pictures—one target picture, a phonological distractor, a visual or semantic distractor, and an unrelated distractor, all drawn in black and white. The child is instructed to point to the picture corresponding to the word spoken by the translator. In Kenyan samples, the Kilifi distinguished school-attending from non-school-attending children, was negatively correlated with behavioral problems, and demonstrated adequate test-retest reliability (Alcock, Holding, Mung'ala-Odera, & Newton, 2008; Holding et al., 2004). These results were mostly replicated in a Ugandan sample (Nampijja et al., 2010). Each item was assigned 1 point for each correct response. Items were summed so that total scores could range from 0 to 24. The Kilifi was used as a measure of Oral Language skills.

Five Theory of Mind Tasks (Peterson, Wellman, & Liu, 2005)

The five Theory of Mind tasks comprise a 10-minute procedure that assesses the child's awareness of how mental states such as memories, beliefs, desires, and intentions govern the behavior of self and others. This awareness is purported to facilitate the child's social competence. The tasks consist of presenting a series of props (i.e., adult doll, girl and boy doll, toy house, cardboard tea box, a toy pig and cow, a picture of the back of a boy's head, and pictures of a carrot, biscuit, bushes, and hut) that facilitate the interviewer's narration of five brief stories. Each story assesses a different aspect of theory of mind: diverse desires, diverse beliefs, knowledge access, false belief, and hidden emotion. After each story, the interviewer asks the child two or three questions that assess the child's theory of mind. We slightly modified three stories to make them more culturally appropriate. In the diverse beliefs story, we replaced the garage with a hut and the cat with a chicken. In the knowledge access story, we replaced the toy chest with a toy house and the dog with a cow. In the false belief story, we replaced the Band-Aid box with a tea box (a familiar container in all Ugandan households). We believed that these slight modifications would not affect coding. The five Theory of Mind tasks were able to track the different developmental trajectories of theory of mind in children with deafness, autism, and typical development (Peterson et al., 2005; Peterson, Wellman, & Slaughter, 2012).

Each item was assigned 1 point for demonstrating theory of mind in response to the questions presented after each story. Items were summed so that total scores could range between 0 and 5. In the present study, scores ranged between 0 and 4 at Time 1 (every child participant responded incorrectly to the hidden emotion story) and between 0 and 5 at Time 2. The five Theory of Mind tasks were used as a measure of Theory of Mind skills.

Procedure

In January, 2014, we traveled to the rural Ugandan villages of Mpigi and Kabubbu to collect Time 1 data on the caregivers and children. The librarians at the Mpigi Community Library and Kabubbu Community Library as well as our project coordinator recruited participants for a study documenting the impact of the STSA play intervention on caregivers and their children ages 3 to 5 over whom they have primary responsibility. All caregivers and children provided oral or written consent to participate in this IRB-approved study after the scope and procedures of the study were carefully explained.

One of us (VD) and a research assistant independently interviewed caregivers for over one hour in a quiet area of a nearby school in both villages with assistance from two translators, who translated the questions and the caregivers' responses from Luganda to English. Caregivers received a bar of laundry soap and a bag of sugar for their participation. Caregivers were administered an interview that included questions designed to assess caregiver's Educational Level, Quality of Life, Reading Aloud to Target Child, Social Support, and Total Possessions.

At the same time, one of us (GG) and a research assistant independently interviewed the children for over one hour in a separate area from the caregivers with assistance from two translators, who translated the instructions and the children's responses from Luganda to English. Children received a T-shirt and a lollipop for their participation. The three child measures were administered in a fixed order: the BSRA-3, the Kilifi, and the Five Theory of Mind Tasks at both Time 1 and Time 2 (August, 2014) after six months of intervention.

Our project coordinator and his assistant, both trained by one of us (GG), conducted the STSA play intervention and the control intervention at the Mpigi Community Library and the Kabubbu Community Library. In Mpigi, children were randomly assigned to two STSA play intervention groups (n = 16 and n =15) and two control groups (n = 15 and n = 15), which were conducted for one hour twice per week for six months (February to July, 2014). Similarly, in Kabubbu, children were randomly assigned to two STSA play intervention groups (both n =16) and two control groups (both n = 15), which were conducted in exactly the same manner. The four Mpigi groups were conducted on Mondays and Wednesdays for a total of 42 sessions, while the four Kabubbu groups were conducted on Tuesdays and Thursdays for a total of 41 sessions. Some group sessions were canceled because of exam and holiday schedules as well as unscheduled events that interfered (e.g., all children from a village attending a child's funeral).

The STSA play intervention was described earlier. Both the STSA children and the control children received a story reading time (in Luganda) followed by a series of questions to assess their story comprehension and stimulate them to reflect on the storyline and the reasons why the characters behaved as they did. The children were then given paper and crayons to draw anything they wished on both front and back. The STSA children dictated their stories during their drawing time, followed by the acting out of these stories by the group.

RESULTS

Descriptive Statistics by Group

Table 1 displays the descriptive statistics and mean differences between the STSA and control groups. Results indicate that random assignment did not prevent the STSA children from being almost four months older than the control children. In addition, the STSA children scored higher than the control children at Time 1 on the Numbers/Counting subtest, Shapes subtest, BSRA-3 Total Scores, and Theory of Mind Total Scores. Four subsequent analyses of covariance (ANCOVAs) indicated age accounted for these four significant differences.

Between-Group Differences in Change Scores

Table 2 displays the mean differences in change scores between the STSA and control groups. Results indicate that the STSA children scored higher than the control children on the Colors subtest of the BSRA-3. No other differences in change scores were significant.

Within-Group Differences in the Total Sample

Because there was only one significant difference between the STSA and control children on the Emergent Literacy, Oral Language, and Theory of Mind variables reported on, we analyzed Time 1 to Time 2 change on these variables in the total sample. Table 3 displays the mean differences between Time 1 and Time 2 on all the variables of interest. A series of paired-samples t-tests was conducted, and all mean differences were highly significant, $p < .001$, except for the Theory of Mind Total Scores, which were significant, $p < .05$. Children in both groups dramatically improved their Emergent Literacy, Oral Language, and Theory of Mind scores.

Within-Group Differences in the STSA Group

We wanted to analyze Time 1 to Time 2 change on these variables in each group in isolation. Table 4 displays the mean differences between Time 1 and Time 2 on all the variables of interest. A series of paired-samples t-tests was conducted, and all mean differences were highly significant, $p < .001$, except for the Shapes subtest, which was significant, $p < .01$, and the Theory of Mind Total Scores, which were nonsignificant. STSA children dramatically improved their Emergent Literacy and Oral Language scores.

Within-Group Differences in the Control Group

Table 5 displays the mean differences between Time 1 and Time 2 on all the variables of interest. A series of paired-samples t-tests was conducted, and all mean differences were highly significant, $p < .001$, except for the Theory of Mind Total Scores, which were significant, $p < .05$. Control children dramatically improved their Emergent Literacy, Oral Language, and Theory of Mind scores.

Exploratory Analyses

Gender as a Moderator of Change

We were interested in exploring whether gender moderated the changes in Emergent Literacy, Oral Language, and Theory of Mind scores between Time 1 and Time 2. In an ANCOVA controlling for age, gender moderated the Kilifi Time 1 Total Scores on Time 2 Total Scores (see Figure 1). The figure suggests that for the lowest scoring children at Time 1, the girls performed better in receptive vocabulary skills than the boys at Time 2, $F(1,116) = 6.43$, $p < .05$.

Caregiver Correlates of Emergent Literacy, Oral Language, and Theory of Mind Scores at Time 1

We were also interested in exploring caregiver variables that correlated with their children's Emergent Literacy, Oral Language, and Theory of Mind scores at Time 1. These caregiver variables included caregiver's Quality of Life, Total Possessions, Social Support, and Educational Level. Table 6 displays the descriptive statistics of the caregiver variables and mean differences between the STSA and control groups. Table 7 displays the correlation matrix between these caregiver variables and their children's Emergent Literacy, Oral Language, and Theory of Mind variables. Caregiver's Quality of Life (higher scores denote lower Quality of Life) was negatively correlated with the Colors subtest of the BSRA-3, $p < .01$, and the Letters and Numbers/Counting subtests of the BSRA-3, the BSRA-3 Total Scores, and the Kilifi Total Scores, $p < .05$. Caregiver's Total Possessions was positively correlated with the Kilifi Total Scores, $p < .001$. Caregiver's Social Support was positively correlated with the Kilifi Total Scores, $p < .05$. Caregiver's Educational Level was positively correlated with the Colors and Letters subtests of the BSRA-3, $p < .05$, the Sizes/Comparisons subtest of the BSRA-3, $p < .001$, the BSRA-3 Total Scores, the Kilifi Total Scores, $p < .01$, and the Theory of Mind Total Scores, $p < .05$. Three multiple regression analyses were conducted, with BSRA-3 Total Scores, Kilifi Total Scores, and Theory of

Figure 1.

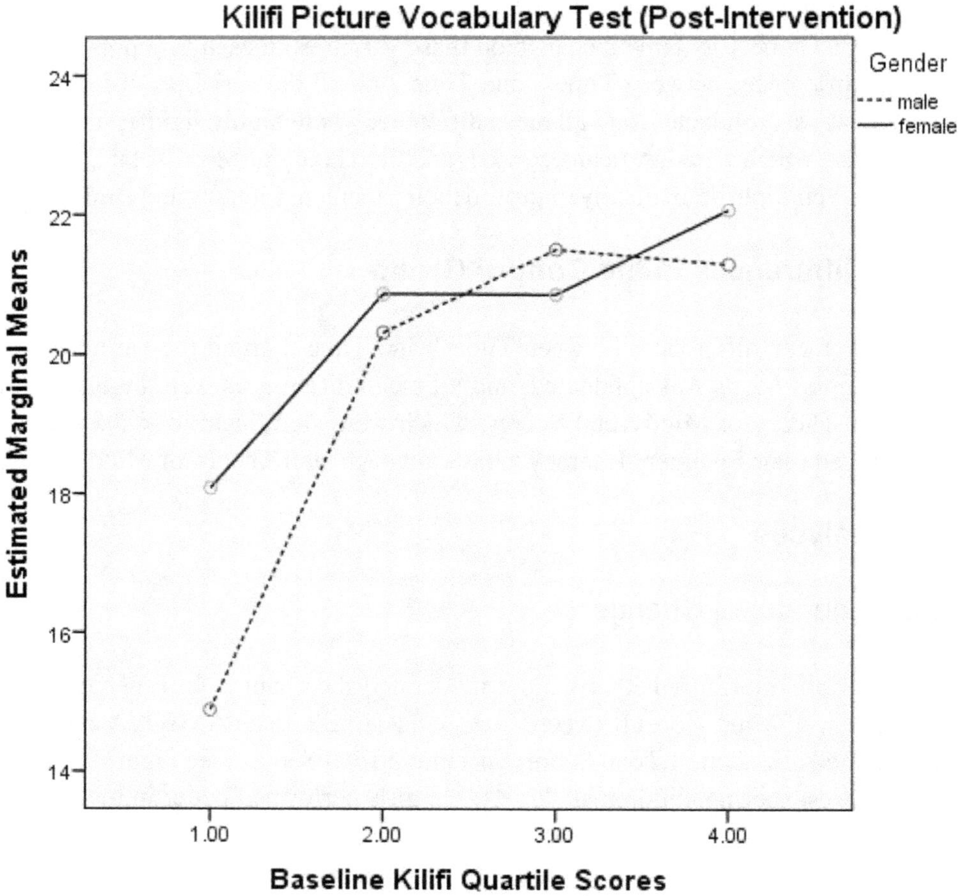

Mind Total Scores taking turns as the dependent variable. Of the four caregiver predictor variables, caregiver's Educational Level predicted the BSRA-3 Total Scores, $\beta = .23$, $p < .05$. Caregiver's Total Possessions and Educational Level predicted the Kilifi Total Scores, $\beta = .31$, $p < .01$, and $\beta = .20$, $p < .05$, respectively. Caregiver's Educational Level predicted the Theory of Mind Total Scores, $\beta = .20$, $p < .05$. The results suggest that caregivers play an important role in the development of their children's Emergent Literacy, Oral Language, and Theory of Mind skills.

Caregiver Correlates of Emergent Literacy, Oral Language, and Theory of Mind Change Scores

Caregiver's Quality of Life was positively correlated with their children's Kilifi Change Scores, $r = .22$, $p < .05$, and caregiver's Total Possessions were negatively correlated with their children's Kilifi Change Scores, $r = -.31$, $p < .001$. The results suggest that children whose caregivers had the lowest Quality of Life and fewest Total Possessions experienced the greatest gains in their oral language skills. It appears that group intervention benefits most the children living in the most disadvantageous family environments.

Caregiver Reading Habits as Correlates of Emergent Literacy, Oral Language, and Theory of Mind Scores at Time 1

We were also interested in exploring caregiver reading habits that correlated with their children's Emergent Literacy, Oral Language, and Theory of Mind scores at Time 1. These variables included Reading Aloud to Target Child and Frequency of Reading Aloud to Target Child. Table 8 displays the correlation matrix between caregiver reading habits and their children's Emergent Literacy, Oral Language, and Theory of Mind variables. Caregiver's Reading Aloud to Target Child was positively correlated with the Sizes/Comparisons subtest of the BSRA-3 and the Kilifi Total Scores, $p < .01$, the Colors subtest of the BSRA-3, the BSRA-3 Total Scores, and the Theory of Mind Total Scores, $p < .05$. Caregiver's Frequency of Reading Aloud to Target Child was positively correlated with the Colors and Sizes/Comparisons subtests of the BSRA-3 and the Theory of Mind Total Scores, $p < .01$, the Letters subtest of the BSRA-3, the BSRA-3 Total Scores, and the Kilifi Total Scores, $p < .05$. Three multiple regression analyses were conducted, with BSRA-3 Total Scores, Kilifi Total Scores, and Theory of Mind Total Scores taking turns as the dependent variable. Of the four caregiver predictor variables and Frequency of Reading Aloud to Target Child, none of these variables predicted the BSRA-3 Total Scores. Caregiver's Total Possessions predicted the Kilifi Total Scores, $\beta = .36$, $p < .001$. Frequency of Reading Aloud to Target Child predicted the Theory of Mind Total Scores, $\beta = .20$, $p < .05$. The results suggest that caregiver reading habits differentially predict children's Theory of Mind scores.

Caregiver and Child Time 1 Correlates of Session Attendance and Total STSA Stories Told

Finally, we were also interested in exploring caregiver and child variables at Time 1 that correlated with the total number of group sessions attended by all the children and the total number of stories told by the STSA children. Table 9 displays the correlation matrix between the caregiver and child variables and Session Attendance and Total Stories Told (in the STSA group). Session Attendance was positively correlated with the Kilifi Total Scores, $p < .05$. Total Stories Told was negatively correlated with caregiver's Quality of Life (higher scores denote lower Quality of Life), $p < .05$, and positively correlated with the BSRA-3 Total Scores and Frequency of Reading Aloud to Target Child, $p < .05$. The results suggest that caregiver and child variables assessed at Time 1 predict Session Attendance and Total Stories Told during the STSA play intervention.

DISCUSSION

This study tested the effectiveness of the STSA play intervention on Ugandan preschoolers' Emergent Literacy, Oral Language, and Theory of Mind in two rural Ugandan community libraries. With a literacy rate of 79% for men and 58% for women in Uganda (UNICEF, 2013), we were interested in using the rural community library as a convenient vehicle for delivering a play-based group intervention twice per week for six months that has been shown to improve emergent literacy, oral language, and social competence in preschoolers in the US (Nicolopoulou et al., 2015). STSA children scored higher than the control children on the Colors subtest of the BSRA-3. Perhaps children were primed for learning colors by using colored crayons to draw pictures after the library assistant's storytelling time and during the children's story dictation time. Perhaps the colors that the children used in their drawings found their way into the stories they dictated, which helped them to remember the color names. Control children also drew pictures with colored crayons, but they did not have the opportunity to use color names in story dictation; thus, they did not rehearse them in dictated stories. We could determine whether the STSA children used color names in their story dictation by counting the frequency of the use of such words in their stories. The translation of every child's STSA story has just been completed, thus allowing us to complete word frequency counts.

Contrary to expectations, however, the STSA play intervention did not produce any other significant benefits in Emergent Literacy, Oral Language, or Theory of Mind skills. Instead, both the STSA and control children showed highly significant improvement in most of the child variables measured. Why did the STSA children not demonstrate significantly more improvement in Emergent Literacy, Oral Language, and Theory of Mind skills than the control children? The preschool children participating in this study were pulled one hour twice a week from preschool classrooms that contained over 60 children with only two teachers to join a group of only 15 children with two facilitators. The study children often received individualized attention from these facilitators, who sometimes let them sit in their laps while they were drawing or, in the case of the STSA children, dictating their stories. In addition to small group size and individualized attention, both groups of children were exposed to a storytelling time with the facilitator asking comprehension questions afterward. One group of children told and acted out stories, while the other group continued working on their drawings, but otherwise, the two groups were identical. It is quite plausible that both groups benefited from these interventions and that the STSA play intervention did not add incrementally to this exposure to attention, oral language through story reading, and story comprehension.

Given the adverse learning conditions in their preschool classrooms, perhaps any intervention that included small group size, individualized attention, freestyle drawing, story reading, and story comprehension could have produced similar outcomes on Emergent Literacy, Oral Language, and Theory of Mind skills. Perhaps a higher frequency of the STSA play intervention than twice per week or longer duration than six months is necessary to produce a significant effect. It is also possible that a "sleeper effect" (Muratori, Picchi, Bruni, Patarnello, & Romagnoli, 2003) on children's outcomes might be assessed at a later follow-up assessment. STSA children might reap benefits from this play intervention later in development that could distinguish them from control children. We also did not directly assess children's expressive vocabulary skills. Because the STSA play intervention forces children to rehearse their expressive vocabulary skills, we might have detected significant differences between the STSA and control children on this particular set of skills so crucial to later academic and occupational success. Even with changes to the assessment protocol, however, the study was probably underpowered with only 123 participants to detect significant differences between the two conditions.

Having tested the effectiveness of the STSA play intervention on Ugandan preschoolers' Emergent Literacy, Oral Language, and Theory of Mind, we decided to conduct a series of exploratory analyses on the total sample ($N = 123$) to determine whether gender moderates change on the outcome variables and whether any caregiver variables predict the child outcome variables at Time 1. Interestingly, controlling for age, gender moderated the Kilifi Time 1 Total Scores on Time 2 Total Scores. Figure 1 suggests that for the lowest scoring children at Time 1, the girls performed better in receptive vocabulary skills than the boys at Time 2. We believe that the lowest scoring boys might have lower emotional investment in these activities than the lowest scoring girls and thus did not pay as much attention to the story reading, the drawings, or, in the case of the STSA boys, the story dictation or story-acting. By the end of the six-month intervention period, these boys' receptive vocabulary scores did not improve as much as the girls' scores. In this extreme patriarchal society, listening to and telling stories might not be considered a masculine activity for boys. Previous research from our lab (Fanciullo et al., 2013) suggests gender-coded differences in children's implicit perception of familial social roles in this culture. The fact that these boys were also far behind in their receptive vocabulary skills probably also made these activities difficult for them and further eroded any interest they might have otherwise had.

Four caregiver variables—Quality of Life, Total Possessions, Social Support, and Educational Level—were correlated with the child outcome variables at Time 1. When entered simultaneously in a multiple regression analysis, caregiver's Educational Level predicted the BSRA-3 Total Scores and Theory of Mind Total Scores, and caregiver's Total Possessions and Educational Level predicted the Kilifi Total Scores. Prior to intervention, we were able to predict children's Emergent Literacy, Oral Language, and Theory of Mind scores from their caregiver's educational level and wealth. The fact that caregiver wealth (as measured by total number of possessions) was identified as a significant predictor of their children's receptive vocabulary skills is particularly striking because so little variation exists in these caregivers' income levels. Caregiver's wealth and educational level play a large role in the development of their children's Emergent Literacy, Oral Language, and Theory of Mind skills, suggesting that any play intervention targeting these outcomes must also simultaneously target caregiver, family, and community needs. The social context plays an outsized role in the development of emergent literacy (Bus, 1994). Quicken Trust (www.quickentrust.com), a UK-based private charity in Uganda, sponsors programs such as Adopt-a-Granny that provide material support to Ugandan matriarchs who often provide much of the direct care to children. This charity builds and furnishes new homes that provide shelter for these children. The Uganda Community Libraries Association (UgCLA) sponsors the Family Literacy Project (Parry, Kirabo, & Nakyato, 2014) in which caregivers get together once per week to learn how to read and to discuss how to start a business. Participants have not only become literate but have also learned how to raise chickens, cattle, and other livestock to provide for their families. Successful intervention must involve caregivers as well as children. Perhaps caregivers can also be offered graduate equivalency educational and vocational opportunities and be trained to read or tell stories to their children at home. Work with caregivers and families increases the odds that play-based group interventions such as STSA could benefit these children in the long term.

It was also encouraging to observe that children whose caregivers had the lowest Quality of Life and fewest Total Possessions experienced the greatest gains in their Oral Language skills. It appears that group intervention benefits most those children living in the most disadvantageous family environments. Perhaps educational resources need to focus particularly on these children because they seem to derive the greatest benefit from group intervention.

Unsurprisingly, caregiver's Reading Aloud to Target Child and Frequency of Reading Aloud to Target Child were positively correlated with the BSRA-3 Total Scores, Kilifi Total Scores, and Theory of Mind Total Scores. After controlling for the four caregiver variables, only Frequency of Reading Aloud to Target Child predicted the Theory of Mind Total Scores. Frequent exposure to stories told by the caregiver helps children to develop a theory of one's own and others' minds over and above the caregiver's Quality of Life, Total Possessions, Social Support, and even Educational Level. Mar and his colleagues (2010) reported similar findings in a US sample after controlling for child's age and gender, receptive vocabulary skills, and parental income. Our findings suggest that supporting caregivers' reading aloud to their children (if they are themselves literate) might facilitate theory of mind development even in the presence of social-contextual risk factors such as poverty, lack of social support, poor quality of life, and even educational level. Mothers must know how to read, however, and so programs such as the Family Literacy Project are instrumental in helping caregivers to acquire literacy skills, not only to help them develop their own businesses but also to facilitate theory of mind skills in their young children.

Mar and his colleagues (2010) suggested two possible mechanisms for this finding. First, reading stories aloud to the child allows the caregiver to engage in conversation about the story characters and their beliefs, intentions, and feelings. Through such conversation, the child develops an increasingly nuanced understanding of the mental states of self and others—both similarities and differences between the mind of the self and the minds of others. Second, reading stories aloud to the child provides opportunities for the child to simulate the events depicted in his or her mind by adopting the visuospatial perspective of story characters. This mental simulation is believed to be associated with the development of imagination and pretense, which in turn predict theory of mind skills and ultimately, social competence in children (Garner, Curenton, & Taylor, 2005; Seja & Russ, 1999; Taylor & Carlson, 1997).

We collected videos of the caregivers in our sample reading a wordless story book to their children; we are now coding and analyzing these data to discover whether caregivers who read aloud to their children at home more frequently and thus have children with more highly developed theory of mind skills are also more likely to engage these children in discussions of mental state talk around the story characters. We believe that children whose caregivers engage them in discussions of mental state talk while reading a wordless story book are more likely to simulate the depicted events in the story, develop the capacity to interpret the behaviors of story characters as expressions of their mental states, and ultimately, reproduce these simulations in their own dictated stories, which they also act out in the STSA play intervention. We suggest that "playing around" with mental representations of story characters' intentions and behaviors can facilitate "playing around" with words and actions in the context of the STSA play intervention. This playing around capacity might also predict later flexibility in understanding peers' intentions and behaviors and thus enhance social competence so crucial for later relationship and occupational success. Preliminary evidence for this position comes from our finding that caregiver's Frequency of Reading Aloud to Target Child was positively correlated with Total Stories Told in the STSA play intervention. Listening to stories from the caregiver at home, possibly discussing them and simulating the events depicted in these stories in the child's mind, facilitates the child's own symbolization and storytelling ability. These storytelling experiences provide further differentiation, integration, and complexity to the child's developing mental structure, which permits deeper emotional understanding of oneself and others (Goodman, 2010).

Limitations

This study's limitations serve to qualify the conclusions that can be drawn. Translators assisted with the caregiver and child assessments. Although trained by the researchers to translate responses as accurately as possible, some responses might have got lost in translation. Administration of these measures by Ugandans without the need for translation would be ideal.

Some of the caregivers and children had never interacted with a foreigner ("*mzungu*") before. Reactions among the villagers varied widely from curiosity to fear. Although no one in this study refused to participate, some caregivers and children were more inhibited in their responses than others, thus introducing a potential confounding variable. Participants also needed to adjust to using a translator to communicate with the interviewers. All four translators, who grew up in the general area of Mpigi and Kabubbu, made every effort to build rapport with participants and remove social inhibitions. They used humor and friendly interactions with the interviewers, observed by the participants, to emphasize that the translators and interviewers were friends. The interviewers also made every effort to establish rapport directly with the participants. For example, one of us (GG) used fist-bumping ("*bonga*"), a common greeting among children in the villages, to make the child participants smile and to facilitate interactions with him. In spite of such efforts, it is not known to what extent the interviewers' presence might have confounded the results. Native interviewers might have obtained different results.

Caregivers sometimes lied about their children's birthdates to gain entry into the participant pool. In rural Uganda, it is surprisingly easy to succeed at lying about a child's age because most children have no birth records. A culturally based lack of emphasis on birthdates also accounts for the imprecision encountered in caregivers' memory of birthdates. A few caregivers could not even remember the year in which their child was born. If a child whose mother could not remember his or her birthdate appeared to fall outside the age criteria, we excluded that child from the study. In spite of these efforts, the children's ages might be inaccurate.

No information was collected about ancillary caregivers who have both indirect and direct impacts on the child. For example, assessment of the amount and quality of contact with the father could facilitate our understanding of the developmental pathways of school readiness skills in this population. Information about other caregivers could also serve to augment the emerging socioemotional picture of these preschool children.

Finally, in accordance with the correlational nature of this study, the authors took advantage of the significant correlations between the caregiver and child variables of interest to test six predictions. Future research should test these models *a priori*.

Future Directions for Research

One possibility raised earlier is that the STSA play intervention implemented for two additional years might improve children's outcomes and be detected at a later follow-up assessment. The children in this study from Kabubbu have continued to receive the STSA play intervention twice per week in the intervening two years, while the STSA play intervention in Mpigi, the other targeted village, was discontinued after six months. Perhaps an intervention period of two and a half years might differentiate the STSA children from the control children on the identified outcomes of Emergent Literacy, Oral Language, and Theory of Mind. We are also coding and analyzing data from our videos of caregivers reading a wordless story book to their children. We hope to identify one of the mediators of Frequency of Reading Aloud to Target Child on Theory of Mind Total Scores: the use of mental state talk (Bekar, 2014) in discussing these stories with their children.

We also collected attachment data on these children using the Attachment Story-Completion Task (Bretherton, Biringen, Ridgeway, Maslin, & Sherman, 1989; Bretherton, Prentiss, & Ridgeway, 1990; Bretherton, Ridgeway, & Cassidy, 1990). We expect children's quality of attachment to mediate the relation between the caregiver variables and child outcomes of Emergent Literacy, Oral Language, and Theory of Mind skills because previous research on Western samples suggests that securely attached preschoolers are more likely to attend to their caregivers' reading aloud to them and to experience less anxiety in such interactive learning contexts (Bus, 2001, 2003). The caregiver-child relationship provides the necessary emotional context in which emergent literacy can flourish or flounder. It is also possible that an anxiously attached child can make the reading process unpleasant for the caregiver, who in turn avoids reading to the child to reduce conflict. The bidirectional nature of the caregiver-child relationship must be examined in relation to literacy acquisition in future studies.

Literacy programs targeting young adults of reproductive age must emphasize reading aloud to their children. These programs can then be evaluated for their effectiveness in improving literacy, and follow-up studies can evaluate the success of these programs in persuading these young adults to read aloud to their future children. The two hours per week spent reading aloud to children in small groups did improve Emergent Literacy, Oral Language, and Theory of Mind skills. If librarians can be trained to read aloud to children and encourage children to tell stories and act them out, the literacy rate in Uganda might increase, accompanied by a drop in the poverty rate.

Table 1. Child descriptive statistics by group

Variable	STSA Group (1)				Control Group (2)				Significance	
	M		*SD*		*M*		*SD*			
	Pre	Post	Pre	Post	Pre	Post	Pre	Post	Pre	Post
Group size	$n = 63$	$n = 63$			$n = 60$	$n = 58$				
Child age (months)[a]	60.33	--	7.80	--	56.47	--	9.14	--	1 > 2*	--
Child gender (% male)	42.9				45.0				--	--
Total attendance		30.56		10.42		30.38		9.19		--
Total STSA stories told[b]		7.84		6.50		--		--		
School Readiness Skills (BSRA-3)										
Colors (subtest 1)	2.27	3.79	2.96	3.52	2.00	2.16	2.71	2.95	--	1 > 2**
Letters (subtest 2)	6.84	10.44	5.66	5.18	5.12	7.78	5.79	5.74	--	1 > 2**
Numbers/counting (subtest 3)	7.21	10.21	7.02	6.93	4.58	7.31	5.90	6.99	1 > 2*	1 > 2*
Sizes/comparisons (subtest 4)	8.87	12.00	6.28	5.93	7.33	10.29	5.02	5.01	--	--
Shapes (subtest 5)	7.70	9.65	5.68	5.09	5.12	8.66	4.39	5.20	1 > 2**	--
Total scores	32.89	46.10	23.59	22.12	24.15	36.19	19.39	22.21	1 > 2*	1 > 2*
Receptive Vocabulary (Kilifi)										
Total scores	19.02	20.37	3.34	2.75	17.83	19.74	3.95	2.88	--	--
Theory of Mind										
Total scores	2.40	2.54	.89	.98	2.05	2.38	.98	.91	1 > 2*	--

Note. $N = 123$ pre-intervention. $N = 121$ post-intervention. BSRA-3 = Bracken School Readiness Assessment-III. Kilifi = Kilifi Picture Vocabulary Test. *M* = mean. Pre = Pre-intervention. Post = Post-intervention. *SD* = standard deviation. STSA = Storytelling/Story-Acting play intervention.

[a]One child in the STSA group had just turned 6 years old at baseline.[b]Only children in the STSA group ($n = 63$) told stories.

$^{*}p < .05$. $^{**}p < .01$.

Table 2. Between-group differences in change scores

Variable	STSA Group (1)		Control Group (2)		Significance
	M	*SD*	*M*	*SD*	
School Readiness Skills (BSRA-3)					
Colors (subtest 1)	1.52	2.30	.24	2.19	1 > 2**
Letters (subtest 2)	3.60	4.03	2.76	4.62	--
Numbers/counting (subtest 3)	3.00	4.28	2.78	4.28	--
Sizes/comparisons (subtest 4)	3.13	5.64	3.19	4.67	--
Shapes (subtest 5)	1.95	5.31	3.71	5.25	2 > 1†
Total scores	13.21	13.44	12.67	12.06	--
Receptive Vocabulary (Kilifi)					
Total scores	1.35	2.90	2.02	3.50	--
Theory of Mind					
Total scores	.14	1.09	.33	1.07	--

Note. N = 123 pre-intervention. N = 121 post-intervention. BSRA-3 = Bracken School Readiness Assessment-III. Kilifi = Kilifi Picture Vocabulary Test. M = mean. SD = standard deviation. STSA = Storytelling/Story-Acting play intervention.

†$p < .10$. **$p < .01$.

Table 3. Within-group differences (total sample)

Variable	*M*		*SD*		Significance
	Pre (1)	**Post (2)**	**Pre**	**Post**	
School Readiness Skills (BSRA-3)					
Colors (subtest 1)	2.10	3.01	2.80	3.35	2 > 1***
Letters (subtest 2)	5.97	9.17	5.75	5.59	2 > 1***
Numbers/counting (subtest 3)	5.93	8.82	6.65	7.08	2 > 1***
Sizes/comparisons (subtest 4)	8.02	11.18	5.71	5.55	2 > 1***
Shapes (subtest 5)	6.38	9.17	5.23	5.15	2 > 1***
Total scores	28.40	41.35	21.97	22.63	2 > 1***
Receptive Vocabulary (Kilifi)					
Total scores	18.40	20.07	3.69	2.82	2 > 1***
Theory of Mind					
Total scores	2.23	2.46	.95	.95	2 > 1*

Note. N = 121 post-intervention. BSRA-3 = Bracken School Readiness Assessment-III. Kilifi = Kilifi Picture Vocabulary Test. M = mean. Pre = Pre-intervention. Post = Post-intervention. SD = standard deviation.

*$p < .05$. ***$p < .001$.

Table 4. Within-group differences (STSA group)

Variable	*M*		*SD*		Significance
	Pre (1)	Post (2)	Pre	Post	
School Readiness Skills (BSRA-3)					
Colors (subtest 1)	2.27	3.79	2.96	3.52	2 > 1***
Letters (subtest 2)	6.84	10.44	5.66	5.18	2 > 1***
Numbers/counting (subtest 3)	7.21	10.21	7.02	6.93	2 > 1***
Sizes/comparisons (subtest 4)	8.87	12.00	6.28	5.93	2 > 1***
Shapes (subtest 5)	7.70	9.65	5.68	5.09	2 > 1**
Total scores	32.89	46.10	23.59	22.12	2 > 1***
Receptive Vocabulary (Kilifi)					
Total scores	19.02	20.37	3.34	2.75	2 > 1***
Theory of Mind					
Total scores	2.40	2.54	.89	.98	--

Note. $N = 121$ post-intervention. BSRA-3 = Bracken School Readiness Assessment-III. Kilifi = Kilifi Picture Vocabulary Test. M = mean. Pre = Pre-intervention. Post = Post-intervention. SD = standard deviation. STSA = Storytelling/Story-Acting play intervention.
$^{**}p < .01$. $^{***}p < .001$.

Table 5. Within-group differences (control group)

Variable	*M*		*SD*		Significance
	Pre (1)	Post (2)	Pre	Post	
School Readiness Skills (BSRA-3)					
Colors (subtest 1)	1.91	2.16	2.64	2.95	--
Letters (subtest 2)	5.02	7.78	5.75	5.74	2 > 1***
Numbers/counting (subtest 3)	4.53	7.31	5.98	6.99	2 > 1***
Sizes/comparisons (subtest 4)	7.10	10.29	4.91	5.01	2 > 1***
Shapes (subtest 5)	4.95	8.66	4.30	5.20	2 > 1***
Total scores	23.52	36.19	19.10	22.21	2 > 1***
Receptive Vocabulary (Kilifi)					
Total scores	17.72	19.74	3.96	2.88	2 > 1***
Theory of Mind					
Total scores	2.05	2.38	.13	.12	2 > 1*

Note. $N = 121$ post-intervention. BSRA-3 = Bracken School Readiness Assessment-III. Kilifi = Kilifi Picture Vocabulary Test. M = mean. Pre = Pre-intervention. Post = Post-intervention. SD = standard deviation.
$^{*}p < .05$. $^{***}p < .001$.

Table 6. Caregiver descriptive statistics by group (pre-intervention)

Variable	STSA Group (1)		Control Group (2)		Significance
	M	*SD*	*M*	*SD*	
Caregiver age (years)[a]	34.29	8.99	29.90	5.61	1 > 2**
Caregiver gender (% female)	95.2		96.7		--
Educational level (years)[a]	6.80	3.43	6.78	3.08	--
Quality of life[b]	25.48	5.86	26.22	5.74	--
Social support	2.67	.80	2.60	.85	--
Total possessions	5.76	2.48	4.88	2.81	--
Reading aloud to target child (% yes)	68.25		60.00		--
Frequency of reading aloud	2.46	1.20	2.37	1.23	--

Note. $N = 123$ pre-intervention. M = mean. SD = standard deviation. STSA = Storytelling/Story-Acting play intervention.
[a]$N = 121$. [b]Higher scores denote lower quality of life.
$^{**}p < .01$.

Table 7. Caregiver correlates of theory of mind, emergent literacy, and receptive vocabulary scores at Time 1

Variable	1(*r*)	2(*r*)	3(*r*)	4(*r*)
Caregiver				
1. Education	--			
2. Quality of life (COOP Charts)[a]	-.13	--		
3. Social support	.28**	-.37***	--	
4. Total possessions	.22*	-.36***	.27**	--
Child				
School Readiness Skills (BSRA-3)				
Colors (subtest 1)	.20*	-.20*	.06	.07
Letters (subtest 2)	.19*	-.21*	.07	.12
Numbers/counting (subtest 3)	.16	-.23**	.01	.11
Sizes/comparisons (subtest 4)	.33***	-.11	.11	.18
Shapes (subtest 5)	.17	-.14	.08	.09
Total scores	.25**	-.21*	.08	.14
Receptive Vocabulary (Kilifi)				
Total scores	.29**	-.22*	.20*	.39***
Theory of Mind				
Total scores	.20*	-.17	.02	.09

Note. $N = 123$ pre-intervention. BSRA-3 = Bracken School Readiness Assessment-III. Kilifi = Kilifi Picture Vocabulary Test.
[a]Higher scores denote lower quality of life.
$^{*}p < .05$. $^{*}p < .01$. $^{***}p < .001$.

Table 8. Caregiver reading habits as correlates of theory of mind, emergent literacy, and receptive vocabulary scores at Time 1

Variable	1(*r*)	2(*r*)
Caregiver		
1. Reading aloud to target child	--	
2. Frequency of reading aloud	.87***	--
Child		
School Readiness Skills (BSRA-3)		
Colors (subtest 1)	.22*	.24**
Letters (subtest 2)	.17	.21*
Numbers/counting (subtest 3)	.15	.14
Sizes/comparisons (subtest 4)	.25**	.28**
Shapes (subtest 5)	.11	.08
Total scores	.21*	.22*
Receptive Vocabulary (Kilifi)		
Total scores	.27**	.22*
Theory of Mind		
Total scores	.20*	.25**

Note. $N = 123$ pre-intervention. BSRA-3 = Bracken School Readiness Assessment-III. Kilifi = Kilifi Picture Vocabulary Test.
$^{*}p < .05$. $^{**}p < .01$. $^{***}p < .001$.

CONCLUSION

The STSA play intervention in general did not perform better than the control group on the child outcomes of Emergent Literacy, Oral Language, and Theory of Mind skills. Both groups included a reading time with comprehension questions, small group size, and individualized attention. Children in both groups improved dramatically on all three indices of school readiness. Boys with the lowest receptive vocabulary levels did not improve as much as girls with the same levels. Caregiver's Educational Level predicted the child's Emergent Literacy, Oral Language, and Theory of Mind skills at Time 1. Caregiver's Total Possessions also predicted the child's Oral Language skills at Time 1. Caregiver's Frequency of Reading Aloud to the Target Child predicted the child's Theory of Mind skills at Time 1 and was positively correlated with the total number of stories the child told during the STSA play intervention.

Caregivers provide the underlying context for children's school readiness skills. We expect that improvements in caregivers' educational level, wealth, and time to read aloud to their children daily will facilitate their children's development of the skills necessary for school entry. It might also be true that such improvements will prepare children to take fuller advantage of library-based children's activities such as story reading and the STSA play intervention. Widespread dissemination of rural village libraries with cost-effective caregiver and child programs focusing on the development of school readiness skills carries the potential to restore the Pearl of Africa to its original luster.

Table 9. Caregiver and child Time 1 correlates of session attendance and total STSA stories told

Variable	1(*r*)	2(*r*)[a]
1. Session attendance	--	
2. Total STSA stories told[a]	.52***	--
Caregiver		
Education	-.08	.24
Quality of life (COOP Charts)[b]	-.01	-.27*
Social support	.05	.10
Total possessions	-.04	.07
Reading aloud to target child	.08	.08
Frequency of reading aloud	.09	.27*
Child		
School Readiness Skills (BSRA-3)		
Colors (subtest 1)	.07	.24
Letters (subtest 2)	.15	.23
Numbers/counting (subtest 3)	.10	.20
Sizes/comparisons (subtest 4)	.12	.25
Shapes (subtest 5)	.10	.24
Total scores	.13	.27*
Receptive Vocabulary (Kilifi)		
Total scores	.19*	.22
Theory of mind		
Total scores	.10	.17

Note. $N = 123$ pre-intervention. BSRA-3 = Bracken School Readiness Assessment-III. Kilifi = Kilifi Picture Vocabulary Test.
[a]$n = 63$. [b]Higher scores denote lower quality of life.
*$p < .05$. ***$p < .001$.Figure 1. Baseline Kilifi picture vocabulary test scores X gender interaction effect

ACKNOWLEDGMENT

This research was supported by two grants awarded to the authors by the J. William Fulbright Foreign Scholarship Board, Bureau of Educational and Cultural Affairs, US Department of State. The authors wish to acknowledge the following persons for their assistance with this study: the caregiver interviewers (Karen Gubert, Daniel Gubert, Jamie Lynn Forzato, Harriet Namigadde, Patrick Okapero Kokas), caregiver translators (Harriet Namigadde, Patrick Okapero Kokas), child interviewers (Michelle Fanciullo, Julius Ssentume), child translators (Habib Gayonga, Julius Ssentume), Ugandan Project Coordinator (Julius Ssentume), American Project Coordinators (Michelle Fanciullo, Tina Lo), participant recruiter (Julius Ssentume), materials design (Tina Lo, Dustin Kahoud), data entry (Dori Brender), STSA and control group facilitators (Julius Ssentume—project coordinator, Habib Gayonga—associate coordinator), caregiver and child video transcribers (Faye Bourie, Fran Dalis, Abigail Frawley, Erin Fults, Christina Garcia, Yonina Goldberg, Kaylene Irizarry, Seerat Kapani, Jessica Kozakowski, Jenae Richardson, Anna Rivera, Adama Toure, Angel Vidal, Cassandra Walker), drivers (Andrew Ssekyewa, Peter Kabiito), babysitters (Margaret "Maggie" Namugenyi, Grace Nabbanja), Mpigi Community Library (Joeria Namuddu, Librarian), and Kabubbu Community Library (Augustine Timothy Napagi, Librarian). The authors also gratefully acknowledge the cooperation of the children and caregivers who participated in this study. For more information about this research, please visit http://www.rurallibrariesresearchnetwork.com.

REFERENCES

Aber, J. L., Jones, S. M., & Cohen, J. (2000). The impact of poverty on the mental health and development of very young children. In C. H. Zeanah (Ed.), *Handbook of infant mental health* (2nd ed.; pp. 113–128). New York: Guilford Press.

Adams, M. J. (1990). *Beginning to read: Thinking and learning about print.* Cambridge, MA: MIT Press.

Aikens, N. L., & Barbarin, O. A. (2008). Socioeconomic differences in reading trajectories: The contribution of family, neighborhood, and school contexts. *Journal of Educational Psychology, 100*(2), 235–251. doi:10.1037/0022-0663.100.2.235

Alcock, K. J., Holding, P. A., Mungala-Odera, V., & Newton, C. R. J. C. (2008). Constructing tests of cognitive abilities for schooled and unschooled children. *Journal of Cross-Cultural Psychology, 39*(5), 529–551. doi:10.1177/0022022108321176

Artadi, E., & Sala-i-Martin, X. (2003). *The economic tragedy of the XXth century: Growth in Africa.* NBER Working Paper No. 9865. Retrieved from http://www.nber.org/papers/w9865.pdf

Barnett, W. S., Jung, K., Yarosz, D. J., Thomas, J., Hornbeck, A., Stechuk, R., & Burns, S. (2008). Educational effects of the Tools of the Mind curriculum: A randomized trial. *Early Childhood Research Quarterly, 23*(3), 299–313. doi:10.1016/j.ecresq.2008.03.001

Bekar, O. (2014). *Mental state talk in mothers' and preschool children's narratives: Relation to children's social-emotional functioning and maternal stress* (Unpublished doctoral dissertation). New School for Social Research, New York, NY.

Belsky, J., & Fearon, R. M. (2002). Early attachment security, subsequent maternal sensitivity, and later child development: Does continuity in development depend upon continuity of care giving? *Attachment & Human Development, 4*(3), 361–387. doi:10.1080/14616730210167267 PMID:12537851

Blair, C., Knipe, H., Cummings, E., Baker, D. P., Gamson, D., Eslinger, P., & Thorne, S. L. (2007). A developmental neuroscience approach to the study of school readiness. In R. C. Pianta, M. J. Cox, & K. L. Snow (Eds.), *School readiness and the transition to kindergarten in the era of accountability* (pp. 149–174). Baltimore, MD: Paul H. Brookes.

Bracken, B. A. (2007). Bracken school readiness assessment: Examiner's manual (3rd ed.). San Antonio, TX: Pearson.

Bretherton, I., Biringen, Z., Ridgeway, D., Maslin, C., & Sherman, M. (1989). Attachment: The parental perspective. *Infant Mental Health Journal, 10*(3), 203–221. doi:10.1002/1097-0355(198923)10:3<203::AID-IMHJ2280100307>3.0.CO;2-8

Bretherton, I., Prentiss, C., & Ridgeway, D. (1990). Family relationships as represented in a story-completion task at thirty-seven and fifty-four months of age. *New Directions for Child Development, 48*(48), 85–105. doi:10.1002/cd.23219904807 PMID:2216013

Bretherton, I., Ridgeway, D., & Cassidy, J. (1990). Assessing internal working models of the attachment relationship: An attachment story completion task for 3-year-olds. In M. T. Greenberg, D. Cicchetti, & E. M. Cummings (Eds.), *Attachment in the preschool years: Theory, research, and intervention* (pp. 273–308). Chicago: University of Chicago Press.

Bronson, M. B. (2000). *Self-regulation in early childhood: Nature and nurture*. New York: Guilford.

Bus, A. G. (1994). The role of social context in emergent literacy. In E. M. H. Assink (Ed.), *Literacy acquisition and social context* (pp. 9–24). Oxford, UK: Harvester Wheatsheaf/Prentice Hall.

Bus, A. G. (2001). Parent-child book reading through the lens of attachment theory. In L. Verhoeven & C. Snow (Eds.), *Literacy and motivation: Reading engagement in individuals and groups* (pp. 39–53).

Bus, A. G. (2003). Social-emotional requisites for learning to read. In On reading books to children: Parents and teachers (pp. 3-15). Mahwah, NJ: Lawrence Erlbaum Associates.

Catts, H. W., Fey, M. E., Zhang, X., & Tomblin, J. B. (1999). Language basis of reading and reading abilities: Evidence from a longitudinal investigation. *Scientific Studies of Reading, 3*(4), 331–361. doi:10.1207/s1532799xssr0304_2

Coolahan, K., Fantuzzo, J., Mendez, J., & McDermott, P. (2000). Preschool peer interactions and readiness to learn: Relationships between classroom peer play and learning behaviors and conduct. *Journal of Educational Psychology, 92*(3), 458–465. doi:10.1037/0022-0663.92.3.458

Crockenberg, S. (1981). Infant irritability, mother responsiveness, and social support influences on the security of infant-mother attachment. *Child Development, 52*(3), 857–865. doi:10.2307/1129087 PMID:7285658

Dent, V. F. (2006). Observations of school library impact at two rural Ugandan schools. *New Library World, 107*(9/10), 403–421. doi:10.1108/03074800610702598

Dent, V. F. (2007). Local economic development in Uganda and the connection to rural community libraries and literacy. *New Library World, 108*(5/6), 203–217. doi:10.1108/03074800710748777

Dent, V. F., Goodman, G., & Kevane, M. (2014). *Rural community libraries in Africa: Challenges and impacts*. Hershey, PA: IGI Global. doi:10.4018/978-1-4666-5043-5

Dickinson, D. K., & Neuman, S. B. (Eds.). (2006). *Handbook of early literacy research* (Vol. 2). New York: Guilford.

Fanciullo, M., Yellin, E., Blake, B., Chu, D., Schroeder, M., Fults, E., . . . Goodman, G. (2013, June). *An examination of rural Ugandan preschool children's implicit perceptions of familial social roles.* Paper presented at the meeting of the New York State Psychological Association, New York, NY.

Fantuzzo, J., Sekino, Y., & Cohen, H. L. (2004). An examination of the contributions of interactive peer play to salient classroom competencies for urban Head Start children. *Psychology in the Schools*, *41*(3), 323–335. doi:10.1002/pits.10162

Felitti, V. J., Anda, R. F., Nordenberg, D., Williamson, D. F., Spitz, A. M., Edwards, V., & Marks, J. S. et al. (1998). Relationship of childhood abuse and household dysfunction to many of the leading causes of death in adults: The Adverse Childhood Experiences (ACE) Study. *American Journal of Preventive Medicine*, *14*(4), 245–258. doi:10.1016/S0749-3797(98)00017-8 PMID:9635069

Ferguson, P., Jimerson, S. R., & Dalton, M. J. (2001). Sorting out successful failures: Exploratory analyses of factors associated with academic and behavioral outcomes of retained students. *Psychology in the Schools*, *38*(4), 327–341. doi:10.1002/pits.1022

Fonagy, P., Gergely, G., Jurist, E. L., & Target, M. (2002). *Affect regulation, mentalization, and the development of the self.* New York: Other Press.

Fonagy, P., & Target, M. (2005). Bridging the transmission gap: An end to an important mystery of attachment research? *Attachment & Human Development*, *7*(3), 333–343. doi:10.1080/14616730500269278 PMID:16210243

Garner, P. W., Curenton, S. M., & Taylor, K. (2005). Predictors of mental state understanding in preschoolers of varying socioeconomic backgrounds. *International Journal of Behavioral Development*, *29*(4), 271–281. doi:10.1177/01650250544000053

Goodman, G. (2010). *Therapeutic attachment relationships: Interaction structures and the processes of therapeutic change*. Lanham, MD: Jason Aronson.

Grienenberger, J., Kelly, K., & Slade, A. (2005). Maternal reflective functioning, mother-infant affective communication, and infant attachment: Exploring the link between mental states and observed caregiving behavior in the intergenerational transmission of attachment. *Attachment & Human Development*, *7*(3), 299–311. doi:10.1080/14616730500245963 PMID:16210241

Hart, B., & Risley, T. R. (1999). *The social world of children: Learning to talk.* Baltimore, MD: Paul H. Brookes Publishing.

Hecht, S. A., Burgess, S. R., Torgesen, J. K., Wagner, R. K., & Rashotte, C. A. (2000). Explaining social class differences in growth of reading skills from beginning kindergarten through fourth-grade: The role of phonological awareness, rate of access, and print knowledge. *Reading and Writing*, *12*(1/2), 99–127. doi:10.1023/A:1008033824385

Holding, P. A., Taylor, H. G., Kazungu, S. D., Mkala, T., Gona, J., Mwamuye, B., & Stevenson, J. et al. (2004). Assessing cognitive outcomes in a rural African population: Development of a neuropsychological battery in Kilifi District, Kenya. *Journal of the International Neuropsychological Society*, *10*(02), 246–260. doi:10.1017/S1355617704102166 PMID:15012845

Human Development Reports Uganda. (2014). Retrieved from http://hdr.undp.org/en/countries

Hungi, N., & Thuku, F. (2010). Variations in reading achievement across 14 southern African school systems: Which factors matter? *International Review of Education*, *56*(1), 63–101. doi:10.1007/s11159-009-9148-x

Kagan, S. L., & Lowenstein, A. E. (2004). School readiness and children's play: Contemporary oxymoron or compatible option? In E. F. Zigler, D. G. Singer, & S. J. Bishop-Josef (Eds.), *Children's play: The roots of reading* (pp. 59–76). Washington, DC: Zero to Three Press.

Kranich, N. (Ed.). (2001). *Libraries and democracy: The cornerstones of liberty*. Chicago: American Library Association.

Lakner, C., & Milanovic, B. (2013). *Global income distribution: From the fall of the Berlin Wall to the Great Recession.* Policy Research Working Paper, World Bank. Retrieved from http://www-wds.worldbank.org/external/default/WDSContentServer/IW3P/IB/2013/12/11/000158349_20131211100152/Rendered/PDF/WPS6719.pdf)

Mar, R. A., Tackett, J. L., & Moore, C. (2010). Exposure to media and theory-of-mind development in preschoolers. *Cognitive Development*, *25*(1), 69–78. doi:10.1016/j.cogdev.2009.11.002

Meins, E. (1997). *Security of attachment and the social development of cognition*. Hove, UK: Psychology Press.

Meins, E., Fernyhough, C., Wainwright, R., Gupta, M. D., Fradley, E., & Tuckey, M. (2002). Maternal mind-mindedness and attachment security as predictors of theory of mind understanding. *Child Development*, *73*(6), 1715–1726. doi:10.1111/1467-8624.00501 PMID:12487489

Muratori, F., Picchi, L., Bruni, G., Patarnello, M., & Romagnoli, G. (2003). A two-year follow-up of psychodynamic psychotherapy for internalizing disorders in children. *Journal of the American Academy of Child and Adolescent Psychiatry*, *42*(3), 331–339. doi:10.1097/00004583-200303000-00014 PMID:12595787

Nampijja, M., Apule, B., Lule, S., Akurut, H., Muhangi, L., Elliott, A. M., & Alcock, K. J. (2010). Adaptation of Western measures of cognition for assessing 5-year-old semi-urban Ugandan children. *The British Journal of Educational Psychology*, *80*(1), 15–30. doi:10.1348/000709909X460600 PMID:19594989

Nelson, E., Wasson, J., Kirk, J., Keller, A., Clark, D., Dietrich, A., & Zubkoff, M. et al. (1987). Assessment of function in routine clinical practice: Description of the COOP Chart method and preliminary findings. *Journal of Chronic Diseases*, *40*(S1), 55S–63S. doi:10.1016/S0021-9681(87)80033-4 PMID:3597698

Nicolopoulou, A. (2002). Peer-group culture and narrative development. In S. Blum-Kulka & C. E. Snow (Eds.), *Talking to adults: The contribution of multiparty discourse to language acquisition* (pp. 117–152). Mahwah, NJ: Lawrence Erlbaum Associates.

Nicolopoulou, A., & Cole, M. (2010). Design experimentation as a theoretical and empirical tool for developmental pedagogical research. *Pedagogies*, *5*(1), 61–71. doi:10.1080/15544800903406316

Nicolopoulou, A., de Sá, A. B., Ilgaz, H., & Brockmeyer, C. (2010). Using the transformational power of play to educate hearts and minds: From Vygotsky to Vivian Paley and beyond. *Mind, Culture, and Activity*, *17*, 1–17.

Nicolopoulou, A., Schnabel Cortina, K., Ilgaz, H., Brockmeyer Cates, C., & de Sá, A. B. (2015). Using narrative- and play-based activity to promote low-income preschoolers oral language, emergent literacy, and social competence. *Early Childhood Research Quarterly*, *31*, 147–162. doi:10.1016/j.ecresq.2015.01.006 PMID:25866441

Nuwagaba-Biribonwoha, H., Mayon-White, R. T., Okong, P., Brocklehurst, P., & Carpenter, L. M. (2012). The impact of HIV on maternal morbidity in the pre-HAART era in Uganda. *Journal of Pregnancy*, *2012*, 1–6. doi:10.1155/2012/508657 PMID:22013532

Nuwagaba-Biribonwoha, H., Mayon-White, R. T., Okong, P., Carpenter, L. M., & Jenkinson, C. (2006). The impact of HIV on maternal quality of life in Uganda. *AIDS Care*, *18*(6), 614–620. doi:10.1080/09540120500359298 PMID:16831790

Oyserman, D., Bybee, D., Mowbray, D., & MacFarlane, P. (2002). Positive parenting among African American mothers with a serious mental illness. *Journal of Marriage and the Family*, *64*(1), 65–77. doi:10.1111/j.1741-3737.2002.00065.x

Paley, V. G. (1990). *The boy who would be a helicopter: The uses of storytelling in the classroom*. Cambridge, MA: Harvard University Press.

Parry, K. (2007, August). *A library for learning: Experiences of students in Uganda*. Paper presented at the provincial conference of the Education Library Information and Technology Services, Port Shepstone, KwaZulu, South Africa.

Parry, K. (2014). Exploring secondary school student factors and academic outcomes at the Kitengesa Community Library. In V. F. Dent, G. Goodman, & M. Kevane (Eds.), *Rural community libraries in Africa: Challenges and impacts*. Hershey, PA: IGI Global.

Parry, K., Kirabo, E., & Nakyato, G. (2014). Working with parents to promote childrens literacy: A family literacy project in Uganda. *Multilingual Education*, *4*(1), 1–15. doi:10.1186/s13616-014-0013-2

Peterson, C. C., Wellman, H. M., & Liu, D. (2005). Steps in theory-of-mind development for children with deafness or autism. *Child Development*, *76*(2), 502–517. doi:10.1111/j.1467-8624.2005.00859.x PMID:15784096

Peterson, C. C., Wellman, H. M., & Slaughter, V. (2012). The mind behind the message: Advancing theory-of-mind scales for typically developing children, and those with deafness, autism, or Asperger syndrome. *Child Development*, *83*, 469–485. PMID:22304467

Pullen, P. C., & Justice, L. M. (2003). Enhancing phonological awareness, print awareness, and oral language skills in preschool children. *Intervention in School and Clinic*, *39*(2), 87–98. doi:10.1177/10534512030390020401

Quicken Trust. (2016). Retrieved from www.quickentrust.com

Quirk, M., Mayworm, A., Furlong, M. J., Grimm, R., & Rebelez, J. (2015). Dimensionality and measurement invariance of a school readiness screener by gender and parent education levels. *International Journal of School and Educational Psychology*, *3*(3), 167–177. doi:10.1080/21683603.2015.1053644

Raver, C. C., Garner, P. W., & Smith-Donald, R. (2007). The roles of emotion regulation and emotion knowledge for children's academic readiness: Are the links causal? In R. C. Pianta, M. J. Cox, & K. L. Snow (Eds.), *School readiness and the transition to kindergarten in the era of accountability* (pp. 121–147). Baltimore, MD: Paul H. Brookes.

Sachs, J. D., McArthur, J. W., Schmidt-Traub, G., Kruk, M., Bahadur, C., Faye, M., & McCord, G. (2004). Ending Africa's poverty trap. In W. C. Brainard & G. L. Perry (Eds.), *Brookings papers on economic activity* (pp. 117–240). Washington, DC: Brookings Institution Press.

Schady, N. (2011). Parents education, mothers vocabulary, and cognitive development in early childhood: Longitudinal evidence from Ecuador. *American Journal of Public Health, 101*(12), 2299–2307. doi:10.2105/AJPH.2011.300253 PMID:22021308

Schaefer, C., Coyne, J. C., & Lazarus, R. S. (1981). The health-related functions of social support. *Journal of Behavioral Medicine, 4*(4), 381–406. doi:10.1007/BF00846149 PMID:7338894

Seja, A. L., & Russ, S. W. (1999). Childrens fantasy play and emotional understanding. *Journal of Clinical Child Psychology, 28*(2), 269–277. doi:10.1207/s15374424jccp2802_13 PMID:10353085

Sheppard, M. (2009). High thresholds and prevention in childrens services: The impact of mothers coping strategies on outcome of child and parenting problems—six month follow-up. *British Journal of Social Work, 39*(1), 46–63. doi:10.1093/bjsw/bcm088

Simons, R., Beaman, J., Conger, R., & Chao, W. (1993). Stress, support, and antisocial behavior trait as determinants of emotional well-being and parenting practices among single mothers. *Journal of Marriage and the Family, 55*(2), 385–398. doi:10.2307/352809

Slade, A., Grienenberger, J., Bernbach, E., Levy, D., & Locker, A. (2005). Maternal reflective functioning, attachment, and the transmission gap: A preliminary study. *Attachment & Human Development, 7*(3), 283–298. doi:10.1080/14616730500245880 PMID:16210240

Snow, C. E. (1991). The theoretical basis for relationships between language and literacy in development. *Journal of Research in Childhood Education, 6*(1), 5–10. doi:10.1080/02568549109594817

Snow, C. E., & Dickinson, D. K. (1990). Social sources of narrative skills at home and at school. *First Language, 10*(29), 87–103. doi:10.1177/014272379001002901

Snow, C. E., & Dickinson, D. K. (1991). Skills that aren't basic in a new conception of literacy. In E. M. Jennings & A. C. Purves (Eds.), *Literate systems and individual lives: Perspectives on literacy and schooling* (pp. 179–191). Albany, NY: State University of New York Press.

Sroufe, L. A., Egeland, B., Carlson, E. A., & Collins, W. A. (2005). *The development of the person: The Minnesota study of risk and adaptation from birth to adulthood.* New York: Guilford Press.

Stilwell, C. (1989). Community libraries: A brief review of their origins and nature with particular reference to South Africa. *Journal of Librarianship, 21*(4), 260–269. doi:10.1177/096100068902100403

Stilwell, C. (1991). Community libraries: A viable alternative to the public library in South Africa? *Progressive Librarian, 4*, 17–27.

Storch, S. A., & Whitehurst, G. J. (2002). Oral language and code-related precursors to reading: Evidence from a longitudinal structural model. *Developmental Psychology, 38*(6), 934–947. doi:10.1037/0012-1649.38.6.934 PMID:12428705

Tamis-LeMonda, C. S., Bornstein, M. H., & Baumwell, L. (2001). Maternal responsiveness and childrens achievement of language milestones. *Child Development, 72*(3), 748–767. doi:10.1111/1467-8624.00313 PMID:11405580

Tanser, F., Hosegood, V., Bärnighausen, T., Herbst, K., Nyirenda, M., Muhwava, W., & Newell, M. et al. (2008). Cohort Profile: Africa Centre Demographic Information System (ACDIS) and population-based HIV survey. *International Journal of Epidemiology, 37*(5), 956–962. doi:10.1093/ije/dym211 PMID:17998242

Taylor, M., & Carlson, S. M. (1997). The relationship between individual differences in fantasy and theory-of-mind. *Child Development, 68*(3), 436–455. doi:10.2307/1131670 PMID:9249959

United Nations Children's Fund (UNICEF). (2013). *Uganda country statistics*. Retrieved from http://www.unicef.org/infobycountry/uganda_statistics.html

United Nations Educational, Scientific and Cultural Organization (UNESCO). (2007). *Youth (15-24) and adult (15+) literacy rates by country and by gender for 2000-2004*. UNESCO Institute for Statistics. Retrieved from http://stats.uis.unesco.org/unesco/ReportFolders/ReportFolders.aspx

United Nations Educational, Scientific and Cultural Organization (UNESCO). (2014). *Literacy data chart/Africa*. Retrieved from http://www.unesco.org/new/en/dakar/education/literacy

van IJzendoorn, M. H., Dijkstra, J., & Bus, A. G. (1995). Attachment, intelligence and language: A meta-analysis. *Social Development, 4*(2), 115–128. doi:10.1111/j.1467-9507.1995.tb00055.x

Weiland, C., & Yoshikawa, H. (2013). Impacts of a pre kindergarten program on childrens mathematics, language, literacy, executive function, and emotional skills. *Child Development, 84*(6), 2112–2130. doi:10.1111/cdev.12099 PMID:23534487

Wells, G. (1985). Preschool literacy-related activities and success in school. In D. R. Olson, N. Torrance, & A. Hildyard (Eds.), *Literacy, language, and learning: The nature and consequences of reading and writing* (pp. 229–255). New York: Cambridge University Press.

Wells, G. (1986). *The meaning makers: Children learning language and using language to learn*. Portsmouth, NH: Heinemann.

Westby, C. E. (1991). Learning to talk—talking to learn: Oral-literate language differences. In C. Simon (Ed.), *Communication skills and classroom success: Therapy methodologies for language learning disabled students* (pp. 181–218). San Diego, CA: College-Hill Press.

Whitehurst, G. J., & Lonigan, C. J. (2001). Emergent literacy: Development from prereaders to readers. In S. B. Neuman & D. K. Dickinson (Eds.), *Handbook of early literacy research* (pp. 11–29). New York: Guilford.

World Bank. (2014). *Fighting HIV/AIDS in Uganda*. Retrieved from https://www.worldbank.org/progress/uganda.html

World Bank Country Statistics. (2014). Retrieved from http://data.worldbank.org/country/uganda

World Bank Literacy Indicators Female. (2014). Retrieved from http://data.worldbank.org/indicator/SE.ADT.LITR.FE.ZS

World Bank Literacy Indicators Male. (2014). Retrieved from http://data.worldbank.org/indicator/SE.ADT.1524.LT.MA.ZS

World Bank Sub-Saharan Africa Statistics. (2014). Retrieved from http://data.worldbank.org/region/SSA

You, D., Hug, L., & Chen, Y. (2014). *Levels and trends in child mortality 2014*. Retrieved from http://siteresources.worldbank.org/ICPEXT/Resources/Levels-and-Trends-in-Child-Mortality-Report-2014.pdf

Zigler, E. F., Singer, D. G., & Bishop-Josef, S. J. (Eds.), *Children's play: The roots of reading*. Washington, DC: Zero to Three Press.

KEY TERMS AND DEFINITIONS

Cross-Cultural Psychology: Researchers engage in the study of the human mind across cultural contexts. Cultural context shapes both the development and the functioning of the human mind; thus, it is important to understand what these cultural influences are and how they exert their influences on the human mind.

Emergent Literacy Skills: Children need to acquire this set of skills before learning how to read. These skills include knowledge of 1) colors, 2) letters, 3) numbers/counting, 4) sizes/comparisons, and 5) shapes.

Oral Language Skills: Children need to know how to speak a language fluently before entering a school context. These skills include knowledge of receptive and expressive vocabulary words.

Play-Based Intervention: Children are engaged in an activity that includes the use of their own creativity and imagination and is largely self-directed rather than therapist or teacher-directed.

School Readiness Skills: To be ready to enter a school context, children need to have three skill sets: emergent literacy skills, oral language skills, and social competence (specifically, theory of mind skills). Secure attachment to a caregiver facilitates the acquisition of all three skill sets.

STSA: The Storytelling/Story-Acting play-based intervention includes 1) a storytelling phase in which the child tells a story to a facilitator who records it verbatim and 2) a story-acting phase in which the child author selects other children to act out the story read to them by the facilitator.

Theory of Mind Skills: Children need to know how to read the social cues of the teacher and classmates before entering a school context. These skills include the understanding that the contents of people's minds differ from one person to the next and that one's own perceptions might differ from the perceptions of others.

Chapter 12
Ethics in Play Therapy Consultation and Supervision

Jeffrey S. Ashby
Georgia State University, USA

Laura Wood
Georgia State University, USA

Sarah Kiperman
Georgia State University, USA

ABSTRACT

Ethics in play therapy consultation and supervision can be complex because of the "layered" nature of the relationships involved in each of these indirect services. In this chapter, we discuss the differential obligations the play therapy consultant or supervisor owes to the consulate/supervisee and the client. The ethical constructs of informed consent, competence, confidentiality, and dual relationships are discussed in relationship to the consultee/supervisee and the client. While the obligations are similar in these indirect services, there are also different obligations in each of these areas.

ETHICS IN PLAY THERAPY SUPERVISION AND CONSULTATION

Do the right thing. - Spike Lee

Ethics is ultimately doing the right thing. This can be straightforward in clinical practice and may be a relatively easy path to find. Our codes (e.g., American Counseling Association [ACA, 2014], American Psychological Association [APA, 2010]) and practice guidelines (e.g., Association of Play Therapy [APT, 2012]) give guidance that help us practice ethically, such as providing services within the boundaries of our competence and protecting client confidentiality. The codes (ACA, 2014) also recommend incorporating Kitchner's (1984) five ethical principles into all aspects of practice: autonomy (fostering a client's independence and right to control the direction of his/her life), nonmaleficence (not cause harm to others), beneficence (doing good unto others and promote human welfare), justice (fairness and

DOI: 10.4018/978-1-5225-2224-9.ch012

equal treatment), and fidelity (commitment to demonstrate faithfulness and loyalty to the professional relationship at hand). The additional principle, veracity (dealing truthfully with clients) is also provided in the code of ethics (ACA, 2014).

Ethics in play therapy, however, is complicated by an obligation not limited to the child, but to additional stakeholders such as parents/guardians, teachers, and other professionals. Navigating these relationships often requires professionals to seek consultation or supervision. While a number of resources offer guidance in play therapy ethics (e.g., APT, 2012; Ashby & Clark, 2015), delineate conceptual differences among supervision and consultation (e.g., Knoff, 1988), discuss ethics as they relate to consultation (e.g., Doughtery, 1992; Newman, 1993) and supervision, (e.g., Herlihy, Gray, & McCollum, 2002; Ladany, Lehrman-Waterman, Molinaro, & Wolgast, 1999), limited information is available on how these topics function together. Many professionals question 'when should I seek consultation', 'does this require supervision', or 'what are my obligations as a supervisor or consultant?'. This chapter aims to address these questions and discuss the ethics of these indirect play therapy services with additional stakeholders in consultation and supervision.

In this chapter, we attempt to help the reader understand the layered ethical obligations inherent to indirect play therapy services. Keeping in mind the ultimate responsibility to the child client, the chapter will address the ethical obligations to attain informed consent, practice within the boundaries of one's competence, protect confidentiality, and manage potential dual relationships with the consultee/supervisee, the child client, and the client's parents/guardians. These familiar issues can take on greater complexity in the layered application of play therapy consultation/supervision. The goal of this chapter is to help clarify the differential obligations we hold so that we can ultimately do the right thing.

WHO'S WHO? THE ROLES INVOLVED IN INDIRECT PLAY THERAPY SERVICES

Understanding the ethical and legal obligations in play therapy consultation and supervision can be complicated, in large part because these indirect play therapy services are made up of a tripartite relationship among at least three parties: the indirect play therapy service provider (e.g., supervisor, consultant), the direct play therapy service provider (e.g., supervisee, consultee), and the client (e.g., child and their family, system). Because of the layered nature endemic to indirect services (e.g., supervisor, supervisee, supervisee's client) there are varied and various parties to whom the play therapist supervisor or consultant owes an ethical duty. In addition, with regard to ethical obligations, it may be helpful to treat supervision and consultation as discrete areas of specialization with differential ethical obligations (Thomas, 2010).

In play therapy supervision, the play therapist supervisor owes a direct ethical obligation to the supervisee and an indirect ethical obligation to the supervisee's clients (ACA, 2014). The play therapist supervisor is ethically obligated to meet a reasonable standard of care in providing supervision (Russell-Chapin & Chapin, 2011). The supervisor may take on a number of roles in supervision including teaching, mentoring, evaluating, and providing guidance and direction. The supervisor is ethically obligated to provide a reasonable standard of care. That standard of care is consistent with the ethical obligations in direct service to clients (e.g., informed consent, competence, confidentiality, dual relationships). In addition to the ethical obligation the play therapy supervisor has to the supervisee, the supervisor also has an ethical obligation to the supervisee's clients (Knapp & VandeCreek, 1997). Play therapists generally seek play therapy supervision when they cannot practice competently without supervision (e.g., are not yet licensed, are practicing in a new area). The supervisor takes responsibility for the supervisees' practice with clients in these relationships, meaning play therapy supervisors are responsible for their actions as supervisors, their supervisee's treatment of clients and ensuring the client receives a reasonable standard of care.

Consultation, like supervision, includes at least three parties: the consultant, the consultee, and the consultee's dependent, client, or client system (Remley & Herlihy, 2016). The role of a play therapy consultant differs from a supervisor in various ways, which accounts for their different ethical obligations to both the consultee and the party who is the focus of the consultation (e.g., client, client system, student, dependent child). While play therapy supervision generally takes place between two clinicians (supervisor and supervisee), a play therapist might provide consultation with several entities including, but not limited to, another play therapist or licensed clinician, parents, teachers, and or/other school personnel. While there are similarities between supervision and consultation, the ethical obligation the play therapist consultant owes to the consultee and the child or system that is the focus of the consultation differs from the obligations in supervision. In consultation, the play therapist consultant is ethically obligated to provide a reasonable standard of care to the consultee (e.g., competence, confidentiality).

The role of consultant is similar to the role of supervisor in that both roles may include teaching, mentoring, and providing guidance and direction. However, consultation is nonhierarchical and the roles of consultant and consultee share coordinate status (Sandoval, 2014). The role of consultant does not typically include evaluation, and the guidance and direction offered by the consultant may be considered and ultimately rejected by the consultee. In the case of a play therapist seeking play therapy consultation, the consultee is generally understood to be practicing within the bounds of competence and is seeking additional information, guidance, expertise, and/or perspective on a case or cases. While the consultant does owe an ethical obligation to the party for whom the consultee has sought consultation, the consultant is not typically viewed as responsible for the actions of the consultee in providing services or intervening with the child or system that is the focus of the consultation (Jacob, Decker, & Timmerman Lugg, 2016). As a result, the consultant typically does not have the role of evaluator and is not viewed as responsible for the consultee's actions with children or systems.

Understanding the similarities and distinctions between the roles of play therapist supervisor and play therapist consultant can aid in differentiating distinct ethical obligations owed in these rather complex, layered relationships. As we consider the application of the ethical constructs of informed consent, competence, confidentiality, and dual relationships, it will be important to acknowledge that they are fairly interdependent.

INFORMED CONSENT IN PLAY THERAPY SUPERVISION AND CONSULTATION

The ACA code of ethics (ACA, 2014, p. 20) defines informed consent as "a process of information sharing associated with possible actions clients may choose to take, aimed at assisting clients in acquiring a full appreciation and understanding of the facts and implications of a given action or actions." Ultimately, informed consent refers to clients acknowledging their comprehensive awareness of the services they receive. In play therapy, service providers (the supervisee/consultee) are responsible for providing their clients with access to adequate information so they are informed consumers (Beahrs & Gutheil, 2001). The goal of informed consent is to prevent situations where clients would not have consented to a provided service had they known information prior to beginning treatment. Traditional informed consent practice includes three important components to ensure this goal is met: (1) *capacity*, (2) *comprehension*, and

(3) *voluntariness* (Dekraai, Sales, & Hall, 1998). *Capacity* refers to a client's ability to make rational decisions. *Comprehension* ensures clients have all of the information that they need in a comprehensible form. V*oluntariness* refers to the client giving consent willingly, without coercion and their ability to withdraw from service at any time. These three components apply to informed consent in indirect service and should always be considered in evaluating the consent of clients, supervisees, and consultees

Informed Consent for Indirect Service Providers and the Clients of Their Consultees/Supervisees

Informed consent in traditional settings is typically enacted between supervisees/consultees and their clients. Ashby & Clark (2015) offer an overview of the appropriate topics to cover in informed consent with a client and a play therapist. They also highlight that informed consent is typically sought from the parents or guardians of the child client, with developmentally appropriate assent gathered from the child. However, when direct service providers seek supervision and/or consultation, additional information may need to be shared for clients to be able to give truly informed consent. For clients to demonstrate full understanding and comprehension of services, they must be made aware that by consenting to treatment, they are doing so with the understanding that other professionals (e.g., indirect service providers) will be involved in their case through supervision or consultation.

Direct service providers who have sought supervision need to make sure that their clients understand the nature and implications of the supervisory relationship. For instance, informed consent with the client should include the information that the play therapist can only provide competent care under the supervision of another professional and, without that supervision, would not be competent to provide a direct clinical service (Bernard & Goodyear, 1998). In addition, informed consent should clarify that the play therapist will be systematically sharing the client's confidential information with the supervisor and that the supervisor, just like the treating clinician, has an ethical mandate to keep client information confidential except in special circumstances (e.g., legally mandated to disclose). Because supervisors are vicariously responsible for all of the actions of their supervisees (Goodyear & Rodolfa, 2012), supervisors have the responsibility to make sure that their supervisees have gathered appropriate informed consent from clients.

As previously noted, the practice of consultation differs somewhat from the indirect service of supervision. Consistent with this distinction, informed consent in the practice of consultation is somewhat different than the process in supervision. When a direct service provider seeks consultation, the direct service provider fully anticipates providing competent care to clients but is typically seeking to be as expert as possible (Kurpius & Fuqua, 1993). In addition, while the play therapist consultee may disclose confidential information about a client, the information is typically not adequate to make the client identifiable. As a result, it may be a best practice for play therapists to acknowledge (in informed consent with clients) that they regularly consult with other professionals about cases to provide the best possible care. Play therapists might also clarify that consultation will only occur with qualified professionals and confidentiality will be guarded.

Informed Consent for Indirect Service Providers and Their Consultees/Supervisees

When play therapists are providing indirect services, informed consent between a play therapist and the supervisee or consultee can help frame the service provided and the expectation of each party (Jacob et al., 2016). In consultation, formal documentation of informed consent may not be necessary given the equal relationship and demonstrated competence of the consultee. The formal nature of supervision calls for a signed informed consent according to the Ethical Standards for Counseling Supervisors from the Association for Counselor Education, and Supervision (1993). This consent may include several of the issues typically addressed in informed consent for treatment including anticipated length of service, limits to privacy, any fees, risks and benefits, and storage of records (Thomas, 2007). Informed consent in supervision is designed to prevent supervisees from saying they would not have consented to receiving supervision had they been more aware prior to entering the supervisory relationship (Beahrs & Gutheil, 2001).

It is expected that supervisees and consultees should have the capacity for judgement and decision making for informed consent (Dekraai, Sales, & Hall, 1998). Though, in the case of both supervision and consultation, supervisors and consultants should assess for capacity. If supervisees or consultees are impaired to the degree that they lack capacity for decision making (e.g., whether or not to engage in indirect services with a play therapist supervisor/consultant) then informed consent cannot be obtained and supervision/consultation should not occur. This lack of capacity might well imply impairment on the part of the supervisee/consultee that could bring harm to clients and, consequently, the play therapist supervisor/consultant might need to take action (e.g., report to a clinic director or ethics board). Indirect service providers may want to consider whether the supervisee/consultee presents as using substances, with impairment of memory or thought process, or with an altered state of consciousness, all of which would undermine the capacity of the person to give consent and to provide competent care for clients.

The second component of informed consent, comprehension, is required in both supervision and consultation informed consent. While comprehension in consultation is often informally accounted for, comprehension should be explicitly addressed and documented in supervision, so the supervisee has a clear understanding of all aspects of supervision (McCarthy et al., 1995). McCarthy and colleagues (1995) and Thomas (2007) provided a list of issues to address in informed consent among supervisors and supervisees. Some examples of information Thomas (2007) suggests including are a supervisor's credentials, the time commitment and documentation of supervision, supervisor's responsibilities, confidentiality limits, financial interests, benefits and risks associated with supervision, and evaluation methods. This list gives a general overview of the kinds of information that can help potential supervisees make an informed decision about entering into a supervisory relationship. Comprehension in informed consent for consultation includes some of the same components as supervision, but may also be more limited (Jacob et al., 2016). Potential consultees should have comprehension of the consultant's areas of competence and expertise before consenting to consultation.

Voluntariness in informed consent assumes that consultees and supervisees have willingly consented to their received services (Corey, Haynes, Moulton, & Muratori, 2010). In consultation, the intentional act of choosing the consultant can imply the enactment of voluntariness, as the consultee usually actively initiated the consultation. In supervision, signing an informed consent form provides formal documentation that the supervisee voluntarily agrees to enter the supervision experience. However, supervision often happens in the context of a formal training experience and as a result, supervisees are often obligated to have supervision since it is required for progress in an academic training program or in the pursuit of certification or licensure. The implication in supervision is that one can always choose not to pursue a particular training program and adequate information about the requirements of supervision must be made clear before a trainee begins the program.

Withdrawing from supervision or consultation involves consultees and supervisees acknowledging the benefits of the service on which they will miss out (e.g., a second opinion in consultation or formally documented hours of supervision). While consultees can willingly terminate their consultation, continue practicing, and seek help from another professional, supervisees should stop seeing the clients for whom they sought supervision until they have access to a qualified supervisor.

COMPETENCE IN PLAY THERAPY CONSULTATION AND SUPERVISION

Fairburn and Cooper (2011) defined competence as "the extent to which a therapist has the knowledge and skill required to deliver a treatment to the standard needed for it to achieve its expected effects" (p. 375). The ethical mandate of competence suggests that practitioners should only use the skills they know how to use. The directive for competence is made clear in several ethical codes. For example, ACA states, "Counselors practice only within the boundaries of their competence, based on their education, training, supervised experience, state and national professional credentials, and appropriate professional experience" (2014, C.2.a, p. 8).

There are various aspects to consider when accounting for competency. Licensure or certification as a counselor or mental health professional presents as a broad acknowledgement of the skills one has as a competent service provider. However, determining individual areas of competence are typically left to the discretion of the practitioner. Pope and Vasquez (2010) propose that formal academic training, professional training, and supervised experience may be the best standard for the establishment and defense of the boundaries of competence. In delivering indirect play therapy services, practitioners have to consider whether they are competent in their skillset as a play therapist to work with the client of the supervisee or consultant as well as in their skills as a consultant or supervisor.

Competence in Treating the Clients of the Supervisees and Consultees

It is important to be competent in play therapy skills as indirect service provision assumes the supervisor and consultant are competent in areas and for clients for which they provide consultation and supervision. Competence for play therapists spans knowing *about* particular treatments, populations, and presenting problems and knowing *how* to deliver these services to clients from diverse backgrounds in specific settings (Ashby & Clark, 2015). Practitioners should have documented formal instruction, training, and supervised experiences in the areas in order to be considered competent. Questions practitioners may ask in evaluating whether they are competent to supervise or consult on a case include: (1) am I competent in working with children; (2) am I competent to conduct play therapy; (3) am I competent to address the presenting concern; (4) am I competent in working with diverse clients; and (5) do I have adequate training and supervision to provide care to this client.

1 and 2: Am I Competent in Working with Children and Conducting Play Therapy?

Play therapy is generally considered a "limited-domain intervention" (Barber, Sharpless, Klostermann, & McCarthy, 2007), which requires specialization in order to practice. The practice of play therapy assumes a competence in child therapy. Exhibiting competence in working with children can be achieved via academic course training in child development and child psychopathology, as well as in supervised experience working with child clients. Competence in the specialty area of play therapy may be established most easily through formal training and supervised experience. One way to demonstrate competence as a play therapist is to become a Registered Play Therapist (RPT). The APT (2015) notes that becoming a RPT does not infer one's achieved knowledge or competency, but it conveys certain education and training requirements have been met within the area of play therapy. Beyond training, one should be able to competently conceptualize a case within a theoretical framework, build a relationship, evoke change with certain activities or practices, and terminate treatment when necessary in order to be a competent play therapist.

3: Am I Competent to Address the Presenting Concern?

Addressing the presenting concerns of a client must be within one's competence, as treating a condition with inappropriate methods could lead to a worsened condition. While specialized trainings are required to gain competence in addressing certain presenting concerns such as these, general training, supervision, and consultation may be sufficient for competency in other areas (e.g., children coping with divorce or loss of a parent). Play therapists may regularly consult on cases to assure competence and should seek supervision or refer when they are confronted with cases outside the boundaries of their competence (Sweeney, 2001).

4: Am I Competent in Working with Diverse Clients?

Play therapists work with diverse clients in every session. While we may assume competence applies to clients who are culturally different from ourselves (e.g., different race/ethnicity, nationality, religious background) we must challenge ourselves to have awareness for the client's comprehensive culture (O'Connor, 2005). It is inevitable that clients' cultures will differ from our own, especially as we work with children – a culture in and of itself! In addition, clients can present with different values, languages, religions, ethnicities, and experiences. We are ethically obligated (ACA, 2014) to practice in a culturally competent manner (i.e., the continued effort of practitioners to exhibit effective work within the cultural context of the client [Campinha-Bacote, 2002]). Cultural competence involves having an awareness of one's own culture and biases and understanding the cultural experience of the client. To exhibit competence, practitioners should seek to educate themselves with supervision, training, coursework, and ongoing self-reflection (Gil, 2005).

5: Do I Have Adequate Training and Supervision to Provide Care to This Client?

Because play therapist supervisors and consultants should only provide this indirect service in areas where they are competent, they should consistently ask themselves if they have enough training and supervision to provide direct service to the client with adequate care. A good way to account for this is to assess the amount of documented training and supervision hours that specifically relate to the area of competency being assessed.

Competence in the Practice of Consultation and Supervision

Play therapist must also be competent in providing supervision or supervision in order to ethically provide indirect service to clients and systems (Pope & Vasquez, 2010). Indirect service providers are typically viewed as experts when assuming the role of supervisor or consultant. In supervision, the indirect service provider takes on the role of expert as the person receiving supervision is working outside the boundaries of their competence. In this situation, play therapist supervisees work under a competent play therapist (the supervisor) to develop their competencies and the supervisor assumes responsibility for the client being seen by the supervisee. Consultants are viewed as competent play therapists who can trouble-shoot scenarios, consider different options, test hypotheses, and ask relevant questions. The consulting relationship is often more informal than supervision and is a service provided to competent individuals (e.g., a practitioner, parent, teacher) in collaboration to yield effective ideas to benefit the client. While the indirect service provider is being approached in consultation due to their exhibited competence, the person seeking consultation is also viewed as competent and the client ultimately remains the primary responsibility of the consultee (Jacob et al., 2016).

Although the degree of responsibility and the expectations for competency differ for consultants versus supervisors, the areas of competency are similar for both. Beyond the questions of competency related to the specific client, helpful questions of competency to ask yourself when entering into the role of an indirect play therapy service provider include: (1) do I have adequate preparation and training in consultation or supervision methods and techniques; and (2) am I aware of and able to address the multicultural and diversity issues present across relationships.

1: Do I Have Adequate Preparation and Training in Consultation or Supervision Methods and Techniques?

Similar to competency related specifically to the client, indirect play therapy service providers must have training and experience with the methods and techniques associated with consultation or supervision. This may include graduate level course work, simulated supervision or consultation, supervised experiences of supervision or consultation (i.e., meta-supervision), and continuing education activities (APT, 2015; Newman, 2013). These trainings should be focused both on general supervision and consultation as well as specific play therapy consultation and supervision (APT, 2015). While competency cannot be defined by certification, APT does offer credentialing as a Registered Play Therapist-Supervisor (RPT-S) to demonstrate that a certain level of training has been met. The RPT-S certification requires additional hours of general clinical and play therapy experiences compared to the hours attained as an RPT, as well as specific supervisor training (APT, 2015).

2: Am I Aware of and Able to Address the Multicultural and Diversity Issues Present across Relationships?

The ACA Code of Ethics (2014) highlights the importance of being aware of and able to address any multicultural and diversity issues that may be present across relationships. Due to the indirect nature of supervision and consultation, this includes the indirect play therapy service provider (i.e., supervisor or consultant), the direct service provider (i.e., supervisee or consultee), the client, and the general context (e.g., school, clinic, home). Robinson, Bradley, and Hendricks (2000) suggested a four-step process for developing multicultural supervision competence. The first step is to develop awareness of how cultural issues affect counseling processes. In the second step, supervisors identify how cultural dynamics have an impact on supervision relationships. The third step is characterized by an exploration of cultural limitations and contributions of counseling theories. Finally, in the fourth step, supervisors integrate multicultural issues into existing supervision models.

Ingraham (2000) provided a multicultural consultation framework specifically for schools that can be adapted and applied to consultation across settings as well as to the supervision relationship. The following five components are included in the Multicultural School Consultation (MSC) framework and have been adapted to apply to the provisions of indirect play therapy services:

1. **Indirect Service Provider Learning and Development:** Knowledge and skill in areas such as understanding one's own culture and the impact it has on others, understanding individual differences within cultures, understanding of rapport building across cultures
2. **Direct Service Provider Learning and Development:** Knowledge and skill in areas such as decreasing the use of a "color-blind" approach, improving confidence
3. **Cultural Variations in the Indirect Provider-Direct Provider-Client Constellation:** Considering the similarities and differences between the consultant, consultee, and client
4. **Contextual and Power Influences:** Knowledge and awareness of the cultural context of the system, disruptions to balance of power and the impact
5. **Hypothesized Methods for Supporting Direct Service Provider and Client Success:** Using multiple perspectives to frame the problem, modeling bridging between cultures, seeking feedback from others

By following the Robinson et al.'s (2000) model and the guidelines provided by Ingraham (2000), the indirect service provider can continue developing their competency when working within diverse settings with culturally diverse clients.

When assessing competence in indirect play therapy services, the play therapist may ask a number of questions. The potential indirect play therapy service provider might ask (1) "Am I competent in the practice of supervision or consultation?"; (2) "If I am generally competent in the practice of supervision/consultation, am I competent in the area in which I would be providing that service in this situation (e.g., problem focus area, client population, or system)?"; and (3) "If questioned, could I easily defend my competence in each of these areas through education, training, and supervised experience?"

CONFIDENTIALITY IN PLAY THERAPY CONSULTATION AND SUPERVISION

Sommers-Flanagan and Sommers-Flanagan (2015) noted that confidentiality is one of the most important ethical considerations in mental health practice and Slack and Wassenaar (1999) found that issues of confidentiality were among the most common ethical dilemmas reported by clinicians around the world. Confidentiality refers to the ethical and legal obligation of a mental health provider to protect private information shared by a client in a therapeutic setting (Sweeney, 2001). The importance of confidentiality is rooted in the need for a sense of trust between the client and the therapist as an essential grounding of any therapeutic relationship. As further emphasized by the ACA code of ethics (2014, pg. 4), "Trust is the cornerstone of the counseling relationship, and counselors have the responsibility to respect and safeguard the client's right to privacy and confidentiality." However, confidentiality is not as straightforward as simply promising to never repeat what has been discussed. There are instances when confidentiality may legally or ethically be breached, such as when the client gives permission or when it is mandated by law.

The issue of confidentiality is further complicated in the practice of play therapy (APT, 2012; Carmichael, 2006). Although the legal obligation of confidentiality is reserved for the individual that provides informed consent (typically the parent or legal guardian of the play therapy client), the importance of trust in the therapeutic relationship remains equally important between a therapist and a child client. Finding the balance between respecting the child's right to privacy with the legal right of the parent or guardian to remain informed can be challenging (Sweeney, 2001). Serving in the role of supervisor or consultant, the picture of confidentiality becomes even more complex as one considers the issues of confidentiality related to child clients as well as supervisees and consultees.

Honoring the Confidentiality of the Supervisees' and Consultants' Clients

The obligation of confidentiality for information disclosed by or about the child receiving play therapy is an important consideration of the indirect service provider. However, the specific boundaries of confidentiality differ somewhat depending on the role of either supervisor or consultant. According to ACA (2014), one of the primary roles of the supervisor is to "monitor the services provided by supervisees" (p. 12). This process of monitoring naturally involves access to the client information disclosed by the supervisee and there is little about the client that will remain confidential between a supervisor and supervisee. It is the responsibility of the supervisor to protect the privacy of the child beyond the supervisory relationship. This is done both by not sharing confidential information with others and ensuring that the supervisee is aware of the obligation of confidentiality (Borders & Brown, 2005).

The consultation relationship differs from the relationship of supervisor and supervisee, which affects the structure of confidentiality. According to ACA (2014), information shared in a consulting relationship is discussed for professional purposes only and should not reveal identifying information whenever possible. This may be more difficult in settings such as schools where descriptions of a student's behavior (e.g., a fight in the hallway that is public knowledge in the school) or a personal attribute important to the consultation (e.g., a physical attribute that is resulting in bullying) may reveal the identity of the child. As a consultant, one can limit the amount of identifying information requested by asking, "Why am I seeking this information?" If it is not to help the presenting professional concern, it should remain confidential.

In both supervision and consultation, the child and legal client (e.g., parent, guardian) must be informed that information may be shared with other professionals, including supervisors and consultants. Furthermore, they must be informed that there are limits to confidentiality beyond these relationships. The limits of confidentiality for client information are the same for the indirect service provider as they are for the direct service provider, including (a) the legal client (e.g., parent) gives permission for information to be disclosed to a third party; or (b) it is required or permitted by law (Fisher, 2013).

Permission

The parent or guardian has the right to give permission for information to be shared with others (Remley & Herlihy, 2016). One common reason a parent may give permission is so that pertinent information can be shared with other professionals, such as teachers, who may need to know how best to work with the child. In cases such as these, it is important to protect the privacy and autonomy of the child as much as possible by allowing the child to have a voice in what information is to be shared. Other instances when permission may be given to breach confidentiality include needing to inform insurance policies about diagnoses or progress and transferring records between therapists or school systems. Again, all parties should be informed about what information is to be disclosed and to whom.

Required or Permitted by Law

Indirect play therapy service providers are regarded as mandated reporters. Therefore, when we take the role of a supervisor or consultant, we are legally and ethically required to breach confidentiality when there is a threat of harm to the child or other individuals. The supervisor is likely to play a direct role and even model for the supervisee this process, especially if it is a new domain for the supervisee. As a consultant, the indirect play therapy service provider can still support the process of mandated reporting without needing to be aware of the child's identity. Both in consultation and supervision, the indirect play therapy service provider should work with the direct play therapy service provider to make a plan of how to breach confidentiality. It is recommended that the child and the parent or guardian be included in or informed of the process when appropriate (Taylor & Adelman, 1989).

Honoring the Confidentiality of the Consultee and Supervisee

Just as trust is the cornerstone of a therapeutic relationship between the child and the play therapist, the foundation of trust is essential to the professional relationship between the indirect and direct service providers (Corey et al., 2010). Therefore, when we discuss confidentiality as an indirect play therapy provider, it is important to recognize the need to protect the privacy of the direct service provider in order to create a safe and supportive environment. It is not uncommon for supervisees and consultees to divulge personal information that arises for them as they work with clients. Care should be taken to ensure that both sides are clear about the guarantees and limits of confidentiality before the delivery of an indirect service. The limits of confidentiality in a supervisory or consultation relationship are similar to those in direct therapeutic relationships, including when permission has been given by the direct service provider and when it is ethically or legally required or permitted to breach confidentiality.

Permission

There may be instances where an indirect service provider is given permission to share information related to the direct service provider discussed during the supervision or consultation. For example, supervisees typically give consent for their supervisors to share evaluation information with other entities (e.g., state licensure boards, university practicum instructors). This consent is often required before supervision is undertaken and as Cobia and Boes (2000) note, should be explicitly outlined in the informed consent between supervisor and supervisee. In both supervision and consultation, the supervisee or consultee may also give permission for the indirect service provider to disclose information for the purposes of recommendations for jobs or further training opportunities. In each case, consent for the disclosures should be clearly documented.

Required or Permitted by Law

As a mental health professional, the indirect play therapy service provider remains a mandated reporter. If there is any reason to believe that the direct service provider is engaging in harmful behavior towards the client, such as physical abuse, it is legally mandated that the behavior be reported immediately to the appropriate authorities. In many cases though, the boundary of harmful behavior is not as clear as physical abuse. For example, imagine a consultation situation in which the direct service provider is working with a child who he/she is not professionally competent to serve. Through consultation, it becomes clear to you as a consultant that the professional is practicing outside the boundaries of his/her competence. In situations such as these, where you believe the professional has violated their ethical obligations but it has not as of yet caused or threatened to cause substantial harm, ACA (2014) recommends first attempting to resolve the issue informally by approaching the colleague about your concerns. In this case, it would not be your ethical or legal obligation to immediately breach confidentiality. While these two situations demonstrate instances where the indirect play therapy service provider should and should not immediately breach confidentiality, it can often be less clear cut what it means to cause "substantial harm" (ACA, 2014). In those situations, it is often helpful to consult with other professionals without needing to reveal identifying information.

When assessing confidentiality in indirect play therapy services, the play therapist may ask a number of questions. The play therapy consultant or supervisor might ask, "Am I keeping information about the consultee or supervisee private and confidential?" "If I am disclosing information about the consultee or supervisee, do I have permission (e.g., signed release for disclosure of evaluation information from a supervisee to a licensure board) or am I ethically required to do so (e.g., with a seriously impaired consultee with whom I have not been able to resolve the situation informally)?" Because the play therapist providing indirect services has an ethical obligation to the consultee or supervisee and the client, the play therapy consultant or supervisor might also ask, "Am I keeping information about the client private and confidential?" "If I am disclosing information about the client, do I have permission (e.g., signed release for disclosure to teachers or systems) or am I ethically required to do so (e.g., as a mandatory reporter)?"

DUAL RELATIONSHIPS IN PLAY THERAPY CONSULTATION AND SUPERVISION

A dual role is generally understood as when a mental health service provider has a professional role with a person along with another role or relationship with the same person or a with a person closely associated with the person (Moleski & Kiselica, 2005). "This may involve assuming more than one professional role (such as instructor and therapist) or blending professional and non-professional relationships (such as a counselor and friend or counselor and business partner)" (Corey, Corey, & Callanan, 1998, p. 225).

The ACA code of ethics (2014) frames the discussion of dual relationships as "Managing and Maintaining Boundaries and Professional Relationships". The question becomes how far can boundaries be ethically extended? The answer differs depending on the type of indirect serviceprovided (consultation vs. supervision). The answer also depends on the other party in the potential dual relationship (the consultee/supervisee or the client of the consultee/supervisee). Again, the layered nature of indirect service provision adds complexity to decision-making when navigating potential dual relationships and ethical extensions of boundaries.

Managing Boundaries with Consultees' and Supervisees' Clients

Play therapists providing these indirect services must also manage boundaries with the clients on whose behalf indirect services are sought. For the clients of supervisees, the management of boundaries is very similar to the process used in navigating the boundaries between a counselor and a client. Because the supervisor is vicariously responsible for the client, the relationship to the client of the supervisee is similar to that of the counselor. In evaluating whether to engage in a dual relationship with the client of a supervisee, the recommendations of Younggren and Gottlieb (2004) seem instructive. The authors suggest that, before engaging in a dual relationship with a client, the professional ask and answer several questions. These include: Is entering into a relationship in addition to the professional one necessary, or should I avoid it? Can this relationship potentially cause harm to the client? If harm seems unlikely, would the additional relationship prove beneficial? Is there a risk that the dual relationship could disrupt the therapeutic relationship? Can I evaluate this matter objectively? The answers to these questions, in consultation with another professional, can aid in managing boundaries in an ethical manner.

Managing boundaries with clients of consultees may also be an ethical challenge. However, the consultant may not know the identity of the client. The ACA (2014) code notes that in consulting with colleagues, clinicians "disclose information only to the extent necessary to achieve the purposes of consultation." The indirect service provider engaging in this type of consultation would not have a dual role with the client, because the client was not identified to the consultant. Other forms of consultation (e.g., parent consultation, teacher consultation) offer additional challenge such as the client being typically identifiable and, as a result, the boundaries with the client should be managed. Nevertheless, the ethical boundaries with a consultation client may be different from the ethical boundaries with a supervision client. When the type of consultation client may differ significantly (e.g., the child of a parent with whom you are consulting but who you are, or are not, treating in play therapy, the student of a teacher with whom you are consulting but who you are, or are not, treating in play therapy, an administrator with whom you are consulting about a system), there are few rules that can be universally applied. Play therapists consultants may consider the proximity of the client of the consultee to the play therapist consultant, and apply Younggren and Gottlieb's (2004) method of evaluation. The answers to their questions may differ depending on the proximity of the consultant to the client (e.g., consulting with a teacher about a student who is not being treated by the play therapist but who attends the same school as the children of the play therapist).

Managing Boundaries with Consultees and Supervisees

Because the roles of supervisor and consultant are distinct, the management of boundaries differs for the play therapist providing these different indirect services. The role of supervisor is a professional role that typically involves some form of evaluation (e.g., letter of recommendation, licensure evaluation form, academic grade). As a result, the role of supervisor is likely incompatible with traditionally social roles (e.g., friend, family member) because the social role has the capacity to undermine the objectivity and effectiveness of the supervision (e.g., it's hard to give my friend or family member a less than stellar evaluation) (ACA, 2014). However, unlike the traditional counselor-client relationship, the supervisor-supervisee relationship is typically time-limited and is unlikely to be resumed at a future date. Since a therapy client might return for therapy at another time, it may be unwise to begin a personal relationship with the client after initial termination of therapy since that personal relationship with the client would preclude the counselor from seeing the client in future (Pritchett & Fall, 2001). Unlike counseling relationships, supervision relationships are not typically resumed in future but are limited to a particular case or cases, pre-licensure period, or academic term. In contrast to work with counseling clients, supervisees often develop into colleagues with whom the past supervisor would welcome a personal or business relationship. Nevertheless, the ACA code of ethics (2014) emphasizes the evaluation and gatekeeping roles of supervisors and warns against supervising any individual "with whom they have an inability to be objective" (p. 13).

Managing boundaries as a consultant is somewhat less straightforward. The role of consultant does not typically involve evaluation (Jacob et al., 2016). As a result, an existing social relationship with a consultee (e.g., friend, family member) may be less likely to undermine the objectivity and effectiveness of the consultation. In addition, professionals often seek consultation from other professionals who they know personally (e.g., through similar professional involvement, business arrangements). Some aspect of a personal relationship may be the basis for consultation (e.g., knowing the person has an area of expertise and a style that appeals to the potential consultee).

Managing boundaries and potential dual relationships in indirect services can be particularly challenging and call for higher ordered thinking on the part of the indirect service provider. Understanding the role of the provider (consultant vs. supervisor) and, if consultation is being provided, the type of consultation, can inform the decision-making process.

CONCLUSION

In ethics, the primary goal is to *"do the right thing"* (Spike Lee). This chapter has provided a brief overview of four important ethical issues relevant to the indirect play therapy services of supervision and comprehension: informed consent, competence, confidentiality, and dual/multiple relationships. The application of these issues in play therapy supervision and consultation is complex and the above discussion is not a comprehensive list of the ethical issues relevant to these indirect services. The goal was to guide the reader in understanding how these issues apply when the ethical obligation of the play therapist is to both the supervisee or consultee and to the client of the supervisee or consultee.

As Sweeney (2001) has noted, ethical actions are "more than a professional mandate", they are "an extension of the play therapist's commitment to children" (p. 75). While it is not possible to address all ethical dilemmas that indirect service providers may experience, this chapter discusses topics that require heightened ethical awareness. Honoring the values of informed consent, competence, confidentiality, and dual relationships can help the play therapy consultants and supervisees fulfill their commitment to improving the lives of children.

REFERENCES

American Counseling Association. (2014). *ACA code of ethics.* Retrieved from https://www.counseling.org/resources/aca-code-of-ethics.pdf

American Psychological Association. (2010). *Ethical principles of psychologists and code of conduct.* Retrieved from http://www.apa.org/ethics/code/principles.pdf

Ashby, J., & Clark, K. M. (2015). Ethics in play therapy. In D. A. Crenshaw & A. L. Stewart (Eds.), *Play therapy: A comprehensive guide to theory and practice* (pp. 511–523). New York, NY: The Guilford Press.

Association for Counselor Education and Supervision. (1993). *Ethical guidelines for counseling supervisors.* Retrieved from: http://www.liberty.edu/media/1152/School%20Counseling%20ACES%20Ethical%20Guidelines.pdf

Association for Play Therapy. (2012). *Play therapy best practices.* Retrieved from http://c.ymcdn.com/sites/www.a4pt.org/resource/resmgr/Publications/Play_Therapy_Best_Practices.pdf

Association for Play Therapy. (2015). *Credentialing guide: Registered Play Therapist (RPT) & Supervisor (RPT-S).* Retrieved from: http://c.ymcdn.com/sites/www.a4pt.org/resource/ resmgr/RPT_and_RPT-S_Credentials/RPTS_Guide_December_2015.pdf

Barber, J. P., Sharpless, B. A., Klostermann, S., & McCarthy, K. S. (2007). Assessing intervention competence and its relation to therapy outcome: A selected review derived from the outcome literature. *Professional Psychology, Research and Practice*, *38*(5), 493–500. doi:10.1037/0735-7028.38.5.493

Beahrs, J. O., & Gutheil, T. G. (2001). Informed consent in psychotherapy. *The American Journal of Psychiatry*, *158*(1), 4–10. doi:10.1176/appi.ajp.158.1.4 PMID:11136625

Bernard, J. M., & Goodyear, R. G. (1998). *Fundamentals of Clinical Supervision* (2nd ed.). Needham Heights, MA: Allyn & Bacon.

Borders, L. D., & Brown, L. L. (2005). *The new handbook of counseling supervision.* Mahwah, NJ: Lawrence Erlbaum Associates.

Campinha-Bacote, J. (2002). The process of cultural competence in the delivery of healthcare services: A model of care. *Journal of Transcultural Nursing*, *13*(3), 181–184. doi:10.1177/10459602013003003 PMID:12113146

Carmichael, K. D. (2006). Legal and ethical issues in play therapy. *International Journal of Play Therapy*, *15*(2), 83–99. doi:10.1037/h0088916

Cobia, D. C., & Boes, S. R. (2000). Professional disclosure statements and formal plans for supervision: Two strategies for minimizing the risk of ethical conflicts in post-masters supervision. *Journal of Counseling and Development*, *78*(3), 293–296. doi:10.1002/j.1556-6676.2000.tb01910.x

Corey, G., Corey, M. S., & Callanan, P. (1998). *Issues and ethics in the helping professions.* Belmont, CA: Brooks/Cole.

Corey, G., Haynes, R., Moulton, P., & Muratori, M. (2010). *Clinical supervision in the helping professions: A practical guide* (2nd ed.). Alexandria, VA: American Counseling Association.

Dekraii, M., Sales, B., & Hall, S. (1998). Informed consent, confidentiality, and duty to report laws in the conduct of child therapy. In T. R. Kratochwill & R. J. Morris (Eds.), *The practice of child therapy* (3rd ed., pp. 540–559). Boston, MA: Allyn & Bacon.

Dougherty, A. M. (1992). Ethical issues in consultation. *Elementary School Guidance and Counseling*, *26*, 214–220.

Fairburn, C. G., & Cooper, Z. (2011). Therapist competence, therapy quality, and therapist training. *Behaviour Research and Therapy*, *49*(6-7), 373–378. doi:10.1016/j.brat.2011.03.005 PMID:21492829

Fisher, M. A. (2013). *The ethics of conditional confidentiality: A practice model for mental health professionals*. New York, NY: Oxford University Press. doi:10.1093/med:psych/9780199752201.001.0001

Gil, E. (2005). From sensitivity to competence in working across cultures. In E. Gil & A. A. Drewes (Eds.), *Cultural issues in play therapy* (pp. 3–25). New York, NY: Guilford Press.

Goodyear, R. K., & Rodolfa, E. (2012). *Negotiating the complex ethical terrain of clinical supervision*. In S. J. Knapp, M. C. Gottlieb, M. M. Handelsman, & L. D. VandeCreek (Eds.), APA handbook of ethics in psychology (Vol. 2, pp. 261–275). Washington, DC: American Psychological association. doi:10.1037/13272-013

Herlihy, B., Gray, N., & McCollum, V. (2002). Legal and ethical issues in school counselor supervision. *Professional School Counseling*, *6*, 55–60.

Ingraham, C. L. (2000). Consultation through a multicultural lens: Multicultural and cross-cultural consultation in schools. *School Psychology Review*, *29*, 320–343.

Jacob, S., Decker, D. M., & Timmerman Lugg, E. (2016). *Ethics and law for school psychologists*. Hoboken, NJ: John Wiley & Sons.

Kitchener, K. S. (1984). Intuition, critical evaluation and ethical principles: The foundation for ethical decisions in counseling psychology. *The Counseling Psychologist*, *12*(3), 43–55. doi:10.1177/0011000084123005

Knapp, S., & VandeCreek, L. (1997). Ethical and legal aspects of clinical supervision. In C. E. Watkins (Ed.), *Handbook of psychotherapy supervision* (pp. 589–599). New York, NY: Wiley.

Knoff, H. M. (1988). Clinical supervision, consultation, and counseling: A comparative analysis for supervisors and other educational leaders. *Journal of Curriculum and Supervision*, *3*(3), 240–252.

Kurpius, D. J., & Fuqua, D. R. (1993). Fundamental issues in defining consultation. *Journal of Counseling and Development*, *71*(6), 598–600. doi:10.1002/j.1556-6676.1993.tb02248.x

Ladany, N., Lehrman-Waterman, D., Molinaro, M., & Wolgast, B. (1999). Psychotherapy supervisor ethical practices: Adherence to guidelines, the supervisory working alliance, and supervisee satisfaction. *The Counseling Psychologist*, *27*(3), 443–475. doi:10.1177/0011000099273008

Lee, S. (Producer), & Lee, S. (Director). (1989). *Do the right thing* [Motion picture]. United States: Universal Pictures.

McCarthy, P., Sugden, S., Koker, M., Lamendola, F., Maurer, S., & Renninger, S. (1995). A practical guide to informed consent in clinical supervision. *Counselor Education and Supervision*, *35*(2), 130–138. doi:10.1002/j.1556-6978.1995.tb00217.x

Moleski, S. M., & Kiselica, M. S. (2005). Dual relationships: A continuum ranging from the destructive to the therapeutic. *Journal of Counseling and Development*, *8*(1), 3–11. doi:10.1002/j.1556-6678.2005.tb00574.x

Newman, C. F. (2013). Training cognitive behavioral therapy supervisors: Didactics, simulated practice, and meta-supervision. *Journal of Cognitive Psychotherapy: An International Quarterly*, *27*(1), 5–18. doi:10.1891/0889-8391.27.1.5

Newman, J. L. (1993). Ethical issues in consultation. *Journal of Counseling and Development*, *72*(2), 148–156. doi:10.1002/j.1556-6676.1993.tb00914.x

OConnor, K. (2005). Addressing diversity issues in play therapy. *Professional Psychology, Research and Practice*, *36*(5), 566–573. doi:10.1037/0735-7028.36.5.566

Pope, K. S., & Vasquez, M. J. T. (2010). *Ethics in psychotherapy and counseling: A practice guide*. San Francisco: Jossey-Bass.

Pritchett, S., & Fall, K. A. (2001). Post-termination non-sexual dual relationships: Dynamics and assessment. *Texas Counseling Association Journal*, *29*, 72–79.

Remley, T. P., & Herlihy, B. P. (2016). *Ethical, Legal, and Professional Issues in Counseling* (5th ed.). Boston: Pearson.

Robinson, B., Bradley, L. J., & Hendricks, C. B. (2000). Multicultural counseling supervision: A four-step model toward competency. *International Journal for the Advancement of Counseling*, *22*(2), 131–141. doi:10.1023/A:1005567609258

Russell-Chapin, L. A., & Chapin, T. (2011). *Clinical supervision: Theory and practice*. Pacific Grove, CA: Brooks/Cole.

Sandoval, J. (2014). Best practices in school-based mental health/consultee-centered consultation by school psychologists. In P. L. Harrison & A. Thomas (Eds.), *Best practices in school psychology: Data-based and collaborative services* (pp. 493–507). Bethesda, MD: National Association of School Psychologists.

Slack, C. M., & Wassenaar, D. R. (1999). Ethical dilemmas of South African clinical psychologists: International comparisons. *European Psychologist*, *4*(3), 179–186. doi:10.1027//1016-9040.4.3.179

Sommers-Flanagan, R., & Sommers-Flanagan, J. (2015). *Becoming an ethical helping professional: Cultural and philosophical foundations*. Hoboken, NJ: John Wiley & Sons, Inc.

Sweeney, D. S. (2001). Legal and ethical issues in play therapy. In G. L. Landreth (Ed.), *Innovations in play therapy: Issues, processes, and special populations* (pp. 65–82). Burlington, MA: Taylor & Francis.

Taylor, L., & Adelman, H. (1989). Reframing the confidentiality dilemma to work in childrens best interests. *Professional Psychology, Research and Practice*, *20*(2), 79–83. doi:10.1037/0735-7028.20.2.79

Thomas, J. T. (2007). Informed consent through contracting for supervision: Minimizing risks, enhancing benefits. *Professional Psychology, Research and Practice*, *38*(3), 221–231. doi:10.1037/0735-7028.38.3.221

Thomas, J. T. (2010). *The ethics of supervision and consultation: Practical guidelines for mental health professionals*. Washington, DC: American Psychological Association. doi:10.1037/12078-000

Younggren, J. N., & Gottlieb, M. C. (2004). Managing risk when contemplating multiple relationships. *Professional Psychology, Research and Practice*, *35*(3), 255–260. doi:10.1037/0735-7028.35.3.255

Chapter 13
Integrating Play Therapy and Mental Health Consultation

Krystal Vaughn
LSUHSC New Orleans, USA

Erin Dugan
LSUHSC New Orleans, USA

ABSTRACT

Many parents and teachers are often confounded when it comes to figuring out a child's presenting issues. Mental health consultants are able to note the frequency, proximity, duration and intensity of and in which the behavior(s) occur (American Psychological Association, 2013; Henderson & Martin, 2014). These professionals are equipped with the tools, education, and experience and are able to gather information, observe, and assess the challenging behaviors or presenting issues in order to formulate and conceptualize a treatment plan for the child, their parent(s), and/or the school/center based setting. Additionally, mental health consultants may offer valuable feedback; increase of knowledge, skills and awareness; development of treatment plans; and implementation of the necessary interventions. This chapter seeks to provide professionals with the definitions, differences, structure, and implementation of a mental health consultation model.

INTRODUCTION

Many parents(caregivers), as well as teachers, are often confounded when it comes to figuring out their child's presenting issues and/or challenging behaviors. Parents often turn to their primary support systems, which tend to include: their own parents, siblings, friends, as well as their child's teacher(s), school, guidance counselor, or principal/director. These individuals and caregivers may work together to collect information about the child including their strengths and areas for growth. All parties may seek to develop a sound rationale for the child's challenging behaviors/presenting issues, in order to help the child develop appropriate behaviors which allow the child to function better in their environment(s).

The child's place of work (school) and his/her home environment are important settings to observe the child's behaviors and note antecedents (happenings prior to the behaviors) and consequences (events

DOI: 10.4018/978-1-5225-2224-9.ch013

after the behaviors). Additionally, consultants may note the frequency, proximity, duration, and intensity of identified behaviors (American Psychological Association, 2013; Henderson & Martin, 2014). Many parents and teachers reach out to mental health consultants who may be trained as psychologists, counselors, social workers, early interventionists, or psychiatrists to conduct consultative services.

Mental health professionals may be better equipped to observe behaviors noting the factors involved including strengths and areas of growth, including those that may hinder the child's functioning. Additionally, mental health consultants are equipped with the tools, education, and experience to gather information, observe, and assess young children. Consultants may work with involved parties to develop a mutually agreed upon treatment plan. After the treatment plan is developed, the consultant can work to implement the necessary behavioral interventions.

Once interventions are set in place, consultants may work with parents, teachers, and school officials to ensure successful implementation and amend interventions, when necessary. While working to fine tune behavioral interventions and supports, consultants may offer feedback to increase knowledge, skills and awareness for the teachers and caregivers. This chapter seeks to provide professionals with the definition, differences, structure, and implementation of a mental health consultation model in both child-centered and center-based environments.

CHILD-CENTERED AND CENTER-BASED CONSULTATION

Mental health consultation is generally requested in one of two forms: case consultation (child-centered) or program consultation (center-based). When a request for case consultation is received, it is typically on behalf of the individual child. This request for services may come directly from the caregiver or school around a challenging behavior or concern for impairment and/or at functioning level. For example, Abigail, a 3-year-old female in a private preschool, presents with social difficulties, such as taking turns with her peers as well as aggressive behaviors. The school reportedly informed Abigail's single mother that she is not engaging with her peers appropriately and at times displays aggressive behaviors on the playground if another child has a desired object. Additionally, the teachers reported that she appears overstimulated by activity and noises in the gym. They describe Abigail as agitated in the gym, unable to play with peers, yelling, and, at times, covering her hears when the noise level rises. Perplexed by this presentation, as mom reportedly does not see such behavior in the home, she is referred for consultation to support the child's social development within the classroom and school setting.

Program consultation may be more inclusive and comprise the entire program or school. Georgetown University's Early Childhood Mental Health Consultation program (2015) states that center-based consultation is indirect and provides assistance to the caregivers to support young children's development, especially in the domain of social and emotional development. This relationship is collaborative and relationship-based, but delivered by a trained mental health consultant who understands the importance of infant and early childhood mental health (Georgetown University, 2015). For example, Abigail's preschool, ABC Schoolhouse, recently applied and received funding to provide care for young children of single mothers as part of a community outreach program aimed at improving outcomes for children in poverty. However, shortly after admitting three children as part of the grant, the staff acknowledged they were unprepared to meet the needs of children from improvised backgrounds. They recognized that they were unaware of the effects of poverty, specifically, of social-emotional ramifications. The director enlisted the services of a mental health consultant to increase the staff and administrators' knowledge and understanding of the social-emotional effects of poverty and requested didactics focused how to meet the children's needs in a developmentally appropriate manner, while incorporating the children into the play-based center's routines.

Consultation elements mirror many of the founding principles set forth by Axline in 1947 (Axline, 1947) which include: (1)Must develop a warm and friendly relationship with the child; (2) Accepts the child as she or he is; (3) Establishes a feeling of permission in the relationship, so that the child feels free to express his or her feelings completely; (4) Is alert to recognize the feelings the child is expressing and reflects these feelings back in such a manner that the child gains insight into his/her behavior; (5) Maintains a deep respect for the child's ability to solve his/her problems and gives the child the opportunity to do so; the responsibility to make choices and to institute change is the child's, so the therapist (6) Does not attempt to direct the child's actions or conversations in any manner; the child leads the way, the therapist follows and (7) Does not hurry the therapy along; It is a gradual process and must be recognized as such by the therapist, who (8) Only establishes those limitations necessary to anchor the therapy to the world of reality and to make the child aware of his/her responsibility in the relationship.

While Johnston and Brinamen (2006) proposed understanding another's subjective experience, Axline encouraged play therapists to accept the whole child. Both promote a greater understanding of the child's experience. This may include hearing what it is like for the caregiver or teacher to work with the identified child and how the challenges affect their teacher-student relationship. As consultants allow the partners to share their subjective experience(s), professionals may learn more about how their personal histories, attachment styles, beliefs, or attitudes affect the teacher-student relationship. From this place, a mental health consultant is able to promote the acceptance of the child and begin to strengthen the teacher-student relationship. This also allows the teacher and the child to feel secure, thus facilitating growth and development for the child. Regardless of the approach to consultation, it is important that all parties understand the process and the interventions proposed. Play therapy is one such approach often recommended to both teachers and parents.

According to Schottelkorb, Swan, and Ogawa (2015), "Child-centered play therapy (CCPT) is an evidence-based humanistic therapeutic intervention for your children" (p.221). Play therapy facilitates not only the child's progression and overall development, but also the parents' acceptance of their child, fostering understanding and the promotion of the effective attainment of skills and techniques needed to support the child-parent relationship. Likewise, play therapists are able to work similarly with teachers, encouraging the acquisition of skills and understanding educators may need to foster teacher-student relationship with the identified client. However, many key elements have to be considered in the development of the therapist-caregiver relationship as well as the consultant-center relationship.

When caregivers are uninformed, misinformed, or have differing expectations, play therapy or the consultation relationship may be terminated early—prior to the goals being met in relationship to the therapeutic treatment plan. Therefore, Dugan, Swanson, and Short (2011) recommended caregiver consultations focus on the child, provide education to the parents, and allow for collaboration—this may occur over the course of several consultation visits. These consultation visits will ideally include the therapist as well as the parent(s)/caregiver(s). Focusing specifically on the beginning phases of parental consultation, Cates, Paone, Packman, and Margolis (2006) recommended that parent consultations, specifically when play therapy is being recommended, provide an overview of the prescribed approach, the therapeutic goals, structure of the sessions, fees, length of sessions, ongoing parental consultations, and rationale for the identified services. They also encouraged concise sharing of information and allowing time for parental questions and/or concerns. Their consultation intake also addressed the limits of confidentiality, ethical, and legal issues (Cates, Paone & Margolis, 2006). Professionals may have limited time in initial intake consultations, due to the parent(s)/caregiver(s)'s need as well as their report of their child's presenting issues and the parent(s)'s concern(s). Therefore, professionals may wish to develop and utilize a checklist with such components to ensure all recommendations are provided and openly discussed between the therapist and the parent(s)/caregiver(s).

The consultation structure used may vary by theoretical orientation or consultation program. For example, Schottelkorb, Swan, and Ogawa (2015) proposed a child-centered parent consultation model that includes five elements: (a) forming and maintaining relationships; (b) demonstrating awareness (c) respecting parents as experts in their children; (d) sharing relevant knowledge, and (e) teaching therapeutic skills. This structure may vary by clinical setting. However, Lolan (2011) found that play therapists agreed that engaging parents leads to a positive treatment outcome. Depending on orientation, consultation model, or clinical setting, some play therapists may meet with caregivers monthly, while others may meet with parents on an as-needed basis. Regardless, caregivers should be informed of the process and structure of consultation visits. Additionally, the scheduling of consultations should be implemented into the child's treatment plan.

Kottman (2003) encouraged information sharing on the importance of caregiver involvement across environments, including school, home, and social, to benefit the child. Ongoing parental consults can provide updates on the child's progress, treatment goals, education, and ultimately termination (Cates, Paone & Margolis, 2006). In some clinics, caregiver consultation is part of the treatment plan and is discussed during the initial intake. Parents are often scheduled for their first parent consultation following their child's third or fourth session (Dugan, Swanson & Short, 2011). This allows for the therapist to support, educate, monitor progress, and collaborate with the parents. However, consultations may need to be scheduled at an earlier time due to the presenting behaviors of the child during sessions, intensity of the child's internalizing or externalizing behaviors at home/school, or the need to consult with the parent(s). These early or unplanned consultation visits may allow the therapist to implement and/or follow up on a recommended intervention. Ray (2011) also noted that if weekly parental requests continue, this may indicate a need for personal counseling, and a referral for such should be made.

INTAKE

The intake comprises several important dimensions including request for services, review of the child's presenting issue(s), referral source(s), treatment planning, and, possibly, record requests. A request for child-centered consultation services often comes from the parent(s), but may also be driven by third parties, such as the school, pediatrician, psychologist, psychiatrist, or hospital. In child-centered consultation the child is the identified client. However, in center-based consultation the school may be the identified client. This is especially important to note, as the American Counseling Association (2014) points out the information shared must be specific to the identified client. Therefore, if center-based consultation is provided, the consultant may not discuss a specific child in that center without appropriate parental authorization and consent.

When a request for services is center-driven, it is important for the consultant to maintain a professional and ethical dialogue with the school. However, appropriate authorization and consent and/or release of information must be obtained from the child's legal guardian (American Counseling Association, 2014). Additionally, it is important for the play therapists to obtain information in reference to the identified client. Professional collaborations may be appropriate and beneficial for clients. In some instances, children may be receiving services from multiple providers and it may be necessary to consult with those professionals (e.g., speech therapists, occupational therapists, audiologists, learning specialists, etc.). This may allow mental health consultants to formulate the child's treatment plan, as well as confer with professionals on a regular basis in order to provide continuity of care and best practices.

In a child-centered consultation model initial sessions may include the caregivers and play therapist, but typically not the young child. Ray (2011) believed the main objective during the first parent meeting was to establish a relationship with the parent. However, during the first session several tasks may be accomplished: discussions of confidentiality, parental concerns, importance of consistency, play therapy process and structure, information gathering (i.e., developmental, medical, educational, family histories) and recommendations for assessments, if applicable. Therefore, this first meeting may last anywhere from 1 to 2 hours, depending on the presenting issues, including an overview of the frequency, duration, intensity and proximity of the child's presenting behaviors (Ray, 2011). During this timeframe, parents may also need to be educated on the importance and benefits of play therapy, ages and stages of child development, typical versus atypical behavior, and appropriate interventions.

When surveying play therapists, Lolan and Dugan (2010) found that one of the most common questions play therapists are asked by parents is: "What is play therapy and how will it help my child?". While play therapy awareness campaigns have increased in recent years, some parents may still be unsure of the benefits of play therapy. Thus, Schottelkorb, Swan, and Ogawa (2015) suggested providing the parents with the brochure *Child-Centered Play Therapy: A Parent's Guide* to further facilitate the understanding of the effectiveness of play therapy. Besides, parents may be directed to the *Association of Play Therapy*'s website, where they promote understanding of play therapy through videos. *Play Therapy Works!* is a 7.5-minute video to increase understanding of the value of play therapy, *History Speaks* is a 15-minute video with significant figures in the field of play therapy, and *Andrew* is a public service announcement (PSA) that describes play therapy in a simplest way (available in English and Spanish). Lastly, a recent evidence-based practice statement published by the *Association for Play Therapy* (Ray & McCullough, 2015) may offer parents a general understanding of the field of play therapy.

At the conclusion of the intake session, parents may be educated on the logistics, including policies and procedures of the agency/clinic. For many parents, this may be the first time they receive mental health or, specifically, play therapy services, so they may have questions. If other professionals are to be consulted, how will this occur? How are appointments made, how often are children seen, and when do ongoing consultation meetings occur?

SETTING UP THE CONTRACT/TREATMENT PLAN

Each child should receive an individualized treatment plan, in addition to the best type of service (e.g., play therapy, filial therapy, group play therapy, family play therapy, etc.). This is essential and considered "best practice." Likewise, setting up a contractual treatment plan with the parents is equally important and may be essential in providing services to any child of any age. This plan provides both the parent(s) and therapist(s) an agreement of services that will be provided to the child (identified client) based on the presenting issue(s), goals, types of services, and interventions. This plan will also allow the parent(s), other caregiver(s), teacher(s), other professional(s), as well as the clinician an overview of their responsibilities. This plan may include treatment goals and objectives, specific strategies, and methods of treatment, schedule for accomplishing the goals and objectives, and later the current status and progress made by the child based on the services/interventions. Treatment plans may house information including, but not limited to, the child's name, age, date of birth, date of treatment plan, presenting issues, goals/objectives, recommended interventions, proposed length of service(s), responsible party (e.g., client, parent, teacher), and setting (individual, group, parent consultation) in which the intervention should be carried out (Ray, 2011). For example, Abigail's mother presents with concerns (reported by the teacher). She reports that in the preschool environment her daughter has social difficulties, aggression, difficulties with turn taking, and overstimulation. In this treatment plan, the therapist could include the presenting issues—difficulties with turn taking, aggression, and emotional expression. The treatment plan goals may be identified as increasing appropriate turn taking skills, verbal emotional expression, and self-regulation. Finally, the identified interventions could include behavior modification (school and home), group therapy (clinic), and parent education (clinic).

ONGOING PARENTAL CONSULTATION

Research indicated play therapists acknowledge two factors are necessary for positive play therapy outcomes: the relationship between child and therapist and caregiver involvement in treatment (Phillips & Landreth, 1998). As a result, ongoing parental consultation is essential in order to monitor progress, educate the parents, and continue the collaborative relationship. Many play therapy parent consultation models advised therapists to provide parental consultation every 3 to 5 visits (Ray, 2011; Schottelkorb, Swan & Ogawa, 2015). However, this may present logistical issues for some clinical settings. For example, does the therapist provide parental consultation immediately after the child's session? If so, does this reduce the time allowed for the child's session? Moreover, if consultation occurs in a larger clinic, who provides care for the child during the parental consultation? Ray (2011) acknowledged that the ideal situation would allow for one-hour parental consultation separate from the child's visit—allowing for fewer distractions. This initial consultation as well as ongoing consultations would also ideally involve all caregivers. At times, play therapists may schedule the consultation in addition to the child's weekly scheduled session or in lieu of the child's scheduled session for that week.

Due to the changing world, many children are cared for by more than their biological parents; therefore, parental consultation should involve all caregivers, such as biological parents, grandparents, and stepparents. Nevertheless, logistically, this may be unlikely. For this reason, the therapist should consider alternative means of caregiver communication allowing for collaboration with all caregivers. For example, weekly caregiver reports, telephone consultations, or email updates (with appropriate legal consent). Furthermore, the therapist may consider if providing parental consultations to all caregivers at once is productive or if separate parental consultations are necessary (e.g., logistics, custody issues, legal reasons, etc.). These intervening and supporting consultations are important to the child's ongoing therapy as these sessions allow all parties to contribute to the child's wellbeing, identify responsibility for implementing strategies and methods, and discuss the child's progress based on the treatment plan.

During these ongoing parental consultations, play therapists may inquire about the child's progress, provide education (parenting skills), and update the parent on progress in the play therapy sessions, including, but not limited to, identifying and discussing themes in the child's play therapy sessions. Schottelkorb, Swan, and Ogawa recommend asking specifically about how the child is doing at school and home, thereby keeping the focus on the child. However, Ray (2011) acknowledged that parents often bring multiple and minor problems to light during this time. Thus, the therapist must use clinical decision-making skills to determine if the parent should be moved on to the next phase of consultation or if supporting the parent in the here and now would benefit the client more (Ray, 2011). The therapists may also utilize information gained from session with the child to determine what support to offer the caregiver. For example, Kottman (2011) advised that the play in the dollhouse, puppet, and sand tray work may offer valuable information on where parents need support. Once the decision to move on to parental concerns is determined, the therapist can discuss concerns that were presented in the initial intake session, reflecting on progress since that time. Yet, it is important to remember that parents can be nervous or feel inferior, blaming themselves for the child's presenting issues (Kottman, 2011). Clinical skills are necessary to provide a united consultation environment that conveys the message that the parent is the expert in his/her child.

This collaborative and flexible approach to consultation allows the play therapist to tailor the skills or education to the presenting problem (Schottelkorb, Swan & Ogawa). Also, Dugan, Swanson, and Short (2011) acknowledged that the "skills" are typically based on the caregiver's concerns, therapeutic goals, and therapeutic recommendations—based on needs detected in the parent-child relationship. Allowing the parents to reflect on their concerns, progress, or changes prior to the parent consult may also be beneficial.

Dugan, Swanson, and Short (2011) encouraged the use of a caregiver feedback form allowing caregivers to share written information weekly. Their caregiver feedback form included requests for information regarding new insights, changes, areas of concern, and observed needs. They recognized that play therapists have limited interaction with the client—typically once a week for 45 minutes. Thus, the caregiver and other professionals are key to relevant information regarding new insights or changes. This may also foster the collaborative approach and allow the therapist opportunities to reframe parental thought patterns, if necessary. While this weekly caregiver form provides the caregiver the opportunity to contribute weekly, the therapists may also generate a reflective practice of their own.

The use of a therapist's feedback form to guide the therapist's consultation and communication about the child is recommended by Dugan, Swanson, and Short (2011). This form may present the play therapist the opportunity to reflect on the child's strengths, patterns of play, play themes, points of discussion, disclosures, areas of growth, and needed professional consultations. When play therapists are able to communicate or focus attention on strengths or what the child is "doing right", they allow for the parent's contemplation of positive growth (Landreth, 2006). Furthermore, play therapists may use the caregiver form to reflect on the patterns of play or play themes, which allows for client conceptualization (Benedict, Hastings, Ato, Carson & Nash, 1998). Through client conceptualization, the therapists may determine which points to discuss (e.g., changes in thoughts, feelings, or behaviors) with the parents. These may also include disclosures made by the child, which necessitate additional information (Dugan, Swanson & Short, 2011). However, if the therapist chooses to provide this information, Ray (2011) suggested using a transitional statement to move the consultation from parent-driven to therapist's observations. Lastly, the therapist may offer to provide parenting education or skills benefiting the child.

For example, Abigail's mother would utilize the weekly caregiver feedback form to document her turn taking and emotional expression each week as she brings her in for her group therapy. This form, housed in a separate "caregiver folder", allows for Abigail's mother to document, continually, based on the week prior, her progress (worse, same, or better). This allows the clinician to receive information based on her mother's report of Abigail's behaviors at home and/or school. Abigail's mother would utilize the caregiver consultation feedback form to document over the past three to four weeks Abigail's progress (strengths, areas for growth, resources needed, changes of concern, stressors evident in the parent's life, what the parent is learning about her child and herself, what the parent would like to discuss at the consultation, what the parent is doing to contribute or hinder the child's growth, what the parent's part in the process is currently, what changes have been made, parental needs and desires, and addresses parental self-care). Likewise, the therapist may utilize a feedback from to prepare for the parent's consultation, which includes reflection on patterns of the play behaviors and play themes, points of discussion, reports and/or disclosures made by the child, the child's strengths, areas of growth for the child, skills needed to be discussed at home, professionals and/or family members that need to be consulted, and any feedback that the parents, family members, or partnering professional have provided.

The play therapist may choose to teach a play-based skill or provide parent education. It is advised that parents only be provided one skill at a time, otherwise they can feel overwhelmed. Dugan, Swanson, and Short (2011) advocated for consideration of primary skills, such as reflecting feelings, returning responsibility, limit setting, and choice giving. Limit setting may be especially important to parents of preschoolers who are focused on autonomy and exploration. These new childhood behaviors may present new challenges for parents who need more education and support on limit setting. During these consultations, parents may be educated on parenting styles that include love, warmth, and appropriate limits (Nash & Schaefer, 2010). Furthermore, connecting the parent to the child's session can assist with facilitation, reduce barriers to success, and increase parental accountability for goals (McGuire & McGuire, 2001). In addition to parent consultation, some parents may also benefit from parent training classes, wherein behavior modification techniques and relationship enhancement increase parents' ability to properly discipline and build positive relationships (Nash & Schaefer, 2010). After all, the ultimate goal of therapy would be for the child to meet the identified treatment goals and begin to function with the least amount of ongoing restrictions across environments. Moreover, caregivers who have more confidence in parenting skills, a greater understanding of development, and a positive parent-child relationship may be better advocates for their child.

SCHOOL-BASED CONSULTATION

School Consultation with Parents

Vernon (2009) stated that school counselors may provide parental counseling, education, or consultation. She further described counseling as work with a parent on personal matters, education as psycho-educational, and consultation as follow up to skills training or for parents whose children have specific difficulties or require more concentrated guidance. Vernon believed that consultation was more triadic in nature, stating it provides support or skills to the caregiver instead of working specifically on the parent's personal issues. Similarly, Gibson (2004) stated consultation is an indirect process wherein a counselor works with the parent indirectly to effect change in the child/client. While providing consultation services to parents, Vernon proposed school counselors working with the following values in mind: improved parent-child relationships, improved behaviors (home and school), improved responsibility acceptance, increase parental involvement at school, and improved school achievements. However, she acknowledged that some parents come with irrational beliefs, such as unrealistic demands, self-downing, catastrophizing, and low frustration tolerance. Awareness of parents' skill levels, belief system, and parenting style may provide the consultant with additional knowledge. Thereby, allowing the consultant to reinforce specific skills and improve parental understanding in other areas, this consultative process may occur in phases.

Vernon proposed consultation services in schools occur in five different phases. She stated the process includes (1) phase in, (2) problem identification, (3) implementation, (4) evaluation, and (5) termination. During the phasing in process, the goal of consultation would be to build the relationship through the use of basic counseling skills, such as listening, empathy, and understanding. Phase 2, problem identification, allowed the consultant to gain clarity about the presenting issue. During the problem identification phase, counselors may use paraphrasing, restating, and goals settings to clarify and define the specific identified concern. Kottman (2011) stated that parents can provide a wealth of knowledge regarding the presenting issue and past interventions, if applicable. After gathering the information, consultants may move into phase 3, wherein the consultant and caregiver may consider alternative strategies. Additionally, the consultant may give feedback during this phase, as the plan of action is implemented across sessions. This allows the consultant to work with the caregiver to fine tune the strategies to best fit the family. In phase 4, the consultant works with the caregiver to determine the level of success with the implemented strategies. The parties may discuss successes and areas for growth. It is especially important that the consultant positively reinforces the successes, regardless of the magnitude. This specific phase may last several sessions with the caregiver, fine tuning the skills or strategies utilized by the caregiver. Lastly, phase 5 allows for termination of the consultation process. This phase allows for closure, focusing on the successes and challenges throughout the consultation process, emphasizing the positive progress (Vernon, 2010). Along with these consultative services, some parents may participate in general education and support groups.

In the case of Abigail, once she starts school, the consultant may work with parents to transition her into the new school setting. At that time, the consultant may schedule an intake appointment to gather information and hear what has worked for the family in the past and what successes were experienced in the preschool program. As Abigail enters the school, the consultant may work with the parent and teacher(s) to develop activities to increase positive peer interactions. This may include offering teacher directed opportunities to transition from mother to engaging peer activities in the morning. After Abigail has settled into her routine at school, the consultant may work with the teachers and parents on identified problems such as peer aggression to decrease the frequency, duration, and intensity of such maladaptive behaviors. The consultant will then work with parties involved to implement specific plans to meet the child's needs. Upon implementation of the plan, the consultant will work with the teacher and parent to evaluate and amend the prescribed plan to increase the rate of success. Keeping in mind that Abigail's plans may occasionally need to be amended, the consultant can work with the parent(s) and teacher(s) on strategies that allow each of the caregivers to be the facilitators of change for Abigail. As Abigail's transition into the school year becomes smoother and her aggression has decrease considerably and more positive peer interactions are noted, the consultant will enter into the termination phase with Abigail's parent(s) and teacher(s).

In addition to consultation services, Vernon stated that school counselors may embed parenting support or education groups into their practice. These sessions may be focused on general parenting, such as communication, child development, discipline, and parental involvement. Alternatively, school counselors may offer education to parents on specific topics, such as ADHD, learning disabilities, eating disorders, or chronic illness. However, some parents may not have specific concerns, but still benefit from knowledge of general development discussions, such as preschoolers' separation anxiety, positive peer relationships, puberty, and transition to next grade (Vernon, 2010). While these may or may not be part of a consultation, this approach allows the counselor to offer targeted support and education to parents who may not be willing, able, or available for longer term parent consultation services.

School Consultation with Administrators, Faculty, and Staff

School-based consultation should be grounded in a strengths-based approach. Johnston and Brinamen (2006) identified ten elements they consider essential to consultation: (1) mutuality of endeavor; (2) avoiding the position of expert; (3) wondering instead of knowing; (4) understanding another's subjective experience; (5) considering all levels of influence; (6) hearing and representing all voices-especially the child's; (7) the centrality of the relationship; (8) parallel process as an organizing principle; (9) patience; and (10) holding hope. These guiding principles to early childhood mental health consultation ring true throughout numerous educational settings (e.g., childcare, preschool, and early elementary schools). As mental health professionals, we are able to consider multiple perspectives. As consultants, this skill is especially important. We may consider what it would be like to parent this child, teach this child, or be friends with this child. This allows us the ability to "hold hope" that we can work with other important individuals in the child's life to facilitate healthier relationships.

As with parental consultation, school-based consultation should begin with the relationship building phase (Kottman, 2011). Then, the consultant may gather information about the teacher-child relationship, classroom dynamics or practices, and presenting issues. It is important for the teacher to believe these endeavors are part of a collaborative approach; after all, the teacher typically spends 5 days a week with the child and may resent the therapist conveying position of expert. While working with the teacher, it is critical that the consultant are aware of the teacher's own personal issues that may arise presenting challenges in the relationship with the child or in classroom management techniques (Kottman). As with parents, the focus should remain on the child; if the teacher's personal issues are becoming the focus of consultation, it may be appropriate and necessary to refer the teacher for counseling.

Consultation with teachers, school counselors, or principals/directors may focus on a variety of topics, such as the child's relationships, classroom discipline strategies, improved teacher-child relationship, or family dynamics (Kottman, 2011). This work should begin with parental permission, teacher rapport, information gathering, understanding of the process, and consultation goals (Kottman, 2011). For example, who will be included in the consultation? How long will services last? And what will be included with the services? Are the services purely consultative in the school or will you provide play therapy or social skills groups?

As with parent consultation, teachers, school counselors, or principals/directors will need to provide information on the presenting issue, what was used to resolve or prevent the issue in the past, and other relevant information. Teachers, school counselors, or principals/directors may be able to provide educational, developmental, and family histories, too. Kottman (2011) recommended having the teacher, school counselors, or principals/directors provide information on behavioral, emotional, and academic functioning. Then, she stated that she uses active listening to support and encourage the individuals involved in consultation.

Teachers, school counselors, or principals/directors can provide a wealth of knowledge about children; after all, they interact with children for a large portion of the day. Additionally, teachers, school counselors, or principals/directors are able to observe many different types of behaviors (persistence to task, social interactions, frustration tolerance, etc.). As mental health consultants, it is important to tap into this valuable resource. Play therapists may ask teachers, school counselors, or principals/directors to track behaviors each week, utilizing a teacher report form. This form may include items such as behavior rating scales, child's mood, experience teaching the child (stressful vs. enjoyable), or notable occurrences.

Preschool teachers are especially valuable, as the early years lay the foundation for social emotional development. Gioia and Tobin (2010) reminded clinicians social play quickly progresses from parallel play to make believe play in a few short years. Teachers may enhance development by adding pretend play throughout the preschool day. This may lead to increases in the child's language development, social development, and emotional awareness (Gioia & Tobin, 2010). As children continue to develop at differing rates, teachers may need to scaffold early childhood play. For example, the teacher may need to embed him/herself into center-based play assisting children in developing pretend play. This may be done through the use of puppets, dramatic play materials, or animal figures. Consultants may work with teachers on child-centered language that facilitates child lead pretend play. Additionally, consultants may assist teachers in "wondering" with children to aid in increased abilities to engage peers in pretend play. While some teachers may have extensive experience working with young children, in childcare centers it is not uncommon to have teachers with limited child development knowledge. In a study for the National Association for the Education of Young Children Snow (2013) reported that 39% of child care teachers have a bachelor's degree and 19% have a high school diploma or less. Consequently, it is imperative that consultants consider the level of child development knowledge and training of the child care teacher. However, Johnson and Brinamen (2006) recommend that, when working with early child care teachers, professionals should enter into the relationship avoiding the position of expert. These teachers spend an abundant amount of time with the child, therefore they have knowledge related to the child's presenting behavior(s), even if they lack formal education on child development.

At times, consultation work with the teacher, school counselor, or principal/director may include didactics to increase teachers' knowledge, skills, or awareness. Teachers, school counselors, or principals/directors may be asked by a consultant to note client changes within the school environment, allowing for teacher reflection prior to scheduled consultation visit. These notations may include positive or negative changes, new insights, important interactions, engagements or areas the teacher wishes to discuss in upcoming consultations. In these consultations, play therapists may gather additional information, address concerns, or educate teachers on skills to improve the child's functioning within the environment. McGuire and McGuire (2001) noted tracking, accepting, understanding, encouraging, and limit setting as important skills for teachers to develop. They believed that those skills could foster growth beyond the play therapy session, into the classroom, and potentially to the outside environment. However, at times, while working with the caregivers, teacher, school counselor, or principal/director or other staff, it may become necessary to make additional referrals as the child needs additional services or support.

REFERRAL SOURCES

Consultation services may include collaboration with a variety of professionals: school counselors, speech therapist, occupational therapist, learning specialists, pediatricians, or psychiatrists. These consultations may include an initial referral for evaluation or an ongoing relationship benefiting the child. Some children may present for play therapy services with other professionals already working with the child; if so, a consent to collaborate would be necessary (American Counseling Association, 2014). However, many times, it is while providing play therapy or a screening during intake that a clinician determines that a child may benefit from additional evaluations or services. This requires the play therapist to have a network of referral sources. A play therapist may also need to consider the client or family needs, available appointment times of the referral source, insurance acceptability, or general waitlist time. A parent may feel comfortable seeking additional services if the play therapist was able to professionally and ethically speak to the collegial relationship or past consultation successes of working with a specific referral source(s).

Local school counselors are often part of the consultation process for play therapists who offer services in a clinic or agency. These clients may present for services, but also experience difficulties in school environments. When parents request school consultation visits or the therapist recommends a school consultation, play therapists may also provide child-centered consultation services. These services begin with an intake session with the parents, a phone consultation to gather information from the school staff/faculty, an observational assessment gathering sessions, and outside consultation with other working professionals, such as occupational therapists, physical therapists, speech therapist, and learning specialists.

CHALLENGES IN PLAY THERAPY CONSULTATION

Play therapists may be inundated by numerous challenges while providing parental consultation: engaging reluctant caregivers, parental consistency, legal issues, early termination, and overwhelmed parents. Nash and Schaefer (2010) also noted that parents of preschool children may experience persistent behavioral problems when the following are present: ineffective parenting, family dysfunction, and vulnerabilities (2010). Therefore, parents should be informed during the initial intake of the importance of consistent and predictable attendance for play therapy sessions. Logistics such as scheduling of appointments may also be stressful for caregivers. For example, clinics may schedule appointments in a variety of ways (week to week, reoccurring, based on availability, etc.). However, regularly reoccurring appointments may reduce the absentee rate of clients. Legal issues such as custody may also provide challenges to those who provide services to young children. While state laws differ, play therapists may minimize parental frustrations by keeping the parents informed of the progress.

Often parents may not feel that play therapy is "helping" and terminate services early. While play therapists may not eliminate this feeling, through education and collaboration play therapists may be able to empathically discuss the perception with parents. Specifically, parents may benefit from education on the idea or notion that children may "get worse, before they get better" and by the play therapist building an open collaborative relationship with parents. Collaborative relationships may foster honest discussions about the current progress of their child, frustrations, and perceived barriers. It is also important that play therapist note and address parental request skills building or behavior modification plans during the initial consultation. Nonetheless, Ray (2011) warned against educating on specific skills during the initial consultation visit as the relationship is not fully formed. The initial consultation visit may be overwhelming for many parents, a lot of information has been exchanged (developmental history, parental concerns, confidentiality, etc.). Furthermore, Ray reminds that the child has not been observed at this point.

Alternative arrangements may be needed to get the child to session on a consistent and regular basis. This may include transportation by a grandparent, friend, or childcare provider. McGuire and McGuire (2001) advised that the adult bringing the child to session must have the authority or permission of the legal guardian. A document may be kept in the client file showing such permission was granted. However, in these situations, there may be less access to parents. In this regard, McGuire and McGuire remind us that legal consent for treatment must be obtained from the legal guardian and communication may only be with those who have authority (2001). This may be especially challenging if services are provided in a school, wherein there are numerous adults interacting with the child throughout the day. These individuals may want to be involved or informed to benefit the child and the school environment, especially if there are disruptive behaviors. While presented with these challenges and others, play therapists may overcome barriers by following Steen's stages of parental consults (2010).

Throughout parent consults, challenges may arise. If play therapists are aware of the developmental stages of the consultation relationship, though, they may be equipped to meet the parents' needs. Steen (2010) defined four stages to parent consultation: engagement, cooperation, incorporation, and termination. In parental engagement, parents may experience a myriad of emotions, ranging from defensiveness to uncertainty. Here play therapists must meet the parent where they are and engage through empathy. During the second stage, play therapists may see parents become more active participants, seeking advice (Steen, 2010). Once cooperation occurs, the therapists may begin to see parents exhibiting insight. The third phase of parent consultation is active; parents begin to incorporate skills and knowledge. Steen stated in this stage parents begin to take responsibility and changes begin to occur in the environment. This insight and incorporation of skills generally leads to termination of parent consults. This phase may be very similar to therapeutic termination (Steen, 2010).

Regardless of the working stage of parent consultation, it is important to remember that parents may move at different paces and occasionally regress when presented with new challenges. Play therapists should also be aware of entering working stages that are incongruent with the parents' progress. For example, Steen stated that parents may not be able to take responsibility early in the incorporation stage (2010).

ETHICAL CONSIDERATIONS

As play therapists are multidisciplinary, they should familiarize themselves with their personal codes of ethics, the state laws, other regulatory bodies (professional organizations, certifications, or registrations). Many similarities may be found between the governing bodies, such as American Counseling Association (ACA), American Association of Marriage and Family Therapists (AAMFT), and American Psychological Association (APA). However, slight differences occur. Additionally, the Association for Play Therapy offers *Play Therapy Best Practices*, that is a guiding document offering information on topics such as instruction, supervision, and practices (Kottman, 2011). The document is further divided into the following sections: therapeutic relationship; parents and family; confidentiality; professional responsibility; relationships with other professionals; evaluation, assessment, and interpretation; teaching, training, and supervision; research and publication; and use of technology (Association for Play Therapy, 2016).

Specific to the issue of informed consent, Kottman (2011) advised that the custodial parent must sign giving consent for treatment or consultation services (if applicable). Landreth (1991) also reminded that the adult requesting services may not have legal custody of the child and that assumption should not be made. Besides, the legal guardian must authorize consultation services. Play therapists may not discuss a child with significant individuals (teachers, caregivers, school officials, etc.) without parental permission (Landreth, 1991). This may be especially important to remember if the provider is also employed by the school or viewed as part of the team (Landreth, 1991).

The custodial parent/caregiver is the individual who is able to make decisions about treatment plans, confidentiality, release of information, videotaping, and termination of services. However, each state has its own laws regarding parental rights, so it is important to understand each parent's rights in the practitioner's state of practice. Kottman also advised play therapists to request a copy of the divorce decree and have the custodial parent sign a release of information if the non-custodial parent requests sharing of information. McGuire and McGuire (2001) went a step further, advising therapists to request the "most recent" copy of the divorce decree acknowledging that some parents are in back to back court proceedings. McGuire and McGuire also recommended therapists to document that the request was made for the most up- to-date legal documentation. Additionally, one may request the birth certificate of a child who only has one caregiver.

CONCLUSION

Mental health consultation, whether child-centered or center-based, may provide both parents and teachers effective means to provide support to the child. In addition to the mental health consultant, the array of caregivers, including parent(s) and teacher(s), professionals, and paraprofessionals working together to support the child, must have opportunities to collaborate and recommend interventions. In addition to case conceptualization, collaboration with the therapeutic team is necessary to develop, assess, and guide the child's treatment.

REFERENCES

American Counseling Association. (2014). *ACA Code of Ethics*. Alexandria, VA: Author.

American Psychiatric Association. (2013). *Diagnostic and statistical manual of mental disorders: DSM-5*. Washington, DC: American Psychiatric Association.

Association for Play Therapy. (2012). *Play therapy best practices*. Retrieved from: http://c.ymcdn.com/sites/a4pt.site-ym.com/resource/resmgr/Publications/Play_Therapy_Best_Practices.pdf

Axline, V. (1947). *Play therapy*. New York: Houghton-Mifflin.

Block, P. (2000). *Flawless consulting: A guide to getting your expertise used*. San Francisco: Joseey-Bass/Pfeiffer.

British Association of Play Therapists. (2008). Retrieved from www.bapt.info/

Brown, Pryzwansky, & Schulte. (2001). *Psychological consultation* (5th ed.). Boston, MA: Allyn and Bacon.

Cates, J., Paone, T., Packman, J., & Margolis, D. (2006). Effective parent consultation in play therapy. *International Journal of Play Therapy*, *15*(1), 87–100. doi:10.1037/h0088909

CMHS-SVP0151. (n.d.). Rockville, MD: Center for Mental Health Services, Substance Abuse and Mental Health Services Administration.

Cohen, E., & Kaufmann, R. K. (2000). *Early childhood mental health consultation*. DHHS Pub. No.

Cohen, E., & Kaufmann, R. K. (2005). *Early childhood mental health consultation. DHHS Pub. No. CMHS-SVP0151* (Rev. Ed.). Rockville, MD: Center for Mental Health Services, Substance Abuse and Mental Health Services Administration.

Drewes, A. A., & Schaefer, C. E. (2010). *School-based play therapy.* New York, NY: Routledge. doi:10.1002/9781118269701

Dugan, E., Swanson, K. & Short, E. (2011). Play therapy caregiver consultations. *Playtherapy,* 22-23.

Duran, F., Hepburn, K., Kaufmann, R., Le, L., Allen, M. D., Brennan, E. M., & Green, B. (no date). *Research synthesis: Early childhood mental health consultation*. Nashville, TN: Vanderbilt University, The Center on the Social and Emotional Foundations for Early Learning. Retrieved July 9, 2012 from www.vanderbilt.edu/csefel

Georgetown University. (2015). *Early childhood mental health consultation*. Center for Child and Human Development. Retrieved from: http://gucchd.georgetown.edu/67637.html

Gioia, K., & Tobin, R. (2010). The role of sociodramatic play in promoting self regulation. In Play therapy for preschool children (pp. 181-198). Washington, DC: American Psychological Association. doi:10.1037/12060-009

Henderson, S.W., & Martin, A. (2014). Case formulation and integration of information in child and adolescent mental health. In *IACAPAP e-textbook of child and adolescent mental health*. Geneva: International Association for Child and Adolescent Psychiatry and Allied Professions.

Johnston, K., & Brinamen, C. (2006). *Mental health consultation in child care: Transforming relationships among directors, staff and families*. Washington, DC: ZERO TO THREE Press.

Kottman, T. (2011). *Play therapy basics and beyond*. Alexandria, VA: American Counseling Association.

Landreth, G. (1991). *Play therapy: The art of the relationship*. Florence, KY: Accelerated Development.

Lolan, A., & Dugan, E. (2010). Engaging caregivers in play therapy: A review of common questions and misconceptions posed by caregivers to play therapists in Louisiana. *Play Therapy*, *5*, 20–23.

McGuire, D. K., & McGuire, D. E. (2001). *Linking parents to play therapy: A practical guide with application, interventions, and case studies*. New York, NY: Routledge.

Nash, J., & Schaefer, C. (2010). Clinical and developmental issues in psychotherapy with preschool children: Laying the groundwork for play therapy. In Play therapy for preschool children (pp. 15-45). Washington, DC: American Psychological Association.

O'Connor, K. J., & Braverman, L. D. (2009). *Play therapy theory and practice: Comparing theories and techniques*. Hoboken, NJ: John Wiley & Sons, Inc.

Phillips, R., & Landreth, G. (1995). Play therapists on play therapy: II. Clinical issues in play therapy. *International Journal of Play Therapy*, *7*(1), 1–24. doi:10.1037/h0089416

Ray, D., & McCullough, R. (2015). *Evidence-based practice statement: play therapy*. Association for Play Therapy. Retrieved from: https://c.ymcdn.com/sites/a4pt.siteym.com/resource/resmgr/About_APT/APT_Evidence_Based_Statement.pdf

Ray, D. C. (2011). *Advanced play therapy: Essential conditions, knowledge, and skills for child practice*. New York, NY: Routledge.

Schaefer, C. (2010). *Play therapy for preschool children*. Washington, DC: American Psychological Association. doi:10.1037/12060-000

Schottelkorb, A., Swan, K., & Ogawa, Y. (2015). Parent consultation in child-centered play therapy: A model for research and practice. *International Journal of Play Therapy*, *24*(4), 221–233. doi:10.1037/a0039609

Snow, K. (2013). *Who is the Early Child Care and Education Workforce?* National Association for the Education of Young Children. Retrieved from: http://www.naeyc.org/blogs/gclarke/2013/11/who-early-care-and-education-workforce-0

Steen, R.L. (2010). *Parent consultation: Beyond engagement*. Association for Play Therapy October Mining Report.

Vernon, A. (2009). *Counseling children & adolescents*. Denver, CO: Love Publishing Company.

KEY TERMS AND DEFINITIONS

Center Based Consultation: "An indirect, problem-solving service involving a collegial relationship between the consultant and consultee in which the consultant acquires and communicates psychological date germane to the consultee's problem as well as the psychological principles that will enable the consultee to utilize the data" (Brown, Pryzwansky & Schulte, 2001, p. 48).

Challenging Behavior(S): Any behavior that is observed to impair or interfere with the child's functioning in the child's environment (school, home, social, etc.).

Child-Centered Play Therapy: "Play therapy is the dynamic process between child and Play Therapist in which the child explores at his or her own pace and with his or her own agenda those issues, past and current, conscious and unconscious, that are affecting the child's life in the present. The child's inner resources are enabled by the therapeutic alliance to bring about growth and change. Play therapy is child-centered, in which play is the primary medium and speech is the secondary medium." (British Association of Play Therapists. [updated 2008]).

Consultant: A person who makes recommendations to an individual or group (center), but cannot require or hold power to make changes (Block, 2000).

Early Childhood Mental Health Consultation: "The developing capacity of infants, toddlers, and young children to experience, manage, and express emotion; form close, secure relationships; and actively explore the environment and learn (adapted from ZERO TO THREE, www.zerotothree.org)." (Duran, F., Hepburn, K., Kaufmann, R., Le, L., Allen, M.D., Brennan, E. M., & Green, B. (no date).

Mental Health Consultation: "Mental health consultation is a service provided to caregiving professionals such as doctors, nurses, teachers, lawyers, welfare workers, probation officers, police, and clergy to assist them in dealing with the psychological aspects of a current work problem and, most important, to deal more effectively with similar problems in the future" (Brown, Pryzwansky & Schulte, 2001, p. 19).

Programmatic Consultation: "Improving the overall quality of the program and/or assisting the program to solve a specific issue that affects more than one child, staff member, and/or family" (Cohen & Kaufmann, 2005, p. 8).

Chapter 14
Multicultural Considerations in Play Therapy Caregiver Consultation

Kristy A. Brumfield
Immaculata University, USA

Rheta LeAnne Steen
Loyala University New Orleans, USA

Celita J. Owens
Immaculata University, USA

Renee M. Floer
Loyola University New Orleans, USA

ABSTRACT

The purpose of this chapter is to review the literature regarding parent consultation and to address special considerations when working across cultures and ethnicities. Understanding privacy expectations and how to meet the needs of families, without discouraging the caregivers or unintentionally breaking cultural guidelines, will be explored. This chapter is extremely important because mental health professionals must adhere to the diversity guidelines and ethical standards of practice in complex cases, with many involved caregivers at times. When consulting with caregivers from culturally diverse backgrounds, consultants need to consider the impact of culture on the caregiver, the child client, and on the consultation process.

MULTICULTURAL CONSIDERATIONS IN PLAY THERAPY CAREGIVER CONSULTATION

According to Colby and Ortman (2014) in a 2014 report of National Population Projections, more than half of the nation's children are expected to be from a minority race or ethnic group by the 2020 census. By 2060, 36 percent of children (people under 18) will be white, as compared to 52 percent today. The U.S. Census Bureau (2010) also states the Hispanic population increased by 15.2 million between 2000 and 2010, accounting for over half of the 27.3 million increase in the total population of the United States. Professionals who work with children and their caregivers must attempt to develop an understanding of various cultures and the roles of the caregivers and children within these cultures. Although there is an increasing diversity in referrals, demographic surveys indicate that white females continue to dominate

DOI: 10.4018/978-1-5225-2224-9.ch014

the fields of play therapy and counseling.(Haslam & Harris, 2011; Kranz, Kottman, & Lund, 1998; Phillips & Landreth, 1995; Ryan, Gomory, & Lacasse, 2002).

It is challenging, if not impossible, to summarize the breadth of information necessary when considering the specific needs of every cultural subgroup the play therapist encounters in their role as a play therapy caregiver consultant (PTCC). However, competence in working with a variety of clients is essential and ethically mandated. In fact, according to the American Counseling Association (ACA) Code of Ethics, counselors are expected to be capable of working with diverse populations and must gain training and supervision when confronted with limitations in their scope of practice, especially when confronted with underrepresented or marginalized populations (American Counseling Association, 2014).

In an investigation of play therapists' self-reported multicultural competence, subjects indicated a need for specific multicultural education as well as ongoing supervision to maximize, "attitudes and beliefs, knowledge, skills, and action" (Penn & Post, 2012, p. 3). In this chapter, we attempt to provide useful guidelines for consideration when working with culturally diverse clients and their caregivers, without assuming that there is an exact answer or a "cookbook recipe approach" all too often used in multicultural or diversity-focused chapters. We present historical and up-to-date information on multicultural considerations for the PTCC, including practical implications for practice in engaging caregivers as a culturally competent play therapist. This information is based on and extensive literature review, research gained from clinical work, and current consultation with PTCCs in the field. It should be noted that the relative lack of research on both multicultural considerations in play therapy and caregiver consultation in general are significant limitations in the scope and breadth of this chapter.

Multicultural Competence

The Association for Multicultural Counseling and Development (AMCD) published Multicultural Competencies on their website, www.multiculturalcounseling.org, which outlines specific standards and serves as a resource for counselors to increase their cultural competence (Arredondo, P., Toporek, M. S., Brown, S., Jones, J., Locke, D. C., Sanchez, J. and Stadler, H., 1996). Additionally, the ACA published Multicultural and Social Justice Counseling Competencies that offer developmental domains the PTCC can utilize to become more culturally competent (www.counseling.org/knowledge-center/competencies). These guidelines outline self-awareness, other-awareness, and rapport in addition to specific interventions. Exploring and understanding the guidelines challenges the counselor to acknowledge the pursuit of social justice while embracing multicultural competencies as a lifelong endeavor (Ratts, Singh, Nassar-McMillan, Butler, & McCullough, 2015). Of particular relevance to PTCCs, is the recommendation to recognize similarities and differences both within and between cultural groups. Finally, as a guideline for understanding client worldview, the fact that culture influences communication styles for both the caregiver and the consultant. As such, the consultant must "acquire culturally responsive cross-cultural communication skills to interact with [caregivers]" (Ratts, Singh, Nassar-McMillan, Butler, & McCullough, 2015).

In addition to the ACA and the AMCD, The Association for Play Therapy also published best practice guidelines to assist PTCCs in providing the highest level of care for their clients (www.a4pt.org/?page=Research). Concepts such as boundaries of competence, non-discrimination, and sensitivity to individual vs. group differences are all areas where cultural competence is considered a necessary skill. Concerning issues of diversity and training, best practices specify:

Play therapists actively participate in a process by which they strive to 1) become and remain aware of their own cultural backgrounds, influences, and biases including, but not limited to, religion, gender, sexual orientation, ethnicity, and race; 2) acquire and continuously seek knowledge about how cultural backgrounds, influences, and biases operate in the lives of their clients; and 3) demonstrate culturally responsive therapeutic skills. (p. 13)

Clearly, the ethically responsible PTCC must continually develop, practice, and maintain skills around cultural awareness and sensitivity.

The Importance of Play and Play Therapy

From ancient philosophy to modern scientific research, play is an integral component in learning and child development (Fisher, Hirsh-Pasek, Golinkoff & Gryfe, 2008). Play is a ubiquitous part of the lives of all children that holds no bounds. Landreth (2012) indicated that play is the "native language" of children, an innate and universal method of communication through which children converse in an open and direct way. In recent years there has been an increased consideration for physical health and nutrition through outdoor activities with national campaigns like the NFL's Play 60 and First Lady Michelle Obama's "Let's Move!". These contributions are necessary and essential elements of keeping children motivated to maintain their health through physical activity, but a focus on play as a component to mental and emotional health is missing.

In spite of the evidence of the positive developmental benefits of play, there has been a significant decline in the amount of time allotted for free and unstructured play in today's society. In one study, researchers examined filial play across cultures and found that parent subjects confirm a trend toward decreased outdoor play and increased sedentary indoor activities (Roopnarine & Davidson, 2015). Play is redefined as a trivial exercise that is a placeholder for nonacademic activities. The importance of play in the school setting has diminished as the demands of children's academic performance in school has significantly increased (Pellegrini, 2008; Pellegrini & Blatchford, 2002; Pellegrini & Holmes, 2006; Ramstetter, Murray, & Garner, 2010; Slater, Nicholson, Chriqui, Turner, & Chaloupka, 2012).

Caregiver's Concept of Play

The effectiveness of play therapy is a researched and reliable form of therapy when used with multiple populations, yet the phenomenon of play continues to be seen as an abstruse process (Ray, Bratton, Rhines, & Jones, 2001). Given that beliefs evolve in part through cultural and personal experiences, caregivers and experts may hold different beliefs about the nature of play itself (Fisher et al., 2008). The definition of play can vary across cultures, yet we use the term in a general sense. Examining other cultures' and populations' definition of play and specific play activities can yield positive feedback within the therapeutic alliance. Additionally, identifying the thematic perceptions of play in various cultures leads to a more informed approach when collaborating with caregivers. As caregivers begin to explore therapy as an option, it is imperative to understand the challenges faced by various populations that can affect their openness to play.

Caregivers' beliefs surrounding play and its purpose provide further implication to the function of play in the home. Understanding the use and typical nature of play in the home sheds light on how an introduction of play in a therapeutic setting will be received and understood. For caregivers from diverse backgrounds and experiences, the PTCC must be willing to acknowledge that his or her perspective may not be aligned with that of the caregiver, and time spent exploring perceptions of play and expectations for treatment should not be hurried.

Caregivers Concept of Play Therapy and Consultation

Despite efforts by the Association for Play Therapy to educate the public about play therapy, caregivers remain largely uniformed about the importance of play in counseling with children. Shale (2004) concluded that, although parents recognized the developmental value of play therapy and perceived it as helpful, they were unclear about *what* play therapy was. This is one of many areas where culturally sensitive caregiver consultation can fill the gap of missing information and increase caregivers' comfort with the process.

Unless skilled and qualified clinicians take the time to explain what play therapy is and how techniques will be employed with their children, caregivers may simply not know or understand what play therapy is and how it can be implemented in counseling with children, adolescents, and families. These and other factors may contribute to a sobering statistic reported by Lolan (2011), who found that only 35.9% of play therapists believe caregivers are willing to participate regularly in the therapeutic process. This statistic may increase when caregivers are culturally different from the consultant (Chang, Ritter, & Hays, 2005).

Caregiver perceptions of play therapy are colored by a number of factors, which contribute to the overall counseling experience (Crane, 2001). Caregivers' educational level, the circumstances that caused them to seek counseling, and whether or not participation is voluntary can all affect the counseling process. Previous experiences with counseling may also influence caregiver perceptions regarding the therapeutic process in general. Other important factors include the family's socioeconomic status in relation to the perceived "worth" of counseling. Finally, caregivers' thoughts about play and the value of play for children can have a direct impact on what they think about the therapeutic use of play as a tool for addressing their parental concerns (Brumfield & Christensen, 2011; Muhammad, 2009). After considering all of the above factors and their potential influence on the counseling experience, it becomes clear that the therapist's ability to explain play therapy and to engage with caregivers is of utmost importance.

Cultural Misrepresentation in Research

Direct accounts of caregiver attitudes regarding play are limited in the research. In a phenomenological study of African American parents' perceptions of play therapy, Brumfield and Christensen (2011) found "… African American parents' perceptions of play, counseling, and play therapy revealed information consistent with two main themes: (1) value of play, and (2) receptivity to counseling. Parents identified *developmental learning* and *release* as two of the main values surrounding play." It appears evident from their findings that African American parents' perceptions are consistent with the idea that play is central to childhood development and release. This implies that there is time delegated for this activity, since it is recognized as important.

Historically, however, researchers have published accounts without sensitivity to cultural differences. Bracey (2012) discussed the prominence of a deficit-based or ethnocentric perspective, the tendency to overgeneralize African American families, and the tendency to pathologize and misinterpret cultural norms as influencing parenting practices in the research history of this population (Boykin & Toms,

1985; Cain & Combs-Orme, 2005; Carter-Black, 2003; Dodson, 1995; Gomes & Mabry, 1991). For example, researchers studying children from low-income African American families found that they engage in less significant amounts of pretend play in comparison to other groups. Additional researchers indicated that middle-income children in preschool and the early primary grades engage in more pretend play than low-income (often African American) children (e.g., Rosen, 1974; Smilansky, 1968; White, 1978). Further, while addressing the negative hypothesis regarding pretend play in this population, McLoyd (1985) stated the assumption that low-income children engage in less frequent, lower-quality pretend play or play that is characteristically unimaginative and desultory, and is widely accepted in the available literature (Lovinger, 1974; Murphy, 1972; Singer, 1973; Smilansky, 1968). It is crucial to note the disparaging research. With a staggering amount of focus on deficits rather than strength-based assumptions, combating these popular subgroup issues when addressing caregiver perception is of significant importance.

Play Therapy through a Culturally Sensitive Lens

It has become a putative notion that African American families do not seek counsel from mental health workers or agencies; however, there is limited exploration into this perceived phenomenon. Brumfield and Christensen (2011) noted specific factors that facilitated or encouraged African American parents to pursue counseling, which pertained to how reliable the referral source was, as well as the perceived support parents experience from their family, community, and society, in general. Similarly, in a study examining counseling with Hispanic families, Kossak (2005) suggested that Hispanic clients are more willing to consider and adhere to services when they have a sense of being understood and have developed trust in the counselor.

Bridges, de Arellano, Rheingold, Danielson, and Silcott (2010) have identified many reasons why members of the Hispanic population are less likely to receive mental health services, including: not understanding the value of the services to language barriers, limited financial resources, social consequences of accessing care, lack of culturally responsive practices, immigration status, and the use of alternative healers and methods to treat mental health concerns (Bornsheuer & Polonyi, 2010; Bridges et al., 2010; Costantino, Malgady, & Primavera, 2009; Garza, 2004; Garza & Watts, 2010). Careful consideration needs to be taken when discussing cultures' preferred methods of treatment in all populations, and the Hispanic population is no exception. Garza and Watts (2010) stated that, historically, Hispanics have eschewed unwanted attention and the social stigma that often accompany mental health treatment. Additionally, they found that Hispanic individuals typically prefer addressing problems within the boundaries of the family. It is a common cultural practice to seek help from the primary care physician for physical conditions, but is less common to address mental health issues as they arise. Cultural values that can incite Hispanic families to engage in therapy have been identified in a previous study that examined filial therapy and Hispanic values. Garza and Watts (2010) proposed four Hispanic values that, when interfaced with play therapy, help facilitate effective culturally responsive treatment: (1) the importance *offamilismo* (family), (2) *respeto* (respect), (3) *personalismo* (personal relationships), and (4) *confianza* (trust). PTCCs should keep these in mind when working to engage Hispanic families.

Caregivers can have a hard time understanding the benefits of play therapy; what it is, or how it can be helpful. They may find it difficult distinguishing play therapy from play at home or at school. To address this issue, the Association for Play Therapy (2015) clarifies the difference for potential clients and caregivers stating, "Play therapy differs from regular play in that the therapist helps children to address and resolve their own problems." Working with a child may not require a heavy concentration on cultural sensitivity during the act of play, but collaborating with parents without acknowledging the norms of that culture can impede the alliance. Hinman (2003) suggested that Hispanic parents may expect a problem-focused approach from the therapist and that any deviation from that will need clarification in order for the parent to have a better understanding of the therapeutic process. Explaining the function of play and play therapy in ways that families will understand and based on cultural correlations can increase their openness to the process of play therapy.

In addition to being agents of consent for clients who are minors, parents and primary caregivers play an integral part in the efficacy of play therapy and counseling with children and adolescents (Axline, 1993; Cates, Paone, Packman, & Margolis, 2006; Kottman, 2011; McGuire & McGuire, 2001; Post, Ceballos, & Penn, 2012; Timberlake & Cutler, 2001; VanFleet, Sywulak & Sniscak, 2010). The ability to *engage caregivers* in the process of play therapy from intake to termination is often daunting for the novice PTCC. Newly trained therapists may not feel adequately prepared for systemic work or may be otherwise intimidated by interactions outside of the individual work with the child (Cates et al., 2006; LeBlanc & Ritchie, 1999; Lolan, 2011; Post, 2014; Ray, Bratton, Rhine, & Jones, 2001, Steen, 2010).

Adding a diversity aspect to the PTCC relationship may further intimidate beginning therapists and delay the development of a therapeutic alliance with the caregivers. Fortunately, according to the literature, this reluctance is transient. Researchers found as many as 90% of play therapists are comfortable working alone with caregivers (Haslam & Harris, 2011). Play therapists acknowledge the value and importance of including caregivers (Cates et al., 2006; LeBlanc & Ritchie, 1999; Lolan, 2011; Post, 2014; Ray, Bratton, Rhine, & Jones, 2001, Steen, 2010) and even specifically cite parent consultation as a necessary aspect of treatment (Ray, 2011; Scotelkorb, Swan, & Ogawa, 2015). While educating caregivers on the process of play therapy, the PTCC must model open discussion and be patient with a variety of cultural norms in order to help facilitate their engagement.

Involving Caregivers

In non-dominant cultures, individuals frequently utilize internal and collaborative resources and supports such as church and family (Bethea-Whitfield, 2005; Boyd-Franklin, 2003; Dixon & Vaz, 2005; Harley, 2005). A consequence of these cultural factors is the perception of the PTCC as an outsider and an increased possibility that counseling only becomes an option when the situation becomes extreme—resulting in increased frustration for caregivers PTCCs need to be aware of this potential frustration so that caregiver needs can be adequately addressed. Further research found that parents from non-dominant cultures seek referrals from schoolteachers, school counselors, church leaders, and medical professionals (Brumfield & Christensen, 2011). Providing play therapy educational brochures or information sessions at parenting groups, churches, school meetings, or other events where caregivers congregate can increase awareness and decrease frustration. During consultation, clinicians can demonstrate understanding by acknowledging the feedback caregivers may have already received from other stakeholders and allowing room for diverse perspectives.

Ray (2011) identifies six play therapist attitudes that are essential in working with parents: (1) respect for the parent's role, (2) respect for the parents' knowledge of the child, (3) affection for the parent as a person, (4) patience, (5) clear focus on the child as the client, and (6) therapist as expert. With culturally diverse caregivers, it may be important to be more overt in the expression of respect for the caregiver's role and knowledge. The consultant should be careful to avoid blame or judgment, which are likely to result in defensiveness, mistrust, and ultimately caregiver disengagement. The consultant may need to empower clients to share their own stories if they've had prior experiences suggesting their perspective was unwanted or unwelcome. It may take more time in order to establish rapport with caregivers who are reluctant or uncertain about the process, and the competent consultant will respect this need for increased time. In order to facilitate caregiver empowerment, Holcomb-McCoy and Bryan (2010) recommend PTCCs recognize the inherent power differential that exists between consultants and caregivers, diminish their own role as experts, and include consultees as mutual experts in the process.

PTCCs should be intentional as they help caregivers brainstorm potential goals and action steps for themselves and their children, specifically addressing methods for countering any oppression or micro-aggressions they are currently experiencing. Further, caregivers should be encouraged to take responsibility for their own learning and to make connections in their own communities. Empowering caregivers in this way will increase their confidence and empower them to develop tactics that can meet their individual needs (Brumfeld & Christensen, 2011).

Children are very perceptive, and their affect is often influenced by their caregivers' verbal and non-verbal cues (Timberlake & Cutler, 2001). For this reason, ongoing caregiver consultation is essential. If caregivers are skeptical or concerned about counseling, then children may share such skepticism and concern. On the contrary, if caregivers are excited about and open to the process, then children are likely more engaged (Carmichael, 2006). Overall, it is safe to assume that most caregivers truly want what is best for their children and that they are willing to cooperate with the PTCC (Brumfield & Christensen, 2011; Crane, 2001; McGuire & McGuire, 2001; VanFleet et al., 2010; Wachtel, 1994). Involving the parents is essential.

Guidelines for Competent Practice

Culturally Specific Skills

PTCCs working with caregivers from non-dominant or underrepresented cultures must maintain an awareness of the client's need to trust that the clinician is qualified, and has experience working with diverse children and families. This reassurance is particularly necessary if the clinician does not resemble the client phenotypically. The ability of both parties to see eye to eye in order to develop the trusting relationship that is key in caregiver consultation. Despite the fact that PTCC may view cultural differences as the "problem" (Holcomb-McCoy & Bryan, 2010), most helping professionals acknowledge that the client as an expert on his or her own life and/or experiences. The PTCC can honor those experiences in many covert ways, particularly through the implementation of a few familiar basic helping skills and the core conditions (Steen, 2010).

There is support in the literature for the application of multicultural competence to play therapy and counseling children (Gil, 2005; Hinman, 2003; Jayne, Stulmaker, & Purswell, 2013; O'Connor, 2005; Penn & Post, 2012; Ritter & Chang, 2002). However, the PTCC's level of cultural awareness may interfere with their working relationships. PTCCs who are unable to understand traditional family interaction patterns in culturally diverse family and cross-cultural communication styles will be unable to adequately address caregiver concerns (Cain & Combs-Orme, 2005; Holcomb-McCoy & Bryan, 2010). The PTCC should be aware of any cultural differences in play behavior and parenting style in order to increase the perceived usefulness of feedback given to caregivers, improve interpretation and diagnosis, and avoid misunderstandings or errors in communication.

Additionally, there is a great deal literature focused on the role of culture in the process of consultation. Frequently the PTCC conceptualization of an identified problem stems from cultural differences. For example, the culturally unaware therapist might determine that a child's problem is related to various demographic factors such as membership in a marginalized racial group, coming from a socioeconomically disadvantaged household, or parents' marital status (Holcomb-McCoy & Bryan, 2010; Ingraham, 2000, 2003; Tarver-Behring & Ingraham, 1998). In a qualitative study of low-income African American mothers, Kalyanpur and Rao (1991) identified three aspects of negative experiences with professionals; disrespect, focus on deficits, and discounting parenting style differences, which are likely related to preconceived notions based on these demographic factors.

The PTCC should also consider the overrepresentation of certain non-dominant or minority groups in special education populations and be sensitive to the academic needs of the child or adolescent client concurrent with any social, emotional, or behavioral needs that might be present. It should also be considered that some children may be the recipients of numerous multidisciplinary services, and caregivers may be overwhelmed with the well-intentioned support from a bevy of providers.

Franklin and Boyd-Franklin (1985) contend that traditional African values and beliefs have been transmitted from generation to generation and continue to influence African American parenting. Perceptions of play are intrinsically tied to the values and beliefs that influence parenting. Some parents embrace play as essential, whereas others are less impressed by the fact that play could be a contributing factor in childhood development (Roopnarine, Shin, Jung, & Hossain, 2003). The idea is not to convince those caregivers who believe the latter, but to have an understanding of how what they believe is affecting their child's development. Corresponding with all therapeutic approaches, it is imperative to have a comprehensive background of the caregivers, as this relationship directly affects the child. Although trans-generational influences undoubtedly affect parenting, environment, socioeconomic status, and personal experiences also have a significant impact. Examining those domains in correlation to play is complex, as a lack of research exists in this specific area; however, implications can be made based on existing research (Boykin & Toms, 1985; Cain & Combs-Orme, 2005; Carter-Black, 2003; Dodson, 1995; Gomes & Mabry, 1991).

Caregiver as Expert

Caregivers may feel powerless or question their parenting abilities when they have to seek outside help (Vernon & Clemente, 2005). This powerlessness can come across as anger or resentment for the children, other family members, the counselors, or the referring agencies (Timberlake & Cutler, 2001). Throughout their clinical experience, the authors have observed that often, when children are in crisis, so are their caregivers.

A caregiver consultation model to be used in conjunction with child-centered play therapy has been proposed that encompasses key components of the relational approach most frequently cited by PTCCs subscribing to a specific therapeutic orientation. The five components include: 1) forming and maintaining the caregiver–therapist relationship through demonstration of core relationship conditions, 2) demonstrating present awareness to listen and respond, 3) respecting caregivers as experts on their own children, 4) sharing relevant knowledge, and 6) teaching therapeutic skills (Schottelkorb et al., 2015).

Holcomb-McCoy and Bryan (2010) propose an advocacy and empowerment approach to caregiver consultation. They encourage consultants to recognize and acknowledge the almost daily challenges encountered by most families of color and those from lower socioeconomic backgrounds. The caregiver should be considered appropriately in the context of culturally diverse and historically oppressed backgrounds. The consultant should validate the strengths demonstrated for survival under these circumstances. This model suggests four components of caregiver consultation, including: 1) statement of the problem; 2) the consideration of cultural, familial, and political factors that are influencing the problem; 3) the development of critical consciousness; and 4) the use of problem-solving strategies (p. 265). Using these strategies should facilitate engagement with caregivers of diverse and oppressed backgrounds.

DISCUSSION

Models for Culturally Competent Engagement

We suggest the following general guidelines for culturally competent caregiver consultation: 1) explain the process clearly and thoroughly, allowing time for questions should they arise; 2) give caregivers a tour of your space, as well as culturally relevant audio-visual and/or reading materials. 3) determine a predictable and consistent schedule for consultation meetings (weekly, monthly, as needed); 4) consider your space: Do your decorations, magazines, waiting areas, and child therapy areas all paint a picture of inclusiveness; 5) typical attending skills used in counseling (active listening, showing empathy/understanding); 6) caregivers want resources and it is the job of PTCCs to provide them.

Many PTCCs find comfort in approaching work with caregivers from a theoretical standpoint similar to that used in therapy. In the first decade of this century emerged a prevalence of three models of caregiver consultation: conjoint behavioral consultation, Adlerian parent consultation, and values-based consultation (Bornsheuer & Polonyi, 2010; Holcomb-McCoy & Bryan, 2010). More recently, child/caregiver-centered approaches have been suggested (Schottelkorb et al., 2015). These strategies can be broken into two main categories: psychoeducational and relational.

Psychoeducational Approach to Play Therapy

In psychoeducational caregiver consultation, the primary goal is teaching caregivers, imparting information, or sharing ideas. These PTCCs typically ascribe to cognitive behavioral or behavioral theories, whereas those in the latter are more likely humanistic (i.e., person-centered, existential, gestalt).

The psychoeducational approach can be problematic if the consultant is insensitive to cultural factors. Holcomb-McCoy and Bryan (2010) specifically note the potential conflict between African American caregivers and certain behavior modification techniques. These behaviorally informed strategies may also overlook psychosocial factors such as cultural values, family dynamics, patterns of social interaction, and learned coping mechanisms. PTCCs must be careful to consider that Hispanic and Asian families traditionally involve extended family members, such as grandparents, in family and child-rearing decisions more than their European counterparts. Learned coping mechanisms are sometimes misunderstood as resistance, or even pathologized and diagnosed, rather than considered in the context of necessary adaptations to surviving in hostile environments. The overrepresentation of certain non-dominant cultures for various diagnoses (e.g., African American and Latin American children diagnosed with emotional and behavioral disorders) warrants caregiver consideration prior to assuming accuracy of past records. A behavioral approach may also miss the source of perceived maladaptive behaviors such as frustration, anger, or insecurity due to culturally related environmental factors.

Relational Approach to Play Therapy

In relational approaches, the relationship between caregiver and consultant is the identified change agent, and information or interventions are not deemed sufficient (Holcomb-McCoy & Bryan, 2010). The relational approach assumes that a warm and caring relationship, wherein the PTCC demonstrates unconditional positive regard for the caregiver, will provide the atmosphere for growth and change in the caregiver and, by extension, in the child client. Unfortunately, the underpinnings of such humanistic approaches assume that each participant in the relationship (caregiver and PTCC) has the ability to elude prejudices, assumptions, and preconceived notions. Another typical core belief in humanistic approaches is the role of the caregiver, rather than the consultant, as expert. This may conflict with cultural beliefs that value deference to authority figures and see relationships as hierarchical (Holcomb-McCoy & Bryan, 2010). This may also be the case for some Asian caregivers to expect the PTCC to give direction and provide "coaching", rather than take a more egalitarian and/or supportive stance. Conscious and unconscious perceptions may cause African American clients to anticipate racial prejudice and discrimination from white therapists. These assumptions may be the cause of resistance or reluctance to share openly in consultation or even in early termination of the counseling and consultation relationship (Boyd-Franklin, 2003).

REFERENCES

American Counseling Association. (2014). *ACA Code of Ethics*. Alexandria, VA: Author.

Arredondo, P., Toporek, M. S., Brown, S., Jones, J., Locke, D. C., Sanchez, J., & Stadler, H. (1996). *Operationalization of the Multicultural Counseling Competencies*. AMCD.

Association for Play Therapy, Inc. (2015). Play therapy makes a difference. In *Why Play Therapy?* Retrieved from http://www.a4pt.org/?page=PTMakesADifference

Axline, V. M. (1993). *Play therapy* (33rd ed.). Boston, MA: Houghton Mifflin.

Bethea-Whitfield, P. (2005). African American women and mental health. In D. A. Harley & J. M. Dillard (Eds.), *Contemporary mental health issues among African Americans* (pp. 35–47). Alexandria, VA: American Counseling Association.

Bornsheuer, J., & Polonyi, M. A. (2010). Adlerian counseling with Hispanic clients and families. *Professional Issues in Counseling*. Retrieved from http://www.shsu.edu/piic/AdlerianCounselingwithHispanicClientsandFamilies.htm

Boyd-Franklin, N. (2003). *Black families in therapy: Understanding the African American experience* (2nd ed.). New York, NY: Guilford Press.

Boykin, A. W., & Toms, F. D. (1985). Black child socialization: A conceptual framework. In H. P. McAdoo & J. L. McAdoo (Eds.), *Black children: Social, environmental, and parental environments* (pp. 35–51). Newbury Park, CA: Sage Publications.

Bracey, J. R. (2012). Socializing race: Parental beliefs and practices in two African American families. *Dissertation Abstracts International*, *72*(7-B), 4363.

Bridges, A. J., de Arellano, M. A., Rheingold, A. A., Danielson, C. K., & Silcott, L. (2010). Trauma exposure, mental health, and service utilization rates among immigrant and United States-born Hispanic youth: Results from the Hispanic family study. *Psychological Trauma: Theory, Research, Practice, and Policy*, *2*(1), 40–48. doi:10.1037/a0019021

Brumfield, K. A., & Christensen, T. M. (2011). Discovering African American parents perceptions of play therapy: A phenomenological approach. *International Journal of Play Therapy*, *20*(4), 208–223. doi:10.1037/a0025748

Cain, D. S., & Combs-Orme, T. (2005). Family structure effects on parenting stress and practices in the African American family. *Journal of Sociology and Social Welfare*, *32*(2), 19–40.

Carmichael, K. D. (2006). *Play therapy: An introduction*. Upper Saddle River, NJ: Pearson Education.

Carter-Black, J. (2003). The myth of the tangle of pathology: Resilience strategies employed by middle-class African American families. *Journal of Family Social Work*, *6*(4), 75–100. doi:10.1300/J039v06n04_06

Cates, J., Paone, T., Packman, J., & Margolis, D. (2006). Effective parent consultation in play therapy. *International Journal of Play Therapy*, *15*(1), 87–100. doi:10.1037/h0088909

Chang, C. Y., Ritter, K. B., & Hays, D. G. (2005). Multicultural trends and toys in play therapy. *International Journal of Play Therapy*, *14*(2), 69–85. doi:10.1037/h0088903

Colby, S. L., & Ortman, J. M. (2014). Projections of the size and composition of the U.S. population: 2014 to 2060. In Current population reports (pp. 25–1143). Washington, DC: U.S. Census Bureau; Retrieved from https://www.census.gov/content/dam/Census/library/publications/2015/demo/p25-1143.pdf

Costantino, G., Malgady, R. G., & Primavera, L. H. (2009). Congruence between culturally competent treatment and cultural needs of older Latinos. *Journal of Consulting and Clinical Psychology*, *77*(5), 941–949. doi:10.1037/a0016341 PMID:19803573

Crane, J. (2001). The parents' part in the play therapy process. In G. L. Landreth (Ed.), *Innovations in play therapy: Issues, process, and special populations* (pp. 83–95). New York, NY: Brunner-Routledge.

Dixon, C. G., & Vaz, K. (2005). Perceptions of African Americans regarding mental health counseling. In D. A. Harley & J. M. Dillard (Eds.), *Contemporary mental health issues among African Americans* (pp. 163–174). Alexandria, VA: American Counseling Association.

Dodson, J. E. (1995). Conceptualizations of Black families. In N. R. Goldberger & J. B. Veroff (Eds.), *The culture and psychology reader* (pp. 276–291). New York, NY: New York University Press.

Fisher, K. R., Hirsh-Pasek, K., Golinkoff, R. M., & Gryfe, S. G. (2008). Conceptual split? Parents and experts perceptions of play in the 21st century. *Journal of Applied Developmental Psychology*, *29*(4), 305–316. doi:10.1016/j.appdev.2008.04.006

Franklin, A. J., & Boyd-Franklin, N. (1985). A psycho-educational perspective on Black parenting. In H. P. McAdoo & J. L. McAdoo (Eds.), *Black children: social, educational & parental environments*. Beverly Hills, CA: Sage Publications.

Garza, Y. (2004). *Effects of culturally responsive child-centered play therapy compared to curriculum-based small group counseling with elementary-age Hispanic children experiencing externalizing and internalizing behavior problems: A preliminary study* (Unpublished doctoral dissertation). University of North Texas, Denton, TX.

Garza, Y., & Watts, R. E. (2010). Filial therapy and Hispanic values: Common ground for culturally sensitive helping. *Journal of Counseling and Development*, *88*(1), 108–113. doi:10.1002/j.1556-6678.2010.tb00157.x

Gil, E. (2005). From sensitivity to competence in working across cultures. In E. Gil & A. A. Drewes (Eds.), *Cultural issues in play therapy* (pp. 3–25). New York, NY: Guilford Press.

Gomes, P. G., & Mabry, C. A. (1991). Negotiating the world: The developmental journey of African American children. In J. E. Everett, S. S. Chipungu, & B. R. Leashore (Eds.), *Child welfare: An Africentric perspective* (pp. 156–182). New Brunswick, NJ: Rutgers University Press.

Harley, D. A. (2005). The Black church: A strength-based approach in mental health. In D. A. Harley & J. M. Dillard (Eds.), *Contemporary mental health issues among African Americans* (pp. 191–203). Alexandria, VA: American Counseling Association.

Haslam, D., & Harris, S. (2011). Integrating play and family therapy methods: A survey of play therapists attitudes in the field. *International Journal of Play Therapy*, *20*(2), 51–65. doi:10.1037/a0023410

Hinman, C. (2003). Multicultural considerations in the delivery of play therapy services. *International Journal of Play Therapy*, *12*(2), 107–122. doi:10.1037/h0088881

Holcomb-McCoy, C., & Bryan, J. (2010). Advocacy and empowerment in parent consultation: Implications for theory and practice. *Journal of Counseling and Development*, *88*(3), 259–268. doi:10.1002/j.1556-6678.2010.tb00021.x

Ingraham, C. L. (2000). Consultation through a multicultural lens: Multicultural and cross-cultural consultation in schools. *School Psychology Review*, *29*(3), 320–343.

Ingraham, C. L. (2003). Multicultural consultee-centered consultation: When novice consultants explore cultural hypotheses with experienced teacher consultees. *Journal of Educational & Psychological Consultation*, *14*(3/4), 329–362. doi:10.1080/10474412.2003.9669492

Jayne, K. M., Stulmaker, H. L., & Purswell, K. E. (2013). Multicultural dimensions in child counseling research: A systematic review. *Journal of Professional Counseling, Practice, Theory, & Research*, *40*(2), 15–32.

Kalyanpur, M., & Rao, S. S. (1991). Empowering low-income Black families of handicapped children. *The American Journal of Orthopsychiatry*, *61*(4), 523–532. doi:10.1037/h0079292 PMID:1836108

Kossak, S. N. (2005). Exploring the elements of culturally relevant service delivery. *Families in Society*, *86*(2), 189–195. doi:10.1606/1044-3894.2454

Kottman, T. (2011). *Play therapy: Basics and beyond* (2nd ed.). Alexandria, VA: American Counseling Association.

Kranz, P. L., Kottman, T., & Lund, N. L. (1998). Play therapists opinions concerning the education, training, and practice of play therapists. *International Journal of Play Therapy*, *7*(1), 73–87. doi:10.1037/h0089419

Landreth, G. L. (2012). *Play therapy: The art of the relationship* (3rd ed.). New York, NY: Brunner-Routledge.

LeBlanc, M., & Ritchie, M. (1999). Predictors of play therapy outcomes. *International Journal of Play Therapy*, *8*(2), 19–29. doi:10.1037/h0089429

Lolan, A. R. (2011). *Play therapists' practice patterns and perceptions of the factors that influence caregiver engagement in play therapy* (Doctoral dissertation). University of New Orleans. Retrieved from http://scholarworks.uno.edu/cgi/viewcontent.cgi?article=2411&context=td

Lovinger, S. L. (1974). Socio-dramatic play and language development in preschool disadvantaged children. *Psychology in the Schools*, *11*(3), 313–320. doi:10.1002/1520-6807(197407)11:3<313::AID-PITS2310110315>3.0.CO;2-L

McGuire, D. K., & McGuire, D. E. (2001). *Linking parents to play therapy: A practical guide with applications, interventions, and case studies*. New York, NY: Routledge.

McLoyd, V. C. (1985). Are toys (just) toys? Exploring their effects on pretend play of low-income preschoolers. In M. B. Spencer, G. K. Brookins, W. R. Allen, M. B. Spencer, G. K. Brookins, & W. R. Allen (Eds.), *Beginnings: The social and affective development of black children* (pp. 81–100). Hillsdale, NJ: Lawrence Erlbaum Associates, Inc.

Muhammad, Y. J. (2009). Low-income African American parents' views about the value of play for their preschool age children in Head Start. *Dissertation Abstracts International*, *71*(3-A), 911.

Murphy, L. B. (1972). Infants' play and cognitive development. In M. W. Piers (Ed.), *Play and cognitive development*. New York, NY: Norton.

OConnor, K. (2005). Addressing diversity issues in play therapy. *Professional Psychology, Research and Practice*, *36*(5), 566–573. doi:10.1037/0735-7028.36.5.566

Pellegrini, A. D. (2008). The Recess Debate: A Disjuncture between Educational Policy and Scientific Research. *American Journal of Play*, *1*(2), 181–191.

Pellegrini, A. D., & Blatchford, P. (2002). The developmental and educational significance of recess in schools. *Early Rep*, *29*(1), 1–7.

Pellegrini, A. D., & Holmes, R. M. (2006). *The role of recess in primary school. Play= learning: How play motivates and enhances children's cognitive and social-emotional growth*. Oxford, UK: Oxford University Press.

Penn, S. L., & Post, P. B. (2012). Investigating various dimensions of play therapists self-reported multicultural counseling competence. *International Journal of Play Therapy*, *21*(1), 14–29. doi:10.1037/a0026894

Phillips, R., & Landreth, G. (1995). Play therapists on play therapy I: A report of methods, demographics and professional practices. *International Journal of Play Therapy*, *4*(1), 1–26. doi:10.1037/h0089404

Post, P. B. (2014, August 25). Involving parents in child-centered play therapy. *Counseling Today*. Retrieved from http://ct.counseling.org/2014/08/involving-parents-in-child-centered-play-therapy/

Post, P. B., Ceballos, P. L., & Penn, S. L. (2012). Collaborating with parents to establish behavioral goals in child-centered play therapy. *The Family Journal (Alexandria, Va.)*, *20*(1), 51–57. doi:10.1177/1066480711425472

Ramstetter, C. L., Murray, R., & Garner, A. S. (2010). The crucial role of recess in schools. *The Journal of School Health*, *80*(11), 517–526. doi:10.1111/j.1746-1561.2010.00537.x PMID:21039550

Ratts, M. J., Singh, A. A., Nassar-McMillan, S., Butler, S. K., & McCullough, J. R. (2015). *Multicultural and social justice counseling competencies*. Retrieved from http://www.multiculturalcounseling.org/index.php?option=com_content&view=article&id=205:amcd-endorses-multicultural-and-social-justice-counseling-competencies&catid=1:latest&Itemid=123

Ray, D., Bratton, S., Rhine, T., & Jones, L. (2001). The effectiveness of play therapy: Responding to the critics. *International Journal of Play Therapy*, *10*(1), 85–108. doi:10.1037/h0089444

Ray, D. C. (2011). *Advanced play therapy: Essential conditions, knowledge, and skills for child practice*. New York, NY: Routledge.

Ritter, K. B., & Chang, C. Y. (2002). Play therapists self-perceived multicultural competence and adequacy of training. *International Journal of Play Therapy*, *11*(1), 103–113. doi:10.1037/h0088859

Roopnarine, J. L., & Davidson, K. L. (2015). Parent-child play across cultures: Advancing play research. *American Journal of Play*, *7*(2), 228–252.

Roopnarine, J. L., Shin, M., Jung, K., & Hossain, Z. (2003). Play and early development and education: The instantiation of parental belief systems. In *Contemporary perspectives in early childhood education* (pp. 115–132). Greenwich, CT: Information Age Publishing, Inc.

Rosen, C. E. (1974). The effects of sociodramatic play on problem-solving behavior among culturally disadvantaged preschool children. *Child Development*, *45*(4), 92CL927.

Ryan, S. D., Gomory, T., & Lacasse, J. R. (2002). Who are we? Examining the results of the Association for Play Therapy membership survey. *International Journal of Play Therapy*, *11*(2), 11–41. doi:10.1037/h0088863

Schottelkorb, A. A., Swan, K. L., & Ogawa, Y. (2015). Parent consultation in child-centered play therapy: A model for research and practice. *International Journal of Play Therapy*, *24*(4), 221–233. doi:10.1037/a0039609

Shale, N. C. (2004). Perceptions of Black parents regarding play therapy (Unpublished master's thesis). Pretoria, South Africa: University of Pretoria. Retrieved from http://upetd.up.ac.za/thesis/available/etd-02102005-135343/unrestricted/00dissertation.pdf

Singer, J. (1973). Observing imaginative play: Approaches to recording, rating, and categorizing. In J. Singer (Ed.), *The child's world of make-believe: Experimental studies of imaginative play*. New York: Academic Press.

Slater, S. J., Nicholson, L., Chriqui, J., Turner, L., & Chaloupka, F. (2012). The impact of state laws and district policies on physical education and recess practices in a nationally representative sample of US public elementary schools. *Archives of Pediatrics & Adolescent Medicine*, *166*(4), 311–316. doi:10.1001/archpediatrics.2011.1133 PMID:22147763

Smilansky, S. (1968). *The effects of sociodramatic play on disadvantaged preschool children*. New York: Wiley.

Steen, R. L. (2010). *Parent consultation: Beyond engagement*. Association for Play Therapy October Mining Report. Retrieved from www.a4pt.org

Tarver-Behring, S., & Ingraham, C. L. (1998). Culture as a central component of consultation: A call to the field. *Journal of Educational & Psychological Consultation*, *9*(1), 57–72. doi:10.1207/s1532768xjepc0901_3

Timberlake, E. M., & Cutler, M. M. (2001). *Developmental play therapy in clinical social work*. Needham Heights, MA: Allyn and Bacon.

U.S. Census Bureau. (2003). *Young, diverse, urban*. Retrieved from http://www.census.gov/Press-Release/www/ releases/archives/hispanic_origin_population/001130.html

U.S. Census Bureau. (2010). *2010 Census Summary File*. Author.

U.S. Census Bureau. (2015). *New Census Bureau report analyzes U.S. population projections* (Release No. CB15-TPS.16). Retrieved from https://www.census.gov/newsroom/press-releases/2015/cb15-tps16.html

VanFleet, R., Sywulak, A. E., & Sniscak, C. C. (2010). *Child-centered play therapy*. New York, NY: Guilford.

Vernon, A., & Clemente, R. (2005). *Assessment and intervention with children and adolescents: Developmental and multicultural approaches* (2nd ed.). Alexandria, VA: American Counseling Association.

Wachtel, E. F. (1994). *Treating troubled children and their families*. New York, NY: Guilford.

White, B. (1978). *Experience and environment: Major influences on the development of young children* (Vol. 2). Englewood Cliffs, NJ: Prentice-Hall.

KEY TERMS AND DEFINITIONS

Caregiver: Primary adult responsible for caretaking for the child or adolescent client. This term may refer to a biological, adoptive, or foster parent; a legal guardian; a grandparent or other family member; or any other person with whom the counselor, therapist, or clinician regularly consults regarding the child client's treatment.

Cultural Competence: Counselors who engage the lifelong process of developing cultural and diversity competence through trainings, readings, and advocating for social justice.

Multicultural: Relating to any of the various components of an individual's or group's cultural identity. Including but not limited to race/ethnicity, gender, sexual/affectional orientation, age, religious affiliation, socioeconomic status, and disability status.

Play Therapist: Person who is training in play therapy and practices working with children and their families. This person understands that children communicate through play and use toys to express themselves.

Play Therapy Caregiver Consultant (PTCC): The competent play therapist must include the caregiver in the play therapy process via consistent consultations. These consultations allow an alliance to form, offer support and parenting assistance to the parent, and ultimately help adjust the system, as needed to a more functional form.

Chapter 15
Consultation Strategies for Working with Professionals Supporting Foster Families

Kim Coggins
Austin Peay State University, USA

Kristie Opiola
UNC Charlotte, USA

Kara L. Carnes-Holt
University of Wyoming, USA

ABSTRACT

Children and families involved in the foster care system present with unique needs requiring support from diverse professionals. Because of the range of stakeholders involved with children and families in the foster care system, play therapists must become knowledgeable and skillful consultants and collaborators to best facilitate holistic wellness for these families. Through this chapter, the authors seek to provide play therapists with a strong foundation of knowledge and skills to draw upon when working with this population. First, readers are introduced to the mental health needs faced by foster care children and families. The authors then describe the diverse roles frequently fulfilled by play therapists as consultants and collaborators within various systems impacting children in foster care. Finally, a case study is included to provide a practical description of how play therapists can integrate a greater use of consultation, collaboration, and advocacy into their work to bet meet the needs of foster care children and families within their care.

DOI: 10.4018/978-1-5225-2224-9.ch015

INTRODUCTION

Through their work, play therapists have the opportunity to work with many distinctive populations. One such population includes children and families involved with the foster care system. These children and families face unique challenges and diverse needs, requiring support from various professionals. Because of the range of stakeholders involved with children and families in the foster care system, play therapists must become knowledgeable and skillful consultants and collaborators to best facilitate holistic wellness for these families.

In this chapter, the authors first examine the current status of children in the foster care system and explore some of the unique mental health needs faced by these children. This information helps cultivate an understanding of the need for specialized consultation and training for play therapists and other important stakeholders. Important terms related to the foster care, the legal systems, and consultation interventions are included and defined to provide foundational knowledge necessary for understanding and working within this system. Next, the authors describe numerous roles that play therapists enact with essential stakeholders in foster children's lives. These stakeholders include parents and caregivers, caseworkers, legal professionals, and other professionals providing care for foster children and families. These roles are further explained through a clinical case example to provide an opportunity for readers to explore how a play therapist can integrate a greater use of consultation, collaboration, and advocacy to best meet the needs of children and families in their care.

CURRENT STATUS OF CHILDREN AND THE FOSTER CARE SYSTEM

Rates of children in the welfare system vary per year. In 2015, the United States foster care system served over 670,000 children including those who remained in foster care from previous years and those who entered during the course of the year (U.S Department of Health and Human Services, Administration for Children and Families, Administration on Children, Youth and Families, Children's Bureau, 2016a, p. 2). Children enter the foster care system for various reasons including abuse or neglect, severe behavioral problems, and parental illness, substance abuse, or death (American Academy of Pediatrics [AAP], 2016). These children frequently experience trauma and early attachment disruptions prior to entering the foster care system and experience further trauma within the system through disrupted placements, inconsistent care, and extended time spent in foster care (Klain & White, 2013). Fortunately, the child welfare system has made progress in reducing the length of time children spend in foster care by improving the timeliness of adoptions and permanent placements. Currently less than 26% of children remain in the foster care system for more than 2 years (U.S Department of Health and Human Services, Administration for Children and Families, Administration on Children, Youth and Families, Children's Bureau, 2016b, p. 2). Reasons for discharge from the foster care system include reunification with primary caregivers, kinship placements, adoption, emancipation, legal guardianship, death of the child, running away or transfer to another agency (U.S Department of Health and Human Services, Administration for Children and Families, Administration on Children, Youth and Families, Children's Bureau, 2016b, p. 3).

Mental Health Needs

Play therapists working with children in the foster care system must be aware of the unique mental health needs of this population in order to effectively provide therapeutic services through consultation for these children and their support systems. Children in foster care are at substantial risk for developing developmental, behavioral, and emotional problems due to chaotic and unpredictable early lives (Litrownik, 2012; Pecora, Jensen, Romanelli, Jackson, & Ortiz, 2009). Before the age of 18, many foster children have experienced frequent changes in caregivers, homes, and schools. In addition, their home placements are inconsistent as other foster children move in and out of the home and children may have exposure to further violence or disruptive behaviors from other children in foster care. This instability in their environments puts them at an increased risk for mental health disorders (Litrownik, 2012; Pecora et al., 2009).

Youth in foster care and foster care alumni have disproportionately high prevalence of emotional and behavioral disorders. Up to 80% of youth in foster care display behavioral or mental health problems and foster care children are commonly diagnosed with mental health disorders at rates higher than the general population of youth and young adults (Pecora et al., 2009). In addition, youth in the foster care system are at greater risk for co-occurring diagnoses (Pecora et al., 2009), and are twice as likely to have chronic medical problems. The impact of poor mental health is not isolated to their stay in foster care. Young adult foster care alumni frequently have poor mental health outcomes with a higher prevalence of anxiety, social problems, drug abuse, and panic disorder which may contribute to lifelong difficulties, such as unemployment and poor educational outcomes (Pecora et al., 2005). According to the Northwest Alumni Study in 2005, approximately 20% of foster alumni demonstrated higher rates of three or more psychiatric disorders.

Overall, welfare providers determined mental health services are key to helping youth recover from their early life experiences. However, only approximately one-quarter of youth in foster care receive regular mental health services despite the high rates of emotional and behavioral concerns in this population (Burns et al., 2004). Children and youth in foster care have an increased risk for experiencing trauma and disruptions in attachment development, increasing the prevalence for unique mental health concerns with this population. Unfortunately, problematic behaviors are often addressed first without exploring the experiences that influence those behaviors. Play therapists need a specialized understanding of the unique needs of foster care children related to trauma and attachment concerns in order to provide holistic care for the children and wrap around support for caregivers and interdisciplinary professionals working to meet the needs of foster care children (Brodinsky, 2013; Perry & Salavitz, 2006; Purvis Cross, & Sunshine, 2007; Siegel & Hartzell, 2003).

Trauma Concerns

Children in the foster care system experience a higher prevalence of complex trauma, mental health issues, and severe posttraumatic stress symptomology (Greeson et al., 2011). In fact, the varying levels of trauma and poly-victimization (multiple type of violence, abuse and crime) that foster children encounter both before entering the system and within the foster care system can increase their risk of mental health disorders by up to tenfold (Klain & White, 2013). In addition to the effects of any traumatic events leading to children's removal from their primary caregiver, by entering the foster care system, these children experience the additional traumas of separation from family, community, and friends and facing an uncertain future (Klain & White, 2013).

Children's reaction to trauma is dependent on their age and resiliency. Research shows the earlier a child experiences trauma the more debilitating the impact on children's health and development (Perry & Szalavitz, 2006; National Child Traumatic Stress Network [NCTSN]; van der Kolk, 2005). Young children who do not have a positive, caring caregiver, such as foster children, are at a greater risk for negative effects from trauma due to their underdeveloped sense of self, limited life experiences and understanding of others, and underdeveloped coping behaviors (Klain & White, 2013). Their lack of psychological resources places young foster children at greater risk for long-term harm (NCTSN). Responsive mental health care is imperative to help foster children recover from early trauma. Placement into a home with a safe and responsive caregiver is important to help foster children recover from their early life experiences. Without a combination of mental health, responsive caregiving and psychosocial interventions, foster children endure complex trauma that can leave a lasting impact on their holistic development and growth (Klain & White, 2013).

Attachment Development

Another important determinant of children's emotional well-being and social development is a secure attachment between children and their primary caregivers. Humans are organized to attach to their caregivers in order to connect with others and seek safety and protection (Bowlby, 1988; Siegel, 2001). The role of primary caregivers is essential in building the child's attachment schema. Infants' attachment styles are created through their interactions with their primary caregivers, range along a continuum from secure to insecure, and impact all domains of their development (Siegel, 2001). Relationships that promote secure attachments are characterized by consistent and predictable communication patterns and interactions between caregiver and child, interaction patterns that display emotional availability, and caregivers who are perceptive and responsive to their child's needs (Siegel, 2012; Siegel & Hartzell, 2003). Children who develop secure attachments with their primary caregiver have a foundation of safety and security from which the child can explore their world and other relationships and interpret their own needs and the behaviors and feelings of others (Beijersbergen, Jeffer, Bakermans-Kranenburg, & van Ijzendoorn, 2012; Siegel, 2012). Furthermore, secure attachments enable children to seek closeness to their caregivers, pursue comfort from caregivers in time of distress, and internalize the caregiver-child relationship as an internal working model of a secure base (Bowlby, 1988).

Unfortunately, many foster children did not experience an attuned and supportive primary caregiver and therefore were removed from their parents and placed in temporary households to provide safer environments. Instead of connection, safety, and protection, foster children's early experiences included neglect, frequent changes in caregivers, periods of isolation, and abuse causing children to feel confused and in doubt of the parent-child relationship and placing them at risk for developing an insecure style of attachment (Brodzinsky, 2013; Hughes, 2006; Siegel, 2012). Children who form insecure attachments often create defensive strategies to maintain personal safety and control and protect themselves from their desire to attach and connect with others around them (Perry, 1994; Siegel & Hartzell, 2003); however, these defensive strategies can manifest as problematic behaviors in foster homes and other settings.

Children with insecure attachments tend to view others and the world around them as harsh, unreliable, and filled with uncertainty (Siegel & Hartzell, 2003). This negative perception of the world can lead these children to avoid closeness to their new caregivers, have feelings of anxiety and uncertainty when they need to depend on their caregivers, and be unsure of what to expect from their caregivers (Bowlby, 1980; Perry, 1994). Due to past experiences with trauma and attachment disruptions, foster children can be reactive which makes forming relationships challenging for foster parents because the child is easily triggered (Perry & Szalavitz, 2006; Purvis et al., 2007; van der Kolk, 2005). Children who form insecure attachments perceive that, in order to be safe, they must control their own environment and this control may manifest itself through behaviors such as extreme tantrums, aggression, indiscriminate affection, and isolation from others (Hughes, 1999). A child who lacked attentive and protective parenting is continually searching for a way to achieve a felt sense of safety, commonly manifesting as hypervigilance (Perry, 1994). Increased fear, sensory processing issues, difficulty self-regulating, disorder of memory, and short-term memory loss are some of the consequences present in the lives of children who have experienced attachment breaks and trauma (Forbes & Post, 2006; Purvis et al., 2007; Siegel & Hartzell, 2003).

Although children's attachment styles are created at the beginning of life, they can be altered or changed when new, compassionate, and consistent people are in their life (Siegel & Hartzell, 2003; Zilberstein, 2013). Mental health interventions that focus on caregiver-child relationships and provide core conditions that build predictable, safe and secure relationships for foster children and are essential for foster children to recover from their early life traumas. Perry and Szalavitz (2006) suggest loving and responsive foster parents can have a major influence on preventing long-term negative outcomes for young foster children. Therefore, understanding the needs of children who experience early trauma and attachment disruptions can help foster parents care for their children and provide needed support to assist children toward healing. Furthermore, play therapists working with families involved in the foster care system need to establish a comprehensive understanding of the interrelationship between trauma and attachment in order to provide holistic care for the family and to appropriately coordinate care with other stakeholders in the child's extended system.

Foster Parent Training and Support

Foster parent support and training requirements are set by individual state licensing division of family and protective services. Each state has unique criteria and specific requirements are found on individual state family services websites. The authors explored four department of family services state-specific websites (Texas, New York, Ohio, and Washington) and found some similarities in training guidelines (New York State Office of Children and Family Services, n.d; Ohio Department of Job and Family Services, 2014; Texas Adoption Resource Exchange, n.d.; Washington State Department of Social and Health Services, n.d.). Common training topics included understanding the child welfare system, common experiences of children in care, child development, strategies and techniques for working with foster youth, trauma informed care, constructive guidance and discipline, Cardiopulmonary Resuscitation (CPR), First Aid, dispensing medication, and emergency behavior interventions. Foster parents are required to receive annual continuing education and ongoing training. States vary widely on their continuing training requirements and base decisions regarding requirements on children's level of care. In addition to training, foster parents are provided with a range of support services including formal and informal visits with caseworkers, psychological services (counseling, therapy, psychiatry), support groups, and online trainings and resources. All support services vary by state and proximity to foster family; therefore, there can be inconsistency in services and current services are not sufficient to meet the complex needs of families involved in the foster care system.

Foster parents benefit from an array of services since many foster children enter foster homes without the foundational skills to engage in healthy communication, cooperation, respect, and problem solving (AAP, 2016). Foster parents have frequently reported that they feel uninformed and unprepared for the level of care and problematic behaviors their foster child displays. Many foster children experience behavioral and emotional dysregulation and caregiver-child interactions can be challenging causing foster parents to encounter significant family stress and feel discouraged, withdrawn, and unresponsive to the child's needs (Carnes-Holt & Bratton, 2014; Purvis et al., 2007). Youth in foster care need positive relationships with foster parents and foster parents need help navigating the tricky role of repairing foster children's early and continual trauma. Mental health services that include parental involvement are necessary to empower caregivers and provides caregivers with the tools to manage children's challenging behaviors and emotional needs and can help parents become change agents in the lives of foster youth and positively impact the long-term sustainability of caregiver-child relationships (Horwitz, Chamberlain, Landsverk, & Mullican, 2010; Price, Chamberlain, Landsverk, Reid, Leve, & Laurent, 2008).

Multicultural Dimensions

Children in foster care represent a wide range of diverse ethnic and cultural backgrounds. According to the Child Welfare Information Gateway (2016), in 2014 the majority of children in foster care were White (42%) followed by Black (24%), Latino (22%), and multiracial and Native American (10%). Since 2005, the numbers of Black children in foster care have decreased, while the numbers of White, Latino, multiracial and Native American children have increased. Children in foster care system have distinctive histories and upbringings that are likely to differ than their foster family. These differences can provide unique challenges in the ways foster families and other helping professionals connect and understand foster children's behaviors and needs (AAP, 2016).

Play therapists are often charged with a unique and important task of helping children in foster care cope and recover from placement in foster system and less than ideal early life experiences. Mental health providers, such as play therapists and counselors, must be responsive to the cultural influences in the child's life and make an effort to gain awareness of the importance of each child's culture within self and the environment in order to understand their unique worldview (Post & Tillman, 2015). Culturally responsive therapists assess for cultural influences and consistently reexamine "how such [cultural] factors may influence the therapeutic relationship, engagement in treatment, and treatment outcomes" (Post & Tillman, 2015, p. 496). The ability of play therapists to assess for foster children's cultural factors may be a challenge because of the limited information foster parents received about their foster child (AAP, 2016). Culture and ethnicity can still be explored through several different avenues including consultations. For older children, therapists may find it helpful to discuss what is important to the child and how things are different, ways to integrate important cultural influences in their new environments and relationships, and how to have cultural discussions with their foster families. Through intentional consultations with foster parents, biological parents, and caseworkers, play therapists can gather additional information about pertinent cultural factors and ethnic histories. This knowledge can help play therapists discover overt and covert factors that may influence the child's interactions with caregivers and other systems and develop culturally responsive approaches to therapy and consultation.

NAVIGATING THE FOSTER CARE SYSTEM

Play therapists are uniquely situated to positively impact many facets of the foster care system. However, in order to be effective advocates and collaborators, play therapists must strive to understand the complexities inherent in this system and the impacts of this system on families involved in the foster care system (McWey, Henderson & Tice, 2006). In this section, the authors first examine some standard terms that play therapists will encounter when navigating the foster care system. Next, the authors address the numerous roles play therapists can fulfill through consultations with various stakeholders in the foster care system including parents and caregivers, caseworkers, legal professionals, and other professionals. Finally, the various ethical and legal complications inherent in working and consulting within the foster care system are explored. Best practices for providing comprehensive care for children in foster care can only be achieved through dedicated interprofessional collaboration and this section provides foundational information necessary for forging these vital professional relationships (Britner & Mossler, 2002; McWey et al., 2006; World Health Organization [WHO], 2010).

Standard Definitions of Terms to Understand

A multitude of terminology is connected to navigating multiple systems of working with children in the foster care system. Often it is assumed that caregivers and professionals understand the numerous roles and terms. However, many of these terms vary from state to state such as Department of Family Services (DFS) versus Child Protective Services (CPS). For continuity within this chapter, authors use the term "Department of Human Services" or DHS to refer to the department housing the foster care system. Below are a few key terms and operational definitions that are important to know when working with systems of care for children and families in foster care:

- **Petition for Emergency Custody:** The report that is filed with the court after a child is removed from the home due to concerns of abuse.
- **Department of Human Services Attorney:** The attorney that is responsible for presenting evidence of harm to a child that resulted in entering the foster care system.
- **Guardian/Custodian's Attorney:** The attorney who represents the "accused" caregivers and their interests and rights concerning the child that has been placed in care.
- **Attorney Ad Litem:** The child's attorney that is appointed by the court. They will be present at all court hearing and may speak to the child directly about their thoughts, feelings, and experience. The attorney is to represent the child's best interest. They must tell the court what the child's desires are even if the attorney ad litem does not agree that these are in the best interest of the child.
- **Caseworker:** This professional is appointed to work with children and families and make sure that appropriate services are provided to keep children safe. The caseworker should help biological parents understand the legal process and outline a case plan of what they must achieve to regain custody of the child in foster care. A copy of the case plan must be given to the biological parents.
- **Court Appointed Special Advocate (CASA):** A trained volunteer that is appointed by the judge to develop a relationship with the child and related caregivers and share information on what they believe is best for the child.

- **Emergency Hearings:** This hearing is for the judge to determine if there is a reason to continue to have the child in foster care or other placement or if child should be returned home. This decision is based in the child's safety and best interest. If child does not return home, then the judge makes a ruling about visitation rights and additional services provided to the family.
- **Adjudication Hearing/Trial:** The purpose of this trial is for the judge to determine if the child has been abused or neglected. This can involve numerous witnesses and any other information deemed relevant to the case. The judge dismisses the case if abuse/neglect is not founded. If the case is substantiated, then the judge outlines what needs to happen for the child to be returned back to caregivers. This decision is referred to at the disposition.
- **Disposition Hearing:** This hearing is held after the adjudication hearing or soon after. The judge approves a case plan for the child and family and requires the involvement of the Department of Human Services (DHS). The judge can hold caregivers in contempt of course for not complying with the case plan.
- **Review Hearing:** The purpose of the review hearing is for the judge to make sure that all parties are complying with the court orders and case plan, and determine the current status and well-being of the child.
- **Permanency Planning Hearing:** The judge listens to all relevant information about what has happened since the first court appearance. The DHS caseworker shares what they believe to be in the best interest of the child, and other professionals involved in case may also speak during this hearing. The judge then decides on which permanent placement is best for the child such as:
    - Return child to parent custody.
    - Continue the goal of child-family reunification if the judge determines that positive progress is being made.
    - Approve a plan for termination of parental rights and move towards placing the child for adoption.
    - Approve plan for child to be in the permanent custody of another party.
    - Extend foster care placement and focus on independent living skills for child as they age out of the system.
- **Termination of Parental Rights:** The purpose of this hearing is for the judge to decide whether to sever the legal relationship be parent and child. The DHS attorney or the attorney ad litem file this petition. The termination of parental rights involves the Judge determining that the parent is unfit and termination of parental rights is in the best interest of the child. If termination of parental rights is awarded this means that the DHS is now in full legal control of child and parent has lost all rights including visitation, communication, and access to any information. This termination also means that everyone in the child's biological family is no longer legally related to this child. After termination of parental rights is granted the child is typically available for adoption.
- **Filial Therapy:** Filial therapy, pioneered by Bernard and Louise Guerney, is a relationship-focused mental health intervention used to help meet the needs of both parents and children by empowering parents to serve as the therapeutic agent of change (Guerney, 1964; Landreth 2012; Landreth & Bratton 2006). Parents learn principles and methodology of child-centered play therapy in a small group format utilizing didactic instruction, supervision of video recorded play sessions, and role playing (Guerney, 1964; Landreth 2012).

- **Child Parent Relationship Therapy (CPRT):** CPRT is a manualized filial therapy model grounded in the attitudes and principles of child-centered play therapy. In CPRT, parents receive training and supervision in basic child-centered play therapy skills and principles including tracking behaviors, reflecting content and feeling, facilitating decision-making, providing encouragement, and setting limits. By using these skills, parents learn to be with their children in non-judgmental and accepting ways that support development of a healthy parent-child relationship. This positive relationship provides the foundation for personal growth and change in the child and the parent (Landreth & Bratton, 2006). A protocol for CPRT can be found in the treatment manual *Child-parent relationship therapy (CPRT) treatment manual: A 10-session filial therapy model for training parents* (Bratton, Landreth, Kellam, & Blackard, 2006).

The Role of the Play Therapist

Play therapy is "the systematic use of a theoretical model to establish and interpersonal process where in trained play therapists use the therapeutic powers of play to help clients prevent or resolve psychosocial difficulties and achieve optimal growth and development" (Schafer & Peabody, 2016, p. 23). Play therapy techniques provide a developmentally responsive means of engaging with children using their primary language of play (Landreth, 2012). A play therapist is a licensed mental health professional who has earned an additional play therapy credential through a national play therapy association (Association for Play Therapy [APT], 2016a; Schafer & Peabody, 2016). Members of many different mental health professions can be licensed as a play therapist including counselors, marriage and family therapists, psychologists, and social workers (APT, 2016a). In child counseling, not all mental health professionals seek or obtain the additional certification as a play therapist; nonetheless, for simplicity and continuity, the term "play therapist" is used throughout this chapter to refer to any mental health professional providing services for children and families within the foster care system.

Play therapists' roles as consultants within in the foster care system typically fall under one of these categories: teaching and training, providing direct evaluation and treatment, advocating, and collaborating with others to support children's mental and overall health and well-being (Milam-Miller, 2009). Throughout the entire process, play therapists recognize and respond to the importance of increased communication, training, and collaboration across all stakeholders in the foster care system (Britner & Mossler, 2002; McWey et al., 2006). These stakeholders include individuals from varied professions and backgrounds with different bodies of knowledge. When serving as consultants within the foster care system, play therapists strive to engage in collaborative practice in which individuals from "two or more professions learn about, from, and with each other" to improve collaboration and quality of care (WHO, 2010, p. 7).

This section specifically explores play therapists' roles with regards to parents, guardians, and caregivers; caseworkers and professionals in the foster care system; legal professionals including judges, attorneys ad litem, and court appointed special advocates (CASAs); and other professionals including teachers, occupational therapists, physical therapists, speech therapists, medical professionals, and others. By joining together with other individuals committed to the well-being of children and adolescents in the foster care system, play therapists can extend their impact far beyond that afforded through traditional client care (Ko et al., 2008; Milam-Miller, 2009).

Role with Parents, Guardians, and Caregivers

Families involved in the foster care system have wide-ranging needs that are unique to this population. Children in the foster care system often face multiple temporary placements and long waits for permanent placements increasing their risk of experiencing interpersonal trauma, insecure attachment, and other mental health struggles (Congressional Coalition on Adoption Institute [CCAI], 2014; Lanius, Vermetten, & Pain, 2010; Nelson, Bos, Gunner & Sonuga-Burke, 2011; Litrownik, 2012). Individuals providing foster care frequently struggle to form relationships with these children and may feel ill-equipped to manage their children's significant behavior problems and high levels of relational stress (Brodzinsky, 2013; Carnes-Holt & Bratton, 2014; Hughes, 2006; Purvis et al., 2007). In 2015, caseworkers listed reunification of the family as the primary goal for over half of the children in foster care, emphasizing that, despite having children placed in out-of-home care, the biological parents continue to play a central role in their children's past and future (Molin & Palmer, 2005; U.S. Health & Human Services Administration for Children & Families, 2016a). In these cases, repairing the parent-child relationship becomes a critical piece of therapy (Molin & Palmer, 2005). Furthermore, parents and foster parents are regularly struggling to navigate both the foster care and legal systems while simultaneously working to support their children's growth, development, and wellness.

Unfortunately, foster parents and biological parents are often overlooked or excluded from their children's treatment, minimizing the extent of their role with the children, failing to provide essential information for supporting their children's health and wellness, and invalidating the struggles that these caregivers face when caring for their children (Molin & Palmer, 2005). By consulting directly with these parents, guardians, and caregivers, play therapists can provide crucial information and support while empowering the families to effectively serve as agents of change in their children's lives (Bratton et al., 2006; Ornelas, Silverstein, & Tan, 2007).

Play therapists consulting with families involved in the foster care system should be knowledgeable about child development, attachment and the effects of trauma, as well as the processes involved in both the legal and foster care systems. Providing psychoeducational support for families regarding the practical steps and the mental health struggles present in foster care cases helps to shift the focus from the professional to the family as the agent of change (Ornelas et al., 2007). Many times, by helping caregivers to understand the social-emotional and behavioral needs of children who experience early trauma, play therapists can help equip them to provide a relationship that promotes secure attachment and healing (Carnes-Holt & Bratton, 2014; Perry & Szalzvitz, 2006; Purvis et al., 2007).

Furthermore, interventions that involve caregivers in the therapeutic process are key for addressing the unique needs of children in the foster care system (Carnes-Holt & Bratton, 2014; James, 1994; Perry & Szalavitz, 2006; Purvis et al., 2007). By using relationship enhancing interventions that include caregiver participation, play therapists can help children repair insecure attachments and more toward more healthy ways of functioning (Purvis, Cross, & Pennings, 2009; Siegel & Hartzell, 2003; Zilberstein, 2013). Healthy attachment enhances the foster child's ability to feel safe and secure, self-regulate, explore their environment, and take risks (Bowlby, 1980). Caregivers that promote secure parent-child relationships help foster children exhibit curiosity in their world, display flexibility, and have the ability to organize their thoughts, emotions, and behaviors (Siegel & Hartzell, 2003). Together, the child and caregiver form strategies to maintain closeness and assess the child's physical and emotional safety. If a break in the parent-child relationship occurs, the caregiver seeks to repair the break by recognizing the child's emotional state, helping the child understand what happened, and soothing the child back to an emotionally balanced and secure state.

Child-Parent Relationship Therapy

Child-Parent Relationship Therapy (CPRT) is one such intervention that specifically addresses the underlying mental health concerns surrounding early trauma and disrupted attachments while empowering caregivers to serve as the agents of change for children in their care (Bratton et al., 2006; Bratton, Opiola, & Dafoe, 2015; Landreth & Bratton, 2006). CPRT is grounded in the theoretical principles of child-centered play therapy (CCPT) and person-centered philosophy and is predicated on the belief that a secure relationship between caregiver and child is necessary for children's healthy development and overall well-being (Landreth & Bratton, 2006). This intervention is traditionally delivered in a small, support group format through ten weekly two hour meetings (Landreth & Bratton, 2006); however, the information can be adapted for use in individual and dyad caregiver sessions or consultations. Using a training format consisting of didactic, supportive, and supervision experiences, caregivers are taught CCPT attitudes and skills as means to becoming a healing mediator for their foster child during supervised, weekly caregiver-child play sessions. Caregivers use play to gain understanding of child's past experiences and associated feelings (Bratton et al., 2015). Furthermore, caregiver-child playtimes provide a unique and developmentally responsive means to help foster parents attune to and understand their foster child's underlying needs, respond more empathically to their foster child's behavioral and emotional difficulties, and facilitate their foster child's ability to co-regulate.

CPRT is a filial therapy treatment model with over 50 studies investigating its process and outcomes. Thirty-five published, controlled outcome studies involving over 1000 participants have examined the effectiveness of CPRT on increasing parental empathy, decreasing stress in the parent-child relationship, and reducing children's behavior problems. Previous studies show the efficacy of CPRT across diverse populations, variety of presenting issues, varying age ranges, and its transportability across real-world settings. Comprehensive systematic reviews (Bratton et al., 2010; Lindo, Bratton, & Landreth, 2015) and meta-analyses (Bratton, Ray, Rhine, & Jones, 2005; Lin & Bratton, 2015) conducted over the past decade support and strengthen the findings from individual CPRT studies. Six studies have examined the effectiveness of CPRT specific to children who have experienced interpersonal trauma with their primary caregivers (Carnes-Holt & Bratton, 2014; Costas & Landreth, 1999; Harris & Landreth, 1997; Landreth & Lobaugh, 1998; Opiola & Bratton, in process; Smith & Landreth, 2003). Results from the six studies indicate that parents who participated in CPRT had more positive and stronger outcomes than parents who participated in waitlist control groups and treatment as usual.

Two of these six studies examined the effectiveness of CPRT specific to foster care and adopted children (Carnes-Holt & Bratton, 2014; Opiola & Bratton, in review). Carnes-Holt and Bratton's (2014) research examined the effectiveness of CPRT as an intervention to support and respond to the unique needs of foster and adoptive families and 48% of the children included in the study were adopted from foster care. When compared to the waitlist control group, parents who participated in the 10-week CPRT intervention reported statistically significant improvements in children's problem behaviors and parental empathy. Carnes-Holt and Bratton (2014) concluded that CPRT offers hope to families struggling to connect and has the potential to disrupt negative trajectories associated with early childhood behavioral struggles. Opiola and Bratton (in revew) explored the effects of CPRT for foster and adoptive families who reported concerns related to attachment, children's behaviors, and parental stress and 53% of the children included in the study were adopted from foster care. This study replicated and confirmed Carnes-

Holt and Bratton's (2014) research while adding to the methodological rigor of the study by including a treatment as usual group instead of a waitlist control group for comparison. Compared to parents in the treatment as usual group, parents who participated in CPRT reported statistically significant improvements in child behavior problems, parent-child relationship stress, and parental empathy.

Combined, the results from these two studies provide compelling support for CPRT as a responsive intervention for foster and adoptive children and families. Recently, the Donaldson Adoption Institute (DAI) evaluated empirical support for various interventions that specifically target the unique struggles of children who experience attachment disruptions. The report identified CPRT, Dyadic Developmental Psychotherapy (DDP; Hughes, 1997), and Theraplay (Booth & Jernberg, 2009) as the most promising parent-child adoption specific interventions. Furthermore, the report identified CPRT as the parent-child intervention that demonstrates the most robust empirical support for helping adopted children and their families (Brodzinsky, 2013). Due to the shortage of professionals equipped to provide interventions for families and children that are responsive to foster care and adoption issues, plays therapists fulfill a vital role with parents, guardians, and caregivers by providing them with the skills to effectively support the mental health of the children in their care (Ornelas et al., 2007). Furthermore, by utilizing empirically supported interventions involving parents and caregivers, play therapist are prepared to empower families as the therapeutic agent of change for children experiencing disrupted attachments and trauma (Bratton et al., 2006; Carnes-Holt & Bratton, 2014; Landreth & Bratton, 2006).

Role with Caseworkers and the Foster Care System

Consultation with caseworkers and other professionals within the foster care system are central to any therapeutic work with children involved with the foster care system. Because these children are placed in out-of-home care, caseworkers often exercise legal custody of children in foster care (Molin & Palmer, 2005). This means that play therapists must work together with foster care professionals to obtain informed consent and to coordinate mental health care for these children. However, caseworkers are often unsure of their role in monitoring treatment of the children under their care (Molin & Palmer, 2005). Play therapists have a responsibility to ensure that caseworkers responsible for providing informed consent consistently have the information necessary to provide consent. This means therapists must update the caseworker frequently regarding shifts in modality, potential issues involved with treatment, changes in diagnoses or providers, and other major changes in treatment (Molin & Palmer, 2005). Additionally, since it is the responsibility of the caseworker to coordinate care from diverse service providers or for multiple family members, play therapists need to be proactive in consulting with caseworkers in order to help facilitate comprehensive care for children in the foster care system (Molin & Palmer, 2005).

Caseworkers can be vital sources of information about children's histories in and before placement in the foster care system. Play therapists and caseworkers must seek to learn from each other and with each other to best serve the needs of the children in their care (Ko et al., 2008; WHO, 2010). Often, caseworkers and other professionals in the foster care system are acutely aware of the traumas that brought children into the system, but significantly less aware of the impact of children's trauma histories on their current behavioral and emotional responses (Ko et al., 2008). Play therapists can facilitate cross-disciplinary trainings that help to fill gaps in knowledge for these professionals to ensure that children receive trauma-informed care across settings and systems (Day, Somers, Darden, & Yoon., 2014; Ko et al., 2008).

Role Within the Legal System

Within the legal system, play therapists play crucial roles as consultants to legal professionals and resources for families involved with the legal and foster care system. Judges facing more cases involving children, adolescents, and their families are increasingly seeking consultations from mental health professionals specifically as it relates to child development and attachment concerns (Bartol & Bartol, 2015). Whereas judges and other legal professionals receive extensive training regarding law, they do not often have training specific to family systems, mental health, or child development. Play therapists working with families involved in the foster care system can be called upon to provide relevant information about research related to child development, attachment, effects of trauma, and other issues related to foster care and adoption. Educating judges, attorneys ad litem, CASAs, and other legal professionals regarding children's mental wellness and development serves as a vital way to advocate for the well-being and holistic care for children and adolescents in the foster care system. Furthermore, play therapists working with families involved in the foster care system can serve as an important resource for these families by becoming knowledgeable about the legal system and providing support and guidance for them as they navigate this complex system.

Role with Other Professionals

Because of the developmental risks and educational needs of children within the foster care system, these children often require support from diverse professionals to promote academic success and holistic health (Day et al., 2014; Lanius et al., 2010; Nelson et al., 2001; Newton, Litrownik, & Landsverk, 2000). Interdisciplinary teams can be comprised of diverse professionals including, but not limited to, health professionals (pediatricians, nutritionists, etc.), therapists (physical, occupational, speech, etc.), school professionals (classroom teachers, special education teachers, school counselor, etc.), and mental health professionals (psychiatrist, psychologist, play therapist, etc.). These professionals provide care and implement interventions to address developmental delays, physical and mental health, academic functioning, and the overall health of the child (Day et al., 2014). Unfortunately, without adequate communication, the interventions from this diverse group of individuals could become compartmentalized and disjointed, failing to provide continuous comprehensive care. Cross-system consultation is vital for providing holistic care for children in the foster care system, and play therapists can play an important role in advocating for and organizing the necessary communication and coordination. By maintaining consistent communication and collaboration among various treatment providers, the interdisciplinary team can more effectively address comprehensive goals across distinct settings, including home, school, and in the playroom.

Furthermore, play therapists can serve as a crucial source of information related to child development and the impact of attachment disruptions and early trauma on children's development. Diverse professionals are well informed with regards to their individual disciplines, but are often unaware of the far-reaching influences of traumatic histories on current physical, emotional, and behavioral development and responses (Ko et al., 2008). Cross disciplinary trainings are important to address knowledge gaps with professionals who provide care for children involved in the foster care system and equip them to meet the unique needs inherent with this population (Day et al., 2014). Ideally, each system that interacts with the child, from the foster care system to court and legal systems as well as the educational and family systems, can collaborate effectively to provide holistic, trauma and attachment informed care for children and families (Ko et al., 2008).

Ethical and Legal Considerations

When working and consulting within the foster care system, play therapists must be aware of unique ethical and legal considerations they will face within their role as therapist. Furthermore, play therapists acting as consultants within the legal field face the additional responsibility of maintaining the ethical and professional standards of the mental health profession within an arena with very different rules, responsibilities, and ethics (Lee & Nachlis, 2011). Because play therapists working within the foster care system frequently fulfill multiple roles within diverse systems, it is vital to be aware of the ethical issues inherent in different systems in order to expertly and effectively work in the best interests of the child being served. Two ethical issues that are especially pertinent when working with children and families involved in the foster care system are those of consent and confidentiality (Molin & Palmer, 2005).

Informed consent allows individuals to make informed choices about their mental health care and is required by most therapist accreditation entities (American Association for Marriage and Family Therapy [AAMFT], 2012, 1.2; American Counseling Association [ACA], 2014, A.2, B.5; American Psychological Association [APA], 2010, 3.10, 10.01; Association for Play Therapy [APT], 2016b, A.3; American School Counselor Association [ASCA], 2016, A.2.b,c). Children are legally incapable of giving informed consent due to their age, and in treatment with children, therapists obtain consent from the child's legal guardians. In the case of children in the foster care system, the caseworker typically acts as the child's legal guardian and provides consent for counseling services, unless another legal representative is appointed (Molin & Palmer, 2005). Play therapists have the responsibility to ensure the legal guardian receives adequate information throughout the course of treatment to maintain the standards of informed consent. This consent applies to all aspects of the therapeutic process including, but not limited to, initiation of treatment, assessments, consultations with other stakeholders, and other changes in the course of care (Molin & Palmer, 2005). The initial informed consent as well as subsequent discussions regarding continued consent must be clearly documented in the client's file (AAMFT, 2012, 1.2; ACA, 2014, A.2.a; APA, 2010, 3.10; Molin & Palmer, 2005).

Because of the numerous people involved in the children's care, issues of confidentiality often arise when working with children in the foster care system. In the therapist-client relationship, trust is vital and therapists are responsible for protecting the confidentiality of their clients by only disclosing information with appropriate consent or when ethically or legally mandated (AAMFT, 2012, 2; ACA, 2014, B.1: APA, 2010, 4; APT, 2016b, C.1; ASCA, 2016, A.2). When working with children in the foster care system, therapists must obtain consent for most disclosures from the child's legal guardian, frequently the caseworker (Molin & Palmer, 2005). This includes disclosures made to biological parents, foster parents, and other professionals with whom the therapist may wish to consult. Furthermore, therapists are expected to maintain reasonable confidentiality even when consulting with other professionals (AAMFT, 2012, 2.3, ACA, B.7.b, APA, 2010, 4.06; APT, 2016b, C.1).

Whereas issues of consent and confidentiality can be complex in cases with families involved with the foster care system, therapists have an ethical obligation to work to overcome those struggles and engage in appropriate consultation and collaboration. The Association for Play Therapy Best Practices (2016b) suggests that "whenever possible or feasible play therapists...consult other professional providers to develop clear agreements over coordination of treatment planning" (A.4). Due to the diverse professionals providing services for the child, these consultations help to prevent redundant services or missing necessary services (APT, 2016b, A.4). Furthermore, the American Psychological Association (APA, 2010) asserts that therapists are to cooperate with other professionals to provide effective and appropriate services for their clients (3.09). The American Counseling Association (ACA, 2014) provides direction concerning therapists' interactions both with parents or caregivers (B.5.b) and with interdisciplinary teams (D.1.c). In all of these organizations, therapists are ethically obligated to seek to build appropriate collaborative relationships with family members and other interdisciplinary professionals in order to draw on diverse perspectives and expertise to best support the overall well-being of the child.

CLINICAL CASE EXAMPLE

This clinical case example provides an opportunity for the reader to explore possible ways a play therapist can incorporate intentional consultation into work with a child and family involved with the foster care system. Identifying information has been significantly altered to maintain parent/child confidentiality.

Sam is an approximately six-year-old male of African American descent who resides with his foster parents, both of whom are of Anglo descent. Sam lived with his biological mother who was diagnosed with bipolar disorder and often neglected Sam when she was in her depressed or manic phases. This behavior led to Sam's removal from his biological mother's care at age 2. According to his case worker, his mother was unpredictable and neglectful of Sam's physical, mental, and emotional needs. In addition, Sam's biological mother does not stay on her medication and Department of Human Service is working on terminating her rights. Sam is the only child in his foster parents', Laura and Steve, home. Laura and Steve hope to adopt Sam when his biological parent's rights are terminated.

During an initial consultation with Sam's foster parents, they reported concerns about his mood swings, violent outbursts, intense anger, and heightened sensitivity after supervised visits with his mother. Laura also reported Sam refuses to let her leave home without him. Laura and Steve shared that Sam frequently has lengthy "melt downs" and is difficult to console. Furthermore, they expressed that these outbursts are often unpredictable. Laura stated "at times I feel like he is intentionally disobeying me." She reported that when he is in a "rage" that she physically restrains him until he calms down, adding that Sam generally wanted her to continue to hold him and "cuddle" after an episode. Laura and Steve informed the counselor that Sam is currently on ADHD and anxiety medication.

Laura reported that Sam wants to discuss his biological mother and struggles to feel safe in their family. Laura and Steve worked to incorporate many of Sam's cultural components in their home, however they expressed that Sam misses his family and he feels like an "outsider." Socially, Sam was described by parents and teacher as "acting younger than his age" and often is hyperactive or unresponsive during teaching times. However, Sam's teacher expressed that he was only slightly behind from an educational perspective. During this initial consultation, the therapist believed that she had forged a strong connection with Sam's parents and that they would be active partners in the therapeutic process. Laura and Steve agreed Sam would benefit from play therapy and potentially family therapy.

Role with Parents, Guardians, and Caregivers

Laura and Steve seem to recognize that Sam's behavior stems from his early experiences and genuinely want to understand how to help him, but both parents struggle to understand Sam's emotional state and how his early experiences may impact his current reactions/ behaviors. Because of these concerns, the therapist plans to have frequent parent consultations with Laura and Steve to provide support and education regarding the unique needs foster and adopted children often present. The therapist also plans to incorporate CPRT weekly session topics into consultation sessions to help Laura and Steve be responsive to Sam and respond to his behaviors and emotional needs in an attuned and empathic manner so Sam will feel safe, understood and accepted.

- What other topics may be important to discuss in consultations with Laura and Steve?
- What multicultural dimensions are present in this family and how could a play therapist work with Laura and Steve to help address these concerns?

Role with Caseworkers and the Foster Care System

Prior to initiation of treatment and throughout the process, the therapist contacts Sam's caseworker to obtain appropriate consent for therapy and disclosures related to consultations. The therapist also seeks to establish a consistent means for maintaining contact with the caseworker to allow for updates concerning Sam's well-being and maintaining current consent.

- What information could be important for a play therapist to learn from Sam's caseworker during consultations?
- What information could be important for a play therapist to discuss with Sam's caseworker during consultations?

Role within the Legal System

At this time, the therapist chooses not to engage in consultations with legal professionals serving Sam; however, the therapist actively provides written materials as well as training sessions for DHS employees, caseworkers, and legal professionals concerning the impact of trauma and attachment disruptions on children's mental and physical health.

- What type of information may be important to include in written or in-person training sessions for these professionals?
- What information regarding the legal system could Sam's play therapist be aware to help support Laura, Steve, and Sam through the legal processes or parental rights termination and adoption?

Role with Other Professionals

Since Sam appears to be experiencing some socioemotional and behavioral struggles in the classroom, the therapist also discusses the importance of helping his teacher understand his early life experiences and providing specific interventions that can help him be successful in a school environment. Engaging in continued consultation with his teacher and other school personnel can provide the therapist with the opportunity to gain information about progress or ongoing struggles Sam experiences at school and to provide support to school professionals providing care and instruction to Sam.

- How can Sam's play therapist invite the teacher to be an active participant in Sam's care?
- What other professionals are involved in Sam's care with whom the play therapist may wish to consult?

CONCLUSION

Children in the foster care system display unique and diverse needs and are frequently at risk for experiencing negative outcomes related to developmental, behavioral, and emotional problems (Pecora et al., 2009). However, by engaging the various caregivers and professionals involved in the care of foster children using active consultation and learning, play therapists are able to invite these stakeholders to collaboratively support the child and family in ways that responsive to the specific needs faced by children in foster care. Through strong collaborative relationships with family members and other interdisciplinary professionals, play therapists are able to benefit from diverse wisdom and expertise in order to determine how each invested individual can best support the overall well-being and development of the child (Ko et al., 2008; Milam-Miller, 2009). Intentional consultation among stakeholders provides the foundation for comprehensive care for foster children and offers hope for reducing risk, healing relational trauma, and positively impacting children's long term development and wellness.

REFERENCES

American Academy of Pediatrics (AAP). (n.d.). *Healthy foster care America: Mental and behavioral health.* Retrieved from https://www.aap.org

American Association for Marriage and Family Therapy (AAMFT). (2012). *AAMFT code of ethics.* Alexandria, VA: Author.

American Counseling Association (ACA). (2014). *ACA code of ethics.* Alexandria, VA: Author.

American Psychological Association (APA). (2010). *Ethical principles of psychologists and code of conduct.* Washington, DC: Author.

American School Counselor Association (ASCA). (2016). *ASCA ethical standards for school counselors.* Alexandria, VA: Author.

Association for Play Therapy (APT). (2016a). *Credentialing guide: Registered play therapist (RPT) and supervisor (RPT-S).* Clovis, CA: Author.

Association for Play Therapy (APT). (2016b). *Play therapy best practices: Clinical, professional, & ethical issues.* Clovis, CA: Author.

Bartol, C. R., & Bartol, A. M. (2015). *Psychology and law: Research and practice.* Los Angeles, CA: Sage Publications, Inc.

Beijersbergen, M. D., Jeffer, F., Bakermans-Kranenburg, M. J., & van IJzendoorn, M. H. (2012). Remaining or becoming secure: Parental sensitive support predicts attachment continuity from infancy to adolescence in a longitudinal adoption study. *Developmental Psychology, 48*(5), 1277–1282. doi:10.1037/a0027442 PMID:22369333

Booth, P. B., & Jernberg, A. M. (2009). *Theraplay: Helping parents and children build better relationships through attachment-based play* (3rd ed.). San Francisco, CA: Josey-Bass.

Bowlby, J. (1980). *Attachment and loss*. New York, NY: Basic Books.

Bowlby, J. (1988). *A secure base: Parent-child attachment and healthy human development*. New York: Basic Books.

Bratton, S. C., Landreth, G., Kellum, T., & Blackard, S. (2006). *Child parent relationship therapy (CPRT) treatment manual: A ten session filial therapy model for training parents*. New York: Routledge.

Bratton, S. C., Opiola, K., & Dafoe, E. (2015). Child-parent relationship therapy: A 10 session filial therapy model. In D. A. Crenshaw & A. L. Stewart (Eds.), *Play therapy: A comprehensive guide to theory and practice* (pp. 129–140). New York, NY: Guilford Press.

Bratton, S. C., Ray, D. C., Rhine, T., & Jones, L. D. (2005). The efficacy of play therapy with children: A meta-analytic review of treatment outcomes. *Professional Psychology, Research and Practice*, *36*(4), 376–390. doi:10.1037/0735-7028.36.4.376

Britner, P. A., & Mossler, D. G. (2002). Professionals decision-making about out-of-home placements following instances of child abuse. *Child Abuse & Neglect*, *26*(4), 317–332. doi:10.1016/S0145-2134(02)00311-3 PMID:12092801

Brodzinsky, D. M. (2013). *A need to know: Enhancing adoption competence among mental health professionals. Policy Perspective*. New York, NY: Donaldson Adoption Institute.

Burns, B. J., Phillips, S. D., Wagner, H. R., Barth, R. P., Kilko, D. J., Campbell, Y., & Landsverk, J. (2004). Mental Health Need and Access to Mental Health Services by Youths Involved with Child Welfare: A National Survey. *Journal of the American Academy of Child and Adolescent Psychology*, *43*(8), 960–970. doi:10.1097/01.chi.0000127590.95585.65 PMID:15266190

Carnes-Holt, K., & Bratton, S. C. (2014). The efficacy of child parent relationship therapy for adopted children with attachment disruptions. *Journal of Counseling and Development*, *92*(3), 328–337. doi:10.1002/j.1556-6676.2014.00160.x

Child Welfare Information Gateway. (2016). *Foster Care Statistics 2014*. Retrieved from www.childwelfare.gov

Congressional Coalition on Adoption Institute. (2014). *Facts and statistics*. Retrieved from http://www.ccainstitute.org/index.php?option=com_content&view=category&layout=blog&id=25&Itemid=43

Costas, M., & Landreth, G. (1999). Filial therapy with non-offending parents of children who have been sexually abused. *International Journal of Play Therapy*, *8*(1), 43–66. doi:10.1037/h0089427

Day, A. G., Somers, C., Darden, J. S., & Yoon, J. (2015). Using cross-system communication to promote educational well-being of foster children: Recommendations for a national research, practice, and policy agenda. *Children & Schools*, *37*(1), 54–62. doi:10.1093/cs/cdu027

Forbes, H., & Post, B. (2006). *Beyond consequences logic, and control: A love based approach to helping attachment-challenged children with severe behaviors*. Orlando, FL: Beyond Consequences Institute, LLC.

Greeson, J. K., Briggs, E. C., Kisiel, C. L., Layne, C. M., Ake, G. S. III, Ko, S. J., & Fairbank, J. A. et al. (2011). Complex Trauma and Mental Health in Children and Adolescents Placed in Foster Care: Findings from the National Child Traumatic Stress Network. *Child Welfare*, *90*(6), 91–108. PMID:22533044

Guerney, B. G. (1964). Filial therapy: Description and rationale. *Journal of Consulting Psychology*, *28*(4), 304–310. doi:10.1037/h0041340 PMID:14198792

Harris, Z. L., & Landreth, G. L. (1997). Filial therapy with incarcerated mothers: A five-week model. *International Journal of Play Therapy*, *6*(2), 53–73. doi:10.1037/h0089408

Horwitz, S. M., Chamberlain, P., Landsverk, J., & Mullican, C. (2010). Improving the mental health of children in Child Welfare through the implementation of evidence-based parenting. *Administration and Policy in Mental Health*, *37*(1-2), 27–39. doi:10.1007/s10488-010-0274-3 PMID:20143150

Hughes, D. A. (1997). *Facilitating developmental attachment: The road to emotional recovery and behavioral change in foster and adopted children*. Lanham, MD: Rowman & Littlefield.

Hughes, D. A. (1999). Adopted children with attachment problems. *Child Welfare*, *78*(5), 541–561. PMID:10501012

Hughes, D. A. (2006). *Building the bonds of attachment: Awakening love in deeply troubled children* (2nd ed.). Lanham, MD: Rowman & Littlefield.

James, B. (1994). *Handbook for treatment of attachment-trauma problems in children*. Lexington, MA: Lexington Books.

Klain, E. J., & White, A. R. (2013). *Implementing trauma-informed practices in child welfare*. State Policy Advocacy and Reform Center. Retrieved from http://childwelfaresparc.org/wp-content/uploads/2013/11/Implementing-Trauma-Informed-Practices.pdf

Ko, S. J., Ford, J. D., Kassam-Adams, N., Berkowitz, S. J., Wilson, C., Wong, M., & Layne, C. M. et al. (2008). Creating trauma-informed systems: Child welfare, education, first responders, health care, juvenile justice. *Professional Psychology, Research and Practice*, *39*(4), 396–404. doi:10.1037/0735-7028.39.4.396

Landreth, G. L. (2012). *Play Therapy: The art of the relationship* (3rd ed.). New York, NY: Routledge.

Landreth, G. L., & Bratton, S. C. (2006). *Child parent relationship therapy (CPRT): A 10-session filial therapy model*. New York, NY: Routledge Taylor & Francis Group.

Landreth, G. L., & Lobaugh, A. F. (1998). Filial therapy with incarcerated fathers: Effects on parental acceptance of child, parental stress, and child adjustment. *Journal of Counseling and Development*, *6*(2), 53–73.

Lanius, R. A., Vermetten, E., & Pain, C. (Eds.). (2010). *The impact of early life trauma on health and disease: The hidden epidemic*. Cambridge, UK: Cambridge University Press. doi:10.1017/CBO9780511777042

Lee, S. M., & Nachlis, L. S. (2011). Consulting with attorneys: An alternative hybrid model. *Journal of Child Custody*, *8*(1), 84–102. doi:10.1080/15379418.2010.547448

Lin, Y. D., & Bratton, S. C. (2015). A meta-analytic review of child-centered play therapy approaches. *Journal of Counseling and Development*, *93*(1), 45–58. doi:10.1002/j.1556-6676.2015.00180.x

Lindo, N. A., Bratton, S. C., & Landreth, G. L. (2015). Child parent relationship therapy: Theory, research, and intervention process. In L. A. Reddy, T. M. Files-Hall, & C. E. Schaefer (Eds.), *Empirically based play interventions for children* (2nd ed.; pp. 241–261). Washington, DC: American Psychological Association.

Litrownik, A. J. (2012, Winter). A longitudinal perspective on mental health services for foster youth: Continued risk and the challenge of chaotic caregiving environments. *American Psychological Association: CYF News*, 17-19.

McWey, L. M., Henderson, T. L., & Tice, S. N. (2006). Mental health issues and the foster care system: An examination of the impact of the adoption and safe families act. *Journal of Marital and Family Therapy*, *32*(2), 195–214. doi:10.1111/j.1752-0606.2006.tb01600.x PMID:16676896

Milam-Miller, S. (2009). The psychiatrist as consultant: Working within schools, the courts, and primary care to promote childrens mental health. *The Psychiatric Clinics of North America*, *32*(1), 165–176. doi:10.1016/j.psc.2008.10.002 PMID:19248923

Molin, R., & Palmer, S. (2005). Consent and participation: Ethical issues in the treatment of children in out-of-home care. *The American Journal of Orthopsychiatry*, *75*(1), 152–157. doi:10.1037/0002-9432.75.1.152 PMID:15709858

National Child Traumatic Stress Network. (n.d.). Retrieved from www.nctsnet.org

Nelson, C. A. III, Bos, K., Gunnar, M. R., & Sonuga-Barke, E. J. S. (2001). Children without permanent parents: Research, practice, and policy. V. The neurobiological toll of early human deprivation. *Monographs of the Society for Research in Child Development*, *76*(4), 127–146. doi:10.1111/j.1540-5834.2011.00630.x PMID:25018565

New York State Office of Children and Family Services. (n.d.). *Become a foster parent: Requirements to become a foster parent.* Retrieved from http://ocfs.ny.gov/main/fostercare/requirements.asp

Newton, R. R., Litrownik, A. J., & Landsverk, J. A. (2000). Children and youth in foster care: Disentangling the relationship between problem behaviors and number of placements. *Child Abuse & Neglect*, *24*(10), 1363–1374. doi:10.1016/S0145-2134(00)00189-7 PMID:11075702

Ohio Department of Job and Family Services. (2014). *Fact sheet: Foster care.* Retrieved from http://jfs.ohio.gov/factsheets/fostercare.pdf

Opiola, K., & Bratton, S. C. (in review). The effects of child-parent relationship therapy (CPRT) for adoptive families. *Submitted to Journal of Counseling and Development.*

Ornelas, L. A., Silverstein, D. N., & Tan, S. (2007). Effectively addressing mental health issues in permanency-focused child welfare placement. *Child Welfare*, *86*(5), 93–112. doi:10.1037/t05563-000 PMID:18422050

Pecora, P. J., Jensen, P. S., Romanelli, L. H., Jackson, L. J., & Ortiz, A. (2009). Mental health services for children placed in foster care: An overview of current challenges. *Child Welfare*, *88*(1), 5–26. PMID:19653451

Pecora, P. J., Kessler, R. C., Williams, J., O'Brien, K., Downs, A. C., English, D., & Holmes, K. et al. (2005). *Improving family foster care: Findings from the northwest foster care alumni study*. Seattle, WA: Casey Family Programs.

Perry, B. D. (1994). Neurobiological sequelae of childhood trauma. Post-traumatic disorders in children. In M. Murburg (Ed.), *Catecholomine function in posttraumatic stress disorder: Emerging concepts* (pp. 253–276). Washington, DC: American Psychiatric Press.

Perry, B. D., & Szalavitz, M. (2006). *The boy who was raised as a dog: and other stories from a child psychiatrist's notebook*. Philadelphia, PA: Basic Books.

Post, P., & Tillman, K. S. (2015). Cultural issues in play therapy. In D. A. Crenshaw & A. L. Stewart (Eds.), *Play therapy: A comprehensive guide to theory and practice* (pp. 496–510). New York, NY: Guilford Press.

Price, J. M., Chamberlain, P., Lansverk, J., Reid, J. B., Leve, L. D., & Laurent, H. (2008). Effects of a foster parent training intervention on placement changes of children in foster care. *Child Maltreatment*, *13*(1), 64–75. doi:10.1177/1077559507310612 PMID:18174349

Purvis, K., Cross, D., & Pennings, J. (2009). Trust-based relational intervention: Interactive principles for adopted children with special social-emotional needs. *The Journal of Humanistic Counseling, Education and Development*, *48*(1), 3–22. doi:10.1002/j.2161-1939.2009.tb00064.x

Purvis, K. B., Cross, D. R., & Sunshine, W. L. (2007). *The connected child: For parents who have welcomed children from other countries and cultures, from troubled backgrounds, with special behavioral or emotional needs*. New York, NY: McGraw-Hill.

Ray, D. (2011). *Advanced play therapy: Essential conditions, knowledge, and skills for child practice*. New York, NY: Routledge.

Schafer, C. E., & Peabody, M. A. (2016). Glossary of play therapy terms. *Play Therapy*, *11*(2), 20–24.

Siegel, D. J. (2001). Toward an interpersonal neurobiology of the developing mind: Attachment relationships, mindsight, and neural integration. *Infant Mental Health Journal*, *22*(1-2), 67–94. doi:10.1002/1097-0355(200101/04)22:1<67::AID-IMHJ3>3.0.CO;2-G

Siegel, D. J. (2012). *Pocket guide to interpersonal neurobiology: An integrative handbook of the mind*. New York, NY: W.W. Norton & company.

Siegel, D. J., & Hartzell, M. (2003). *Parenting from the inside out: How a deeper self- understanding can help you raise children who thrive*. New York, NY: Tarcher/Penguin.

Smith, N., & Landreth, G. (2003). Intensive filial therapy with child witnesses of domestic violence: A comparison with individual and sibling group play therapy. *International Journal of Play Therapy*, *12*(1), 67–88. doi:10.1037/h0088872

Texas Adoption Resource Exchange (TARE). (n.d.). *Requirements for foster/adopt families*. Retrieved from https://www.dfps.state.tx.us/Adoption_and_Foster_Care/Get_Started/requirements.asp

The Annie E. Casey Foundation. (2009). *The 2009 KIDS COUNT data book: State profiles of child well-being*. Baltimore, MD: Author.

U. S. Department of Health and Human Services, Administration for Children and Families, Administration on Children, Youth and Families, Children's Bureau. (2016a). *Trends in foster care and adoption: FY 2006- FY 2015*. Retrieved from www.acf.gov/default/files/cb/trends_fostercare-adoption2015.pdf

U. S. Department of Health and Human Services, Administration for Children and Families, Administration on Children, Youth and Families, Children's Bureau. (2016b). The AFCARS report FY 2015 data
van der Kolk, B. A. (2005). Developmental trauma disorder. *Psychiatric Annals*, *35*, 401–408.

Washington State Department of Social and Health Services. (n.d.). *Training requirements*. Retrieved from https://www.dshs.wa.gov/ca/foster-parenting/training-requirements

World Health Organization. (2010). *Framework for action on interprofessional education and collaborative practice*. Geneva: WHO Press. Available at http://apps.who.int/iris/bitstream/10665/70185/1/WHO_HRH_HPN_10.3_eng.pdf?ua=1

Zilberstein, K. (2013). The use and limitations of attachment theory in child psychotherapy. *Psychotherapy (Chicago, Ill.)*, *51*(1), 93–103. doi:10.1037/a0030930 PMID:23398037

KEY TERMS AND DEFINITIONS

Attorney Ad Litem: The child's attorney that is appointed by the court. They will be present at all court hearing and may speak to the child directly about their thoughts, feelings, and experience. The attorney is to represent the child's best interest. They must tell the court what the child's desires are even if the attorney ad litem does not agree that these are in the best interest of the child.

Caseworker: This professional is appointed to work with children and families and make sure that appropriate services are provided to keep children safe. The caseworker should help biological parents understand the legal process and outline a case plan of what they must achieve to regain custody of the child in foster care. A copy of the case plan must be given to the biological parents.

Child Parent Relationship Therapy (CPRT): CPRT is a manualized filial therapy model grounded in the attitudes and principles of child-centered play therapy. In CPRT, parents receive training and supervision in basic child-centered play therapy skills and principles including tracking behaviors, reflecting content and feeling, facilitating decision-making, providing encouragement, and setting limits. By using these skills, parents learn to be with their children in non-judgmental and accepting ways that support development of a healthy parent-child relationship. This positive relationship provides the foundation for personal growth and change in the child and the parent (Landreth & Bratton, 2006). A protocol for CPRT can be found in the treatment manual *Child-parent relationship therapy (CPRT) treatment manual: A 10-session filial therapy model for training parents* (Bratton, Landreth, Kellam, & Blackard, 2006).

Court Appointed Special Advocate (CASA): A trained volunteer that is appointed by the judge to develop a relationship with the child and related caregivers and share information on what they believe is best for the child.

Department of Human Services (DHS): The government agency responsible for housing the foster care system within state government offices. In different states, this agency may fall under different titles including Department of Family Services (DFS) or Child Protective Services (CPS).

Department of Human Services Attorney: The attorney that is responsible for presenting evidence of harm to a child that resulted in entering the foster care system.

Filial Therapy: Filial therapy, pioneered by Bernard and Louise Guerney, is a relationship-focused mental health intervention used to help meet the needs of both parents and children by empowering parents to serve as the therapeutic agent of change (Guerney, 1964; Landreth 2012; Landreth & Bratton 2006). Parents learn principles and methodology of child-centered play therapy in a small group format utilizing didactic instruction, supervision of video recorded play sessions, and role playing (Guerney, 1964; Landreth 2012).

Guardian/Custodian's Attorney: The attorney who represents the "accused" caregivers and their interests and rights concerning the child that has been placed in care.

Stakeholders for Children in Foster Care: Individuals who have an active role in providing care for children in the foster care system. Stakeholders include, but are not limited to, biological parents, foster parents, caseworkers, legal professionals (e.g. attorneys, judges, CASAs, etc.), health professionals (pediatricians, nutritionists, etc.), therapists (physical, occupational, speech, etc.), school professionals (classroom teachers, special education teachers, school counselors, etc.), and mental health professionals (psychiatrists, psychologists, play therapists, etc.).

Chapter 16
Teachers Can Play Too:
Teacher-Child Relationships, Social-Emotional Development, and Academic Engagement

Szu-Yu Chen
Central Michigan University, USA

Natalya A. Lindo
University of North Texas, USA

ABSTRACT

Positive teacher-child relationships are key factors for children's social-emotional development and academic success in schools. Teachers' ability to provide children with emotional support and understand children's unique needs may improve challenging behaviors in the classroom. Play-based teacher intervention training models provide teachers opportunities to become therapeutic agents and learn how to use humanistic play therapy skills and language to communicate with children and respond to their unique needs. In this chapter, the authors introduce four play-based teacher intervention training models: Kinder Training, Child-Teacher Relationship Training, Relationship Enhancement for Learner and Teacher, and Teacher-Child Relationship Building. The authors also illustrate these models' goals, training structure, research support for their effectiveness with teacher-child relationships, children's behavioral issues, academic engagement, and teachers' classroom management skills.

INTRODUCTION

According to the Center for Disease Control and Prevention (2015), approximately 5.4 percent of U.S. children age 5 to 17 were reported by a parent to exhibit social, emotional, or behavioral difficulties. Children with emotional or behavioral problems may have difficulty managing their emotions, focusing on tasks, and/or regulating their behavior (New Freedom Commission on Mental Health, 2003). Thus, good emotional and behavioral health is a key component to children's healthy development and may facilitate academic achievement (Center for the Study of Social Policy, 2012).

DOI: 10.4018/978-1-5225-2224-9.ch016

Research has shown that the teacher-child relationship has long-lasting effects on children's social-emotional development and academic success in schools (Rimm-Kaufman, 2011). Children's social-emotional or behavioral difficulties may cause significant stressors for teachers and impact their ability to provide children with emotional support. Additionally, teachers' responses to children's behaviors may affect children's psychological, social, and cognitive development, as well as academic engagement and achievement (Baker, 2006; Pianta, 1999; Ray, 2007). Hence, it appears beneficial for teachers to receive professional development training aimed at improving teacher-child relationships, managing students' challenging behaviors, and responding to students' emotional needs. In addition, providing teachers support and helping them develop effective ways of communicating with children may increase their confidence in managing children's behaviors and emotional difficulties, reduce teaching stress, and improve overall job satisfaction (White et al., 1997).

THE IMPACT OF TEACHER-CHILD RELATIONSHIP

Children's primary relationships with significant adults, such as parents, caregivers, and teachers are highly influential in young children's lives and can greatly influence their development (Draper, Siegel, White, Solis, & Mishna, 2009; Guerney, 2000; Hamre & Pianta, 2005; Landreth & Bratton, 2006). Pianta (1999) discussed the impact of inadequate attachment with significant adults on children's lifelong developmental outcomes. Specifically, children who have experienced unstable and negative relationships in early childhood have a higher risk for challenges in social, emotional, and cognitive development and therefore have the potential to exhibit poor school performance and classroom adjustment (Janson & King, 2006; Perry, 2001; Pianta & Stuhlman, 2004).

Children's relationships with their teachers are among the most important relationships they establish in the school environment (Birch & Ladd, 1997). Given the large amount of time teachers spend with students, teachers can be significant role models in children's lives (Stulmaker, 2012). Researchers have suggested that children's developmental outcomes largely depend on the quality of teacher-child relationships (Birch & Ladd, 1997, 1998; Pianta, 1999; Pianta & Stuhlman, 2004; Hamre & Pianta, 2001, 2005). Research also has shown that healthy teacher-child relationships may enhance children's social-emotional development and academic success. Positive teacher-child relationships encourage children's active participation in learning and peer relationships, contributing to a functional classroom environment (Baker, 2006; Birch & Ladd, 1997; Howes, 2000; Hamre & Pianta, 2005). However, negative teacher-child relationships have been linked to children's poor behavioral and academic outcomes as well as negative attitudes about school (Birch & Ladd, 1997; Decker, Dona, & Christenson, 2007; Garner & Waajid, 2008).

Birch and Ladd (1997) categorized the nature of the teacher-child relationship as one of the three categories of close, conflictual, and dependent. They examined the relationship between the closeness, dependency, and conflict features of teacher-child relationships in 206 kindergarten children's school adjustment.

Birch and Ladd (1997) found that close teacher-child relationships were strongly linked with academic performance as well as school liking and self-directedness. In close teacher-child relationships, teachers provide emotional security, facilitate open communication, and create stable environments that may function as a support for children in the school setting. Children may therefore have positive attitudes toward school, experience successful academic performance, and foster healthy social-emotional development

(Birch & Ladd, 1997). In addition, Pianta (2001) argued that children who build secure relationships with their teachers during their early years are more likely to have successful relationships with peers and teachers in the future. Children in close teacher-child relationships tend to view teachers as a secure base for facilitating self-direction and autonomy, contributing to regulation of emotional experience and social behavior, and engendering prosocial skills and emotional understanding (Birch & Ladd, 1997, 1998; Howes, 2000; Pianta, 1999).

On the other hand, children having conflictual relationships with teachers tended to avoid or dislike school, be less self-directed, and be less cooperative and engaged in classroom activities (Birch & Ladd, 1997). Conflictual teacher-child relationships may cause children to continuously engage in discordant interactions with teachers and be unable to perceive teachers as a secure base for learning and growth (Birch & Ladd, 1997). This can function as a stressor for children in the school environment and negatively impact their school adjustment. Such difficulties in teacher-child relationships may increase children's negative feelings about or attitudes toward school. The resulting feelings of insecurity may further lead to isolation, depression and anxiety that may also be related to poor academic achievement and performance (Birch & Ladd, 1997; Meesters & Muris, 2002; Pianta, 1999; Saltali, 2013).

The results of Birch and Ladd's study (1997) indicated that dependent teacher-child relationships were strongly associated with school adjustment difficulties in academic performance, learning attitudes, and engagement with the school environment. Children in dependent teacher-child relationships tend to show a high degree of overdependence on their teachers. Children may overly rely on teachers as a source of support, and this may interfere with children's school adjustment. Children may show feelings of loneliness and negative attitudes toward school. The dependency in this relationship may restrict these children's curiosity, learning, and development of healthy peer relationships (Birch & Ladd, 1997).

Baker (2006) further proposed that children's behavior, social-emotional development, and academic achievement may be reciprocally associated and greatly influenced by the quality of teacher-child relationships. Additionally, Yost and Mosca (2002) indicated that when teachers feel increased stress, they are more likely to respond to children in ways that perpetuate rather than prevent children's problematic behaviors. Both teachers and children may therefore experience the school environment negatively because of the continuity of a negative cycle of interaction (Helker & Ray, 2009; Myers & Pianta, 2008).

CLASSROOM BEHAVIOR

Various researchers described the reciprocal interactions among teacher-child relationships, children's behavior, teachers' perceptions of children's behavior, and teachers' behaviors. For example, in a longitudinal study, Birch and Ladd (1998) examined the relationship between kindergarten children's behavioral orientations and their first-grade teacher-child interactions and suggested that teacher-child relationships may be a potential moderator of children's behavior. Birch and Ladd categorized children into three behavioral orientations. Children who exhibited aggressive and disruptive behavior were characterized as moving against others. Children who lacked an interest in connecting with other children were characterized as moving away from others, and children who showed cooperative and helpful behavior were characterized as moving toward others. Participants of this study included 199 kindergarten children and 17 teachers. Researchers interviewed children's kindergarten teachers during the first year of the study, and then interviewed participating children's first grade teachers in the next year of the study. The results indicated that the quality of the teacher-child relationship was associated with children's changes in their behavioral orientation or school adjustment over time. They concluded that children's early behavioral styles in the classroom have concurrent and long-term relevance to teacher-child relationships or peer relationships.

Pianta (1999) used the term *filters* to explain how an adult's perceptions of a child potentially leads to the adult's distorted interpretations of the child's behavior. In any adult-child relationship, the adult tends to hold particular perceptions of the child's characteristics. Pianta argued that when the adult believes the child is bright, lazy, or manipulative, the adult automatically and unconsciously filters the child's behavior through the specific perception the adult holds. The adult then interprets the child's behavior according to the filter and mirrors these filtered perceptions of the child. Accordingly, the adult's filtered interpretations of the child's behavior may influence the adult's behavior more than the child's actual behavior. For example, if a teacher holds the perception that a particular child is lazy, she or he may then see that the child is reluctant to engage in a group activity. Instead of trying to understand the child's reluctance, the teacher may attribute the lack of involvement as confirmation of the child's laziness. Subsequently, the teacher may respond negatively, resulting in discouraging the child. However, if the teacher perceives the reluctant child as anxious, the teacher may interpret the child's behavior as stemming from timidity and respond with gentle support or encouragement.

Based on Pianta's (1999) filter concept, Dobbs and Arnold (2009) examined the relationships between teachers' perceptions of children's behavior and teachers' behaviors toward children. The results indicated that teachers tended to give more commands to children who they reported as having more total behavior problems and more externalizing problems. Dobb and Arnold concluded that a better understanding of teachers' experiences, perceptions, and needs in their relationships with children may reduce teachers' difficulties with children's classroom behavior. Hence, it is essential to address both the teacher-child relationship and teacher behavior in intervention programs (Dobb & Arnold, 2009).

Consistent with previous findings, Gonzales (2012) presented the relationship reciprocal cycle (RRC) and pointed out that a lack of training in responding to children's emotional and behavioral needs may cause teachers and children to be caught in a never-ending cycle of poor responses. When the cycle is allowed to repeat between a child and teacher the following outcomes occur: (a) the child shows disruptive behaviors stemming from emotional disturbance, (b) the teacher feels challenged and ineffective due to the child's disruptive behavior, (c) the teacher's feelings create a strain on the teacher-child relationship, (d) the teacher develops a negative perception of the child, (e) the teacher responds to the child in a negative way that may include threats or punishments, and (f) the teacher's negative responses create more emotional disturbance within the child, influencing the child to display additional disruptive behaviors.

Pianta (1999) indicated that children demonstrating problematic behavior are embedded within a system of family factors, life stressors, and childhood characteristics. In context, children often face numerous stressors such as parental divorce, single parenthood, child abuse and neglect, and grief and loss (White et al., 1997). Early in development, children's emotions are expressed behaviorally (Pianta, 1999). Thus, when children struggle with emotional stress, they may display behavioral concerns and maladjustment to school that impedes learning and development (White et al., 2000). Because teachers spend a great deal of time with the children in their classrooms each week, teachers are likely to encounter the various and negative effects of children's stressful lives (White et al., 2000). Ray (2007) noted that most teachers lack necessary skills for effectively responding to children's social-emotional needs when children exhibit challenging behavior in the classroom. This highlights the importance of developing professional development training models that provide teachers with child development resources and effective communication tools.

SOCIAL-EMOTIONAL DEVELOPMENT

Research has delineated the importance for teachers to build consistent and nurturing relationships with children to meet children's emotional needs and promote positive outcomes (Perry, 2001; Pianta, 1999). Various research studies provided evidence of the impact of teacher-child relationships on children's social-emotional development. For instance, Pianta and Stuhlman (2004) examined the correlations between teacher-child relationships and 490 young children's social and academic skills over a 3-year period. Preschool, kindergarten, and first-grade teachers reported their perceptions of their relationships with the participant children using the short form of the Student-Teacher Relationship Scale (STRS; Pianta, 2001). The results indicated moderate correlations among teachers' rating of conflictual teacher-child relationships and slightly lower correlations among teachers' rating of close teacher-child relationships across three years. Pianta and Stuhlman (2004) also found that the conflict and closeness within teacher-child relationships might significantly predict first grade children's academic achievement and social competence.

In order to gather a comprehensive picture of the impact of teacher-child relationships on children's behavioral development in and outside of the school setting, Pianta and Stuhlman (2004) also investigated both mothers' and teachers' ratings of children's internalizing and externalizing problem behavior. The results showed that mothers' reports of children's internalizing behavior (e.g., depression and anxiety) were related to pre-school and first grade teachers' report of conflict in their teacher-child relationships. Mothers' ratings of children's externalizing behavior (e.g., aggression and hyperactivity) were associated with pre-school teachers' relational conflict reports. Moreover, teachers' ratings of children's behavioral problems were associated with their concurrent perceptions of their relationships with the children. More teacher-child conflicts were associated with higher levels of perceived child behavior problems. This finding appears consistent with Pianta's (1999) filter concept as well.

Furthermore, emotional support from teachers who help children establish positive and emotionally secure relationships with adults may predict a broad range of social and task-orientation competencies (Hamre & Pianta, 2005; Howes et al., 2008; Pianta, 1999). For example, teachers who demonstrate warmth, care, respect, child-centeredness, sensitivity, and appropriate communication may promote children's positive responses toward teachers and the ability to develop healthy peer relationships (Hamre & Pianta, 2005).

ACADEMIC ENGAGEMENT AND ACHIEVEMENT

Researchers have found a strong link between the quality of teacher-child relationships and children's academic engagement. Learning in the classroom is significantly dependent on a child's relationship with the teacher (Greene, 1995, 1996; Pianta, 1998). For many children, the motivation to learn and put effort into learning tasks is related to the quality of the teacher-child relationship (Abidin, Greene, & Konold, 2004). Hence, lack of positive interactions between teachers and children may interfere with children's academic learning and development (Birch & Ladd, 1998). Unfortunately, many children do not have satisfactory relationships with their teachers leading to the need for researchers to examine the impact of the teacher-child relationship on students' learning behaviors and academic engagement.

Ladd and Burgess's (2001) observed 400 children and their teachers from kindergarten through the completion of first grade. The results indicated that children with behavioral problems were less likely both to cooperate in the classroom and engage in academic tasks. Children who had negative relationships with teachers and peers were less likely to enjoy school and engage in classroom activities and more likely to show more severe disruptive behaviors, thought problems, and attention problems by the completion of the first grade. Ladd and Burgess concluded that at-risk children experiencing ongoing strained relationships with teachers are at greater risk of developing psychological maladjustment that prevents them from enjoying academic success, benefitting from learning, and developing academic competency.

Additionally, in a longitudinal study with 880 children from birth to third grade, O'Connor and McCartney (2007) found that the quality of the teacher-child relationship is highly associated with student academic achievement. They indicated that the quality of the teacher-child relationship significantly changed from preschool to third grade and indicated that children whose relationships with teachers were on an increasingly negative trajectory from preschool to third grade demonstrated lower achievement performance in the third grade. However, children who built increasingly positive relationships with teachers demonstrated higher achievement performance. Therefore, the quality of the teacher-child relationship can predict and foster children's academic achievement. Moreover, they found that the quality of the teacher-child relationship was correlated with students' engagement in the classroom, indicating that students who have positive teacher-child relationships tend to be more engaged and attentive in the classroom. Finally, O'Connor and McCartney suggested that interventions aimed to improve children's academic achievement should focus on the teacher-child relationship.

Researchers have recognized the impact of a positive emotional climate on at-risk children's self-regulation and academic outcomes (Hamre & Pianta, 2005; Ladd & Burgess, 2001; Myers & Pianta, 2008). Teachers tend to determine students' level of engagement based on the degree of classroom participation (Hamre & Pianta, 2005), and researchers have focused on examining relationships between teacher emotional support and students' class participation rates. For example, Pianta, La Paro, Payne, Cox, and Bradley (2002) observed the quality of kindergarten classrooms to examine the relationships among classroom quality, teachers' classroom management skills, and target children's behaviors. The results indicated that among 223 kindergarteners, children who experienced an emotional, child-centered classroom climate showed more on-task and learning behavior than children who experienced an instructional and teacher-directed classroom. Specifically, when teachers demonstrated warmth and caring, the children exhibited more on-task behavior. Additionally, when teachers provided a more child-centered classroom climate that allowed children more freedom and choice, children tended to display positive support and interactions with peers as well as increased on-task behavior and engagement in learning (Pianta et al., 2002).

Hamre and Pianta (2005) used data from a national prospective study of 910 children to examine if children's high risk for school failure could be moderated by support from first-grade teachers. Specifically, they examined whether children who were academically at risk while in kindergarten and later had first-grade teachers exhibiting strong instructional and emotional support demonstrated higher achievement than other at-risk children who did not receive emotional support from teachers. The results showed that at-risk children who received strong instructional and emotional support in the first-grade classroom had higher achievement scores and better relationships with their teachers. Hamre and Pianta concluded that school-based prevention and intervention focused on improving the social and emotional climate of classrooms can facilitate children's academic, social, and behavioral development. Additionally, school-based interventions that target improvements in the quality of teacher-child interactions can improve children's positive outcomes (Hamre & Pianta, 2005).

Patrick, Ryan, and Kaplan (2007) examined the correlation between early adolescents' perceptions of the classroom environment and their engagement in the classroom. Participants in this study included 602 fifth grade children. The findings demonstrated a strong positive relationship between students' perception of the classroom environment as being supportive and their levels of motivation and engagement. Patrick et al. concluded that when students perceive that they receive emotional support and encouragement from teachers, they are more likely to be on-task in the classroom and use self-regulating strategies.

Evidently, these findings emphasize that the quality of the teacher-child relationship has a critical impact on children's academic development and academic engagement in the classroom. Children who experience negative relationships with teachers are at greater risk for developing behavioral problems and refusing to engage in learning (Pianta et al., 2002). In contrast, teachers who provide children with emotional support and are responsive to children's emotional needs tend to show a higher level of awareness of children's academic needs as well as concern for children's interests, strengths, and views (Birch & Ladd, 1997; Helker & Ray, 2009; Pianta, 1999). As a result, it is vital that teachers foster healthy relationships with children to decrease children's risk factors and promote their academic success. Furthermore, researchers suggested that interventions focused on enhancing teacher-child relationships and training teachers to respond more appropriately to children's social-emotional needs and problem behavior appear necessary in the school setting, particularly for young children identified as academically at-risk (Bennett & Bratton, 2011). Moreover, strengthening teacher-child relationships may direct children toward healthy socio-emotional outcomes, and improve teachers' ability to better understand their students' development, and ultimately break the negative reciprocal relationship cycle (Adelman & Taylor, 2012; Gonzales, 2012; Helker & Ray, 2009; Pianta, 1999Stulmaker, 2013; White et al., 2000).

In summary, research indicates that the teacher-child relationship may serve as a contributing factor in children's social-emotional development and academic success (Baker, 2006; Hamre & Pianta, 2001; Rimm-Kaufman, 2011). The quality of the relationship is individualized to each dyad and dependent on the characteristics of the particular teacher and child involved (Ray, 2007). Children's problematic behaviors may result in significant stressors for teachers and challenge teachers' ability to provide children with emotional support; however, teachers' responses to children's behaviors may impact children's psychological, social, and cognitive development as well as academic engagement and achievement (Baker, 2006; Pianta, 1999; Ray, 2007). As a result, teachers may benefit from professional development training aimed at enhancing teacher-child relationships, managing students' challenging behaviors, and responding to students' emotional needs. Providing teachers support and helping them develop effective responses to children may help increase their confidence in managing children's misbehaviors and emotional difficulties and improve their overall job satisfaction (White et al., 1997).

Given the uniqueness of the classroom environment and the high degree of relational processes that occur between teachers and children, the quality of teacher-child relationships may strongly influence children's behavior, social and emotional development, and academic engagement (Baker, 2006; Pianta, 1999). The research has suggested an increasing need for effective school mental health programs to address the teacher-child relationship and children's social-emotional, behavioral, and mental health development. As a result, more and more mental health professionals have noted the importance of implementing professional development training programs from developmentally appropriate approaches, such as play-based teacher interventions, to facilitate improvements in teacher-child relationships as well as foster children's learning and growth (Lindo et al., 2014).

PLAY-BASED PROFESSIONAL DEVELOPMENT TRAINING MODELS

The Therapeutic Power of Play

Play has been viewed as the way children are able to naturally communicate and learn about themselves, others, and the world (Erickson, 1963; Landreth, 2012; Piaget, 1962; Ray, 2011; Vygotsky, 1966). According to Landreth (2012), play and activity are the natural modes of communication for children. Children communicate through spontaneous play rather than expressing themselves verbally because they feel more comfortable with play (Kottman, 2003; Landreth, 2012; Ray, 2011). Similarly, play is crucial in the development of emotional, cognitive, language, motor, and social skills (Carlson, Watts, & Maniacci, 2006; Landreth, 2012; Ray, 2011). The fundamental importance of play to children's healthy development is evident. Children do not need to be taught how to play nor do they need to be shown how to play. Play is a spontaneous, enjoyable, voluntary, and non-goal-directed activity for children. Children play out their life experiences as a natural dynamic and self-healing process (Landreth, 2012). Play demonstrates numerous therapeutic factors that may cause beneficial outcomes for children. For instance, play provides a developmentally responsive way to enhance children's self-expression, relationship-building, competence, self-control, reality testing, social skills, and coping skills (Landreth, 2012; Schaefer, 1993; Schaefer & Drewes, 2009). Hence, play has the power not only to facilitate normal development but also to reduce problematic behaviors across contexts (Schaefer, 1993). This seems to suggest that play has the potential to improve social-emotional and behavioral problems in the classroom as well and may positively influence children's academic experiences in the school setting.

Researchers argued that the use of play in therapy is based on the principle that children are best understood from a developmental perspective and provides a variety of advantages for children (Wilson & Ryan, 2005). For example, play provides fun to the therapeutic process, can decrease children's resistance to the therapeutic relationship, and offers an expressive experience to children with several conflicts and struggles in daily life (Landreth, 2012; Ray, 2011). The use of play as a therapeutic modality allows children to express themselves symbolically while they work through their issues. Moreover, play promotes children's communication with therapists and enhances children's social motivation and skill development (Landreth, 2012; Ray, 2011).

Children can develop a sense of control and competency through play in the therapeutic process (Landreth, 2012; Ray, 2011). Children can utilize the play therapy room as a safe place for them to release energy and express themselves (Landreth, 2012; Ray, 2011). Schaefer (1993) described some of the values associated with play in therapy. For instance, play therapy encourages children's creativity and flexibility and provides children opportunities to develop problem-solving skills. Children can explore new behaviors and evaluate the consequences of behaving in new ways through role playing. By using stories, artwork, or fantasy play, children can create new ways of understanding and develop additional alternative solutions (Schaefer, 1993). Children can reestablish feelings of secure attachment and benefit from the positive aspects of relationships through shared fun and fantasy play with play therapists. Play can help children enhance positive relationships with others as play therapists create a safe and nurturing environment for children by showing unconditional acceptance, warmth, and respect (Schaefer, 1993). Given the power of play and its potential benefit for children's learning and development in the therapeutic setting, the application of play-based models to the school system may serve as an effective intervention for children who experience social, emotional and academic difficulties.

Teachers as Therapeutic Agents

Play therapy has been successfully utilized in the school environment and researchers have indicated the effectiveness of school-based play therapy for children exhibiting a variety of presenting problems (Bratton, 2010; Ray et al., 2007). To increase children's access to play therapy services in schools and to have the most positive impact on the mental health needs of young children, mental health professionals advocated for school-based play therapy services to address children's social-emotional and academic needs (Bratton, 2010; Galassi, Griffin, & Akos, 2008). Due to the significance of the caregiver-child relationship, research findings have shown that the involvement of parents and other significant caregivers, especially teachers trained and supervised by mental professionals in play-based interventions, demonstrated a larger treatment effect size than play therapy interventions provided by mental health professionals (Bratton, 2010; Bratton et al., 2005; Landreth & Bratton, 2006).

Given that elementary-aged children have unique cognitive, social, and emotional development needs (Carlson, Dinkmeyer, & Johnson, 2008; White et al., 1999; White, Draper, Flynt, & Jones, 2000), involving teachers in children's therapeutic process and providing teacher consultation is likely to be the most effective way to facilitate teachers' understanding of their students and to help students become successful learners in the school environment (Dinkmeyer & Carlson, 2006; White, Flynt, & Jones, 1999). Teachers are primarily responsible for students' achievement and behavior in the school environment; they can utilize knowledge about students' unique developmental needs to build positive teacher-child relationships and serve as therapeutic agents for their students' growth (Carlson et al., 2008; White et al., 1999, 2000). As a result, counselors might consider training teachers to use play therapy skills, providing consultation services aimed at enhancing teacher-child relationships and optimizing children's social-emotional and academic development.

Hamre and Pianta (2005) indicated that students are likely to become successful learners in school if they participate in interventions aimed at improving teacher-child relationships. Draper et al. (2001) specifically noted that teachers are significant adults in children's lives, highlighting the importance of involving teachers in interventions focused on improving children's social, emotional, and academic concerns. Hence, interventions designed to improve teacher-child relationships may improve children's classroom behavior and strengthen their developmental competencies as well.

Based on the benefits of using play as a therapeutic modality and involving teachers in children's process of learning and growing, various play-based interventions have been developed to increase access to play therapy services in preschools and elementary schools (Stulmaker, 2013). Play-based teacher interventions allow counselors to train teachers in basic play therapy skills and assist teachers in gaining awareness of children's emotional needs. Moreover, these interventions provide teachers an opportunity to utilize developmentally appropriate skills to facilitate children's social, emotional and academic growth.

Play-Based Teacher Intervention Models

Guerney (1964) developed filial therapy, a play-based counseling intervention grounded in the principles and philosophies of child-centered play therapy. Mental health professionals usually conduct filial therapy in a group format. The weekly group meetings provide parents didactic and dynamic elements that support parents' abilities to learn basic child-centered play therapy skills, apply the skills with their children in one-on-one play sessions, process the parent-child play sessions, and share their stories about their relationships with and concerns about their children (Guerney, 1964). The goals of filial therapy are to help parents meet children's psychological needs while strengthening the parent-child relationship, helping children communicate their needs, feelings, and thoughts, and increasing children's self-esteem (Guerney, 1964). Filial therapy has been regarded as an effective treatment modality for a wide range of families' concerns (Coufal & Brock, 1979; Guerney, 2000; Guerney & Stover, 1971; Oxman, 1972; Stover & Guerney, 1967). For instance, children showed significant improvement in behavior and social adjustment and parents demonstrated an increase in empathic interactions with their emotionally disturbed children after parents received 12 to 18 months of filial therapy (Stover & Guerney, 1967).

Based on the initial positive outcomes of the filial therapy model, Bach (1968) suggested that teachers could benefit from learning filial therapy as well. Bach hypothesized that teachers could use play therapy techniques to facilitate improvements in children's emotional and behavioral problems and teachers' classroom management skills. Andronico and Guerney (1969) discussed the potential application of filial therapy to the school setting. Given the significant amount of time that children spend with their teachers, Andronico and Guerney believed that teachers using the filial therapy approach would be better able to understand children's behavior, effectively attend to children's emotional needs in the classroom, and improve their classroom environments. Additionally, children would receive benefits similar to what they would receive in traditional mental health services through making emotional connections with teachers in the classroom, and as a result, children could increase their levels of self-esteem and self-responsibility (Andronico & Guerney, 1969).

Guerney and Fluman (1970) later proposed that in order to foster healthy teacher-child relationships and promote the social-emotional health of children in the classroom, counselors can train teachers to become therapeutic agents and provide them with supervision in the utilization of basic play therapy skills with children. Guerney and colleague trained 11 elementary school teachers in the filial therapy model for 20 weeks and provided supervision for teachers who each conducted 14 individual play sessions with withdrawn students. The results indicated that teachers could implement the play therapy skills effectively and accurately in the play sessions with their students (Guerney & Fluman, 1970). Moreover, all nine of the students in the treatment group showed consistent improvement in assertiveness.

Given the initial results from Guerney and Fluman's study delineating the benefits of training teachers to be therapeutic agents for children, the idea of utilizing the filial therapy model with teachers has led to the creation of counseling-based professional development training models including: (a) Kinder Training developed by White, Flynt, and Draper (1997), (b) Child-teacher Relationship Training (CTRT) developed by Bratton, Morrison, and Ray (2009), (c) Relationship Enhancement for Learner and Teacher (RELATe) developed by Ray, Muro, and Schumann (2004), and (d) Teacher-child Relationship Building (TCRB) developed by Lindo et al. (2014). The goals of these four play-based teacher interventions are to train teachers to use basic humanistic play therapy skills, involve teachers directly in the intervention by training them to become therapeutic change agents, strengthen teacher-child relationships, and promote students' social-emotional and academic development.

Kinder Training

White, Flynt, and Draper (1997) developed kinder therapy, a play-based professional development training model, later renamed kinder training. It is based on filial therapy (Guerney, 1964) and the theoretical constructs of Individual Psychology. Given the reported effectiveness of filial therapy, White et al. deemed the structure of filial therapy appropriate for application to teachers.

In addition, White et al. (1997) indicated that the basic tenets of Individual Psychology are confluent with fostering positive relationships between adults and children, so the incorporation of Individual Psychology tenets may be helpful for teachers to gain a better understanding of how children perceive themselves and interact with others as well as build meaningful relationships with children.

Goals and Structure of Kinder Training

The goals of the kinder training model are for counselors to involve teachers directly in the intervention by training teachers to become play therapy agents as they improve their relationships with children (White et al., 2000). Kinder training is designed to enhance teachers' ability to connect with children, help children make better adjustments to their classrooms, and ultimately improve children's academic and social skills as well as their relationships with teachers (White et al., 2000).

White et al. (2000) outlined five basic steps for implementing kinder training in a school. First, the counselor conducts a 2-day in-service workshop to train teachers in the basic principles of non-directive play therapy, including encouragement with tracking, reflection of feelings, logical consequences, limit setting, and goal identification and disclosure. In addition, teachers learn important Adlerian principles of (a) lifestyle, (b) social interest, (c) creative self, (d) mistaken goals of behavior, (e) private logic, (f) encouragement, (g) logical consequences, (h) family atmosphere, and (i) psychological birth order. The counselor also presents an overview of children's social, cognitive, and moral development, and describes different types of play, including play for pleasure, play for mastery, and play to deal with traumatic events, to help teachers understand children's play in the playroom and classroom.

The structure of the workshop consists of didactic lecture, demonstration of individual play sessions, role play, and group discussion. After the in-service kinder training, the counselor schedules weekly teacher-directed play sessions with each teacher and a child of focus. Next, each teacher conducts a 30-minute individual play session with their child of focus once a week for six weeks. Teachers choose a target child based on concerns about the child's social, emotional, or academic skills. The counselor may participate in the teacher-led play sessions to the extent needed to help the teacher become familiar with their new role. The counselor videotapes the sessions or unobtrusively observes from the same room or from another room using a live video-feed or two-way mirror.

During each individual supervision session, the counselor provides the teacher with feedback in the form of education and retraining to improve the teacher-child relationship in the classroom as well as to prepare the teacher for the next individual play session with the child of focus. Depending on the teacher's schedule, this can take place right after the play session, during teachers' daily lesson planning time, conference time, or after school. The counselor uses this time to discuss issues related to the teacher-child relationship and uses encouragement by addressing the teacher's strengths and efforts as well as by providing a better understanding of the child. The counselor then connects Adlerian principles to the play therapy skills and assists teachers' transfer of skills from the playroom to the classroom. Finally, the counselor provides follow-up sessions to support teachers who wish to continue applying the model after the completion of the intervention. The number of follow-up sessions varies depending on the teacher and child's needs and the teacher's ability to assimilate kinder training concepts.

White et al. (2000) proposed a 2-day training followed by six individual play sessions. Given the hectic and sometimes unpredictable nature of the school setting and the unique needs of individual teachers, White et al. (2000) also pointed out the possibility for counselors to adapt this model to various formats. For example, kinder training may be conducted in an individual format or utilize a single day of training.

Based on the first author's experience conducting individual kinder training, the counselor may use one 4-hour session or two 2-hour sessions after school. The first component would be devoted to an overview of Adlerian principles and child development and the second component to the teaching of non-directive play techniques and role play. In addition, the individualized format appears to allow flexibility to meet each teacher's unique needs by tailoring the kinder training and addressing individual concerns regarding children of focus. Moreover, the counselor is better able to build an individual relationship with each teacher throughout the kinder training, providing the counselor an opportunity to understand and support each teacher's emotional needs and learning.

The counselor can also consider conducting a one-day training if time is limited and the number of teacher participants are small. The counselor may introduce the Adlerian principles and teach basic play therapy skills during the morning session. Teachers can then practice play therapy skills in the afternoon (White et al., 2000).

Research Support for Kinder Training

While research on the use of kinder training has been limited, the available studies provided evidence of the model's effectiveness (Chen, 2015; Draper, White, O'Shaughnessy, Flynt, & Jones, 2001; Draper, 2009; Edwards, Varjas, White, & Stokes, 2009; Solis, 2005; White et al., 1997; White, Flynt, & Jones 1999). For example, White et al. (1997) conducted a case study to illustrate the application of kinder therapy with a school counselor, a kindergarten teacher, and one Hispanic child struggling with issues of control and school anxiety. The application of kinder therapy with the school counselor-teacher-child triad led to improvements in the child's presenting problems (White et al., 1997). In addition, the school counselor reported having the ability to maximize her effectiveness by involving the teacher in the therapeutic process. The researchers concluded that mental health practitioners and school counselors could find the kinder training model helpful when working with discouraged teachers and children.

White, Flint, and Jones (1999) conducted a pilot study with six kindergarten teachers and children. Teachers received 1 day of training in basic play therapy skills and Adlerian principles and conducted six weekly supervised play sessions with a child of focus. White and colleagues utilized pre- and post-tests to evaluate the effects of kinder training on the teachers' use of encouragement, limit-setting, and goal disclosure statements. They examined the teachers' perceptions of the children's levels of encouragement, language arts, math skills, social interactions, and behaviors. The results indicated changes in teacher-child interactions in the classroom as evidenced by teachers' triple increase in encouraging and goal-disclosure statements and double increase in logical consequences. The teachers' use of ineffective verbal responses decreased by two thirds (White et al., 1999). Teachers perceived an increase in children's positive social skills and a decrease in negative social behaviors, such as hyperactivity, aggressiveness, and attention-related behavior. Finally, all six children demonstrated improvements in math and language arts skills.

Draper et al. (2001) conducted a single-case design to examine the effects of kinder training on children's behavior, social skills, and early literacy. The participants included kindergarten and first-grade teachers ($n = 14$) and their selected students ($n = 14$). Teachers received a 2-day training and conducted six play sessions with their children of focus. After completion of the training, teachers reported positive changes in their students' classroom behaviors. Specifically, students demonstrated improvements in early literacy skills, increases in adaptive behaviors, and decreases in problem behavior. Independent raters also observed positive changes in teachers' classroom behavior as teachers demonstrated increases in their numbers of encouragement, limit setting, and facilitative statements. Results suggested that kinder training is possibly an effective prevention or intervention program for improving students' behavioral problems and enhancing teachers' relationship-building techniques (Draper et al., 2001).

Draper et al. (2009) utilized a waitlist control group design to examine the effects of kinder training on teacher-child relationships with 60 preschool children and teachers. Teachers of preschoolers participated in a 1-day group training with weekly coaching and dyadic consultation. Teachers were asked to practice basic play therapy skills with children in school settings. They reported that teachers perceived positive changes in children's problem behaviors compared to children in the waitlist control group and concluded that kinder training may be an effective treatment for young children exhibiting a downward trend in their problematic behavior.

Edwards, Varjas, White, and Stokes (2009) utilized a qualitative approach to examine the acceptability, integrity, and perceived effectiveness of kinder training for a group of elementary school teachers. In addition to utilizing transcribed and analyzed teacher consultation sessions, the researchers conducted in-depth pre and post-intervention interviews with five teachers who participated in kinder training. The teachers reported improved classroom management skills, student classroom behavior, and teacher-child relationships. Additionally, the teachers not only demonstrated an understanding of the training content, such as tracking, empathy, encouragement, and limit-setting, but also reported a positive view of the training structure. Teachers perceived kinder training to be an effective training model and observed its positive impact on their communication skills, the quality of their teacher-student relationships, classroom management skills, and students' behaviors.

Chen (2015) utilized an experimental single-case methodology and a multiple baseline across subjects design to investigate the impact of kinder training on early elementary children's on-task behavior. Three elementary school teacher participants conducted weekly individual play sessions with two preschool students and one first grade student who were identified as frequently exhibiting off-task behavior. The child participants' on-task behavior was repeatedly assessed using the Direct Observation Form (DOF; McConaughy & Achenbach, 2009) throughout the baseline and intervention phases. Results demonstrated that all child participants showed improvement in on-task classroom behavior. Visual analysis revealed that all child participants demonstrated a positive change in on-task behavior during the intervention phase. All teacher participants reported observing improvement in the child participants' on-task behavior and teacher-child relationships. Teachers' post-intervention reports supported the notion of reciprocal interactions among teacher-child relationships, understanding of children's lifestyle and goals of misbehavior, and children's on-task behavior.

The kinder training studies conducted to date demonstrated increases in teachers' facilitative statements, encouragement, and effective limit-setting (Draper et al., 2001; White et al., 1999), improved confidence in teaching (Solis, 2005), and awareness of children's needs (Solis, 2005). Students also improved their social skills, enhanced their self-esteem, reduced their problem behaviors (Draper et al., 2001; Edwards et al., 2009; White et al., 1997, 1999), and increased their on-task behavior (Chen, 2015). Consequently, kinder training appears to be a play-based teacher intervention model that systematically addresses teacher-child relationships, children's cognitive and social development, children's lifestyle, children's social-emotional and behavioral issues, as well as teachers' classroom management skills.

Strengths and Challenges in Kinder Training Implementation

Kinder training provides counselors flexibility to adapt the model to various formats. In addition to conducting a 2-day training, counselors may choose to provide teachers with individual training or a single day of training. This may lessen both counselors and teachers' time commitment. Regarding the accessibility, kinder training has been successfully conducted with preschool children and early elementary school children. The authors consider it necessary for counselors to build rapport with school personnel and administrators to maximize support during the training. Given that kinder training is based on the philosophy of Individual Psychology, the authors also recommend that counselors understand and practice the tenets of Individual Psychology so that they are be better positioned to help teachers gain an understanding of children from an Adlerian perspective, and apply play therapy skills and language accordingly.

Given that the ultimate goal of kinder training is to help teachers generalize the learned techniques, counselors are expected to assist teachers in transferring kinder training language and skills to the classroom context through in-class modeling. In addition, during weekly supervision counselors continue to provide consultation and help teachers make modifications as necessary.

Child-Teacher Relationship Training (CTRT)

Bratton, Morrison, and Ray adapted kinder training, and incorporated child-centered play therapy principles and procedures of the 10-session model of child-parent relationship therapy (CPRT; Bratton, Landreth, Kellam, & Blackard, 2006) to develop child-teacher relationship training (CTRT). Moreover, Landreth (2002) argued that CTRT may be an effective intervention model for increasing the quality of the teacher-child relationship and decreasing behavioral problems of children. Since its development, various research findings have indicated the effectiveness of CTRT (Gonzales, 2012; Helker & Ray, 2009; Morrison & Bratton, 2011; Pronchenko-Jain, 2012; Sepulveda, Garza, & Morrison, 2011).

Goals and Structure of CTRT

The goal of CTRT is to help teachers establish positive relationships with students and reduce children's emotional and behavioral challenges (Helker & Ray, 2009; Morrison & Bratton, 2011; Sepulveda, Garza, & Morrison, 2011). CTRT is divided into two phases based on the classroom setting, school schedule, and teacher in-service training schedule (Helker & Ray, 2009). The first phase of treatment consists of an intensive 2.5 day training session conducted by a CTRT trained therapist. The counselor trains teachers to demonstrate child-centered play therapy skills, such as reflective listening, reflection of child's feelings, therapeutic limit setting, facilitating creativity/spontaneity, facilitating decision making, returning responsibility, and structuring weekly play sessions (Helker & Ray, 2009). During CTRT Phase I, teachers choose a child of focus from their classrooms based on teachers' concerns of children's emotional or behavioral challenges, and conduct seven weekly 30-minute videotaped play sessions (Helker & Ray, 2009). Teachers then participate in a weekly supervision group led by CTRT therapists to discuss the videotaped play sessions and the training content. During this phase, therapists introduce teachers to the facilitation of encouragement and self-esteem building responses. At the end of the seven weeks of play sessions and training/supervision, teachers begin the second phase of training (Helker & Ray, 2009).

Phase II lasts for 10 weeks with an emphasis on generalizing CTRT skills to the classroom environment. In this phase, teachers conduct child teacher relationship time (CTR Time) three times per week. This involves a 30-minute time slot, three times a week based on teachers' daily schedules. CTR time usually involves children's participation in small groups during center time or other unstructured classroom period. The CTRT therapists initially model the use of CTRT skills with a small group of children in the classroom. Gradually, the teachers play a more active role and the CTRT therapists provide coaching that enables teachers to continue practicing CTRT skills with different groups of children so that teachers can build relationships with all children in their classroom. Teachers and CTRT therapists continue weekly training and supervision groups over the course of CTRT Phase II to discuss challenges of implementing CTRT skills with small groups of children in the classroom (Helker & Ray, 2009).

Research Support for CTRT

Helker and Ray (2009) and in a companion study, Morrison and Bratton (2010) conducted preliminary studies of CTRT with the Head Start population. Helker and Ray (2009) examined the effectiveness of CTRT on 12 teachers' and classroom aides' use of relationship-building skills in their classrooms and on 19 students' classroom behaviors. The results showed that teachers learned and maintained CTRT skills through Phase III. Children who scored in the borderline or clinical range on at least one syndrome scale on the Caregiver-Teacher Report Form (C-TRF; Achenbach & Rescorla, 2000) demonstrated improvement in their externalizing problems after participating in CTRT; moreover, children's decreases in externalizing problems correlated with teachers' frequent use of relationship-building skills.

In a companion study, Morrison and Bratton (2010) examined the effect of CTRT on 11 children scoring in the borderline or clinical range on at least one syndrome scale on the C-TRF prior to the intervention. The researchers found that children who participated in CTRT demonstrated improvements in their externalizing behavior problems and total problems. The results showed CTRT to be an effective teacher-intervention model with the Head Start population (Morrison & Bratton, 2010).

Sepulveda, Garza, and Morrison (2011) conducted a qualitative study to explore 10 Head Start teachers' perceptions of participating in CTRT after completion of Phase I and II. Overall teachers had a positive experience with CTRT and perceived a strengthened relationship with their children of focus as well as improvements in the children's behaviors. In addition, teachers reported feeling increased confidence with classroom management.

Gonzales (2012) conducted an exploratory study to examine the effectiveness of CTRT with 20 Head Start at-risk preschool children exhibiting disruptive behavior. The results showed that children whose teachers received the CTRT intervention demonstrated a statistically significant decrease in externalizing behavior on the Caregiver-Teacher Report Form (C-TRF) and total problems on the Direct Observation Form (DOF) from pre- to mid- to post-test. The results indicated that CTRT was an effective intervention for at-risk preschool children exhibiting disruptive classroom behavior (Gonzales, 2012). Gonzales further suggested that CTRT may serve as an early mental health intervention for at-risk populations.

To explore the impact of CTRT on teacher's ability to provide students emotional support in the classroom, teachers' use of relationship-building skills, and teachers' level of stress, Pronchenko-Jain (2012) conducted CTRT with 11 Head Start teachers/ aides and 8 children. The results revealed that CTRT demonstrated large effects over time on the Classroom Assessment Scoring System (CLASS) and the Child Teacher Relationship Skills Checklist (CTRT-SC). The findings provided support for CTRT as an effective intervention for increasing teachers' ability to provide at-risk students emotional and relational support in the classroom (Pronchenko-Jain, 2012).

The CTRT studies conducted to date demonstrated increases in teachers' emotional support toward students (Pronchenko-Jain, 2012), improved confidence in classroom management, and reduced teaching stress (Pronchenko-Jain, 2012; Sepulveda et al., 2011). Students also decreased their problem behaviors (Gonzales, 2012; Helker & Ray, 2009; Morrison & Bratton, 2010). As a result, CTRT seems to be a play-based teacher intervention model that focuses on improvement in teacher-child relationships and enhancing students' emotional and behavioral issues.

Strengths and Challenges in CTRT Implementation

CTRT requires counselors and teachers to dedicate a significant time commitment and allow for flexibility in classroom schedules. A lack of an alternative training format may limit the implementation of CTRT in elementary schools that do not have the classroom structure and teaching aide support that often exists in early learning academies and pre-school settings. Hence, the authors suggest that counselors establish relationships with school personnel and administrators to receive additional support. It is also essential for counselors to collaborate with teachers to schedule the training, CTR time, and weekly supervision. Similarly to Kinder Training, one of the strengths of CTRT is that counselors have opportunities to enter the classroom and model the skills in a group setting which can support teachers in generalizing the skills from the playroom to the classroom environment. It also appears to help teachers effectively increase their classroom management skills as they receive counselors' immediate support and feedback.

CTRT demonstrates a unique component in its supervision model. Unlike other training models, CTRT uses a group supervision format for teachers to process their play sessions with students and facilitate group learning. However, counselors might feel challenged to address each teacher's specific needs, and teachers may have difficulty scheduling group supervision time around their other teaching responsibilities. Counselors have successfully implemented CTRT in early childhood centers and early elementary schools (Gonzales, 2012; Helker & Ray, 2009; Morrison & Bratton, 2010; Pronchenko-Jain, 2012; Sepulveda et al., 2011) because of the teaching aide support that these schools provide. Additionally, counselors implementing CTRT require an understanding of child-centered play therapy philosophy, non-directive play therapy skills and language, and a belief that the relationship is a necessary and essential factor for children's growth.

Relationship Enhancement for Learner and Teacher (RELATe)

Similar to CTRT, relationship enhancement for learner and teacher (RELATe) therapy is an adaptation of Landreth's (2002) 10-week CPRT model. It engages the principles of child-centered play therapy to train elementary school teachers.

Goals and Structure of RELATe

The primary goal of RELATe is to facilitate improvements in teachers' interpersonal skills in order to strengthen their relationships with children. RELATe training takes place in a 3-6 hour class consisting of lectures, video demonstration, role-play, and live practice with children. Play therapists train teachers in basic child-centered play therapy skills, including tracking, reflection of feelings, returning responsibility, limit setting, and choice giving (Ray et al., 2004).

As part of conducting RELATe training, and based on teachers' concerns for children's emotional or behavioral difficulties, teachers conduct weekly 20-minute play sessions with a child of focus. After each play session, RELATe therapists provide approximately 10 minutes of feedback to teachers as they discuss play session progress. The teachers may select a time that accommodates their teaching schedule and is least disruptive to the child's schedule (i.e., not during lunchtime, recess, or a critical academic instruction time). Ray et al., (2004) found that most teachers seemed to prefer to use a portion of their lesson preparation hour for training. As a result, Ray and colleagues decreased the educational training time of RELATe to incorporate one-on-one live supervision and suggested that training can be implemented by a single school counselor to increase applicability to elementary schools.

Research Support for RELATe

Ray et al. (2004) conducted a pilot study to examine the effectiveness of RELATe using volunteer teachers. They found that teachers considered the model beneficial and rewarding for them and the children of focus. The teacher participants reported gaining an awareness of the differences in their teaching and communication styles and becoming more nondirective when interacting with children. Teachers reported increases in their self-awareness, the development of new perceptions of children, and their sensitivity to children.

Carlson (2011) conducted a single-case design study to examine the effectiveness of RELATe on elementary school teachers' interpersonal skills and their relationships with students in their classroom. Participants included eight teachers. The results demonstrated overall positive effects; 5 out of 8 teachers showed increases in responsiveness and all teachers decreased their level of criticism. In addition, 5 out 8 teachers indicated positive changes in teacher-child relationships.

Strengths and Challenges in RELATe Implementation

RELATe is a relatively time efficient training model. Because RELATe aims to increase its applicability to elementary schools, the training period is comparatively shorter. However, it can be applied to early childhood centers as well. One of the strengths of RELATe is its flexibility in terms of training time and individual supervision that may increase teachers' willingness to participate in the training and practice play therapy skills with the target child. Counselors do not conduct in-class modeling of play therapy skills and language in the classroom setting. Thus, they need to heavily rely on teachers' motivation to gradually transition from working with one child to utilizing the play therapy language and skills with all children in the classroom. Given that RELATs is adapted from CTRT, the authors suggest that counselors be familiar with the child-centered play therapy philosophical underpinnings. It is also critical for counselors to believe that strengthening the teacher-child relationship is key to children's learning and growth.

Teacher-Child Relationship Building (TCRB)

Teacher-child relationship building (TCRB) is a play-based professional development model adapted from kinder training (White et al., 1997) and filial therapy (Guerney, 1964) with a goal to use teacher-child relationships to promote teachers' and children's positive outcomes (Lindo et al., 2014). TCRB is designed to strengthen teacher-child relationships, improve students' behaviors, enhance students' academic involvement, and develop teachers' classroom management skills (Lindo et al., 2014).

Goals and Structure of TCRB

TCRB includes two major training modules of play session training and supervision and classroom training. The primary goal for the first module is to help the teacher develop a relationship with an identified student through practicing child-centered play therapy skills. During the second module, the counselor then helps the teacher transfer child-centered play therapy skills into the classroom. The second module is designed to assist teachers' development of a healthy classroom climate, improvement in all teacher-student relationships, and development of classroom management skills.

During the first module, trainers conduct a 2-day in-service training that involves lecture, group discussion, videotapes, and role-plays. Teachers learn basic child-centered play therapy skills and child development concepts. The specific child-centered play therapy skills include tracking/acknowledging child's nonverbal language, reflection of feelings and content, facilitating decision-making, returning responsibility, self-esteem building, and therapeutic limit setting. The child development components include age-specific typical play and classroom behaviors. After the 2-day training, teachers conduct four weekly 30-minute play sessions with identified children. Trainers then provide approximately 15 minutes of weekly supervision to discuss feedback regarding the teachers' skill demonstration and personal awareness and help teachers make connections between children's playroom and classroom behaviors.

During the second module, trainers provide four weekly classroom training sessions during a 30-minute informal instruction period. During this time, the trainers model the application of child-centered play therapy skills in the classroom, and teachers receive opportunities to practice child-centered play therapy skills in classroom situations under their trainer's direct supervision.

Research Support for TCRB

Lindo et al. (2014) conducted a phenomenological study with 18 early education teachers exploring their perceptions of the initial implementation of TCRB. They examined acceptability and perceived effectiveness as well as teachers' perceptions of the content and structure of the TCRB model. Teachers considered TCRB informative, well organized, and structured (Lindo et al., 2014). Teachers also believed TCRB was effective in enhancing teacher-child relationships, developing classroom management skills, and reducing children's behavioral problems (Lindo et al., 2014).

Strengths and Challenges in TCRB Implementation

TCRB is a newly developed play-based professional development training model that adapts the kinder training format and is based on the philosophy of child-centered play therapy. The strengths of TCRB include its one-on-one supervision that can ensure teachers' unique needs are met. Teachers also have opportunities to observe how counselors apply play therapy skills and language during instruction time, and to practice these skills under counselors' live supervision in order to improve their classroom management skills. Unlike other training models, TCRB includes child development resources adapted to meet the needs of the specific grade level of the teacher participants. The TCRB structure appears comprehensive and less of a time commitment; however, to date, there has only been one research study conducted in an early learning academy. Lindo et al. (2014) suggested making changes to the training format in order to accommodate the unique structure of elementary schools where teaching aide support may be limited. Participants in the pilot study indicated the desire for additional play sessions with their children of focus in order to further develop the teacher-child relationship. Thus, the authors recommend that counselors consider increasing the number of play sessions based on teachers' time and schedules.

The above overview presented examples of play-based professional development training models designed for implementation with children by teachers in early childhood centers or elementary schools. Kinder training aligns with the Adlerian principles of egalitarian relationships, the art of encouragement, children's mistaken goals of behavior, logical consequences, and social interest. Kinder training fosters a holistic understanding of children as part of facilitating change. CTRT, RELATe, and TCRB incorporate child-centered play therapy principles with an emphasis on understanding children's feelings, experience, and needs through play behavior and using the teacher-child relationship as the therapeutic factor in promoting children's healthy development. Because of the similarities and differences among these models, it is important for school counselors or other mental health professionals to determine which model would be most appropriate and effective for implementing in specific school settings (see Table 1).

CONCLUSION

The number of young children exhibiting behavioral problems has significantly increased in recent years (Powell, Dunlap, & Fox, 2006). Behavioral challenges not only reduce children's engagement in learning (Lane, Wehby, & Cooley, 2006; Luiselli, Putnam, Handler, & Feinbergl, 2005) but also increase teaching stress and cause strained teacher-child relationships (White et al., 2000; Ray, 2007). Thus, children's challenging classroom behavior has become one of the most common reasons for teachers' referrals to school counselors (Roberts, 2011). Research indicated that teachers who lack training in effectively at-

Table 1. Comparison of four play-based professional development training models

	Kinder Training	Child-Teacher Relationship Training (CTRT)	Relationship Enhancement for Learner and Teacher (RELATe)	Teacher-Child Relationship Building (TCRB)
Theoretical Orientation	Non-directive play therapy with Adlerian principles	Child-centered play therapy	Child-centered play therapy	Child-centered play therapy
Training Structure	2-day in-service training with six weekly 30-minute play sessions, in-class modeling, and follow-up sessions.	Phase I: 10 weeks with seven weekly 30-minute individual play sessions Phase II: 10 weeks of three weekly 30-minute, child teacher relationship (CTR) classroom sessions	3-6 training hours with weekly 20-minute individual play sessions	Module 1: 2-day in-service training with four weekly 30-minute play sessions Module 2: four weekly 30-minute classroom training sessions
Training Content	Basic non-directive play therapy skills, child development, and Adlerian principles	Basic child-centered play therapy skills	Basic child-centered play therapy skills	Basic child-centered play therapy skills and child development
Supervision of Teachers	Weekly 20-minute individual supervision	Weekly 1-hour group supervision	Weekly 10-minute individual supervision	Weekly 15-minute individual supervision
Ideal School Setting	Preschool and early elementary school	Preschool	Preschool and elementary school	Preschool and early elementary school

tending to children's emotional and behavioral needs may negatively respond to children's behavior and unintentionally exacerbate children's emotional disturbance and problem behaviors (Gonzales, 2012). Given the benefits of using play as a modality for promoting children's socio-emotional development in schools, several play-based teacher intervention training models have been developed to help teachers improve their relationships with students and learn to communicate and effectively respond to students' needs.

Although research on humanistic play-based professional development training models has been limited, the available studies all provide support for the models' effectiveness with children's social-emotional and behavioral problems, as well as academic engagement. Additionally, each play-based professional development model possesses unique strengths and challenges related to implementation in the school setting. Hence, it appears important for mental health professionals or school counselors to consider the feasibility of program implementation, the particular needs of teachers and children, and the counselors' theoretical orientations. The presented models help teachers learn basic play therapy skills and language and understand how to communicate with children in a developmentally appropriate way. Most importantly, teachers learn how to strengthen their relationships with children and effectively respond to their emotional and behavioral needs through therapeutic skills.

REFERENCES

Adelman, H. S., & Taylor, L. (2012). Mental health in schools: Moving in new directions. *Contemporary School Psychology*, *16*, 9–18.

Andronico, M., & Guerney, B. G. Jr. (1967). The potential application of filial therapy to the school situation. *Journal of School Psychology*, *6*(1), 2–7. doi:10.1016/0022-4405(67)90057-X

Bach, A. (1968). *Pupil discovery training: The application of filial therapy to teacher-student relationship*. Washington, DC: U.S. Department of Health, Education, and Welfare, Office of Education.

Baker, J. (2006). Contributions of teacher-child relationships to positive school adjustment during elementary school. *Journal of School Psychology*, *44*(3), 211–229. doi:10.1016/j.jsp.2006.02.002

Bennett, M. O., & Bratton, S. C. (2011). The effects of child teacher relationship training on children of focus: A pilot study. *International Journal of Play*, *20*(4), 193–207. doi:10.1037/a0025833

Birch, S. H., & Ladd, G. W. (1997). The teacher-child relationship and childrens early school adjustment. *Journal of School Psychology*, *35*(1), 61–79. doi:10.1016/S0022-4405(96)00029-5

Birch, S. H., & Ladd, G. W. (1998). Childrens interpersonal behaviors and the teacher-child relationship. *Developmental Psychology*, *34*(5), 934–946. doi:10.1037/0012-1649.34.5.934 PMID:9779740

Bratton, S. C. (2010). Meeting the early mental health needs of children through school-based play therapy. In A. A. Drewes & C. E. Schaefer (Eds.), *School-based play therapy* (2nd ed.; pp. 17–58). Hoboken, NJ: John Wiley & Sons, Inc.

Bratton, S. C., Ray, D., Rhine, T., & Jones, L. (2005). The efficacy of play therapy with children: A meta-analysis review of treatment outcomes. *Professional Psychology, Research and Practice*, *36*(4), 376–390. doi:10.1037/0735-7028.36.4.376

Carlson, J., Dinkmeyer, D., & Johnson, E. (2008). Adlerian teacher consultation: Change teachers, change students! *Journal of Individual Psychology*, *64*(4), 480–493.

Carlson, J., Watts, R. E., & Maniacci, M. (2006). *Adlerian therapy: Theory and practice*. Washington, DC: American Psychological Association. doi:10.1037/11363-000

Carlson, S. E. (2011). *Effects of a Play-Based Teacher Consultation (PBTC) Program on Interpersonal Skills of Elementary School Teachers in the Classroom* (Doctoral dissertation). Retrieved from http://libproxy.library.unt.edu:2279/

Center for the Study of Social Policy. (2012). *Results-based public policy strategies for promoting children's social, emotional, and behavioral health.* Retrieved from http://www.cssp.org/policy/papers/Promote-Childrens-Social-Emotional-and-Behavioral-Health.pdf

Centers for Decease Control and Prevention, National Center for Health Statistics, National Health Interview Survey. (2015). *Mental health.* Retrieved from http://www.cdc.gov/nchs/data/hus/2015/035.pdf

Coufal, J. D., & Brock, G. W. (1979). Parent child relationship enhancement: A skills training approach. In N. Stinnett, B. Chesser, & J. DeFrain (Eds.), *Building family strengths: Blueprints for action* (Vol. 1, pp. 196–221). Lincoln, NE: University of Nebraska Press.

Decker, D. M., Dona, D. P., & Christenson, S. L. (2007). Behaviorally at-risk African American students: The importance of student-teacher relationships for student outcomes. *Journal of School Psychology*, *45*(1), 83–109. doi:10.1016/j.jsp.2006.09.004

Dinkmeyer, D. C. Jr, & Carlson, J. (2006). *Consultation: Creating school-based interventions* (3rd ed.). New York, NY: Routledge.

Dobbs, J., & Arnold, D. H. (2009). Relationship between preschool teachers reports of childrens behavior and their behavior toward those children. *School Psychology Quarterly*, *24*(2), 95–105. doi:10.1037/a0016157 PMID:20431714

Draper, K., Siegel, C., White, J., Solis, C. M., & Mishna, F. (2009). Preschoolers, parents, and teachers (PPT): A preventive intervention with and at risk population. *International Journal of Group Psychotherapy*, *59*(2), 221–242. doi:10.1521/ijgp.2009.59.2.221 PMID:19441968

Draper, K., White, J., OShaughnessy, T. E., Flynt, M., & Jones, N. (2001). Kinder training: Play-based consultation to improve the school adjustment of discouraged kindergarten and first grade students. *International Journal of Play Therapy*, *10*(1), 1–30. doi:10.1037/h0089441

Edwards, N. A., Varjas, K. M., White, J. F., & Stokes, S. A. (2009). Teachers perceptions of kinder training: Acceptability, integrity, and effectiveness. *International Journal of Play Therapy*, *18*(3), 129–146. doi:10.1037/a0015170

Galassi, J., Griffin, D., & Akos, P. (2008). Strengthen-based school counseling and the ASCA National Model. *Professional School Counseling*, *12*(2), 176–181. doi:10.5330/PSC.n.2010-12.176

Garner, P. W., & Waajid, B. (2008). The associations of emotions knowledge and teacher-child relationships to preschool childrens school-related developmental competence. *Journal of Applied Developmental Psychology*, *29*(2), 89–100. doi:10.1016/j.appdev.2007.12.001

Gonzales, T. L. (2012). *Child teacher relationship training as a Head Start early mental health intervention for children exhibiting disruptive behavior* (Doctoral dissertation). Retrieved from http://digital.library.unt.edu/ark:/67531/metadc149553/

Guerney, B. Jr. (1964). Filial therapy: Description and rationale. *Journal of Counseling Psychology*, *28*, 304–310. PMID:14198792

Guerney, B., & Flumen, A. B. (1970). Teachers as psychotherapeutic agents for withdrawn children. *Journal of School Psychology*, *8*(2), 107–113. doi:10.1016/0022-4405(70)90029-4

Guerney, B. G., & Stover, L. (1971). *Filial therapy: Final report to NIMH, Grant 1826401*. University Park, PA: The Pennsylvania State University.

Guerney, L. G. (2000). Filial therapy into the 21st century. *International Journal of Play Therapy*, *9*(2), 1–17. doi:10.1037/h0089433

Hamre, B. K., & Pianta, R. C. (2001). Early teacher-child relationships and the trajectory of childrens school outcomes through eighth grade. *Child Development*, *72*(2), 625–638. doi:10.1111/1467-8624.00301 PMID:11333089

Hamre, B. K., & Pianta, R. C. (2006). Can instructional and emotional support in the first-grade classroom make a difference for children at risk of school failure. *Child Development*, *76*(5), 949–967. doi:10.1111/j.1467-8624.2005.00889.x PMID:16149994

Helker, W. P., & Ray, D. C. (2009). The impact of child teacher relationship training on teachers and aides use of relationship-building skills and the effect on student classroom behavior. *International Journal of Play Therapy*, *18*(2), 70–83. doi:10.1037/a0014456

Howes, C. (2000). Social-emotional classroom climate in child care, child-teacher relationships, and childrens second grade peer relations. *Social Development*, *9*(2), 191–204. doi:10.1111/1467-9507.00119

Howes, C., Burchinal, M., Pianta, R., Bryant, D., Clifford, R., & Barbarin, O. (2008). Ready to learn? Childrens pre-academic achievement in pre-Kindergarten programs. *Early Childhood Research Quarterly*, *23*(1), 27–50. doi:10.1016/j.ecresq.2007.05.002

Janson, G. R., & King, M. A. (2006). Emotional security in the classroom: What works for young children. *Journal of Family and Consumer Sciences*, *98*(2), 70–74.

Kottman, T. (2003). *Partners in play: An Adlerian approach to play therapy* (2nd ed.). Alexandra, VA: American Counseling Association.

Ladd, G., & Burgess, K. (2001). Do relational risks and protective factors moderate the linkages between childhood aggression and early psychological and school adjustment? *Child Development*, *72*(5), 1579–1601. doi:10.1111/1467-8624.00366 PMID:11699688

Landreth, G. L. (2012). *Play therapy: The art of the relationship* (3rd ed.). New York, NY: Brunner-Routledge.

Landreth, G. L., & Bratton, S. C. (2006). *Child-parent relationship therapy: A 10-week filial therapy model*. Springfield, IL: Thomas Books.

Lane, K. L., Wehby, J. H., & Cooley, C. (2006). Teacher expectations of students classroom behavior across the grade span: Which social skills are necessary for success. *Exceptional Children*, *72*(2), 153–167. doi:10.1177/001440290607200202

Lindo, N. A., Dillman Taylor, D., Meany-Walen, K. K., Purswell, K., Jayne, K., Gonzales, T., & Jones, L. (2014). Teachers as therapeutic agents: Perceptions of a school-based mental health initiative. *British Journal of Guidance & Counselling*, *42*(3), 284–296. doi:10.1080/03069885.2014.896452

Luiselli, J. K., Putnam, R. F., Handler, M. W., & Feinberg, A. B. (2005). Whole-school positive behaviours support: Effects on student discipline problems and academic performance. *Educational Psychology*, *25*(2-3), 183–198. doi:10.1080/0144341042000301265

McConaughy, S. H., & Achenbach, T. M. (2009). *Manual for the ASEBA direct observation form*. Burlington, VT: University of Vermont, Research Center for Children, Youth, & Families.

Myers, S. S., & Pianta, R. C. (2008). Development commentary: Individual and contextual influences on student-teacher relationships and childrens early problem behaviors. *Journal of Clinical Child and Adolescent Psychology*, *17*(3), 600–608. doi:10.1080/15374410802148160 PMID:18645750

New Freedom Commission on Mental Health. (2003). *Achieving the promise: Transforming mental health care in America. Final report (DHHS Pub. No. SMA-03-3832)*. Rockville, MD: Department of Health and Human Services.

OConnor, E., & McCartney, K. (2007). Examining teacher-child relationships and achievement as part of an ecological model of development. *American Educational Research Journal*, *44*(2), 340–369. doi:10.3102/0002831207302172

Oxman, L. (1972). *The effectiveness of filial therapy: A controlled study* (Doctoral dissertation). *Dissertation Abstracts International*, *31B*(11), 6656.

Patrick, H., Ryan, A. M., & Kaplan, A. (2007). Early adolescents perceptions of the classroom social environment, motivational beliefs, and engagement. *Journal of Educational Psychology*, *99*(1), 83–98. doi:10.1037/0022-0663.99.1.83

Perry, B. D. (2001). Attachment: The first core strength. *Early Childhood Today*, *16*, 28–30.

Piaget, J. (1962). *Play, dreams, and imitation in childhood*. New York, NY: Rutledge.

Pianta, R. C. (1999). *Enhancing relationships between children and teachers*. Washington, DC: American Psychological Association. doi:10.1037/10314-000

Pianta, R. C., La Paro, K. M., Payne, C., Cox, M. L., & Bradley, R. (2002). The relation of kindergarten classroom environment to teacher, family, and school characteristics and child outcomes. *The Elementary School Journal*, *102*(3), 225–238. doi:10.1086/499701

Pianta, R. C., & Stuhlman, M. W. (2004). Teacher-child relationships and children's success in the first years of school. *School Psychology Review*, *33*(3), 444–458.

Powell, D., Dunlap, G., & Fox, L. (2006). Prevention and intervention for the challenging behaviors of toddlers and preschoolers. *Infants and Young Children*, *19*(1), 25–35. doi:10.1097/00001163-200601000-00004

Pronchenko-Jain, Y. (2012). *Child teacher relationship training (CTRT) with children exhibiting disruptive behavior: Effects on teacher's ability to provide emotional and relational support to students and on student-teacher relationship stress* (Doctoral dissertation). Retrieved from http://libproxy.library.unt.edu:2279/ark:/67531/metadc149655/

Ray, D. (2007). Two counseling interventions to reduce teacher-child relationship stress. *Professional School Counseling*, *10*(4), 428–440. doi:10.5330/prsc.10.4.x340302242715705

Ray, D. (2011). *Advanced play therapy: Essential conditions, knowledge, and skills for child practice*. New York, NY: Routledge.

Ray, D., Muro, J., & Schumann, B. (2004). Implementing play therapy in the schools: Lessons learned. *International Journal of Play Therapy*, *13*(1), 79–100. doi:10.1037/h0088886

Rimm-Kaufman, S. (2011). Improving students' relationships with teachers to provide essential supports for learning. Washington, DC: American Psychological Association. Retrieved from http://www.apa.org/education/k12/relationships.aspx

Roberts, M. (2011). *Off-task behavior in the classroom: Applying FBA and CBM: NASP toolkit*. Retrieved from http://www.nasponline.org/communications/spawareness/Off-Task%20Behavior.pdf

Schaefer, C., & Drewes, A. (2009). The therapeutic powers of play and play therapy. In A. Drewes (Ed.), *Blending play therapy with cognitive behavioral therapy: Evidence-based and other effective treatment and techniques* (pp. 3–15). Hoboken, NJ: Wiley.

Schaefer, C. E. (1993). What is play and why is it therapeutic? In C. E. Schaefer (Ed.), *The therapeutic power of play* (pp. 1–15). New York, NY: Aronson.

Sepulveda, C., Garza, Y., & Morrison, M. O. (2011). Child teacher relationship training: A phenomenological study. *International Journal of Play Therapy*, *20*(1), 12–25. doi:10.1037/a0021938

Solis, C. (2005). Implementing kinder training as a preventive intervention: African American preschool teacher perceptions of the process, effectiveness, and acceptability (Doctoral dissertation). *Dissertation Abstracts International*, *66B*, 2488.

Stover, L., & Guerney, B. G. (1967). The efficacy of training procedures from mothers in filial therapy. *Psychotherapy (Chicago, Ill.)*, *4*(3), 110–115. doi:10.1037/h0087950

Stulmaker, H. (2013). Counseling-based teacher interventions: Defining, exploring, and differentiating. *International Journal of Play Therapy*, *22*(1), 2–12. doi:10.1037/a0030195

Vygotsky, L. (1966). Play and its role in the mental development of the child. *Voprosy Psihologii*, *12*, 6–18.

White, J., Draper, K., Flynt, M., & Jones, N. P. (2000). *Kinder training: Play-based teacher consultation to promote the adjustment and achievement of discouraged students*. Norcross, GA: KidChoice.

White, J., Flynt, M., & Draper, K. (1997). Kinder therapy: Teachers as therapeutic agents. *International Journal of Play Therapy*, *6*(2), 33–49. doi:10.1037/h0089407

White, J., Flynt, M., & Jones, N. P. (1999). Kinder therapy: An Adlerian approach for training teachers to be therapeutic agents through play. *Journal of Individual Psychology*, *55*(3), 365–382.

Wilson, K., & Ryan, V. (2005). *Play therapy: A non-directive approach for children and adolescents* (2nd ed.). Oxford, UK: Elsevier.

Yost, D. S., & Mosca, F. J. (2002). Beyond behavior strategies: Using reflection to manage youth in crisis. *ERIC Clearinghouse*, *75*, 264–268.

KEY TERMS AND DEFINITIONS

Child-Centered Play Therapy: A nondirective approach working with children that is consistent with person-centered principles. Children express and explore themselves for optimal growth and development through play. Counselors believe therapist-child relationship is the primary healing factor for children's change.

Child-Teacher Relationship Training: A play-based professional training model that incorporates child-centered play therapy principles and techniques and follows the procedures of the 10-session model of child-parent relationship therapy. CTRT aims to help teachers build positive relationships with children and decrease children's emotional and behavioral difficulties.

Filial Therapy: A play-based counseling intervention based on the principles and philosophies of child-centered play therapy. Counselors train parents in basic play therapy skills and apply them with their children. The goals include helping parents improve the parent-child relationship and understand children's need, and helping children communicate their needs, feelings, and thoughts.

Humanistic Play Therapy: Nondirective play therapy interventions.

Kinder Training: A play-based professional training model that counselors train teachers to utilize nondirective play therapy techniques and Adlerian principles with a child in a play setting. Kinder Training systematically addresses teacher-child relationships, children's social-emotional and academic development, children's lifestyle, and teachers' classroom management skills.

Play-Based Professional Development Training: Counselors train teachers in basic play therapy skills and involve teachers directly in the therapeutic intervention. Counselors assist teachers in using play as modality to strengthen teacher-child relationships, gain understanding of children's needs, and promote children's social-emotional and academic growth.

Relationship Enhancement for Learner and Teacher: A play-based professional training model adapted from Child-Teacher Relationship Training. Counselors train teachers in basic child-centered play therapy skills and enhance teacher-child relationships through facilitating improvements in teachers' interpersonal skills.

Teacher-Child Relationship Building: A play-based professional development model adapted from kinder training and filial therapy. Counselors train teachers in basic child-centered play therapy skills and child development concepts with a goal to use teacher-child relationships to promote teachers' and children's positive outcomes.

Chapter 17
Play and Speech Therapy in Schools:
Toward a Model of Interprofessional Collaborative Practice

Suzan E. Weishof
International School of Hamburg, Germany

ABSTRACT

Research over the past eight decades has demonstrated strong correlations between the development of play and the development of language in young children. Play and speech therapists share a common child-centered, play-based approach to therapeutic interventions. The growing trend of service delivery within the school setting, along with professional ethical requirements, has led to the necessity of play therapists, speech therapists, teachers, and parents to work collaboratively in promoting holistic, comprehensive intervention plans that serve children's best interests. Based on the healthcare field's model of interprofessional collaborative practice, the purpose of this chapter is to define areas of common practice among speech and play therapists and to propose a model of interprofessional collaborative practice within a school-based context.

THE CONNECTION BETWEEN PLAY AND LANGUAGE DEVELOPMENT

The child does not, in the first instance, communicate with his fellow beings in order to share thoughts and reflections; he does so in order to play. (Jean Piaget, 1959, p. 27)

The substantial body of research in the field of play and language has firmly established an incontrovertible connection between play and the acquisition of language in children's development. As early as 1933, Vygotsky described symbolic play as the critical "pivot" that allows children to develop symbolic speech. Martin (1981, p. 49) described play as "an essential precursor to language," and Formaad (1974, p. xii) posited that "play is powerfully at work in the growth process of the child and is related most closely to the motivation and exercise of speech." Since the 1970s, the substantial body of research

DOI: 10.4018/978-1-5225-2224-9.ch017

outcomes derived from both the play therapy and speech and language pathology fields has highlighted the relationship of symbolic play to children's acquisition of receptive and expressive language, and how these two areas of child development appear to be inextricably intertwined.

Both play and language are symbolic in nature; in play, a child uses one object to represent another (a stick becomes a car), and in language, sounds and words represent internal meanings relating to the real world. McCune (1995, p.198) described this burgeoning cognitive function of the child as *mental representation*—the "internal component that supports the expression of meaning in various modalities." Mental representation is the ability of the child to understand that an object (termed a *signifier*) can represent an object that is not present (the *signified*). In an example provided by Leslie (1987), a child's perception that "this is a banana" illustrates the normal representational system. However, when a child can "decouple" this perception from its literal meaning and make the cognitive leap to the pretend perception that "this banana is a telephone," one begins to see the observable behavior found in symbolic play. The development of a child's capacity for mental representation is theorized to be a direct contributor to both language acquisition as well as the development of symbolic play.

Play and language both advance through well-defined stages of ever-increasing complexity. Piaget (1962) outlined the seven levels of symbolic play development (beginning at approximately 16-20 months of age):

1. **Enactive Representation:** A child shows understanding through gesture (i.e., shaking the hand as if it is holding a rattle).
2. **Symbolic Schema:** A child pretends to engage in normal activities (i.e., using an empty cup to pretend he/she is drinking).
3. **Single Schema:** A child pretends an object engages in normal activities (i.e., covering a truck with a blanket and putting it "to sleep") or the child pretends to engage in normal activities of others or other objects (i.e., pretending to be a dog).
4. **Single Schema Combinations:** A child plays at only one action, but expands it to various objects or people (i.e., feeding dolls and stuffed animals).
5. **Multi-Schema Combinations:** A child plays at more than one action (i.e., feeding the stuffed dog, then brushing its hair, then putting it to sleep).
6. **Planned Single Schema Symbolic Play:** A child plans the play activity (level 4) in advance.
7. **Combinations with Planned Elements:** A child plans multi-schema play sequences that tend toward realistic scenes.

Bowen (1998) explained how Roger Brown's (1973) stages of syntactic and morphological development (expressive language) similarly delineates the sequence in which children learn and use grammatical structures (from approximately 15-52 months of age):

Stage 1: A child uses one or two words to express operations of reference (i.e., that car, birdie go) or semantic relations (i.e., push car, food hot).
Stage 2: A child uses the present progressive (i.e., she goi*ng*) and plurals (i.e., my block**s**).
Stage 3: A child uses the irregular past tense (i.e., me *fell* down) and possessives (i.e., doll**'s** hair).
Stage 4: A child uses articles (i.e., *a* dot on *the* dress), the regular past tense (i.e., he *jumped*), and the third person regular (i.e., the dog *eats* it).

Stage 5: A child uses the third person irregular (i.e., he *does*), uncontractible auxiliary (i.e., he was doing it, not me), contractible copula (i.e., they're happy), and contractible auxiliary (i.e., I'm hiding).

One of the leading authorities on play and language, McCune (1981, 1995, 2010) examined how the developmental stages of children's language acquisition coincided with Piaget's symbolic play stages, specifically noting the changes in a child's ability to form signifier-signified relationships between objects. Her findings led to the conclusion that children's symbolic play levels were a significant predictor of linguistic behavior. Three specific relationships illustrate this predictive effect: (a) the development of single-word utterances with the onset of Piaget's Level 2, (b) the development of multi-word utterances with the onset of Level 4, and (c) the development of syntax in language with the onset of Level 5-7. McCune (1995) carefully pointed out, however, that causal relationships were not implied, and reasserted that mental representation is the underlying cognitive structure supporting both the development of symbolic play and language.

Ample research evidence contributes to the contention that symbolic play may be considered a strong indicator of linguistic development in young children. With Westby's development of the Symbolic Play Scale in 1980, professionals working with children were provided a common tool with which to draw observational conclusions about the correlations between play and language development in a clinical setting. In the scale's initial use, Westby (1980) determined that no meaningful use of language fell above the corresponding symbolic play level. In a correlational study of 16 normally developing, 16 mentally retarded and 16 autistic children, Sigman and Ungerer (1984) concluded that none of the non-verbal children in the comparison groups demonstrated symbolic play at any level. In a review of the literature up until the mid-1980's, Pellegrini (1985) suggested that children who demonstrated more decontextualized play (Level 2) also demonstrated a higher incidence of elaborated noun phrases and use of past-tense/future-tense verbs.

Throughout the 1990's, correlational research studies that observed and recorded developments in the play behaviors of children provided further insights into the play-language connection, specifically the relationship between symbolic play and expressive language development. Rescorla and Goossens (1992) studied 20 children aged 2 years with specific language impairment and found that in comparison with children with typical language development, children with language impairment demonstrated significantly less sequencing and symbolism in their play. Similarly, Tamis-LeMonda and Bornstein (1994) conducted a study of 41 young children (13-20 months) and discovered that symbolic play was a significant predictor of a child's speech diversity (use of varied sentence structure and vocabulary). Scherer and D'Antonio (1997) reported that amongst six children born with a cleft palate, their mean length of utterance (MLU) significantly coincided with the length of their symbolic play sequences.

More recent studies with international populations have highlighted the predictive attributes of symbolic play on the linguistic development in young children. Utilizing standardized tools such as the Test of Pretend Play and the Symbolic Play Test in conjunction with a variety of standardized measurements of language development and analysis of videotape, researchers have highlighted specific areas of linguistic development that appear to be correlated with symbolic play. In central Finland, P. Lyytinen, Poikkeus, Laakso, Eklund and H. Lyytinen (2001) studied 106 children with a family history of dyslexia to investigate whether or not these children were more likely to develop delayed language than children from families with no history of dyslexia. Families were interviewed and completed a questionnaire, and children were assessed longitudinally at 14, 24, 30 and 42 months using the Symbolic Play Test in videotaped play sessions. Results of this investigation yielded the conclusion that symbolic play skills assessed at 14 months were found to be a reliable predictor of receptive (r=.50) and expressive (r=.62) language at the age of 3.5 years. In southern Ireland, O'Toole (2005) conducted a correlational study of 21 two to six-year old children with Down Syndrome and determined that symbolic play and language development were significantly correlated (r=.83) at two to three years of age, but gradually diverged as the children in the study grew older (four to five years of age). In central England, Kirkham, Stewart and Kidd (2013) investigated the relationships between language, graphic symbolism and symbolic play among 60 three to four-year old children and found that measures of language production was the strongest significant predictor of symbolic play as compared to measures of age, non-verbal abilities or graphic symbolism. Additionally, in an urban center of Israel, Orr and Geva (2015) studied 14 children aged 6 to 14 months with normal development. After analyzing videotaped play sessions, the researchers concluded that the age at which children initiated single-object symbolic play was significantly correlated (r=.86) with the age at which children initiated audio-vocal output (babbling).

Despite the prevalent caveats from most scholars who research the connections between play and language that causation cannot be inferred from their findings (namely, that a child's ability to engage in symbolic play directly triggers the attainment of language skills or vice-versa), it is nevertheless evident that certain language abilities coincide in a parallel fashion with children's symbolic play behaviors. Practitioners may be encouraged to reflect on the possibility that "by helping a child's imaginative play we can lay the foundations of his language development" (McConkey, 1976).

THE USE OF PLAY IN CHILD-CENTERED PLAY THERAPY AND SPEECH THERAPY IN SCHOOLS

Play Therapy

Given the strong connections between play and language development, it is not surprising that both play therapists and speech therapists rely on the inherent power of play in their therapeutic work with young children, particularly in the school setting. Perhaps more than any other single researcher, Garry Landreth has described the therapeutic effects of play, specifically non-directive, child-centered play. In child-centered play therapy, children are not required or even pointedly encouraged to express themselves through language. The therapeutic relationship is instead established through the process of the child playing with the toys in the playroom in a self-directed manner as the therapist responds to the child's play in accepting, sensitive, and receptive ways. Play is believed to be the child's natural way of communicating; it is considered to be "the child's language, and toys are their words" (Landreth, 2002). In his book, *Play Therapy: The Art of the Relationship* (pp. 90-92), Landreth outlines the areas of "intuitive learning" that children experience through this type of play:

1. Self-control and responsible freedom of expression,
2. Respect for self,
3. Responsible control of feelings,
4. Acceptance of feelings,
5. Responsible choice-making,
6. Creativity and resourcefulness in confronting problems,
7. Self-direction, and

8. Gradual self-acceptance.

The school setting provides a culturally sensitive, flexible, and time-effective environment in which child-centered play therapy services can be provided for children with mental health issues. Indeed, the Centers for Disease Control and Prevention (Perou, Bitsko, Blumberg, Pastor, Ghandour, Gfroerer, et al., 2013), President Barack Obama (United States 2013), the Center for School Mental Health Assistance (CSMHA, 2002), and the former U.S. Surgeon General (UDHHS, 2000) have all highlighted the urgent need for schools to address the ever-increasing need for mental health service delivery within a collaborative, school-based context. Despite Ray, Armstrong, Warren, and Balkin's (2005) findings that out of 381 school counselors surveyed nationally, 62% indicated that they use play therapy only three hours or less per week in schools, Bratton (2010) provides resounding empirical support for the efficacy of play therapy in schools in her summary of 51 studies conducted since 1990.

Landreth, Ray, and Bratton (2009) outlined specific benefits of the use of child-centered play therapy in a school setting, including the flexible use of space and mobility of toys, convenience of scheduling sessions within the school day, the option of using short-term intensive formats, and the facilitation of professional consultation with teachers. Lamanna (2005, p. 10) noted that schools are comforting, predictable environments for children, and that identification of children's mental health needs can be achieved more readily and timely through school personnel than if left up to parents who may not be aware that their children are in need of services. Additionally, play therapy in a school setting provides more cost-effective, consistent access to mental health services for children (Drewes, 2001).

Although the findings of Ebrahim, Steen, and Paradise (2012) revealed that lack of training was the primary barrier to implementing play therapy in school settings, Perryman and Doran (2010) defined several factors regarding the use of play therapy in schools that contribute to successful implementation, most notably those that involve professional collaboration with school boards, administration, teachers, other school-based professionals, and parents. The ethical standards for school counselors outlined by the American School Counselor Association (ASCA, 2010), specifically Section F4 states:

School counselors and school counseling program directors/supervisors collaborate with special educators, school nurses, school social workers, school psychologists, college counselors/admissions officers, physical therapists, occupational therapists, and speech pathologists to advocate for optimal services for students and all other stakeholders. (ASCA, 2010, p. 6)

It appears that a critical element to the successful use of play therapy in schools is the role of the trained play therapist in engaging and adeptly managing the collaborative process.

Speech Therapy

Similar to the use of non-directive play in child-centered play therapy, speech therapists have also advocated for the use of play in their work with children with speech and language impairment (SLI). The Individuals with Disabilities Education Act (2004) officially defines speech and language impairment as "a communication disorder such as stuttering, impaired articulation, a language impairment, or a voice impairment that adversely affects a child's educational performance". Most recently the American Speech-Language-Hearing Association (ASHA, 2012) has recommended an exclusion of the term "specific language impairment" from the fifth edition of the *Diagnostic and Statistical Manual of*

Mental Disorders due to the fact that a child's non-verbal IQ is required to make a diagnosis. For the purposes of this chapter, the term "speech and language impairment" (SLI) will be used as defined by the Individuals with Disabilities Education Act.

Documented reference to the effective use of non-directive play in the field of speech therapy appears as early as the 1940's; this approach was implemented with a five-year-old selectively mute girl and results showed the child was voluntarily expressive with strangers after 18 months (Reymert, 1946). Improvements in intelligibility of speech (Dupont, Landsman & Valentine, 1953; Jeffree & McConkey, 1974), stuttering (Smathers & Tirnauer, 1959; Andronico & Blake, 1971), selective mutism (Post, 2001) and articulation (Sokoloff, 1959; Kupperman, Bligh & Goodman, 1980; Broen & Westman, 1990) have been demonstrated through case studies and pre-post design research utilizing play therapy interventions. Bouillion (1973) found that in an intensive 14-week program, non-directive group play therapy was "the most efficient remediator" (p. 47) of dysfluency and articulation errors as compared to individual speech therapy, group speech lessons, physical-motor training, and the control group.

The majority of research outcomes relating to the use of play with children with speech difficulties have been derived from case studies utilizing a range of play-based interventions including Theraplay (Kupperman, Bligh & Goodban, 1980), filial therapy (Broen & Westman, 1990), and the Natural Incidental Language Treatment model (Donahue-Kilburg, 1992). However, a small number of experimental group design studies have yielded encouraging outcomes that suggest the specific use of child-centered group play therapy can have significant treatment effects for children with SLI. Wakaba (1983) conducted a study with three Japanese boys aged four to five years who stuttered; after 21 sessions of non-directive group play therapy, instances of anxiety and aggressive behavior during play sessions decreased, as did instances of stuttering. A follow-up survey administered six months and again five years after therapy revealed improvements in both stuttering and social adjustment. In an experimental group design study, Danger and Landreth (2003) conducted 25 sessions of child-centered group play therapy with children aged 4 to 6 years identified as having articulation and expressive language delays in addition to their regular speech therapy sessions; children in the control group received only speech therapy. Results indicated that child centered group play therapy had a large practical significance in improving children's expressive language, and revealed an increase in overall verbal expression among the children in the experimental group.

Cogher (1999) described how play is used in speech therapy sessions. Play is not used to focus on the specific development of individual skills such articulation, fluency, vocabulary development, or syntax. It is used to provide an optimal learning environment for the child that provides "experiences of language and communication strategies that are powerful and effective" (Cogher, 1999, p. 7). In this approach, children play with the toys in a self-directed manner and the speech therapist plays alongside the child while modeling linguistically and contextually appropriate commentary on the child's play.

Elements of child-centered play in speech therapy include:

1. Establishing joint attention between the child and the speech therapist to an object or action initiated by the child to which spoken language refers.
2. Establishing play routines initiated by the child which provide a scaffold for joint attention and language modeling.
3. Establishing access to simple, repeated language input that is related to self and interpretable at the child's current level of ability.
4. Developing confidence in children who are demand- or failure-avoidant.

In the literature of the field, speech and language pathologists have long advocated for the inclusion model of service delivery in which speech therapists provide speech therapy within the school setting as opposed to a clinical setting. The Virginia Department of Education (CVDE, 2011) outlined best practices for speech pathologists working in schools and noted the clear advantages of conducting speech therapy services in a school setting: (a) the ease with which therapists can collaborate with educational professionals, (b) the ability to observe the general educational environment and address the social implications that speech difficulties present to children during the school day, (c) the availability of school-based data that can inform comprehensive assessment and program planning for a child, and (d) the opportunity to contribute to school-based early prevention programs. Hartas (2004) suggested that changes in the focus of language development theories from the discrete to the holistic have led to the belief that children with speech difficulties "should be included in the mainstream classrooms so that they are exposed to diverse linguistic inputs and social behaviors by listening to language modeled by their peers and adults" (p. 35).

The American Speech-Language-Hearing Association (ASHA, 1991) published a position paper outlining the move away from the provision of traditional pull-out speech therapy during the school day and toward a more collaborative model of service delivery involving trans-disciplinary teams consisting of teachers, school-based professionals such as nurses and counselors, paraprofessionals, and parents. Collaborative service delivery re-defines the role of the speech therapist in a school setting; instead of attending monthly school-based meetings to merely report on an individual student's progress in speech therapy sessions, the speech therapist collaborates on an interprofessional team to make holistic and meaningful decisions about student assessment, goal-setting, planning programs, and monitoring progress.

Strikingly similar to school counselors, speech language pathologists (SLPs) working in schools are bound to their professional association's guidelines for ethical practice:

SLPs' unique contributions complement and augment those made by other professionals who also have unique perspectives and skills. Working collegially with general education teachers who are primarily responsible for curriculum and instruction is essential. SLPs also work closely with reading specialists, literacy coaches, special education teachers, occupational therapists, physical therapists, school psychologists, audiologists, guidance counselors, and social workers, in addition to others. (ASHA, 2010, p. 3)

Therefore, the role of collaborative practice for both play therapists and speech therapists can be seen as a fundamental component of ethical support service models in school settings.

SPEECH AND LANGUAGE IMPAIRMENT AND SOCIAL/EMOTIONAL COMORBIDITIES

Language, both receptive and expressive, is strongly interwoven into the fabric of the social and emotional lives of children. It is the means by which children learn to identify and describe the world around them, express their understanding of the world to significant others, and the socially expected way in which they label and communicate their feelings. When a child experiences or displays strong emotion, it is usually the case that the child will be immediately asked, "What is wrong? What happened? Why are you upset?" A child's inability to effectively meet these requests for a spoken response can be "a frustrating and blocking experience that generates almost intolerable tensions within the child" (Axeline, 1947, p. 58).

A recent study at the University of California, Los Angeles (Lieberman, Eisenberger, Crockett, Tom, Pfeifer & Way, 2007) investigated the conventional wisdom that putting feelings into words (affect labeling) actually helps to manage negative emotions; researchers found that activation of the area of the brain (specifically, the right ventrolateral prefrontal cortex) that takes place when a person linguistically labels an emotion actually dampens and diminishes the functioning of the amygdalae – the area of the brain that processes emotional reactions and is strongly connected to emotional learning. While some may argue that diminished emotional responses are therapeutic, those with a child-centered, humanistic theoretical approach to therapy may contend that utilizing techniques that block emotional learning may be counter-productive to the true expression of the child's inner emotions as they are expressed through the medium of play.

The international body of research documenting the comorbidity of SLI and social/emotional problems is extensive. In the United States, Baker and Cantwell (1987) noted that 44% of speech-impaired children were found to have some psychiatric illness diagnosed in accordance with the *Diagnostic and Statistical Manual of Mental Disorders*. In the United Kingdom, Conti-Ramsden, Mok, Pickles & Durkin (2013) asserted that 28% of adolescents with speech and language impairments (n=139) reported borderline/abnormal emotional problems on the Strengths and Difficulties Questionnaire, as compared to 6.6% of adolescents (n=124) with no history of speech or language impairment. In New Zealand, Silva, Williams and McGee studied 1,037 children and found that children with language delays at age 3 had significantly higher behavioral problems at ages 7, 9, and 11 as compared with children whose language developed normally. In Croatia, Gregl, Kirigin, Bilać, Sućeska, Ligutićić, Jakšić & Jakovljević (2014) reported that preschool children with SLI (n=97) had significantly ($p<0.01$) higher behavioral problems and significantly ($p<0.05$) higher affective problems than the control group (n=60). In the Netherlands, Muris, Steerneman, Merckelbach, Holdrinet & Meesters (1998) conducted a study with 44 children (mean age 9.7 years) with pervasive developmental disorders, including communication skills, and concluded that 84.1% of the children met the full criteria for at least one anxiety disorder.

Research has also indicated that the emotional impacts of language impairments identified in childhood are observed well into adolescence. Lindsay, Dockrell and Strand (2007) conducted a 4-year study that measured the stability of behavior, emotional and social difficulties in children with SLI at age 8 through to age 12. They concluded that "behavioral difficulties in school are related to earlier language difficulties at 8 years and that this relationship persists over the period 8-12 years" (p. 823). A meta-analysis conducted by Yew and O'Kearney (2013) concluded that children diagnosed with SLI between the ages of 3 and 8.8 years (n=553) were more than twice as likely to meet the criteria for clinical levels of behavioral difficulties (conduct disorders, oppositional defiant disorder, or ADHD) at a follow-up between a period of 2 to 12 years as compared with children of the same age with typical language development. This analysis also found that SLI children were 1.84 times as likely to meet the criteria for clinical levels of emotional problems (anxiety or mood disorders) into adolescence than children with typical language development. Specific results from this analysis also suggested that impairments in receptive language (the ability to understand spoken or written language) were more strongly associated with emotional problems, and that boys with SLI were more strongly associated with conduct problems.

The link between a child's impaired ability to understand spoken language and comorbid emotional problems has also been explored by Toppelberg and Shapiro (2000) in their review of research conducted between 1990 and 2000. They concluded that "the presence of receptive or comprehension language disorders has proven to be the single most important consideration, as they are a high-risk indicator of . . . psychiatric comorbidity, worsening social competence and hyperactivity over the years and they are often not suspected or detected" (p. 151). Alarmingly, Im-Bolter and Cohen (2007) highlighted a study conducted by Cohen, Barwick, Horodezky, Vallance and Im (1998) that revealed of 380 children referred solely for psychological services, a full 40% had an undetected, undiagnosed language impairment. They have termed children's receptive language impairment as "the invisible handicap" (p. 531). It is clearly evident why numerous SLI researchers have urged children's mental health professionals to increase their awareness of speech and language impairments, to understand the indicators, and to work in collaborative professional teams with SLP's in order to provide comprehensive, holistic interventions (Gregl et al, 2014; Toppelberg & Shaprio, 2000; Conti-Ramsden et al, 2013; Pinborough-Zimmerman et al, 2007; Im-Bolter & Cohen, 2007; Yew & O'Kearney, 2013).

THE ROLE OF CONSULTATION AND COLLABORATION IN PLAY AND SPEECH THERAPY IN SCHOOLS

Play Therapists

Based on the above body of research, the emerging recommendation for play therapists to explore the benefits of a collaborative model of interprofessional practice bears consideration. However, in comparison to the extensive body of research publications demonstrating the efficacy of play therapy interventions for children with a variety of presenting problems, play therapy scholars have touched only marginally on the topic of the importance of consultation in the therapeutic process; research on the topic of play therapists' collaborative practice with speech therapists is virtually non-existent. The studies by Wakaba (1983) and Danger & Landreth (2003) specifically addressing therapeutic interventions of both play and speech therapists make no mention of interprofessional collaboration, outside of consultation for the purposes of sharing standardized language testing results. An online search of PsychNET, ERIC, Google Scholar, Pubpsych and JSTOR using the search terms "play therapy", "speech therapy", "collaboration" and/or "multidisciplinary" and/or "interprofessional" yielded only one academic article specifically addressing the issue of collaboration between play and speech therapists. Peabody and Demanchick (2016) examined the model of interprofessional collaborative practice currently advocated in the healthcare field (Panel, I.E.C.E., 2011) as it relates to the future roles of play therapists and other professionals working in schools. Of particular note is their assertion that "best practice suggests that creating collaborative relationships among and across [these] professions provides opportunities for mutual learning, planning, and feedback that lead to rich understandings of young children and families" (p. 2). Despite the dearth of attention play and speech therapy collaboration has received in the professional literature, the underlying implication that play therapists begin to reflect on a broader "community of practice" orientation is gradually gaining ground.

Somewhat more ample is the available research regarding collaboration between play therapists and classroom teachers, specifically with regards to the sharing of therapeutic response skills with teachers and assistants working in schools. Bratton (2010) outlined ten studies conducted since 1999 in which play therapists provided a series of training sessions in child-centered therapeutic response skills for teachers in public schools and Head Start programs utilizing the Child-Parent Relationship training model (Bratton, Landreth, Kellam & Blackard, 2006), the Filial Therapy model (Van Fleet, 1994) or the Kinder

Training model (White, Flynt & Draper, 1997). Outcomes of these consultative training sessions resulted in decreases in children's disruptive behaviors, increases in teachers' empathic communication skills, and children's increased social competence. Brown (2000) similarly reported statistically significant gains in teacher trainees' empathy, their ability to allow children's self-direction, and communication of acceptance. Helker and Ray (2009) reported that as a result of 10 weeks of training using a modified version of the Child-Parent Relationship training model, followed by 10 weeks of coaching with 24 teachers and teaching assistants working with children at a Head Start center, a significant relationship was found between teacher's use of relationship-building skills and children's decrease of externalizing behaviors in the classroom. Similarly, Morrison and Bratton (2009) reported significant improvements in children's externalizing behaviors after conducting training sessions with Head Start teachers in an economically disadvantaged community.

By far the most ample body of research regarding play therapists' consultative process addresses the dynamic of the therapist's role in supporting parents. Building upon the work of Cates, Paone, Packman, and Margolis (2006) and Bornsheuer and Watts (2012), Schottelkorb Swan, and Ogawa (2015) describe parent consultation as the practice of sharing information with caregivers about a child's progress during the course of play therapy and teaching appropriate response and limit-setting skills—all within the context of a therapist-led intervention. The proposed child-centered parent consultation (CCPC) model consists of five components:

1. Establishing the core conditions for building a relationship as outlined by Rogers (1957).
2. Maintaining a "present-focus" with the caregiver and utilizing therapeutic responses—reflecting content and feeling, esteem-building, facilitating responsibility and limit-setting—as delineated by Landreth (2002).
3. Respecting the parent as an expert on his/her own child.
4. Sharing knowledge about the child-centered play therapy process and child development, as well as the child's progress in therapy.
5. Teaching and modeling basic therapeutic skills.

This focus on creating positive, genuine, and empathic relationships with parents as partners in the process is reflected in Ray's (2011) descriptions of the six essential attitudes that play therapists should possess in order for the consultative process to be successful. This includes respect for parents' unique role, knowledge of their child, and parents' basic humanness. Post (2014) further highlights the importance of fostering a strong therapist-parent alliance and educating parents as part of an effective consultation process.

Nevertheless, to date, there have been few experimental design studies that investigate the impact of parent consultation on play therapy outcomes. One quantitative research study that indirectly relates to this topic is the doctoral dissertation Q-methodological investigation by Lee (Ray, 2014), which examined the services and processes of play therapy that were most valued by parents. This study revealed the most important factor to parents about the play therapy process was the *play therapist's active engagement in gathering information and collaborating with other professionals at the child's school, with a focus on behavioral, academic, social, and medical issues*.

Not to diminish the established research involving play therapists serving in a consultative role with teachers and parents – indicating the potential for these approaches to positively impact therapeutic interventions - it is worthwhile to note a subtle distinction between *consultation* and *collaboration*. As early as 1974, Pryzwansky delineated a clear difference between these two forms of professional interaction. He described the characteristics of the consultative relationship as focused on expert advice-giving and skills-teaching, which suggests consultees assume a passive position in which they are "free to accept, modify or reject" (Pryzwansky, 1974, p. 581) the strategies offered by the consultant. In contrast, characteristics of the collaborative relationship include mutual goal-setting, joint development of the elements of an intervention plan, and mutual responsibility for implementation and evaluation of outcomes (Panel, 2011). Indeed, the Association for Play Therapy (2012) advocates that play therapists work together with "other professional providers to develop clear agreements over coordination of treatment planning" (A.4) and "are aware and acknowledge traditions and practices of other professional disciplines" (D.6).

Speech Therapists

The aforementioned lack of research regarding play and speech therapy collaboration, as well as collaborative models that include children's mental heath professionals in general, is startling, given the clearly established links between speech and language impairment and social/emotional problems in young children. This exclusion notwithstanding, the field of speech and language pathology has made comparative strides in exploring, designing, implementing and reflecting upon models of interprofessional collaborative practice with both teaching professionals and parents.

The National Center for Education Statistics (Kena, Musu-Gillette, Robinson, Wang, Rathbun, Zhang, et al., 2015) reported that 21% of all American children receiving special services under the Individuals with Disabilities in Education Act possess some form of speech or language impairment. Of these children, a full 87% receive their intervention services within the context of the school setting. Recognizing this increasing trend, SLPs appear to be somewhat further along the collaborative road, as evidenced by several research studies that examine the effects of teacher-SLP collaborative practice on the therapeutic progress of children with speech and language impairment (Ellis, Schlaudecker, & Regimbal1995; Farber & Klein, 1999; Throneburg Calvert, Sturm, Paramboukas, & Paul, 2000;Van Kleek, Gillam, & McFadden, 1998; Wilcox, Kouri, & Caswell, 1991), all of which found positive effects for children's communication development.

A school survey report from the American Speech-Language-Hearing Association (ASHA, 2012) stated that a full 21% of all SLPs in the United States indicate they are moving to a collaborative model of service delivery within the context of the school setting. Published models of teacher-therapist collaboration for speech and language service delivery include many similar elements to those of play therapy:

- Child-centered, genuineness, empathy, trustworthiness, sharing of expertise (Flynn & Power-deFur, 2013).
- Profession-specific contributions, the nature of the relationship between the speech therapist and the teacher, mutual respect for expertise (Tollerfield, 2003).
- Sharing and exchanging skills, compatibility in beliefs, the importance of "chemistry" and respect for "personality" (Hartas, 2004).

Recent survey research on professional perceptions of the effectiveness of the collaborative model between SLPs and classroom teachers has yielded important descriptive data on early implementations. Leonard and Leonard (2003) conducted a follow-up survey of 101 teachers from 45 schools in northern Louisiana and reported that collaboration training, common planning time, listening to teachers' suggestions, and administrative support were the primary factors that teachers suggested would promote positive collaborative practice. Glover, McCormack, and Smith-Tamaray (2015) surveyed 36 SLPs working in New South Wales, Australia regarding their views on collaborative practice. The results of their findings indicated, most importantly, that teachers and SLPs desire knowledge and training in collaborative approaches, as well as more regular opportunities to collaborate within the school setting. Hartas (2004) surveyed 25 teachers and 17 SLPs in the United Kingdom and found that more than 90% of SLPs and teachers believe that collaborative practice positively influences them at an individual level, a client level, and a professional level, and that a shared understanding of the process of collaboration is crucial. Finally, Baxter, Brookes, Bianchi, Rashid, and Hay (2009) surveyed 250 SLPs and teachers from 25 schools in northern England; among other outcomes, it was reported that only 17% of staff had participated in courses in the collaborative approach.

A common theme appears to emerge from a cursory review of current survey-based research, namely, that training and education in collaborative practices appears to be high on the list of positive contributing factors to an acceptance of the collaborative model amongst SLPs and teachers. Once again, the American Speech-Language-Hearing Association (ASHA, 2015) is leading the way in interprofessional education (IPE) in its *Envisioned Future 2025* by setting the strategic outcome that "academic programs employ IPE approaches to personnel preparation and both students and ASHA members engage in interprofessional collaborative practice" (p. 3).

The crucial role that parents play in the language development of their children has long been recognized in the field of speech therapy. Finley (2012) states, "The therapist-centered model is being replaced by a family-centered model, which is now considered the best practice" (p. 1). Within these family-centered models, such as Enhanced Milieu Teaching (Kaiser & Hancock, 2013), Parent-Child Interaction Therapy (Allen & Marshall, 2011), and PLAY – Play and Language for Autistic Youngsters (Solomon, Van Egeren, Mahoney, Huber, & Zimmerman, 2014), speech therapists train parents and caregivers to implement strategies that support children's language growth in their daily routines at home. Notably, Cheslock & Kahn (2011) summarized the growing research evidence that suggests family-based speech therapy interventions are as effective as clinician-implemented interventions in obtaining positive language development outcomes.

Considered to be one of the more effective collaborative models, Allen & Marshall (2011) described the elements of Parent-Child Interaction Therapy as being comprised not only of parental education and training by speech therapists, but also of the parent becoming "an integral part of the intervention team" (p. 8). Similar to the Child-Parent Relationship training model in play therapy, elements of this collaborative model include:

- A focus on the parent's shared role in service delivery,
- The parent's role in gathering observational data through videotaped sessions in which skills such as responsiveness to non-verbal gestures, turn-taking and reinforcement of language gains are practiced,
- Reflective sessions with the speech therapist in which the videotapes are analyzed and common goals are identified,
- A concluding session in which the parent is recognized and credited for their child's language gains, and future management strategies are discussed.

The encouraging trend in the field of speech and language pathology to consider interprofessional collaboration as a central element of best practice, not only by practitioners and researchers, but by state and national professional organizations indicates a positive shift in practice and sets the stage for the increased inclusion of all professionals who support the development of young children in the school setting.

Teachers

Not to be forgotten, the role of the classroom teacher in elementary schools is a pivotal one and plays a critical role in the collaborative process. The field of education is experiencing an ever-increasing necessity for professional collaboration, and these demands are growing as the population of children requiring school-based services for educational as well as medical, social, behavioral and emotional needs are expanding. Data generated by the National Center for Educational Statistics (Kena et al., 2015) revealed that in 2013-2014, 6.5 million children aged 3-21 received special educational services, or approximately 13% of all public student students in the United States.

Historically, classroom teachers worked in self-contained, individual classrooms and autonomously delivered the academic curriculum to their students, sharing student progress with parents at pre-determined times (usually twice during a school year) and reporting to administrators when summoned. Gradually, teachers began to engage in professional dialogue with fellow grade-level teachers, music, art, sport and site-based teaching specialists as the delivery of the curriculum began to diversify. In recent years, this group has significantly expanded to include school counselors, school psychologists, learning support specialists, diagnosticians, occupational therapists, speech therapists, health care professionals, social workers, mental health professionals and instructional coaches. With little training in university-level preparation programs and few standardized models of how teachers should manage this web of discourse within the school day, it is no wonder that today's elementary classroom teacher is experiencing increasing levels of stress and burnout that may have a significant negative impact on the students they strive to serve (Aloe, Amo & Shanahan, 2014).

Nevertheless, teachers are bound by professional ethical standards and have defined roles and responsibilities within their profession. Specifically relating to collaboration, the National Board for Professional Teaching Standards explicitly states:

Accomplished teachers also participate in the coordination of services to students. Today's schools include a wide variety of educational specialists, and with increasing specialization has come the need for coordination, lest pupils' educational experiences become fragmented ... National Board Certified teachers are adept at identifying students who might benefit from such special attention and at working in tandem with specialists. (NBPTS, 2014, p. 12)

One promising framework that concretely outlines specific structures for collaborative practice in the field of education has been developed by Dettmer, Thurston & Dyck (2005). Prominent elements of this framework include:

- The importance of delineation and clarification of professional roles included on collaborative teams.
- A well-defined structure of meetings that prioritizes time allocation to collaboration.

- Team evaluation of the effectiveness of collaboration on attaining goals for student progress.
- A commitment on the part of all members to actively engage in needs assessments, planning, data gathering, feedback and evaluation.

Ideally, identifying and synthesizing the common elements found within the various consultation and collaboration models in the fields of play therapy, speech therapy and education will ultimately lead to a more cohesive, conjoint and practical model for interprofessional collaborative practice - thereby advancing the quality of holistic interventions that support children's overall well being in school-based settings.

TOWARD A MODEL OF INTERPROFESSIONAL COLLABORATIVE PRACTICE

In light of the play-language connection in children's cognitive development, a shared value of the use of play in therapeutic interventions in schools, the comorbidity of social, emotional and behavioral problems and language impairments, and the ethical expectations for professional practice, one can conclude that reflective consideration of a shift toward interprofessional collaborative practice for play therapists, SLPs, and teachers working in school settings is decidedly warranted. As described by Peabody and Demanchick (2016, p. 2), "with evidentiary support of collaborative practices growing, it is important for play therapists to consider opportunities for interprofessional collaboration."

The World Health Organization (WHO) and the Interprofessional Education Collaborative (Panel, 2011) defined both the model and the core competencies for interprofessional collaborative practice in the healthcare field. Its aim was to define best practices for how "multiple healthcare workers from different professional backgrounds work together with patients, families, carers and communities to deliver the highest quality of care" (p. 13). The Center for Mental Health in Schools organization at the University of California, Los Angeles (2006, p. 4) states that the purpose of the collaborative model is "to align systems and ensure the promise of a comprehensive, highly effective system for children and youth and their families." The Center for School Mental Health Assistance (2002, p. 4) also describes the shift to collaborative practice as moving "to the transdisciplinary framework where professionals actively teach, learn, and work with other service providers across discipline boundaries." Inspired by the WHO model, and based on both published models of consultation and collaboration in the fields of education, play therapy and speech and language pathology, a preliminary model emerges that illustrates the critical elements of interprofessional collaborative practice for play therapists, speech therapists, teachers, and parents within the context of school settings.

Hypothetical Case Example

For descriptive purposes, the following hypothetical case example is offered as a means of illustrating how an interprofessional collaborative process between play therapists, speech therapists, teachers and parents might optimally proceed:

Alicia is a five-and-one-half-year old girl attending public school in a suburb of a large metropolitan area in the United States. Her family consists of her full-time working mother and her two-year-old younger brother. At age four, Alicia was diagnosed with an SLI - specifically, an expressive language delay accompanied by articulation difficulties. After several weeks of navigating the health care and insurance bureaucracy, Alicia's mother was able to arrange for Alicia to attend a local speech therapy

Figure 1. A model of interprofessional collaborative practice

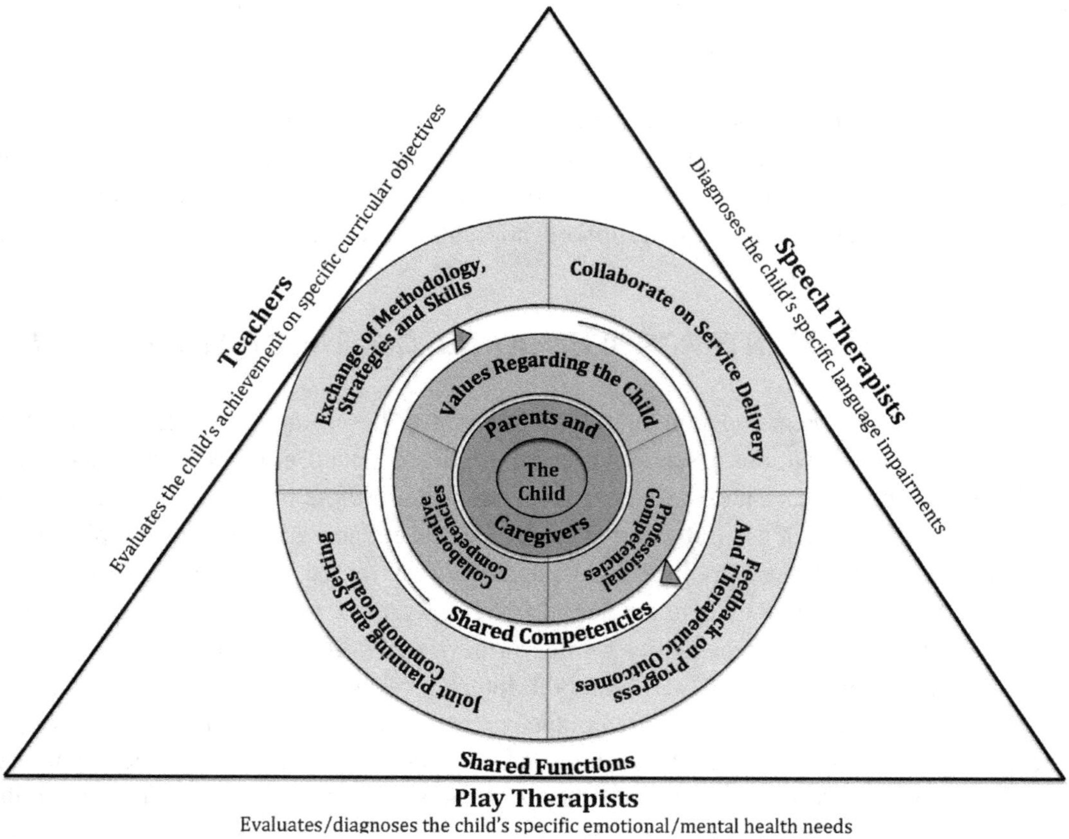

clinic once a week, using a combination of directive multiple exemplar training and non-directive play-based techniques. When her brother was born, Alicia began showing mild indications of separation anxiety, which her mother managed by allowing Alicia to sleep in her mother's bed at night. When Alicia entered kindergarten at age five, she began showing elevated signs of separation anxiety and was emotionally distressed (crying, clinging to the teacher) for up to 40 minutes each school morning after her mother departed. Her speech therapist noticed a slight regression in Alicia's ability to articulate the specific speech sounds they had been working on; at the consultation session, Alicia's mother informed the speech therapist that Alicia had been having extreme difficulty separating from her at school in the morning; the speech therapist consequently referred Alicia to a play therapist who worked at a neighboring clinic. At the kindergarten's parent-teacher conference session, Alicia's teacher shared with the mother her increasing concerns about Alicia's continued inability to separate in the morning and how this seemed to be negatively affecting her social interactions with other classmates. Alicia's mother informed the kindergarten teacher that Alicia was in her third week of sessions with a local play therapist. After learning the details of Alicia's current situation at the first parent consultation session, the play therapist obtained permission from Alicia's mother to contact the speech therapist and the kindergarten teacher and arranged for the first interprofessional collaborative meeting to take place in the conference room of the school after school hours.

The Child, Parents, and Caregivers

Placed at the center of the model, the child, parents, and caregivers represent the enduring focus of interprofessional collaborative practice. The process embraces the child as a whole person, as well as the caregiving system in which the child lives. The application of shared competencies, the implementation of shared functions, and the discipline-specific contributions that each professional brings to the collaborative process are uniformly directed toward advocating for the well-being and healthy development of the child and the family.

Phase One

Shared Competencies: Values Regarding the Child

The start of the collaborative process begins with the recognition that essential to the successful functioning of the professional team is a shared set of values and competencies relating to the child. In the case example, the play therapist might begin by describing the purpose of the team meeting – to establish the basic framework for a comprehensive "team approach" to intervention that will most effectively meet Alicia's needs. The first element of this process consists of identifying and articulating the shared values and beliefs about children held by each member of the team. The play therapist may express her belief in the child's innate capacity for positive growth; the speech therapist may describe his valuing of non-directive approaches to intervention; the teacher may delineate her strongly held belief in the importance of successful peer interactions in the educational development of children, and the parent may express the importance placed on her child's right to privacy in relation to members of the school administration. Ensuring a shared understanding of the underlying values and beliefs regarding the child is a key factor in setting the stage for productive communication and goal-setting. Team members specify and confirm these values as a springboard for all further collaborative work.

Shared Competencies: Collaborative Competencies

Similar to the core conditions of establishing therapeutic relationships, core competencies in the process of collaboration are vital for team members to understand and actively demonstrate. The Interprofessional Education Collaborative (Panel, 2011) have defined specific skills that professionals need when engaging in interprofessional collaboration, including:

- Develop a trusting relationship with patients, families, and other team members.
- Act with honesty and integrity in relationships with patients, families, and other team members.
- Communicate one's roles and responsibilities clearly to patients, families, and other professionals.
- Organize and communicate information in a form that is understandable, avoiding discipline-specific terminology when possible.
- Listen actively and encourage ideas and opinions of other team members.
- Use respectful language appropriate for a given difficult situation, crucial conversation, or interprofessional conflict.
- Develop consensus on ethical principles.

Given their specialized training and expertise in this area, play therapists are well suited to assume a leading role in establishing these collaborative competencies and advocating adherence to these elements during the process by all members of the team. In the case example, the play therapist might elicit a discussion of these core principles by prompting the members of the team to offer suggestions as to how their respective training programs have informed their approach to sharing information about Alicia's challenges with her mother. Contributions from each member of the team could be reflected and summarized by the play therapist, who subsequently guides the team to a shared commitment to observe these principles.

Shared Competencies: Professional Competencies

Play therapists, speech therapists, and teachers are bound by their professional ethical standards to maintain up-to-date knowledge and an understanding of current research in their specific fields. All professional members of the team should expressly commit to the use of evidence-based practice throughout the collaborative process.

Phase Two

Shared Functions: Joint Planning and Setting Common Goals

With shared values and competencies defined and confirmed, the next phase of the process entails enfolding the discipline-specific goals determined by each team member into the establishment of a comprehensive, well-aligned and holistic plan of intervention—with the child as the focus. Each team member contributes their own professional knowledge and assessment outcomes of the child; Hartas (2004, p. 34) described this as *coordination*, where specialists remain "within their existing professional boundaries," but engage in a dialogue with the aim of bringing their work into closer alignment. The IPE advises that team members strive to avoid the use of discipline-specific terminology and jargon. The aim of this shared function is the creation of collective, transdisciplinary goals that will support the holistic positive development of the child.

In the hypothetical example, the play therapist may outline her initial observations that Alicia's play themes suggest the therapeutic goal of Alicia developing a deeper sense of mastery, safety and security. The speech therapist may share his therapeutic goal of fostering Alicia's ability to hear the differences between sounds in speech (phonological discrimination) and her ability to pronounce the ending sounds of words that end in the letters b, d and m (accurate sound production of vocalized ending consonants). The kindergarten teacher may explain her primary instructional goal of teaching Alicia the pre-literacy skill of constructing simple verbal narratives related to play, as well as developing an interest in stories and books. She may also share the goal of teaching Alicia the social interaction skill of inviting another child to join her in a self-selected play activity; through the team discussion, the teacher might also come to learn that she shares not only the speech therapist's goal of supporting Alicia's developing phonological discrimination, since this is a key skill children need to develop before learning to read, but also the play therapist's goal of facilitating Alicia's sense of mastery. Alicia's mother might describe her goal of reducing the time it takes Alicia to separate from her in the mornings (a goal no doubt shared by the teacher) as well as a personal goal of reducing the stress this places on her as a working mother – a goal also sought by the play and speech therapists in recognition of the supporting role parents play in the therapeutic process. Alicia's mother may also come to realize that she shares the kindergarten teacher's goal of helping Alicia to make and enjoy friendships with her classmates at school. The shared function of contributing discipline-specific goals through such a dialogue can clearly facilitate the identification, articulation and consensus of common goals.

Shared Functions: Exchange of Methodologies, Strategies, and Skills

Once common goals are set, the collaborative team can then initiate a dialogue concerning methods, strategies, and skills that serve to advance these goals. A primary element of both play therapy and speech therapy models of consultation is the sharing of skills used by therapists with parents and other school-based professionals working with special-population children. Watts, Hawthorn, Hoffbrand, Jackson, and Spurling (1997) describes this process as *crossfertilization*, in which basic intervention skills are taught and exchanged amongst professionals with the aim of empowering all members of a collaborative team to think and work across professional boundaries. Hall (2005) asserts that in this phase of interprofessional collaborative practice, it is essential that team members "foster a status-equal basis" (p. 192) when sharing intervention strategies, and be mindful of traditional professional cultures that dictate hierarchical power structures and expertise. She also advises caution regarding the phenomenon of "role blurring" (p. 192), which can create confusion amongst members of the team regarding "where one's practice boundaries begin and end" and may lead to resistance on the part of team members who are used to assuming the role of expert. The concept of exchanging methodologies must be viewed in light of ethical guidelines regarding working outside areas of professional expertise and is intended to include only those basic skills normally taught in the context of parent consultation.

In the case example, the play therapist may wish to share the CONNECT model (Helker, Schottelkorb, & Ray, 2007) with team members. This model includes seven therapeutic skills that play therapists teach to parents during parent consultation sessions and may serve to foster Alicia's growing sense of mastery and safety in contexts outside of the play therapy room:

- Convey acceptance through words and actions.
- Offer understanding by acknowledging feelings and wishes.
- Notice children's behaviors and actions.
- Negotiate choices.
- Encourage self-esteem.
- Communicate limits by ACTing (*A*cknowledging the child's feelings, *C*ommunicate the limit, *T*arget an alternative).
- Trust yourself to be genuine.

The speech therapist may wish to share the multiple exemplar technique (Bowen & Cupples, 1999) with team members, which consists of activities that serve to promote Alicia's ability to distinguish phonological structures:

- **Say the Word That Rhymes with the One I Say:** The therapist may say the word "plane" and point to a picture of a plane, then show the child a picture of a train and the child says "train".
- **Silly Sentences:** The therapist makes a statement such as, "I flew to New York on a pane" and the child determines if the sentence is accurate or "silly".

- **Walk When you Hear the Two-Steps:** The therapist may show a picture of a plane, a pirate and a puppy, and the child must "walk" his fingers across the table when they hear and see the picture with the consonant cluster /pl/.

The kindergarten teacher may wish to share various play-based literacy strategies used in the classroom setting (Saracho, 2013) that may serve to foster Alicia's development of pre-literacy skills, such as:

- Language modeling techniques,
- Storytelling techniques,
- Songs and chants that reinforce mastery of rhyming patterns,
- Use of encouragement for proximal zones of development, and
- Recording the child's narrative dialogue during self-selected play activities and playing it back to the child, stopping periodically to summarize, model target vocabulary or allow the child to finish a phrase when the recording is paused.

Shared Functions: Collaborate on Service Delivery

The professional learning resulting from the open and mutually beneficial sharing of strategies to address children's needs serves as the basis for the next step in the collaborative process, service delivery. In addition to each professional implementing his/her discipline-specific interventions with children in a therapeutic setting or in the classroom, a raised awareness of the skills used by other team members can expand the repertoire of responses used by professionals during the course of their work with children.

For example, Alicia's kindergarten teacher may be engaged in a play-based literacy lesson in which she is guiding and supporting students' ability to construct a simple narrative about self-selected play activities. The teacher notices Alicia demonstrating excitement about a tower she built with wooden blocks; Alicia's body language and facial expression communicate that she has made a realization about her tower that excited her, but she is completely non-verbal. The teacher may first use the strategy of questioning associated with the teaching of pre-literacy skills by asking, "How did you build your tower?"—a strategy designed to promote the goal of narrative-building skills. Noticing that Alicia does not respond verbally to the question, but excitedly points to the top of the tower and the top of her own head, the teacher can employ the play therapy strategy of reflecting the child's actions and feelings by stating, "You are excited about your tower! You built it all by yourself (promoting the goal of mastery). You noticed something about it and you pointed to the top of your head." The teacher can then utilize the speech therapy technique of *Silly Sentences* by stating "You noticed that the ower is aller than the op of your ead. Was a that a real sentence or a silly sentence?" (promoting the goal of phonological awareness). This alignment and consistency of simple intervention strategies used by team members can serve to promote the transdisciplinary goals defined by the collaborative team which, in turn, supports the integrated, holistic and positive development of the child.

Shared Functions: Feedback on Progress and Therapeutic Outcomes

Finally, regular collaborative sessions with play therapists, speech therapists, teachers, and parents can facilitate the sharing of observations that demonstrate progress toward the attainment of common goals, keeping in mind the shared value of recognizing confidentiality boundaries. Regular collaborative sessions also allow for a process of modification or redefining of goals, as well as setting a timeline and preparing for termination of services.

In the hypothetical example, the play therapist may report back to the collaborative team her observations that Alicia's play themes reflecting mastery have gradually declined over time during the course of play therapy sessions, and the need for limit setting to end her sessions has markedly diminished. She might outline the projected termination timeline for Alicia's play sessions and alert the kindergarten teacher to the possibility of an increased need for using empathic statements in the classroom once play therapy has terminated. The speech therapist might report gains in Alicia's most recent results from standardized articulation testing and celebrate her success in mastering word-ending articulation. He may further encourage Alicia's mother to occasionally revisit the *Silly Sentences* game with Alicia during routine family activities with the new goal of isolating singular /b/ and /d/ sounds at the beginning of words. The teacher might share updated information about Alicia's progress in initiating social play on the playground and during lunchtime, and share examples of successful use of the phonological awareness activities shared by the speech therapist. Alicia's mother may describe the degree to which her personal levels of stress have reduced as a result of the collaborative process, and inquire of the team their predictions of when she might reasonably expect Alicia to separate from her in the mornings with complete confidence. At this stage, the play therapist can bring the process to closure by facilitating suggestions from the team as to the needed frequency of future collaborative meetings, the preferred channels of communication to report periodic feedback, and the processes by which future team meetings might be arranged on an as-needed basis.

SUPPORTING ELEMENTS AND BARRIERS TO INTERPROFESSIONAL COLLABORATIVE PRACTICE

Ultimately the true measure of the effectiveness of interprofessional collaborative practice amongst play therapists, speech therapists, teachers and parents will lie in the degree to which the children in their care experience positive growth in language skills, social, emotional and behavioral stability, and holistic well-being. Simply stated, professional trust and respect are the essential factors that underlie all successful collaborative endeavors (Hall, 2005).

Supporting Elements to Interprofessional Collaborative Practice

The majority of professional literature that delineates the supporting elements of interprofessional collaborative practice in comprehensive detail, not surprisingly, comes from the medical and health care fields. San Martin-Rodgriguez, Beaulieu, D'Amour & Ferrada-Videla (2005) have identified three main categories of determinants that may positively influence interprofessional collaborative processes:

- *Interactional determinants,* which reflect team members' communication skills, levels of trust, mutual respect and willingness to collaborate.
- *Organizational determinants,* which reflect the need for horizontal as opposed to hierarchical structures, the provision of meeting space and time, shared understandings of rules and protocols, and division of work.

- *Systemic determinants,* which reflect the degree to which social factors such as perceived power differences (i.e. nurses being viewed as subordinate to doctors), or cultural stereotypes (i.e. male v. female authority) are detected on the team, as well as the openness and flexibility of the professional systems under which the team members operate.

In light of these determinants, play therapists will need to consider the avenues by which, as professionals in human communication, they can support and foster the establishment of trust, respect and openness amongst team members, while being mindful of not over-asserting leadership or managing the group in a directive manner. Implementing techniques through which social factors or cultural stereotypes might gently be recognized and discussed lie well within the professional skill set of play therapists; hesitancy to bring these potentially uncomfortable issues to light might have unanticipated negative impacts on the collaborative process. More practical factors that play therapists should reflect upon include ensuring that meeting locations provide a reasonable expectation of confidentiality so that the likelihood of meetings being inadvertently interrupted by school or clinic personnel is minimized, establishing positive relationships with school administrative personnel in order to engage their cooperation in providing release time for teachers and speech therapists working on site to participate in collaborative meetings, and facilitating a clear understanding of the progressive steps in the interprofessional collaborative process by all members of the team.

Barriers to Interprofessional Collaborative Practice

Additional researchers have further specified the conditions under which interprofessional collaborative practice is least successful, identifying potential barriers to the process (Flynn & Power-deFur, 2013; Glover et al., 2015; Hartas, 2004; Leonard & Leonard, 2003; Lolan, 2011; Tollerfield, 2003; Whitmire, 2002). For example, Daly (2004) notes that failure to establish procedures for quality record-keeping of collaborative meetings can lead to "inactive collaboration" (p. 78) amongst team members who may not see it as their role to initiate or delegate the task of recording shared goals, intervention planning, team member feedback or modifications of goals. Tollerfield (2003) cautions that expanding caseloads within the school setting can impact the availability of speech therapists to attend interprofessional collaborative meetings, and professional cultural factors such as a therapist's tendency to conceptualize herself as "specialist" as opposed to "learner" can lead to resistance to participating in the shared function of service delivery. Oandasan & Reeves (2005) caution that staff turnover can have a potentially damaging influence on the outcomes of collaborative practice. Relocation, promotion, personal leave, burn-out or re-assignment of teachers and therapists can disrupt the working process and set the momentum of the working group back considerably, as well as necessitating the introduction and orientation of new professionals to the team. They note, "When group turnover occurs, an initiative is likely to wither away" (p. 41).

The factors outlined above should be explored and considered as play and speech therapists reflect on the opportunities that interprofessional collaborative practice offers for establishing comprehensive, holistic models of intervention for children with language and socio/emotional issues.

SUMMARY AND FUTURE CONSIDERATIONS

Interprofessional collaborative practice is a developing model that therapeutic professionals working with children in schools may benefit from exploring. Practitioners of play and speech therapy have much in common in regard to their perspectives on children's development, their use of play as a mode of intervention, and their successful work in school settings. The current trend toward inclusion-based models of intervention suggests that play therapists, speech therapists, teachers, and parents will need to develop collaborative competencies that will make the process of comprehensive goal-setting and integrated service delivery productive and successful.

University graduate-level training programs play a pivotal role in preparing professionals who work with children to develop the necessary skill sets that will enable them to proficiently function on interprofessional collaborative teams. Using the core competencies outlined by the World Health Organization, experts in the fields of speech and play therapy working in universities may wish to consider defining collaborative competencies for speech and play therapists, and incorporating these competencies into their respective programs of study. Interprofessional education (IPE) programs have already been established in the field of counseling psychology through Boston College (Brabek, Walsh, Kenny & Comilang (1997), medicine and health care through the University of Toronto, Canada and South Bank University, London (Oandasan & Reeves, 2005), the University of Florida, the University of Washington and Rosalind Franklin University of Medicine and Science (Bridges, Davidson, Odegard, Maki & Tomkowiak, 2011) and professional psychology through the Workgroup on Consultation and Interdisciplinary Relationships (Arrendondo, Shealy, Neale & Winfrey, 2004). These established post-graduate programs may serve as a template for speech and play therapy professors to define future interprofessional collaborative competencies as part of their university preparation programs.

The issues outlined in this chapter suggest implications for future research by those working in the play and speech therapy fields. Most prominently, there is an imperative need to define and empirically research the mechanisms by which the social, emotional and behavioral needs of children with SLI can be addressed and supported through speech and play therapy collaborative interventions. Experimental research in the field of play therapy on the efficacy of parent consultation models and their effects on therapeutic outcomes would contribute to the evidence base for the collaborative model, as would survey-based research on the perspectives and attitudes of play therapists and teachers toward working as part of collaborative teams. Play therapists, speech therapists, teachers and parents are at the cusp of seizing the opportunity to create innovative, holistic and collaborative pathways to improve service delivery, and may potentially enter a new phase of professional practice that offers exciting possibilities for the mutual support of children's development and holistic well-being.

REFERENCES

Allen, J., & Marshall, C. R. (2011). Parent-child interaction therapy in school-aged children with SLI. *International Journal of Language & Communication Disorders*, *46*, 397–410.

Aloe, A. M., Amo, L. C., & Shanahan, M. E. (2014). Classroom management self-efficacy and burnout: A multivariate meta-analysis. *Educational Psychology Review*, *26*(1), 101–126.

American School Counselor Association. (2010). *Ethical standards for school counselors*. Retrieved from https://wvde.state.wv.us/institutional/Counselors/ASCAEthicalStandards.pdf

American Speech-Language-Hearing Association. (2012). Asha's recommended revisions to the dsm-5. Retrieved from www.asha.org/uploadedFiles/*DSM-5-Final-Comments.pdf*

American Speech-Language-Hearing Association (ASHA). (1991). *A model for collaborative service delivery for students with language-learning disorders in the public schools*. Retrieved from http://www.asha.org/policy/rp1991-00123/

American Speech-Language-Hearing Association (ASHA). (2010). *Roles and responsibilities of speech-language pathologists in schools*. Retrieved from http://www.asha.org/policy/PI2010-00317/

American Speech-Language-Hearing Association (ASHA). (2012). *Schools survey report: SLP workforce/work conditions*. Retrieved from http://www.asha.org/uploadedFiles/Schools-2012-SLP-Workforce.pdf

American Speech-Language Hearing Association (ASHA). (2015). *Strategic pathway to excellence*. Retrieved from http://www.asha.org/About/Strategic-Pathway/

Andronico, M. P., & Blake, I. (1971). The application of filial therapy to young children with stuttering problems. *The Journal of Speech and Hearing Disorders*, *36*(3), 377–381. doi:10.1044/jshd.3603.377 PMID:5566117

Arrendondo, P., Shealy, C., Neale, M., & Winfrey, L. L. (2004). Consultation and Interprofessional collaboration: Modeling for the future. *Journal of Clinical Psychology*, *60*(7), 787–800.

Association for Play Therapy. (2012). *Play therapy best practices*. Retrieved from http://www.a4pt.org/resource/resmgr/Publications/Play_Therapy_Best_Practices.pdf

Axeline, V. M. (1947). *Play Therapy*. New York: Ballantine.

Baker, L., & Cantwell, D. P. (1987). A prospective psychiatric follow-up of children with speech/language disorders. *Journal of the American Academy of Child and Adolescent Psychiatry*, *26*(4), 546–553. doi:10.1097/00004583-198707000-00015 PMID:3654509

Baxter, S., Brookes, C., Bianchi, K., Rashid, K., & Hay, F. (2009). Speech and language therapists and teachers working together: Exploring the issues. *Child Language Teaching and Therapy*, *25*(2), 215–234. doi:10.1177/0265659009102984

Bjork, R. A., Dunlosky, J., & Kornell, N. (2013). Self-regulated learning: Beliefs, techniques, and illusions. *Annual Review of Psychology*, *64*(1), 417–444. doi:10.1146/annurev-psych-113011-143823 PMID:23020639

Bornsheuer, J. N., & Watts, R. E. (2012). Play therapy and parent consultation: A review of best practices. *ACA Vistas 2012*.

Bouillion, K. R. (1973). The comparative efficacy of nondirective group play therapy with preschool, speech or language delayed children. *Dissertation Abstracts International*, *35*, O1B.

Bowen, C. (1998). *Brown's stages of syntactic and morphological development*. Retrieved from www.speech-language-therapy.com/index.php?option=com_content&view=article&id=33

Bowen, C., & Cupples, L. (1999). Parents and children together (PACT): A collaborative approach to phonological therapy. *International Journal of Language & Communication Disorders*, *34*(1), 35–55.

Bratton, S. (2010). Meeting the early mental health needs of children through school-based play therapy. In C.E. Schaefer & A.A. Drewes (Eds.), School-Based Play Therapy (pp. 17-58). Wiley.

Bratton, S. C., Landreth, G. L., Kellam, T., & Blackard, S. (2006). *Child parent relationship therapy (CPRT) treatment manual: A 10-session filial therapy model for training parents*. Routledge.

Bridges, D. R., Davidson, R. A., Odegard, P. S., Maki, I. V., & Tomkowiak, J. (2011). Interprofessional collaboration: Three best practice models of interprofessional education. *Medical Education Online*, 16.

Broen, P. A., & Westman, M. J. (1990). Project Parent: A preschool speech program implemented through parents. *The Journal of Speech and Hearing Disorders*, *55*(3), 495–502. doi:10.1044/jshd.5503.495 PMID:2381191

Brown, C. J. (2000). *Filial therapy with undergraduate teacher trainees; child-teacher relationship training* (Doctoral dissertation, University of North Texas).

Brown, R. (1973). *A first language: The early stages*. London: George Allen & Unwin. doi:10.4159/harvard.9780674732469

Cates, J., Paone, T., Packman, J., & Margolis, D. (2006). Effective parent consultation in play therapy. *International Journal of Play Therapy*, *15*(1), 87–100. doi:10.1037/h0088909

Center for Mental Health in Schools. (2006). *The current status of mental health in schools: A policy and practice analysis*. Retrieved from http://smhp.psych.ucla.edu/pdfdocs/currentstatusmh/currentstatus.pdf

Center for School Mental Health Assistance (CSMHA). (2002). *Developing collaborative ESMH programs*. Downloaded from www.schoolmentalhealth.org/.../ESMH/developing_collabor_2002.pdf

Charman, T., Ricketts, J., Dockrell, J. E., Lindsay, G., & Palikara, O. (2015). Emotional and behavioural problems in children with language impairments and children with autism spectrum disorders. *International Journal of Language & Communication Disorders*, *50*(1), 84–93. doi:10.1111/1460-6984.12116 PMID:25039810

Cheslock, M. A., & Kahn, S. J. (2011). Supporting families and caregivers in everyday routines. *The ASHA Leader*, *16*, 10–13.

Cogher, L. (1999). The use of non-directive play in speech and language therapy. *Child Language Teaching and Therapy*, *15*(1), 7–16. doi:10.1191/026565999670736631

Cohen, N. J., Barwick, M. A., Horodezky, N. B., Vallance, D. D., & Im, N. (1998). Language, achievement, and cognitive processing in psychiatrically disturbed children with previously identified and unsuspected language impairments. *Journal of Child Psychology and Psychiatry, and Allied Disciplines*, *39*(06), 865–877.

Commonwealth of Virginia Department of Education (CVDE). (2011). *Speech-language pathology services in schools: Guidelines for best practice.* Retrieved from http://sbo.nn.k12.va.us/sped/documents/speech-pathology-handbook.pdf

Conti-Ramsden, G., Mok, P. L., Pickles, A., & Durkin, K. (2013). Adolescents with a history of specific language impairment (SLI): Strengths and difficulties in social, emotional and behavioral functioning. *Research in Developmental Disabilities*, *34*(11), 4161–4169. doi:10.1016/j.ridd.2013.08.043 PMID:24077068

Conti-Ramsden, G., Mok, P. L., Pickles, A., & Durkin, K. (2014). Longitudinal trajectories of peer relations in children with specific language impairment. *Journal of Child Psychology and Psychiatry, and Allied Disciplines*, *55*(5), 516–527. doi:10.1111/jcpp.12190 PMID:24410167

Daly, G. (2004). Understanding the barriers to multiprofessional collaboration. *British Medical Journal*, *323*(7303), 28–31.

Danger, S., & Landreth, G. (2005). Child-centered group play therapy with children with speech difficulties. *International Journal of Play Therapy*, *14*(1), 81–102. doi:10.1037/h0088897

Dettmer, P., Thurston, L. P., & Dyck, N. J. (2005). Consultation, Collaboration, And Teamwork For Students With Special Needs. Pearson. Retreived from http://www.ablongman.com/html/productinfo/dettmer5e/0205435238_ch2.pdf

Donahue-Kilburg, G. (1992). *Family-centered early intervention for communication disorders: Prevention and treatment. Excellence in Practice Series*. Gaithersburg, MD: Aspen Publishers.

Drewes, A. A. (2001). The possibilities and challenges in using play therapy in schools. In C. E. Schaefer, L. J. Carey, & A. A. Drewes (Eds.), School-based Play Therapy (pp. 41-62). Wiley.

Dupont, H. J., Landsman, T., & Valentine, M. (1953). The treatment of delayed speech by client-centered therapy. *Journal of Consulting Psychology*, *17*(2), 122–125. doi:10.1037/h0058713 PMID:13044886

Ebrahim, C., Steen, R. L., & Paradise, L. (2012). Overcoming school counselors barriers to play therapy. *International Journal of Play Therapy*, *21*(4), 202–214. doi:10.1037/a0029791

Ellis, L., Schlaudecker, C., & Regimbal, C. (1995). Effectiveness of a collaborative consultation approach to basic concept instruction with kindergarten children. *Language, Speech, and Hearing Services in Schools*, *26*(1), 69–74. doi:10.1044/0161-1461.2601.69

Farber, J. G., & Klein, E. R. (1999). Classroom-based assessment of a collaborative intervention program with kindergarten and first-grade students. *Language, Speech, and Hearing Services in Schools*, *30*(1), 83–91. doi:10.1044/0161-1461.3001.83 PMID:27764293

Finley, V. B. (2012). Parental involvement in speech-language intervention. University of Southern Mississippi Honors Thesis. Paper 75. Retrieved from http://aquila.usm.edu/cgi/viewcontent.cgi?article=1074&context=honors_theses

Flynn, P., & Power-deFur, L. (2013). *Collaboration in schools: Let the magic begin.* Presentation at the American Speech-Language and Hearing Association Schools Conference. Retrieved from http:// www.asha.org/events/convention/handouts/2013/1403-flynn/

Formaad, W. (1974). *Articulation therapy through play: A multi-sensory approach.* Gled Ridge, NJ: Exceptional Press.

Glover, A., McCormack, J., & Smith-Tamaray, M. (2015). Collaboration between teachers and speech and language therapists: Services for primary school children with speech, language and communication needs. *Child Language Teaching and Therapy*, *31*(3), 363–382. doi:10.1177/0265659015603779

Gregl, A., Kirigin, M., Bilać, S., Sućeska Ligutićić, R., Jakšić, N., & Jakovljević, M. (2014). Speech comprehension and emotional/behavioral problems in children with specific language impairment (SLI). *Collegium Antropologicum*, *38*(3), 871–877.

Hall, P. (2005). Interprofessional teamwork: Professional cultures as barriers. *Journal of Interprofessional Care, 19*(sup1), 188-196.

Hartas, D. (2004). Teacher and speech-language therapist collaboration: Being equal and achieving a common goal. *Child Language Teaching and Therapy*, *20*(1), 33–54. doi:10.1191/0265659004ct262oa

Helker, W. P., & Ray, D. C. (2009). Impact of child teacher relationship training on teachers' and aides' use of relationship-building skills and the effects on student classroom behavior. *International Journal of Play Therapy*, *18*(2), 70.

Helker, W. P., Schottelkorb, A. A., & Ray, D. (2007). Helping students and teachers CONNECT: An intervention model for school counselors. *Journal of Professional Counseling, Practice, Theory, & Research*, *35*, 31–45.

Im-Bolter, N., & Cohen, N. J. (2007). Language impairment and psychiatric comorbidities. *Pediatric Clinics of North America*, *54*(3), 525–542.

Irwin, E. C., & McWilliams, B. J. (1974). Play therapy for children with cleft palates. *Children Today*, *3*(3), 18–22. PMID:4464044

Jackson, L. (1950). Non-speaking children. *The British Journal of Medical Psychology*, *23*(1-2), 87–100. doi:10.1111/j.2044-8341.1950.tb00373.x PMID:14801378

Jeffree, D., & McConkey, R. (1974). Extending language through play. *Special Education: Forward Trends*, *1*(3), 13. PMID:4282762

Kaiser, A., & Hancock, T. (2013). Teaching parents new skills to support their young childrens development. *Infants and Young Children*, *16*(1), 9–21. doi:10.1097/00001163-200301000-00003

Kena, G., Musu-Gillette, L., Robinson, J., Wang, X., Rathbun, A., Zhang, J., & Velez, E. D. V. (2015). *The Condition of Education 2015. NCES 2015-144*. National Center for Education Statistics.

Kirkham, J., Stewart, A., & Kidd, E. (2013). Concurrent and longitudinal relationships between development in graphic, language and symbolic play domains from the fourth to the fifth year. *Infant and Child Development*, *22*(3), 297–319. doi:10.1002/icd.1786

Kupperman, P., Bligh, S., & Goodban, M. (1980). Activating articulation skills through theraplay. *The Journal of Speech and Hearing Disorders*, *45*(4), 540–548. doi:10.1044/jshd.4504.540 PMID:7442168

Lamanna, J. E. (2005). *Child-centered play therapy in elementary schools* (Counselor Education Master's Thesis). State University of New York.

Landreth, G. L. (2002). *Play therapy: The art of the relationship* (2nd ed.). Routledge.

Landreth, G. L., Ray, D. C., & Bratton, S. C. (2009). Play therapy in elementary schools. *Psychology in the Schools*, *46*(3), 281–289. doi:10.1002/pits.20374

Leonard, L., & Leonard, P. (2003). The continuing trouble with collaboration: Teachers talk. *Current Issues in Education, 6*(15).

Leslie, A. (1987). Pretense and representation: The origins of theory of mind. *Psychological Review*, *94*(4), 412–426. doi:10.1037/0033-295X.94.4.412

Lieberman, M. D., Eisenberger, N. I., Crockett, M. J., Tom, S. M., Pfeifer, J. H., & Way, B. M. (2007). Putting feelings into words: Affect labeling disrupts amygdala activity in response to affect stimuli. *Association for Psychological Science*, *18*(5), 421–428.

Lillard, A. S., Lerner, M. D., Hopkins, E. J., Dore, R. A., Smith, E. D., & Palmquist, C. M. (2013). The impact of pretend play on childrens development: A review of the evidence. *Psychological Bulletin*, *139*(1), 1–34. doi:10.1037/a0029321 PMID:22905949

Lindsay, G., Dockrell, J. E., & Strand, S. (2007). Longitudinal patterns of behaviour problems in children with specific speech and language difficulties: Child and contextual factors. *The British Journal of Educational Psychology*, *77*(4), 811–828.

Lolan, A. R. (2011). *Play therapists' practice patterns and perceptions of the factors that influence caregiver engagement in play therapy* (Doctoral dissertation). Retrieved from http://scholarworks.uno.edu/td/1352/

Lyytinen, P., Poikkeus, A. M., & Laakso, M. L. (1997). Language and symbolic play in toddlers. *International Journal of Behavioral Development*, *21*(2), 289–302. doi:10.1080/016502597384875

Lyytinen, P., Poikkeus, A. M., Laakso, M. L., Eklund, K., & Lyytinen, H. (2001). Language development and symbolic play in children with and without familial risk for dyslexia. *Journal of Speech, Language, and Hearing Research: JSLHR*, *44*(4), 873–885. doi:10.1044/1092-4388(2001/070) PMID:11521780

Martin, J. A. (1981). *Voice, speech and language in the child: Development and disorder*. New York: Springer-Verlag. doi:10.1007/978-3-7091-7042-7

McConkey, R. (1976). Extending language through play. *Journal of Child Psychology and Psychiatry, and Allied Disciplines*, *17*, 189–197.

McCune, L. (1995). A normative study of representational play at the transition to language. *Developmental Psychology*, *31*(2), 198–206. doi:10.1037/0012-1649.31.2.198

McCune, L. (2010). Symbolic transformation: The mind in movement through culture and society. In B. Wagoner (Ed.), *Symbolic Transformation* (pp. 193–209). London: Routledge Press.

McCune-Nicolich, L. (1981). Toward symbolic functioning: Structures of early pretend games and potential parallels with language. *Child Development*, *52*(3), 785–797. doi:10.2307/1129078

Morrison, M. O., & Bratton, S. C. (2010). Preliminary investigation of an early mental health intervention for Head Start programs: Effects of child teacher relationship training on children's behavior problems. *Psychology in the Schools*, *47*(10), 1003–1017.

Muris, P., Steerneman, P., Merckelbach, H., Holdrinet, I., & Meesters, C. (1998). Comorbid anxiety symptoms in children with pervasive developmental disorders. *Journal of Anxiety Disorders*, *12*(4), 387–393.

National Board for Professional Teaching Standards. (2014). *What teachers should know and be able to do*. Retrieved from www.nbpts.org/sites/default/files/what_teachers_should_know.pdf

O'Toole, C. (2005). The relationship between preverbal behaviours and language development: Investigating symbolic play and language development in children with Down Syndrome. *Questions of Quality*, 241.

Oandasan, I., & Reeves, S. (2005). Key elements of interprofessional education. Part 2: Factors, processes and outcomes. *Journal of Interprofessional Care, 19*(sup1), 39-48.

Orr, E., & Geva, R. (2015). Symbolic play and language development. *Infant Behavior and Development*, *38*, 147–161. doi:10.1016/j.infbeh.2015.01.002 PMID:25658200

Panel, I. E. C. E. (2011). *Core competencies for interprofessional collaborative practice: Report of an expert panel*. Interprofessional Education Collaborative Expert Panel.

Peabody, M. A., & Demanchick, S. P. (2016). Interprofessional opportunities: Understanding roles in collaborative practice. *International Journal of Play Therapy*. doi:10.1037/pla0000013

Pellegrini, A. D. (1985). Relations between preschool children's symbolic play and literate behavior. *Play, language and stories: The development of children's literate behavior*, 79-97.

Perou, R., Bitsko, R. H., Blumberg, S. J., Pastor, P., Ghandour, R. M., Gfroerer, J. C., & Parks, S. E. (2013). Mental health surveillance among children—United States, 2005–2011. *MMWR. Surveillance Summaries*, *62*(Suppl 2), 1–35. PMID:23677130

Perryman, K., & Doran, J. (2010). Guidelines for incorporating play therapy in the schools. *School-Based Play Therapy*, 61.

Piaget, J. (1959). *The language and thought of the child*. New York: Humanities.

Piaget, J. (1962). *Play dreams, and imitation in childhood*. New York: W.W. Norton.

Pinborough-Zimmerman, J., Satterfield, R., Miller, J., Bilder, D., Hossain, S., & McMahon, W. (2007). Communication disorders: Prevalence and comorbid intellectual disability, autism, and emotional/behavioral disorders. *American Journal of Speech-Language Pathology*, *16*(4), 359–367.

Post, P. (2001). Play Therapy with Selective Mute Children. In G. Landreth (Ed.), *Innovations in Play Therapy* (pp. 303–321). Routledge.

Post, P. (2014). Involving parents in child-centered play therapy. *Counseling Today*. Retrieved from http://ct.counseling.org/2014/08/involving-parents-in-child-centered-play-therapy/

Pryzwansky, W. B. (1974). A reconsideration of the consultation model for delivery of school-based psychological services. *The American Journal of Orthopsychiatry*, *44*(4), 579–583. doi:10.1111/j.1939-0025.1974.tb00912.x PMID:4844029

Ray, D. (2011). *Advanced play therapy: Essential conditions, knowledge, and skills for child practice*. Taylor & Francis.

Ray, D. C. (2014). *Child-centered play therapy parent services: A Q-methodological investigation* (Doctoral dissertation). University of North Texas.

Ray, D. C., Armstrong, S. A., Warren, E. S., & Balkin, R. S. (2005). Play therapy practices among elementary school counselors. *Professional School Counseling*, 360–365.

Rescorla, L., & Goossens, M. (1992). Symbolic play development in toddlers with expressive specific language impairment (SLI-E). *Journal of Speech, Language, and Hearing Research: JSLHR*, *35*(6), 1290–1302. doi:10.1044/jshr.3506.1290 PMID:1283611

Reymert, M. L. (1946). Play therapy of Mooseheart. *Journal of Exceptional Children*, *13*(1), 2. PMID:20277977

Rogers, C. (1957). The necessary and sufficient conditions of therapeutic personality change. *Journal of Consulting Psychology*, *21*(2), 95–103. doi:10.1037/h0045357 PMID:13416422

San Martín-Rodríguez, L., Beaulieu, M. D., D'Amour, D., & Ferrada-Videla, M. (2005). The determinants of successful collaboration: a review of theoretical and empirical studies. *Journal of Interprofessional Care, 19*(sup1), 132-147.

Saracho, O. N. (2013). *An integrated play-based curriculum for young children*. Routledge.

Scherer, N. J., & DAntonio, L. (1997). Language and play development in toddlers with cleft lip and/or palate. *American Journal of Speech-Language Pathology*, *6*(4), 48–54. doi:10.1044/1058-0360.0604.48

Schottelkorb, A. A., Swan, K. L., & Ogawa, Y. (2015). Parent consultation in child-centered play therapy: A model for research and practice. *International Journal of Play Therapy*, *24*(4), 221–233. doi:10.1037/a0039609

Sigman, M., & Ungerer, J. (1984, March). Cognitive and language skills in autistic, mentally retarded, and normal children. *Developmental Psychology*, *20*(2), 293–302. doi:10.1037/0012-1649.20.2.293

Silva, P. A., Williams, S., & McGee, R. (1987). A longitudinal study of children with developmental language delay at age three: Later intelligence, reading and behaviour problems. *Developmental Medicine and Child Neurology*, *29*(5), 630–640.

Smathers, S., & Tirnauer, L. (1959). Speech-play therapy. *The Journal of Speech and Hearing Disorders*, *24*(1), 59–61. doi:10.1044/jshd.2401.59 PMID:13631694

Sokoloff, M. A. (1959). A comparison of gains in communicative skills, resulting from group play therapy and individual speech therapy, among a group of non-severely dysarthric, speech handicapped cerebral palsied children (PhD diss., New York University). *Dissertation Abstracts International*, *20*(02), B803.

Solomon, R., Van Egeren, L. A., Mahoney, G., Huber, M. S. Q., & Zimmerman, P. (2014). PLAY Project Home Consultation intervention program for young children with autism spectrum disorders: A randomized controlled trial. *Journal of Developmental and Behavioral Pediatrics*, *35*(8), 475.

Tamis-LeMonda, C. S., & Bornstein, M. H. (1994). Specificity in mother-toddler language-play relations across the second year. *Developmental Psychology*, *30*(2), 283–292. doi:10.1037/0012-1649.30.2.283

Thiemann-Bourque, K. S., Brady, N. C., & Fleming, K. K. (2012). Symbolic play of preschoolers with severe communication impairments with autism and other developmental delays: More similarities than differences. *Journal of Autism and Developmental Disorders*, *42*(5), 863–873. doi:10.1007/s10803-011-1317-7 PMID:21720725

Thomas, R. M., & Kaipa, R. (2016). Speech and language deficits in separation anxiety disorder. *Advances in Pediatric Research, 3*(7).

Throneburg, R. N., Calvert, L. K., Sturm, J. J., Paramboukas, A. A., & Paul, P. J. (2000). A comparison of service delivery models effects on curricular vocabulary skills in the school setting. *American Journal of Speech-Language Pathology*, *9*(1), 10–20. doi:10.1044/1058-0360.0901.10

Tollerfield, I. (2003). The process of collaboration within a special school setting: An exploration of the ways in which skills and knowledge are shared and barriers are overcome when a teacher and speech and language therapist collaborate. *Child Language Teaching and Therapy*, *19*(1), 67–84. doi:10.1191/0265659003ct244oa

Toppelberg, C. O., & Shapiro, T. (2000). Language disorders: A 10-year research update review. *Journal of the American Academy of Child and Adolescent Psychiatry*, *39*(2), 143–152.

United States Department of Health and Human Services. (2000). *Report of the Surgeon General's Conference on Children's Mental Health: A national action agenda*. Author.

United States President Obama. (2013). *Now is the Time: The President's Plan to Protect Our Children and Our Communities by Reducing Gun Violence*. White House.

Van Kleeck, A., Gillam, R. B., & McFadden, T. U. (1998). A study of classroom-based phonological awareness training for preschoolers with speech and/or language disorders. *American Journal of Speech-Language Pathology*, *7*(3), 65–76. doi:10.1044/1058-0360.0703.65

VanFleet, R. (1994). *Filial therapy: Strengthening parent–child relationships through play*. Professional Resource Press/Professional Resource Exchange.

Vygotsky, L. (1933). Play and its role in the mental development of the child. In J. S. Bruner, A. Jolly, & K. Sylva (Eds.), *Play* (pp. 537–555). New York: Basic Books.

Wakaba, Y. Y. (1983). Group play therapy for Japanese children who stutter. *Journal of Fluency Disorders*, *8*(2), 93–118. doi:10.1016/0094-730X(83)90023-2

Watts, A. G., Hawthorn, R., Hoffbrand, J., Jackson, H., & Spurling, A. (1997). Developing local lifelong guidance strategies. *British Journal of Guidance & Counselling*, *25*(2), 217–227. doi:10.1080/03069889708253803

Werner, L. S. (1945). Treatment of a child with delayed speech. *The Journal of Speech Disorders*, *10*(4), 329–334. doi:10.1044/jshd.1004.329 PMID:21004357

Westby, C. E. (1980). Assessment of cognitive and language abilities through play. *Language, Speech, and Hearing Services in Schools*, *11*(3), 154–168. doi:10.1044/0161-1461.1103.154

White, J., Flynt, M., & Draper, K. (1997). Kinder therapy: Teachers as therapeutic agents. *International Journal of Play Therapy*, *6*(2), 33.

Whitmire, K. (2002). The evolution of school-based speech-language services: A half century of change and a new century of practice. *Communication Disorders, 23*(2), 68-76.

Wilcox, M. J., Kouri, T. A., & Caswell, S. B. (1991). Early Language language InterventionA intervention: A Comparison comparison of Classroom classroom and Individual individual Treatmenttreatment. *American Journal of Speech-Language Pathology*, *1*(1), 49–62. doi:10.1044/1058-0360.0101.49

Yew, S. G. K., & O'Kearney, R. (2013). Emotional and behavioural outcomes later in childhood and adolescence for children with specific language impairments: Meta-analyses of controlled prospective studies. *Journal of Child Psychology and Psychiatry, and Allied Disciplines*, *54*(5), 516–524.

Chapter 18
The Play Therapist in the Courtroom:
Preparing Yourself and Your Client for Court

Jeffrey M. Sullivan
Sam Houston State University, USA

Sinem Akay
Sam Houston State University, USA

ABSTRACT

This chapter addresses what is often the most anxiety inducing experience most play therapists will encounter in their professional career: appearing in court. Play therapists who work with cases of child abuse face a higher chance of appearing in court on behalf of their child client. The purpose this chapter is to detail some ways play therapists can best prepare for the court process, which often begins at the moment the client relationship is established, how to prepare for court once a subpoena is received, and best practices for testifying in court on behalf of the child client. Finally, this chapter discusses the effects of court on the child and how to best help children recover from courtroom experiences.

INTRODUCTION

Child Protective Services (CPS) received around 3.4 million child abuse and neglect reports in 2012. Among these referrals, 9.2 per 1,000 children were victims of abuse; of which 78% were neglect, 18% were physical abuse, and 9% were sexual abuse (U.S. Department of Health and Human Services, Administration for Children and Families, Administration on Children and Families, Children's Bureau, 2012). According to Finkelhor, Shattuck, Turner, and Hamby (2014), 1 in 4 children living in the U.S. experience some form of abuse during their childhood years. Equally distressing is a recent meta-analytic review of childhood neglect in the U.S., which revealed that the overall estimated prevalence for physical neglect of children was 163 per 1,000, while the prevalence of emotional neglect numbered 184 per

DOI: 10.4018/978-1-5225-2224-9.ch018

1,000 (Stoltenborg, Bakermans-Kranenburg, & Ijzendoorn, 2013). Clearly there are an alarming number of abuse cases in the U.S., and probably even more that go unreported.

These numbers, however, only capture cases at the time of report, and fail to capture what happens to children once their abuse is reported. The events that follow the reporting of abuse are every bit as challenging for children as dealing with the abuse itself because the abuse is now in the open, and should children be called on to appear in court, testify in their own defense, and face their abuser directly, this experience may leave a scar almost as deep as the abuse itself. And if this child is a client in play therapy, then the play therapist often feels challenged in ways that they rarely feel prepared to face.

Play therapists provide children with developmentally appropriate treatments to deal with trauma and are invaluable resources for children to recover from trauma related to neglect and abuse. However, most play therapists are equipped to work with children and caregivers to provide trauma treatment, but are underprepared for being subpoenaed to testify in court. The courtroom is far removed from the warmer confines of the therapeutic relationship. When going to court, expectations change and the role of the play therapist shifts from therapeutic ally of the child to objective witness of the facts.

While the legal system over the past 10 years has continued to recognize play therapy as an appropriate method for counseling children (Snow, 2016), play therapists appearing in court may still experience systematic scrutiny of their records, manner of practice, and professional credibility. Play therapists unaccustomed to this level of scrutiny may experience what feels like an attack on their personal and professional integrity. Moreover, upon completing a courtroom experience as a witness, play therapists may be left wondering whether their testimony actually helped or possibly even harmed their client's case, leaving them feeling dejected, guilty, and even traumatized. Most certainly, going to court is a scary experience, as the authors of this chapter will attest, and it's common to feel lost, vulnerable, and isolated when summoned to appear in court.

The purpose of this chapter is to shed light on an aspect of play therapy practice that many play therapists don't understand or acknowledge until the subpoena arrives at their doorstep. It will help play therapists prepare for the day of court, which can be emotionally and professionally overwhelming. The information provided in this chapter will help play therapists better understand the legal process, from reporting child abuse to going to court. Play therapists will understand their roles in court when called to testify on behalf of their clients, and know ethical ways of working with attorneys during court preparation. Additionally, this chapter will include tips for play therapists to help prepare their clients for court, as well as process the aftermath of appearing in court, so they can avoid further traumatization. Our ultimate goal is to help play therapists feel better orientated and prepared for the courtroom experience.

Finally, it is important to note that because this chapter is written for a United States audience, it is written in general terms that will apply to most states. However, as always, play therapists are encouraged to familiarize themselves with relevant state laws regarding the legal process and abuse reporting and prevention, as well as relevant codes of professional ethics (e.g. licensed professional counselor, social worker, licensed marriage and family therapist, psychologist, etc.).

BEST PRACTICES TO GET PREPARED FOR COURT

Reporting Abuse and Neglect

In the U.S., approximately 48 states designate professionals who are mandated by law to report child abuse and neglect (Child Welfare Information Gateway, 2013). Mandatory reporters are typically people who have frequent contact with children, such as mental health care professionals, childcare providers, law enforcement officers, medical examiners, social workers, and teachers. Additionally, in 18 states, all citizens, regardless of their profession, are required to report child maltreatment.

Like other mental health professionals, play therapists are mandated to report abuse and neglect of children when it comes to their attention. Play therapists are required to use the appropriate reporting phone numbers or websites assigned for each state by the government any day and time to report maltreatment of children (Child Welfare Information Gateway, 2016). For play therapists who testify in court in cases of abuse, the process of being an effective witness begins with the report of abuse. It cannot be overstated the importance of making a timely and detailed report of abuse when abuse is suspected, and knowing the appropriate professional boundaries to respect when questioning child clients about suspected abuse.

In most cases, play therapists will encounter one of two scenarios that necessitate making a report to a child protective agency: 1) the caregiver states that their child reported being maltreated, or 2) a child makes a spontaneous and suspicious statement during the session (Kuehnle & Connell, 2010). Signs that abuse is taking place might include (HelpGuide.org, 2016):

- **Signs of Physical Abuse:**
  - Frequent injuries or unexplained bruises, welts, or cuts
  - Child always being watchful and on alert
  - Injuries appear to have a pattern such as marks from a hand or belt
  - Shying away from touch, flinches at sudden movements, and seems afraid to go home
  - Wears inappropriate clothing to cover up injuries, such as long sleeved shirts on hot days
- **Signs of Sexual Abuse:**
  - Trouble walking or sitting
  - Displays knowledge or interest in sexual acts inappropriate to his or her age, or even seductive behavior
  - Makes strong efforts to avoid a specific person, without an obvious reason
  - Runs away from home
- **Signs of Neglect:**
  - Clothes are ill-fitting, filthy, or inappropriate for the weather
  - Hygiene is consistently bad (unbathed, matted and unwashed hair, noticeable body odor)
  - Untreated illnesses and physical injuries
  - Is frequently unsupervised or left alone or allowed to play in unsafe situations and environments
  - Is frequently late or missing from school

Considering the importance of thorough child abuse reports, the authors believe that play therapists may need to set aside their theoretical approach, which may caution play therapists from asking direct questions, so they may ask open-ended and non-leading questions to ensure child's safety. If a child makes a spontaneous and suspicious statement during the session, play therapists need to ensure child's safety by asking one or two open ended questions, such as "Tell me more about how your dad touched your pee pee" or "Tell me more about who left these bruises on you" (Kuehnle & Connell, 2010). This way the play therapist can gain enough information to report the abuse or neglect, and help child protection agencies to make an informed decision about safety of the child. Also, this will help therapist to understand context of reported action; whether or not it can be categorized as abuse. As an example, in order to make an accurate report, play therapists need to know if a father touched his 3 year-old son's genitals in the bathtub to help him clean or it was a sexualized act. And because child protection agencies frequently prioritize their cases according to immediacy of danger, their response times often differ from one case to another. In other words, child protection agencies will act faster if the alleged perpetrator of the child is their primary caregiver when compared to an alleged perpetrator who is a distant uncle and currently in jail. If the play therapist needs to talk with the caregiver after a child makes an outcry to help ensure the child's safety, it is important to encourage the caregiver not to ask the child any questions. Having discussions regarding the abuse may cause errors in memory due to leading and misleading questions (Principe & Schindewolf, 2012; Warren & Peterson, 2014), which may cause to the child to provide inaccurate information during the forensic interview.

After therapists report child abuse or neglect, the child protection agency will typically visit the child at home or school to confirm the presence of abuse. Should there be enough evidence to suggest the presence of abuse, the victimized children typically go through an interview led by trained forensic interviewers who work to elicit the most accurate information from children (Kuehnle & Connell, 2010). In order to avoid unwilling shaping and reinforcing of erroneous statements during the therapy process, legal professionals prefer children to complete a forensic interview before starting or continuing the process of therapy.

It is of the upmost importance for play therapists to understand that their role is to *report* suspected abuse, and not to *investigate* suspected abuse. When factors such as suggestive questioning or interview bias occur in play session because of the therapist's leading questions (e.g., "Was it your dad who touched your private part?"), child's memories may become tainted (Kuehnle & Connell, 2010), which may lead to the case becoming more difficult to prosecute. Additionally, play therapists continually questioning their clients in play sessions to gather more information regarding alleged abuse deprives children of therapeutic support that is exhibited within a relationship that relies on neutrality and unconditional acceptance of the child.

The *investigation* of suspected abuse relies on other professionals, such as trained child abuse investigators or forensic interviewers, who bring their expertise to the task (Kuehnle & Connell, 2010). This expertise includes both clinical and forensic skills, and these forensic skills are usually beyond the purview of play therapists, and include knowledge of interview techniques that elicit the most accurate information, knowledge about ways children's reports may be tainted or preserved, and advantages and disadvantages of special accommodations for children's testimony. Without specialized training in forensic skills, play therapists should in no way attempt to investigate abuse beyond what is needed to make an official abuse report. Doing so may interfere with information later collected from the child by trained officials and could jeopardize a criminal case against the alleged perpetrator.

It is highly recommended that play therapists familiarize themselves with the child abuse reporting process in their state to know specifically what information needs to be collected if a child makes an outcry in session. Many states now have an option for online reporting that play therapists can download and study to know what types of information to obtain when gathering information about abuse. Also, it is common to feel unsure whether the information a child reports actually rises to legal levels of abuse. It is recommended that when in doubt, play therapists call the state's child protection agency and ask whether making an official report is needed. Because reporting child abuse is the law in every state, if there are any doubts, it is always better to err on the side of caution and inquire as to whether a report is required.

Play Therapy after a Report of Abuse

In the legal context, it is important for therapists to be aware of most the appropriate time to provide services for children who are allegedly abused or neglected (Cheung, 2012). If the outcry or report of abuse occurs after the initiation of play therapy, the play therapist may need to take important steps to protect the integrity of the investigation. For instance, should the investigation proceed to the forensic interview, the authors recommend consulting with the forensic interviewer and other officials investigating the case to determine whether to suspend play therapy services until the interview is completed so that children's eyewitness statements can be preserved without fear of contamination.

If children have to wait for the interview and are in need of immediate treatment, play therapists may need to start or continue treatment before the forensic interview. In this case, play therapists need to make sure that they do not bias future disclosures by distorting children's view of their experience (e.g., talking about forgiveness, discussing possible punishments for the alleged perpetrator, talking about uncertainties related to the child's placement if the alleged perpetrator is the primary caregiver) (Cheung, 2012). If play therapy begins after the reporting of abuse and during the investigation, such as when a caregiver seeks play therapy to help a child recover from the effects of the abuse, play therapists should work closely with primary caregivers and investigating officials to determine the status of the case and the potential role of the play therapist as the investigation continues. The best practice for play therapists is to focus on emotional and behavioral symptoms in session and help children cope with these symptoms without prompting children to talk about details of the abuse or neglect.

Play Therapists' Role in the Criminal Justice System

Prosecutors in the United States need to meet the "beyond reasonable doubt" standard of evidence in order to convict an alleged perpetrator (Staller & Vandervort, 2010). This standard requires prosecutors to provide strong evidence, as well as convince the jury or judge of the alleged perpetrator's guilt beyond doubt. However, children are at a great disadvantage in the criminal justice system because it relies heavily on their verbal statements during forensic interview to verify abuse allegations, as in sexual abuse cases where delayed outcries are common and thus the evidence is limited (Azzopardi, Madigan, & Kirkland-Burke, 2014), In order to overcome this disadvantage, prosecutors often request a court order for therapy notes and subpoena play therapists as witnesses in court.

Session Notes and Documentation

Thorough but concise documentation is an important part of being an ethically and legally prepared therapist (Harris et al., 2009). Combined with an explanation of play therapy, children's developmentally appropriate ways to express themselves, and clients' background information, play therapists' documentation can be used in court as a supportive evidence. Play therapy documentation may include children's emotional, cognitive, and behavioral assessment results, their progress throughout the therapy process, and children's and their parent's clinically important statements during sessions. Being thorough with documentation also means that play therapists document their interactions with other professionals that are involved in the child's life such as doctors, child protection agencies, caseworkers, child advocates, law enforcement officers, and attorneys. This will help play therapists go back to the file and refresh their memories related to that specific case when necessary. Play therapists need to remember that different states and licensing boards may have different rules and regulations on clinical documentation (Harris et al., 2009). In order to avoid disciplinary actions, play therapists need to be aware of specific regulations that apply to them.

While thorough documentation is an important part of ethical practice, giving too much detail in the session notes may jeopardize confidentiality of the therapeutic relationship as well as integrity of the client (Harris et al., 2009). If play therapists can learn to be brief, but comprehensive, play therapy notes can be both thorough and concise. For example, if a child tells her play therapist that the punching bag is her alleged perpetrator, then beats up the punching bag and screams "I hate you for what you did to me," the play therapist can be thorough and concise by writing the following statement in his session note: "The client worked on her anger towards the alleged perpetrator. She expressed her anger both verbally and behaviorally in the playroom." This statement serves to protect the child's confidentiality by not focusing on the specific behaviors or statements, but focusing on the clinically important feelings and behaviors.

For play therapists who are subpoenaed to provide documentation or witness statements for court, thorough documentation will allow them to show a jury or judge that they did not say or do anything in session to bias children's reports related to alleged abuse or neglect. When a child makes an outcry in session, it is important to document exact initial comment of the child, the follow up questions of play therapist, and the child's responses (Kuehnle, 1996). If a child reports during a play session that his uncle touched his genitals, the play therapist may write following statement in the session note: "The client was playing with the dollhouse when he volunteered the information that his uncle touched his "pee-pee" when they were playing hide and seek together at the client's house. When the therapist asked the client to show where his "pee-pee" was, the client pointed to his penis." This type of documentation is different than concise session notes, as detailed information about the outcry will help show jury the validity of child's statements.

If the child does not make a full outcry using verbal communication, play behaviors of the child in session are important when recognizing child abuse or neglect. Thus, in addition to documenting clinically significant verbal interactions, play therapists need to document play behaviors as well. If the child undresses two dolls (identified by the child as "me and my uncle") and puts them in the same bed, the play therapist will need to document this play with a detailed description. The play therapist also needs to document the questions that he or she asked following sexualized play (e.g., "The play therapist asked the client to tell more about what happened after they were in bed.") If the child does not talk, but rather conveys the experience using the dolls, the play therapist will need to describe the play again in detail in session documentation (e.g., "The client put the doll that he identified as his uncle on top of the doll that he identified as himself.")

Receiving Calls or Letters from Attorneys

When attorneys contact play therapists regarding a client, play therapists need to gather more information about the request before sending attorneys any paperwork, letters, or giving attorneys details about the case over the phone. This will include questions about the person they represent (client or alleged perpetrator), nature of proceedings, type of information that they want to gather, time frame, and format of requested information (Barsky & Gould, 2002). The play therapist should not confirm that they know the client until the attorney sends a signed release of information showing the custodian of the child grants permission for the play therapist to provide this information to the attorney. Doing so is important to ensure the client's confidentiality. If more than one adult has custody of the child, then the play therapist should obtain signatures from all parties involved. However, in the cases where a primary caregiver is the alleged abuser, the play therapist can obtain signatures only from non-offending caregivers who have custodial rights over the child.

Barsky and Gould (2002) suggested a statement that clinicians can give to attorneys, which has been adjusted by the authors to meet the needs of play therapists:

The policy of my agency (or private practice) requires that I first gather information about the nature of your request. Out of respect for client confidentiality, I cannot tell you whether this person is a client of this agency. If the person is a client, I will need to speak with his or her custodian and obtain a written release of confidential information. I will call you by [date] to let you know whether I have a consent to talk to you about this client.

If the primary custodian of the child does not want to sign a release of information form, then the play therapist will need to hold on to the requested information unless legally required by a subpoena or court order to disclose the information. Furthermore, it is important for play therapists not to discuss important information over the phone, as it may be used in court without the play therapist's knowledge, and play therapists may be called to testify in court regarding these statements (Barsky & Gould, 2002). Offering to give requested information in the form of a letter may allow play therapists to think through their statements that may be used in court, but such a letter may only be sent after obtaining permission from the primary custodian of the child.

Being Subpoenaed and Witnessing in Court

One of the more stressful experiences a play therapist can go through is being subpoenaed, which is the beginning of their legal involvement in court. It is when play therapists often feel most vulnerable as professionals, in large part because their credibility and license are subject to scrutiny by lawyers whose job it is to take apart their report of experiences to determine what they consider the best version of the events that transpired. There are many nuances to responding to a subpoena, understanding the role you will play in the court proceedings, and working with the different parties involved. Without some understanding of these nuances, play therapists often feel lost and unsure of how to best represent themselves and their clients in court.

Types of Witnesses

Play therapists who appear as witnesses in court, but who are unfamiliar with the courtroom process, often don't understand that there are two roles for witnesses in court: fact witness and expert witness (Children's Law Center, 2010), and that they are often mutually exclusive. But because courtroom dramas on television and movies depict witnesses who are experts in their field and on their client, and who deliver testimony upon which the entire case hangs in the balance, many play therapists new to the court experience feel tremendous pressure to "win the case" for their client by delivering testimony that will produce the best outcome for their client and the community. However, for most play therapists, the truth about testifying as a witness is much more dry. Most play therapists are called to testify as fact witnesses, asked to deliver "just the facts", and keep their opinions to themselves.

Fact witnesses testify based on their direct personal knowledge and observation (Children's Law Center, 2010). They avoid introducing any of their own opinions about the client or case and stick only to what they have directly witnessed while working with the client. In other words, play therapists who serve as fact witnesses may only talk about the information that they themselves gathered in sessions, and only report on what they observed. This standard of testimony for fact witnesses is true whether appearing in civil or criminal court. For instance, as a fact witness, the play therapist may testify that her child client attended 16 play therapy sessions, the child client reported in session that the she was sexually abused, that the client's mother reported that she was sexually abused, and that the client presented as traumatized as evidenced by her rumination over specific instances of being sexually abused and self-description that she did something wrong.

Notice how as a fact witness, most statements begin with "The client reported…", "The client presented…", and "The client described…", as well as "…as evidenced by the client." These qualifiers are crucial to the play therapist's testimony as a fact witness and suggest an objective stance, as though the play therapist is reporting only what was observed without subjective opinion or bias. If not directly asked, fact witnesses are required to stay away from offering subjective opinions in court that are not based on facts.

Mental health clinicians, including play therapists, have been accused of not being able to differentiate facts from subjective opinions or observations (Barsky & Gould, 2002), in large part because clinicians *do* operate in the realm of interpretation. One of the main principles behind all play therapy approaches is that children express themselves best through play, a symbolic medium, and play therapists have the specialized knowledge and skill to understand a child's play in therapeutic terms. Moreover, play therapists are used to making educated assumptions and informal assessments by looking at children's feelings, thoughts, and behaviors, as well as family dynamics. However, in court, attorneys are interested in observable and documented facts, such as what happened, what was said, and how many times something occurred, rather than subjective meanings attributed to specific situations (Bond & Sandhu, 2005).

Play therapists' tendency to look beyond the facts may cause problems for them in court if they bring too much interpretation to their courtroom testimony as a fact witness. Thus, play therapists need to put additional effort to think outside of their training and stick to the facts while they are on the stand as fact witnesses. If the attorney asks a play therapist what she saw and heard in session, the play therapist can talk about the nonverbal and verbal communication by the child and the child's play, such as "Jimmy picked two dolls and said that one of them was him and the other was his uncle. Then he took their clothes off and put them in the same bed next to each other." By responding in this way, the play therapist talks strictly about the facts rather than talking about her own opinions about what was the meaning that Jimmy attributed to her play. Were the play therapist to say, "Jimmy picked up the two dolls and put them in the same bed next to each other, *which suggests that he may have conflicted feelings about his abuser,*" this would be going beyond the observable facts.

Thus, among the most important things to know as a fact witness is to stay only within what is known as directly observable fact. When testifying, if an attorney asks, "Based on your sessions with Jimmy, how many times was Jimmy sexually assaulted by his uncle?" and the answer in unknown by the play therapist, the play therapist must simply say "I don't know" or "That information is beyond what I learned in our sessions." What happens sometimes, however, is play therapists don't want to appear incompetent when asked about something they don't know as a fact witness, and will reach into interpretation to sound like they know the answers (Vaughan-Eden, 2008). Possible interpretative answers to the questions above might be, "Bases on Jimmy's play, he seems like he was victimized multiple times by his uncle." Because these statements are not supported by observable facts from the play therapy sessions, they are interpretative and go beyond the role of fact witness. The danger here is that the defense attorneys could discredit the entire testimony of the play therapist as interpretive, which they would support by stating the play therapist does not know the difference between facts and interpretation.

Sticking only to the facts can be a real challenge for play therapists. It goes against much of play therapy training, which includes looking for themes and patterns (Ray, 2011). It also is a skill that takes practice, and for play therapists lacking sufficient practice in reporting only the facts, it can be challenging to recognize the line between an observable fact and an interpretative opinion. Working closely with the attorneys in the case is perhaps the best way to clarify the play therapist's role, and a qualified and diligent attorney will spend time with play therapists to prep them for testifying in court and educate them about the difference between fact and interpretation. Also effective is for play therapists to get into the habit of describing and documenting their cases in terms of "The client reported…," "The client described…," and "…as evidenced by…," which will preserve the play therapists' objective reports of past sessions and present a fact-based documentation by the play therapist should his or her records ever be subpoenaed as court documents.

Contrary to fact witnesses, play therapists testifying as expert witnesses are actually allowed, if not encouraged, to provide education and opinions in court regarding the meaning behind facts and research. Play therapists as expert witnesses testify about their knowledge related to topics such as child development, trauma, impacts of trauma on children's emotional, cognitive, and behavioral wellbeing, grooming (discussed at the end of this chapter), recanting, and social and family dynamics in regards to abuse and neglect. Because expert witnesses are testifying based on their expert opinion, they are held to a different standard than fact witnesses. While fact witnesses stick to what is directly observable and reportable, and can be discredited for offering inappropriate interpretation, expert witnesses are there almost exclusively to offer their interpretation of research and facts.

To be credible as an expert witness, the play therapist must have the necessary credentials, be up to speed with current research, and have a high standing in the professional community (Vaughan-Eden, 2008). Opinions that are offered cannot simply be anecdotal, such as saying, "Based on my experience with a similar client," the opinions and interpretations need to be grounded in research and evidence-based practice. For instance, beginning responses with phrases such as, "Current research suggests (with cited sources)," and "Previous cases similar to this one reveal that… (with exemplar cases)" offer substantive credibility to expert witness testimony. Play therapists who are called to be expert witnesses need to ensure objectivity regardless of being paid by one party or another (Bond & Sandhu, 2005). If therapists who are called as expert witnesses also are the client's play therapist, they need to adopt an impartial perspective, remembering that their role is to educate jurors and facilitate a fair decision.

To be an expert witness, a play therapist does not need to be directly involved in the case. For instance, unlike fact witnesses, who are generally called to court because of their direct involvement as the child's play therapist, expert witnesses are frequently called to help judges and juries make sense of testimony, to bring a professional, educated, and specialized opinion, and to highlight areas of importance in the testimony of others (Vaughan-Eden, 2008). A criminal case involving child trauma might include the district attorney calling a play therapist as an expert witness to talk about how trauma symptoms present through play. Attorneys sometimes use fact witnesses and expert witnesses together to weave a more substantial case, such as calling the play therapist of the child as a fact witness to describe the specific details of what transpired in play therapy, and then calling another play therapist as an expert witness to offer education of the fact witness' testimony. Conversely, expert witnesses may also be called to refute the testimony of another fact or expert witness by offering a contrary opinion.

The majority of play therapists who are summoned to testify in court will be summoned as fact witnesses. They will be serving or will have had served as the child's play therapist, and have knowledge about the case that the attorneys or judge believe is valuable. Fewer play therapists will be called as expert witnesses, and these play therapists will often have a more distinguished position in the professional community and specific knowledge, education, and background experience to suggest their opinion is credible. In addition, expert witnesses are also often paid by one side involved in the case to deliver testimony seen as beneficial to that side, whereas fact witnesses are in court to describe as accurately and objectively as possible what transpired. Because of the great disparity in expectations between fact and expert witness, it is essential that play therapists know which role they are being summoned to fulfill and their specific responsibilities within this role. Knowing this will go a long way to helping the play therapist present as a credible and trustworthy witness.

Types of Court

Two sets of lawyers, the people they represent, and a judge. Taken together, you have a pretty accurate courtroom scene. Add a jury and you have the courtroom scene commonly depicted in the media. Courtrooms typically include one person or party who is bringing a complaint or suit (the plaintiff) against another person or party (the defendant). Attorneys for each side provide legal representation (unless one or both parties insist on self-representation), and both sides may call witnesses to help support their case. Juries, an assembled group of the defendant's peers, may or may not be part of the court process. If a jury is assembled, the jury decides some or all portions of the case, and if there is no jury, then the judge decides the case in what is called a bench trial, so named because where the judge sits is commonly referred to as the "bench." In most cases, the judge presides over the courtroom to maintain order and oversee the proceedings.

Within this typical courtroom structure, however, there are important differences that concern the type complaint, the person or entity bringing the complaint, and the age of the person receiving the complaint. For play therapists about to appear in court, it is important to know what type of court setting they are entering. The three general types of court settings are criminal court, juvenile court, and civil court.

Criminal court, the first type of court setting, convenes when the government is prosecuting a person who they believe has broken the law. The government, whether local, state, or federal, is always the plaintiff, and the attorneys representing them are known as district attorneys, state's attorneys, or federal prosecutors, depending upon whether the case is at the district, state, or federal level. The person charged with the crime is known as the defendant, and is guaranteed by United States law the right to an attorney for legal representation. However, in some instances, defendants may waive their right to an attorney and represent themselves. For defendants who cannot afford an attorney, they have legal access to representation by a public defender, a specialized attorney hired by the government to represent individuals who cannot afford or acquire legal representation. Examples of criminal cases in which a play therapist might be involved are physical or sexual abuse cases against a child, neglect cases, and possibly assault cases (if a child client assaults another individual).

If a person appears as a defendant in criminal court in the Unites States, they have certain rights and privileges. They have the right to an attorney, the right to confront and cross-examine witnesses, the privilege again self-incrimination, and the right to notice of charges. In addition, the prosecution must provide proof of the charges beyond a reasonable doubt before a judge or jury can convict a person. Should the defendant be found guilty, they will face punishment, and punishments can range from fines, probation, to jail or prison time. In the United States, only adults can be charged with crimes. Children under the age of 18 cannot be charged with crimes and are instead charged with delinquent acts, and their cases are heard in juvenile court.

While criminal court and juvenile court both involve the government accusing someone of breaking the law, there are several important differences between criminal court and juvenile court that extend beyond the age of the defendant. Unlike adults in criminal court, minors appearing in juvenile court are charged with delinquent acts rather than crimes, and are not "convicted", but rather found *delinquent*. Should a minor be found delinquent, the goal is to provide opportunities for rehabilitation in the best interests of the minor so they can become contributing members of society, rather than to punish, as would be the goal in criminal court.

Importantly, juveniles possess the same rights and privileges as adults in criminal court including: the right to an attorney, the right to confront and cross-examine witnesses, the privilege again self-incrimination, and the right to notice of charges. However, juveniles do not have the right to a jury trial, and must have their case heard before a judge in what is called an adjudication hearing. And juveniles are protected by the same burden of proof standard that applies in criminal court, in that the prosecution must prove beyond a reasonable doubt that the juvenile is guilty of the charged delinquent act.

The third type of court setting, civil court, differs from criminal and juvenile court in that the government is not the plaintiff. Instead, the plaintiff is one individual bringing a complaint against another individual. In civil court, the plaintiff may ask for either monetary relief, such as a cash award to remedy the situation, or equitable relief, in which the plaintiff asks the court to order the other party to do or not do something. Civil cases may include a jury, but not usually. And the burden of proof is much different in civil court than criminal or juvenile court. In civil court, a preponderance of evidence is sufficient in most cases to earn a favorable ruling.

A specialized form of civil court is family court, and is a setting where play therapists might find themselves called to testify quite frequently. Family law deals with issues that emerge when intimate relationships and marriages break down, and involve the division of property, money, and debt. Unlike in civil court, in family court there may not be a clear plaintiff or defendant, as both parties may be seeking monetary or equitable relief from the other. Moreover, custody cases in which a child protection agency is involved often take play in family court. Child protection agencies may also subpoena play therapists to appear in court as witnesses to help determine custody arrangements.

Court Process

When play therapists get subpoenaed to attend court as expert or fact witnesses, first they will need to get in touch with the attorney that requested the subpoena. This will help to gain a better understanding of the type of witness required, any documents that they need to bring to court, and the type of questions that they will hear from the attorney who requested the subpoena (Stern, Vaughan-Eden, & Coslett, 2016). This is an important first step towards preparation for court. Considering that play therapists may have clients scheduled for the court date, another important step is to contact the attorney when the court date gets closers to ask whether or not the court date is postponed and at what time they need to be in court. Maintaining contact with the attorney in this way helps to plan better and avoids unnecessary cancellations for time needed in court.

It is natural for people to experience anxiety when it is time to be on the stand and answer questions. However, it is best practice for play therapists to find ways to relax as much as possible and not let their anxiety interfere with giving clear statements. Giving clear answers, having good eye-contact with attorneys and jury, and presenting a relaxed posture conveys professionalism and credibility.

Play therapists going to the trial should try to be in court earlier than the scheduled time, as stress about running late will add to their already existing anxiety (Sidebotham, 2014). When arrived at court, play therapists should introduce themselves to the court usher. Play therapists can ask the usher's advice regarding the way they should address the judge, as judges are addressed differently in different levels of court. Play therapists then will be asked to wait outside the courtroom until it is their time to be on the witness stand. Depending on the state, play therapists may be given options to take an oath or an affirmation on the stand before they start answering questions. As they answer questions, they should face the judge or the jury as their audience. Play therapists may bring copies of previously subpoenaed clinical documents in order to answer questions more accurately. Additionally, it is best practice for therapists to bring a copy of their vitae to court (Vaughan-Eden, 2008), as defense attorneys may ask detailed questions about the play therapists' experience and qualifications with an attempt to disqualify them as witnesses.

If play therapists are asked about a particular document, they can look at the copy that they already have on the stand with them or ask the attorney to show them the document (Vaughan-Eden, 2008). Unless play therapists clearly state to the judge that they exhausted their memories, they may not be allowed to look at notes and records. Vaughan-Eden suggests therapists to turn documents over to the attorney and ask to review them when necessary, as any documentation on the stand are subject to review by the attorneys.

When it is time to be on the stand, Barsky and Gould (2002) suggested ten rules for witnesses to follow regardless of which attorney is asking the questions. The following is a summary of ten rules that play therapists can follow to be effective witnesses:

1. **Tell the Truth:** Each individual who play a role in court as a witness gives an oath to tell the truth and only the truth as they step on the stand. Play therapists may feel the urge to reflect well on themselves and their clients. However, no matter what the truth is and how bad it may sound, play therapists are required to tell the whole truth.
2. **Convey Professionalism:** Although court experience can be unfamiliar for play therapists, they should remember that they have the clinical and research background to be effective witnesses. They also have skills to convey their message in an interesting and warm manner in order to get

jury's attention. Another thing to remember is that regardless of defense attorney's attitude and negative statements during cross-examination, play therapists need to keep calm and stay away from arguing or getting defensive with the attorney.

3. **Respect Formalities of the Tribunal:** Play therapists need to be aware of the unwritten rules around respect for the court and the judge. Dressing in a conservative and professional manner is one way to show this respect. Additionally, play therapists should show respect towards judges by calling them "Your Honor," and show respect to others by using only professional titles and designations.
4. **Speak Loud, Slow, and without Hesitation:** Considering that the information given during testimonies is recorded, play therapists should try to talk slower and louder than usual, and spell out unusual words when necessary. It is also best practice to take a moment before answering the questions to give attorneys time to object and provide more time to think through the answer. If play therapists need more time to formulate their answers, they can always ask for extra time to think. This will also allow them not to look hesitant or rushed.
5. **Give Concise and Clear Answers:** Although some questions can be difficult to answer with a simple "Yes" or "No," most attorneys want witnesses to answer close-ended questions as such. However, if the question is complicated or contains double negatives, it is better to follow yes or no with a brief statement such as "Yes, he told me that it was his uncle." Play therapists should also try to avoid statements such as "I guess" and "So far as I know," as these ambiguous statements will weaken the impact of their testimonies. Another important point is to gear level of language to the jury, as they may not know some terms that you use as a therapist.
6. **Let the Attorneys be in Charge:** Therapists may be used to facilitating communication through questions or statements. However, in the examination process, attorneys are in charge of asking questions and play therapists cannot facilitate additional conversations regardless of the importance of information they want to provide.
7. **Just the Facts:** Most play therapists will go to court as fact witnesses and they can only testify about the facts. Only expert witnesses can provide court with evidence based on their expert opinions. Thus, play therapists who are fact witnesses need to focus on concrete and specific information.
8. **Keep Calm:** During cross-examination by defense attorneys, it can be difficult for play therapists to keep their composure and just answer the questions to their best knowledge. Defense attorneys are trained to be adversarial in order to reach their goals. So, play therapists should try not to take the attacks personally and use relaxation techniques to keep calm during the examination process.
9. **Maintain Good Eye-Contact:** There are different opinions regarding who witnesses should look at while they are answering questions. Best practice is to have eye-contact with the person who is asking questions, and occasionally glancing at the jury or others in the room to look more natural while answering questions.
10. **Use Notes and Documents to Recall Specific Information:** Considering that play therapists see many clients during their careers, it is not reasonable to expect them to remember details about their client's behaviors or statements. Play therapists can use notes and documents in court to refresh their memories by asking permission to refer to the paperwork.

Considering that play therapists do not have extensive training regarding testifying in court and most of them do not testify often, attorneys will be understanding of any questions or concerns that therapists may have before court. Additionally, if play therapists follow some of the suggestions listed in this chapter, they will find it easier to get through the testifying process as effective witnesses.

CHILDREN IN COURT

Impacts of Court Experience on Children

Symptoms of the trauma experienced early in life through neglect, as well as sexual and physical abuse, often extend into adulthood, increasing the likelihood of issues such as poor medical health, Post-Traumatic Stress Disorder, substance abuse, anxiety, and depression (Hovens et al., 2012; Fairbank, 2008). When abuse is reported, either by the child victim or another concerned individual, dealing with the aftermath of the abuse may cause the child to be vulnerable to further distress and possible trauma. The secret that the child has been keeping about the abuse, sometimes for fear of shame or threat by the abuser should the child tell anyone, is now being addressed in public, possibly among family or other formally safe places, such as school, church, or circles of friends. The child may feel shame or even fear as a result of having the authorities investigating or prosecuting the abuser. Early interventions are needed for treatment of trauma in children in order to prevent life-long emotional problems (Kramer & Landolt, 2011), including the potential trauma that may emerge form the legal process that ensues.

According to a longitudinal study, sexual abuse victims aged 4 to 17 when their criminal case began predicted poorer adjustment approximately 12 years later as compared to participants in a control group (Quas et al., 2005). In addition, compared to matched control group individuals with no child sexual abuse experience, children who repeatedly testified in childhood, or testified in cases where the alleged perpetrator received a light sentence, predicted poorer mental health outcomes. Additionally, children who were younger when the legal case began had higher levels of externalizing problems in the future. Externalizing problems included difficulties with interpersonal relationships, rule breaking, and aggressive behaviors (Achenbach, 1999).

Quas et al. (2005) also indicated that children who had to testify in court repeatedly and whose cases resulted in a severe sentence for the perpetrator exhibited higher levels of emotional problems compared to children who did not have to testify and whose cases resulted in severe sentencing. They speculated that having to testify might offset any positive mental health effects of positive case outcome.

Although testifying in court is likely to have negative impacts on children, in many cases it is not possible to exclude them from their roles of being present for court to provide evidence (Cheung, 2012). Thus, it is important to take children's needs into consideration as they are getting prepared for this stressful event. Considering the potential impact of testifying in court on children's emotional wellbeing, it is important for play therapists to know how to prepare children for their upcoming court experience. This preparation includes using play therapy techniques to teach children age-appropriate details about court to give them a sense of control, using play therapy skills to normalize children's anxiety and fear related to going to court and potentially facing their perpetrators, and helping children to improve their coping skills to handle this stressful situation.

Preparing Children for Court

Considering the possible negative impact of court experience on children as discussed in previous section, play therapists may need to help children to become cognitively and emotionally prepared to testify in court. However, when preparing children for court, play therapists need to take precaution against possible accusations by defense attorneys that the child was biased by the play therapist's views (Cheung, 2012). One of the main things to be avoided by play therapists is helping children prepare written court testimonies. Written testimonies prepared by children in session may cause the jury to see children's testimonies as biased.

Play therapists can use play and activities to approach children at their developmental level during court preparation. Most play therapists have toys in their playrooms such as dollhouses, dolls, cars, puppets, and animals. These toys can be used in play sessions to demonstrate the courtroom and the court process. Play therapists can use dollhouse furniture and other materials in the playroom to show children how the courtroom will look when they walk in and where they will sit during their testimony. If children have high anxiety, play therapist can give them the option to use animals rather than dolls to demonstrate people in court. This may help children to gradually process the upcoming stressful event through use of symbols. It will also be helpful for children to play out the day of court step by step in the playroom using toys. Play therapists can encourage children to use toys to demonstrate the events that will take place such as waking up, having breakfast, getting in the car, going to the court house, walking into the court room, sitting on the stand, seeing family members sitting in the room, confronting the perpetrator, answering questions asked by attorneys, being done with testifying, and going back home. Knowing what is going to happen step by step will give children a sense of control.

Play therapists can also use other activities and books to help children get prepared to testify in a fun and developmentally appropriate way. Below is a list of resources that may help prepare children for court:

- Kids Go to Court Coloring Book by District Attorney Offices in the State of Alaska. Play therapists can download this book for free through website http://www.law.alaska.gov
- Let's Go to Court Booklet for children by British Columbia Ministry of Public Safety and Solicitor General. Play therapists can download this booklet for free through website http://www2.gov.bc.ca
- You are not Alone video and the Super Hero Island game prepared by the Canadian Society for Investigation of Child Abuse to help children gain more information about court. Play therapists can go to website http://www.childcourtprep.com to access the game and the video.

Regardless of the toys, games, and activities that play therapists use, children need to learn some basic concepts before they are in the courtroom. First, children need to know that there are rules that need to be followed in court, such as answering the questions and telling the truth at all times (Copen, 2000). Play therapists can use different activities to help children understand the difference between truth and lie or fiction. One example for related activities is playing out different scenarios using puppets and asking the child whether or not the puppets are telling the truth.

Children also need to know that they can correct any mistake that they make in court (Copen, 2000). Play therapists and children can role-play making mistakes and correcting them by saying "Sorry, it is not what really happened" and telling the true story. Play therapists can also use dolls, animals, and puppets to make this practice more interesting for young children.

Play therapists should also work with children to help reduce their anxiety before and during the testimony, such as teaching children how to do deep breathing exercises using bubbles. Play therapists need to first demonstrate deep breathing by counting to four with their fingers as they take a deep breathe, holding their breathe in for a few seconds, and then making a big bubble by exhaling very slowly into the bubble stick. If children can practice deep breathing in session using bubbles, they can use this skill in courtroom without the need for blowing bubbles. Play therapists can also work with children to make a small good luck charm that they can put in their pockets when they are in court.

If children are scared of going to court because they don't feel safe being in the same room with their abusers, play therapists can talk with their caregivers to get in touch with Bikers Against Child Abuse (B.A.C.A.). This organization's goal is to create a feeling of safety for children who experienced abuse by adult perpetrators (Sawyer & Judd, 2012). If requested, B.A.C.A can go to court with children to provide them a sense of protection in the courtroom.

Some children may be developmentally or emotionally unable to handle the stress related to facing their perpetrators in court. Consider a six-year-old child who was sexually abused by her father many times since she was three years old. Her father told this child repeatedly that he would hurt her if she talked about the abuse. This child goes to court before completing the play therapy process and she is still scared of getting hurt by her father. During the trial, she sits on the witness stand and faces her father who stares at her with anger the whole time she is there. This scenario is not uncommon for children to experience in the courtroom and it is not unusual for children to shut down when they face their perpetrators. Thus, depending on the child's age, developmental level, and emotional readiness to face the perpetrator, closed-circuit testimony may be needed to ensure the best outcome for the case and the child's emotional wellbeing. In closed-circuit testimony, the child testifies outside the courtroom using closed circuit television. The Supreme Court's decision allows children to testify using closed-circuit television in some cases (Mulkey, 2015). However, attorneys may be reluctant to get permission from court to use alternative methods of testimony. Thus, play therapists may need to advocate for their clients when there are developmental or emotional barriers for the child to testify in the courtroom.

Helping Children to Recover from Courtroom Experiences

After children are done with their eyewitness testimonies, play therapists should congratulate them for their achievement to testify in court. It is highly recommended for play therapists to have a session within a couple days of testifying in order to help children to process their feelings and thoughts. Again, toys and activities can be used with children to help them play out and talk about their experiences. Play therapists should look for irrational beliefs or thoughts that children may have related to their court experience such as "I made my uncle go to jail" or "I made my uncle's family cry." Play therapists can use books for psychoeducation related to abuse and punishment to help children correct their irrational thoughts.

IMPORTANT INFORMATION FOR EXPERT WITNESSES

In a trial, most jurors will not be knowledgeable in child abuse and neglect, but acquiring this knowledge during the trial is critical to their decision making process (Cossins, Goodman-Delahunty, & O'Brien, 2009). In almost every child abuse case, defense attorneys will put effort on undermining the victim's credibility, sometimes using the myths related to child abuse and neglect (e.g. If a child misses his alleged perpetrator, it means the abuse did not happen; if there are inconsistencies in the child's report, it means the outcry was inaccurate; the child would not have waited for 5 years to have an outcry if the abuse actually happened). Considering the likelihood of jurors holding misconceptions related to abused or neglected children's emotions and behaviors (Quas, Thompson, & Clarke-Stewart, 2005), play therapists who testify as expert witnesses need to have knowledge of most recent research on children's common behaviors and emotional reactions after experiencing abuse (Vaughan-Eden, 2008). The following section includes the main topics that play therapists may need to discuss in court as expert witnesses. The research included in this section is not inclusive and play therapists should do their own literature review before court in order to find the most recent information.

Grooming and Delayed Outcry

Perpetrators of sexual abuse tend to use secrecy and shame in order to keep their victims silent (Azzopardi et al., 2014). Grooming behaviors, the acts that perpetrators exhibit to gain access to children and prepare them to comply with abuse, is one way to achieve secrecy, shame, and fear in order to avoid sexual abuse outcries (Bennett & O'Donohue, 2014). Examples of grooming behaviors include sexualized conversations not permissible given adult-child relationship (e.g., a neighbor talking about his sex life with a 12 year-old girl), exposing the child to materials that are sexually explicit (an adult asking a child to watch porn together), socially inappropriate gift giving (e.g., lingerie bought by a couch), inappropriate nonsexual conversations (e.g., an uncle telling an 8-year-old that she is the only one who understands him), inappropriate touching (e.g., asking the child to sit on one's lap), bribing for physical contact (e.g., giving money to the child after sexualized touching), asking the child to keep secrets regarding inappropriate contact, and threatening the child to not disclose. Other factors that delay children's sexual abuse outcries include fear of rejection, mistrust in others, belief in significance of obeying adults, developmental limitations, emotional impact of trauma, unsupportive caregivers, and fear of the perceived repercussions of disclosure (Azzopardi et al., 2014; Somer & Szwarcberg, 2001).

Children's Mixed Feelings towards Their Perpetrators and Recantation

Although research related to feelings of children towards their perpetrators is very limited, some authors emphasize the importance of children's previous or existing relationships with their perpetrators to understand their emotional and behavioral reactions after getting involved in the criminal system (Cohen, 2000; Plach, 2008). Children who were abused by people who showed them attention, bought them presents, and made them feel special, may have mixed feelings towards their perpetrators (Cohen, 2000). Children may believe that their outcry caused them to lose maybe the only person in their lives who was attentive and caring. They may miss having their perpetrators in their lives even though that person also caused them physical and emotional pain. When asked about these feelings in court, play therapists need to be prepared to educate the judge and the jury regarding normalcy of mixed feelings related to perpetrators who played both positive and negative roles in children's lives.

For play therapists going to court as expert witnesses, it is also necessary to understand the dynamics that may lead to recanting, or the withdrawal of a previously made outcry. Plach (2008) suggested several factors that may influence children towards recantation. One of the main factors is the lack of support from the child's primary caregiver or even an active pressure to recant. Children's strong need to be loved and protected by their caregivers may result in taking their statements back regarding the outcry in order to regain their caregiver's attention or avoid being in an unsafe environment. Additionally, in cases in which alleged perpetrators are related to victimized children, problems such as bitterness and hostility within family members may occur (Copen, 2000). Such unhealthy dynamics may cause children to feel guilty about having the outcry, which may result in recanting. Play therapists also need to remember the role of culture in understanding and explaining children's behaviors. Cultures in which loyalty to family is strongly emphasized may also have an impact on children's feelings of guilt that result in recantation (Plach, 2008).

Another major factor that plays a role in children's recantation is participating in criminal justice system and child protection agencies (Plach, 2008). Being involved with child protection agencies as well as going through the steps of criminal justice system may be overwhelming for both caregivers and children. For the families who already have strong negative views about these systems, being involved in them especially may come with great fear and frustration. Children who experience these negative feelings may recant as an attempt to end the tension.

Suggestibility and Memory

In court, suggestibility is a common discussion for child abuse cases when evaluating children's eyewitness reports. Suggestibility refers to the influence of social and psychological factors on children's memory and reports of the events (Ceci & Bruck, 1993). Considering that most children are alone with the alleged perpetrator when abuse takes place, cases heavily rely on children's own statements. Thus, play therapists who are in court as expert witnesses need to be knowledgeable about research results concerning children's suggestibility and memory issues.

According to Malloy and Quas (2009), one factor that predicts children's accuracy as witnesses is age at the time of abuse. According to Bauer, Burch, Scholin, and Guler (2007), older children may have difficulty remembering events that occurred in infancy or toddlerhood. However, young children are more likely to remember experiences they had as infants or toddlers because their memories have had less time to fade or disappear.

Age at the time of the interview also predicts children's accuracy in their statements (Malloy & Quas, 2009) According to recent research studies, younger children are more likely to have false memories compared to older children and adults (Bruer & Pozzulo, 2014; Eisen, Qin, Goodman, & Davis, 2002; Otgaar, Howe, Peters, Smeets, & Moritz, 2014; Schaaf, Alexander, & Goodman, 2008). These researchers supported the idea that children's accuracy to retrieve memories of their experiences and resisting suggestions from others improve by age due to improved cognitive skills. Even though there is an increased number of research studies regarding false memories and suggestibility of children, these results do not disqualify children's outcries of abuse or neglect. While children's memory systems continue to improve by age, young children can still provide accurate and detailed information regarding their past experiences (Klemfuss & Ceci, 2012).

Additionally, there is controversy in literature as to whether or not inconsistent statements of children indicate inaccuracy of the outcry (Malloy & Quas, 2009). Ghetti, Qin, and Goodman (2002) suggested that when children experience repeated exposure to abuse, providing consistent statements across different interviews may become more challenging due to having to focus on a unique event out of a set of repeated incidents.

According to Friedman and Ceci (2015), children who go through cross-examination in court may appear inconsistent in their statements, as the logic of cross examination is to disregard accuracy of testimonies by using statements such as "You have said that X is true, but you also testified to the truth of Y, and these two statements cannot be true at the same time, so you must not be telling the truth when you said X or Y." According to the authors, failure of children to be consistent with their statements in court may not be related to their flawed original statements, but it may be related to the child's inability or unwillingness to answer cross-examiner's questions. In support, Bettenay, Ridley, Henry, and Crane (2015) conducted a research study with children ages 4-11, which showed that a cross-examination style of asking questions cause increased anxiety levels in children. According to the authors, high anxiety levels predict susceptibility and increase the number of changed responses during questioning. The authors suggested appropriate court preparation for children might improve their emotional wellbeing as well as accuracy of their answers during cross-examination.

Other researchers suggested that sexually abused children are highly vulnerable to suggestibility during questioning, especially if there is interrogative pressure (Vagni, Maiorano, Pajardi, & Gudjonsson, 2015). Researchers added that children who were abused by a family member are more vulnerable to suggestibility, as these children are likely to experience higher relational and emotional distress because of the feeling of betraying their family member's trust and the consequences of having an outcry on their family system.

CONCLUSION

Most play therapists do not receive formal education regarding court process and preparation. Considering that the court system promotes impaneling of jurors who have no information about the subject matter of the trial (Stern et al., 2016), even play therapists who do not have their Registered Play Therapist status or who are still working towards their licensure can be qualified as witnesses. New play therapists and interns in mental health programs should do all necessary preparations to act as witnesses in court and trust that they have more knowledge and experience in mental health than the jurors. Thus, It is important for play therapists to seek additional sources to learn how to prepare themselves and their clients for court. This chapter aimed to provide basic information for therapists to know the steps towards ethical and effective practices in court preparation. This chapter can be the first step for many play therapists towards gaining better understanding related to legal involvement in court. Considering that there is growing literature regarding court testimonies of children and practitioners, play therapists should continue to expand their knowledge by following up with related literature.

REFERENCES

Achenbach, T. (1999). The child behavior checklist and related instruments. In M. E. Maruish (Ed.), *The use of psychological testing for treatment planning and outcome assessment* (pp. 429–466). Mahwah, NJ: Lawrence Erlbaum Associates.

Azzopardi, C., Madigan, S., & Kirkland-Burke, M. (2014). Extended sexual abuse forensic evaluation with young children: Program outcomes and disclosure correlates. *Journal of Child Custody*, *11*, 304–324. doi:10.1080/15379418.2014.988901

Barsky, A. E., & Gould, J. (2002). *Clinicians in court: A guide to subpoenas, depositions, testifying, and everything else you need to know*. New York, NY: Guilford.

Bauer, P. J., Burch, M. M., Scholin, S. E., & Güler, O. E. (2007). Using cue words to investigate the distribution of autobiographical memories in childhood. *Psychological Science*, *18*(10), 910–916. doi:10.1111/j.1467-9280.2007.01999.x PMID:17894609

Bennett, N., & ODonohue, W. (2014). The construct of grooming in child sexual abuse: Conceptual and measurement issues. *Journal of Child Sexual Abuse*, *23*(8), 957–976. doi:10.1080/10538712.2014.960632 PMID:25258355

Bettenay, C., Ridley, A. M., Henry, L. A., & Crane, L. (2015). Changed responses under cross-examination: The role of anxiety and individual differences in child witnesses. *Applied Cognitive Psychology*, *29*(3), 485–491. doi:10.1002/acp.3125

Bond, T., Sandhu, A., & British Association for Counselling. (2005). *Therapists in Court: Providing Evidence and Supporting Witnesses*. London: SAGE Publications Ltd.

Bruer, K., & Pozzulo, J. D. (2014). Influence of eyewitness age and recall error on mock juror decision-making. *Legal and Criminological Psychology*, *19*(2), 332–348. doi:10.1111/lcrp.12001

Ceci, S. J., & Bruck, M. (1993). Suggestibility of the child witness: A historical review and synthesis. *Psychological Bulletin*, *113*(3), 403–439. doi:10.1037/0033-2909.113.3.403 PMID:8316609

Cheung, M. (2012). *Child sexual abuse: Best practices for interviewing and treatment*. Chicago, IL: Lyceum Books.

Child Welfare Information Gateway. (2016). *State Child Abuse and Neglect Reporting Numbers*. Retrieved April, 13, 2016, from https://www.childwelfare.gov/organizations/?CWIGFunctionsaction=rols:main.dspROL&rolType=Custom&RS_ID=%205

Children's Law Center. (2010). *Fact sheet: Working with child witnesses*. Retrieved April, 29, 2016, from http://www.childrenslawcenter.org/sites/default/files/Fact%20Sheet%20Child%20Witnesses%28July%202015%29.pdf

Copen, L. M. (2000). *Preparing children for court: A practitioner's guide*. Thousand Oaks, CA: Sage.

Cossins, A., Goodman-Delahunty, J., & OBrien, K. (2009). Uncertainty and misconceptions about child sexual abuse: Implications for the criminal justice system. *Psychiatry, Psychology and Law*, *16*(3), 435–452. doi:10.1080/13218710902930234

Eisen, M. L., Qin, J., Goodman, G. S., & Davis, S. L. (2002). Memory and suggestibility in maltreated children: Age, stress arousal, dissociation, and psychopathology. *Journal of Experimental Child Psychology*, *83*(3), 167–212. doi:10.1016/S0022-0965(02)00126-1 PMID:12457859

Fairbank, J. A. (2008). The epidemiology of trauma and trauma related disorders in children and youth. *PTSD Research Quarterly*, *19*(1), 1–8.

Finkelhor, D., Shattuck, A., Turner, H. A., & Hamby, S. L. (2014). The Lifetime Prevalence of Child Sexual Abuse and Sexual Assault Assessed in Late Adolescence. *The Journal of Adolescent Health*, *55*(3), 329–333. doi:10.1016/j.jadohealth.2013.12.026 PMID:24582321

Friedman, R. D., & Ceci, S. J. (2015). The Child Quasi Witness. *The University of Chicago Law Review. University of Chicago. Law School*, *82*(1), 89–111.

Ghetti, S., Qin, J., & Goodman, G. S. (2002). False memories in children and adults: Age, distinctiveness, and subjective experience. *Developmental Psychology, 38*(5), 705–718. doi:10.1037/0012-1649.38.5.705 PMID:12220049

Harris, S. M., Brown, A., Dakin, J. B., Lucas, B., Riley, L., & Bulham, R. (2009). Are clinical records really that important? The dearth of research and practice guidelines in MFT literature. *The American Journal of Family Therapy, 37*(5), 373–387. doi:10.1080/01926180902754729

HelpGuide.org. (2016). *Understanding child abuse and neglect.* Retrieved July 30, 2016 from http://www.helpguide.org/articles/abuse/child-abuse-and-neglect.htm

Hovens, J. M., Giltay, E. J., Wiersma, J. E., Spinhoven, P., Penninx, B. H., & Zitman, F. G. (2012). Impact of childhood life events and trauma on the course of depressive and anxiety disorders. *Acta Psychiatrica Scandinavica, 126*(3), 198–207. doi:10.1111/j.1600-0447.2011.01828.x PMID:22268708

Klemfuss, J. Z., & Ceci, S. J. (2012). Legal and psychological perspectives on childrens competence to testify in court. *Developmental Review, 32*(3), 268–286. doi:10.1016/j.dr.2012.06.005

Kramer, D. N., & Landolt, M. A. (2010). Characteristics and efficacy of early psychological interventions in children and adolescents after single trauma: A meta-analysis. *European Journal of Psychotraumatology*, 11-24. doi:10.3402/ejpt.v2i0.7858

Kuehnle, K. (1996). *Assessing allegations of child sexual abuse*. Sarasota, FL: Prefessional Resource Press.

Kuehnle, K., & Connell, M. (2010). Child sexual abuse suspicions: Treatment considerations during investigation. *Journal of Child Sexual Abuse, 19*(5), 554–571. doi:10.1080/10538712.2010.512554 PMID:20924910

Malloy, L. C., & Quas, J. A. (2009). Children's suggestibility: Areas of consensus and controversy. In K. Kuehnle & M. Connell (Eds.), *The evaluation of child sexual abuse allegations: A comprehensive guide to assessment and testimony* (pp. 267–297). Hoboken, NJ: John Wiley & Sons.

Mulkey, E. A. (2015). Confronting Legal and Technological Incongruity: Remote Testimony for Child Witnesses. *Vanderbilt Journal Of Entertainment & Technology Law, 17*(2), 463–492.

Otgaar, H., Howe, M. L., Peters, M., Smeets, T., & Moritz, S. (2014). The production of spontaneous false memories across childhood. *Journal of Experimental Child Psychology*, 12128–12141. doi:10.1016/j.jecp.2013.11.019 PMID:24448519

Plach, T. (2008). *Investigating allegations of child and adolescent sexual abuse: An overview for professionals*. Springfield, IL: Charles C Thomas Publisher, LTD.

Principe, G. F., & Schindewolf, E. (2012). Natural conversations as a source of false memories in children: Implications for the testimony of young witnesses. *Developmental Review, 32*(3), 205–223. doi:10.1016/j.dr.2012.06.003 PMID:23129880

Quas, J. A., Goodman, G. S., Ghetti, S., Alexander, K. W., Edelstein, R., Redlich, A. D., & Jones, D. P. H. et al. (2005). Childhood sexual assault victims: Long-term outcomes after testifying in criminal court. *Monographs of the Society for Research in Child Development, 70*(2), vii-145. PMID:16159360

Quas, J. A., Thompson, W. C., & Clarke-Stewart, K. A. (2005). Do jurors know what isnt so about child witnesses? *Law and Human Behavior*, *29*(4), 425–456. doi:10.1007/s10979-005-5523-8 PMID:16133948

Ray, D. (2011). *Advanced play therapy: Essential conditions, knowledge, and skills for child practice*. New York, NY: Routledge.

Sawyer, C., & Judd, R. G. (2012). Counselors and Bikers Collaborate to Empower Abused Children. *Journal of Creativity in Mental Health*, *7*(1), 35–48. doi:10.1080/15401383.2012.661243

Schaaf, J. M., Alexander, K. W., & Goodman, G. S. (2008). Childrens false memory and true disclosure in the face of repeated questions. *Journal of Experimental Child Psychology*, *100*(3), 157–185. doi:10.1016/j.jecp.2007.09.002 PMID:18061609

Sidebotham, P. (2014). Giving evidence in court. *Paediatrics and Child Health (Oxford)*, *24*(12), 562–566. doi:10.1016/j.paed.2014.01.009

Snow, M. S. (2016, July). *Play therapy goes to court: Ethical and legal issues*. PowerPoint presented at the Center for Play Therapy Summer Institute, Denton, TX.

Somer, E., & Szwarcberg, S. (2001). Variables in delayed disclosure of childhood sexual abuse. *The American Journal of Orthopsychiatry*, *71*(3), 332–341. doi:10.1037/0002-9432.71.3.332 PMID:11495335

Staller, K. M., & Vandervort, F. E. (2010). Child sexual abuse: Legal burdens and scientific methods. Seeking justice in child sexual abuse: shifting burdens and sharing responsibilities. In K. M. Staller & K. C. Faller (Eds.), *Seeking justice in child sexual abuse* (pp. 1–34). New York, NY: Columbia University Press.

Stern, P., Vaughan-Eden, V., & Coslett, G. (2016, June). *Preparing and presenting expert testimony*. Paper presented at 24th Annual American Professional Society on the Abuse of Children Colloquium, New Orleans, LA.

Stoltenborgh, M., Bakermans-Kranenburg, M. J., & van IJzendoorn, M. H. (2013). The neglect of child neglect: A meta-analytic review of the prevalence of neglect. *Social Psychiatry and Psychiatric Epidemiology*, *48*(3), 345–355. doi:10.1007/s00127-012-0549-y PMID:22797133

U.S. Department of Health and Human Services, Administration for Children and Families, Children's Bureau. (2012). *Child maltreatment*. Retrieved February 5, 2014, from http://www.acf.hhs.gov/sites/default/files/cb/cm2012.pdf

Vagni, M., Maiorano, T., Pajardi, D., & Gudjonsson, G. (2015). Immediate and delayed suggestibility among suspected child victims of sexual abuse. *Personality and Individual Differences*, *79129-133*. doi:10.1016/j.paid.2015.02.007

Vaughan-Eden, V. (2008, Summer-Fall). Key points to testifying in child abuse cases. *APSAC Advisor*, 23-26.

Warren, K. L., & Peterson, C. (2014). Exploring Parent-Child Discussions of Crime and their Influence on Childrens Memory. *Behavioral Sciences & the Law*, *32*(6), 686–701. doi:10.1002/bsl.2144 PMID:25393638

Compilation of References

Aber, J. L., Jones, S. M., & Cohen, J. (2000). The impact of poverty on the mental health and development of very young children. In C. H. Zeanah (Ed.), *Handbook of infant mental health* (2nd ed.; pp. 113–128). New York: Guilford Press.

Abidin, R. R. (1995). Parenting Stress Index: Professional Manual (3rd ed.). Odessa, FL: Psychological Assessment Resources, Inc.

Abidin, R., Greene, R., & Konold, T. (2004). *Index of teacher stress: Professional manual*. Lutz, FL: Psychological Assessment Resources.

Achenbach, T. (1999). The child behavior checklist and related instruments. In M. E. Maruish (Ed.), *The use of psychological testing for treatment planning and outcome assessment* (pp. 429–466). Mahwah, NJ: Lawrence Erlbaum Associates.

Achenbach, T. M., & Rescorla, L. A. (2001). *Manual for the ASEBA school-age forms & profiles*. Burlington, VT: University of Vermont, Research Center for Children, Youth, & Families.

Ackerman, P. T., Newton, J. O., McPherson, W. B., Jones, J. G., & Dykman, R. A. (1998). Prevalence of post traumatic stress disorder and other psychiatric diagnoses in three groups of abused children (sexual, physical, and both). *Child Abuse & Neglect*, *22*(8), 759–774. doi:10.1016/S0145-2134(98)00062-3 PMID:9717613

Ackerman, T. (2005). The puppet as a metaphor. In M. Bernier & J. O'Hare (Eds.), *Puppetry in education and therapy* (pp. 5–11). Bloomington, IL: Authorhouse.

Adams, M. J. (1990). *Beginning to read: Thinking and learning about print*. Cambridge, MA: MIT Press.

Adelman, H. S., & Taylor, L. (2012). Mental health in schools: Moving in new directions. *Contemporary School Psychology*, *16*, 9–18.

Adler, A. (1998). *Understanding human nature*. Academic Press. (Original work published 1927)

Adler, A. (1998). *Understanding human nature*. London: Oneworld Publications. (Original work published 1927)

Adler-Tapia, R. (2012). *Child psychotherapy: Integrating developmental theory into clinical practice*. New York, NY: Springer.

Aikens, N. L., & Barbarin, O. A. (2008). Socioeconomic differences in reading trajectories: The contribution of family, neighborhood, and school contexts. *Journal of Educational Psychology*, *100*(2), 235–251. doi:10.1037/0022-0663.100.2.235

Ainsworth, M. D. (1969). Object Relations, dependency and attachment: A theoretical review of the infant mother relationship. *Child Development*, *40*(4), 969–1025. doi:10.2307/1127008 PMID:5360395

Akay, S. (2013). *The effects of Adlerian play therapy on maladaptive perfectionism and anxiety in children* (Unpublished doctoral dissertation). University of North Texas, Denton, TX.

Akos, P., & Milsom, A. (2007). Introduction to special issue: Group work in K-12 schools. *Journal for Specialists in Group Work*, *32*(1), 5–7. doi:10.1080/01933920600977440

Alcock, K. J., Holding, P. A., Mungala-Odera, V., & Newton, C. R. J. C. (2008). Constructing tests of cognitive abilities for schooled and unschooled children. *Journal of Cross-Cultural Psychology*, *39*(5), 529–551. doi:10.1177/0022022108321176

Allen, J., & Marshall, C. R. (2011). Parent-child interaction therapy in school-aged children with SLI. *International Journal of Language & Communication Disorders*, *46*, 397–410.

Aloe, A. M., Amo, L. C., & Shanahan, M. E. (2014). Classroom management self-efficacy and burnout: A multivariate meta-analysis. *Educational Psychology Review*, *26*(1), 101–126.

American Academy of Pediatrics (AAP). (n.d.). *Healthy foster care America: Mental and behavioral health*. Retrieved from https://www.aap.org

American Association for Marriage and Family Therapy (AAMFT). (2012). *AAMFT code of ethics*. Alexandria, VA: Author.

American Counseling Association (ACA). (2014). *ACA code of ethics*. Alexandria, VA: Author.

American Counseling Association. (2014). *ACA Code of Ethics*. Alexandria, VA: Author.

American Counseling Association. (2014). *ACA code of ethics*. Retrieved from https://www.counseling.org/resources/aca-code-of-ethics.pdf

American Counseling Association. (2014). *Code of ethics and standards of practice*. Alexandria, VA: Author.

American Psychiatric Association. (2013). *Diagnostic and statistical manual of mental disorders* (5th ed.). Washington, DC: American Psychiatric Association.

American Psychiatric Association. (2013). *Diagnostic and statistical manual of mental disorders: DSM-5*. Washington, DC: American Psychiatric Association.

American Psychological Association (APA). (2010). *Ethical principles of psychologists and code of conduct*. Washington, DC: Author.

American Psychological Association. (2010). *Ethical principles of psychologists and code of conduct*. Retrieved from http://www.apa.org/ethics/code/principles.pdf

American School Counselor Association (ASCA). (2016). *ASCA ethical standards for school counselors*. Alexandria, VA: Author.

American School Counselor Association. (2010). *Ethical standards for school counselors*. Retrieved from https://wvde.state.wv.us/institutional/Counselors/ASCAEthicalStandards.pdf

American School Counselor Association. (2013). *Ethical standards for school counselors*. Alexandria, VA: Author.

American Speech-Language Hearing Association (ASHA). (2015). *Strategic pathway to excellence*. Retrieved from http://www.asha.org/About/Strategic-Pathway/

American Speech-Language-Hearing Association (ASHA). (1991). *A model for collaborative service delivery for students with language-learning disorders in the public schools*. Retrieved from http://www.asha.org/policy/rp1991-00123/

American Speech-Language-Hearing Association (ASHA). (2010). *Roles and responsibilities of speech-language pathologists in schools*. Retrieved from http://www.asha.org/policy/PI2010-00317/

American Speech-Language-Hearing Association (ASHA). (2012). *Schools survey report: SLP workforce/work conditions.* Retrieved from http://www.asha.org/uploadedFiles/Schools-2012-SLP-Workforce.pdf

American Speech-Language-Hearing Association. (2012). Asha's recommended revisions to the dsm-5. Retrieved from www.asha.org/uploadedFiles/*DSM-5-Final-Comments.pdf*

Anda, R. F., Felitti, V. J., Bremner, D. J., Walker, J., Whitefield, J. D., Perry, B. D., & Giles, W. G. (2006). The enduring effects of childhood abuse and related experiences. *European Archives of Psychiatry and Clinical Neuroscience*, *256*(3), 174–186. doi:10.1007/s00406-005-0624-4 PMID:16311898

Andronico, M. P., & Blake, I. (1971). The application of filial therapy to young children with stuttering problems. *The Journal of Speech and Hearing Disorders*, *36*(3), 377–381. doi:10.1044/jshd.3603.377 PMID:5566117

Andronico, M., & Guerney, B. G. Jr. (1967). The potential application of filial therapy to the school situation. *Journal of School Psychology*, *6*(1), 2–7. doi:10.1016/0022-4405(67)90057-X

Arredondo, P., Toporek, M. S., Brown, S., Jones, J., Locke, D. C., Sanchez, J., & Stadler, H. (1996). *Operationalization of the Multicultural Counseling Competencies*. AMCD.

Arrendondo, P., Shealy, C., Neale, M., & Winfrey, L. L. (2004). Consultation and Interprofessional collaboration: Modeling for the future. *Journal of Clinical Psychology*, *60*(7), 787–800.

Artadi, E., & Sala-i-Martin, X. (2003). *The economic tragedy of the XXth century: Growth in Africa.* NBER Working Paper No. 9865. Retrieved from http://www.nber.org/papers/w9865.pdf

Ashby, J., & Clark, K. M. (2015). Ethics in play therapy. In D. A. Crenshaw & A. L. Stewart (Eds.), *Play therapy: A comprehensive guide to theory and practice* (pp. 511–523). New York, NY: The Guilford Press.

Ashdown, D. M., & Benard, M. E. (2012). Can explicit instruction in social and emotional learning skills benefit the social-emotional development, well-being, and academic achievement of young children? *Early Childhood Education Journal*, *39*(6), 379–405. doi:10.1007/s10643-011-0481-x

Association for Counselor Education and Supervision. (1993). *Ethical guidelines for counseling supervisors.* Retrieved from: http://www.liberty.edu/media/1152/School%20Counseling%20ACES%20Ethical%20Guidelines.pdf

Association for Play Therapy (APT). (2016a). *Credentialing guide: Registered play therapist (RPT) and supervisor (RPT-S).* Clovis, CA: Author.

Association for Play Therapy (APT). (2016b). *Play therapy best practices: Clinical, professional, & ethical issues.* Clovis, CA: Author.

Association for Play Therapy, Inc. (2015). Play therapy makes a difference. In *Why Play Therapy?* Retrieved from http://www.a4pt.org/?page=PTMakesADifference

Association for Play Therapy. (2012). *Play therapy best practices.* Retrieved from http://c.ymcdn.com/sites/www.a4pt.org/resource/resmgr/Publications/Play_Therapy_Best_Practices.pdf

Association for Play Therapy. (2012). *Play therapy best practices.* Retrieved from http://www.a4pt.org/resource/resmgr/Publications/Play_Therapy_Best_Practices.pdf

Association for Play Therapy. (2012). *Play therapy best practices.* Retrieved from: http://c.ymcdn.com/sites/a4pt.site-ym.com/resource/resmgr/Publications/Play_Therapy_Best_Practices.pdf

Association for Play Therapy. (2015). *Credentialing guide: Registered Play Therapist (RPT) & Supervisor (RPT-S).* Retrieved from: http://c.ymcdn.com/sites/www.a4pt.org/resource/ resmgr/RPT_and_RPT-S_Credentials/RPTS_Guide_December_2015.pdf

Association for Play Therapy. (2016, March). *Play therapy defined.* Retrieved from http://www.a4pt.org/ps.playtherapy.cfm?ID=1158

Association for Play Therapy. (n.d.). *What is play therapy?* Retrieved from http://www.a4pt.org/?page=PTMakesADifference

ATF. (2016a). *Brady law*. Washington, DC: Bureau of Alcohol, Tobacco, Firearms and Explosives. Retrieved from https://www.atf.gov/rules-and-regulations/brady-law

ATF. (2016b). *Gun Control Act*. Washington, DC: Bureau of Alcohol, Tobacco, Firearms and Explosives. Retrieved from https://www.atf.gov/rules-and-regulations/gun-control-act

ATF. (2016c). *National Firearms Act*. Washington, DC: Bureau of Alcohol, Tobacco, Firearms and Explosives. Retrieved from https://www.atf.gov/rules-and-regulations/national-firearms-act

Axeline, V. M. (1947). *Play Therapy*. New York: Ballantine.

Axline, V. (1964). *Dibs in search of self.* New York, NY: Random House Publisher.

Axline, V. M. (1947). *Play therapy*. New York, NY: Ballantine.

Axline, V. M. (1964). *Dibs: In search of self - personality development in play therapy*. Boston, MA: Houghton Mifflin.

Azzopardi, C., Madigan, S., & Kirkland-Burke, M. (2014). Extended sexual abuse forensic evaluation with young children: Program outcomes and disclosure correlates. *Journal of Child Custody*, *11*, 304–324. doi:10.1080/15379418.2014.988901

Bach, A. (1968). *Pupil discovery training: The application of filial therapy to teacher-student relationship*. Washington, DC: U.S. Department of Health, Education, and Welfare, Office of Education.

Badenoch, B. (2008). *Being a brain-wise therapist: A practical guide to interpersonal neurobiology*. New York, NY: Norton.

Badenoch, B., & Kestly, T. (2015). Exploring the neuroscience of healing play at every age. In D. Crenshaw & A. Stewart (Eds.), *Play therapy: A comprehensive guide to theory and practice* (pp. 524–538). New York, NY: Guildford Press.

Baggerly, J., & Landreth, G. (2001). Training children to help children: A new dimension in play therapy. *Peer Facilitator Quarterly*, *18*(1), 6–14.

Baggerly, J., Ray, D., & Bratton, S. (2010). *Child-centered play therapy research: The evidence base for effective practice*. Hoboken, NJ: John Wiley & Sons. doi:10.1002/9781118269626

Baird, B. (1965). *The art of the puppet*. New York, NY: The Macmillan Company.

Baker, J. (2006). Contributions of teacher-child relationships to positive school adjustment during elementary school. *Journal of School Psychology*, *44*(3), 211–229. doi:10.1016/j.jsp.2006.02.002

Baker, L., & Cantwell, D. P. (1987). A prospective psychiatric follow-up of children with speech/language disorders. *Journal of the American Academy of Child and Adolescent Psychiatry*, *26*(4), 546–553. doi:10.1097/00004583-198707000-00015 PMID:3654509

Balaban, V. (2006). Psychological assessment of children in disasters and emergencies. *Disasters*, *30*(2), 178–198. doi:10.1111/j.0361-3666.2006.00314.x PMID:16689917

Bales, S. N., Fisher, P. A., Greenough, W., Knudsen, E., Phillips, D., & Roineck, A. J. (2010). *Early experiences can alter gene expression and affect long-term development.* Working paper no. 10. National Scientific Council on the Developing Child. Retrieved from www.developingchild.net

Barber, J. P., Sharpless, B. A., Klostermann, S., & McCarthy, K. S. (2007). Assessing intervention competence and its relation to therapy outcome: A selected review derived from the outcome literature. *Professional Psychology, Research and Practice, 38*(5), 493–500. doi:10.1037/0735-7028.38.5.493

Barnett, W. S., Jung, K., Yarosz, D. J., Thomas, J., Hornbeck, A., Stechuk, R., & Burns, S. (2008). Educational effects of the Tools of the Mind curriculum: A randomized trial. *Early Childhood Research Quarterly, 23*(3), 299–313. doi:10.1016/j.ecresq.2008.03.001

Barsky, A. E., & Gould, J. (2002). *Clinicians in court: A guide to subpoenas, depositions, testifying, and everything else you need to know.* New York, NY: Guilford.

Bartol, C. R., & Bartol, A. M. (2015). *Psychology and law: Research and practice.* Los Angeles, CA: Sage Publications, Inc.

Bauer, P. J., Burch, M. M., Scholin, S. E., & Güler, O. E. (2007). Using cue words to investigate the distribution of autobiographical memories in childhood. *Psychological Science, 18*(10), 910–916. doi:10.1111/j.1467-9280.2007.01999.x PMID:17894609

Baumeister, R. F., & Leary, M. R. (1995). The need to belong: Desire for interpersonal attachments as a fundamental human motivation. *Psychological Bulletin, 117*(3), 497–529. doi:10.1037/0033-2909.117.3.497 PMID:7777651

Baxter, S., Brookes, C., Bianchi, K., Rashid, K., & Hay, F. (2009). Speech and language therapists and teachers working together: Exploring the issues. *Child Language Teaching and Therapy, 25*(2), 215–234. doi:10.1177/0265659009102984

Beahrs, J. O., & Gutheil, T. G. (2001). Informed consent in psychotherapy. *The American Journal of Psychiatry, 158*(1), 4–10. doi:10.1176/appi.ajp.158.1.4 PMID:11136625

Beck, L. E. (2008). *Infants and children: Prenatal through middle childhood* (6th ed.). Boston, MA: Pearson Education.

Beijersbergen, M. D., Jeffer, F., Bakermans-Kranenburg, M. J., & van IJzendoorn, M. H. (2012). Remaining or becoming secure: Parental sensitive support predicts attachment continuity from infancy to adolescence in a longitudinal adoption study. *Developmental Psychology, 48*(5), 1277–1282. doi:10.1037/a0027442 PMID:22369333

Bekar, O. (2014). *Mental state talk in mothers' and preschool children's narratives: Relation to children's social-emotional functioning and maternal stress* (Unpublished doctoral dissertation). New School for Social Research, New York, NY.

Belskey, J., & de Hann, M. (2011). Parenting and children's brain development. *Journal of Child Psychology and Psychiatry, and Allied Disciplines, 52*, 409–429. doi:10.1111/j.1469-7610.2010.02281.x PMID:20626527

Belsky, J., & Fearon, R. M. (2002). Early attachment security, subsequent maternal sensitivity, and later child development: Does continuity in development depend upon continuity of care giving? *Attachment & Human Development, 4*(3), 361–387. doi:10.1080/14616730210167267 PMID:12537851

Bennett, L., Shiner, S., & Ryan, S. (2006, October). Using Theraplay in shelter settings with mothers & children who have experienced violence in the home. *Journal of Psychosocial Nursing and Mental Health Services, 44*(10), 38–48. PMID:17063889

Bennett, M. O., & Bratton, S. C. (2011). The effects of child teacher relationship training on children of focus: A pilot study. *International Journal of Play, 20*(4), 193–207. doi:10.1037/a0025833

Bennett, N., & ODonohue, W. (2014). The construct of grooming in child sexual abuse: Conceptual and measurement issues. *Journal of Child Sexual Abuse*, *23*(8), 957–976. doi:10.1080/10538712.2014.960632 PMID:25258355

Bernard, J. M., & Goodyear, R. G. (1998). *Fundamentals of Clinical Supervision* (2nd ed.). Needham Heights, MA: Allyn & Bacon.

Bernier, M. (2005a). Introduction to puppetry in therapy. In M. Bernier & J. O'Hare (Eds.), *Puppetry in education and therapy* (pp. 109–115). Bloomington, IL: Authorhouse.

Bernier, M. (2005b). Psychopuppetry: Animated symbols in therapy. In M. Bernier & J. O'Hare (Eds.), *Puppetry in education and therapy* (pp. 125–133). Bloomington, IL: Authorhouse.

Bethea-Whitfield, P. (2005). African American women and mental health. In D. A. Harley & J. M. Dillard (Eds.), *Contemporary mental health issues among African Americans* (pp. 35–47). Alexandria, VA: American Counseling Association.

Bettenay, C., Ridley, A. M., Henry, L. A., & Crane, L. (2015). Changed responses under cross-examination: The role of anxiety and individual differences in child witnesses. *Applied Cognitive Psychology*, *29*(3), 485–491. doi:10.1002/acp.3125

Birch, S. H., & Ladd, G. W. (1997). The teacher-child relationship and childrens early school adjustment. *Journal of School Psychology*, *35*(1), 61–79. doi:10.1016/S0022-4405(96)00029-5

Birch, S. H., & Ladd, G. W. (1998). Childrens interpersonal behaviors and the teacher-child relationship. *Developmental Psychology*, *34*(5), 934–946. doi:10.1037/0012-1649.34.5.934 PMID:9779740

Bjork, R. A., Dunlosky, J., & Kornell, N. (2013). Self-regulated learning: Beliefs, techniques, and illusions. *Annual Review of Psychology*, *64*(1), 417–444. doi:10.1146/annurev-psych-113011-143823 PMID:23020639

Blair, C., Knipe, H., Cummings, E., Baker, D. P., Gamson, D., Eslinger, P., & Thorne, S. L. (2007). A developmental neuroscience approach to the study of school readiness. In R. C. Pianta, M. J. Cox, & K. L. Snow (Eds.), *School readiness and the transition to kindergarten in the era of accountability* (pp. 149–174). Baltimore, MD: Paul H. Brookes.

Blanco, P. J. (2009). *The impact of school-based child centered play therapy on academic achievement, self-concept, and teacher-child relationship stress* (Doctoral Dissertation). University of North Texas.

Blanco, P. J., Ray, D. C., & Holliman, R. (2012). Long-term child centered play therapy and academic achievement of children: A follow-up study. *International Journal of Play Therapy*, *21*(1), 1–13. doi:10.1037/a0026932

Blanco, P., Muro, J., Holliman, R., Stickley, V., & Carter, K. (2015). Effect of child-centered play therapy on performance anxiety and academic achievement. *Journal of Child and Adolescent Counseling*, *1*(2), 66–80. doi:10.1080/23727810.2015.1079117

Blanco, P., & Ray, D. (2011). Play therapy in the schools: A best practice for improving academic achievement. *Journal of Counseling and Development*, *89*(2), 235–242. doi:10.1002/j.1556-6678.2011.tb00083.x

Block, P. (2000). *Flawless consulting: A guide to getting your expertise used.* San Francisco: Joseey-Bass/Pfeiffer.

Blyth, D. A., & Traeger, C. M. (1995). The self-concept and self-esteem of early adolescents. *Theory into Practice*, *22*(2), 91–98. doi:10.1080/00405848309543045

Bond, T., Sandhu, A., & British Association for Counselling. (2005). *Therapists in Court: Providing Evidence and Supporting Witnesses*. London: SAGE Publications Ltd.

Booth, P., & Jernberg, A. (2010). *Theraplay: Helping parents and children build better relationships through attachment-based play* (3rd ed.). San Francisco, CA: Jossey-Bass.

Borders, L. D., & Brown, L. L. (2005). *The new handbook of counseling supervision*. Mahwah, NJ: Lawrence Erlbaum Associates.

Bornsheuer, J. N., & Watts, R. E. (2012). Play therapy and parent consultation: A review of best practices. *ACA Vistas 2012*.

Bornsheuer, J., & Polonyi, M. A. (2010). Adlerian counseling with Hispanic clients and families. *Professional Issues in Counseling*. Retrieved from http://www.shsu.edu/piic/AdlerianCounselingwithHispanicClientsandFamilies.htm

Bouillion, K. R. (1973). The comparative efficacy of nondirective group play therapy with preschool, speech or language delayed children. *Dissertation Abstracts International*, *35*, O1B.

Bowen, C. (1998). *Brown's stages of syntactic and morphological development*. Retrieved from www.speech-language-therapy.com/index.php?option=com_content&view=article&id=33

Bowen, C., & Cupples, L. (1999). Parents and children together (PACT): A collaborative approach to phonological therapy. *International Journal of Language & Communication Disorders*, *34*(1), 35–55.

Bowlby, J. (1969). Attachment and loss: Vol 1 Attachment. New York, NY: Avery (Penguin Group).

Bowlby, J. (1980). *Attachment and loss*. New York, NY: Basic Books.

Bowlby, J. (1988). *A secure base: Parent-child attachment and healthy human development*. New York: Basic Books.

Boyd-Franklin, N. (2003). *Black families in therapy: Understanding the African American experience* (2nd ed.). New York, NY: Guilford Press.

Boykin, A. W., & Toms, F. D. (1985). Black child socialization: A conceptual framework. In H. P. McAdoo & J. L. McAdoo (Eds.), *Black children: Social, environmental, and parental environments* (pp. 35–51). Newbury Park, CA: Sage Publications.

Bracey, J. R. (2012). Socializing race: Parental beliefs and practices in two African American families. *Dissertation Abstracts International*, *72*(7-B), 4363.

Bracken, B. A. (2007). Bracken school readiness assessment: Examiner's manual (3rd ed.). San Antonio, TX: Pearson.

Bratton, S. (2010). Meeting the early mental health needs of children through school-based play therapy. In C.E. Schaefer & A.A. Drewes (Eds.), School-Based Play Therapy (pp. 17-58). Wiley.

Bratton, S. C., Dafoe, E., Swan, A., Opiola, K., McClintock, D., & Barcenas, G. (2015). *Play Therapy Outcome Research Database*. Retrieved from http://evidencebasedchildtherapy.com/research/

Bratton, S. (2010). Meeting the early mental health needs of children through school based play therapy: A review of outcome research. In A. A. Drewes & C. E. Schaefer (Eds.), *School based play therapy* (2nd ed.; pp. 17–58). New York, NY: John Wiley & Sons. doi:10.1002/9781118269701.ch2

Bratton, S. C. (2010). Meeting the early mental health needs of children through school-based play therapy. In A. A. Drewes & C. E. Schaefer (Eds.), *School-based play therapy* (2nd ed.; pp. 17–58). Hoboken, NJ: John Wiley & Sons, Inc.

Bratton, S. C. (2015). Evidence Base for Play Therapy: Strengths and Limitations. In K. J. O'Conner, C. E. Schaefer, & L. D. Braverman (Eds.), *Handbook of Play Therapy* (2nd ed.). Hoboken, NJ: John Wiley & Sons. doi:10.1002/9781119140467.ch35

Bratton, S. C., Ceballos, P. L., & Ferebee, K. W. (2009). Integration of structured expressive activities within a humanistic group play therapy format for preadolescents. *Journal for Specialists in Group Work*, *34*(3), 251–275. doi:10.1080/01933920903033487

Bratton, S. C., Landreth, G. L., Kellam, T., & Blackard, S. (2006). *Child parent relationship therapy (CPRT) treatment manual: A 10-session filial therapy model for training parents*. Routledge.

Bratton, S. C., Landreth, G., Kellum, T., & Blackard, S. (2006). *Child parent relationship therapy (CPRT) treatment manual: A ten session filial therapy model for training parents*. New York: Routledge.

Bratton, S. C., Landreth, G., & Lin, D. (2010). Child parent relationship therapy (CPRT): A review of controlled outcome research. In J. N. Baggerly, D. C. Ray, & S. C. Bratton (Eds.), *Child-centered play therapy research: The evidence base for effective practice* (pp. 267–294). Hoboken, NJ: John Wiley & Sons.

Bratton, S. C., Opiola, K., & Dafoe, E. (2015). Child-parent relationship therapy: A 10 session filial therapy model. In D. A. Crenshaw & A. L. Stewart (Eds.), *Play therapy: A comprehensive guide to theory and practice* (pp. 129–140). New York, NY: Guilford Press.

Bratton, S., Ceballos, P., Sheely-Moore, A., Meany-Walen, K., Pronchenko, Y., & Jones, L. (2013). Head start early mental health intervention: Effects of child-centered play therapy on disruptive behaviors. *International Journal of Play Therapy*, *22*(1), 28–42. doi:10.1037/a0030318

Bratton, S., Landreth, G., Kellam, T., & Blackard, S. (2006). *Child-parent relationship therapy (CPRT) treatment manual: A 10-session filial therapy model for training parents*. New York, NY: Taylor & Francis Group.

Bratton, S., & Ray, D. (2000). What the research shows about play therapy. *International Journal of Play Therapy*, *9*(1), 47–88. doi:10.1037/h0089440

Bratton, S., Ray, D., Rhine, T., & Jones, L. (2005). The efficacy of play therapy with children: A meta-analytic review of treatment outcomes. *Professional Psychology, Research and Practice*, *36*(4), 376–390. doi:10.1037/0735-7028.36.4.376

Bremner, J. D., Randall, P., Scott, T. M., Bronen, R. A., Seibyl, J. P., Southwick, S. M., & Innis, R. B. et al. (1995). MRI-based measurement of hippocampal volume in patients with combat-related posttraumatic stress disorder. *The American Journal of Psychiatry*, *152*(7), 973–981. doi:10.1176/ajp.152.7.973 PMID:7793467

Bresin, K., & Gordon, K. H. (2013). Aggression as affect regulation: Extending catharsis theory to evaluate aggression and experiential anger in the laboratory and daily life. *Journal of Social and Clinical Psychology*, *32*(4), 400–423. doi:10.1521/jscp.2013.32.4.400

Bretherton, I., Biringen, Z., Ridgeway, D., Maslin, C., & Sherman, M. (1989). Attachment: The parental perspective. *Infant Mental Health Journal*, *10*(3), 203–221. doi:10.1002/1097-0355(198923)10:3<203::AID-IMHJ2280100307>3.0.CO;2-8

Bretherton, I., Prentiss, C., & Ridgeway, D. (1990). Family relationships as represented in a story-completion task at thirty-seven and fifty-four months of age. *New Directions for Child Development*, *48*(48), 85–105. doi:10.1002/cd.23219904807 PMID:2216013

Bretherton, I., Ridgeway, D., & Cassidy, J. (1990). Assessing internal working models of the attachment relationship: An attachment story completion task for 3-year-olds. In M. T. Greenberg, D. Cicchetti, & E. M. Cummings (Eds.), *Attachment in the preschool years: Theory, research, and intervention* (pp. 273–308). Chicago: University of Chicago Press.

Bridges, A. J., de Arellano, M. A., Rheingold, A. A., Danielson, C. K., & Silcott, L. (2010). Trauma exposure, mental health, and service utilization rates among immigrant and United States-born Hispanic youth: Results from the Hispanic family study. *Psychological Trauma: Theory, Research, Practice, and Policy*, *2*(1), 40–48. doi:10.1037/a0019021

Bridges, D. R., Davidson, R. A., Odegard, P. S., Maki, I. V., & Tomkowiak, J. (2011). Interprofessional collaboration: Three best practice models of interprofessional education. *Medical Education Online*, 16.

British Association of Play Therapists. (2008). Retrieved from www.bapt.info/

Britner, P. A., & Mossler, D. G. (2002). Professionals decision-making about out-of-home placements following instances of child abuse. *Child Abuse & Neglect, 26*(4), 317–332. doi:10.1016/S0145-2134(02)00311-3 PMID:12092801

Brodzinsky, D. M. (2013). *A need to know: Enhancing adoption competence among mental health professionals. Policy Perspective*. New York, NY: Donaldson Adoption Institute.

Broen, P. A., & Westman, M. J. (1990). Project Parent: A preschool speech program implemented through parents. *The Journal of Speech and Hearing Disorders, 55*(3), 495–502. doi:10.1044/jshd.5503.495 PMID:2381191

Brofenbrenner, U. (1979). *The ecology of human development: Experiments by nature and design.* Cambridge, MA: Harvard University Press.

Bromfield, R. (1995). The use of puppets in play therapy. *Child & Adolescent Social Work Journal, 12*(6), 435–444. doi:10.1007/BF01875812

Bronson, M. B. (2000). *Self-regulation in early childhood: Nature and nurture.* New York: Guilford.

Brooks, S., & Patterson, G. (2011). Using contact work in interactions with adults with learning disabilities and autistic spectrum disorders. *British Journal of Learning Disabilities, 39*(2), 161–166. doi:10.1111/j.1468-3156.2010.00643.x

Brown, C. J. (2000). *Filial therapy with undergraduate teacher trainees; child-teacher relationship training* (Doctoral dissertation, University of North Texas).

Brown, Pryzwansky, & Schulte. (2001). *Psychological consultation* (5th ed.). Boston, MA: Allyn and Bacon.

Brown, R. (1973). *A first language: The early stages.* London: George Allen & Unwin. doi:10.4159/harvard.9780674732469

Bruer, K., & Pozzulo, J. D. (2014). Influence of eyewitness age and recall error on mock juror decision-making. *Legal and Criminological Psychology, 19*(2), 332–348. doi:10.1111/lcrp.12001

Brumfield, K. A., & Christensen, T. M. (2011). Discovering African American parents perceptions of play therapy: A phenomenological approach. *International Journal of Play Therapy, 20*(4), 208–223. doi:10.1037/a0025748

Burneikaite, S. (2009). Possibilities of puppet therapy and their use in puppeteers projects. *Socialinis Ugdymas, 7*(18), 112–122.

Burns, B. J., Phillips, S. D., Wagner, H. R., Barth, R. P., Kilko, D. J., Campbell, Y., & Landsverk, J. (2004). Mental Health Need and Access to Mental Health Services by Youths Involved with Child Welfare: A National Survey. *Journal of the American Academy of Child and Adolescent Psychology, 43*(8), 960–970. doi:10.1097/01.chi.0000127590.95585.65 PMID:15266190

Bus, A. G. (2003). Social-emotional requisites for learning to read. In On reading books to children: Parents and teachers (pp. 3-15). Mahwah, NJ: Lawrence Erlbaum Associates.

Bus, A. G. (1994). The role of social context in emergent literacy. In E. M. H. Assink (Ed.), *Literacy acquisition and social context* (pp. 9–24). Oxford, UK: Harvester Wheatsheaf/Prentice Hall.

Bus, A. G. (2001). Parent-child book reading through the lens of attachment theory. In L. Verhoeven & C. Snow (Eds.), *Literacy and motivation: Reading engagement in individuals and groups* (pp. 39–53).

Bushman, B. J., Baumeister, R. F., & Stack, A. D. (1999). Catharsis, aggression, and persuasive influence: Self-fulfilling or self-defeating prophecies? *Journal of Personality and Social Psychology, 76*(3), 367–376. doi:10.1037/0022-3514.76.3.367 PMID:10101875

Butler, S., Guterman, J. T., & Rudes, J. (2009). Using puppets with children in narrative therapy to externalize the problem. *Journal of Mental Health Counseling*, *31*(3), 225–233. doi:10.17744/mehc.31.3.f255m86472577522

Byers, J. (2013). Integrating play and expressive art therapy into communities: A multimodal approach. In E. J. Green & A. A. Drewes (Eds.), *Integrating expressive arts and play therapy with children and adolescents* (pp. 283–301). Somerset, NJ: John Wiley & Sons.

Byers, J. G. (2016). Expressive arts in play therapy. In K. J. O'Connor, C. E. Schaefer, & L. D. Braverman (Eds.), *Handbook of Play Therapy* (pp. 277–288). Hoboken, NJ: John Wiley & Sons.

Caffo, E., & Belaise, C. (2003). Psychological aspects of traumatic injury in children and adolescents. *Child and Adolescent Psychiatric Clinics of North America*, *12*(3), 493–535. doi:10.1016/S1056-4993(03)00004-X PMID:12910820

Cain, D. S., & Combs-Orme, T. (2005). Family structure effects on parenting stress and practices in the African American family. *Journal of Sociology and Social Welfare*, *32*(2), 19–40.

California Evidence-Based Clearinghouse for Child Welfare. (2016). *CEBC Program Registry.* Retrieved on July 24, 2016 from http://www.cebc4cw.org/

Campinha-Bacote, J. (2002). The process of cultural competence in the delivery of healthcare services: A model of care. *Journal of Transcultural Nursing*, *13*(3), 181–184. doi:10.1177/10459602013003003 PMID:12113146

Carlson, S. E. (2011). *Effects of a Play-Based Teacher Consultation (PBTC) Program on Interpersonal Skills of Elementary School Teachers in the Classroom* (Doctoral dissertation). Retrieved from http://libproxy.library.unt.edu:2279/

Carlson, J., Dinkmeyer, D., & Johnson, E. (2008). Adlerian teacher consultation: Change teachers, change students! *Journal of Individual Psychology*, *64*(4), 480–493.

Carlson, J., & Slavik, S. (1997). *Techniques in Adlerian Psychology*. New York, NY: Routledge.

Carlson, J., Watts, R. E., & Maniacci, M. (2006). *Adlerian therapy: Theory and practice*. Washington, DC: American Psychological Association. doi:10.1037/11363-000

Carlson, N. R. (2010). *Physiology of behavior* (10th ed.). Boston, MA: Allyn and Bacon.

Carmichael, K. D. (2006). Legal and ethical issues in play therapy. *International Journal of Play Therapy*, *15*(2), 83–99. doi:10.1037/h0088916

Carmichael, K. D. (2006). *Play therapy: An introduction.* Upper Saddle River, NJ: Pearson Education.

Carmicheal, K. D. (1993). Play therapy and children with disabilities. *Issues in Comprehensive Pediatric Nursing*, *16*(165), 165–173. doi:10.3109/01460869309078273 PMID:8119836

Carnes-Holt, K., & Bratton, S. (2014). The efficacy of child parent relationship therapy for adopted children with attachment disruptions. *Journal of Counseling and Development*, *92*(3), 328–337. doi:10.1002/j.1556-6676.2014.00160.x

Carter-Black, J. (2003). The myth of the tangle of pathology: Resilience strategies employed by middle-class African American families. *Journal of Family Social Work*, *6*(4), 75–100. doi:10.1300/J039v06n04_06

Carter, R. B., & Mason, P. S. (1998). The selection and use of puppets in counseling. *Professional School Counseling*, *1*(5), 1–13.

Cartwright-Hatton, S., Tschernitz, N., & Gomersall, H. (2005). Social anxiety in children: Social skills deficit or cognitive distortion? *Behaviour Research and Therapy*, *43*(1), 131–141. doi:10.1016/j.brat.2003.12.003 PMID:15531358

Cates, J., Paone, T., Packman, J., & Margolis, D. (2006). Effective parent consultation in play therapy. *International Journal of Play Therapy*, *15*(1), 87–100. doi:10.1037/h0088909

Catts, H. W., Fey, M. E., Zhang, X., & Tomblin, J. B. (1999). Language basis of reading and reading abilities: Evidence from a longitudinal investigation. *Scientific Studies of Reading*, *3*(4), 331–361. doi:10.1207/s1532799xssr0304_2

Ceballos, P., & Bratton, S. (2010). Empowering Latino families: Effects of a culturally-responsive intervention for low-income immigrant Latino parents on childrens behaviors and parental stress. *Psychology in the Schools*, *47*(8), 761–775. doi:10.1002/pits.20502

Ceci, S. J., & Bruck, M. (1993). Suggestibility of the child witness: A historical review and synthesis. *Psychological Bulletin*, *113*(3), 403–439. doi:10.1037/0033-2909.113.3.403 PMID:8316609

Center for Mental Health in Schools. (2006). *The current status of mental health in schools: A policy and practice analysis.* Retrieved from http://smhp.psych.ucla.edu/pdfdocs/currentstatusmh/currentstatus.pdf

Center for School Mental Health Assistance (CSMHA). (2002). *Developing collaborative ESMH programs.* Downloaded from www.schoolmentalhealth.org/.../ESMH/developing_collabor_2002.pdf

Center for the Study of Social Policy. (2012). *Results-based public policy strategies for promoting children's social, emotional, and behavioral health.* Retrieved from http://www.cssp.org/policy/papers/Promote-Childrens-Social-Emotional-and-Behavioral-Health.pdf

Centers for Decease Control and Prevention, National Center for Health Statistics, National Health Interview Survey. (2015). *Mental health.* Retrieved from http://www.cdc.gov/nchs/data/hus/2015/035.pdf

Centers for Disease Control. (2013). *Children's mental health – New report.* Retrieved on July 24, 2016 from http://www.cdc.gov/Features/childrensmentalhealth/

Chaffin, M., Hanson, R., & Saunders, B. E. (2006). Report of the APSAC Task Force on attachment therapy, reactive attachment disorder, and attachment problems: Reply to letters. *Child Maltreatment*, *11*(4), 381–386. doi:10.1177/1077559506292636 PMID:17043315

Chambless, D. L., & Ollendick, T. H. (2001). Empirically supported psychological interventions: Controversies and evidence. *Annual Review of Psychology*, *52*(1), 685–716. doi:10.1146/annurev.psych.52.1.685 PMID:11148322

Champagne, F. A. (2015). Epigentics of the developing brain. *Zero to Three*, *35*, 2–8. Retrieved from http://search.ebscohost.com.proxy.wichita.edu/login.aspx?direct=true&db=cmh&jid=QQT&site=chc-live

Chang, C. Y., Ritter, K. B., & Hays, D. G. (2005). Multicultural trends and toys in play therapy. *International Journal of Play Therapy*, *14*(2), 69–85. doi:10.1037/h0088903

Charman, T., Ricketts, J., Dockrell, J. E., Lindsay, G., & Palikara, O. (2015). Emotional and behavioural problems in children with language impairments and children with autism spectrum disorders. *International Journal of Language & Communication Disorders*, *50*(1), 84–93. doi:10.1111/1460-6984.12116 PMID:25039810

Cheng, Y., & Ray, D. C. (2016). Child-centered group play therapy: Impact on social-emotional assets of kindergarten children. *Journal for Specialists in Group Work*, *41*(3), 209–237. doi:10.1080/01933922.2016.1197350

Cheslock, M. A., & Kahn, S. J. (2011). Supporting families and caregivers in everyday routines. *The ASHA Leader*, *16*, 10–13.

Cheung, M. (2012). *Child sexual abuse: Best practices for interviewing and treatment.* Chicago, IL: Lyceum Books.

Child Abuse Treatment and Prevention Act. (2010). *As Amended by P. L. 111-320 The CAPTA Reauthorization Act of 2010. U. S. Department of Health and Human Services.* Retrieved from https://www.acf.hhs.gov/sites/default/files/cb/capta2010.pdf

Child Welfare Information Gateway. (2013). *What is child abuse and neglect? Recognizing the signs and symptoms.* Washington, DC: U.S. Department of Health and Human Services, Children's Bureau.

Child Welfare Information Gateway. (2016). *Foster Care Statistics 2014.* Retrieved from www.childwelfare.gov

Child Welfare Information Gateway. (2016). *State Child Abuse and Neglect Reporting Numbers.* Retrieved April, 13, 2016, from https://www.childwelfare.gov/organizations/?CWIGFunctionsaction=rols:main.dspROL&rolType=Custom&RS_ID=%205

Children's Law Center. (2010). *Fact sheet: Working with child witnesses.* Retrieved April, 29, 2016, from http://www.childrenslawcenter.org/sites/default/files/Fact%20Sheet%20Child%20Witnesses%28July%202015%29.pdf

Chinekesh, A., Kamalian, M., Eltemasi, M., Chinekesh, S., & Alavi, M. (2014). The effect of group play therapy on socio-emotional skills in pre-school children. *Global Journal of Health Science, 6*(2), 163–167. PMID:24576376

Chorpita, B., Daleiden, E., Ebesutani, C., Young, J., Becker, K., Nakamura, B., & Starace, N. et al. (2011). Evidence-based treatments for children and adolescents: An updated review of indicators of efficacy and effectiveness. *Clinical Psychology: Science and Practice, 18*(2), 154–172. doi:10.1111/j.1468-2850.2011.01247.x

Clemens, E. (2007). Developmental counseling and therapy as a model for school counselor consultation with teachers. *Professional School Counseling, 10*(4), 352–359. doi:10.5330/prsc.10.4.t142010klu723434

Cloitre, M., Stolbach, B. C., Herman, J. L., van der Kolk, B., Pynoos, R., Wang, J., & Petkova, E. (2009). A developmental approach to complex PTSD: Childhood and adult cumulative trauma as predictors of symptom complexity. *Journal of Traumatic Stress, 22*(5), 399–408. doi:10.1002/jts.20444 PMID:19795402

CMHS-SVP0151. (n.d.). Rockville, MD: Center for Mental Health Services, Substance Abuse and Mental Health Services Administration.

Cobia, D. C., & Boes, S. R. (2000). Professional disclosure statements and formal plans for supervision: Two strategies for minimizing the risk of ethical conflicts in post-masters supervision. *Journal of Counseling and Development, 78*(3), 293–296. doi:10.1002/j.1556-6676.2000.tb01910.x

Cogher, L. (1999). The use of non-directive play in speech and language therapy. *Child Language Teaching and Therapy, 15*(1), 7–16. doi:10.1191/026565999670736631

Cohen, E., & Kaufmann, R. K. (2000). *Early childhood mental health consultation.* DHHS Pub. No.

Cohen, E., & Kaufmann, R. K. (2005). *Early childhood mental health consultation. DHHS Pub. No. CMHS-SVP0151* (Rev. Ed.). Rockville, MD: Center for Mental Health Services, Substance Abuse and Mental Health Services Administration.

Cohen, J. A., & Mannarino, A. P. (2008). Trauma-focused cognitive behavioral therapy for children and parents. *Child and Adolescent Mental Health, 13*(4), 158–162. doi:10.1111/j.1475-3588.2008.00502.x

Cohen, J. A., Mannarino, A. P., & Deblinger, E. (Eds.). (2012). *Trauma focused CBT for children and adolescents: Treatment applications.* New York, NY: The Guilford Press.

Cohen, J. A., Perel, J. M., Debellis, M. D., Friedman, M. J., & Putnam, F. W. (2002). Treating traumatized children: Clinical implications of the psychobiology of posttraumatic stress disorder. *Trauma, Violence & Abuse, 3*(2), 91–108. doi:10.1177/15248380020032001

Cohen, J. A., & Scheeringa, M. S. (2009). Post-traumatic stress disorder diagnosis in children: Challenges and promises. *Dialogues in Clinical Neuroscience*, *11*(1), 91–99. PMID:19432391

Cohen, N. J., Barwick, M. A., Horodezky, N. B., Vallance, D. D., & Im, N. (1998). Language, achievement, and cognitive processing in psychiatrically disturbed children with previously identified and unsuspected language impairments. *Journal of Child Psychology and Psychiatry, and Allied Disciplines*, *39*(06), 865–877.

Colby, S. L., & Ortman, J. M. (2014). Projections of the size and composition of the U.S. population: 2014 to 2060. In Current population reports (pp. 25–1143). Washington, DC: U.S. Census Bureau; Retrieved from https://www.census.gov/content/dam/Census/library/publications/2015/demo/p25-1143.pdf

Collie, K., Backos, A., Malchiodi, C., & Spiegel, D. (2006). Art therapy for combat-related PTSD: Recommendations for research and practice. *Art Therapy: Journal of the American Art Therapy Association*, *23*(4), 157–164. doi:10.1080/07421656.2006.10129335

Commonwealth of Virginia Department of Education (CVDE). (2011). *Speech-language pathology services in schools: Guidelines for best practice.* Retrieved from http://sbo.nn.k12.va.us/sped/documents/speech-pathology-handbook.pdf

Congressional Coalition on Adoption Institute. (2014). *Facts and statistics.* Retrieved from http://www.ccainstitute.org/index.php?option=com_content&view=category&layout=blog&id=25&Itemid=43

Conners, C. K., Sitarenios, G., Parker, J. D. A., & Epstein, J. N. (1998). Revision and restandardization of the Conners Teacher Rating Scale (CTRS-R): Factor structure, reliability, and criterion validity. *Journal of Abnormal Child Psychology*, *26*(4), 279–291. doi:10.1023/A:1022606501530 PMID:9700520

Conti-Ramsden, G., Mok, P. L., Pickles, A., & Durkin, K. (2013). Adolescents with a history of specific language impairment (SLI): Strengths and difficulties in social, emotional and behavioral functioning. *Research in Developmental Disabilities*, *34*(11), 4161–4169. doi:10.1016/j.ridd.2013.08.043 PMID:24077068

Conti-Ramsden, G., Mok, P. L., Pickles, A., & Durkin, K. (2014). Longitudinal trajectories of peer relations in children with specific language impairment. *Journal of Child Psychology and Psychiatry, and Allied Disciplines*, *55*(5), 516–527. doi:10.1111/jcpp.12190 PMID:24410167

Cook, A., Spinazzola, J., Ford, J., Lanktree, C., Blaustein, M. B., Cloitre, M., & van der Kolk, B. (2005). Complex trauma in children and adolescents. *Psychiatric Annals*, *35*(5), 390–398.

Cook, L., & Friend, M. (1995). Co-teaching: Guidelines for creating effective practices. *Focus on Exceptional Children*, *28*(3), 1–16.

Coolahan, K., Fantuzzo, J., Mendez, J., & McDermott, P. (2000). Preschool peer interactions and readiness to learn: Relationships between classroom peer play and learning behaviors and conduct. *Journal of Educational Psychology*, *92*(3), 458–465. doi:10.1037/0022-0663.92.3.458

Cooper, M., O'Hara, M. O., Schmid, P. F., & Wyatt, G. (2007). Preface. In M. Cooper, M. O'Hara, P. Schmid, & G. Wyatt (Eds.), The handbook of person-centered psychotherapy and counseling (pp. xxi-xxiv). New York, NY: Palgrave Macmillan.

Copen, L. M. (2000). *Preparing children for court: A practitioner's guide.* Thousand Oaks, CA: Sage.

Copple, C., & Bredekamp, S. (2009). *Developmentally appropriate practice in early childhood programs serving children from birth through age 8* (3rd ed.). Washington, DC: National Association for the Education of Young Children.

Corey, G. (2013). *Theory and practice of counseling and psychotherapy* (9th ed.). New York: Brooks/Cole Publishing Company.

Corey, G., Corey, M. S., & Callanan, P. (1998). *Issues and ethics in the helping professions.* Belmont, CA: Brooks/Cole.

Corey, G., Haynes, R., Moulton, P., & Muratori, M. (2010). *Clinical supervision in the helping professions: A practical guide* (2nd ed.). Alexandria, VA: American Counseling Association.

Cort, L., & Rowley, E. (2015, September). A case study evaluation of a Theraplay intervention to support mothers and preschool children following domestic abuse. *Debate., 156*, 33–41.

Cossins, A., Goodman-Delahunty, J., & OBrien, K. (2009). Uncertainty and misconceptions about child sexual abuse: Implications for the criminal justice system. *Psychiatry, Psychology and Law, 16*(3), 435–452. doi:10.1080/13218710902930234

Costantino, G., Malgady, R. G., & Primavera, L. H. (2009). Congruence between culturally competent treatment and cultural needs of older Latinos. *Journal of Consulting and Clinical Psychology, 77*(5), 941–949. doi:10.1037/a0016341 PMID:19803573

Costas, M., & Landreth, G. (1999). Filial therapy with non-offending parents of children who have been sexually abused. *International Journal of Play Therapy, 8*(1), 43–66. doi:10.1037/h0089427

Coufal, J. D., & Brock, G. W. (1979). Parent child relationship enhancement: A skills training approach. In N. Stinnett, B. Chesser, & J. DeFrain (Eds.), *Building family strengths: Blueprints for action* (Vol. 1, pp. 196–221). Lincoln, NE: University of Nebraska Press.

Cozolino, L. (2010). *The neuroscience of psychotherapy.* New York: Norton.

Cozolino, L. (2010). *The neuroscience of psychotherapy: Healing the social brain* (2nd ed.). New York, NY: W. W. Norton & Co.

Crane, J. (2001). The parents' part in the play therapy process. In G. L. Landreth (Ed.), *Innovations in play therapy: Issues, process, and special populations* (pp. 83–95). New York, NY: Brunner-Routledge.

Creeden, K. (2009). How trauma and attachment can impact neurodevelopment: Informing our understanding and treatment of sexual behaviors problems. *Journal of Sexual Aggression, 15*(3), 261–273. doi:10.1080/13552600903335844

Crenshaw, D. A., & Kenney-Noziska, S. (2014). Therapeutic presence in play therapy. *International Journal of Play Therapy, 23*(1), 31–43. doi:10.1037/a0035480

Crockenberg, S. (1981). Infant irritability, mother responsiveness, and social support influences on the security of infant-mother attachment. *Child Development, 52*(3), 857–865. doi:10.2307/1129087 PMID:7285658

Dahir, C. A., Burnham, J. J., & Stone, C. (2009). Listen to the voices: School counselors and comprehensive school counseling programs. *Professional School Counseling, 12*(3), 182–192. doi:10.5330/PSC.n.2010-12.182

Daly, G. (2004). Understanding the barriers to multiprofessional collaboration. *British Medical Journal, 323*(7303), 28–31.

DAndrea, W., Stolbach, B., Ford, J., Spinazzola, J., & van der Kolk, B. A. (2012). Understanding interpersonal trauma in children: Why we need a developmentally appropriate trauma diagnosis. *The American Journal of Orthopsychiatry, 2*(2), 187–200. doi:10.1111/j.1939-0025.2012.01154.x PMID:22506521

Danger, S., & Landreth, G. (2005). Child-centered group play therapy with children with speech difficulties. *International Journal of Play Therapy, 14*(1), 81–102. doi:10.1037/h0088897

Day, A. G., Somers, C., Darden, J. S., & Yoon, J. (2015). Using cross-system communication to promote educational well-being of foster children: Recommendations for a national research, practice, and policy agenda. *Children & Schools, 37*(1), 54–62. doi:10.1093/cs/cdu027

De Bellis, M. D. (2001). Developmental traumatology: The psychobiological development of maltreated children and its implications for research, treatment, and policy. *Development and Psychopathology*, *13*(3), 539–564. doi:10.1017/S0954579401003078 PMID:11523847

De Bellis, M. D., Keshavan, M. S., Clark, D. B., Casey, B. J., Giedd, J. N., Boring, A., & Ryan, N. D. (1999). Developmental traumatology part II: Brain development. *Society of Biological Psychiatry*, *45*(10), 1271–1284. doi:10.1016/S0006-3223(99)00045-1 PMID:10349033

Decker, D. M., Dona, D. P., & Christenson, S. L. (2007). Behaviorally at-risk African American students: The importance of student-teacher relationships for student outcomes. *Journal of School Psychology*, *45*(1), 83–109. doi:10.1016/j.jsp.2006.09.004

Dekker, M. C., Koot, H. M., Ende, J., & Verhulst, F. (2002). Emotional and behavioral problems in children and adolescents with and without intellectual disability. *Journal of Child Psychology and Psychiatry, and Allied Disciplines*, *43*(8), 1087–1098. doi:10.1111/1469-7610.00235 PMID:12455929

Dekraii, M., Sales, B., & Hall, S. (1998). Informed consent, confidentiality, and duty to report laws in the conduct of child therapy. In T. R. Kratochwill & R. J. Morris (Eds.), *The practice of child therapy* (3rd ed., pp. 540–559). Boston, MA: Allyn & Bacon.

Delany, R. J. (1994). *Fostering changes: Treating attachment-disordered foster children.* Fort Collins, CO: Walter J. Corbett Publishing.

Delima, M. D., & Vimpani, G. (2011). The neurobiological effects of childhood maltreatment: An often overlooked narrative related to long term effects of early childhood trauma? *Family Matters (Melbourne, Vic.)*, *89*, 42–52.

Dent, V. F. (2006). Observations of school library impact at two rural Ugandan schools. *New Library World*, *107*(9/10), 403–421. doi:10.1108/03074800610702598

Dent, V. F. (2007). Local economic development in Uganda and the connection to rural community libraries and literacy. *New Library World*, *108*(5/6), 203–217. doi:10.1108/03074800710748777

Dent, V. F., Goodman, G., & Kevane, M. (2014). *Rural community libraries in Africa: Challenges and impacts.* Hershey, PA: IGI Global. doi:10.4018/978-1-4666-5043-5

Dettmer, P., Thurston, L. P., & Dyck, N. J. (2005). Consultation, Collaboration, And Teamwork For Students With Special Needs. Pearson. Retreived from http://www.ablongman.com/html/productinfo/dettmer5e/0205435238_ch2.pdf

DeVre, R. (1992). *Prouty's Pre-Therapy* (Master's Thesis). Department of Psychology, University of Ghent, Belgium.

Dhaese, M. (2011). Holistic Expressive Play Therapy: An integrative approach to helping maltreated children. In A. A. Drewes, S. C. Bratton, & C. E. Schaefer (Eds.), *Integrative play therapy* (pp. 75–93). Hoboken, NJ: John Wiley & Sons Inc.; doi:10.1002/9781118094792.ch5

Dickinson, D. K., & Neuman, S. B. (Eds.). (2006). *Handbook of early literacy research* (Vol. 2). New York: Guilford.

Dillman Taylor, D., Nelson, K. M., Gungor, A., & Meany-Walen, K. K. (2016). *Group Adlerian play therapy with children with externalizing behaviors.* Manuscript submitted for publication.

Dillman Taylor, D., & Bratton, S. C. (2014). Developmentally appropriate practice: Adlerian play therapy with preschool children. *Journal of Individual Psychology*, *70*(3), 205–219. doi:10.1353/jip.2014.0019

Dillman Taylor, D., & Meany-Walen, K. (2015). Investigating the effectiveness of Adlerian Play Therapy (AdPT) with children with disruptive behaviors: A single-case research design. *Journal of Child and Adolescent Counseling*, *1*(2), 81–99. doi:10.1080/23727810.2015.1081519

Dinacci, A. (2001). Objective evaluation criterion for the Pre-Therapy interview. *International Pre-Therapy Review*, *1*(1), 21–30.

Dinkmeyer, D. C. Jr, & Carlson, J. (2006). *Consultation: Creating school-based interventions* (3rd ed.). New York, NY: Routledge.

Dinkmeyer, D., Dinkmeyer, D. Jr, & Sperry, L. (1987). *Adlerian counseling and psychotherapy* (2nd ed.). Columbus, OH: Merrill.

Dixon, C. G., & Vaz, K. (2005). Perceptions of African Americans regarding mental health counseling. In D. A. Harley & J. M. Dillard (Eds.), *Contemporary mental health issues among African Americans* (pp. 163–174). Alexandria, VA: American Counseling Association.

Dobbs, J., & Arnold, D. H. (2009). Relationship between preschool teachers reports of childrens behavior and their behavior toward those children. *School Psychology Quarterly*, *24*(2), 95–105. doi:10.1037/a0016157 PMID:20431714

Dodson, J. E. (1995). Conceptualizations of Black families. In N. R. Goldberger & J. B. Veroff (Eds.), *The culture and psychology reader* (pp. 276–291). New York, NY: New York University Press.

Donahue-Kilburg, G. (1992). *Family-centered early intervention for communication disorders: Prevention and treatment. Excellence in Practice Series*. Gaithersburg, MD: Aspen Publishers.

Dougherty, A. M. (1992). Ethical issues in consultation. *Elementary School Guidance and Counseling*, *26*, 214–220.

Dozier, M., Bick, J., & Bernard, K. (2011). Attachment-based treatment for young, vulnerable children. In J. Osofsky (Ed.), *Clinical Work with Traumatized Young Children* (pp. 75–95). New York: Guilford.

Draper, K., Siegel, C., White, J., Solis, C. M., & Mishna, F. (2009). Preschoolers, parents, and teachers (PPT): A preventive intervention with and at risk population. *International Journal of Group Psychotherapy*, *59*(2), 221–242. doi:10.1521/ijgp.2009.59.2.221 PMID:19441968

Draper, K., White, J., OShaughnessy, T. E., Flynt, M., & Jones, N. (2001). Kinder training: Play-based consultation to improve the school adjustment of discouraged kindergarten and first grade students. *International Journal of Play Therapy*, *10*(1), 1–30. doi:10.1037/h0089441

Dreikurs, R., & Soltz, V. (1964). *Children: The challenge.* Hawthorn Dutton.

Drewes, A. A. (2001). The possibilities and challenges in using play therapy in schools. In C. E. Schaefer, L. J. Carey, & A. A. Drewes (Eds.), School-based Play Therapy (pp. 41-62). Wiley.

Drewes, A. (2008). Bobo revisited: What the research says. *International Journal of Play Therapy*, *17*(1), 52–56. doi:10.1037/1555-6824.17.1.52

Drewes, A. A., & Schaefer, C. E. (2010). *School-based play therapy.* New York, NY: Routledge. doi:10.1002/9781118269701

Dube, S. R., Feletti, V. J., Dong, M., Giles, W. H., & Anda, R. F. (2003). The impact of adverse childhood experiences on health problems: Evidence from four birth cohorts dating back to 1900. *Preventive Medicine*, *37*(3), 268–277. doi:10.1016/S0091-7435(03)00123-3 PMID:12914833

Dugan, E., Swanson, K. & Short, E. (2011). Play therapy caregiver consultations. *Playtherapy,* 22-23.

Dupont, H. J., Landsman, T., & Valentine, M. (1953). The treatment of delayed speech by client-centered therapy. *Journal of Consulting Psychology*, *17*(2), 122–125. doi:10.1037/h0058713 PMID:13044886

Duran, F., Hepburn, K., Kaufmann, R., Le, L., Allen, M. D., Brennan, E. M., & Green, B. (no date). *Research synthesis: Early childhood mental health consultation*. Nashville, TN: Vanderbilt University, The Center on the Social and Emotional Foundations for Early Learning. Retrieved July 9, 2012 from www.vanderbilt.edu/csefel

Dykens, E. M. (2000). Annotation: Psychopathology in children with intellectual disability. *Journal of Child Psychology and Psychiatry, and Allied Disciplines*, *41*(4), 407–417. doi:10.1111/1469-7610.00626 PMID:10836671

Ebrahim, C., Steen, R. L., & Paradise, L. (2012). Overcoming school counselors barriers to play therapy. *International Journal of Play Therapy*, *21*(4), 202–214. doi:10.1037/a0029791

Edwards, N. A., Varjas, K. M., White, J. F., & Stokes, S. A. (2009). Teachers perceptions of kinder training: Acceptability, integrity, and effectiveness. *International Journal of Play Therapy*, *18*(3), 129–146. doi:10.1037/a0015170

Edwards, V. J., Holden, G. W., Felitti, V. J., & Anda, R. F. (2003). Relationship between multiple forms of childhood maltreatment and adult mental health in community respondents: Results from the adverse childhood experiences study. *The American Journal of Psychiatry*, *160*(8), 1453–1560. doi:10.1176/appi.ajp.160.8.1453 PMID:12900308

Eigsti, I. M., & Cicchetti, D. (2004). The impact of childmaltreatment on expressive syntax at 60 months. *Developmental Science*, *7*(1), 88–10. doi:10.1111/j.1467-7687.2004.00325.x PMID:15323121

Eisen, M. L., Qin, J., Goodman, G. S., & Davis, S. L. (2002). Memory and suggestibility in maltreated children: Age, stress arousal, dissociation, and psychopathology. *Journal of Experimental Child Psychology*, *83*(3), 167–212. doi:10.1016/S0022-0965(02)00126-1 PMID:12457859

Elias, M. (2006). The connection between academic and social-emotional learning. In M. Elias & H. Arnold (Eds.), The Educator's guide to emotional intelligence and academic achievement (pp. 4-14). Thousand Oaks, CA: Corwin Press.

Elkind, D. (2001). *The hurried child: Growing up too fast too soon* (3rd ed.). Cambridge, MA: Perseus.

Ellis, L., Schlaudecker, C., & Regimbal, C. (1995). Effectiveness of a collaborative consultation approach to basic concept instruction with kindergarten children. *Language, Speech, and Hearing Services in Schools*, *26*(1), 69–74. doi:10.1044/0161-1461.2601.69

Erickson, F. (1963). Viewpoints on children in hospitals. *Hospitals*, *1*, 37–47.

Eyberg, S., Nelson, M., & Boggs, S. (2008). Evidence based psychological treatments for children and adolescents with disruptive behavior. *Journal of Child and Adolescent Psychology*, *37*(1), 215–237. doi:10.1080/15374410701820117 PMID:18444059

Fairbank, J. A. (2008). The epidemiology of trauma and trauma related disorders in children and youth. *PTSD Research Quarterly*, *19*(1), 1–8.

Fairburn, C. G., & Cooper, Z. (2011). Therapist competence, therapy quality, and therapist training. *Behaviour Research and Therapy*, *49*(6-7), 373–378. doi:10.1016/j.brat.2011.03.005 PMID:21492829

Fall, M., Navelski, L., & Welch, K. (2002). Outcomes of a play intervention for children identified for special education services. *International Journal of Play Therapy*, *11*(2), 91–106. doi:10.1037/h0088866

Fanciullo, M., Yellin, E., Blake, B., Chu, D., Schroeder, M., Fults, E., . . . Goodman, G. (2013, June). *An examination of rural Ugandan preschool children's implicit perceptions of familial social roles*. Paper presented at the meeting of the New York State Psychological Association, New York, NY.

Fang, X., Brown, D. S., Florence, C. S., & Mercy, J. A. (2012). The economic burden of child maltreatment in the United States and implications for prevention. *Child Abuse & Neglect*, *36*(2), 156–165. doi:10.1016/j.chiabu.2011.10.006 PMID:22300910

Fantuzzo, J., Sekino, Y., & Cohen, H. L. (2004). An examination of the contributions of interactive peer play to salient classroom competencies for urban Head Start children. *Psychology in the Schools*, *41*(3), 323–335. doi:10.1002/pits.10162

Farahzadi, M., Bahramabadi, M., & Mohammadifar, M. (2011). Effectiveness of gestalt play therapy in decreasing social phobia. *Journal of Iranian Psychologists*, *7*, 387–395.

Farber, J. G., & Klein, E. R. (1999). Classroom-based assessment of a collaborative intervention program with kindergarten and first-grade students. *Language, Speech, and Hearing Services in Schools*, *30*(1), 83–91. doi:10.1044/0161-1461.3001.83 PMID:27764293

Feldman, R. S. (2014). *Development across the life span* (7th ed.). Upper Saddle River, NJ: Prentice Hall.

Felitti, V. J., Anda, R. F., Nordenberg, D., Williamson, D. F., Spitz, A. M., Edwards, V., & Marks, J. S. et al. (1998). Relationship of childhood abuse and household dysfunction to many of the leading causes of death in adults: Adverse Childhood Event Study. *American Journal of Preventive Medicine*, *14*(4), 245–258. doi:10.1016/S0749-3797(98)00017-8 PMID:9635069

Fenner, L. B. (2016). Constructing the self: Three-dimensional form. In D. E. Gussak & M. L. Rosal (Eds.), *The Wiley handbook of art therapy* (pp. 154–162). Chichester, UK: John Wiley & Sons, Ltd.

Ferguson, P., Jimerson, S. R., & Dalton, M. J. (2001). Sorting out successful failures: Exploratory analyses of factors associated with academic and behavioral outcomes of retained students. *Psychology in the Schools*, *38*(4), 327–341. doi:10.1002/pits.1022

Findling, J. H., Bratton, S. C., & Henson, R. K. (2006). Development of the trauma play scale: An observation-based assessment of the impact of trauma on play therapy behaviors of young children. *International Journal of Play Therapy*, *15*(1), 7–36. doi:10.1037/h0088906

Finkelhor, D., Shattuck, A., Turner, H. A., & Hamby, S. L. (2014). The Lifetime Prevalence of Child Sexual Abuse and Sexual Assault Assessed in Late Adolescence. *The Journal of Adolescent Health*, *55*(3), 329–333. doi:10.1016/j.jadohealth.2013.12.026 PMID:24582321

Finley, V. B. (2012). Parental involvement in speech-language intervention. University of Southern Mississippi Honors Thesis. Paper 75. Retrieved from http://aquila.usm.edu/cgi/viewcontent.cgi?article=1074&context=honors_theses

Fisher, K. R., Hirsh-Pasek, K., Golinkoff, R. M., & Gryfe, S. G. (2008). Conceptual split? Parents and experts perceptions of play in the 21st century. *Journal of Applied Developmental Psychology*, *29*(4), 305–316. doi:10.1016/j.appdev.2008.04.006

Fisher, M. A. (2013). *The ethics of conditional confidentiality: A practice model for mental health professionals*. New York, NY: Oxford University Press. doi:10.1093/med:psych/9780199752201.001.0001

Fisher, P., Masia-Warner, C., & Klein, R. (2004). Skills for social and academic success: A school-based intervention for social anxiety disorder in adolescents. *Clinical Child and Family Psychology Review*, *7*(4), 241–249. doi:10.1007/s10567-004-6088-7 PMID:15648278

Flahive, M., & Ray, D. (2007). Effects of group sandtray therapy with preadolescents. *Journal for Specialists in Group Work*, *32*(4), 362–382. doi:10.1080/01933920701476706

Flanagan, R., Allen, K., & Henry, D. J. (2010). The impact of anger management treatment and rational emotive behavior therapy in a public school setting on social skills, anger management, and depression. *Journal of Rational-Emotive & Cognitive-Behavior Therapy, 28*(2), 87–99. doi:10.1007/s10942-009-0102-4

Flett, G. L., Hewitt, P. L., Boucher, D. J., Davidson, L. A., & Munro, Y. (2002). *The Child–Adolescent Perfectionism Scale: Development, validation, and association with adjustment.* Unpublished manuscript.

Flynn, P., & Power-deFur, L. (2013). *Collaboration in schools: Let the magic begin.* Presentation at the American Speech-Language and Hearing Association Schools Conference. Retrieved from http:// www.asha.org/events/convention/handouts/2013/1403-flynn/

Foa, E. B., Keane, T. M., Friedman, M. J., & Cohen, J. A. (Eds.). (2009). *Effective treatments for PTSD: Practice guidelines from the International Society for Traumatic Stress Studies* (2nd ed.). New York, NY: The Guilford Press.

Fonagy, P. (1999). Psychoanalytic Theory from the viewpoint of attachment theory and research. In J. Cassidy & P. Shaver (Eds.), *Handbook of attachment theory and research* (pp. 595–624). New York: Guilford Press.

Fonagy, P., Gergely, G., Jurist, E. L., & Target, M. (2002). *Affect regulation, mentalization, and the development of the self.* New York: Other Press.

Fonagy, P., & Target, M. (2005). Bridging the transmission gap: An end to an important mystery of attachment research? *Attachment & Human Development, 7*(3), 333–343. doi:10.1080/14616730500269278 PMID:16210243

Forbes, H., & Post, B. (2006). *Beyond consequences logic, and control: A love based approach to helping attachment-challenged children with severe behaviors.* Orlando, FL: Beyond Consequences Institute, LLC.

Formaad, W. (1974). *Articulation therapy through play: A multi-sensory approach.* Gled Ridge, NJ: Exceptional Press.

Franklin, J., Moore, E., Howard, A., Purvis, K., Cross, D., & Lindaman, S. (2007). *An Evaluation of Theraplay Using a Sample of Children Diagnosed with Pervasive Developmental Disorder (PDD) or Mild to Moderate Autism.* Poster presentation at the American Psychological Association Conference, San Francisco, CA.

Franklin, A. J., & Boyd-Franklin, N. (1985). A psycho-educational perspective on Black parenting. In H. P. McAdoo & J. L. McAdoo (Eds.), *Black children: social, educational & parental environments.* Beverly Hills, CA: Sage Publications.

Fredrickson, B. L., Grewen, K. M., Coffey, K. A., Algoe, S. B., Firestine, A. M., Arevalo, J. G., & Cole, S. W. et al. (2013). A functional genomic perspective on human well-being. *Proceedings of the National Academy of Sciences of the United States of America, 110*(33), 13684–13689. doi:10.1073/pnas.1305419110 PMID:23898182

Friedman, R. D., & Ceci, S. J. (2015). The Child Quasi Witness. *The University of Chicago Law Review. University of Chicago. Law School, 82*(1), 89–111.

Fuhrman, K., & Franz, D.A. (2010, March). Toy guns in the playroom: Yes or No? *Play Therapy*, p. 5.

Fuller, W. (1995). Theraplay as treatment for autism in a school-based day treatment setting. *Continuum. Journal of the American Association for Partial Hospitalization, 2*(2), 89–93.

Galassi, J., Griffin, D., & Akos, P. (2008). Strengthen-based school counseling and the ASCA National Model. *Professional School Counseling, 12*(2), 176–181. doi:10.5330/PSC.n.2010-12.176

Gallo-Lopez, L., & Schaefer, C. E. (Eds.). (2005). *Play therapy with adolescents.* New York: Jason Aronson.

Garner, B. P. (1998). Play development from birth to age four. In D. Fromberg & D. Bergen (Eds.), *Play from birth to twelve and beyond: Contexts, perspectives, and meanings* (pp. 137–153). New York: Garland.

Garner, P. W., Curenton, S. M., & Taylor, K. (2005). Predictors of mental state understanding in preschoolers of varying socioeconomic backgrounds. *International Journal of Behavioral Development, 29*(4), 271–281. doi:10.1177/01650250544000053

Garner, P. W., & Waajid, B. (2008). The associations of emotions knowledge and teacher-child relationships to preschool childrens school-related developmental competence. *Journal of Applied Developmental Psychology, 29*(2), 89–100. doi:10.1016/j.appdev.2007.12.001

Garza, Y. (2004). *Effects of culturally responsive child-centered play therapy compared to curriculum-based small group counseling with elementary-age Hispanic children experiencing externalizing and internalizing behavior problems: A preliminary study* (Unpublished doctoral dissertation). University of North Texas, Denton, TX.

Garza, Y., & Bratton, S. (2005). School-based child-centered play therapy with Hispanic children: Outcomes and cultural considerations. *International Journal of Play Therapy, 14*(1), 51–79. doi:10.1037/h0088896

Garza, Y., & Watts, R. E. (2010). Filial therapy and Hispanic values: Common ground for culturally sensitive helping. *Journal of Counseling and Development, 88*(1), 108–113. doi:10.1002/j.1556-6678.2010.tb00157.x

Gaskill, R., & Perry, B. (manuscript in preparation). *NMT guided play, play therapy and activities for children who won't talk.*

Gaskill, R. L., & Perry, B. D. (2012). Child sexual abuse, traumatic experiences, and their impact on the developing brain. In P. Goodyear-Brown (Ed.), *Handbook of child sexual abuse: Identification, assessment, and treatment* (pp. 30–47). Hoboken, NJ: John Wiley & Sons, Inc.

Gaskill, R., & Perry, B. (2014). The neurobiological power of play: Using the Neurosequential Model of Therapeutics™ to guide play in healing process. In C. Malchoidi & D. Crenshaw (Eds.), *Creative arts & play therapy for attachment trauma*. New York: Guilford Press.

Geller, S. M. & Porges, S. W. (2014). Therapeutic presence: neurophysiological mechanisms mediating feeling safe in therapeutic relationships. *Journal of Psychotherapy Integration, 24*(3), 178-192.

Geller, S., & Porges, S. (2014). Therpeutic presence: Neurophysiological mechanisms mediating feeling safe in therapeutic relationships. *Journal of Psychotherapy Integration, 24*(3), 178–192. doi:10.1037/a0037511

Georgetown University. (2015). *Early childhood mental health consultation.* Center for Child and Human Development. Retrieved from: http://gucchd.georgetown.edu/67637.html

Gerhardt, S. (2004). *Why Love Matters: How affection shapes a baby's brain* (2nd ed.). New York: Routledge.

Gerity, L. (2005). Trauma, puppet making, and narrative: Creating moments of reprieve. In M. Bernier & J. O'Hare (Eds.), *Puppetry in education and therapy* (pp. 139–146). Bloomington, IL: Authorhouse.

Ghetti, S., Qin, J., & Goodman, G. S. (2002). False memories in children and adults: Age, distinctiveness, and subjective experience. *Developmental Psychology, 38*(5), 705–718. doi:10.1037/0012-1649.38.5.705 PMID:12220049

Gilbertson, M. W., Shenton, M. E., Ciszewski, A., Kasai, K., Lasko, N. B., Orr, S. P., & Pitman, R. K. (2002). Smaller hippocampal volume predicts pathologic vulnerability to psychological trauma. *Nature Neuroscience, 5*(11), 1242–1247. doi:10.1038/nn958 PMID:12379862

Gil, E. (2005). From sensitivity to competence in working across cultures. In E. Gil & A. A. Drewes (Eds.), *Cultural issues in play therapy* (pp. 3–25). New York, NY: Guilford Press.

Gil, E. (2006). *Helping abused and traumatized children: Integrating directive and nondirective approaches*. New York, NY, US: Guilford Press.

Gioia, K., & Tobin, R. (2010). The role of sociodramatic play in promoting self regulation. In Play therapy for preschool children (pp. 181-198). Washington, DC: American Psychological Association. doi:10.1037/12060-009

Gladding, S. T. (2012). *Counseling a group specialty* (6th ed.). Upper Saddle River, NJ: Pearson.

Glover, A., McCormack, J., & Smith-Tamaray, M. (2015). Collaboration between teachers and speech and language therapists: Services for primary school children with speech, language and communication needs. *Child Language Teaching and Therapy*, *31*(3), 363–382. doi:10.1177/0265659015603779

Gold, A. L., Shin, L. M., Orr, S. P., Carson, M. A., Rauch, S. L., Macklin, M. L., & Pitman, R. K. et al. (2011). Decreased regional cerebral blood flow in medial prefrontal cortex during trauma-unrelated stressful imagery in Vietnam veterans with post-traumatic stress disorder. *Psychological Medicine*, *41*(12), 2563–2572. doi:10.1017/S0033291711000730 PMID:21733221

Goldstein, A. P., & McGinnis, E. (1997). *Skillstreaming the adolescent: New strategies and perspectives for teaching prosocial skills*. Champaign, IL: Research Press.

Gomes, P. G., & Mabry, C. A. (1991). Negotiating the world: The developmental journey of African American children. In J. E. Everett, S. S. Chipungu, & B. R. Leashore (Eds.), *Child welfare: An Africentric perspective* (pp. 156–182). New Brunswick, NJ: Rutgers University Press.

Gonzales, T. L. (2012). *Child teacher relationship training as a Head Start early mental health intervention for children exhibiting disruptive behavior* (Doctoral dissertation). Retrieved from http://digital.library.unt.edu/ark:/67531/metadc149553/

Gonzalez, J. E., Nelson, J. E., Gutkin, T. B., Saunders, A., Galloway, A., & Shwery, C. S. (2004). Rational emotive therapy with children and adolescents: A meta-analysis. *Journal of Emotional and Behavioral Disorders*, *12*(4), 222–235. doi:10.1177/10634266040120040301

Goodman, G. (2010). *Therapeutic attachment relationships: Interaction structures and the processes of therapeutic change*. Lanham, MD: Jason Aronson.

Goodman, J. F., & Linn, M. I. (2003). Maladaptive behaviors in the young child with intellectual disabilities: Reconsideration. *International Journal of Disability Development and Education*, *50*(2), 137–148. doi:10.1080/1034912032000089648

Goodyear, R. K., & Rodolfa, E. (2012). *Negotiating the complex ethical terrain of clinical supervision*. In S. J. Knapp, M. C. Gottlieb, M. M. Handelsman, & L. D. VandeCreek (Eds.), APA handbook of ethics in psychology (Vol. 2, pp. 261–275). Washington, DC: American Psychological association. doi:10.1037/13272-013

Grasso, D., Ford, J., & Briggs-Gowan, M. (2013). Early life trauma exposure and stress sensitivity in young children. *Journal of Pediatric Psychology*, *38*(1), 94–103. doi:10.1093/jpepsy/jss101 PMID:23008502

Greenspan, S. (1993). *Playground politics: Understanding the emotional life of your school-aged child*. Reading, MA: Harvard University Press.

Green, V. A., OReilly, M., Itchon, J., & Sigafoos, J. (2004). Persistence of early emerging aberrant behavior in children with developmental disabilities. *Research in Developmental Disabilities*, *26*(1), 47–55. doi:10.1016/j.ridd.2004.07.003 PMID:15590237

Greeson, J. K., Briggs, E. C., Kisiel, C. L., Layne, C. M., Ake, G. S. III, Ko, S. J., & Fairbank, J. A. et al. (2011). Complex Trauma and Mental Health in Children and Adolescents Placed in Foster Care: Findings from the National Child Traumatic Stress Network. *Child Welfare*, *90*(6), 91–108. PMID:22533044

Gregl, A., Kirigin, M., Bilać, S., Sućeska Ligutićić, R., Jakšić, N., & Jakovljević, M. (2014). Speech comprehension and emotional/behavioral problems in children with specific language impairment (SLI). *Collegium Antropologicum*, *38*(3), 871–877.

Gresham, F. M., & Elliot, S. N. (1993). Social skills intervention guide: Systematic approaches to social skills training. *Special Services in the Schools*, *8*(1), 137–158. doi:10.1300/J008v08n01_07

Grienenberger, J., Kelly, K., & Slade, A. (2005). Maternal reflective functioning, mother-infant affective communication, and infant attachment: Exploring the link between mental states and observed caregiving behavior in the intergenerational transmission of attachment. *Attachment & Human Development*, *7*(3), 299–311. doi:10.1080/14616730500245963 PMID:16210241

Grych, J. H., Jouriles, E. N., Swank, P. R., McDonald, R., & Norwood, W. D. (2000). Patterns of adjustment among children of battered women. *Journal of Consulting and Clinical Psychology*, *68*(1), 84–94. doi:10.1037/0022-006X.68.1.84 PMID:10710843

Guerney, B. G. (1964). Filial therapy: Description and rationale. *Journal of Consulting Psychology*, *28*(4), 304–310. doi:10.1037/h0041340 PMID:14198792

Guerney, B. G., & Stover, L. (1971). *Filial therapy: Final report to NIMH, Grant 1826401*. University Park, PA: The Pennsylvania State University.

Guerney, B., & Flumen, A. B. (1970). Teachers as psychotherapeutic agents for withdrawn children. *Journal of School Psychology*, *8*(2), 107–113. doi:10.1016/0022-4405(70)90029-4

Guerney, B. Jr. (1964). Filial therapy: Description and rationale. *Journal of Counseling Psychology*, *28*, 304–310. PMID:14198792

Guerney, L. (1983). Client-centered (nondirective) play therapy. In C. Schaefer & K. J. O'Connor (Eds.), *Handbook of play therapy* (pp. 21–64). New York, NY: Wiley.

Guerney, L. G. (2000). Filial therapy into the 21st century. *International Journal of Play Therapy*, *9*(2), 1–17. doi:10.1037/h0089433

Gun Violence Archive. (2016). *Mass shootings in 2015*. Retrieved from http://www.gunviolencearchive.org/reports/mass-shooting

Gurvits, T. V., Shenton, M. E., Hokama, H., Ohta, H., Lasko, N. B., Gilberton, M. W., & Pitman, R. K. et al. (1996). Magnetic resonance imaging study of hippocampal volume in chronic, combat-related posttraumatic stress disorder. *Biological Psychiatry*, *40*(11), 1091–1099. doi:10.1016/S0006-3223(96)00229-6 PMID:8931911

Gysbers, N. (2001). School guidance and counseling in the 21st century: Remember the past into the future. *Professional School Counseling*, *5*(2), 96–106.

Gysbers, N., & Henderson, P. (2011). *Developing & managing your school guidance program* (5th ed.). Alexandria, VA: American Counseling Association.

Hall, P. (2005). Interprofessional teamwork: Professional cultures as barriers. *Journal of Interprofessional Care, 19*(sup1), 188-196.

Hamre, B. K., & Pianta, R. C. (2001). Early teacher-child relationships and the trajectory of childrens school outcomes through eighth grade. *Child Development*, *72*(2), 625–638. doi:10.1111/1467-8624.00301 PMID:11333089

Hamre, B. K., & Pianta, R. C. (2006). Can instructional and emotional support in the first-grade classroom make a difference for children at risk of school failure. *Child Development*, *76*(5), 949–967. doi:10.1111/j.1467-8624.2005.00889.x PMID:16149994

Hansen, T. W. (2011). Prevention of neurodevelopmental sequelae of jaundice in the newborn. *Developmental Medicine and Child Neurology*, *53*, 24–28. doi:10.1111/j.1469-8749.2011.04059.x PMID:21950390

Harley, D. A. (2005). The Black church: A strength-based approach in mental health. In D. A. Harley & J. M. Dillard (Eds.), *Contemporary mental health issues among African Americans* (pp. 191–203). Alexandria, VA: American Counseling Association.

Harrell, A. W., Mercer, S. H., & DeRosier, M. E. (2008). Improving the social-behavioral adjustment of adolescents: The effectiveness of a social skills group intervention. *Journal of Child and Family Studies*, *18*(4), 378–387. doi:10.1007/s10826-008-9241-y

Harris, S. M., Brown, A., Dakin, J. B., Lucas, B., Riley, L., & Bulham, R. (2009). Are clinical records really that important? The dearth of research and practice guidelines in MFT literature. *The American Journal of Family Therapy*, *37*(5), 373–387. doi:10.1080/01926180902754729

Harris, Z. L., & Landreth, G. L. (1997). Filial therapy with incarcerated mothers: A five-week model. *International Journal of Play Therapy*, *6*(2), 53–73. doi:10.1037/h0089408

Hartas, D. (2004). Teacher and speech-language therapist collaboration: Being equal and achieving a common goal. *Child Language Teaching and Therapy*, *20*(1), 33–54. doi:10.1191/0265659004ct262oa

Hart, B., & Risley, T. R. (1999). *The social world of children: Learning to talk*. Baltimore, MD: Paul H. Brookes Publishing.

Hartup, W. W. (1983). Peer relations. In Handbook of child psychology: Socialization, personality, and social development (vol. 4, pp. 103-196). New York: Wiley.

Hartwig, E. K. (2014). Puppets in the playroom: Utilizing puppets and child-centered facilitative skills as a metaphor for healing. *International Journal of Play Therapy*, *23*(4), 204–216. doi:10.1037/a0038054

Haslam, D., & Harris, S. (2011). Integrating play and family therapy methods: A survey of play therapists attitudes in the field. *International Journal of Play Therapy*, *20*(2), 51–65. doi:10.1037/a0023410

Hayes, J. P., LaBar, K. S., McCarthy, G., Selgrade, E., Nasser, J., Dolcos, F., & Morey, R. A. (2011). Reduced hippocampal and amygdala activity predicts memory distortions for trauma reminders in combat-related PTSD. *Journal of Psychiatric Research*, *45*(5), 660–669. doi:10.1016/j.jpsychires.2010.10.007 PMID:21047644

Hecht, S. A., Burgess, S. R., Torgesen, J. K., Wagner, R. K., & Rashotte, C. A. (2000). Explaining social class differences in growth of reading skills from beginning kindergarten through fourth-grade: The role of phonological awareness, rate of access, and print knowledge. *Reading and Writing*, *12*(1/2), 99–127. doi:10.1023/A:1008033824385

Helker, W. P., & Ray, D. C. (2009). Impact of child teacher relationship training on teachers' and aides' use of relationship-building skills and the effects on student classroom behavior. *International Journal of Play Therapy*, *18*(2), 70.

Helker, W. P., & Ray, D. C. (2009). The impact of child teacher relationship training on teachers and aides use of relationship-building skills and the effect on student classroom behavior. *International Journal of Play Therapy*, *18*(2), 70–83. doi:10.1037/a0014456

Helker, W. P., Schottelkorb, A. A., & Ray, D. (2007). Helping students and teachers CONNECT: An intervention model for school counselors. *Journal of Professional Counseling, Practice, Theory, & Research*, *35*, 31–45.

HelpGuide.org. (2016). *Understanding child abuse and neglect.* Retrieved July 30, 2016 from http://www.helpguide.org/articles/abuse/child-abuse-and-neglect.htm

Hemphill, S. A., & Littlefield, L. (2001). Evaluation of a short-term group therapy program for children with behaviour problems and their parents. *Behaviour Research and Therapy*, *39*(7), 823–841. doi:10.1016/S0005-7967(00)00058-9 PMID:11419613

Henderson, S.W., & Martin, A. (2014). Case formulation and integration of information in child and adolescent mental health. In *IACAPAP e-textbook of child and adolescent mental health.* Geneva: International Association for Child and Adolescent Psychiatry and Allied Professions.

Herlenius, E., & Lagercrantz, H. (2001). Neurotransmitters and neuromodulators during early human development. *Early Human Development*, *65*(1), 21–37. doi:10.1016/S0378-3782(01)00189-X PMID:11520626

Herlihy, B., Gray, N., & McCollum, V. (2002). Legal and ethical issues in school counselor supervision. *Professional School Counseling*, *6*, 55–60.

Himebauch, A., Arnold, R., & May, C. (2008). Grief in children and developmental concepts of death #138. *Journal of Palliative Medicine*, *11*(2), 242–243. doi:10.1089/jpm.2008.9973 PMID:18333739

Hinman, C. (2003). Multicultural considerations in the delivery of play therapy services. *International Journal of Play Therapy*, *12*(2), 107–122. doi:10.1037/h0088881

Hinz, L. D. (2009). *Expressive therapies continuum: A framework for using art in therapy*. New York, NY: Routledge.

Hinz, L. D. (2016). Media considerations in art therapy: Directions for future research. In D. E. Gussak & M. L. Rosal (Eds.), *The Wiley handbook of art therapy* (pp. 135–145). Chichester, UK: John Wiley & Sons, Ltd.

Holcomb-McCoy, C., & Bryan, J. (2010). Advocacy and empowerment in parent consultation: Implications for theory and practice. *Journal of Counseling and Development*, *88*(3), 259–268. doi:10.1002/j.1556-6678.2010.tb00021.x

Holding, P. A., Taylor, H. G., Kazungu, S. D., Mkala, T., Gona, J., Mwamuye, B., & Stevenson, J. et al. (2004). Assessing cognitive outcomes in a rural African population: Development of a neuropsychological battery in Kilifi District, Kenya. *Journal of the International Neuropsychological Society*, *10*(02), 246–260. doi:10.1017/S1355617704102166 PMID:15012845

Holt, R. L., & Mikati, M. A. (2010). Care for child development: Basic science rationale and effects of interventions. *Pediatric Neurology*, *44*(4), 239–253. doi:10.1016/j.pediatrneurol.2010.11.009 PMID:21397164

Hong, R., & Mason, C. (2016). Becoming a neurobiologically-informed play therapist. *International Journal of Play Therapy*, *25*(1), 35–44. doi:10.1037/pla0000020

Horwitz, S. M., Chamberlain, P., Landsverk, J., & Mullican, C. (2010). Improving the mental health of children in Child Welfare through the implementation of evidence-based parenting. *Administration and Policy in Mental Health*, *37*(1-2), 27–39. doi:10.1007/s10488-010-0274-3 PMID:20143150

Hovens, J. M., Giltay, E. J., Wiersma, J. E., Spinhoven, P., Penninx, B. H., & Zitman, F. G. (2012). Impact of childhood life events and trauma on the course of depressive and anxiety disorders. *Acta Psychiatrica Scandinavica*, *126*(3), 198–207. doi:10.1111/j.1600-0447.2011.01828.x PMID:22268708

Howard, S., Shaughnessy, A., Sanger, D., & Hux, K. (1998). Lets talk! Facilitating language in early elementary classrooms. *Young Children, 53*(3), 34–39.

Howes, C. (2000). Social-emotional classroom climate in child care, child-teacher relationships, and childrens second grade peer relations. *Social Development, 9*(2), 191–204. doi:10.1111/1467-9507.00119

Howes, C., Burchinal, M., Pianta, R., Bryant, D., Clifford, R., & Barbarin, O. (2008). Ready to learn? Childrens pre-academic achievement in pre-Kindergarten programs. *Early Childhood Research Quarterly, 23*(1), 27–50. doi:10.1016/j.ecresq.2007.05.002

Hughes, D. A. (1997). *Facilitating developmental attachment: The road to emotional recovery and behavioral change in foster and adopted children*. Lanham, MD: Rowman & Littlefield.

Hughes, D. A. (1999). Adopted children with attachment problems. *Child Welfare, 78*(5), 541–561. PMID:10501012

Hughes, D. A. (1999). Adopting children with attachment problems. *Child Welfare, 78*(5), 541–560. PMID:10501012

Hughes, D. A. (2006). *Building the bonds of attachment: Awakening love in deeply troubled children* (2nd ed.). Lanham, MD: Rowman & Littlefield.

Human Development Reports Uganda. (2014). Retrieved from http://hdr.undp.org/en/countries

Hungi, N., & Thuku, F. (2010). Variations in reading achievement across 14 southern African school systems: Which factors matter? *International Review of Education, 56*(1), 63–101. doi:10.1007/s11159-009-9148-x

Im-Bolter, N., & Cohen, N. J. (2007). Language impairment and psychiatric comorbidities. *Pediatric Clinics of North America, 54*(3), 525–542.

Immordino-Yang, M., & Damasio, A. (2007). We feel, therefore we learn: The relevance of affective and social neuroscience to education. *Mind, Brain, and Education, 1*(1), 3–10. doi:10.1111/j.1751-228X.2007.00004.x

Individuals With Disabilities Education Act, 20 U.S.C. § 1400 (2004).

Ingraham, C. L. (2000). Consultation through a multicultural lens: Multicultural and cross-cultural consultation in schools. *School Psychology Review, 29*, 320–343.

Ingraham, C. L. (2003). Multicultural consultee-centered consultation: When novice consultants explore cultural hypotheses with experienced teacher consultees. *Journal of Educational & Psychological Consultation, 14*(3/4), 329–362. doi:10.1080/10474412.2003.9669492

Irwin, E. C. (2002). Using puppets for assessment. In C. E. Schaefer & D. Cangelosi (Eds.), *Play therapy techniques* (2nd ed., pp. 101–113). Lanham, MD: Jason Aronson.

Irwin, E. C., & McWilliams, B. J. (1974). Play therapy for children with cleft palates. *Children Today, 3*(3), 18–22. PMID:4464044

Ivon, H. (2014). Features of children's play and developmental possibilities of symbolic puppet play. *Croatian Journal Educational / Hrvatski Casopis Za Odgoj I Obrazovanje, 16,* 161-180.

Jackson, L. (1950). Non-speaking children. *The British Journal of Medical Psychology, 23*(1-2), 87–100. doi:10.1111/j.2044-8341.1950.tb00373.x PMID:14801378

Jacob, S., Decker, D. M., & Timmerman Lugg, E. (2016). *Ethics and law for school psychologists*. Hoboken, NJ: John Wiley & Sons.

James, B. (1994). *Handbook for treatment of attachment-trauma problems in children*. Lexington, MA: Lexington Books.

Janson, G. R., & King, M. A. (2006). Emotional security in the classroom: What works for young children. *Journal of Family and Consumer Sciences*, *98*(2), 70–74.

Jayne, K. M., Stulmaker, H. L., & Purswell, K. E. (2013). Multicultural dimensions in child counseling research: A systematic review. *Journal of Professional Counseling, Practice, Theory, & Research*, *40*(2), 15–32.

Jeffree, D., & McConkey, R. (1974). Extending language through play. *Special Education: Forward Trends*, *1*(3), 13. PMID:4282762

Jenkins, R. L., & Beckh, E. (2002). Finger puppets and mask making. In C. E. Schaefer & D. Cangelosi (Eds.), *Play therapy techniques* (2nd ed.; pp. 115–122). Lanham, MD: Jason Aronson.

Jernberg, A. M., & Booth, P. (1999). *Theraplay: Helping Parents and Children Build Better Relationships* (2nd ed.). San Francisco, CA: Jossey Bass.

Johnston, K., & Brinamen, C. (2006). *Mental health consultation in child care: Transforming relationships among directors, staff and families*. Washington, DC: ZERO TO THREE Press.

Jones, E., & Landreth, G. L. (2002). The efficacy of intensive individual play therapy for chronically ill children. *International Journal of Play Therapy*, *11*(1), 117–140. doi:10.1037/h0088860

Jones, L., Rhine, T., & Bratton, S. (2002). High school students as therapeutic agents with young children experiencing school adjustment difficulties: The effectiveness of a filial therapy training model. *International Journal of Play Therapy*, *11*(2), 43–62. doi:10.1037/h0088864

Kagan, S. L., & Lowenstein, A. E. (2004). School readiness and children's play: Contemporary oxymoron or compatible option? In E. F. Zigler, D. G. Singer, & S. J. Bishop-Josef (Eds.), *Children's play: The roots of reading* (pp. 59–76). Washington, DC: Zero to Three Press.

Kaiser, A. P., & Delaney, E. M. (2001). Responsive conversations: Creating opportunities for naturalistic language teaching. In M. Ostrosky & S. Sandall (Eds.), *Young Exceptional Children Monograph Series No. 3: Teaching Strategies: What to do to support Young Children's Development* (pp. 13–23). Longmont, CO: Sopris West.

Kaiser, A., & Hancock, T. (2013). Teaching parents new skills to support their young childrens development. *Infants and Young Children*, *16*(1), 9–21. doi:10.1097/00001163-200301000-00003

Kalmakis, K. A., & Chandler, J. A. (2014). Adverse childhood experiences toward a clear conceptual meaning. *Journal of Advanced Nursing*, *70*(7), 1489–1501. doi:10.1111/jan.12329 PMID:24329930

Kalyanpur, M., & Rao, S. S. (1991). Empowering low-income Black families of handicapped children. *The American Journal of Orthopsychiatry*, *61*(4), 523–532. doi:10.1037/h0079292 PMID:1836108

Kandel, E. (1998). A new intellectual framework for psychiatry. *The American Journal of Psychiatry*, *155*(4), 457–469. doi:10.1176/ajp.155.4.457 PMID:9545989

Kauffman, J. M. (2005). *Characteristics of emotional and behavioral disorders of children and youth* (9th ed.). Upper Saddle River, NJ: Pearson.

Kaufman, B. A. (1994). Day by day: Playing and learning. *International Journal of Play Therapy*, *3*(1), 11–21. doi:10.1037/h0089401

Kayler, H., & Sherman, J. (2009). At-risk ninth grade students: A psychoeducational group approach to increase study skills and grade point averages. *Professional School Counseling*, *12*(6), 434–439. doi:10.5330/PSC.n.2010-12.434

Kena, G., Musu-Gillette, L., Robinson, J., Wang, X., Rathbun, A., Zhang, J., & Velez, E. D. V. (2015). *The Condition of Education 2015. NCES 2015-144*. National Center for Education Statistics.

Kendall, S., & Bloomfield, L. (2005). Developing and validating a tool to measure parenting self-efficacy. *Journal of Advanced Nursing*, *51*(2), 174–181. doi:10.1111/j.1365-2648.2005.03479.x PMID:15963189

Kestley, T. A. (2014). *The Interpersonal Neurobiology of Play*. New York, NY: Norton.

Kestly, T. (2015). Sandtray and storytelling in play therapy. In D. A. Crenshaw & A. L. Stewart (Eds.), *Play therapy: A comprehensive guide to theory and practice* (pp. 156–170). New York, NY: Guilford Press.

Kestly, T. A. (2014). *The interpersonal neurobiology of play: Brain-building interventions for emotional well-being*. New York, NY: W.W. Norton & Company.

Kfir, N. (1981). Impasse/priority therapy. In R. Corsini (Ed.), *Handbook of innovative psychotherapies* (pp. 400–415). New York: Wiley.

Kfir, N. (2011). *Personality and priorities: A typology*. Bloomington, IN: Author House.

Kinniburgh, K. J., Blaustein, M., Spinazzola, J., & van der Kolk, B. A. (2005). Attachment, Self-Regulation, and Competency. *Psychiatric Annals*, *35*(5), 424–430.

Kirkham, J., Stewart, A., & Kidd, E. (2013). Concurrent and longitudinal relationships between development in graphic, language and symbolic play domains from the fourth to the fifth year. *Infant and Child Development*, *22*(3), 297–319. doi:10.1002/icd.1786

Kitchener, K. S. (1984). Intuition, critical evaluation and ethical principles: The foundation for ethical decisions in counseling psychology. *The Counseling Psychologist*, *12*(3), 43–55. doi:10.1177/0011000084123005

Klain, E. J., & White, A. R. (2013). *Implementing trauma-informed practices in child welfare*. State Policy Advocacy and Reform Center. Retrieved from http://childwelfaresparc.org/wp-content/uploads/2013/11/Implementing-Trauma-Informed-Practices.pdf

Kleim, J. A., & Jones, T. A. (2008). Principles of experience-dependent neural plasticity: Implications of rehabilitation after brain damage. *Journal of Speech, Language, and Hearing Research: JSLHR*, *51*(1), 225–239. doi:10.1044/1092-4388(2008/018) PMID:18230848

Klemfuss, J. Z., & Ceci, S. J. (2012). Legal and psychological perspectives on childrens competence to testify in court. *Developmental Review*, *32*(3), 268–286. doi:10.1016/j.dr.2012.06.005

Knapp, S., & VandeCreek, L. (1997). Ethical and legal aspects of clinical supervision. In C. E. Watkins (Ed.), *Handbook of psychotherapy supervision* (pp. 589–599). New York, NY: Wiley.

Knell, S. M. (2009). *Cognitive-behavioral play therapy*. Northvale, NJ: Jason Aronson Inc.

Knill, P. J. (1994). Multiplicity as a tradition: Theories for interdisciplinary arts therapies – An overview. *The Arts in Psychotherapy*, *21*(5), 319–328. doi:10.1016/0197-4556(94)90059-0

Knill, P. J. (2005). Foundations for a theory of practice. In P. J. Knill, E. G. Levine, & S. K. Levine (Eds.), *Principles and practice of expressive arts therapy: Toward a therapeutic aesthetics* (pp. 75–170). Philadelphia, PA: Jessica Kingsley Publishers.

Knoff, H. M. (1988). Clinical supervision, consultation, and counseling: A comparative analysis for supervisors and other educational leaders. *Journal of Curriculum and Supervision*, *3*(3), 240–252.

Koenigs, M., & Grafman, J. (2009). Posttraumatic stress disorder: The role of medial prefrontal cortex and amygdala. *The Neuroscientist*, *15*(5), 540–548. doi:10.1177/1073858409333072 PMID:19359671

Koenigs, M., Huey, E. D., Raymont, V., Cheon, B., Solomon, J., Wassermann, E. M., & Grafman, J. (2008). Focal brain damage protects against post-traumatic stress disorder in combat veterans. *Nature Neuroscience*, *11*(2), 232–237. doi:10.1038/nn2032 PMID:18157125

Ko, S. J., Ford, J. D., Kassam-Adams, N., Berkowitz, S. J., Wilson, C., Wong, M., & Layne, C. M. et al. (2008). Creating trauma-informed systems: Child welfare, education, first responders, health care, juvenile justice. *Professional Psychology, Research and Practice*, *39*(4), 396–404. doi:10.1037/0735-7028.39.4.396

Kossak, S. N. (2005). Exploring the elements of culturally relevant service delivery. *Families in Society*, *86*(2), 189–195. doi:10.1606/1044-3894.2454

Kottman, T. (2009). *Treatment manual for Adlerian play therapy*. Unpublished manuscript.

Kottman, T. (2010). *Play therapy: Basics and beyond* (2nd ed.). Alexandria, VA: American Counseling Association.

Kottman, T. (2011). *Play therapy basics and beyond* (2nd ed.). Alexandria, VA: American Counseling Association.

Kottman, T., & Meany-Walen, K. K. (2016). *Partners in play* (3rd ed.). Alexandria, VA: American Counseling Association.

Kottman, T., & Meany-Walen, K. K. (2016). *Partners in play: An Adlerian approach to play therapy* (3rd ed.). Alexandria, VA: American Counseling Association.

Kramer, D. N., & Landolt, M. A. (2010). Characteristics and efficacy of early psychological interventions in children and adolescents after single trauma: A meta-analysis. *European Journal of Psychotraumatology*, 11-24. doi:10.3402/ejpt.v2i0.7858

Kranich, N. (Ed.). (2001). *Libraries and democracy: The cornerstones of liberty*. Chicago: American Library Association.

Kranowitz, C. S. (2010). *The out-of-sync child*. New York, NY: Tarcher Penguin.

Kranz, P. L., Kottman, T., & Lund, N. L. (1998). Play therapists opinions concerning the education, training, and practice of play therapists. *International Journal of Play Therapy*, *7*(1), 73–87. doi:10.1037/h0089419

Kuehnle, K. (1996). *Assessing allegations of child sexual abuse*. Sarasota, FL: Prefessional Resource Press.

Kuehnle, K., & Connell, M. (2010). Child sexual abuse suspicions: Treatment considerations during investigation. *Journal of Child Sexual Abuse*, *19*(5), 554–571. doi:10.1080/10538712.2010.512554 PMID:20924910

Kupperman, P., Bligh, S., & Goodban, M. (1980). Activating articulation skills through theraplay. *The Journal of Speech and Hearing Disorders*, *45*(4), 540–548. doi:10.1044/jshd.4504.540 PMID:7442168

Kurpius, D. J., & Fuqua, D. R. (1993). Fundamental issues in defining consultation. *Journal of Counseling and Development*, *71*(6), 598–600. doi:10.1002/j.1556-6676.1993.tb02248.x

Kyung, K. Y. (2011). The effect of group Theraplay on self-esteem and depression of the elderly in a day care center. *Korean Journal of Counseling*, *12*(5), 1413–1430.

Ladany, N., Lehrman-Waterman, D., Molinaro, M., & Wolgast, B. (1999). Psychotherapy supervisor ethical practices: Adherence to guidelines, the supervisory working alliance, and supervisee satisfaction. *The Counseling Psychologist*, *27*(3), 443–475. doi:10.1177/0011000099273008

Ladd, G., & Burgess, K. (2001). Do relational risks and protective factors moderate the linkages between childhood aggression and early psychological and school adjustment? *Child Development, 72*(5), 1579–1601. doi:10.1111/1467-8624.00366 PMID:11699688

Lakner, C., & Milanovic, B. (2013). *Global income distribution: From the fall of the Berlin Wall to the Great Recession.* Policy Research Working Paper, World Bank. Retrieved from http://www-wds.worldbank.org/external/default/WDSContentServer/IW3P/IB/2013/12/11/000158349_20131211100152/Rendered/PDF/WPS6719.pdf)

Lamanna, J. E. (2005). *Child-centered play therapy in elementary schools* (Counselor Education Master's Thesis). State University of New York.

Lambert, S. F., LeBlanc, M., Mullen, J. A., Ray, D., Baggerly, J., White, J., & Kaplan, D. (2007). Learning more about those who play in session: The National Play Therapy in Counseling Practices Project (Phase 1). *Journal of Counseling and Development, 85*(1), 42–46. doi:10.1002/j.1556-6678.2007.tb00442.x

Landreth, G. (2002). *Play Therapy: The art of the relationships* (2nd ed.). New York, NY: Brunner-Routledge.

Landreth, G. (2012). *Play therapy: The art of the relationship* (3rd ed.). New York, NY: Routledge.

Landreth, G. (2012). *Play Therapy: The Art of the Relationship* (3rd ed.). New York, NY: Routledge.

Landreth, G. L. (2012). *Play therapy: The art of relationship* (3rd ed.). New York, NY: Routledge.

Landreth, G. L. (2012). *Play Therapy: The art of the relationship* (3rd ed.). New York, NY: Routledge.

Landreth, G. L., & Bratton, S. C. (2006). *Child parent relationship therapy (CPRT): A 10-session filial therapy model.* New York, NY: Routledge Taylor & Francis Group.

Landreth, G. L., & Bratton, S. C. (2006). *Child-parent relationship therapy: A 10-week filial therapy model.* Springfield, IL: Thomas Books.

Landreth, G. L., & Lobaugh, A. F. (1998). Filial therapy with incarcerated fathers: Effects on parental acceptance of child, parental stress, and child adjustment. *Journal of Counseling and Development, 6*(2), 53–73.

Landreth, G. L., Ray, D. C., & Bratton, S. C. (2009). Play therapy in elementary schools. *Psychology in the Schools, 46*(3), 281–289. doi:10.1002/pits.20374

Landreth, G., & Bratton, S. (2006). *Child-parent relationship therapy (CPRT): A 10-session filial therapy model.* New York, NY: Routledge.

Lane, K. L., Wehby, J. H., & Cooley, C. (2006). Teacher expectations of students classroom behavior across the grade span: Which social skills are necessary for success. *Exceptional Children, 72*(2), 153–167. doi:10.1177/001440290607200202

Lanius, R. A., Vermetten, E., & Pain, C. (Eds.). (2010). *The impact of early life trauma on health and disease: The hidden epidemic.* Cambridge, UK: Cambridge University Press. doi:10.1017/CBO9780511777042

Laue, C. E. (2015). *Toy guns in play therapy: Controversy and current practice* (Doctoral Dissertation). Available from ProQuest Dissertations and Theses database. (UMI No. 3688574)

Lebedeva, L. (2012). Animated treatment: The method of art therapy used with children having communication problems. *Social Welfare Interdisciplinary Approach, 2*(1), 123–130.

LeBlanc, M., & Ritchie, M. (1999). Predictors of play therapy outcomes. *International Journal of Play Therapy, 8*(2), 19–29. doi:10.1037/h0089429

LeBlanc, M., & Ritchie, M. (2001). A meta-analysis of play therapy outcomes. *Counselling Psychology Quarterly*, *14*(2), 149–163. doi:10.1080/09515070110059142

Leckman, J. F., & March, J. S. (2011). Editorial: Developmental neuroscience comes of age. *Journal of Child Psychology and Psychiatry, and Allied Disciplines*, *52*(4), 333–338. doi:10.1111/j.1469-7610.2011.02378.x PMID:21410471

Lee, S. (Producer), & Lee, S. (Director). (1989). *Do the right thing* [Motion picture]. United States: Universal Pictures.

Lee, M. Y., & Jonson-Reid, M. (2009). Needs and outcomes for low income youth in special education: Variations by emotional disturbance diagnosis and child welfare contact. *Children and Youth Services Review*, *31*(7), 722–731. doi:10.1016/j.childyouth.2009.01.005 PMID:19714226

Lee, M., & Landreth, G. (2003). Filial therapy with immigrant Korean parents in the United States. *International Journal of Play Therapy*, *12*(2), 67–85. doi:10.1037/h0088879

Lee, S. M., & Nachlis, L. S. (2011). Consulting with attorneys: An alternative hybrid model. *Journal of Child Custody*, *8*(1), 84–102. doi:10.1080/15379418.2010.547448

Lender, D., Booth, P., & Lindaman, S. (2012). The Theraplay treatment program: Description and implementation of an attachment-based play for children and caregivers. In A. Rubin (Ed.), *Programs and Interventions for maltreated children and families at risk*. New York: Wiley and Sons.

Leonard, L., & Leonard, P. (2003). The continuing trouble with collaboration: Teachers talk. *Current Issues in Education, 6*(15).

Leslie, A. (1987). Pretense and representation: The origins of theory of mind. *Psychological Review*, *94*(4), 412–426. doi:10.1037/0033-295X.94.4.412

Lew, A., & Bettner, B. L. (1996). *Responsibility in the classroom: A teacher's guide to understanding motivating students.* Connexions Press.

Lew, A., & Bettner, B. L. (1998). *Responsibility in the classroom: A teacher's guide to understanding and motivating students.* Connexions Press.

Lew, A., & Bettner, B. L. (2000). *A parent's guide to understanding and motivating children.* Connexions Press.

Lew, A., & Bettner, B. S. (2000). *A parent's guide to motivating children.* Connexions Press.

Lewis, T., Amini, F., & Lannon, R. (2000). *A general theory of love*. New York: Random House.

Lieberman, A., Van Horn, P., & Ghosh Ippen, C. (2005). Toward evidence-based treatment: Child-Parent Psychotherapy with preschoolers exposed to marital violence. *Journal of the American Academy of Child and Adolescent Psychiatry*, *44*(12), 1241–1248. doi:10.1097/01.chi.0000181047.59702.58 PMID:16292115

Lieberman, M. D., Eisenberger, N. I., Crockett, M. J., Tom, S. M., Pfeifer, J. H., & Way, B. M. (2007). Putting feelings into words: Affect labeling disrupts amygdala activity in response to affect stimuli. *Association for Psychological Science*, *18*(5), 421–428.

Lillard, A. S., Lerner, M. D., Hopkins, E. J., Dore, R. A., Smith, E. D., & Palmquist, C. M. (2013). The impact of pretend play on childrens development: A review of the evidence. *Psychological Bulletin*, *139*(1), 1–34. doi:10.1037/a0029321 PMID:22905949

Lindo, N. A., Bratton, S. C., & Landreth, G. L. (2015). Child parent relationship therapy: Theory, research, and intervention process. In L. A. Reddy, T. M. Files-Hall, & C. E. Schaefer (Eds.), *Empirically based play interventions for children* (2nd ed.; pp. 241–261). Washington, DC: American Psychological Association.

Lindo, N. A., Dillman Taylor, D., Meany-Walen, K. K., Purswell, K., Jayne, K., Gonzales, T., & Jones, L. (2014). Teachers as therapeutic agents: Perceptions of a school-based mental health initiative. *British Journal of Guidance & Counselling, 42*(3), 284–296. doi:10.1080/03069885.2014.896452

Lindsay, G., Dockrell, J. E., & Strand, S. (2007). Longitudinal patterns of behaviour problems in children with specific speech and language difficulties: Child and contextual factors. *The British Journal of Educational Psychology, 77*(4), 811–828.

Lin, Y., & Bratton, S. (2015). A meta-analysis of child-centered play therapy outcome research. *Journal of Counseling and Development, 93*, 45–58. doi:10.1002/j.1556-6676.2015.00180.x

Litrownik, A. J. (2012, Winter). A longitudinal perspective on mental health services for foster youth: Continued risk and the challenge of chaotic caregiving environments. *American Psychological Association: CYF News*, 17-19.

Lolan, A. R. (2011). *Play therapists' practice patterns and perceptions of the factors that influence caregiver engagement in play therapy* (Doctoral dissertation). Retrieved from http://scholarworks.uno.edu/td/1352/

Lolan, A. R. (2011). *Play therapists' practice patterns and perceptions of the factors that influence caregiver engagement in play therapy* (Doctoral dissertation). University of New Orleans. Retrieved from http://scholarworks.uno.edu/cgi/viewcontent.cgi?article=2411&context=td

Lolan, A., & Dugan, E. (2010). Engaging caregivers in play therapy: A review of common questions and misconceptions posed by caregivers to play therapists in Louisiana. *Play Therapy, 5*, 20–23.

Lovinger, S. L. (1974). Socio-dramatic play and language development in preschool disadvantaged children. *Psychology in the Schools, 11*(3), 313–320. doi:10.1002/1520-6807(197407)11:3<313::AID-PITS2310110315>3.0.CO;2-L

Luiselli, J. K., Putnam, R. F., Handler, M. W., & Feinberg, A. B. (2005). Whole-school positive behaviours support: Effects on student discipline problems and academic performance. *Educational Psychology, 25*(2-3), 183–198. doi:10.1080/0144341042000301265

Lundervold, D. A., & Belwood, M. F. (2000). The best kept secret in counselling: Single-case (*N*=1) experimental designs. *Journal of Counseling and Development, 78*(1), 92–102. doi:10.1002/j.1556-6676.2000.tb02565.x

Lyytinen, P., Poikkeus, A. M., & Laakso, M. L. (1997). Language and symbolic play in toddlers. *International Journal of Behavioral Development, 21*(2), 289–302. doi:10.1080/016502597384875

Lyytinen, P., Poikkeus, A. M., Laakso, M. L., Eklund, K., & Lyytinen, H. (2001). Language development and symbolic play in children with and without familial risk for dyslexia. *Journal of Speech, Language, and Hearing Research: JSLHR, 44*(4), 873–885. doi:10.1044/1092-4388(2001/070) PMID:11521780

MacLean, P. D. (1990). *The triune brain in evolution: Role in paleocerebral functions*. New York, NY: Plenum Press.

Main, M., & Goldwin, R. (1984). Predicting rejection of her infant from mothers representation of her own experience: Implications for the abused/abusing intergenerational cycle. *Journal of Child Abuse & Neglect, 8*(2), 203–217. doi:10.1016/0145-2134(84)90009-7 PMID:6539642

Makela, J., & Vierikko, I. (2005). From heart to heart: Interactive therapy for children in care. Report on the Theraplay project in SOS Children's Villages in Finland 2001-2004. The SOS Children's Villages Association, Finland, Annual Report.

Malchiodi, C. A. (2002). *The Soul's palette: Drawing on art's transformative powers for health and well-being*. Boston, MA: Shambhala.

Malchiodi, C. A. (2007). *The art therapy sourcebook.* New York, NY: McGraw Hill.

Malchiodi, C. A. (Ed.). (2005). *Expressive therapies.* New York, NY: Guilford Press.

Malloy, L. C., & Quas, J. A. (2009). Children's suggestibility: Areas of consensus and controversy. In K. Kuehnle & M. Connell (Eds.), *The evaluation of child sexual abuse allegations: A comprehensive guide to assessment and testimony* (pp. 267–297). Hoboken, NJ: John Wiley & Sons.

Maniacci, M., Sackett-Maniacci, L., & Mosak, H. (2014). Adlerian psychotherapy. In D. Wedding & R. J. Corsini (Eds.), *Current psychotherapies* (10th ed.; pp. 55–94). Belmont, CA: Thomson Brooks/Cole.

Marks-Tarlow, T. (2012). The play of psychotherapy. *American Journal of Play, 4*(3), 352–377.

Mar, R. A., Tackett, J. L., & Moore, C. (2010). Exposure to media and theory-of-mind development in preschoolers. *Cognitive Development, 25*(1), 69–78. doi:10.1016/j.cogdev.2009.11.002

Marshack, M. (1960). A method for assessing child-parent interactions under controlled conditions. *The Journal of Genetic Psychology, 97*(1), 3–22. doi:10.1080/00221325.1960.10534309 PMID:14421486

Martin, J. A. (1981). *Voice, speech and language in the child: Development and disorder.* New York: Springer-Verlag. doi:10.1007/978-3-7091-7042-7

Matson, J. L., Fodstad, J. C., & Rivet, T. T. (2009). The relationship of social skills and problem behaviors in adults with intellectual disability and autism or PDD-NOS. *Research in Autism Spectrum Disorders, 3*(1), 258–268. doi:10.1016/j.rasd.2008.07.001

McCarthy, P., Sugden, S., Koker, M., Lamendola, F., Maurer, S., & Renninger, S. (1995). A practical guide to informed consent in clinical supervision. *Counselor Education and Supervision, 35*(2), 130–138. doi:10.1002/j.1556-6978.1995.tb00217.x

McClelland, M., Morrison, F., & Holmes, D. (2000). Children at risk for early academic problems: The role of learning related social skills. *Early Childhood Research Quarterly, 8*(3), 327–329.

McConachy, J., Bartlett, J., Biddle, D., & Lunken, T. (2013). *Small talk final report: Identifying communication problems in children, developing a problem identification tool.* Richmond, Victoria: Berry Street, Take Two Research Project.

McConaughy, S. H., & Achenbach, T. M. (2009). *Manual for the ASEBA direct observation form.* Burlington, VT: University of Vermont, Research Center for Children, Youth, & Families.

McConaughy, S. H., & Achenbach, T. M. (2009). *Manual for the ASEBA Direct Observation Form.* Burlington, VT: University of Vermont, Research Center for Children, Youth, & Families.

McConkey, R. (1976). Extending language through play. *Journal of Child Psychology and Psychiatry, and Allied Disciplines, 17*, 189–197.

McCune, L. (1995). A normative study of representational play at the transition to language. *Developmental Psychology, 31*(2), 198–206. doi:10.1037/0012-1649.31.2.198

McCune, L. (2010). Symbolic transformation: The mind in movement through culture and society. In B. Wagoner (Ed.), *Symbolic Transformation* (pp. 193–209). London: Routledge Press.

McCune-Nicolich, L. (1981). Toward symbolic functioning: Structures of early pretend games and potential parallels with language. *Child Development, 52*(3), 785–797. doi:10.2307/1129078

McDonald, M. K., Borntrager, C. F., & Rostad, W. (2014). Measuring trauma: Considerations for assessing complex and non-PTSD criterion a childhood trauma. *Journal of Trauma & Dissociation*, *15*(2), 184–203. doi:10.1080/15299732.2014.867577 PMID:24410287

McFarlane, A. C., Policansky, S. K., & Irwin, C. (1987). A longitudinal study of the psychological morbidity in children due to a natural disaster. *Psychological Medicine*, *17*(3), 727–738. doi:10.1017/S0033291700025964 PMID:3628633

McGilchrist, I. (2009). *The master and his emissary: The divided brain and the making of the western world*. New Haven, CT: Yale University Press.

McGinnis, E. (2012). *Skillstreaming the adolescent: A guide for teaching prosocial skills*. Champaign, IL: Research Press.

McGuire, D. K., & McGuire, D. E. (2001). *Linking parents to play therapy: A practical guide with application, interventions, and case studies*. New York, NY: Routledge.

McGuire, D. K., & McGuire, D. E. (2001). *Linking parents to play therapy: A practical guide with applications, interventions, and case studies*. New York, NY: Routledge.

McLoyd, V. C. (1985). Are toys (just) toys? Exploring their effects on pretend play of low-income preschoolers. In M. B. Spencer, G. K. Brookins, W. R. Allen, M. B. Spencer, G. K. Brookins, & W. R. Allen (Eds.), *Beginnings: The social and affective development of black children* (pp. 81–100). Hillsdale, NJ: Lawrence Erlbaum Associates, Inc.

McWey, L. M., Henderson, T. L., & Tice, S. N. (2006). Mental health issues and the foster care system: An examination of the impact of the adoption and safe families act. *Journal of Marital and Family Therapy*, *32*(2), 195–214. doi:10.1111/j.1752-0606.2006.tb01600.x PMID:16676896

Meany-Walen, K. K. & Teeling, S. (2016b). *Effects of Adlerian play therapy on children's off-task behaviors and ADHD symptoms*. Manuscript submitted for publication.

Meany-Walen, K. K. (2015). *Individual and group Adlerian play therapy with children with externalizing behaviors: A single case research design*. Manuscript submitted for publication.

Meany-Walen, K. K., Teeling, S., Davis, A., Artley, G., & Vignovich, A. (2016). *Effects of a play therapy intervention on children's on-task behaviors, total problems, and ADHD symptoms*. Manuscript submitted for publication.

Meany-Walen, K. K., Bullis, Q., Kottman, T., & Dillman Taylor, D. (2015a). Group Adlerian play therapy with children with off-task behavior. *Journal for Specialists in Group Work*, *40*(3), 294–314. doi:10.1080/01933922.2015.1056569

Meany-Walen, K. K., & Teeling, S. (2016a). Adlerian play therapy with children with disruptive behaviors and poor social skills. *International Journal of Play Therapy*, *25*, 64–77. doi:10.1037/pla0000022

Meany-Walen, K., Bratton, S., & Kottman, T. (2014). Effects of Adlerian play therapy on reducing students disruptive behaviors. *Journal of Counseling and Development*, *92*(1), 47–56. doi:10.1002/j.1556-6676.2014.00129.x

Meany-Walen, K., Kottman, T., Bullis, Q., & Dillman Taylor, D. (2015). Effects of Adlerian play therapy on childrens externalizing behavior. *Journal of Counseling and Development*, *93*(4), 418–428. doi:10.1002/jcad.12040

Meins, E. (1997). *Security of attachment and the social development of cognition*. Hove, UK: Psychology Press.

Meins, E., Fernyhough, C., Wainwright, R., Gupta, M. D., Fradley, E., & Tuckey, M. (2002). Maternal mind-mindedness and attachment security as predictors of theory of mind understanding. *Child Development*, *73*(6), 1715–1726. doi:10.1111/1467-8624.00501 PMID:12487489

Meiser-Stedman, R., Smith, P., Glucksman, E., Yule, W., & Dalgleish, T. (2008). The posttraumatic stress disorder diagnosis in preschool- and elementary school-age children exposed to motor vehicle accidents. *The American Journal of Psychiatry*, *165*(10), 1326–1337. doi:10.1176/appi.ajp.2008.07081282 PMID:18676592

Mental Health America. (2013). *Recognizing mental health problems in children*. Retrieved from http://www.mentalhealthamerica.net/farcry/go/information/get-info/children-s-mental-health/recognizing-mental-health-problems-in-children

Mezirow, J. (1995). Transformation Theory of Adult Learning. In M. R. Welton (Ed.), *In defense of the lifeworld* (pp. 39–70). New York, NY: SUNY Press.

Milam-Miller, S. (2009). The psychiatrist as consultant: Working within schools, the courts, and primary care to promote childrens mental health. *The Psychiatric Clinics of North America*, *32*(1), 165–176. doi:10.1016/j.psc.2008.10.002 PMID:19248923

Miller, R., & Dillman Taylor, D. (2016). Does Adlerian theory stand the test of time? Examining individual psychology from a neuroscience perspective. *Journal of Humanistic Counseling*, *55*(2), 111–128. doi:10.1002/johc.12028

Miranda, S. S., Dobson, C., Hogan, L., & Perry, B. D. (1999). *The developmental effects of brief music and movement program at a public preschool: A pilot project* (Abstract). Retrieved from www.childtrauma.org/ctaServices/neigh_artsasp

Miranda, L. A., Arthur, A., Mahoney, O., & Perry, B. D. (1998). The art of healing: The healing arts project, early childhood connection. *Journal of Music and Movement-Based Learning*, *4*, 35–40.

Moleski, S. M., & Kiselica, M. S. (2005). Dual relationships: A continuum ranging from the destructive to the therapeutic. *Journal of Counseling and Development*, *8*(1), 3–11. doi:10.1002/j.1556-6678.2005.tb00574.x

Molin, R., & Palmer, S. (2005). Consent and participation: Ethical issues in the treatment of children in out-of-home care. *The American Journal of Orthopsychiatry*, *75*(1), 152–157. doi:10.1037/0002-9432.75.1.152 PMID:15709858

Moon, B. L. (2007). *The role of metaphor in art therapy: Theory, method, and experience*. Springfield, IL: Charles C Thomas Publisher.

Moon, C. H. (2010). *Materials & media in art therapy: Critical understandings of diverse artistic vocabularies*. New York, NY: Taylor and Francis.

Morgan, A., Pendergast, D., Brown, R., & Heck, D. (2015). Relational ways of being an educator: Trauma-informed practice supporting disenfrancised young people. *International Journal of Inclusive Education*, *19*(10), 1037–1051. doi:10.1080/13603116.2015.1035344

Morrison, M. O., & Bratton, S. C. (2010). Preliminary investigation of an early mental health intervention for Head Start programs: Effects of child teacher relationship training on children's behavior problems. *Psychology in the Schools*, *47*(10), 1003–1017.

Morrison, M., & Bratton, S. (2010). Preliminary investigation of an early mental health intervention for Head Start programs: Effects of Child Teacher Relationship Therapy (CTRT) on childrens behavior problems. *Psychology in the Schools*, *47*(10), 1003–1017. doi:10.1002/pits.20520

Moustakas, C. (1959). *Psychotherapy with children: The living relationship*. Greeley, CO: Carron.

Muhammad, Y. J. (2009). Low-income African American parents' views about the value of play for their preschool age children in Head Start. *Dissertation Abstracts International*, *71*(3-A), 911.

Mulkey, E. A. (2015). Confronting Legal and Technological Incongruity: Remote Testimony for Child Witnesses. *Vanderbilt Journal Of Entertainment & Technology Law*, *17*(2), 463–492.

Muratori, F., Picchi, L., Bruni, G., Patarnello, M., & Romagnoli, G. (2003). A two-year follow-up of psychodynamic psychotherapy for internalizing disorders in children. *Journal of the American Academy of Child and Adolescent Psychiatry*, *42*(3), 331–339. doi:10.1097/00004583-200303000-00014 PMID:12595787

Muris, P., Steerneman, P., Merckelbach, H., Holdrinet, I., & Meesters, C. (1998). Comorbid anxiety symptoms in children with pervasive developmental disorders. *Journal of Anxiety Disorders*, *12*(4), 387–393.

Murphey, G. H., Beadle-Brown, J., Wing, L., Gould, J., Shah, A., & Holmes, N. (2005). Chronicity of challenging behaviors in people with severe intellectual disabilities and/or autism: A total population sample. *Journal of Autism and Developmental Disorders*, *35*(4), 405–418. doi:10.1007/s10803-005-5030-2 PMID:16134027

Murphy, L. B. (1972). Infants' play and cognitive development. In M. W. Piers (Ed.), *Play and cognitive development.* New York, NY: Norton.

Myers, S. S., & Pianta, R. C. (2008). Development commentary: Individual and contextual influences on student-teacher relationships and childrens early problem behaviors. *Journal of Clinical Child and Adolescent Psychology*, *17*(3), 600–608. doi:10.1080/15374410802148160 PMID:18645750

Nampijja, M., Apule, B., Lule, S., Akurut, H., Muhangi, L., Elliott, A. M., & Alcock, K. J. (2010). Adaptation of Western measures of cognition for assessing 5-year-old semi-urban Ugandan children. *The British Journal of Educational Psychology*, *80*(1), 15–30. doi:10.1348/000709909X460600 PMID:19594989

Nash, J., & Schaefer, C. (2010). Clinical and developmental issues in psychotherapy with preschool children: Laying the groundwork for play therapy. In Play therapy for preschool children (pp. 15-45). Washington, DC: American Psychological Association.

National Board for Professional Teaching Standards. (2014). *What teachers should know and be able to do.* Retrieved from www.nbpts.org/sites/default/files/what_teachers_should_know.pdf

National Center for Children in Poverty. (2014). *Children's mental health.* Retrieved from http://nccp.org/publications/pub_929.html

National Center for Education Evaluation, U.S. Department of Education. (2014). *What Works Clearinghouse.* Retrieved from http://ies.ed.gov/ncee/wwc/

National Center for Education Statistics. (2014). *Children 3 to 21 years old served under Individuals with Disabilities Education Act (IDEA), part B, by type of disability: Selected years, 1976-77 through 2012-2013* [Data file]. Retrieved from http://nces.ed.gov/programs/digest/d14/tables/xls/tabn204.30.xls

National Child Traumatic Stress Network. (n.d.). Retrieved from www.nctsnet.org

National Scientific Council on the Developing Child. (2010). *Early experiences can alter gene expression and affect longterm development* (Working paper 10). Retrieved from http://developingchild.harvard.edu/resources/reports_and_working_papers/working_papers/wp10/

Nelson, C. A. (2007). A neurobiological perspective on early human development. *Child Development Perspectives*, *1*(1), 13–18. doi:10.1111/j.1750-8606.2007.00004.x

Nelson, C. A., Fox, N. A., & Zeanah, C. H. (2014). *Romania's abandoned children: Deprivation, brain development, and the struggle for recovery.* Cambridge, MA: Harvard University Press. doi:10.4159/harvard.9780674726079

Nelson, C. A. III, Bos, K., Gunnar, M. R., & Sonuga-Barke, E. J. S. (2001). Children without permanent parents: Research, practice, and policy. V. The neurobiological toll of early human deprivation. *Monographs of the Society for Research in Child Development*, *76*(4), 127–146. doi:10.1111/j.1540-5834.2011.00630.x PMID:25018565

Nelson, E., Wasson, J., Kirk, J., Keller, A., Clark, D., Dietrich, A., & Zubkoff, M. et al. (1987). Assessment of function in routine clinical practice: Description of the COOP Chart method and preliminary findings. *Journal of Chronic Diseases*, *40*(S1), 55S–63S. doi:10.1016/S0021-9681(87)80033-4 PMID:3597698

Neuchterlein, K. H., Ventura, J., Subotnik, K. L., & Hayata, J. N. (2014). Developing a cognitive training strategy for first episode schizophrenia: Integrating bottom-up and top-down approaches. *American Journal of Psychiatric Rehabilitation*, *17*(3), 225–253. doi:10.1080/15487768.2014.935674 PMID:25489275

New Freedom Commission on Mental Health. (2003). *Achieving the promise: Transforming mental health care in America. Final report (DHHS Pub. No. SMA-03-3832)*. Rockville, MD: Department of Health and Human Services.

New Freedom Commission on Mental Health. (2003). Achieving the promise: Transforming mental health care in America. Final Report. DHHS Pub. No. SMA-03-3832. Rockville, MD: Author.

New York State Office of Children and Family Services. (n.d.). *Become a foster parent: Requirements to become a foster parent*. Retrieved from http://ocfs.ny.gov/main/fostercare/requirements.asp

Newman, C. F. (2013). Training cognitive behavioral therapy supervisors: Didactics, simulated practice, and meta-supervision. *Journal of Cognitive Psychotherapy: An International Quarterly*, *27*(1), 5–18. doi:10.1891/0889-8391.27.1.5

Newman, J. L. (1993). Ethical issues in consultation. *Journal of Counseling and Development*, *72*(2), 148–156. doi:10.1002/j.1556-6676.1993.tb00914.x

Newton, R. R., Litrownik, A. J., & Landsverk, J. A. (2000). Children and youth in foster care: Disentangling the relationship between problem behaviors and number of placements. *Child Abuse & Neglect*, *24*(10), 1363–1374. doi:10.1016/S0145-2134(00)00189-7 PMID:11075702

Nezu, A. M., & Nezu, C. M. (2008). *Evidence-based outcome research*. New York: Oxford Press.

Nicolopoulou, A. (2002). Peer-group culture and narrative development. In S. Blum-Kulka & C. E. Snow (Eds.), *Talking to adults: The contribution of multiparty discourse to language acquisition* (pp. 117–152). Mahwah, NJ: Lawrence Erlbaum Associates.

Nicolopoulou, A., & Cole, M. (2010). Design experimentation as a theoretical and empirical tool for developmental pedagogical research. *Pedagogies*, *5*(1), 61–71. doi:10.1080/15544800903406316

Nicolopoulou, A., de Sá, A. B., Ilgaz, H., & Brockmeyer, C. (2010). Using the transformational power of play to educate hearts and minds: From Vygotsky to Vivian Paley and beyond. *Mind, Culture, and Activity*, *17*, 1–17.

Nicolopoulou, A., Schnabel Cortina, K., Ilgaz, H., Brockmeyer Cates, C., & de Sá, A. B. (2015). Using narrative- and play-based activity to promote low-income preschoolers oral language, emergent literacy, and social competence. *Early Childhood Research Quarterly*, *31*, 147–162. doi:10.1016/j.ecresq.2015.01.006 PMID:25866441

Nuwagaba-Biribonwoha, H., Mayon-White, R. T., Okong, P., Brocklehurst, P., & Carpenter, L. M. (2012). The impact of HIV on maternal morbidity in the pre-HAART era in Uganda. *Journal of Pregnancy*, *2012*, 1–6. doi:10.1155/2012/508657 PMID:22013532

Nuwagaba-Biribonwoha, H., Mayon-White, R. T., Okong, P., Carpenter, L. M., & Jenkinson, C. (2006). The impact of HIV on maternal quality of life in Uganda. *AIDS Care*, *18*(6), 614–620. doi:10.1080/09540120500359298 PMID:16831790

O'Conner, K. (2015). Eco-systemic play therapy. In C. Schaefer & L. Braverman (Eds.), *Handbook of play therapy*. New York, NY: Wiley & Sons. doi:10.1002/9781119140467.ch9

O'Toole, C. (2005). The relationship between preverbal behaviours and language development: Investigating symbolic play and language development in children with Down Syndrome. *Questions of Quality*, 241.

Oaklander, V. (2007). *Windows to our children*. Gouldsboro, ME: The Gestalt Journal Press.

Oandasan, I., & Reeves, S. (2005). Key elements of interprofessional education. Part 2: Factors, processes and outcomes. *Journal of Interprofessional Care, 19*(sup1), 39-48.

OConnor, E., & McCartney, K. (2007). Examining teacher-child relationships and achievement as part of an ecological model of development. *American Educational Research Journal, 44*(2), 340–369. doi:10.3102/0002831207302172

OConnor, K. (2005). Addressing diversity issues in play therapy. *Professional Psychology, Research and Practice, 36*(5), 566–573. doi:10.1037/0735-7028.36.5.566

O'Connor, K. J., & Braverman, L. D. (Eds.). (2009). *Play therapy theory and practice: Comparing theories and techniques* (2nd ed.). Hoboken, NJ: John Wiley & Sons.

O'Connor, K., & Schaefer, C. (1994). *Handbook of play therapy: Advances and innovations* (Vol. 2). New York, NY: John Wiley & Sons.

Oehlberg, B. (2008). Why schools need to be trauma informed. *Trauma and Loss Research and Interventions, 8*(2), 1–12.

Ogawa, Y. (2004). Childhood trauma and play therapy intervention for traumatized children. *Journal of Professional Counseling, Practice, Theory, & Research, 32*(1), 19–29.

Ogden, P., Minton, K., & Pain, C. (2006). *Trauma and the body: A sensorimotor approach to psychotherapy*. New York: Norton.

Ohio Department of Job and Family Services. (2014). *Fact sheet: Foster care*. Retrieved from http://jfs.ohio.gov/factsheets/fostercare.pdf

Ojiambo, D., & Bratton, S. (2014). Effects of group activity play therapy on problem behaviors of preadolescent Ugandan orphans. *Journal of Counseling and Development, 92*(3), 355–365. doi:10.1002/j.1556-6676.2014.00163.x

Olff, M., Koch, S. J., Nawijn, L., Frijling, J. L., Van Zuiden, M., & Veltman, D. J. (2014). Social support, oxytocin, and PTSD. *European Journal of Psychotraumatology, 51*. doi:10.3402/ejpt.v5.26513 PMID:25511718

Opiola, K., & Bratton, S. C. (in review). The effects of child-parent relationship therapy (CPRT) for adoptive families. *Submitted to Journal of Counseling and Development.*

Ornelas, L. A., Silverstein, D. N., & Tan, S. (2007). Effectively addressing mental health issues in permanency-focused child welfare placement. *Child Welfare, 86*(5), 93–112. doi:10.1037/t05563-000 PMID:18422050

Orr, E., & Geva, R. (2015). Symbolic play and language development. *Infant Behavior and Development, 38*, 147–161. doi:10.1016/j.infbeh.2015.01.002 PMID:25658200

Osofsky, J. D., Kronenberg, M., Bocknek, E., & Hansel, T. C. (2015). Longitudinal impact of attachment-related risk and exposure to trauma among young children after hurricane Katrina. *Child and Youth Care Forum, 44*(4), 493–510. doi:10.1007/s10566-015-9300-7

Otgaar, H., Howe, M. L., Peters, M., Smeets, T., & Moritz, S. (2014). The production of spontaneous false memories across childhood. *Journal of Experimental Child Psychology*, 12128–12141. doi:10.1016/j.jecp.2013.11.019 PMID:24448519

Oxman, L. (1972). *The effectiveness of filial therapy: A controlled study* (Doctoral dissertation). *Dissertation Abstracts International, 31B*(11), 6656.

Oyserman, D., Bybee, D., Mowbray, D., & MacFarlane, P. (2002). Positive parenting among African American mothers with a serious mental illness. *Journal of Marriage and the Family, 64*(1), 65–77. doi:10.1111/j.1741-3737.2002.00065.x

Pace, C. S., & Zavattini, G. C. (2011). Adoption and attachment theory: The attachment models of adoptive mothers and the revision of attachment patterns of their late-adopted children. *Child: Care, Health and Development, 37*(1), 82–88. doi:10.1111/j.1365-2214.2010.01135.x PMID:20637017

Packman, J., & Bratton, S. (2003). A school-based group play/activity therapy intervention with learning disabled preadolescents exhibiting behavior problems. *International Journal of Play Therapy, 12*(2), 7–29. doi:10.1037/h0088876

Paley, V. G. (1990). *The boy who would be a helicopter: The uses of storytelling in the classroom*. Cambridge, MA: Harvard University Press.

Panel, I. E. C. E. (2011). *Core competencies for interprofessional collaborative practice: Report of an expert panel*. Interprofessional Education Collaborative Expert Panel.

Panksepp, J. (2007). Can play diminish ADHD and facilitate the construction of the social brain? *Journal of the Canadian Academy of Child and Adolescent Psychiatry, 16*(2), 57–66. PMID:18392153

Panksepp, J. (2010). Affective neuroscience of the emotional BrainMind: Evolutionary perspectives and implications for understanding depression. *Dialogues in Clinical Neuroscience, 12*(4), 533–545. Retrieved from http://www.ncbi.nlm.nih.gov/pmc/articles/PMC3181986/pdf/DialoguesClinNeurosci-12-533.pdf PMID:21319497

Panksepp, J., & Biven, L. (2012). *The archaeology of mind: Neuroevolutionary origins of human emotions*. New York, NY: Norton.

Pankseppp, J., & Biven, L. (2012). *The archaeology of the mind: Neuroevolutionary origins of human emotions*. New York, NY: Norton.

Parker, J. G., Rubin, K. H., Erath, S. A., Wojslawowicz, J. C., & Buskirk, A. A. (2006). Peer relationships, child development, and adjustment: A developmental psychopathology perspective. In D. Cicchetti & D.J. Cohen (Eds.), Developmental psychopathology: Theory and methods (2nd ed.; pp. 96-161). New York, NY: Wiley.

Parry, K. (2007, August). *A library for learning: Experiences of students in Uganda*. Paper presented at the provincial conference of the Education Library Information and Technology Services, Port Shepstone, KwaZulu, South Africa.

Parry, K. (2014). Exploring secondary school student factors and academic outcomes at the Kitengesa Community Library. In V. F. Dent, G. Goodman, & M. Kevane (Eds.), *Rural community libraries in Africa: Challenges and impacts*. Hershey, PA: IGI Global.

Parry, K., Kirabo, E., & Nakyato, G. (2014). Working with parents to promote childrens literacy: A family literacy project in Uganda. *Multilingual Education, 4*(1), 1–15. doi:10.1186/s13616-014-0013-2

Patrick, H., Ryan, A. M., & Kaplan, A. (2007). Early adolescents perceptions of the classroom social environment, motivational beliefs, and engagement. *Journal of Educational Psychology, 99*(1), 83–98. doi:10.1037/0022-0663.99.1.83

Peabody, M. A., & Demanchick, S. P. (2016). Interprofessional opportunities: Understanding roles in collaborative practice. *International Journal of Play Therapy*. doi:10.1037/pla0000013

Pecora, P. J., Jensen, P. S., Romanelli, L. H., Jackson, L. J., & Ortiz, A. (2009). Mental health services for children placed in foster care: An overview of current challenges. *Child Welfare, 88*(1), 5–26. PMID:19653451

Pecora, P. J., Kessler, R. C., Williams, J., O'Brien, K., Downs, A. C., English, D., & Holmes, K. et al. (2005). *Improving family foster care: Findings from the northwest foster care alumni study*. Seattle, WA: Casey Family Programs.

Pellegrini, A. D. (1985). Relations between preschool children's symbolic play and literate behavior. *Play, language and stories: The development of children's literate behavior*, 79-97.

Pellegrini, A. D. (2008). The Recess Debate: A Disjuncture between Educational Policy and Scientific Research. *American Journal of Play*, *1*(2), 181–191.

Pellegrini, A. D., & Blatchford, P. (2002). The developmental and educational significance of recess in schools. *Early Rep*, *29*(1), 1–7.

Pellegrini, A. D., & Holmes, R. M. (2006). *The role of recess in primary school. Play= learning: How play motivates and enhances children's cognitive and social-emotional growth*. Oxford, UK: Oxford University Press.

Penn, S. L., & Post, P. B. (2012). Investigating various dimensions of play therapists self-reported multicultural counseling competence. *International Journal of Play Therapy*, *21*(1), 14–29. doi:10.1037/a0026894

Perou, R., Bitsko, R. H., Bloomberg, S. J., Pastor, P., Ganhdour, R. M., Gfroefer, J. C., . . . Huang, L. N. (2013). *Mental Health Survelience Among Children – United States, 2005-2011*. Retrieved from: http://www.cdc.gov/mmwr/preview/mmwrhtml/su6202a1.htm

Perou, R., Bitsko, R. H., Blumberg, S. J., Pastor, P., Ghandour, R. M., Gfroerer, J. C., & Parks, S. E. (2013). Mental health surveillance among children—United States, 2005–2011. *MMWR. Surveillance Summaries*, *62*(Suppl 2), 1–35. PMID:23677130

Perry, B. D., Hogan, L., & Marlin, S. J. (2000, August). Curiosity, pleasure, and play: A neurodevelopmental perspective. *Houston Area Association for the Education of Young Child,* 9–12.

Perry, B. (2014). The neurosequential model of therapeutics: Application of a developmentally sensitive and neurobiologically-informed approach to clinical problem-solving in maltreated children. In K. Brandt, B. Perry, S. Seligman, & E. Tronick (Eds.), *Infant and early childhood mental health: Core concepts and clinical practice*. Washington, DC: American Psychiatric Publishing.

Perry, B. D. (1994). Neurobiological sequelae of childhood trauma. Post-traumatic disorders in children. In M. Murburg (Ed.), *Catecholomine function in posttraumatic stress disorder: Emerging concepts* (pp. 253–276). Washington, DC: American Psychiatric Press.

Perry, B. D. (1997). Incubated in terror: Neurodevelopmental factors in the 'cycle of violence. In J. D. Osofsky (Ed.), *Children in a violent society* (pp. 124–149). New York, NY: Guilford Press.

Perry, B. D. (2001). Attachment: The first core strength. *Early Childhood Today*, *16*, 28–30.

Perry, B. D. (2002). Childhood experience and the expression of genetic potential: What childhood neglect tells us about human development. *Brain and Mind*, *3*(1), 79–100. doi:10.1023/A:1016557824657

Perry, B. D. (2006). Applying principles of neurodevelopment to clinical work with maltreated and traumatized children. In N. B. Webb (Ed.), *Working with traumatized youth in child welfare*. New York, NY: Guilford Press.

Perry, B. D. (2008). Child maltreatment: A neurodevelopmental perspective on the role of trauma and neglect in psychopathology. In T. Beachaine & S. P. Hinshaw (Eds.), *Child and adolescent psychopathology* (pp. 93–129). Hoboken, NJ: John Wiley & Sons.

Perry, B. D. (2009). Examining child maltreatment through a neurodevelopmental lens: Clinical application of the Neurosequential Model of Therapeutics. *Journal of Loss and Trauma*, *14*(4), 240–255. doi:10.1080/15325020903004350

Perry, B. D., & Dobson, C. (2013). The Neurosequential Model (NMT) in maltreated children. In J. Ford & C. Courtois (Eds.), *Treating complex traumatic stress disorders in children and adolescents* (pp. 249–260). New York, NY: Guilford Press.

Perry, B. D., & Hambrick, E. (2008). The neurosequential model of therapeutics. *Reclaiming Childhood and Youth*, *17*(3), 38–43.

Perry, B. D., & Pollard, R. (1998). Homeostasis, stress, trauma, and adaptation: A neurodevelopmental view of childhood trauma. *Child and Adolescent Psychiatric Clinics of North America*, *7*, 33–51. PMID:9894078

Perry, B. D., Pollard, R., Blakley, T., Baker, W., & Vigilante, D. (1995). Childhood trauma, the neurobiology of adaptation and the use-dependent development of the brain. How states become traits. *Infant Mental Health Journal*, *16*(4), 271–291. doi:10.1002/1097-0355(199524)16:4<271::AID-IMHJ2280160404>3.0.CO;2-B

Perry, B. D., & Szalavitz, M. (2006). *The boy who was raised as a dog: and other stories from a child psychiatrist's notebook*. Philadelphia, PA: Basic Books.

Perryman, K., & Doran, J. (2010). Guidelines for incorporating play therapy in the schools. *School-Based Play Therapy*, 61.

Peter P. v. Compton Unified School District et al., Compton, California Case 2:15-cv-03726-MWF-PLA Document 41 (07/09/15)

Peters, H. (1999). Pre-Therapy: A client-centered/experiential approach to mentally handicapped people. *Journal of Humanistic Psychology*, *39*(3), 8–29. doi:10.1177/0022167899394002

Peters, H. (2005). Pre-Therapy from a developmental perspective. *Journal of Humanistic Psychology*, *45*(1), 62–81. doi:10.1177/0022167804269404

Peterson, C. C., Wellman, H. M., & Liu, D. (2005). Steps in theory-of-mind development for children with deafness or autism. *Child Development*, *76*(2), 502–517. doi:10.1111/j.1467-8624.2005.00859.x PMID:15784096

Peterson, C. C., Wellman, H. M., & Slaughter, V. (2012). The mind behind the message: Advancing theory-of-mind scales for typically developing children, and those with deafness, autism, or Asperger syndrome. *Child Development*, *83*, 469–485. PMID:22304467

Pezawas, L., Meyer-Lindenberg, A., Drabant, E. M., Verchinski, B. A., Munoz, K. E., Kolachana, B. S., & Weinberger, D. R. et al. (2005). 5-HTTLPR polymorphism impacts human cingulate-amygdala interactions: A genetic susceptibility mechanism for depression. *Nature Neuroscience*, *8*(6), 828–834. doi:10.1038/nn1463 PMID:15880108

Pfefferbaum, B. (1997). Posttraumatic stress disorder in children: A review of the past 10 years. *Journal of the American Academy of Child and Adolescent Psychiatry*, *36*(11), 1503–1511. PMID:9394934

Phillips, R. D. (2009). How firm is our foundation? Current play therapy research. *International Journal of Play Therapy*.

Phillips, R., & Landreth, G. (1995). Play therapists on play therapy I: A report of methods, demographics and professional practices. *International Journal of Play Therapy*, *4*(1), 1–26. doi:10.1037/h0089404

Phillips, R., & Landreth, G. (1995). Play therapists on play therapy: II. Clinical issues in play therapy. *International Journal of Play Therapy*, *7*(1), 1–24. doi:10.1037/h0089416

Piaget, J. (1951). *Play, dreams, and imitation in childhood*. New York, NY: Norton.

Piaget, J. (1954). *The construction of reality in the child.* New York, NY: Basic Books. doi:10.1037/11168-000

Piaget, J. (1959). *The language and thought of the child.* New York: Humanities.

Piaget, J. (1962). *Play dreams, and imitation in childhood.* New York: W.W. Norton.

Pianta, R. C. (1999). *Enhancing relationships between children and teachers.* Washington, DC: American Psychological Association. doi:10.1037/10314-000

Pianta, R. C., La Paro, K. M., Payne, C., Cox, M. L., & Bradley, R. (2002). The relation of kindergarten classroom environment to teacher, family, and school characteristics and child outcomes. *The Elementary School Journal, 102*(3), 225–238. doi:10.1086/499701

Pianta, R. C., & Stuhlman, M. W. (2004). Teacher-child relationships and children's success in the first years of school. *School Psychology Review, 33*(3), 444–458.

Pinborough-Zimmerman, J., Satterfield, R., Miller, J., Bilder, D., Hossain, S., & McMahon, W. (2007). Communication disorders: Prevalence and comorbid intellectual disability, autism, and emotional/behavioral disorders. *American Journal of Speech-Language Pathology, 16*(4), 359–367.

Plach, T. (2008). *Investigating allegations of child and adolescent sexual abuse: An overview for professionals.* Springfield, IL: Charles C Thomas Publisher, LTD.

Pope, K. S., & Vasquez, M. J. T. (2010). *Ethics in psychotherapy and counseling: A practice guide.* San Francisco: Jossey-Bass.

Porges, S. (2004). Neuroception: A subconscious system for detecting threats and safety. *Zero to Three.*

Porges, S. (2011). *The polyvagal theory: Neurophysiological foundations of emotions, attachment, communication, and self-regulation.* New York, NY: Norton.

Porges, S. (2011). *The polyvagal theory: Neurophysiological foundations of emotions, attachments, communications, self-regulation.* New York: Norton.

Post, P. (2014). Involving parents in child-centered play therapy. *Counseling Today.* Retrieved from http://ct.counseling.org/2014/08/involving-parents-in-child-centered-play-therapy/

Post, P. B. (2014, August 25). Involving parents in child-centered play therapy. *Counseling Today.* Retrieved from http://ct.counseling.org/2014/08/involving-parents-in-child-centered-play-therapy/

Post, P. (2001). Play Therapy with Selective Mute Children. In G. Landreth (Ed.), *Innovations in Play Therapy* (pp. 303–321). Routledge.

Post, P. B., Ceballos, P. L., & Penn, S. L. (2012). Collaborating with parents to establish behavioral goals in child-centered play therapy. *The Family Journal (Alexandria, Va.), 20*(1), 51–57. doi:10.1177/1066480711425472

Post, P., & Tillman, K. S. (2015). Cultural issues in play therapy. In D. A. Crenshaw & A. L. Stewart (Eds.), *Play therapy: A comprehensive guide to theory and practice* (pp. 496–510). New York, NY: Guilford Press.

Powell, D., Dunlap, G., & Fox, L. (2006). Prevention and intervention for the challenging behaviors of toddlers and preschoolers. *Infants and Young Children, 19*(1), 25–35. doi:10.1097/00001163-200601000-00004

President's New Freedom Commission on Mental Health. (2003). *Achieving the promise: Transforming mental health care in America final report (DHHS Publication N. SMA-03-3832).* Rockville, MD: Department of Health and Human Services.

Price, J. M., Chamberlain, P., Lansverk, J., Reid, J. B., Leve, L. D., & Laurent, H. (2008). Effects of a foster parent training intervention on placement changes of children in foster care. *Child Maltreatment*, *13*(1), 64–75. doi:10.1177/1077559507310612 PMID:18174349

Principe, G. F., & Schindewolf, E. (2012). Natural conversations as a source of false memories in children: Implications for the testimony of young witnesses. *Developmental Review*, *32*(3), 205–223. doi:10.1016/j.dr.2012.06.003 PMID:23129880

Pritchett, S., & Fall, K. A. (2001). Post-termination non-sexual dual relationships: Dynamics and assessment. *Texas Counseling Association Journal*, *29*, 72–79.

Pronchenko-Jain, Y. (2012). *Child teacher relationship training (CTRT) with children exhibiting disruptive behavior: Effects on teacher's ability to provide emotional and relational support to students and on student-teacher relationship stress* (Doctoral dissertation). Retrieved from http://libproxy.library.unt.edu:2279/ark:/67531/metadc149655/

Prouty, G. (2001). The practice of Pre-Therapy. *Journal of Contemporary Psychotherapy*, *1*(31), 31–40. doi:10.1023/A:1010226814792

Prouty, G., Van Werde, D., & Portner, M. (1998). *Prae-Therapie*. Stuttgart: Klett-Cotta.

Pryzwansky, W. B. (1974). A reconsideration of the consultation model for delivery of school-based psychological services. *The American Journal of Orthopsychiatry*, *44*(4), 579–583. doi:10.1111/j.1939-0025.1974.tb00912.x PMID:4844029

Pullen, P. C., & Justice, L. M. (2003). Enhancing phonological awareness, print awareness, and oral language skills in preschool children. *Intervention in School and Clinic*, *39*(2), 87–98. doi:10.1177/10534512030390020401

Purswell, K. E., & Ray, D. C. (2014). Research with small samples: Considerations for single case and randomized small group experimental designs. *Outcome Research Design*, *5*, 116–126. doi:10.1177/2150137814552474

Purvis, K. B., Cross, D. R., & Sunshine, W. L. (2007). *The connected child: For parents who have welcomed children from other countries and cultures, from troubled backgrounds, with special behavioral or emotional needs*. New York, NY: McGraw-Hill.

Purvis, K., Cross, D., & Pennings, J. (2009). Trust-based relational intervention: Interactive principles for adopted children with special social-emotional needs. *The Journal of Humanistic Counseling, Education and Development*, *48*(1), 3–22. doi:10.1002/j.2161-1939.2009.tb00064.x

Quas, J. A., Goodman, G. S., Ghetti, S., Alexander, K. W., Edelstein, R., Redlich, A. D., & Jones, D. P. H. et al. (2005). Childhood sexual assault victims: Long-term outcomes after testifying in criminal court. *Monographs of the Society for Research in Child Development*, *70*(2), vii-145. PMID:16159360

Quas, J. A., Thompson, W. C., & Clarke-Stewart, K. A. (2005). Do jurors know what isnt so about child witnesses? *Law and Human Behavior*, *29*(4), 425–456. doi:10.1007/s10979-005-5523-8 PMID:16133948

Quicken Trust. (2016). Retrieved from www.quickentrust.com

Quirk, M., Mayworm, A., Furlong, M. J., Grimm, R., & Rebelez, J. (2015). Dimensionality and measurement invariance of a school readiness screener by gender and parent education levels. *International Journal of School and Educational Psychology*, *3*(3), 167–177. doi:10.1080/21683603.2015.1053644

Ramstetter, C. L., Murray, R., & Garner, A. S. (2010). The crucial role of recess in schools. *The Journal of School Health*, *80*(11), 517–526. doi:10.1111/j.1746-1561.2010.00537.x PMID:21039550

Ratts, M. J., Singh, A. A., Nassar-McMillan, S., Butler, S. K., & McCullough, J. R. (2015). *Multicultural and social justice counseling competencies*. Retrieved from http://www.multiculturalcounseling.org/index.php?option=com_content&view=article&id=205:amcd-endorses-multicultural-and-social-justice-counseling-competencies&catid=1:latest&Itemid=123

Rauch, S. L., Whalen, P. J., Shin, L. M., McInerney, S. C., Macklin, M. L., Lasko, N. B., & Pitman, R. K. et al. (2000). Exaggerated amygdala response to masked facial stimuli in posttraumatic stress disorder: A functional MRI study. *Biological Psychiatry*, *47*(9), 769–776. doi:10.1016/S0006-3223(00)00828-3 PMID:10812035

Raver, C. C., Garner, P. W., & Smith-Donald, R. (2007). The roles of emotion regulation and emotion knowledge for children's academic readiness: Are the links causal? In R. C. Pianta, M. J. Cox, & K. L. Snow (Eds.), *School readiness and the transition to kindergarten in the era of accountability* (pp. 121–147). Baltimore, MD: Paul H. Brookes.

Ray, D. C. (2014). *Child-centered play therapy parent services: A Q-methodological investigation* (Doctoral dissertation). University of North Texas.

Ray, D., & McCullough, R. (2015). *Evidence Based Practice Statement: Play Therapy*. Retrieved from https://c.ymcdn.com/sites/a4pt.site-ym.com/resource/resmgr/About_APT/APT_Evidence_Based_Statement.pdf

Ray, D., & McCullough, R. (2015). *Evidence-based practice statement: play therapy*. Association for Play Therapy. Retrieved from: https://c.ymcdn.com/sites/a4pt.siteym.com/resource/resmgr/About_APT/APT_Evidence_Based_Statement.pdf

Ray, D., Schottelkorb, A., & Tsai, M. (2007). Play therapy with children exhibiting symptoms of attention deficit hyperactivity disorder. *International Journal of Play Therapy, 16*(2), 95-111.

Ray, D. (2007). Two counseling interventions to reduce teacher-child relationship stress. *Professional School Counseling*, *10*(4), 428–440. doi:10.5330/prsc.10.4.x340302242715705

Ray, D. (2011). *Advanced play therapy: Essential conditions, knowledge and skills for child practice*. New York, NY: Routledge.

Ray, D. C. (2011). *Advanced play therapy: Essential conditions, knowledge, and skills for child practice*. New York, NY: Routledge/Taylor & Francis Group.

Ray, D. C. (2015). Single-case research design and analysis: Counselling applications. *Journal of Counseling and Development*, *93*(4), 394–402. doi:10.1002/jcad.12037

Ray, D. C., Armstrong, S. A., Warren, E. S., & Balkin, R. S. (2005). Play therapy practices among elementary school counselors. *Professional School Counseling*, 360–365.

Ray, D. C., Lee, K. R., Meany-Walen, K. K., Carlson, S. E., Carnes-Holt, K. L., & Ware, J. N. (2013). Use of toys in child-centered play therapy. *International Journal of Play Therapy*, *22*(1), 43–57. doi:10.1037/a0031430

Ray, D., Armstrong, S., Balkin, R., & Jayne, K. (2015). Child centered play therapy in the schools: Review and meta-analysis. *Psychology in the Schools*, *52*(2), 107–123. doi:10.1002/pits.21798

Ray, D., Blanco, P., Sullivan, J., & Holliman, R. (2009). An exploratory study of child-centered play therapy with aggressive children. *International Journal of Play Therapy*, *18*(3), 162–175. doi:10.1037/a0014742

Ray, D., & Bratton, S. (2010). What the research shows about play therapy: 21st century update. In J. Baggerly, D. Ray, & S. Bratton (Eds.), *Child-centered play therapy research: The evidence-base for effective practice*. New York, NY: John Wiley.

Ray, D., Bratton, S., Rhine, T., & Jones, L. (2001). The effectiveness of play therapy: Responding to the critics. *International Journal of Play Therapy, 10*(1), 85–108. doi:10.1037/h0089444

Ray, D., Muro, J., & Schumann, B. (2004). Implementing play therapy in the schools: Lessons learned. *International Journal of Play Therapy, 13*(1), 79–100. doi:10.1037/h0088886

Ray, D., Schottelkorb, A., & Tsai, M. (2007). Play therapy with children exhibiting symptoms of attention deficit hyperactivity disorder. *International Journal of Play Therapy, 16*(2), 95–111. doi:10.1037/1555-6824.16.2.95

Ray, D., Stulmaker, H., Lee, K., & Silverman, W. (2013). Child-centered play therapy and impairment: Exploring relationships and constructs. *International Journal of Play Therapy, 22*(1), 13–27. doi:10.1037/a0030403

Reddy, L., Files-Hall, T., & Schaefer, C. (2016). *Empirically based play intervention program* (2nd ed.). Washington, DC: American Psychological Association. doi:10.1037/14730-000

Remley, T. P., & Herlihy, B. P. (2016). *Ethical, Legal, and Professional Issues in Counseling* (5th ed.). Boston: Pearson.

Rescorla, L., & Goossens, M. (1992). Symbolic play development in toddlers with expressive specific language impairment (SLI-E). *Journal of Speech, Language, and Hearing Research: JSLHR, 35*(6), 1290–1302. doi:10.1044/jshr.3506.1290 PMID:1283611

Reymert, M. L. (1946). Play therapy of Mooseheart. *Journal of Exceptional Children, 13*(1), 2. PMID:20277977

Reynolds, C. R., & Richmond, B. O. (2008). *The Revised Children's Manifest Anxiety Scale manual.* Los Angeles, CA: Western Psychological Services.

Reynolds, C., & Kamphaus, R. (2015). *Behavioral Assessment Scales for Children* (3rd ed.). San Antonio, TX: Pearson Assessments.

Rimm-Kaufman, S. (2011). Improving students' relationships with teachers to provide essential supports for learning. Washington, DC: American Psychological Association. Retrieved from http://www.apa.org/education/k12/relationships.aspx

Rinne-Albers, M. A. W., van der Wee, N. J. A., Lamers-Winkelman, F., & Vermeiren, R. R. J. M. (2013). Neuroimaging in children, adolescents and young adults with psychological trauma. *European Child & Adolescent Psychiatry, 22*(12), 745–755. doi:10.1007/s00787-013-0410-1 PMID:23553572

Ritter, K. B., & Chang, C. Y. (2002). Play therapists self-perceived multicultural competence and adequacy of training. *International Journal of Play Therapy, 11*(1), 103–113. doi:10.1037/h0088859

Robbins, A. (1994). *A multi-modal approach to creative art therapy.* Bristol, PA: Jessica Kingsley Publishers.

Roberts, M. (2011). *Off-task behavior in the classroom: Applying FBA and CBM: NASP toolkit.* Retrieved from http://www.nasponline.org/communications/spawareness/Off-Task%20Behavior.pdf

Robinson, B., Bradley, L. J., & Hendricks, C. B. (2000). Multicultural counseling supervision: A four-step model toward competency. *International Journal for the Advancement of Counseling, 22*(2), 131–141. doi:10.1023/A:1005567609258

Robison, M., Lindaman, S., Clemmons, M., Doyle-Buckwalter, K., & Ryan, M. (2009). I Deserve a Family: The evolution of an adolescents behavior and beliefs about himself and others when treated with Theraplay in residential care. *Child & Adolescent Social Work Journal, 26*(4), 291–306. doi:10.1007/s10560-009-0177-x

Rogers, C. (1957). The necessary and sufficient conditions of therapeutic personality change. *Journal of Consulting Psychology, 21*(2), 95–103. doi:10.1037/h0045357 PMID:13416422

Rogers, C. R. (1957). *Client-centered therapy: Its current practice, implications, and theory.* Oxford, UK: Houghton Mifflin.

Rogers, M. A., Yamasue, H., Abe, O., Yamada, H., Ohtani, T., Iwanami, A., & Kasai, K. et al. (2009). Smaller amygdala volume and reduced anterior cingulate gray matter density associated with history of post-traumatic stress disorder. *Psychiatry Research: Neuroimaging, 174*(3), 210–216. doi:10.1016/j.pscychresns.2009.06.001 PMID:19914045

Rogers, N. (1993). *The creative connection: Expressive arts as healing.* Palo Alto, CA: Science & Behavior Books, Inc.

Rogers, S., & Pennington, B. (1991). A theoretical approach to the deficits in infantile autism. *Developmental Psychology, 3*(02), 137–162. doi:10.1017/S0954579400000043

Roopnarine, J. L., & Davidson, K. L. (2015). Parent-child play across cultures: Advancing play research. *American Journal of Play, 7*(2), 228–252.

Roopnarine, J. L., Shin, M., Jung, K., & Hossain, Z. (2003). Play and early development and education: The instantiation of parental belief systems. In *Contemporary perspectives in early childhood education* (pp. 115–132). Greenwich, CT: Information Age Publishing, Inc.

Rosen, C. E. (1974). The effects of sociodramatic play on problem-solving behavior among culturally disadvantaged preschool children. *Child Development, 45*(4), 92CL927.

Rothschild, B. (2003). *The body remembers casebook: Unifying methods and models in the treatment of trauma and PTSD.* New York, NY: W. W. Norton.

Rubin & Tregay. (1989). *Play with them: Theraplay groups in the classroom.* Springfield, IL: Charles Thomas.

Rubin, A. (2008). *Practitioner's guide to using research for evidence-based practice.* Hoboken, NJ: Wiley.

Rubin, A. (2008). *Practitioner's guide to using research for evidenced-based practice.* Hoboken, NJ: John Wiley & Sons, Inc.

Rubin, J. A. (2010). *Introduction to art therapy: Sources & resources.* New York, NY: Taylor & Francis Group.

Rubin, J. A. (2011). *The art of art therapy: What every art therapist needs to know* (2nd ed.). New York, NY: Routledge.

Runyan, D., Wattam, C., Ikeda, R., Hassan, F., & Ramiro, L. (2002). Child abuse and neglect by parents and other caregivers. In *World report on violence and health* (pp. 57–82). Geneva, Switzerland: World Health Organization.

Russell-Chapin, L. A., & Chapin, T. (2011). *Clinical supervision: Theory and practice.* Pacific Grove, CA: Brooks/Cole.

Russ, S., & Niec, L. (2011). *Play in clinical practice: Evidence-based approaches.* New York, NY: Guilford Press.

Ryan, S. D., Gomory, T., & Lacasse, J. R. (2002). Who are we? Examining the results of the Association for Play Therapy membership survey. *International Journal of Play Therapy, 11*(2), 11–41. doi:10.1037/h0088863

Ryan, V., & Needham, C. (2001). Non-directive play therapy with children experiencing psychic trauma. *Clinical Child Psychology and Psychiatry, 6*(3), 437–453. doi:10.1177/1359104501006003011

Sachs, J. D., McArthur, J. W., Schmidt-Traub, G., Kruk, M., Bahadur, C., Faye, M., & McCord, G. (2004). Ending Africa's poverty trap. In W. C. Brainard & G. L. Perry (Eds.), *Brookings papers on economic activity* (pp. 117–240). Washington, DC: Brookings Institution Press.

Sahar, T., Shalev, A. Y., & Porges, S. (2001). Vagal modulation of responses to challenge in PTSD. *Biological Psychiatry, 49*, 635–647. doi:10.1016/S0006-3223(00)01045-3

San Martín-Rodríguez, L., Beaulieu, M. D., D'Amour, D., & Ferrada-Videla, M. (2005). The determinants of successful collaboration: a review of theoretical and empirical studies. *Journal of Interprofessional Care, 19*(sup1), 132-147.

Sandoval, J. (2014). Best practices in school-based mental health/consultee-centered consultation by school psychologists. In P. L. Harrison & A. Thomas (Eds.), *Best practices in school psychology: Data-based and collaborative services* (pp. 493–507). Bethesda, MD: National Association of School Psychologists.

Saracho, O. N. (2013). *An integrated play-based curriculum for young children.* Routledge.

Savin-Williams, R. C., & Berndt, T. S. (1990). Friendship and peer relations. In S. S. Feldman & G. R. Elliot (Eds.), *At the threshold: The developing adolescent* (pp. 277–307). Cambridge, MA: Harvard University Press.

Sawyer, C., & Judd, R. G. (2012). Counselors and Bikers Collaborate to Empower Abused Children. *Journal of Creativity in Mental Health, 7*(1), 35–48. doi:10.1080/15401383.2012.661243

Schaaf, J. M., Alexander, K. W., & Goodman, G. S. (2008). Childrens false memory and true disclosure in the face of repeated questions. *Journal of Experimental Child Psychology, 100*(3), 157–185. doi:10.1016/j.jecp.2007.09.002 PMID:18061609

Schady, N. (2011). Parents education, mothers vocabulary, and cognitive development in early childhood: Longitudinal evidence from Ecuador. *American Journal of Public Health, 101*(12), 2299–2307. doi:10.2105/AJPH.2011.300253 PMID:22021308

Schaefer, C. (2010). *Play therapy for preschool children.* Washington, DC: American Psychological Association. doi:10.1037/12060-000

Schaefer, C. (2011). *Foundations of play therapy.* Hoboken, NJ: John Wiley & Sons.

Schaefer, C. E. (1993). What is play and why is it therapeutic? In C. E. Schaefer (Ed.), *The therapeutic power of play* (pp. 1–15). New York, NY: Aronson.

Schaefer, C. E. (1995). *The therapeutic powers of play.* Northvale, NJ: J. Aronson.

Schaefer, C. E., & Drewes, A. A. (Eds.). (2014). *The therapeutic powers of play: 20 core agents of change.* Hoboken, NJ: Wiley.

Schaefer, C. E., & Mattei, D. (2005). Catharsis: Effectiveness in childrens aggression. *International Journal of Play Therapy, 14*(2), 103–109. doi:10.1037/h0088905

Schaefer, C., Coyne, J. C., & Lazarus, R. S. (1981). The health-related functions of social support. *Journal of Behavioral Medicine, 4*(4), 381–406. doi:10.1007/BF00846149 PMID:7338894

Schaefer, C., & Drewes, A. (2009). The therapeutic powers of play and play therapy. In A. Drewes (Ed.), *Blending play therapy with cognitive behavioral therapy: Evidence-based and other effective treatment and techniques* (pp. 3–15). Hoboken, NJ: Wiley.

Schaefer, C., & O'Connor, K. (1983). *Handbook of play therapy.* John Wiley & Sons.

Schafer, C. E., & Peabody, M. A. (2016). Glossary of play therapy terms. *Play Therapy, 11*(2), 20–24.

Scherer, N. J., & DAntonio, L. (1997). Language and play development in toddlers with cleft lip and/or palate. *American Journal of Speech-Language Pathology, 6*(4), 48–54. doi:10.1044/1058-0360.0604.48

Schieffer, K. (2013). *Sunshine Circles: Interactive playgroups for social skills development and classroom management: Teacher Manual.* Evanston, IL: The Theraplay Institute.

Schore, A. N. (2009). Right-brain affect regulation: An essential mechanism of development, trauma, dissociation and psychotherapy. In D. Fosha, D. J. Siegel, & M. Solomon (Eds.), The healing power of emotion: Affective neuroscience development and clinical practice (pp. 112–114). Academic Press.

Schore, A. N. (2001). The effects of early relational trauma on right brain development, affect regulation, and infant mental health. *Infant Mental Health Journal, 22*(1/2), 201–269. doi:10.1002/1097-0355(200101/04)22:1<201::AID-IMHJ8>3.0.CO;2-9

Schore, A. N. (2012). *The science of the art of psychotherapy*. New York, NY: Norton.

Schore, J. R., & Schore, A. N. (2008). Modern Attachment Theory: The central role of affect regulation in development and treatment. *Clinical Social Work Journal, 36*(1), 9–20. doi:10.1007/s10615-007-0111-7

Schottelkorb, A., Doumas, D., & Garcia, R. (2012). Treatment for childhood refugee trauma: A randomized, controlled trial. *International Journal of Play Therapy, 21*(2), 57–73. doi:10.1037/a0027430

Schottelkorb, A., Swan, K., & Ogawa, Y. (2015). Parent consultation in child-centered play therapy: A model for research and practice. *International Journal of Play Therapy, 24*(4), 221–233. doi:10.1037/a0039609

Schumann, B. (2010). Effectiveness of child centered play therapy for children referred for aggression in elementary school. In J. Baggerly, D. Ray, & S. Bratton (Eds.), *Child-centered play therapy research: The evidence base for effective practice* (pp. 193–208). Hoboken, NJ: Wiley.

Schumann, B. (2010). Effectiveness of child-centered play therapy for children referred for aggression. In J. Baggerly, D. Ray, & S. Bratton (Eds.), *Child-centered play therapy research: The evidence-base for effective practice*. Hoboken, NJ: John Wiley. doi:10.1002/9781118269626.ch11

Schwarz, E. D., & Perry, B. D. (1994). The post-traumatic response in children and adolescents. *The Psychiatric Clinics of North America, 17*(2), 311–326. PMID:7937362

Seja, A. L., & Russ, S. W. (1999). Childrens fantasy play and emotional understanding. *Journal of Clinical Child Psychology, 28*(2), 269–277. doi:10.1207/s15374424jccp2802_13 PMID:10353085

Seltzer, M., & Krauss, M. (2001). Quality of life of adults with mental retardation/developmental disabilities who live with family members. *Mental Retardation and Developmental Disabilities Research Reviews, 7*(2), 105–114. doi:10.1002/mrdd.1015 PMID:11389565

Sepulveda, C., Garza, Y., & Morrison, M. O. (2011). Child teacher relationship training: A phenomenological study. *International Journal of Play Therapy, 20*(1), 12–25. doi:10.1037/a0021938

Shahmoom-Shanok, R. (1997). Giving back future's promise: Working resourcefully with. parents of children who have severe disorders of relating and communicating. *Zero to Three, 17*(5), 37–48.

Shale, N. C. (2004). Perceptions of Black parents regarding play therapy (Unpublished master's thesis). Pretoria, South Africa: University of Pretoria. Retrieved from http://upetd.up.ac.za/thesis/available/etd-02102005-135343/unrestricted/00dissertation.pdf

Shapiro, J. P., Friedberg, R. D., & Bardenstein, K. K. (2006). *Child and adolescent therapy: Science and art*. Hoboken, NJ: Wiley.

Shechtman, Z., & Pastor, R. (2005). Cognitive-behavioral and humanistic group treatment for children with disabilities: A comparison of outcome and process. *Journal of Counseling Psychology, 52*(3), 322–326. doi:10.1037/0022-0167.52.3.322

Sheely-Moore, A., & Bratton, S. (2010). A strengths-based parenting intervention with low income African American families. *Professional School Counseling*, *13*(3), 175–183. doi:10.5330/PSC.n.2010-13.175

Shen, Y. (2002). Short-term group play therapy with Chinese earthquake victims: Effects on anxiety, depression, and adjustment. *International Journal of Play Therapy*, *11*(1), 43–63. doi:10.1037/h0088856

Shen, Y. (2007). Developmental model using gestalt-play versus cognitive-verbal group with Chinese adolescents: Effects on strengths and adjustment enhancement. *Journal for Specialists in Group Work*, *32*(3), 285–305. doi:10.1080/01933920701431784

Sheppard, M. (2009). High thresholds and prevention in childrens services: The impact of mothers coping strategies on outcome of child and parenting problems—six month follow-up. *British Journal of Social Work*, *39*(1), 46–63. doi:10.1093/bjsw/bcm088

Shin, L. M., Wright, C. I., Cannistraro, P. A., Wedig, M. M., McMullin, K., Martis, B., & Rauch, S. L. et al. (2005). A Functional Magnetic Resonance Imaging Study of Amygdala and Medial Prefrontal Cortex Responses to Overtly Presented Fearful Faces in Posttraumatic Stress Disorder. *Archives of General Psychiatry*, *62*(3), 273–281. doi:10.1001/archpsyc.62.3.273 PMID:15753240

Sidebotham, P. (2014). Giving evidence in court. *Paediatrics and Child Health (Oxford)*, *24*(12), 562–566. doi:10.1016/j.paed.2014.01.009

Siegel, D. J. (2014, August 1). *Mindfulness as integration* [blog post]. Retrieved from http://www.drdansiegel.com/blog/2014/08/01/mindfulness-as-integration/

Siegel, D. J. (2001). Toward an interpersonal neurobiology of the developing mind: Attachment relationships, mindsight, and neural integration. *Infant Mental Health Journal*, *22*(1-2), 67–94. doi:10.1002/1097-0355(200101/04)22:1<67::AID-IMHJ3>3.0.CO;2-G

Siegel, D. J. (2009). Mindful awareness, mindsight, and neural integration. *The Humanistic Psychologist*, *37*(2), 137–158. doi:10.1080/08873260902892220

Siegel, D. J. (2010). Commentary on integrating interpersonal neurobiology with group psychotherapy: Reflections on mind, brain, and relationships in group psychotherapy. *International Journal of Group Psychotherapy*, *60*(4), 483–485. doi:10.1521/ijgp.2010.60.4.483 PMID:21028973

Siegel, D. J. (2010). *The mindful therapist: A clinician's guide to mindsight and neural integration*. New York, NY, US: W W Norton & Co.

Siegel, D. J. (2011). *The whole-brain child*. New York: Delacorte Press.

Siegel, D. J. (2012). *Pocket guide to interpersonal neurobiology: An integrative handbook of the mind*. New York, NY: W.W. Norton & company.

Siegel, D. J. (2012). *The developing mind: How relationships and the brain interact to shape who we are* (2nd ed.). New York, NY, US: Guilford Press.

Siegel, D. J., & Bryson, T. P. (2011). *The whole-brain child: 12 revolutionary strategies to nurture your child's developing mind*. New York, NY: Delacorte Press.

Siegel, D. J., & Hartzell, M. (2003). *Parenting from the inside out: How a deeper self- understanding can help you raise children who thrive*. New York, NY: Tarcher/Penguin.

Siegel, D. J., & Hartzell, M. (2003). *Parenting from the inside out: How a deeper self-understanding can help you raise children who thrive*. New York, NY: J. P. Tarcher/Penguin.

Siegel, D., & Payne Bryson, T. (2012). *The whole-brain child: Twelve revolutionary strategies to nurture your child's developing mind*. New York, NY: Delacorte Press.

Sigman, M., & Ungerer, J. (1984, March). Cognitive and language skills in autistic, mentally retarded, and normal children. *Developmental Psychology*, *20*(2), 293–302. doi:10.1037/0012-1649.20.2.293

Silva, P. A., Williams, S., & McGee, R. (1987). A longitudinal study of children with developmental language delay at age three: Later intelligence, reading and behaviour problems. *Developmental Medicine and Child Neurology*, *29*(5), 630–640.

Silverman, W. K., & Hinshaw, S. P. (2008). The second special issue on evidence-based psychosocial treatments for children and adolescents: A 10-year update. *Journal of Clinical Child and Adolescent Psychology*, *37*(1), 1–7. doi:10.1080/15374410701817725

Simons, R., Beaman, J., Conger, R., & Chao, W. (1993). Stress, support, and antisocial behavior trait as determinants of emotional well-being and parenting practices among single mothers. *Journal of Marriage and the Family*, *55*(2), 385–398. doi:10.2307/352809

Singer, J. (1973). Observing imaginative play: Approaches to recording, rating, and categorizing. In J. Singer (Ed.), *The child's world of make-believe: Experimental studies of imaginative play*. New York: Academic Press.

Siu, A. F. Y. (2009). Theraplay in the Chinese world: An intervention program for Hong Kong children with internalizing problems. *International Journal of Play Therapy*, *18*(1), 1–12. doi:10.1037/a0013979

Siu, A. F. Y. (2014). Effectiveness of Group Theraplay on Enhancing Social Skills among Children with Developmental Disabilities. *International Journal of Play Therapy*, *23*(4), 187–203. doi:10.1037/a0038158

Slack, C. M., & Wassenaar, D. R. (1999). Ethical dilemmas of South African clinical psychologists: International comparisons. *European Psychologist*, *4*(3), 179–186. doi:10.1027//1016-9040.4.3.179

Slade, A., Grienenberger, J., Bernbach, E., Levy, D., & Locker, A. (2005). Maternal reflective functioning, attachment, and the transmission gap: A preliminary study. *Attachment & Human Development*, *7*(3), 283–298. doi:10.1080/14616730500245880 PMID:16210240

Slater, S. J., Nicholson, L., Chriqui, J., Turner, L., & Chaloupka, F. (2012). The impact of state laws and district policies on physical education and recess practices in a nationally representative sample of US public elementary schools. *Archives of Pediatrics & Adolescent Medicine*, *166*(4), 311–316. doi:10.1001/archpediatrics.2011.1133 PMID:22147763

Smathers, S., & Tirnauer, L. (1959). Speech-play therapy. *The Journal of Speech and Hearing Disorders*, *24*(1), 59–61. doi:10.1044/jshd.2401.59 PMID:13631694

Smilansky, S. (1968). *The effects of sociodramatic play on disadvantaged preschool children*. New York: Wiley.

Smith, D., & Landreth, G. (2004). Filial therapy with teachers of deaf and hard of hearing preschool children. *International Journal of Play Therapy*, *13*(1), 13–33. doi:10.1037/h0088883

Smith, N., & Landreth, G. (2003). Intensive filial therapy with child witnesses of domestic violence: A comparison with individual and sibling group play therapy. *International Journal of Play Therapy*, *12*(1), 67–88. doi:10.1037/h0088872

Snow, K. (2013). *Who is the Early Child Care and Education Workforce?* National Association for the Education of Young Children. Retrieved from: http://www.naeyc.org/blogs/gclarke/2013/11/who-early-care-and-education-workforce-0

Snow, M. S. (2016, July). *Play therapy goes to court: Ethical and legal issues.* PowerPoint presented at the Center for Play Therapy Summer Institute, Denton, TX.

Snow, C. E. (1991). The theoretical basis for relationships between language and literacy in development. *Journal of Research in Childhood Education*, *6*(1), 5–10. doi:10.1080/02568549109594817

Snow, C. E., & Dickinson, D. K. (1990). Social sources of narrative skills at home and at school. *First Language*, *10*(29), 87–103. doi:10.1177/014272379001002901

Snow, C. E., & Dickinson, D. K. (1991). Skills that aren't basic in a new conception of literacy. In E. M. Jennings & A. C. Purves (Eds.), *Literate systems and individual lives: Perspectives on literacy and schooling* (pp. 179–191). Albany, NY: State University of New York Press.

Society of Clinical Child and Adolescent Psychology. (2014). *Effective Child Therapy*. Retrieved from http://www.effectivechildtherapy.com/

Sokoloff, M. A. (1959). A comparison of gains in communicative skills, resulting from group play therapy and individual speech therapy, among a group of non-severely dysarthric, speech handicapped cerebral palsied children (PhD diss., New York University). *Dissertation Abstracts International*, *20*(02), B803.

Solis, C. (2005). Implementing kinder training as a preventive intervention: African American preschool teacher perceptions of the process, effectiveness, and acceptability (Doctoral dissertation). *Dissertation Abstracts International*, *66B*, 2488.

Solomon, R., Van Egeren, L. A., Mahoney, G., Huber, M. S. Q., & Zimmerman, P. (2014). PLAY Project Home Consultation intervention program for young children with autism spectrum disorders: A randomized controlled trial. *Journal of Developmental and Behavioral Pediatrics*, *35*(8), 475.

Somer, E., & Szwarcberg, S. (2001). Variables in delayed disclosure of childhood sexual abuse. *The American Journal of Orthopsychiatry*, *71*(3), 332–341. doi:10.1037/0002-9432.71.3.332 PMID:11495335

Sommers-Flanagan, R., & Sommers-Flanagan, J. (2015). *Becoming an ethical helping professional: Cultural and philosophical foundations*. Hoboken, NJ: John Wiley & Sons, Inc.

Soomro, S., Abbasi, Z., & Lalani, F. (2014). An indepth insight into child abuse and its impact on personality of victims. *International Research Journal of Art and Humanities*, *10*(40), 53–68.

Spielberg, J. M., Miller, G. A., Warren, S. L., Engels, A. S., Crocker, L. D., Sutton, B. P., & Heller, W. (2012). Trait motivation moderates neural activation associated with goal pursuit. *Cognitive, Affective & Behavioral Neuroscience*, *12*(2), 308–322. doi:10.3758/s13415-012-0088-8 PMID:22460723

Sroufe, L. A., Egeland, B., Carlson, E. A., & Collins, W. A. (2005). *The development of the person: The Minnesota study of risk and adaptation from birth to adulthood*. New York: Guilford Press.

Staller, K. M., & Vandervort, F. E. (2010). Child sexual abuse: Legal burdens and scientific methods. Seeking justice in child sexual abuse: shifting burdens and sharing responsibilities. In K. M. Staller & K. C. Faller (Eds.), *Seeking justice in child sexual abuse* (pp. 1–34). New York, NY: Columbia University Press.

Steen, R. L. (2010). *Parent consultation: Beyond engagement*. Association for Play Therapy October Mining Report. Retrieved from www.a4pt.org

Steen, R.L. (2010). *Parent consultation: Beyond engagement*. Association for Play Therapy October Mining Report.

Steinhardt, L. (1994). Creating the autonomous image through puppet theatre and art therapy. *The Arts in Psychotherapy*, *21*(3), 205–218. doi:10.1016/0197-4556(94)90050-7

Stern, P., Vaughan-Eden, V., & Coslett, G. (2016, June). *Preparing and presenting expert testimony*. Paper presented at 24th Annual American Professional Society on the Abuse of Children Colloquium, New Orleans, LA.

Stern, D. N. (2002). *The first relationship: Infant and mother*. Cambridge, MA: Harvard University Press.

Stewart, A. L., Field, T. A., & Echterling, L. G. (2016). Neuroscience and the magic of play therapy. *International Journal of Play Therapy*, *25*(1), 4–13. doi:10.1037/pla0000016

Stilwell, C. (1989). Community libraries: A brief review of their origins and nature with particular reference to South Africa. *Journal of Librarianship*, *21*(4), 260–269. doi:10.1177/096100068902100403

Stilwell, C. (1991). Community libraries: A viable alternative to the public library in South Africa? *Progressive Librarian*, *4*, 17–27.

Stoltenborgh, M., Bakermans-Kranenburg, M. J., & van IJzendoorn, M. H. (2013). The neglect of child neglect: A meta-analytic review of the prevalence of neglect. *Social Psychiatry and Psychiatric Epidemiology*, *48*(3), 345–355. doi:10.1007/s00127-012-0549-y PMID:22797133

Stone, J., & Bray, S. (2015). Trauma and young children: How the problem plays out. *Discussions on Sensitive Issues: Advances in Early Education and Day Care*, *19*, 177–211. doi:10.1108/S0270-402120150000019012

Stone, W. L., & Yoder, P. J. (2001). Predicting spoken language level in children with autism spectrum disorders. *Autism*, *5*(4), 341–361. doi:10.1177/1362361301005004002 PMID:11777253

Storch, S. A., & Whitehurst, G. J. (2002). Oral language and code-related precursors to reading: Evidence from a longitudinal structural model. *Developmental Psychology*, *38*(6), 934–947. doi:10.1037/0012-1649.38.6.934 PMID:12428705

Stover, L., & Guerney, B. G. (1967). The efficacy of training procedures from mothers in filial therapy. *Psychotherapy (Chicago, Ill.)*, *4*(3), 110–115. doi:10.1037/h0087950

Stulmaker, H. (2013). Counseling-based teacher interventions: Defining, exploring, and differentiating. *International Journal of Play Therapy*, *22*(1), 2–12. doi:10.1037/a0030195

Stulmaker, H., & Ray, D. (2015). Child-centered play therapy with young children who are anxious: A controlled trial. *Children and Youth Services Review*, *57*, 127–133. doi:10.1016/j.childyouth.2015.08.005

Substance Abuse and Mental Health Services Administration, U.S. Department of Health and Human Services. (2014). *National Registry of Evidence-Based Programs and Practices*. Retrieved from http://www.nrepp.samhsa.gov/

Substance Abuse and Mental Health Services Administration. (2014). *SAMHSA's concept of trauma and guidance for a trauma-informed approach.* Retrieved from http://store.samhsa.gov/shin/content/SMA14-4884/SMA14-4884.pdf

Sullivan, H. S. (1953). *The interpersonal theory of psychiatry*. New York, NY: Norton.

Sunderland, M. (2006). *The Science of Parenting*. New York, NY: DK Publishing Inc.

Sunderland, M. (2006). *The science of parenting*. New York, NY: DK Publishing.

Swan, K., & Ray, D. (2014). Effects of child-centered play therapy on irritability and hyperactivity behaviors of children with intellectual disabilities. *Journal of Humanistic Counseling*, *53*(2), 120–133. doi:10.1002/j.2161-1939.2014.00053.x

Swan, K., & Schottelkorb, A. (2014). *Contact work in child centered play therapy: A case study*. Person-Centered and Experiential Psychotherapies.

Sweeney, D. S. (2001). Legal and ethical issues in play therapy. In G. L. Landreth (Ed.), *Innovations in play therapy: Issues, processes, and special populations* (pp. 65–82). Burlington, MA: Taylor & Francis.

Sweeney, D. S., Baggerly, J. N., & Ray, D. C. (2014). *Group play therapy: A dynamic approach*. New York, NY: Routledge.

Sweeney, T. J. (2009). *Adlerian counseling and psychotherapy: A practitioner's approach* (5th ed.). New York, NY: Taylor & Francis.

Szalavitz, M., & Perry, B. D. (2010). *Born for love: Why empathy is essential and endangered*. New York, NY: Harper Collins Publishers.

Tamis-LeMonda, C. S., & Bornstein, M. H. (1994). Specificity in mother-toddler language-play relations across the second year. *Developmental Psychology*, *30*(2), 283–292. doi:10.1037/0012-1649.30.2.283

Tamis-LeMonda, C. S., Bornstein, M. H., & Baumwell, L. (2001). Maternal responsiveness and childrens achievement of language milestones. *Child Development*, *72*(3), 748–767. doi:10.1111/1467-8624.00313 PMID:11405580

Tanser, F., Hosegood, V., Bärnighausen, T., Herbst, K., Nyirenda, M., Muhwava, W., & Newell, M. et al. (2008). Cohort Profile: Africa Centre Demographic Information System (ACDIS) and population-based HIV survey. *International Journal of Epidemiology*, *37*(5), 956–962. doi:10.1093/ije/dym211 PMID:17998242

Tarver-Behring, S., & Ingraham, C. L. (1998). Culture as a central component of consultation: A call to the field. *Journal of Educational & Psychological Consultation*, *9*(1), 57–72. doi:10.1207/s1532768xjepc0901_3

Taylor, L., & Adelman, H. (1989). Reframing the confidentiality dilemma to work in childrens best interests. *Professional Psychology, Research and Practice*, *20*(2), 79–83. doi:10.1037/0735-7028.20.2.79

Taylor, M., & Carlson, S. M. (1997). The relationship between individual differences in fantasy and theory-of-mind. *Child Development*, *68*(3), 436–455. doi:10.2307/1131670 PMID:9249959

Texas Adoption Resource Exchange (TARE). (n.d.). *Requirements for foster/adopt families*. Retrieved from https://www.dfps.state.tx.us/Adoption_and_Foster_Care/Get_Started/requirements.asp

The Annie E. Casey Foundation. (2009). *The 2009 KIDS COUNT data book: State profiles of child well-being*. Baltimore, MD: Author.

Thiemann-Bourque, K. S., Brady, N. C., & Fleming, K. K. (2012). Symbolic play of preschoolers with severe communication impairments with autism and other developmental delays: More similarities than differences. *Journal of Autism and Developmental Disorders*, *42*(5), 863–873. doi:10.1007/s10803-011-1317-7 PMID:21720725

Thomas, R. M., & Kaipa, R. (2016). Speech and language deficits in separation anxiety disorder. *Advances in Pediatric Research, 3*(7).

Thomas, J. T. (2007). Informed consent through contracting for supervision: Minimizing risks, enhancing benefits. *Professional Psychology, Research and Practice*, *38*(3), 221–231. doi:10.1037/0735-7028.38.3.221

Thomas, J. T. (2010). *The ethics of supervision and consultation: Practical guidelines for mental health professionals*. Washington, DC: American Psychological Association. doi:10.1037/12078-000

Throneburg, R. N., Calvert, L. K., Sturm, J. J., Paramboukas, A. A., & Paul, P. J. (2000). A comparison of service delivery models effects on curricular vocabulary skills in the school setting. *American Journal of Speech-Language Pathology*, *9*(1), 10–20. doi:10.1044/1058-0360.0901.10

Timberlake, E. M., & Cutler, M. M. (2001). *Developmental play therapy in clinical social work*. Needham Heights, MA: Allyn and Bacon.

Tollerfield, I. (2003). The process of collaboration within a special school setting: An exploration of the ways in which skills and knowledge are shared and barriers are overcome when a teacher and speech and language therapist collaborate. *Child Language Teaching and Therapy*, *19*(1), 67–84. doi:10.1191/0265659003ct244oa

Toppelberg, C. O., & Shapiro, T. (2000). Language disorders: A 10-year research update review. *Journal of the American Academy of Child and Adolescent Psychiatry*, *39*(2), 143–152.

Trotter, K., Eshelman, D., & Landreth, G. (2003). A place for Bobo in play therapy. *International Journal of Play Therapy*, *12*(1), 117–139. doi:10.1037/h0088875

Trotzer, J. P. (2006). *The counselor and the group* (4th ed.). New York, NY: Routledge.

Tucker, C., Schieffer, K., Willis, T., & Hull, C. (2016). *Teacher-led groups foster social- emotional development in at-risk preschools students.* In process.

U. S. Department of Health and Human Services, Administration for Children and Families, Administration on Children, Youth and Families, Children's Bureau. (2016a). *Trends in foster care and adoption: FY 2006- FY 2015.* Retrieved from www.acf.gov/default/files/cb/trends_fostercare-adoption2015.pdf

U. S. Department of Health and Human Services, Administration for Children and Families, Administration on Children, Youth and Families, Children's Bureau. (2016b). The AFCARS report FY 2015 data van der Kolk, B. A. (2005). Developmental trauma disorder. *Psychiatric Annals*, *35*, 401–408.

U.S. Census Bureau. (2003). *Young, diverse, urban.* Retrieved from http://www.census.gov/Press-Release/www/ releases/archives/hispanic_origin_population/001130.html

U.S. Census Bureau. (2010). *2010 Census Summary File.* Author.

U.S. Census Bureau. (2015). *New Census Bureau report analyzes U.S. population projections* (Release No. CB15-TPS.16). Retrieved from https://www.census.gov/newsroom/press-releases/2015/cb15-tps16.html

U.S. Census Bureau. (2015). *Quick Facts.* Retrieved from https://www.census.gov

U.S. Department of Health and Human Services, Administration for Children and Families, Children's Bureau. (2012). *Child maltreatment.* Retrieved February 5, 2014, from http://www.acf.hhs.gov/sites/default/files/cb/cm2012.pdf

U.S. Department of Health and Human Services, Administration on Children, Youth, and Families, Children's Bureau. (2013). *Child Maltreatment 2012.* Retrieved from http://www.acf.hhs.gov/sites/default/files/cb/cm2012.pdf#page=31

U.S. Public Health Service. (2000). *Report of the surgeon general's conference on children's mental health: A national action agenda.* Washington, DC: U.S. Department of Health and Human Services.

U.S. Public Health Service. (2000). *Report of the Surgeon General's conference on children's mental health: A national action agenda.* Washington, DC: U.S. Public Health Service.

United Nations Children's Fund (UNICEF). (2013). *Uganda country statistics.* Retrieved from http://www.unicef.org/infobycountry/uganda_statistics.html

United Nations Educational, Scientific and Cultural Organization (UNESCO). (2007). *Youth (15-24) and adult (15+) literacy rates by country and by gender for 2000-2004.* UNESCO Institute for Statistics. Retrieved from http://stats.uis.unesco.org/unesco/ReportFolders/ReportFolders.aspx

United Nations Educational, Scientific and Cultural Organization (UNESCO). (2014). *Literacy data chart/Africa.* Retrieved from http://www.unesco.org/new/en/dakar/education/literacy

United States Department of Health and Human Services. (2000). *Report of the Surgeon General's Conference on Children's Mental Health: A national action agenda.* Author.

United States President Obama. (2013). *Now is the Time: The President's Plan to Protect Our Children and Our Communities by Reducing Gun Violence.* White House.

US Department of Health and Human Services, Administration on Children, Youth, and Families, Children's Bureau. (2014). *Child maltreatment.* Retrieved from http://www.acf.hhs.gov/sites/default/files/cb/cm2014.pdf#page=21

Vagni, M., Maiorano, T., Pajardi, D., & Gudjonsson, G. (2015). Immediate and delayed suggestibility among suspected child victims of sexual abuse. *Personality and Individual Differences, 79129-133.* doi:10.1016/j.paid.2015.02.007

van der Kolk, B. (2014). *The body keeps the score: Brain, mind, and body in the healing of trauma.* New York: Viking.

van der Kolk, B. A. (1996). The body keeps score: Approaches to the psychobiology of posttraumatic stress disorder. In B. A. van der Kolk, A. C. McFarlane, L. Weisaeth, B. A. van der Kolk, A. C. McFarlane, & L. Weisaeth (Eds.), *Traumatic stress: The effects of overwhelming experience on mind, body, and society* (pp. 214–241). New York, NY: Guilford Press.

Van der Kolk, B. A. (2001). The psychobiology and psychopharmacology of PTSD. *Human Psychopharmacology: Clinical and Experimental, 16*(S1), 49–64. doi:10.1002/hup.270 PMID:12404535

van der Kolk, B. A. (2002). The assessment and treatment of complex PTSD. In R. Yehuda (Ed.), *Psychological trauma.* Arlington, VA: American Psychological Press.

van der Kolk, B. A. (2005). Developmental Trauma Disorder: Toward a rational diagnosis for children with complex trauma histories. *Psychiatric Annals, 35*(5), 401–408.

Van der Kolk, B. A., & Fisler, R. (2007). Dissociation and the fragmentary nature of traumatic memories: Overview. *British Journal of Psychotherapy, 12*(3), 352–361. doi:10.1111/j.1752-0118.1996.tb00825.x

Van Hooff, M., McFarlane, A. C., Baur, J., Abraham, M., & Barnes, D. J. (2009). The stressor Criterion A-1 and PTSD: A matter of opinion? *Journal of Anxiety Disorders, 23*(1), 77–86. doi:10.1016/j.janxdis.2008.04.001 PMID:18511232

van IJzendoorn, M. H., Dijkstra, J., & Bus, A. G. (1995). Attachment, intelligence and language: A meta-analysis. *Social Development, 4*(2), 115–128. doi:10.1111/j.1467-9507.1995.tb00055.x

Van Kleeck, A., Gillam, R. B., & McFadden, T. U. (1998). A study of classroom-based phonological awareness training for preschoolers with speech and/or language disorders. *American Journal of Speech-Language Pathology, 7*(3), 65–76. doi:10.1044/1058-0360.0703.65

VanFleet, R. (1994). *Filial therapy: Strengthening parent–child relationships through play.* Professional Resource Press/ Professional Resource Exchange.

VanFleet, R., Sywulak, A. E., & Sniscak, C. C. (2010). *Child-centered play therapy.* New York, NY: Guilford.

Vasterling, J. J., & Brewin, C. R. (Eds.). (2005). *Neuropsychology of PTSD: Biological, cognitive, and clinical perspectives.* New York, NY: The Guilford Press.

Vaughan-Eden, V. (2008, Summer-Fall). Key points to testifying in child abuse cases. *APSAC Advisor,* 23-26.

Vernon, A. (2009). *Counseling children & adolescents.* Denver, CO: Love Publishing Company.

Vernon, A., & Clemente, R. (2005). *Assessment and intervention with children and adolescents: Developmental and multicultural approaches* (2nd ed.). Alexandria, VA: American Counseling Association.

Vickers, B. (2002). Cognitive behaviour therapy for adolescents with psychological disorders: A group treatment programme. *Clinical Child Psychology and Psychiatry*, *7*(2), 249–262. doi:10.1177/1359104502007002011

Volpe, R. J., DiPerna, J. C., Hintze, J. M., & Shapiro, E. S. (2009). Observing students in classroom settings: A review of seven coding schemes. *School Psychology Review*, *34*, 454–474.

Vygotsky, L. (1933). Play and its role in the mental development of the child. In J. S. Bruner, A. Jolly, & K. Sylva (Eds.), *Play* (pp. 537–555). New York: Basic Books.

Vygotsky, L. (1966). Play and its role in the mental development of the child. *Voprosy Psihologii*, *12*, 6–18.

Wachtel, E. F. (1994). *Treating troubled children and their families*. New York, NY: Guilford.

Wakaba, Y. Y. (1983). Group play therapy for Japanese children who stutter. *Journal of Fluency Disorders*, *8*(2), 93–118. doi:10.1016/0094-730X(83)90023-2

Walsh, M. E., Barrett, J. G., & DePaul, J. (2007). Dat-to-day activities of school counselors: Alignment with new directions in the field of the ASCA national model. *Professional School Counseling*, *10*(4), 370–378. doi:10.5330/prsc.10.4.47p342040286mw72

Ward, J. (2010). *The student's guide to cognitive neuroscience* (2nd ed.). New York, NY: Psychology Press.

Ware Balch, J., & Ray, D. C. (2015). Emotional assets of children with autism spectrum disorder: A single-case therapeutic outcome experiment. *Journal of Counseling and Development*, *93*(4), 429–439. doi:10.1002/jcad.12041

Warner, C. M., Fisher, P. H., Shrout, P. E., Rathor, S., & Klein, R. G. (2007). Treating adolescents with social anxiety disorder in school: An attention control trial. *Journal of Child Psychology and Psychiatry, and Allied Disciplines*, *48*(7), 676–686. doi:10.1111/j.1469-7610.2007.01737.x PMID:17593148

Warren, K. L., & Peterson, C. (2014). Exploring Parent-Child Discussions of Crime and their Influence on Childrens Memory. *Behavioral Sciences & the Law*, *32*(6), 686–701. doi:10.1002/bsl.2144 PMID:25393638

Washington State Department of Social and Health Services. (n.d.). *Training requirements*. Retrieved from https://www.dshs.wa.gov/ca/foster-parenting/training-requirements

Watson, D. (2007). An early interventions approach for students displaying negative externalizing behaviors associated with childhood depression: A study of the efficacy of play therapy in school. *Dissertation Abstracts International*.

Watts, A. G., Hawthorn, R., Hoffbrand, J., Jackson, H., & Spurling, A. (1997). Developing local lifelong guidance strategies. *British Journal of Guidance & Counselling*, *25*(2), 217–227. doi:10.1080/03069889708253803

Watts-English, T., Fortson, B. L., Gibler, N., Hooper, S., & DeBellis, M. D. (2006). The psychobiology of maltreatment in childhood. *The Journal of Social Issues*, *62*(4), 717–736. doi:10.1111/j.1540-4560.2006.00484.x

Watts, R. E. (2013). Adlerian counseling. In B. J. Irby, G. Brown, R. Lara-Alecio, S. Jackson, B. J. Irby, G. Brown, & S. Jackson (Eds.), *The handbook of educational theories* (pp. 459–472). Charlotte, NC: IAP Information Age Publishing.

Webster-Stratton, C., Reid, M., & Hammond, M. (2004). Treating children with early-onset conduct problems: Intervention outcomes for parent, child, and teacher training. *Journal of Clinical Child and Adolescent Psychology*, *33*(1), 105–124. doi:10.1207/S15374424JCCP3301_11 PMID:15028546

Weiland, C., & Yoshikawa, H. (2013). Impacts of a pre kindergarten program on childrens mathematics, language, literacy, executive function, and emotional skills. *Child Development*, *84*(6), 2112–2130. doi:10.1111/cdev.12099 PMID:23534487

Weir, K. N., Lee, S., Canosa, P., Rodrigues, N., McWilliams, M., & Parker, L. (2013). Whole Family Theraplay: Integrating Family Systems Theory and Theraplay to Treat Adoptive Families. *Adoption Quarterly*, *16*(3-4), 175–200. doi:10.1080/10926755.2013.844216

Weisz, J., & Kazdin, A. (2010). *Evidence-based psychotherapies for children and adolescents*. Guilford Press.

Wells, G. (1985). Preschool literacy-related activities and success in school. In D. R. Olson, N. Torrance, & A. Hildyard (Eds.), *Literacy, language, and learning: The nature and consequences of reading and writing* (pp. 229–255). New York: Cambridge University Press.

Wells, G. (1986). *The meaning makers: Children learning language and using language to learn*. Portsmouth, NH: Heinemann.

Werner, L. S. (1945). Treatment of a child with delayed speech. *The Journal of Speech Disorders*, *10*(4), 329–334. doi:10.1044/jshd.1004.329 PMID:21004357

Westby, C. E. (1980). Assessment of cognitive and language abilities through play. *Language, Speech, and Hearing Services in Schools*, *11*(3), 154–168. doi:10.1044/0161-1461.1103.154

Westby, C. E. (1991). Learning to talk—talking to learn: Oral-literate language differences. In C. Simon (Ed.), *Communication skills and classroom success: Therapy methodologies for language learning disabled students* (pp. 181–218). San Diego, CA: College-Hill Press.

Wettig, H. G., Coleman, A. R., & Geider, F. J. (2011). Evaluating the effectiveness of Theraplay in treating shy, socially withdrawn children. *International Journal of Play Therapy*, *20*(1), 26–37. doi:10.1037/a0022666

Wheeler, N., & Dillman Taylor, D. (2016). Integrating interpersonal neurobiology with play therapy. *International Journal of Play Therapy*, *25*(1), 24–34. doi:10.1037/pla0000018

White, B. (1978). *Experience and environment: Major influences on the development of young children* (Vol. 2). Englewood Cliffs, NJ: Prentice-Hall.

Whitehurst, G. J., & Lonigan, C. J. (2001). Emergent literacy: Development from prereaders to readers. In S. B. Neuman & D. K. Dickinson (Eds.), *Handbook of early literacy research* (pp. 11–29). New York: Guilford.

White, J., Draper, K., Flynt, M., & Jones, N. P. (2000). *Kinder training: Play-based teacher consultation to promote the adjustment and achievement of discouraged students*. Norcross, GA: KidChoice.

White, J., Flynt, M., & Draper, K. (1997). Kinder therapy: Teachers as therapeutic agents. *International Journal of Play Therapy*, *6*(2), 33–49. doi:10.1037/h0089407

White, J., Flynt, M., & Jones, N. P. (1999). Kinder therapy: An Adlerian approach for training teachers to be therapeutic agents through play. *Journal of Individual Psychology*, *55*(3), 365–382.

Whiten, A., & Brown, J. (1998). Imitation and the reading of minds: Perspectives from the study of autism, normal children, and non-human primates. In S. Braten (Ed.), *Intersubjective communication and emotion in early ontogency* (pp. 260–281). Cambridge, UK: Cambridge University Press.

Whitmire, K. (2002). The evolution of school-based speech-language services: A half century of change and a new century of practice. *Communication Disorders, 23*(2), 68-76.

Wilcox, M. J., Kouri, T. A., & Caswell, S. B. (1991). Early Language language InterventionA intervention: A Comparison comparison of Classroom classroom and Individual individual Treatmenttreatment. *American Journal of Speech-Language Pathology*, *1*(1), 49–62. doi:10.1044/1058-0360.0101.49

Willis, A., Walters, L., & Crane, D. (2014). Assessing play-based activities, child talk, and single session outcome in family therapy with young children. *Journal of Marital and Family Therapy*, *40*(3), 287–301. doi:10.1111/jmft.12048 PMID:24118088

Wilson, K., & Ryan, V. (2005). *Play therapy: A non-directive approach for children and adolescents* (2nd ed.). Oxford, UK: Elsevier.

Wilson, L., & Scarpa, A. (2014). Childhood abuse, perceived social support, and posttraumatic stress symptoms: A moderation model. *Psychological Trauma: Theory, Research, Practice, and Policy*, *6*(5), 512–518. doi:10.1037/a0032635

Winnicott, D. W. (2005). *Playing and reality*. New York, NY: Tavistock Publications.

Wolpe, J. (1982). *The practice of behavior therapy* (3rd ed.). Oxford, UK: Pergamon.

World Bank Country Statistics. (2014). Retrieved from http://data.worldbank.org/country/uganda

World Bank Literacy Indicators Female. (2014). Retrieved from http://data.worldbank.org/indicator/SE.ADT.LITR.FE.ZS

World Bank Literacy Indicators Male. (2014). Retrieved from http://data.worldbank.org/indicator/SE.ADT.1524.LT.MA.ZS

World Bank Sub-Saharan Africa Statistics. (2014). Retrieved from http://data.worldbank.org/region/SSA

World Bank. (2014). *Fighting HIV/AIDS in Uganda*. Retrieved from https://www.worldbank.org/progress/uganda.html

World Health Organization. (2010). *Framework for action on interprofessional education and collaborative practice*. Geneva: WHO Press. Available at http://apps.who.int/iris/bitstream/10665/70185/1/WHO_HRH_HPN_10.3_eng.pdf?ua=1

Yalom, I. D., & Leszcz, M. (2005). *The theory and practice of group psychotherapy*. Cambridge, MA: Basic Books.

Yew, S. G. K., & O'Kearney, R. (2013). Emotional and behavioural outcomes later in childhood and adolescence for children with specific language impairments: Meta-analyses of controlled prospective studies. *Journal of Child Psychology and Psychiatry, and Allied Disciplines*, *54*(5), 516–524.

Yost, D. S., & Mosca, F. J. (2002). Beyond behavior strategies: Using reflection to manage youth in crisis. *ERIC Clearinghouse*, *75*, 264–268.

You, D., Hug, L., & Chen, Y. (2014). *Levels and trends in child mortality 2014*. Retrieved from http://siteresources.worldbank.org/ICPEXT/Resources/Levels-and-Trends-in-Child-Mortality-Report-2014.pdf

Younggren, J. N., & Gottlieb, M. C. (2004). Managing risk when contemplating multiple relationships. *Professional Psychology, Research and Practice*, *35*(3), 255–260. doi:10.1037/0735-7028.35.3.255

Yuen, T. C., Landreth, G. L., & Baggerly, J. (2002). Filial therapy with immigrant Chinese parents in Canada. *International Journal of Play Therapy*, *11*(2), 63–90. doi:10.1037/h0088865

Zigler, E. F., Singer, D. G., & Bishop-Josef, S. J. (Eds.), *Children's play: The roots of reading*. Washington, DC: Zero to Three Press.

Zilberstein, K. (2013). The use and limitations of attachment theory in child psychotherapy. *Psychotherapy (Chicago, Ill.)*, *51*(1), 93–103. doi:10.1037/a0030930 PMID:23398037

Zins, J., Weissberg, R., Wang, M., & Walberg, H. (Eds.). (2004). *Building academic success and emotional learning: What does the research say?* New York, NY: Teachers College Press.

About the Contributors

Rheta LeAnne Steen is an Associate Professor in the Department of Counseling. She completed her Ph.D. in Counselor Education at the University of North Texas where she specialized in play therapy, counselor supervision, child-parent relationship therapy (filial therapy), and activity therapy. Dr. Steen is the Director and Founder of the Play Therapy Center for Education & Research at Loyola University New Orleans. Dr. Steen is an Approved Provider of Play Therapy Education. Dr. Steen developed multiple courses in play therapy including Intro to Play Therapy, Child Parent Relationship Therapy, Activity Therapy and Advanced Play Therapy & Theory. Dr. Steen recently acquired (2015) an endowment and a grant for the play therapy center to create both a legacy at Loyola University New Orleans for Play Therapy Education and to develop a Continuing and Professional Education Program at Loyola in Play Therapy. Both the endowment and the grant were from the Heebe Family Fund at Touro Hospital. Dr. Steen is currently the Past-President of the Louisiana Association for Play Therapy (LAPT), and she has been on the LAPT Board since 2006. She also sits on other clinical mental health boards, as a volunteer, to promote counseling and play therapy in New Orleans. Dr. Steen is involved on multiple committees and leadership with the national Association for Play Therapy. Dr. Steen is completing an edited book title, *Emerging Research in Play Therapy, Child Counseling, and Consultation,* which will be published in 2017 by IGI Publishing. She has published multiple research articles and chapters on play therapy and counselor education & supervision during her tenure at Loyola, as well as presented papers at international, national, and regional conferences. Currently, Dr. Steen is working on a research manuscript related to evidence based practices in clinical parent consultation and a pedagogical piece on experiential teaching of the CPRT course. Dr. Steen's research interests include parenting populations, diversity in play therapy, spirituality in play therapy, consultation in play therapy, youthful counselors & supervision, hospitalized children, siblings of hospitalized children, and counselor supervision. In teaching, Dr. Steen enjoys presenting extensively on many topics related to play and activity therapy, child-parent relationship therapy, parent consultation, and clinical play therapy consultation. Dr. Steen maintains a small private practice where she specializes in working with young children, pre-adolescents, parents, and families. Her clinical practice facilitates her ability to teach counseling students while experiencing the actuality of working with children, parents, and families in New Orleans.

* * *

Sinem Akay, PhD, LPC, Registered Play Therapist, Certified Trauma-Focused Cognitive Behavioral Therapist, graduated from the Counseling Program at the University of North Texas, where she specialized in play therapy during her master's and doctoral programs. After she moved to the Houston area,

Sinem started to teach master's level counseling classes at Sam Houston State University as an adjunct professor. She also works at Children's Safe Harbor as a therapist and supervisor, advocating for children and teenagers who experienced sexual and physical abuse. Sinem recently started her private practice in the Woodlands area, working with children and teenagers who struggle with a wide range of emotional and behavioral issues.

Jeff Ashby is a Professor in the Department of Counseling and Psychological Services at Georgia State University. He directs the PhD program in Counseling Psychology and the Georgia State Play Therapy Training Institute. In addition, he is the Co-Director of the Center for the Study of Stress, Trauma, and Resilience.

Sue Bratton, Ph.D., LPC-S, RPT-S, is Professor at the University of North Texas and Director of the UNT Center for Play Therapy with over 25 years of experience as a practitioner and researcher. Sue is nationally and internationally known speaker and author with over 80 publications and 300 professional presentations in the areas of child and family counseling. She is co-author of Child Parent Relationship Therapy (CPRT), the CPRT Treatment Manual, and CPRT in Action, a demonstration video illustrating CPRT with adoptive families, as well as three additional contemporary edited texts. Her research agenda focuses on examining the effectiveness of CPRT, play therapy, and school-based counseling services for young children and their families. Sue is an active member of ACA, AARC, AHC, ACAC, ACES, ASGW, ACC, IAFC, and CSI. She is a Past President of the Association for Play Therapy (APT), recipient of the 2016 APT Lifetime Achievement Award, 2007 APT Outstanding Research Award, the 2011 Chi Sigma Iota Outstanding Practitioner Supervisor Award, the 2013 ACA Best Practice Award, the 2013 AHC Humanistic Educator/ Supervisor Award, the 2014 ACA Extended Research Award, and several UNT teaching, research and service awards. She is an active social advocate for children at the local, national, and international level, particularly underserved children who have experienced traumatic experiences. Her career long passion and record of service is focused on making the world a safer place for these children, one in which they receive the help and nurturing they need to reach their full capacity and lead productive and fulfilling lives.

Susan Stewart Bray is an Assistant Professor of Counseling at Wichita State University. Director of the Wichita State Play Therapy Center.

Kristy A. Brumfield is a counselor educator who joined the faculty at Immaculata University as an Associate Professor in January 2015. Prior to this she was a member of the faculty at Xavier University of Louisiana and had been a counselor working with children and adolescents in New Orleans for over ten years. She is a Licensed Professional Counselor - Supervisor, a Registered Play Therapist - supervisor, and a Nationally Certified Counselor. In addition to play therapy, her professional/research interests include work with preschool age children and families, filial therapy, group therapy with adolescents, and multicultural counseling. She has demonstrated a passion for utilizing creative counseling techniques with clients of all ages and has primarily done work with individuals from 3-22 in various settings.

Julia Gentleman Byers, EdD, ATR-BC, LMHC, Professor Emerita at Lesley University, is currently the Co-Chair of the graduate professional certificate in Play Therapy, Senior Advisor in the PhD in Interdisciplinary Study, School of Education, and the Expressive Therapy PhD program within the Graduate School of Arts and Social Sciences. She has provided Expressive Art and Play therapy workshops in over twenty countries, and provided humanitarian relief for human and natural disasters using play therapy skills and applications. Byers has published multiple articles on integrating alternative expressive modalities.

Kara Carnes-Holt is an associate professor in the counseling program at the University of Wyoming. She is a professional counselor, a registered play therapist, and approved play therapy supervisor (RPT-S). Kara has special interests in utilizing humanistic play therapy and filial therapy interventions for children and families struggling with attachment disruptions and trauma histories.

Szu-Yu Chen, Ph.D., a license professional counselor, national certified counselor, and registered play therapist. She earned her doctoral degree in Counseling from the University of North Texas with a specialization in play therapy. She is an assistant professor and clinic director of Center for Community Counseling and Development at the Central Michigan University. She has worked with diverse population in a variety of settings, including private practice, community agency, psychiatric hospital, and schools. In addition to her clinical experience, she has provided intensive supervision to master's level students. Her research interests include humanistic play therapy, family play therapy, play-based teacher intervention, and multicultural counseling and supervision.

Kim Coggins is an assistant professor in the psychological sciences and counseling program at Austin Peay State University. She has special interests in employing play therapy and expressive arts interventions that utilize the therapeutic relationship as the primary and foundational agent of change and facilitate holistic care for children and families.

Valeda Dent, Ph.D. is Dean, University Libraries and Professor at St. John's University in New York. She holds an M.S.W. and M.I.L.S. from the University of Michigan and a Ph.D. from the Palmer School at Long Island University. Her research interests include the impact of chronic poverty on development, rural libraries in Africa and related literacy and reading habits, ethnographic approaches to understanding the user experience, and information and techno-literacy. She has published a number of books, including Qualitative Research and the Modern Library (2011) and Rural Community Libraries in Africa: Challenges and Impacts (2014) with co-authors Dr. Geoff Goodman and Dr. Michael Kevane. Dr. Dent's longitudinal research on rural village libraries in Uganda and elsewhere in Africa has spanned twelve years. Her work has been published in a wide variety of peer-reviewed journals and presented internationally at conferences in South Africa, China, South Korea, the United Kingdom, and Swaziland. In 2013, Dr. Dent and her husband, Dr. Geoff Goodman, were both awarded the J. William Fulbright Foreign Scholarship and spent eight months in 2014 working in two rural village libraries in Uganda establishing an intervention program to facilitate the development of school readiness skills in preschool children. Dr. Dent and her husband live in New York with their 3 year old daughter Carlyn.

Dalena Dillman Taylor, PhD, LPC, LMHC, RPT, is an assistant professor at the University of Central Florida, past president of the North Texas Association for Play Therapy (2013–2014), the Director of UCF's Center for Play Therapy Training and Research, and play therapy certificate coordinator. Dr. Dillman Taylor is a trained Adlerian play therapist and focuses her research on the effectiveness of Adlerian play therapy with children and adolescents who demonstrate disruptive behaviors or academic difficulties in the classroom and at home.

Erin M. Dugan, Ph.D., is a Licensed Professional Counselor Supervisor and a Registered Play Therapist -Supervisor. She is the Associate Dean of Academic Affairs at Louisiana Health Sciences Center, New Orleans, the Interim Department Head in the Department of Clinical Rehabilitation and Counseling, and the Director of the LSUHSC Child & Family Counseling Clinic. Dr. Dugan has published and presented numerous times on the topic of play therapy.

Suzanne M. Dugger's experience includes 5 years of experience as a school counselor, 3 years as a college counselor, 7 years in private practice, and 25 years as a counselor educator. Her teaching and research interests include career counseling, counseling children, school counseling, the counseling process, diagnosis and treatment planning, and doctoral education.

Laura Fazio-Griffith, Ph.D., NCC, LPC-S, LMFT, Registered Play Therapist-Supervisor, is an associate professor at Southeastern Louisiana University. She is the coordinator of the play therapy program and her research interests include: group work, child and adolescent counseling, and supervision. Prior to coming to Southeastern, she was the clinical director of a counseling and training center in the Greater New Orleans area.

Michele J. Ferro received her MA in Expressive Therapies: Art Therapy with a Specialization in Mental Health Counseling in 2014. She works as a clinician for a Child and Adolescent mental health agency using Play Therapy, Art Therapy, and Sandtray with a humanistic and relational approach. Ferro teaches an Introduction to Play Therapy course as adjunct faculty for Lesley University and William James College. She also leads art therapy groups for children and adolescents at a Partial Hospital Program. She is interested in exploring the interplay between play and the expressive therapies.

Rene Floer is pursuing her Masters in Counseling from Loyola University New Orleans, and plans to graduate in August 2017. She is currently working as a student intern with Family Services of Greater New Orleans, providing substance abuse counseling services for individuals referred through Orleans Parish Drug Court. Renee's research interests include: ethical implications of multicultural counseling, and substance abuse treatment through the lens of attachment theory and affect regulation. In her spare time, Renee likes to hike in the mountains of Montana.

Richard L. Gaskill is an Adjunct Professor of Play Therapy at Wichita State University, Executive Director of Sumner Mental Health Center.

Geoff Goodman, Ph.D., is Associate Professor of Psychology in the Long Island University Clinical Psychology Doctoral Program. He is also a licensed clinical and school psychologist with 24 years of experience in private practice in Forest Hills and New City, New York, treating children and adolescents as well as adults. He is certified by the American Board of Professional Psychology (ABPP) and is certified as both an adult and a child and adolescent psychoanalyst and Fellow of the International Psychoanalytical Association (FIPA). He is also a Certified Sex Therapist (CST), Certified Sex Addiction Therapist and Supervisor (CSAT-S), Certified Multiple Addiction Therapist and Supervisor (CMAT-S), and Registered Play Therapist and Supervisor (RPT-S). Dr. Goodman received a Bachelor of Science degree from M.I.T. in 1983, a Master of Arts degree in Developmental Psychology from Columbia University in 1986, and a Doctor of Philosophy degree in Clinical Psychology from Northwestern University in 1991. He completed a child clinical psychology internship at Babies Hospital, Columbia-Presbyterian Medical Center, in 1991, and a postdoctoral fellowship in the treatment and research of borderline personality disorder at New York Hospital, Cornell University Medical Center, in 1995. He is also a graduate of the Adult and Child Psychoanalysis Programs of the Psychoanalytic Training Institute of the Contemporary Freudian Society. Dr. Goodman is the author of many articles on the development of psychopathology and psychotherapy process in high-risk infants, children, and adults, and has presented internationally at conferences in Brazil, Canada, Chile, England, France, and Uganda. He published The Internal World and Attachment (The Analytic Press) in 2002, and three more books in 2010: Transforming the Internal World and Attachment (Vols. 1 and 2; Jason Aronson) and Therapeutic Attachment Relationships (Jason Aronson). In 2006, Long Island University awarded Dr. Goodman the Trustees Award for Scholarly Achievement for his first book, and in 2016, he received the Phi Delta Kappa Lifetime Research Award. In 2013 and 2014, Dr. Goodman published two more books: Rural Community Libraries in Africa: Challenges and Impacts (with wife Valeda F. Dent & Michael Kevane; IGI Global) and his first children's book, Daddy's Secret Cedar Chest (Tate Publishing). In 2013, Dr. Goodman was awarded the J. William Fulbright Foreign Scholarship by the US Department of State and spent eight months in 2014 establishing and evaluating an intervention program to facilitate the development of school readiness skills in preschool children in two rural village libraries in Uganda. He has taken four students to Uganda, two of whom completed doctoral dissertations based on data they collected there. Dr. Goodman is Director of the Long Island University Children's Institute for Play Therapy and Research, Coordinator of the Long Island University Clinical Psychology Doctoral Program's Applied Child Research Team, and Faculty Advisor of The Participant-Observer, the doctoral student newsletter. He is also Director of the Norbert Freedman Center for Psychoanalytic Research at the Institute for Psychoanalytic Training and Research (IPTAR), and serves on the IPTAR Board of Directors. Dr. Goodman lives in Forest Hills with his wife Valeda and daughter Carlyn.

Cary McAdams Hamilton is a Licensed Mental Health Counselor, Child Mental Health Specialist, and Registered Play Therapy Supervisor with diverse experience working in private practice, non-profit mental health service providers, juvenile justice, public education, residential treatment, and county assistance programs. She is focused on working with children, adolescents, and their families to improve relationships and healing. Cary is the President of Olympia Therapy PLLC and is the director and adjunct professor for the play therapy certification program (an APT approved provider) at Antioch University in Seattle, WA. Cary also holds an adjunct position at Brandman University in Lacey, WA and was previously an adjunct professor at George Fox University in Portland, OR. She presents various educational seminars and trainings, including: An Introduction to Play Therapy; Play Therapy in Educational Settings;

An Examination of Trauma and Healing Through Play Therapy, among other workshops. Additionally, Cary was the 2015-2016 President for the Washington State Association for Play Therapy (WA-APT).

Sarah Kiperman is a doctoral student at Georgia State University in the School Psychology department. Her research interests include understanding social support experiences by LGBTQ youth to develop safe spaces and interventions; and developing effective practice techniques in play therapy. Sarah has practiced school psychology (2 years) and play therapy (1 year) in the schools with supervision. She is excited to contribute to this chapter as an experienced supervisee! Sarah will be completing a play therapy focused internship over the next year.

Terry Kottman, Ph.D., RPT-S, NCC, LMHC, developed Adlerian play therapy and founded The Encouragement Zone, a center where she provides play therapy training, life coaching, "playshops" for women, and play therapy supervision. She regularly presents experiential workshops on play therapy; adventure therapy; activity-based counseling; counseling for children, adolescents, and their parents; consultation with teachers; and coaching adults. Kottman has a number of published chapters, articles, and books on Adlerian play therapy and other subjects.

Natalya A. Lindo, Ph.D., LPC, is an Associate Professor at the University of North Texas with over fifteen years of experience as a researcher and clinician with specialized training in working with children and families, in particular diverse and at-risk populations. Dr. Lindo's primary research areas are School-based Play Therapy, Child Parent Relationship Therapy, and Teacher Child Relationship Building. Consistent with this research agenda, Dr. Lindo regularly conducts action-research projects in the public schools related to Child Parent Relationship Therapy and Teacher Child Relationship Building. With a focus on capacity building, Dr. Lindo collaborates with administrators and school counselors to develop school-wide mental health initiatives targeting children who are at risk for school failure.

Jennifer Austin Main, M.S., LPC, RPT-S, is a doctoral candidate in Counselor Education and Supervision at The University of Mississippi, where she and her therapy dog Rook continue to offer play therapy services through the Counselor Education Clinic for Outreach and Personal Enrichment. Prior to coming to Ole Miss, Jennifer owned and operated a private practice and specialized in play therapy and canine assisted play therapy.

Megan Mansfield is a graduate student at Claremont Graduate University studying applied social psychology and evaluation. Her current research uses both group and interpersonal perspectives to look at how people understand their connections to one another (e.g., psychological sense of community, cohesion), and how these connections shape the social world around us and other outcomes (e.g., performance, health outcomes, and motivation).

Reshelle Marino earned her M.Ed. and Ph.D. from the University of New Orleans. She is a licensed professional counselor/board-approved supervisor, nationally certified counselor, and certified school counselor. She is on a tenure-track as an Assistant Professor in the Counseling Department at Southeastern Louisiana University and serves as the Clinical Coordinator of the School Counseling program. She is currently on the executive board for the Louisiana School Counseling Association in the position of President-Elect, and on the executive board for the Louisiana Association of Counselor Educators and

Supervisors in the position of Treasurer. She is also a member of the American Counseling Association, Louisiana Counseling Association, American School Counselor Association, Association of Counselor Education and Supervision, Southern Association of Counselor Education and Supervision, Chi Sigma Iota, and Phi Kappa Phi. Dr. Marino has previously worked for six years as a middle school counselor in a New Orleans charter school for the recovery school district. She is actively involved at her university by participating in research and grant writing, serving on interdisciplinary committees, and is the back-up chapter advisor for Chi Sigma Iota. She actively presents research at state and national conferences, as well as to local mental health agencies. Dr. Marino received a fully funded Louisiana Board of Regent Enhancement grant for her research on the use of advanced digital video technology for the supervision and instructional purposes of master's level counseling students, and received a leadership award from the Dean of the College of Nursing and Health Sciences for her efforts. Other research topics include: counseling children and adolescents, trauma-related disorders, test anxiety, infusing advocacy for specific populations into counselor education programs, and legal and ethical issues for counselors. In addition, she maintains her clinical passion by providing counseling services in a private practice setting to children, adolescents, adults and families. Dr. Reshelle Marino recently received the national 2015 American Counseling Association Ralph F. Berdie Research Award, and the 2015 Louisiana Counseling Association's Distinguished Professional Service Award.

Kristin K. Meany-Walen, PhD, LMHC, RPT-S, is an Assistant Professor in Counseling at the University of Northern Iowa. She also operates a small private practice in which she uses Adlerian theory with children, adolescents, and adults. Meany-Walen has published a number of book chapters and articles on the use of and effectiveness of Adlerian play therapy. Most recently, she and Terry Kottman co-authored Partners in Play: An Adlerian Approach to Play Therapy (3rd ed.).

Kristie Opiola, Ph. D., LPC, RPT, is an Assistant Professor in the Department of Counseling at the University of North Carolina-Charlotte.

Celita J. Owens is a doctoral student studying Clinical Psychology at Immaculata University. Celita obtained both her Master of Arts in Clinical Mental Health Counseling and her Bachelor of Science in Psychology at Xavier University of Louisiana. During her training as a Counselor, the focal point of her clinical training consisted of interpersonal trauma in children and adults, including emotional abuse, emotional neglect, physical abuse as well as domestic violence, and sexual abuse. Her areas of interest include; childhood interpersonal trauma and its impact throughout the lifespan, and acute and chronic sports related traumatic brain injury. Celita's past clinical experiences include serving as lead consultant to behavioral health providers and teachers in public schools, community-based, non-profit education and multi-service behavioral health facilities throughout Montgomery County. She has extensive training in play therapy and is experienced in facilitating creative experiences with children and families. Celita is currently providing counseling services to individuals ranging in ages across the lifespan experiencing a range of clinical issues, including co-occurring disorders in a non-profit, multi-service community behavioral health center.

Hannah Reas holds a Master of Arts in Clinical Psychology with an Emphasis in Marriage and Family Therapy from Pepperdine University. Her clinical experience includes working with children, adults, and families providing evidence-based treatment interventions. She has worked with a diverse range of presenting difficulties, including attention-deficit hyperactivity disorder, autism spectrum disorder, intellectual disability, obsessive-compulsive disorder, major depressive disorder, and bipolar disorder, as well as fetal alcohol syndrome and cerebral palsy. She has also facilitated social skills groups, as well as conducted Functional Behavior Assessments (FBA) to address specific behavioral, affective, cognitive, and social target goals for her previous clients. Additionally, she gained further experience interning for the International Trauma Treatment Program in Washington State, which promotes multicultural education and effective treatments of complex trauma for survivors of war, terrorism, and natural disasters. Ms. Reas has worked in a mental health private practice as an assistant office manager and is a graduate member of the American Psychological Association, Psi Chi International Honor Society in Psychology, Sigma Xi Honor Society in Research, and Phi Alpha Theta National Honor Society in History. Ms. Reas is a current Clinical Psychology Ph.D. student at Seattle Pacific University, with career goals of providing psychological assessment and treatment to veterans and other trauma-related populations.

Sondra Smith-Adcock holds a PhD in Counseling and Counselor Education from The University of North Carolina at Greensboro. She has taught at the University of Florida for over 15 years in the school and mental health counseling areas. She has 20 years counseling experience in schools and clinical settings and has published approximately 50 scholarly works on counseling related topics, with an emphasis on children and adolescents.

Jennifer P. Stone is an Assistant Professor and Program Coordinator of Early Childhood Unified Education at Wichita State University.

Jeffrey M. Sullivan, Ph.D., LPC-S, RPT, is an assistant professor of counselor education at Sam Houston State University in Huntsville, TX. His research interests include play therapy, parenting interventions, and counselor development. He regularly supervises counseling students during their practicum and internship experiences.

Alyssa Swan is a doctoral student in the Counseling program at University of North Texas, specializing in play therapy. She is a graduate assistant at Center for Play Therapy and works a counselor at Child and Family Resource Clinic in Denton, TX. Her clinical and research interests include children and preadolescents, play therapy, expressive arts in counseling, parent-child relationships, and relationship disruptions/trauma.

Karrie Swan is an Assistant Professor, Department of Psychology, Eastern Washington University.

Catherine Tucker holds a PhD in Counselor Education from the University of Florida. She earned tenure in the counseling area programs at Indiana State University, and is now the Research Director at The Theraplay Institute. She holds school counseling licenses in Indiana, and is a Licensed Mental Health Counselor in Indiana. She is also a registered play therapist supervisor. She has over ten years of direct clinical counseling experience and has authored multiple journal articles and book chapters on counseling related issues. She is President-Elect of the Association for Counseling Children & Adolescents from 2015-2017, a division of the American Counseling Association. She is co-author, with Sondra Smith-Adcock, of an upcoming textbook on counseling children and adolescents from SAGE publishing.

Krystal Vaughn, PhD, LPC-S, RPT-S, NCC, is a Licensed Professional Counselor-Supervisor and a Registered Play Therapist-Supervisor specializing in children ages 2-12. As an Assistant Professor at Louisiana State University Health Sciences Center – New Orleans she enjoys teaching, as well as, providing clinical services. Her research interests are supervision, play therapy, and mental health consultation. Dr. Vaughn has extensive experience providing mental health consultation in childcare centers, private schools, and local charter school systems. Dr. Vaughn also provides supervision to counselor interns seeking licensure as professional counselors. She received specialized training in the fields of infant and early childhood mental health and play therapy, which she presents on locally and nationally. Additionally, she serves on numerous boards and committees to promote professionalism in the fields of play therapy and clinical supervision.

Suzan E. Weishof received her Ph.D in Counseling Education with a specialization in Play Therapy from the University of North Texas in 2003, studying under Dr. Garry Landreth. Since 1995, she has been on the faculty of the International School of Hamburg, Germany, serving as a classroom teacher, learning support specialist and whole-school counselor. She has worked as a play therapist in both school and clinical settings and is currently the Junior School Principal at the International School of Hamburg. She was selected as a National Distinguished Principal by the US State Department Office of Overseas Schools, and is a school accreditation visitor for the Council of International Schools.

Naomi Wheeler is a National Certified Counselor and doctoral student at the University of Central Florida. Prior to pursuing her degree in Counselor Education, Mrs. Wheeler served as Project Director at the UCF Marriage & Family Research Institute, evaluating outcomes and leading service for low income and ethnic minority couples. Additionally, she has experience providing mental health services to children and their families including play therapy intervention.

Amanda Winburn, Ph.D., SB-RPT, NCC, is currently serving as an Assistant Professor at the University of Mississippi within the Department of Leadership and Counselor Education. Dr. Winburn has over a decade of experience working with children in various settings. Dr. Winburn is a licensed educator, counselor, and administrator. She currently serves at the Assessment Coordinator and teaches courses within the School Counseling specialty area. Dr. Winburn also has a strong area of interest in Play Therapy. Over the last 5 years, she has been actively involved in play therapy at the University of Mississippi both at the clinical setting as well as actively conducting research within the field. Other research interest include school counseling and bullying.

Laura Wood, as a doctoral student in School Psychology at Georgia State University, has focused on creating, implementing, and evaluating prevention and intervention programs for children. She has been able to use her training in adventure and play therapy to help promote the well-being and healthy development of children with and without developmental disabilities. Laura is committed to continuing to develop her play therapy skills with a focus on the ways that we can incorporate play therapy and related services into the everyday lives of children.

Index

9 Domains of Integration 60

A

abreaction 91-92, 94, 99
Adlerian Play Therapy (AdPT) 4-5, 15-16, 60-62, 66, 69, 71, 73, 77-78, 80, 100-110
Adlerian theory 60, 71-73, 78, 100-101
Adolescent 2, 13, 15-16, 18, 39, 54, 57-58, 77, 94-95, 97, 104, 109, 125, 127, 130, 137-138, 158, 167, 179, 209, 246, 256, 263-264, 282, 310, 336, 343, 364-365
Affective Emotional Motivational Systems 80
aggression 4, 11, 17, 33, 36, 50, 62, 93, 122, 125-126, 130, 141, 154-157, 175, 179, 237, 240, 269, 292, 310
aggressive toys 91, 141-143, 149-151, 153-155, 157
American School Counseling Association (ASCA) 138
American School Counselor Association 124, 127, 136, 278, 281, 318, 336
anger management 136, 140
Ann Jernberg 42
Art Therapy and Play Therapy 158
attachment 4, 14, 22, 28, 31, 33, 36, 42-50, 53-59, 61-64, 74, 79, 83, 86, 90-91, 95-97, 99, 113, 116, 123, 164-166, 175, 179, 186-187, 199, 206-209, 211-213, 234, 266-269, 274-277, 280-283, 285-286, 289, 295, 310
attachment theory 44, 49, 56-59, 74, 116, 123, 207, 286
attorney ad litem 271-272, 286
attunement 30-31, 43, 50-51, 59, 70, 93, 116, 118, 123
autism 43-44, 56, 112, 122-123, 191, 210, 337, 341-343
Autism Spectrum Disorder 112, 123

B

behavioral challenges 93, 301, 306
Bottom-Up Trauma Treatment 27, 40
bottom-up treatment 27, 40
Bruce D. Perry 20, 41

C

caregiver 12, 22, 29-30, 33, 42-43, 45-47, 51, 53, 59, 63, 74, 123, 185-187, 189-191, 193-199, 203-205, 213, 233-240, 245-246, 249-258, 261, 264, 267-268, 274-275, 323, 340, 347-349, 351, 361
caseworker 271-272, 276, 278, 280, 286
Center Based Consultation 232, 247
challenge 46-48, 58-59, 64-65, 73, 90, 93, 109, 126, 220, 226, 270, 284, 294, 353
Challenging Behavior(S) 247
child abuse 21-22, 35-36, 39, 57, 94, 282, 284, 291, 345-350, 359-360, 362, 364-366
Child Centered Consultation 232
child-centered play therapy 2, 13-18, 77-79, 81, 99, 112-115, 121-123, 156, 234, 236, 247, 256, 260, 262-263, 272-273, 275, 283, 286-287, 296, 301, 303-306, 312-314, 317-318, 323, 339, 341-342
child centered play therapy 17, 35, 76, 87, 123
Child parent relationship therapy (CPRT) 14, 18, 273, 282-283, 286, 337
Child-Parent Relationship training 265, 322-323, 325
Child-Teacher Relationship Training 288, 297, 301, 312-313, 337
Cognitive-behavioral play therapy (CBPT) 124, 128, 131, 138
competence 32-33, 70, 72, 115, 119, 141, 184-185, 187, 191, 195, 198, 210, 213-216, 218-222, 225, 227-229, 249-250, 255, 260-262, 264, 282, 292, 295, 309, 322-323, 365
competencies 127, 177, 208, 221, 249-250, 258, 262, 292, 296, 327, 329-330, 335, 341
confidentiality 74, 91, 214-218, 222-225, 227, 229, 231, 235-236, 243-245, 278-279, 332, 334, 350-351

consultant 214-216, 218-219, 221-227, 233-235, 240-242, 245, 247, 250, 252, 254-255, 257-258, 264, 284, 324
consultation 35, 104, 124, 214-227, 229-250, 252, 254-260, 262-263, 265-267, 270, 276-281, 296, 300-301, 308, 312, 318, 322-323, 327-328, 331, 335-338, 341-342
contact work 112-113, 120, 123
controlled outcome research 4, 14, 18
co-regulation 43, 53, 59, 65
court 32, 245, 265, 271-273, 277, 286, 345-347, 349-366
Court Appointed Special Advocate (CASA) 271, 286
court preparation 345-346, 359, 363
Cross-Cultural Psychology 206, 213
cultural competence 220, 228, 249-250, 264

D

Dan Siegel 60, 86
Department of Human Services Attorney 271, 287
Department of Human Services (DHS) 272, 287
Developmental Trauma 49, 81, 83, 98-99, 286
Disassociation 20
diversity 108, 144, 221, 230, 249-250, 254, 261, 264, 316
dual relationships 214-216, 225-227, 230

E

Early childhood mental health consultation 233, 241, 246-247
early mental health 12, 14, 16, 18, 302, 307, 309, 337, 340
Emergent Literacy 182, 184, 190, 192-197, 199-200, 203-204, 207, 210, 212-213
emergent literacy skills 184, 190, 213
engagement 44-48, 51, 59, 61, 64, 71, 83, 114, 117-118, 131, 165-166, 168-170, 174, 176, 178, 185, 207, 244, 247, 254, 257, 261, 263, 270, 288-290, 292-294, 306-307, 310, 323, 340
ethics 136, 214-216, 218, 221, 223, 225, 227-231, 244-245, 250, 258, 278, 281, 346
evidence-based treatment 1, 16, 18, 54, 108
expert witness 345, 352-354
expressive arts 124, 138, 160-161, 180-181

F

fact witness 345, 352-354
filial therapy 2-5, 12, 14-15, 18, 236, 253, 260, 272-273, 275, 282-283, 285-287, 296-297, 304, 307, 309-310, 312-313, 319, 322, 336-337, 343

G

group counseling 44, 124, 126, 128, 135-136, 138, 260
guardian 62, 131, 135, 223-224, 235, 243-244, 264-265, 271, 278, 287
Guardian ad Litem (GAL) 265
gun control 140, 142, 146, 148-149, 154-155, 157
gun violence 140-142, 146-148, 153-157, 343

H

Hemispheric Integration 81, 84, 89-90, 99
humanistic play therapy 288, 297, 312
hyperarousal 20, 22-23, 30, 83-84
informed consent 93, 143, 167, 214-218, 223-224, 227-231, 244, 276, 278

I

Interpersonal Neurobiology (IPNB) 61, 63, 65, 80

J

John Bowlby 42-43
judge 265, 271-272, 286, 349-350, 354-357, 361

K

kinder training 288, 297-301, 303-306, 308, 311-313, 322
Kottman 10, 15-16, 34, 37, 62, 65-75, 78, 100-105, 107-110, 126, 128, 137, 140-141, 156, 160, 165, 168, 180, 235, 238, 240-241, 244-246, 250, 254, 260-261, 295, 309

L

language development 28, 68, 115, 187, 242, 261, 314, 316-317, 320-321, 325, 340-341
Library 182, 187, 191-192, 195, 206-207, 209-211, 259, 308-309, 311
Limbic Resonance 81, 91, 99
limbic system 26, 41, 50, 81, 84-86, 89-91, 99
limit-setting 140, 143, 149, 152-155, 157, 299-300, 323
literacy 182-184, 187, 190, 192-200, 203-204, 207, 210-213, 299-300, 320, 332

M

Meany-Walen 14, 16, 62, 65-75, 77-78, 100-110, 156,

310
Memory Encoding 61, 63, 80
mental health consultation 232-233, 241, 245-248
meta-analysis 2-3, 15-17, 19, 115, 137, 187, 212, 308, 321, 335, 365
metaphor 67, 69, 101, 158-160, 162, 167, 173, 179-181
Multicultural 177, 221-222, 229-230, 249-250, 255, 258-264, 270, 280

N

neglect 20-22, 24-26, 35-36, 38-39, 49, 51, 54, 57, 81, 83, 94, 266, 268, 272, 282, 284, 291, 345-350, 353, 355, 358, 360, 362, 364-366
neural integration 61, 66, 72, 80-81, 86, 91, 97, 285
neurobiological development 42, 61
neurobiologically informed treatment 82
Neurobiology-Informed Treatment 99
neuroception 47, 49, 51-52, 58
neurodevelopment 20-21, 23-25, 27, 34, 36, 38, 40
Neurodevelopmentally Appropriate Trauma Treatment Approaches 40
Neuroplasticity 61, 65, 72-73, 80
neuroscience 21, 28, 35, 37, 40, 42, 44, 56, 58, 60-63, 65-66, 71-73, 75-80, 95-98, 206
nurture 46-48, 59, 79, 98, 207

O

open carry 146, 149-150, 157
Oral Language 182, 184-185, 188, 190, 192-197, 199-200, 204, 210, 212-213
oral language skills 184-185, 188, 190, 194, 197, 204, 210, 213

P

Person Centered Theory 123
person-centered therapy 112-113
Phyllis Booth 42-43
physical abuse 22, 54, 225, 345, 347, 358
play-based intervention 182-183, 213
play-based interventions 12, 65, 81, 183, 296, 314, 319
play-based professional development training 295, 297, 305-307, 313
play-based teacher intervention training 288, 307
play intervention 15, 17, 182, 185, 187-188, 191-192, 195-204
Playroom Materials 66, 140
Play Therapy Caregiver Consultant (PTCC) 250, 264
polyvagal theory 58, 61, 63-64, 79-80, 97
pre-therapy 112-123
Programmatic Consultation 248
projection 107, 158, 160, 162, 167, 172
pro social skills 124-126, 128, 130, 135, 138-139
psychological contact 113-115, 118-120, 123
puppet 31, 101-102, 158-162, 164-181, 238

R

Race and Ethnicity 249
randomized controlled studies 1, 6, 55
Randomized Controlled Trials 3, 5, 19
RCT 1, 5, 12, 103
Reason Treatment Phase for Traumatized Children 40
Regulate Treatment Phase for Traumatized Children 41
Relate Treatment Phase for Traumatized Children 41
Relationship Enhancement for Learner and Teacher 288, 297, 303, 313

S

school counselors 28, 33, 36, 40, 124, 126-127, 129-131, 135-136, 138, 142, 146, 239-243, 254, 281, 287, 299, 306-307, 318, 320, 326, 336, 338-339, 342
school readiness skills 182, 184-188, 190, 199, 204, 213
school setting 12, 32, 108, 124, 128, 131, 135-136, 233, 240, 251, 289, 292, 294-295, 297-298, 307, 314, 317-318, 320, 324-326, 334, 343
self-efficacy 3, 53, 57, 88, 91, 115, 141, 157, 335
sexual abuse 21-22, 37, 81, 164, 171, 345, 347, 349, 355, 358, 361, 363-366
social interest 60-62, 71-73, 75, 298, 306
social skills deficits 126, 128
social workers 145, 233, 265, 273, 318, 320, 326, 347
Speech-Language Pathology 337, 341-344
Stakeholders for Children in Foster Care 287
Stephen Porges 49, 51
structure 44, 46-48, 59, 66, 85, 109, 124, 141, 157, 159, 161-162, 168, 187, 198, 223, 232-236, 259, 288, 297-298, 300-301, 303, 305, 316, 326, 354
STSA 182, 185, 187-188, 191-193, 195-205, 213
supervision 5, 10, 28, 54, 119, 168, 214-231, 244, 250, 272-273, 275, 286-287, 297-298, 301-305
Susan Knell 138
symbolic play 114-116, 118, 314-317, 339-343
symbolism 158, 168, 316-317

T

Teacher-Child Relationship Building 288, 297, 304, 313
Terry Kottman 60, 100, 108
testimony 345-346, 348, 352-354, 359-360, 365-366
Theory of Mind 182, 184-185, 187, 190-200, 203-204, 209, 213, 340
Theory of Mind skills 184-185, 187, 190-191, 194, 196-200, 204, 213
therapeutic powers of play 5, 97, 99, 273, 311
Theraplay 4-5, 42-59, 140, 276, 281, 319, 339
Top-Down Trauma Treatment 41
Trauma-Informed Play TherapyTM 29, 41
Trauma-InformedTM Play therapy 20
treatment planning 235, 278, 324, 363

V

violence 16, 20-21, 23, 32, 39, 54, 56, 81-82, 92-93, 95-96, 126, 140-142, 146-148, 153-157, 267, 285, 343

W

window of tolerance 47, 49, 52-53, 65

Premier Reference Source
Solutions for High-Touch Communications in a High-Tech World

Premier Reference Source
Advanced Research on Biologically Inspired Cognitive Architectures

Premier Reference Source
Workforce Development Theory and Practice in the Mental Health Sector

Premier Reference Source
Resource Management and Efficiency in Cloud Computing Environments

www.ingramcontent.com/pod-product-compliance
Lightning Source LLC
LaVergne TN
LVHW060356300926
849162LV00006B/1279